Terrorism:

Research, Readings, and Realities

LYNNE L. SNOWDEN, PH.D.
Dept. of Sociology, UNCW
Wilmington, North Carolina 28403-3297

BRADLEY C. WHITSEL, PH.D.
Penn State University-Fayette Campus

PEARSON

Prentice
Hall

Upper Saddle River, New Jersey 07458

Library of Congress Cataloging-in-Publication Data

Terrorism : research, readings, & realities/[edited by] Lynne L. Snowden, Bradley C. Whitsel.
  p. cm.
  Includes bibliographical references and index.
  ISBN 0-13-117373-1 (alk. paper)
 1. Terrorism. 2. Terrorism—United States. 3. Terrorism—Religious aspects.
I. Snowden, Lynne L. II. Whitsel, Bradley C. III. Title.

HV6431.T4953 2004
303.6′25—dc22

                                                        2004026871

Executive Editor: Frank Mortimer, Jr.
Assistant Editor: Mayda C. Broco
Managing Editor: Mary Carnis
Production Management: Pine Tree Composition, Inc.
Production Editor: Linda Duarte
Production Liaison: Brian Hyland
Director of Manufacturing and Production: Bruce Johnson
Manufacturing Buyer: Cathleen Petersen
Design Director: Cheryl Asherman
Senior Design Coordinator: Miguel Ortiz
Printer/Binder: Phoenix
Cover Design: Carey Davies
Cover Illustration: Getty Images/Photodisc Blue

Pearson Education LTD.
Pearson Education Singapore, Pte. Ltd
Pearson Education, Canada, Ltd
Pearson Education–Japan

Pearson Education Australia PTY, Limited
Pearson Education North Asia Ltd
Pearson Educaçion de Mexico, S.A. de C.V.
Pearson Education Malaysia, Pte. Ltd

10 9 8 7 6 5 4 3 2 1
ISBN 0-13-117373-1

Acknowledgments

The authors would like to thank a number of people whose support and assistance have been essential to this project. First, Lynne Snowden wishes to recognize the Department of Sociology & Criminal Justice, University of North Carolina at Wilmington, for its support of this publication and her course on Collective Violence. Thanks especially to Mike Snowden, who helped edit our mistakes, for his assistance with this publication. Brad Whitsel is grateful for the assistance provided by the Pennsylvania State University Commonwealth College in the form of a research development grant for the project and also for a supporting grant from the Pennsylvania State University (Eberly Campus) Swimmer Family Faculty Research Fund. Next, we wish to thank the students, professors, and, most of all, the editors at Prentice Hall who helped us to bring this project to completion.

Table of Contents

experts designated by NATO to study the potential of terrorism attacks on nuclear waste shipments and power plant facilities. In 2002, he testified in both the U.S. House of Representatives and the U.S. Senate on the risk of terrorism attacks on transported nuclear waste products designated for shipment to the Yucca Mountain facility.

Lawrence Becker, Ph.D., is an assistant professor of political science at California State University, Northridge, where he teaches courses on American political institutions, public policy, and public administration. He received his Ph.D. in 2001 from the University of Massachusetts at Amherst. He is the author of a forthcoming book, *Doing the Right Thing,* with Ohio State University Press on the ways in which members of Congress use legislative procedures to overcome collective action problems such as site selection for a high-level nuclear waste facility at Yucca Mountain.

Max L. Bromley, Ph.D., is an Associate Professor in the Department of Criminology at the University of South Florida. He has served as the Associate Director of Public Safety at the University of South Florida and worked in the criminal justice field for almost twenty-five years. In addition to his many years of policing experience, Dr. Bromley also worked as a juvenile probation officer early in his career, which provided him with an understanding and appreciation of this critical part of the criminal justice system. He received his B.S. and M.S. in Criminology from Florida State University and has a Doctorate in Higher Education with an emphasis in Criminal Justice from Nova University. Dr. Bromley has co-authored the college textbook entitled *Crime and Justice in America,* 6th edition. He has co-edited a volume entitled *Hospital and College Security Liability* and was the senior co-author of *College Crime Prevention and Personal Safety Awareness.* In addition, he has written dozens of scholarly articles and technical documents on a variety of campus crime and campus policing issues. Recently Dr. Bromley has been involved in research on community policing. His articles have appeared in *Policing, Police Quarterly, Criminal Justice Policy Review,* and *Journal of Contemporary Criminal Justice.* Dr. Bromley also wrote *Department Self-Study: A Guide for Campus Law Enforcement Administrators,* which is used at over 1,000 institutions of higher education.

Sarah H. Corley, University of Arkansas.

Kelly Damphousse, Ph.D., completed his graduate work under Howard Kaplan, director of the Laboratory for the Studies of Social Deviance at Sam Houston State University (SHSU). His dissertation examining the long-term consequences of drug use by adolescents was completed in 1994. After graduation, he worked as an Assistant Professor in the Department of Justice Sciences at the University of Alabama at Birmingham and as Assistant Professor in the College of Criminal Justice at SHSU. After two years, he took a position in the Department of Sociology at the University of Oklahoma (to work at the home of a national championship football team). He has been there ever since. He directs several research projects, most notably the American Terrorism Study and the Oklahoma City Arrestee Drug Abuse Monitoring project.

Mathieu Deflem, Ph.D., is an Assistant Professor in the Department of Sociology at the University of South Carolina. His main research interests are international policing, counterterrorism, law, and theory. Deflem is author of *Policing World Society: Historical Foundations of International Police Cooperation* (Oxford University Press 2002), and editor of *Terrorism and Counter-Terrorism: Criminological Perspectives* (Elsevier Science 2004) and Habermas, *Modernity and Law* (Sage 1996). He may be reached through his Web site: http://www.mathieudeflem.net/.

James. O. Ellis, III, Ph.D., is the Research and Program Coordinator for The National Memorial Institute for the Prevention of Terrorism (MIPT) in Oklahoma City. Ongoing and future research efforts at the Memorial Institute have and will continue to address several of the gaps in the nation's homeland security system. Many of these concerns cropped up in the MIPT-sponsored report *Dark Winter* and "Bioterrorism: Knowing the Agents, Preventing the Terror," a joint conference with the New York Medical College. *Sooner Spring,* a state-level version of *Dark Winter,* will likely shed light on more concerns at the more immediate levels of emergency response. A provider for first responders and a center for lessons learned, the Memorial Institute remains committed to improving the country's ability to prevent and deter terrorism or to mitigate its effects through sound planning, policy, and preparedness efforts.

Dominic Little is currently working as an instructor at California State University Northridge and president of Harvey Institute for Research & Evaluation (HIRE), a consulting firm specializing in quantitative research. His research interests include technology and society, terrorism, and education.

David C. Lobb, Ph.D., earned his doctorate in American history from the Maxwell School of Citizenship and Public Affairs at Syracuse University. He currently works as a Special Agent for the U.S. Naval Criminal Investigative Service and has performed numerous counterintelligence operations.

Lindsay C. Maybin is a graduate student in the Department of Political Science at the University of South Carolina. Her research interests include the democratic peace theory, democratization, and international cooperation. After completing her master's degree, she plans to pursue a Ph.D. in history in preparation for an academic career.

Robert Moore, Ph.D., is Assistant Professor of Criminal Justice at Delta State University. He received his doctorate in Administration of Justice from The University of Southern Mississippi in 2003. His research interests include the use of technology in criminal activities, the response of the legal system to technology crime, and police training.

Gary R. Perlstein, Ph.D., received his doctorate from Florida State University. He is Professor Emeritus and former chair of the Portland State University Hatfield School of Government's Administration of Justice program and a nationally renowned expert on domestic terrorism. Over the past few years, Dr. Perlstein has shared his terrorism expertise with NPR, *USA Today, Newsweek,* ABC News, the *New York Times,* the *Washington Post,* CNN, and the BBC. He is the author of the book *Perspectives on*

Preface

The contents of *Terrorism: Research, Readings, and Realities* include essays that bring focus to both established issues and new developments in the multidisciplinary field of terrorist studies. While the range of topics is broad, each of the essays provides insights into aspects of the phenomena of terrorism and extremism. Both conceptual and case-study approaches are employed to provide the reader with a variety of theoretical, historical, control-oriented, and descriptive explorations of timely and controversial subjects. (Any articles which were previously published have been retained in their original state.) The breadth and diversity of the researched essays and the inclusion of many new contributions on compelling issues make the volume especially well-suited for student use in courses on terrorism and extremism at the undergraduate and graduate levels. Likewise, scholars will find that the fresh research produced for this edited volume adds to the body of knowledge which has been accumulating in this field.

The peer-review process is critical to the production of scholarly work, and for this reason, the editors wish to thank the evaluators who read and commented upon the manuscript prior to its publication: L. D. Andrews, Missouri Western State College; Paul Becker, University of Dayton; Lloyd Klein, Bemidji State University; John J. Mason, Upper Iowa University; Jill Miller, Missouri Western State College; and Gary Warchol, Northern Michigan University. Their recommendations were greatly valued. Our publisher, Prentice Hall, was entirely supportive throughout the duration of this project and we thank Frank Mortimer and Korrine Dorsey, in particular, for their helpful advice (and gentle deadline reminders) at important times. Thanks also go to the United States Institute of Peace and the Federal Bureau of Investigation for their willingness to allow selected reprint reports to be published and especially to each of the individual contributing authors to *Terrorism: Research, Readings, and Realities,* who gave their time and effort to help bring the project to completion.

SECTION ONE

INTRODUCTION

In the wake of the events of 9/11, terrorism has captured global attention to a degree without historical parallel. In the uncertain world that has emerged since 9/11, intergovernmental organizations, national governments, policy analysts, law enforcement groups, scholars, and society at large are all faced with the arrival of tumultuous times that challenge older notions about international terrorism. At the same time, recent developments on the American scene remind us, despite the unprecedented scope of the 9/11 catastrophes, that "homegrown" terrorism and the extremist beliefs that accompany it remain a threat to public order in the United States.

The editors of this book, *Terrorism: Research, Readings, and Realities,* recognized the need two years ago to begin work on a project that examined unfolding shifts in terrorism and violence-prone extremism from the vantage point of both academics and expert practitioners. The new essays commissioned for inclusion in this work respond to the need for different lenses of analysis in the study of terrorist and extremist groups. While concentrating throughout on the larger context of these groups and their strategies, the broad range of these essays encompasses many aspects of research that heretofore have not been brought together in an edited volume. In order to produce both a contemporary and comprehensive treatment of the subject, efforts were made to develop a multiperspective focus. The insights of the contributing criminologists, political scientists, sociologists, historians, and others working in fields linked with terrorist studies were sought to give readers a set of original essays helping to illuminate the significant developments and trends taking place in terrorism and extremism.

The approach in *Terrorism: Research, Readings, and Realities* is scholarly. However, the overall accessibility of the essays will be attractive to students, academics, and practitioners alike. While the essays represent a blend of theoretical work, timely case studies, and practical assessments of the dynamics of terrorism, the volume's focus steers away from deep immersion in the decades-old definitional morass of what constitutes terrorism. At one time, when terrorism was a less pressing issue, this "debate" was a standard part of many books on the topic, and discussions involving the ongoing (and highly unrealistic) search for a universal definition appeared with some frequency in the literature. Definitions of terrorism continue to spring forth, and they run the gamut from the hundreds of ways that academics describe the term to the

SECTION TWO

Domestic Terrorism

LOOK FOR THESE KEY POINTS:

- Many terrorists share common factors in their belief systems.
- The demographic characteristics of American terrorists who were indicted during the 1980s differ substantially from those indicted in the 1990s.
- The U.S. government must seek the underutilized expertise of the local law enforcement agencies (LLEA) to counteract the threat of domestic terrorism.
- There are no shortcuts to effective counterterrorism: measures that overemphasize any one element, such as military responses, can lead to an undermining of other elements, such as political/diplomatic ties, etc.
- Organizational strategies are extremely important to the modern-day movements of the Earth Liberation Front (ELF) and the Animal Liberation Front (ALF).

Domestic terrorists' goal may be to form a nation or a geopolitical alliance, influence a public policy, or simply challenge state or local authorities. All domestic terrorism is intimately connected to power and legitimacy. Power with the capacity to exert force effectively and legitimacy are the prizes to which many terrorist leaders aspire. Ideology performs diverse functions in domestic terrorist groups. Most domestic terrorists use it to aid in mobilizing their resources and to propose reasons why they should have more resources than others. Beliefs that appeal to a constituency aid in developing coalitions with other groups, in prioritizing subgoals (action), and in uniting one's own group around a particular strategy or tactic. Thus, the ideologies and belief systems of domestic terrorists are what distinguishes them to their supporters. Organization in domestic terrorist groups concentrates on mobilizing resources—both human and nonhuman. Problems in organization often cause violence. While most groups who organize to challenge the established power structure adopt its organizational pattern, a desire for radical decentralization will prevent rebels and terrorist groups from benefitting from its structural benefits. Domestic terrorists use violence if they believe that the probability of success is within their grasp if a show of force is executed successfully (Gamson, 1997). In a study of political violence, Gamson found that about one-quarter of all political challengers eventually use some form of violent activity (Gamson, 1990, 1997). Domestic terrorists do not resort to violence in desperation: rather, it is

The final chapter in this section, by Stoner and Perlstein, analyzes the American ecoterror movement. They compare the social dynamics of the Earth Liberation Front and the Animal Liberation Front. After describing the ELF's formation and goals, Stoner and Perlstein give us a history of splinter-group formation, followed by a discussion of the Earth Liberation Front's beliefs, philosophies, and mission. Next comes a discussion of the group's structure and its leadership and membership. The article concludes with a discussion of organizational strategies, methods, and targets of these groups. An exhaustive study of ecoterror criminal events is included in the article's appendix.

REFERENCES

Gamson, William. 1990. *The Strategy of Social Protest.* 2nd ed. New York: Wadsworth Press.
_____ 1997. "The Success of the Unruly." In *Social Movements,* ed. Doug McAdam and David Snow, 356–364. Los Angeles, CA: Roxbury Publishing Company.
McAdam, Doug. 1982. *The Political Process and the Development of Black Insurgency.* Chicago: University of Chicago Press.
McAdam, Doug, and David Snow, eds. 1997. *Social Movements: Readings on Their Emergence, Mobilization, and Dynamics.* Los Angeles, CA: Roxbury Publishing Company.
Meyer, David, and Sidney Tarrow, eds. 1998. *The Social Movement Society.* Lanham, MD: Rowman & Littlefield Publishers, Inc.

CHAPTER 1

Identity and the Terrorist Threat:

An Interpretative and Explanatory Model

Michael P. Arena
Alliant International University-Fresno

Bruce A. Arrigo, Ph.D. *
Department of Criminal Justice
University of North Carolina at Charlotte

ABSTRACT

Many analysts would agree that terrorism is an ever-changing phenomenon; however, like all forms of human behavior, there are certain sociological and psychological elements that remain constant. One such element is that of identity which can serve to both inform and influence terrorist behavior through one's perception of oneself and the person's environment. This article relies upon symbolic interactionism and five of its organizing concepts (symbols and objects, acts and social acts, meaning, role-taking and role-making, and the emergence of the self) to create an interpretative model for understanding terrorist behavior through identity theory. The conceptual framework is then used to examine the creation and maintenance of identities within three terrorist groups: the Provisional Irish Republican Army, the Hamas, and the Tupamaros. Although these groups do not account for all the terrorist attacks in the world, they do

This article is reproduced by permission of the *International Criminal Justice Review* (Volume 14, 2004)

* Please address all correspondence to: Bruce A. Arrigo, Ph.D., Professor and Chair, Department of Criminal Justice, University of North Carolina at Charlotte, 9201 University City Blvd., Charlotte, NC 28223-0001.

represent three diverse forms of terrorism (i.e. national, religious, and revolutionary) from three distinct regions of the globe (i.e. the West, the Middle East, and Latin America). Therefore, understanding their behavior through the identity prism can help to shed light on other groups that exist and those which have yet to emerge. Implications are proposed in the areas of law enforcement, public policy, research, and the model's general utility in assessing other forms of human behavior.

INTRODUCTION

In the 2002 edition of *Patterns of Global Terrorism,* the U.S. Department of State reported a total of 199 international terrorist attacks which resulted in 725 deaths and 2,013 wounded (U.S. Department of State, 2003). The 2001 edition reported 355 attacks, 3,295 deaths, and 2,283 wounded. In 2000, there were 423 attacks, 405 deaths, and 791 wounded. These figures and those from previous years[1] indicate that terrorism is a pervasive problem experienced in all regions of the world. Indeed, the global data indicate that the international community confronts a daunting challenge, especially if it intends to effectively respond to terrorist activities in the 21st century (e.g., Dershowitz, 2002; Laqueur, 2003; Martin, 2003).

One dimension to this formidable challenge is the changing face of terrorism (Berman, 2003; Emerson, 2002). These changes are attributed to recent trends which have developed, especially in the wake of the "9/11" attacks in New York City, Washington, D.C., and rural Pennsylvania. A few examples of these trends include the emergence of the "freelance" or individual terrorist who has little or no affiliation with an organized group (Kushner, 1998a, 1998b), the potential use of weapons of mass destruction (Marlo, 1999), militant Islamic fundamentalism or Islamists (Emerson, 2002; Pinto, 1999; O'Ballance, 1997), far-right extremism (Dobratz & Shanks-Meile, 1997; Hamm, 1993; Smith, 1994), narcoterrorism, ecoterrorism, and animal liberationists (Laqueur, 1999; Tucker, 2000; Whittaker, 2001).

In addition to the changing "face" of terrorism, these trends have forced researchers, law enforcement personnel, and policy makers to re-examine their existing assumptions concerning this international phenomenon (Kushner, 1998a, 1998b; Hoffman, 1998; Laqueur, 2003). For example, as Kushner (1998b) points out, the individual terrorists are difficult to identify as they do not always fit into the classification systems (see, Flemming & Stohl, 1988) developed within academic, law enforcement, and intelligence circles. To illustrate, French terrorism expert, Xavier Raufer, uses the changing constellation of stars to describe the constant changes among various Islamic terrorist groups. "At any given time, you can take a picture of the worldwide Islamic terrorist infrastructure - but two hours later, the entire constellation will appear radically different" (as cited in Emerson, 1998, p. 36). While identification and explanatory systems of this sort may no longer be as accurate as they were in the past, and while the "new" terrorists of today have radically changed from their forefathers of the 1970s, 80s and 90s, it does not mean that contemporary terrorists completely lack a meaningful connection to their ancestral heritage (Berman, 2003).[2] Indeed, terrorism, like all forms of human behavior, has certain underlying sociological and psychological elements. These elements, like the stars in the sky, remain constant or fixed. After all, the movement of the Earth is responsible for the changing appearance of the constellations not the stars themselves.

There have been a number of efforts from the social science disciplines to identify the various psychological and sociological forces at work in terrorist behavior. Typically, these efforts approach the phenomenon from a psychological (Johnson & Feldmann, 1992; Pearlstein, 1991; Reich, 1998; Taylor, 1991; Taylor & Quayle, 1994), sociological (Gibson, 1994; Wieviorka, 1993), or criminological (Hagan, 1997; Hamm, 1993; Smith, 1994) perspective. These works identify a number of common themes that influence one's decision to engage in terrorist behavior (e.g. cognitive dissonance, conformity, an externalized locus of control, group polarization, hopelessness, justification, labeling, rationalization, and socialization). However, another reoccurring theme is identity. Identity can serve to both inform and influence terrorist conduct through one's perception of oneself and the person's environment.

For example, in a chapter addressing how individuals become and remain involved in the terrorist movement, Taylor and Quayle (1994) state that during an interview with an Irish terrorist, identity was a word that reoccurred over and over again as they discussed his life. In addition, Kushner (1998b, p. 20) states that members of the militant Islamic Fundamentalist group, Hamas, ". . . seek their identity in their Islamic roots, which provide them with structure and self-confidence on the personal and ethnic levels" (see also, Emerson, 2003). Relatedly, in his 1995 testimony in front of the Senate Judiciary Committee, the acting Director of the Central Intelligence Agency, Admiral William Studeman, stated that one of the reasons Islamic terrorist groups have become particularly dangerous is that they "do not have a well-established organizational identity" (as cited in Emerson, 1998: 41).

We contend that many researchers and policy analysts take identity for granted, treating it as though the mere mention of the concept conveys the powerful influence it has on who we are and how it affects behavior. Indeed, as Jenkins (1996: 4) observes, ". . . there is something active about the word [identity] which cannot be ignored. Identity is not 'just there', it must always be established." Recognizing the importance of identity in terrorist violence, Post (1998:26) argues that political violence is driven by internal (i.e. psychological) forces. Utilizing a psychodynamic approach and such social psychological concepts as group behavior, conformity, and attribution, Post determines that terrorism is the result of "the terrorist's search for identity, and that, as he strikes out against the establishment, he is attempting to destroy the enemy within." Furthermore, he states that ". . .the act of joining the terrorist group represents an attempt to consolidate a fragmented psychological identity, to resolve a split and be at one with oneself and with society, and, most important, to belong" (Post, 1988:30-31). In conclusion, Post states that "terrorists whose only sense of significance comes from being terrorists cannot be forced to give up terrorism, for to do so would be to lose their very reason for being" (Post, 1988:38). Summarizing the generalized psychological explanation for terrorism, Martin (2003) reaches a similar conclusion. As he explains, "[p]ressures to conform to the group, combined with pressures to commit acts of violence, form a powerful psychological drive to carry on in the name of the cause, even when victory is logically impossible. These pressures become so prevalent that achieving victory becomes a consideration secondary to the unity of the group" (Martin, 2003 p. 72). Statements such as these lay the groundwork for further examination of this theme in terrorism and how it affects cognitive processes and behavior on a more detailed and systematic level.

The concept of identity finds its roots primarily in the field of psychology (Erickson, 1959), although, some of its staunchest advocates come from the interactionist perspective of sociology. For instance, Goffman (1959) suggested that people present their identities in a manner similar to actors on a stage, managing their appearance by engaging in behaviors that are congruent with a particular image. From this micro-level of analysis, society is understood through a focus on the intimate, day-to-day interaction of individuals and their environment (Schaefer, 2000). Unique to this perspective is the ability to integrate both the human nature and social reality aspects of existence (Weigert, Teitge, & Teitge, 1986; Jenkins, 1996). As Weigert et al. (1986:34) state, "a broad tradition exists for developing this paradigm from the work of 'interpretative' sociologists such as symbolic interactionists, ethnomethodologists, and neo-phenomenologists." Indeed, the development and exploration of a terrorist identity could be examined from a variety of interactionist type approaches such as ethnomethodology (Garfinkel, 1967; Hilbert, 1990; Livingston, 1987), social constructionism (Berger & Luckmann, 1967; Best, 1989; Gergen, 1999; Schutz, 1967), and labeling theory (Goode, 1996; Lemert, 1994). However, because the interactionist perspective and its many variants have emerged from symbolic interactionism, understanding the terrorist identity must begin with a framework that will establish a foundation from which other efforts can build.

Based on the work of Charles Horton Cooley and George Herbert Mead, Herbert Blumer (1969:2) described the study of symbolic interactionism in three basic premises; "[t]he first premise is that human beings act toward things on the basis of the meanings that the things have for them. . . [t]he second premise is that the meaning of such things is derived from, or arises out of, the social interaction that one has with one's fellows. . . [t]he third premise is that these meanings are handled in, and modified through, an interpretative process used by the person in dealing with the things he [she] encounters." From these three premises, Hewitt (1976) extrapolates five key symbolic interactionist concepts: (1) symbols and objects; (2) meanings; (3) acts and social acts; (4) role-taking and role-making; and (5) the emergence of the self. Although Hewitt (1976) clearly identified these five concepts as being the hallmarks of symbolic interactionism, they can also be found in the work of Baldwin (1986), Lauer and Handel (1983), and Meltzer (1978).

This article systematically examines these five organizing concepts and their significance in the creation of a sense of identity in members of three terrorist groups: the Provisional Irish Republican Army (PIRA), the Hamas, and the Tupamaros.[3] These three organizations have been chosen for several reasons. First, they represent very diverse regions of the globe: the West, the Middle East, and Latin America. Second, they represent three major forms of terrorism: nationalist, religious, and revolutionary. Third, all three groups have received a substantial amount of attention in both the popular and academic literature (Berman, 2003; Bell,1997; Coogan, 1994; Emerson, 1998; Gilio, 1972; Horgan & Taylor, 1997; Hroub, 2000; Emerson, 1998; Martin, 2003; McGuire, 1973; Mishal & Sela, 2000; Nüsse, 1998; O'Ballance, 1997; Porzecanski, 1973; Taylor, 1997; Weinstein, 1975; White, 1993; White, 1998; Whittaker, 2001; Wilson, 1974). Such forms of literature are the basis of our analysis regarding identity.

Accordingly, this article intends to advance our knowledge of terrorism and identity theory as it is understood through symbolic interactionism. As emergency response expert Hugh Stephens (as cited in White, 1998) describes, terrorism research can be categorized into three levels. The *Immediate Level* is the most accessible, and includes such dimensions as operational or tactical issues for law enforcement. The *Secondary Level* focuses on emergency response planning, long term operations, and intelligence gathering. The *Contextual Level* consists of information of a more general nature. Although law enforcement and policy analysts may not see the immediate benefit of contextual research, it is designed to further existing knowledge on the rationale behind terrorist behavior. Working at this level, then, the conceptual framework we propose endeavors to advance our understanding of the terrorist identity and, perhaps, other similar social phenomena in which identity plays a strong role (e.g. gang affiliation, religious and political extremism). Aside from the terrorism aspect, the framework serves to reinvigorate the study of symbolic interactionism and its practical implications for comprehending contemporary social behavior. However, in order to properly situate the investigation, we begin with a brief overview of identity theory and the three terrorist organizations to which we refer.

A SYMBOLIC-INTERACTIONIST PERSPECTIVE OF IDENTITY

The term "identity" is one that is commonly used in both the psychological and sociological disciplines (Abrams & Hogg, 1999; Ellemers, Spears, & Doosje, 1999; Jenkins, 1996; Worchel, Morales, Páez, & Deschamps, 1998).[4] Although the two orientations may not exactly agree on the definition of the construct or in how it furthers our knowledge of human existence, there is some consensus within the social psychological perspective of symbolic interactionism. Therefore, it is important to understand how identity is conceptualized within this unique discipline (Weigert et al., 1986)

The theoretical study of identity dates back to the early works of the neo-Freudian psychoanalyst, Erik Erikson, who first began formulating his ideas on what he called the "ego identity" in the early 1940s. Erikson (1959, p. 23) described the ego identity as "the awareness of the fact that there is a self sameness and continuity to the ego's synthesizing methods and that these methods are effective in safeguarding the sameness and continuity of one's meaning for others." Erickson's concept of the ego identity soon began to influence the development of symbolic interactionism. As stated by Weigert et al. (1986:1) "a small group of sociologists working within a version of American pragmatism were trying to develop a more adequate sociological psychology for understanding human action as essentially social; they knew of Erikson's work and quickly adopted his term, but shortened it to 'identity'."

Symbolic interactionism is defined as the way in which "we use and interpret symbols not merely to communicate with one another but to create and maintain impressions of ourselves, to forge a sense of *Self,* and to create and sustain what we experience as the reality of a particular social situation" (Johnson, 1995:144). Although Herbert Blumer coined the phrase symbolic interactionism in the 1930s, the discipline's origins began with the work of Charles Horton Cooley (Pontell, 1996/1902) and George Herbert Mead (Morris, 1967). Cooley (1996/1902, p. 63) used the phrase "looking-glass self" to describe his belief that we learn who we are through social interaction. He theorized that one's self-identity (or what he called a self-idea) is developed through three principle elements: "the imagination of our appearance to the other person, the imagination of his judgment of that appearance, and some sort of self-feeling, such as pride or mortification." Symbolic interactionists have also called this the mirror theory of identity, in that "we are what others' reflections make us" (Weigert et al., 1986:50).

Expounding upon the ideas of Cooley, Mead developed a three stage model of how the self emerges through social interaction (Morris, 1967). The first stage is the preparatory stage, during which a child simply imitates the actions of those in their environment. Throughout this stage the child learns the meanings of symbols and begins to use them in communication. During the play stage, a child learns to pretend to be other people, in a sense taking on the roles of others. During the game stage, the child begins to consider his/her own social position in relation to those around the child and the responsibilities each position entails. Through this process, the self emerges as an object toward which action can be directed. In addition, the child begins to respond to the members of his or her social environment.

Based on the work of Cooley, Mead, and Blumer, we can isolate five key concepts of symbolic interactionism. These include symbols and objects, acts and social acts, meanings, role-taking and role-making, and the emergence of the self (Baldwin, 1986, Hewitt, 1976; Lauer & Handel, 1983; Meltzer, 1978). A symbol can be conceptualized in two ways. The first of which is that a symbol is a concrete object consisting of physical matter that can be referred to, designated, or acted toward. In reference to terrorism, a concrete symbol may be a target such as a bank, embassy, or plane belonging to a national airline carrier which may be symbolic of capitalism or Western influence (Hoffman, 1998). A more abstract interpretation of a symbol is as a social object. In these instances, a social object is a socially constructed thing that may be the goal of action. For example justice, poverty, retribution, or respect could all be considered socially constructed objects. Both concrete and abstract objects are significant in their environment when they are designated by symbols. For many in the United States, the American flag represents a symbol of a socially constructed object; namely, freedom or liberty. As Hewitt (1976: 49) describes; "social objects are created as people engage is social acts . . . social acts depend upon social interaction and interpretation. That is, in order for individuals to cooperate with one another in the creation of social objects, they must orient their conduct to one another."

Another concept within symbolic interactionism is that of the act or social act. Mead conceptualized the act as having four components: impulse, perception, manipulation, and consummation. To understand the act, one must consider all of these as a cohesive unit as opposed to being taken by themselves (Baldwin, 1986). In this case, an example may help to explain the sequence of experiences. If while walking toward her car in a deserted shopping-mall parking lot, a woman sees a man suddenly appear who begins walking toward her, the woman's initial impulse may be to act, perhaps to quickly begin searching for her keys. However, the woman's action is dependent upon her perception of the man's action. For instance, she may perceive the man as simply in a rush to get to his own car that happens to be parked near her own. Hewitt (1976, p. 47) states that "the perception and designation of objects and stimuli are strongly influenced by the condition of the organism, so that the actions it undertakes stem as much from its own internal states as from the presence of external events of stimuli." If the woman had experienced an assault in the past she might be more vigilant in her perception of the man's behavior. The third element in the sequence is manipulation. In an effort to manipulate the situation or get a clearer idea of the individual's intent the woman might call out, "what do you want?" As Hewitt (1976, p. 47) states "this is the overt portion of the act - it is the external manifestation of a process that, until now, has gone on internally." That last component is consummation and it depends on the social response to an act (in this case, the question). If the man responds that he just wanted to return the woman's credit card which she had forgotten at the register and if the woman accepts the card graciously, then the sequence is complete and she may return to her day's activities. The significance of the interaction may result in a social object; namely, confidence in the store's personnel.

The third significant concept within symbolic interactionism is meaning. Every social act and object in an individual's environment has meaning. We are constantly interpreting the meanings of these symbols and responding accordingly. As Hewitt (1976, p. 48) states, ". . . meaning is anchored in behavior. The meaning of an act is neither fixed nor unchanging, but is determined in conduct as individuals act toward objects." Engaging in the interpretation of symbols is essential in the process of assigning meaning to both social acts and objects. Many times the interpretation is focused on the intent of a symbol or object. In the example used above, the woman interprets the man's intent throughout the interaction.

The fourth component of symbolic interactionism is the process of role-taking and role-making. This experience occurs when an individual views himself or herself from the standpoint of another. Lauer and Boardmann (1971) define role-taking as "the process whereby an individual imaginatively constructs the attitudes of the other and thus anticipates the behavior of the other" (as cited in Lauer & Handel, 1983, p. 104). As Hewitt (1976, p. 112) states, "role-taking is a process in which one person 'gets inside' the perspective of another in a particular situation and 'observes' his own conduct from the other's point of view." Only when people take on the role of another can they begin to see themselves as an object in their own social environment. In addition, this perspective provides them with the ability to see the various possibilities for their own actions. Included within this process is the idea of reference others or significant and generalized others. Mead described the generalized other as the collective embodiment of society's attitudes, viewpoints, and expectations (Schaefer, 2000). As Jenkins (1996:21) points out "Mead further insisted that self-consciousness, indeed

Validation can then be understood as a means by which to strengthen one's sense of identity. An example of identity validation and the influence of a situational factor occurs when an individual with racist beliefs becomes involved in a Ku Klux Klan ritual, such as a cross lighting, or a political mobilization, such as a rally. The person's involvement in the activity not only affirms his or her racist beliefs but also validates the individual's identity as a white supremacist and as a member of the larger white supremacist movement (Arena & Arrigo, 2000). Furthermore, those who commit to an identity validated through social interaction are expected to live up to certain expectations.

In sum, then, identity is our understanding of who we are and of who others are, and reciprocally, other people's understanding of themselves and of others (including ourselves). It is the answer to the question: "Who am I?" However, from a symbolic interactionist perspective, there is no one answer that remains true throughout the human life span. The formation of new identities and the maintenance of old identities continually rely upon the influence of symbols and objects, acts and social acts, meaning, role-taking and role-making, and the emergence of the self; hence, one's search for identity is considered a life-long process.

TERRORISM RESEARCH AND A BRIEF OVERVIEW OF THREE TERRORIST ORGANIZATIONS

Before any endeavor of this nature can move forward, it is important to operationally define what is meant by the term terrorism. To those unfamiliar with the extant literature addressing this topic, the definition of terrorism has attracted intense debate over the past several years (e.g. Barkan & Snowden, 2001; Hoffman, 1998; Laqueur, 1999; Kushner, 1998b; Martin, 2003; Tucker, 2000; White, 1998). In an effort to move past this discussion and into the conceptual understanding of identity as it relates to terrorist behavior, we have elected to utilize the definition offered by Harvey Kushner (1998b).[5] He describes terrorism as "the use of force (or violence) committed by individuals or groups against governments or civilian populations to create fear in order to bring about political (or social) change" (Kushner, 1988b: 10). Finally, in order to gain some insight into the socio-economic, political, and religious backgrounds of the three terrorist organizations subsequently discussed, we provide a brief synopsis on them.

Provisional Irish Republican Army (PIRA)

The conflict, or what is euphemistically termed the "troubles" in Ireland, can be traced back hundreds of years to the country's beginnings. Because an adequate coverage of the topic requires more space than is allotted within this article, a brief summary has been provided.[6] Ireland's sectarian division began when the Irish were introduced to Christianity around 500 A.D., after which the Irish became devoted followers (White, 1998). By 1172, the country had been invaded and under the control of the Norman King of England. Religious differences and territorial disputes gave birth to armed conflict. Following the Protestant Reformation of the 1500s, King Henry the VIII attempted to implement a church similar to that of the Church of England. The Catholics vehemently denied this conversion and soon the conflict was not just about religion but also about independence. This conflict over both nationalism and separatism continues on into the 21st century.

By the late 1800s, a group of Irish immigrants calling themselves the Irish Republican Brotherhood (IRB) was formed in New York City in an effort to provide economic relief to their friends and family still living in Ireland (Costigan, 1980). Eventually, the group became a financial supporter for revolution. In the aftermath of the 1916 Easter Rebellion, IRB leader Patrick Pearse drafted a letter outlining his terms of surrender. He signed the letter, the Irish Republican Army, and the IRB had officially transformed itself into a fighting force (Bell, 1997). The years following the surrender in Dublin saw the IRA unleash a violent campaign of terrorism. In 1921, a treaty was ratified that granted southern Ireland independence while retaining Northern Ireland under English protection.

The ratification of the treaty resulted in the emergence of divergent opinions within the IRA. Although many believed that independence should be extended to all Irish including the northerners, the means by which to pursue a unified Ireland differed. Some members believed that with the establishment of a political voice their interests were better served through peaceful means specifically through the political party known as Sinn Féin. While more moderate members wanted to maintain the existence of the IRA as an auxiliary force, others wanted to continue their active role in the armed resistance and splintered from the group. With significantly depleted numbers, the IRA continued its struggle until 1962 when the group declared that due to a lack of interest it could no longer continue the armed struggle to end Britain's control over Northern Ireland. In 1969, following the government of Northern Ireland's rather heavy handed response to the fighting that erupted over the civil rights movement and Protestant demonstrations (i.e. the Apprentice Boy Parade), the Provisional Irish Republican Army (PIRA) or "Provos" was developed from a Republican "old guard" that refused to go away after 1962 (White, 1993:28). Under the banner of the Republican movement, PIRA and Sinn Féin have tirelessly worked toward ending British rule over the north and unifying Ireland (Horgan & Taylor, 1997; Taylor, 1997; U.S. Department of State, 2003; White, 1993).

From 1969 until its acceptance of a ceasefire in 1997, the Provisional Irish Republican Army waged a campaign of urban and rural terrorism against British forces operating in the Irish Republic, Great Britain, mainland western Europe, the Middle East, Africa, and the United States (Horgan & Taylor, 1997). As Horgan and Taylor (1997: 2) indicate,

> The PIRA's *modus operandi* has incorporated bombings, shooting attacks, beatings, high-profile assassinations, and kidnappings. The movement has been extensively involved in extortion and armed robberies, and has a sophisticated financial network not unlike that of any large business. PIRA targets have included members of the security forces in Northern Ireland [i.e. the British Army, the Royal Ulster Constabulary (RUC) - the Ulster police force, the Ulster Defense Regiment (UDR) and Royal Irish Regiment (RIR)] as well as government and private-sector individuals, including senior British government officials and British military targets in the mainland United Kingdom and in western Europe.

PIRA targets have also included innocent civilians in Ireland and abroad, and also members of the security forces in the Republic of Ireland. The organization's militancy has, furthermore, been directed against Northern Irish Protestant paramilitary movements, in the main, groups reactive to the Provisionals' terrorist campaign.

Furthermore, although in its earlier years the group's attacks tended to be fairly indiscriminate, the recognition of Sinn Féin (to which PIRA is aligned) as a viable representative of the Republican electorate did cause the group to become more discriminate in its use of violence.

While the 1997 ceasefire has provided a fragile peace in Northern Ireland, the Good Friday Agreement has provided the best hope for an end to the "troubles." It has served as the backdrop for the creation of a 108-member Assembly and 14-member executive body consisting of both Catholic and Protestant representatives, a scaling back of the British military presence, and the PIRA's decision to begin decommissioning its weapons.[7] Although the island's divisional conflicts still result in sporadic acts of violence, the governments of the Republic of Ireland, Northern Ireland, and Great Britain continue to work toward a peaceful resolution.

Hamas

The Palestinian Covenant of the Islamic Resistance Movement, better known as Hamas, was founded on December 14, 1987 (Mishal & Sela, 2000; O'Ballance, 1997). The word Hamas literally translates to "zeal" or "enthusiasm." However, the group is actually an outgrowth of the Muslim Brotherhood which finds its roots in Egypt, around 1925 (White, 1998). Unhappy with the current status of territorial lines established following World War I, the Brotherhood called for a unified Arab realm under the religious tenets of Islam. During the 1980s when Yasir Arafat and the Palestinian Liberation Organization (PLO) began working toward Palestinian Statehood and self-governance, members of the Brotherhood were outraged. Many within the group believed that any compromise or agreement with Israel served only to recognize Israel as a legitimate entity. Furthermore, such action was perceived as a betrayal of Islam and the Arab people. The group was founded by Ahmad Yasin who is still the spiritual leader of the group (Hroub, 2000; Mishal & Sela, 2000). It was created in direct opposition to the PLO and as an alternative for stone-throwing youths. Those members who believed that circumstances called for a more active militant response, formed the group known as Hamas, following the outbreak of the Intifada[8] in December of 1987 (Hroub, 2000; Nüsse, 1998). As O'Ballance notes (1997:167), "its ultimate aim was the destruction of the state of Israel and the formation of an Islamic Fundamentalist Palestine state" and, if necessary, the demise of all those who chose to support its existence (i.e., the West). For Hamas "the only acceptable outcome . . . is the united realm of Islam" (White, 1998:132).

The membership of Hamas consists of Sunni Palestinians with militant Islamic Fundamentalist beliefs (Emerson, 2002). In order to understand the belief systems at play within this group, these designations need to be systematically examined. Within the Islamic religion there are two sects, Shiaism and Sunni. The members of Hamas are Sunnis who follow an Orthodox interpretation of the Islamic religion. They are also Palestinians. Palestinians can be described as the group of people displaced following the Zionist movement to establish the Jewish state of Israel. Finally, they are Islamic Fundamentalists or Islamists. Author Robin Wright (2000:36) offers some insightful remarks regarding the use of the name Islamic Fundamentalist and what it means.

> "Fundamentalism" is in many ways a misnomer in describing Islamic activism. The term was actually first used in the West to describe a movement among Protestant Christians at the turn of the century. It referred to people who adhered to the literal reading of Scriptures and were passive in accepting their lot in life. They did not seek to change the status quo. In contrast, many of today's Islamic movements are more like Catholicism's Liberation Theology. Many urge active use of religious doctrine to improve the social and political order of temporal existence—usually including greater participation in a country's political and economic life.

In addition, Wright (2000) points out that Iranian writer and philosopher, Abdul Karim Soroush defines a Fundamentalist as "one who uses religion as a form of identity rather than as a set of truths" (as cited in Wright, 2000:37). These individuals are to be separated from those who are "true believers."

In a sense, the fundamentalist and militant fundamentalist views were unleashed following the Iranian Revolution (Emerson, 1998; Kepel, 2002; O'Ballance, 1997). This approach was validated and affirmed when it was largely accepted by the Iranian people. As Kelly (1998:34) explains, "[i]n its [Fundamentalist] latest form, however, it attempts to impose a militant version of the 'straight path,' the way enjoined by the Prophet Muhammad, according to some Muslim intellectuals and political radicals." Militant Islamic Fundamentalists justify the use of violence through religion in a fashion similar to those of the Christian Identity faith who justify hate crimes (Arena & Arrigo, 2000). As Emerson (1998) observes, a religious extremist differs only in the religion he or she invokes to commit a crime.

Hamas' membership is organized into four divisions; administration, charity, politics, and military affairs (Hroub, 2000; Nüsse, 1998). During its initial stages, Hamas worked to disseminate anti-Israel propaganda and provided social and economic support to Palestinians in the occupied territories (O'Ballance, 1997). However, Hamas soon earned a particularly violent reputation for engaging in brutal stabbing attacks and for mutilating their victims in Israel, the Gaza Strip, and the West Bank (Emerson, 1998). Although the group's short-term goal is to disrupt the peace process, its long-term goal is to unite the Arab countries under Islam.

According to the U.S. Department of State (2003), members of Hamas's military wing have engaged in terrorist activity in Israel, the West Bank, and the Gaza Strip. They have been responsible for numerous acts of violence including shootings, stabbings, car-bombings, and suicide bombings. To date, however, no U.S. interests have been targeted directly by Hamas activities; although, several U.S. citizens have been killed in the course of their attacks (Katzman, 2002).[9] In June 2003, Hamas reportedly committed to a ceasefire with Israel, however, they have since renewed their violent campaign (Anderson & Moore, 2003). The 53-day relative calm resulting from the truce to establish a nationalist-socialist government focused on agrarian reform, modernization, and equal income distribution. The third component was their commitment to these actions and to strategy. Their objectives were to be achieved by any means available to them. For the Tupamaros, this meant the use of violence, propaganda, and efforts to mobilize the masses.

By 1970, the group had over 3,000 members (Porzecanski, 1973) and the Tupamaros were waging a large-scale campaign of urban terrorism. In examining 336 Tupamaros captured during 1966 and 1972, one-third were professional or technicians, another third were workers or employees, and 30% were students (Porzecanski, 1973). As White (1998: 71) points out "Although they waged an effective campaign of terrorism, they were never able to capture the hearts of the working class. Most of Montevideo's workers viewed the Tupamaros as privileged students with no real interest in the working class." Eventually, the people of Montevideo felt as though they were living in a world of bombings, kidnappings, assaults, bank robberies, murder, and mayhem. The government's response to Tupamaro activity was repression, and the primary tool of gathering intelligence from suspected collaborators was torture. Contrary to the Marighella philosophy, government repression did not serve to mobilize the masses. In fact, with the people's support, the right-wing government all but eliminated the Tupamaro threat by 1972. This notwithstanding, the legend of the Tupamaros endures. They are known as the masters of urban terrorism and their tactics and structure are still imitated by both right and left "wing terrorist groups around the world. As White (1998, p. 72) suggests ". . . the Tupamaros offer the best example of revolutionary terrorism in the world."

UNDERSTANDING IDENTITY AND THE TERRORIST THREAT

The preceding discussion outlined identity theory and the social and related dynamics surrounding three terrorist organizations. We now address the five interactionist concepts used to interpret the terrorist identity. To facilitate this analysis, Table 1.1 summarizes the relationship between the identity themes and the three terrorist organizations.

Identity and the Provisional Irish Republican Army

Symbols
The symbols of conflict in Ireland are numerous. One such example of the sectarian violence between Catholics and Protestants is the annual Apprentice Boy parade that takes place every August in Derry, Northern Ireland. White (1998:169) describes the history behind the commemoration:

> From 1689 to 1691, James II, the Catholic pretender to the British throne, used Ireland as a base from which to revolt against William of Orange, the English King. In August 1689, Irish Protestant skilled workers, called "Apprentice Boys," were relieved by the English

TABLE 1.1   Identity and the Terrorist Threat: Toward a Symbolic Interactionist Framework

Three International Terrorist Organizations		
PIRA	Hamas	Tupamaros
ELEMENTS		
Symbols		
Annual Apprentice Boy Parade	Symbols of the disenfranchised	Symbols of social stratification based on status and class
Acts & Social Acts		
Bloody Sunday & the Irish hunger strikes	Islamic Jihad & the post-mortem Identity	Intimidation and retaliation
Meaning		
Becoming involved	Islamic fundamentalism	Revolutionary justice
Role-Taking & Role-Making		
Publicity & Propaganda Campaigns	Abandoning the "all or nothing" strategy and the "helping hand"	Ideological modifications and appealing to the generalized other
Emergence of the Self		
Irish identity	Harakat al-Muqawama al-Islamiyya (aka) the Islamic Resistance Movement	The "Robin Hood" personna & changing the name from the National Liberation Movement to the Tupamaros

after defending Derry through a long siege by the pretender. The following year William defeated James at the battle of the Boyne River. . . .

The Protestants have flaunted these victories in the face of the Catholics since 1690. Each year they gather to militantly celebrate the battle of the Boyne and the Apprentice Boys with parades and demonstrations. It fuels the fire of hatred in Northern Ireland and demonstrates the division between Protestants and Catholics (White,1998:169).

The current troubles in Ireland are actually a result of the especially violent fighting which erupted following the August 15, 1969 parade, more specifically the Battle of Bogside. In an effort to quell the violence, the Northern Ireland government responded by deploying the Royal Ulster Constabulary (RUC) and eventually detachments from the British Army (White, 1998). Although sporadic violence had erupted prior to the parade, as Taylor (1997) points out, this flashpoint in particular proved to be an initiation for many young people who would later become active members of the Republican Movement. Tony Miller who was 15 at the time of the event and who would later become an active volunteer of the IRA, stated that:

I was throwing stones, gasoline bombs, bottles, everything. You name it. I remember having a serious hatred for the RUC at the time and just wanting to sort of take revenge because you saw people getting battered and choked with tear gas. I was on top of Rossville Flats with a full view of everything that was going on. There were hundreds of people below and you had a perfect view. On top of the apartments was a thing constructed by the Bogside people at the time. It was like a huge catapult. We could put the gasoline bombs on it and shoot the gasoline right onto the spot where the RUC were actually congregating. It was made out of scaffolding and a tire inner tube that people put the gasoline bombs on. We'd pull the tube back and launch the gasoline bombs. It was a powerful feeling, like you were fighting an armed force. That was my first contact with the RUC. (Taylor, 1997: 64-65)

A symbolic interactionist analysis brings to light the symbols the individuals, specifically the Irish Catholics, responded to with such rage, especially as they influenced their identities as Republican activists. The most salient of these are the concrete objects, such as the colorful orange sashes worn by the parade participants and the banners and flags carried through the streets. The RUC were viewed as Protestant collaborators because just days earlier they had attacked Catholic civil rights demonstrators. Their deployment to the event symbolized an oppressive government's continued attempt to further subjugate the Irish Catholics. All of these symbols contributed to the shared sense of oppression, injustice and hatred which sparked participants' decision to create within themselves a terrorist identity.

Acts and Social Acts

Two events or acts are of particular interest to the study of identity within the members of the PIRA: the Bloody Sunday massacre and the Irish Hunger Strikes. The Bloody Sunday Massacre took place on January 30, 1972 when a group of British paratroopers of the First Battalion, Parachute regiment fired upon an unarmed civil rights processional in Derry, Northern Ireland (Taylor, 1997; Coogan, 1994). The shooting took less than 30 minutes and, in the end, the troopers shot and killed 13 parade marchers (Taylor, 1997). The Nationalist community perceived this to be a terrible injustice. As Taylor (1997, p. 137) explains it:

> The only explanation that makes sense to them, and there remain few voices to the contrary, is that there were orders from on-high to teach the rebels of "Free Derry" a lesson they would never forget. This lesson, as the evidence of their eyes told them, was to send a good number of the marchers back home in boxes.

Following a government inquiry into the shootings, the paratroopers were exonerated of all wrongdoings, claiming that they had been fired upon first and that they had returned fire in fear of their lives (Coogan 1994). However, as Taylor (1997) points out, it is important not to view this event in isolation. As previously stated, Hewitt (1976) notes that the perception of an act is strongly influenced by the organism's condition and situational factors.

The conditions prior to the Bloody Sunday massacre were by no means jovial. Although the British troops were met with warmth after landing in Ireland in 1969, their presence eventually came to be recognized as being a pro-Protestant force that was there to assist the Royal Ulster Constabulary. Republicans perceived the British forces' military deployments as being increasingly hostile and oppressive. As Taylor (1997:137) observes,

> For many months, there had been endless rioting in the city. Every day at tea time, there would be a confrontation at the corner of William Street and Rossville Street between soldiers guarding the entrance to the city center and the rioters operating out of "Free Derry." Day after day soldiers would stand there being pelted by rioters and the stone throwers would get in plenty of practice.

The consummation of the act resulted in an increased sense of injustice which resulted in additional protest and uprisings.

Another act which had a powerful influence on the identities of Provisional Irish Republican Army members was the Irish Hunger Strikes. The strikes took place between 1976 and 1981. As White (1993:108) commented, "When the war started in 1969, political status for IRA prisoners, won during earlier IRA campaigns, was rejected by the authorities." The Republican leadership had agreed that if any of them were arrested they would go on hunger strike in an effort to demand political status as a prisoner of war.

On May 15, 1972, Billy McKee, an IRA leader, who was incarcerated in a northern prison began the first of several hunger strikes to achieve political status. Obtaining the designation of a war prisoner not only entitled IRA members to special treatment but it also served to validate their identities as political activists. To those in the IRA, this classification indicated that they were indeed a bona fide fighting force at war with the government of Northern Ireland and, hence, Great Britain. Following vigils and pickets in support of the strikers, the northern government finally gave in to their demands, granting paramilitary activity political status.

Meanwhile, in the south, similar hunger strikes had begun in an effort to seek comparable recognition; however, political status had yet to be granted. On March 1, 1976, the government of Northern Ireland rescinded its policy of granting "special treatment" to those who were incarcerated for paramilitary activity. By 1975, over 1,100 prisoners in Northern Ireland had "special category status." In an effort to put an end to such treatment, the government of Northern Ireland decided that beginning on March 1, 1976, it would revoke its policy of granting political status to those incarcerated for paramilitary offenses (this included both Republicans and Loyalists). Once again, hunger strikes swept the Republican prison population. Eventually, the strikes were ended but not before the strikers could reach the hearts of the Republican community. After receiving considerable media attention, news of the strikers' horrendous treatment began to spread. Although the series of strikes concluded without substantive success, they did prove to be an effective tool in winning the public support and sympathies of the Republican community in both northern and southern Ireland.

Meaning

The impact of the Bloody Sunday massacre and the Irish Hunger strikes on the Republican movement can be observed in terms of meaning. More specifically, the way in which people interpreted the meaning of the acts and responded to that meaning was crucial to their decision to become involved in the PIRA. Indeed, as White (1993, p. 106) notes, "The concern or 'rage' experienced by Southern Irish people after events such as this is a product of national identity, and identity that emotionally, if not physically, links Southern Irish people to Northern Irish people." In essence, the two events became an impetus for individuals to activate their Irish identities, the sense of similarity between Southern and Northern Irish people, and subsequently as an incentive to become involved in the armed struggle to aid their oppressed brothers and sisters. Moreover, as White (1993:107) explains,

> The potential for recruiting Southern Republicans is at its greatest when the social processes described above [examples of state violence against Irish] - an Irish identity heightened by anti-Irish violence in the North and social connections with Republicans - work in combination. During the Provisional Irish Republican era, this has occurred twice: between August 1969 and Bloody Sunday in 1972, and in 1980-1981, when Republican prisoners in Northern Jails went on hunger strikes for political status.

In regard to recruitment efforts, Taylor (1997:152) states that "'Bloody Sunday' had given the Provisional IRA the biggest boost in its history." With respect to the Hunger Strikes, White (1993) suggests that through their involvement in marches and rallies, southern Irish people were brought into direct contact with the Republican Movement. This contact served as the interaction necessary to become involved in the movement.

Although both White (1993) and Taylor (1997) indicate that the two events did result in increased recruitment numbers and support for the PIRA, an in-depth examination of interview data reveals that the events alone should not be understood as the reason for heightened involvement in the Republican movement. Instead, the meaning the events symbolized for the people was the basis for their participation. More specifically, Bloody Sunday and the Hunger Strikes exemplified the injustices perpetrated against the Irish people. As White (1993:90) noted,

> . . . events are important, but the injustice and grievances associated with specific events do not motivate involvement in Republican politics. The state violence is symptomatic of fundamental political problems that plague Northern Ireland and stem, ultimately, from British involvement in Ireland. People turn to the Republican Movement when they realize that the social, political, and economic systems of Northern Ireland are unjust *and* when they realize that these systems are the direct product of British political policies that are designed to keep Irish people acquiescent.

White's conclusion is supported by a statement made by a man who became involved in the PIRA, following Bloody Sunday, and his subsequent interactions with other people who experienced the same sense of repression.

> [Bloody Sunday] didn't change my attitude and in particular it wasn't an emotional response that, "I hate the Brits and it's about time I did something," you know? It was just

that I'd always been concerned, I'd always been motivated towards things Irish and it was just another—it was just another act of political vandalism on Irish people. . . .

As soon as civil rights started, things started to fall together for me. All the little bits of information and facts of evidence that I had picked up, from whatever source. Be it just casual comments from people around me, just watching people's attitudes. And then going to school through the working-class, the Bogside ghetto, area. From my friends not having things. Just observation. When civil rights began, it all began to gel for me and build up towards some main picture. And the picture was that, my gut feeling and the way I had been brought up to respect other people's rights wasn't being done by the state. And therefore all the stories and mythologies and all the rest of it had to have some foundation. And so I started talking to more people and reading more about it. . . . The Republican Movement, it may have historical background, yes, but essentially it got off the ground because it came out of the community [in Derry], and it was a community that accepted it because it was its own people. And therefore I suppose you could say that it was my contemporaries that, if anybody influenced, would have influenced me to join (White, 1993: 92-93).

This interview and others like them led White (1993:90) to argue that, "IRA involvement does not result from 'injustice' but from an understanding of the *political structure* that permits and sustains the subjugation that Northern Irish Nationalists experience." In line with a symbolic interactionist perspective, it is to the meaning of the event(s) that individuals respond not the event in and of itself. Furthermore, as White (1993:127) concluded,

As their national identity, their sense of Irishness, is aroused, Southern Irish people examine the existence of Northern Ireland and their own place in the Irish nation. This prompts involvement in activities like marches and rallies. These bring them into contact with active Republicans. Personal connections draw them into the Republican Movement.

Role-Taking and Role-Making

The fourth concept influencing and maintaining the identities of members of the PIRA is role-taking. Within this concept, one can examine the image members project of themselves and the creation of that image through the utilization of role-taking. In her autobiography entitled *To Take Arms* (1973), author Maria McGuire discusses her involvement in the PIRA as the organization's publicity officer. The following is her description of the strategy the group used to solicit contributions from Irish Catholics living in the United States.

Like the Officials, we were quite ready to play for all they were worth the new Republican myths that were being created out of the current campaign. And nowhere was it easier to capitalize on them than in the United States, where whole communities of Irish-Americans were watching the struggle in the Six Counties like spectators at a morality play, with right and wrong, good and evil, delineated in black and white. It was in the United States that our main fund-raising efforts were conducted, and the visiting speakers, who included Ruairi and John Kelly, the Dublin arms-trial man, were carefully briefed as to how the audience should be played. There should be copious references to the martyrs of 1916 and 1920-1922, the period most of the audience would be living in. Anti-British sentiment, recalling Cromwell, the potato famine, and the Black and Tans, could be profitably exploited. By no means should anything be said against the Catholic Church. And all references to socialism should be strictly avoided; tell them by all means that the Ireland we were fighting for would be free and united, but say nothing about just what form the new free and united Ireland would take. (McGuire, 1973:119)

Only when the PIRA representatives took on the role of the American people could they develop an effective strategy for how best to solicit contributions. Indeed, once they observed their own behavior through the eyes of Irish-Americans, PIRA operatives realized that mentioning socialism or speaking ill of the Catholic church would drive off any potential support from the Americans.

Another tactic frequently utilized by the PIRA in an effort to gain public support is propaganda. It is frequently defined as "the spreading of ideas or information to further or damage a cause" (Mish, 1997, p. 588). The purpose of propaganda is to convince, to win over, and/or to convert individuals to similar modes of thinking (Taithe & Thornton, 1999). Wright (1991) divides the PIRA's target audience into three categories: the uncommitted, the sympathetic, and the active. Each group requires a distinct strategy in order to persuade it or to maintain its organizational loyalty. In order to devise effective propaganda campaigns, one must take on the perspective of the other and consider the appeal to the generalized other. Subsequently, this process serves to reaffirm the group's own favored ways of thinking and, hence, members' own identities.

Emergence of the Self

The last concept influencing the formation and maintenance of identity in the members of the Provisional Irish Republican Army is the emergence of the self. As all four of these concepts begin to integrate with one another, the product is the creation of a self, followed by an identity. The individual's perception of her or his own self-worth, self-esteem, and self-concept all begin to stem from individual participation, inclusion and/or affiliation with the group and the Republican Movement as a whole. For those who felt a sense of Irish identity through their interactions with other activists during rallies, riots, or protests, they experienced their typified self. As they became more active in the movement, the typified self consumed more of their sense of identity, eventually becoming an integral part of their self-concept, self-worth, and self-definition. The final step in realizing the terrorist identity is the naming of oneself. Whether named political activists, soldiers, or patriots, individuals began to see their selves and their identities as social objects.

Identity and the Hamas

Symbols

Hamas or the Islamic Resistance Movement finds its primary support and membership among Palestinians living in the West Bank, Gaza Strip, and East Jerusalem. Therefore, it is reasonable to assume that many of the symbols and objects which influence the Palestinian identity are similar to those that shape the identity of members of Hamas. In his examination of the history and "reemergence" of the Palestinian identity, author Rashid Khalidi (1997:1) states,

The quintessential Palestinian experience, which illustrates some of the most basic issues raised by Palestinian identity, takes place at a border, an airport, a checkpoint: in short, at any one of those many modern barriers where identities are checked and verified. What happens to Palestinians at these crossing points brings home to them how much they share in common as a people. For it is at these borders and barriers that the six million Palestinians are singled out for "special treatment," and are forcefully reminded of their identity: of who they are, and of why they are different from others.

As illustrated by Khalidi, the tangible symbols which remind Palestinians of their marginalized identities are numerous. The objects of the Israeli power structure take the form of borders, airport checkpoints, and the security agents who ask that Palestinians step out of line and follow them to a special room for interrogation and searches. These objects can also take a more subtle form like refugee camps and deteriorating school buildings. These symbols serve as constant reminders to Palestinians that their status is that of a disenfranchised group, singled out for "special treatment."

In an examination of the conflicting collective identities between Israelis and Arabs living within an Israeli state, Nadim Rouhana (1997) describes the forces that shape the collective identity of Arabs in Israel. These forces are organized into three elements: (1) regional developments; (2) Israel's laws, structure and politics, and (3) changes within the group. Each of these elements are further divided into categories which could all be viewed as abstract symbols or symbolically constructed social objects. For example, within the category of regional developments, Rouhana mentions Arab Nationalism, Palestinian revival, Islamic revolution, and the Middle East peace process. The category of laws, structure and politics addresses the current state of affairs in Israel, the state of the Jewish people, the country's democratic procedures, security measures, and its inclusion or exclusion of Arab citizens. The third category refers to changes within the group, including demography, socio-economics, education, political culture, and religion.

Under closer examination, each of these symbolic representations have a powerful influence on the members of Hamas's felt sense of identity. For instance, with the support of the Israeli government and training from the Central Intelligence Agency, the Palestinian National Authority (PNA) began a fervent campaign to arrest and charge members of Hamas for their violent attacks during the late 1990s (Derfner & Toameh, 2000). This can be interpreted as a symbol of betrayal to Hamas members who feel a shared sense of identity with all Palestinians and could continue to be viewed as such if the PNA was to mount another disarmament campaign.

Although Rouhana (1997) draws a distinction between collective and individual or personal identity, he does state that "the collective identity of the group is intertwined with an individual's personal identity as group membership reflects on the individual's self-value. . . . [I]t is important to indicate that once an individual internalizes a collective identity, group membership becomes a part of self-concept, the core of the individual's identity" (Rouhana,11997:17). As such those symbols listed as forces establishing a collective identity for Arabs living within an Israeli state invariably would have an influence on one's overall sense of identity including one's individual and collective identity.

Acts and Social Acts

Acts and social acts are the second concept within symbolic interactionism that shape the formation of identity in members of Hamas. One of the most salient acts which Hamas members engage in is violence (Hroub, 2000; Kepel, 2002; Nüsse, 1998). For Islamic groups like Hamas, the act of violence is a valuable and powerful component in the struggle for Palestinian freedom (Berman, 2003). The act of violence serves to both express disdain for the current status quo and enhances the group's sense of cohesiveness and the movement's solidarity. Hamas has used a variety of violent acts such as murder, kidnapping, car bombings, beatings, and suicide bombings in an effort to achieve its goals. Chief among them is to disrupt the peace process. However, Hamas's use of violence has not just been physical in nature. They also have employed verbal and written intimidation and propaganda to persuade both their fellow Palestinians and Israeli enemies in an effort to impose compliance with their wishes. In addition, Hamas has used a variety of non-violent forms of protest such as road blocks, throwing stones, writing slogans and directives on walls, strikes, civil disobedience, and staging sit-ins by students and teachers.

There are a variety of ways by which to interpret Israeli-Palestinian violence. For Israeli citizens, the violence represents an attack on their freedom, livelihood, and security. For the Palestinians, these acts of violence symbolize disobedience or empowerment. However, to the religious zealots of Hamas, these displays of violence are acts of faith. Most often, these acts of violence and protest are committed in the hope of starting a holy war between the Islamic people and the Israeli state. The Hamas believe that this war will not only bring about the establishment of a Palestinian state but the resurrection of an Islamic government in the region. Islamic jihad can be understood as both a social act and a social object because as people engage in smaller acts of violence, individuals interpret these acts as leading to a large-scale holy war. One such action which symbolically transforms itself from an act of violence into an act of faith is the suicide bomber.

During the decade of 1990s and with the birth of the 21st century, Hamas has made significant use of the suicide attack. The Palestinian Islamists learned the effectiveness of the suicide attack and the construction of car bombs from the Iranian-backed Lebanese Hezbollah (party of God) (Kushner, 1998b; Mishal & Sela, 2000; O'Ballance, 1997).[10] As Kushner (1998b, p. 33) describes, "suicide bombers leave for their missions directly from their mosques, after completing many days of chanting the relevant scriptures aloud with their spiritual handlers. A favorite verse reads: 'Think not of those who are slain in Allah's way as dead. No, they live on and find sustenance in the presence of their Lord.'" Mishal and Sela (2000, 66) state that ". . . Hamas and the [Palestinian] Islamic Jihad adopted the same procedure of finding a candidate for a suicide operation, training and preparing him psychologically, writing a farewell letter, and making a videotape before his mission".[11] Kushner (1998b) explains how the act of suicide is understood to be one of religious devotion:

Karbala [a historical reference to the act of self-sacrifice] is not an act of suicide; Islam forbids the taking of one's own life. Rather, it symbolizes the supreme willingness to submit to the will of Allah with the understanding that rewards will come after death. Islam emphasizes that life on earth is merely a transition to a better life. A suicide bomber is making a transition that will put him or her alongside the other heroes of Islam and next to Allah. (Kushner, 1998b: 24)

To the Islamist, the act of giving one's life to the cause is not death but simply adopting a new identity. Through this series of rituals, members of Hamas essentially create for themselves a postmortem identity (PMI). Weigert et al. (1986:110) states that, the "postmortem identity is used as a technical term for describing the social essence of the self after death." In essence, the PMI is the self situated in death. Lifton (1976, 1979) describes symbolic immortality as a way in which individuals can shape their re-membered identities so that they have a lasting influence on their biological acquain-tances, history, the immediate past, the present, and the future. Lifton describes two modes by which to achieve this sense of immortality relevant to the suicide bomber. The first is the "theological mode" understood as the belief that death will release the individual from a profane life giving way to a spiritual plane of existence (Weigert et al., 1986). The second is the "creative mode" realized through personal achievement and contri-butions that endure through future generations. As Weigert et al. (1986) suggest, the com-bination of these two modes, termed the "ritualization mode," is best suited to describe the socially constructed immortal identity suicide bombers hope to achieve. The immortal identity of past suicide bombers continues to touch the lives of future bombers in the form of song, prayer, social movements, and symbols of their martyrdom.

Meaning

Meaning is the third influential concept of symbolic interactionism and its relevance to the creation of identity in members of Hamas can be found in religion. In compar-ison to groups like the PLO, ". . . Hamas claims uniqueness because in addition to ma-terial, human, or territorial sources, it is also linked to divinity and faith" (Mishal & Sela, 2000:44). The PLO's charter was created through the use of national, civil, and legal terms. However,

> By contrast, Hamas's charter is anchored in religious principles of holiness, divinity, and eternity, with no option for amendment. Moreover, it has the characteristics of a com-prehensive cultural, social, and moral character, encompassing issues such as the role and status of women in society and the national struggle, the importance of educating the younger generation in regard to religious values, and the roles of culture, literature, and art and their contribution to the liberation campaign. The charter also speaks of so-cial and economic solidarity, support for the poor and needy, human rights in an Islamic society, and the correct attitude toward members of the other monotheistic religions. (Mishal & Sela, 2000:45)

The influence of religion permeates every aspect of a member's day-to-day life. Religion gives members a sense of self-worth and self-importance by teaching them that they are special to Allah and the movement. Not only does this meaning provide the rationale for behavior, it legitimizes the use of violence.

Religion also provides meaning for the member's advocacy and use of violence (Kepel, 2002; Berman, 2003). Hamas believes that a Palestinian state will only be achieved through holy war (jihad). The infusion of these two concepts—securing the territory for a Palestinian state and the armed struggle of holy war—is represented in the Hamas slogan: "To raise the banner of Allah over every inch of Palestine" (Mishal & Sela, 2000:42). In addition, Hamas maintains that this conflict will bring about the resurrection of an Islamic world (Emerson, 2002). As Mishal and Sela (2000) point out, Hamas regards Palestine as an Islamic problem; therefore, it is the responsibility of the Palestinian people, the Arab nations, and the Islamic world. Freeing Palestine and resurrecting an Islamic nation represents the duty of all Muslims.

Role-Taking and Role-Making

The concepts of role-taking and role-making also can be observed in the creation of an identity in individual Hamas members and as a collective group. For example, the concept of role-taking helps shed light on why Hamas chose to modify its once inflexible strategy to a situationally-dependent one. As Mishal and Sela (2000:7) indicate, Hamas has ". . . moved away from dogmatic positions in a quest for innovative and pliable modes of conduct, the opposite of doctrinaire rigidity, ready to respond or adjust to fluid conditions without losing sight of their ultimate objectives." This modification could be understood as stemming from Hamas's ability, to adopt the various roles of those in their environment and adapt their behavior accordingly. For instance, by adopting the role of the Islamic government, the poor Palestinians living in refugee camps, and the Palestinian National Authority, Hamas has been able to see their own conduct from the viewpoint of others.[12] The influence of the role-taking concept on the formation of identity is illustrated by Mishal and Sela (2000:9). As they explain it,

> [Hamas and Islamic movements with similar ideologies] took care not to depict their social and political reality as a cluster of mutually exclusive, diametrically opposed categories, characterized by "either-or" relations. And they refrained from portraying themselves in terms of fixed identities, distinct boundaries, and stable, well-established preferences. In short, they recognized the limits beyond which they could not go in pursuing an "all or nothing" policy to advance their ultimate political goals.

The ability to adjust to a changing political and social climate has enabled Hamas to attract and maintain public support, gain compliance among its rank and file, and act as a power broker for the Palestinian people (Mishal & Sela, 2000).

Another example of role-taking and role-making at work is Hamas's image as a servant of Islam. Hamas has created this image through the adoption of two roles. The fist is by taking on the role of providing charity through the Islamic practice of helping the poor called *zakat*. This is accomplished through community service programs like education, welfare, and health services. Regardless of whether this role was or was not adopted for purely altruistic reasons, it has served to win the hearts of the Palestinian people which in turn has expanded their public support among the needy. In a second role, Hamas extended its service beyond the Palestinian conflict by becoming a servant of Islam. While the Palestinian Liberation Organization (PLO) settles for the concession of territory to be turned into a Palestinian state, Hamas continues to strive for a unified Islamic nation which is rid of the Israeli presence. As Mishal and Sela (2000:ix) note:

> Hamas will be able to continue mobilizing wide popular support and to maintain its public image as a standard bearer of Palestinian national values. And as long as Yasir Arafat and the Palestinian Authority fail to translate Israeli-Palestinian peace negotiations into tangible territorial achievements and economic benefits, Hamas will continue playing its role as the guardian of Islam and the champion of authentic Palestinian aspirations.

By taking on the role of the generalized other (in its variety of forms) Hamas has been able to adapt its strategies and create an image which maximizes its appeal among the Palestinian and the Islamic people.

Emergence of the Self

The emergence of the self is the fifth force influencing the identity of members of Hamas. The emergence of the Hamas identity can be traced back to the emergence of the collective identity of Muslim peoples. This finds its roots in the early days of the Intifada. As Mishal and Sela (2000:34-35) explain,

> The spontaneous riots that erupted on December 9, 1987, in the Jabalia refugee camp in Gaza and rapidly swelled into a popular uprising, soon to be called the Intifada, understood both the power of the ethos of armed struggle against Israel and the social and political conditions, which were ripe for its fulfillment in the occupied territories.

During this time, the Muslim Brotherhood faced pressure from its younger more militant members to "adopt an actively combatant posture, consistent with the Palestinians' public mood and expectations" (p. 35). On December 14, 1987, the leaders of the brotherhood granted their request by adopting a "*jihad* now" policy and by creating a military wing to the brotherhood known as the Islamic Resistence Movement. Eventually adopting the name Hamas (an acronym for Harakat al-Muqawama al-Islamiyya) which translates to "zeal" or "enthusiasm," the group established a new role for itself; namely, the combatant wing of the Muslim Brotherhood. The group then soon began to manage its image as a servant of the people through its community service initiatives.

Identity and the Tupamaros

Symbols

The symbols that were pertinent to the formation and maintenance of the Tupamaro identity are observable in both concrete and abstract form. In the early stages of the country's declining economy, the working and middle classes felt the adverse effects of unemployment, inflation, and poverty. In line with a Marxist perspective, this agreed upon system of social stratification gave rise to resentment toward the bourgeoisie. As a social object, this system of stratification became a symbol for which the National Liberation Movement directed its voice. This voice captured a shared sense of oppression, exploitation, and marginalization among the disenfranchised. Everyday citizens were reminded of their secondary status through their contact with banks, factories, police installations, and the landowners who paid them their menial wages. The move-ment desired the socially constructed object of equality and liberation from the chains of the wealthy class. Indeed, Porzecanski (1973) speculated that Sendic's exclusion from the wealthier middle class was the motivation behind his efforts to organize the Tupamaros. As we previously explained, Sendic's more militant Marxist leanings helped galvanize Uruguayan workers in a protest against the government in 1963. However, Porzecanski believed that Sendic was attempting to improve his own social status by reorganizing the current economic system. This is an excellent example of how Sendic's sense of identity was contingent upon his perception of his own place in the stratifi-cation system and how he attempted to alter this identity as he acted toward it.

As the National Liberation Movement transformed itself into the more militant Tupamaro organization, the symbols of their disenfranchisement became the basis for their selection of targets of violence. Porzecanski (1973) describes three such targets. The first of these included physical symbols of capitalism such as factories, banks, and government establishments. The Tupamaros robbed banks, sabotaged public power fa-cilities, and set fire to factory buildings. The second target was the socially agreed upon object of the "oligarchy." The ruling elite included the landowners, industrialists, mer-chants, business leaders, professional politicians, government officials, those repre-sentatives of nations who exercised a neocolonial influence over Uruguay, and the wealthy in general. The Tupamaros moved against this group, referring to them as the "enemy," and engaged in acts of murder, bombings, and kidnapping (Porzecanski, 1973). The third target was the police and military who served as the primary enforcers of their marginalized identities and protected the interests of the ruling class. Violence was directed against anyone who wore a uniform and the installations which housed their activities.

Acts and Social Acts

The four components (impulse, perception, manipulation, and consummation) of the act are illustrated when examining the Tupamaros' attempts to intimidate the enemy, especially when they retaliated against the government's efforts to suppress their ac-tivities. The authorities' typical response was to use hard-line tactics such as intimi-dation, force, torture, and censorship. The Tupamaros' initial impulse might have been to respond by attacking police and military installations directly; however, they per-ceived the battle for power in Uruguay to be as much a psychological war as a physi-cal one. Thus, the Tupamaros manipulated their tactics and utilized both an "indirect" and "direct" approach. Porzecanski (1973:46) explained the difference between the two perspectives in the following way:

> Direct approach meant that the target of guerilla action was the "guilty" party itself; for instance, a police officer who was accused of being a torturer was shot dead. Indirect ap-proach meant that people related to the "guilty" party were punished precisely because of their association with someone accused of doing something wrong; for instance, the bodyguards of an army or police officer accused of doing his job "too well" were shot. In other words, the purpose of the indirect approach was to isolate specific government and military authorities from their friends, consultants, bodyguards and even relatives.

In addition to murder, the Tupamaros responded by kidnapping and throwing bombs into the homes of those citizens they believed were members of the oligarchy. Another frequently used tactic designed to publicly humiliate a police officer was to ". . . surround a policeman on the street and force him to give up his gun; or they would 'search' a policeman's home, frightening his family and taking with them his uniform, gun, and ammunition" (Porzecanski, 1973, p. 46). Clearly, this was a less violent, albeit powerful, tactic. The consummation of these acts committed by both the Tupamaros and the Uruguayan government resulted in a social object; namely, terror.

Meaning

The third component of the symbolic interactionist framework, influencing the formation of the Tupamaros identity was meaning. Although this concept can be examined in the symbols and social acts described above, it can be further interpreted through the Tupamaros' use of violence, or what they referred to as "revolutionary justice." Those who were active in the group rationalized their use of violence as a necessary means by which to achieve a desired end; equality among the people of Uruguay. For example the Tupamaros robbed banks to finance their revolutionary campaign and also returned the money stolen from the exploited masses. The justification of liberatory justice is conveyed in a statement released by the organization. In pertinent part, it read:

> We must make a clear distinction between what the bourgeoisie's property and the workers' property really is. The former is, beyond doubt, the outcome of workers' exploitation; the latter is the result of work and individual effort. Therefore, the bourgeoisie's property is our natural fountain of resources and we have the right to expropriate it without compensation. [Our] revolution puts to use the surplus of the privileged. (Porzecanski, 1973:41)

Thus, retaliation was considered a justified means in which alleged ill-treatment of arrested guerrillas prompted "revolutionary justice, such as the execution of selected police officers" (Porzecanski, 1973:21).

Every social act and object in an individual's environment has meaning. We are constantly interpreting the meanings of these symbols and responding accordingly. As Hewitt (1976:48) states, ". . . meaning is anchored in behavior. The meaning of an act is neither fixed nor unchanging, but is determined in conduct as individuals act toward objects." Engaging in the interpretation of symbols, then, is essential to the process of assigning meaning to both social acts and objects. Many times, the interpretation is focused on the intent of a symbol or object. In the example used above, the meaning assigned to revolutionary justice legitimized the use of violence.

Role-Taking and Role-Making

Role-making and role-taking is the fourth component of symbolic interactionism and it, too, could be observed in both the individual and collective identity of the Tupamaros. The idea of role-taking was exemplified in the Tupamaros' efforts to modify their political viewpoints, tactics and, subsequently, their social image, in an attempt to win the favor of the Uruguayan people. As previously stated, the Tupamaros represented an organization founded on Marxist theory. However, as White (1998:70) points out, "[r]ather than risk alienating the population with abstract Marxist rhetoric, they wanted to create an economy that would offer opportunities to Montevideo's working class. As they expanded, the Tupamaros constantly stressed that theirs was a working-class revolution, in an effort to attract a following" (White, 1998:70). The Tupamaros were well aware that if they bombarded the people of Uruguay with Marxist ideology it might have served to repel public support. Moreover, as White (1998:73) notes,

> Rather than accepting a standard line of Marxist dogma, the Tupamaros were willing to use national socialism as their political base; this demonstrated just how much they could compromise. According to one of their propaganda statements, they argued for a nationalized economy with guaranteed employment and social security. The export economy would remain intact, but profits would be shared among the people. Although this view hardly represents Marxism, the Tupamaros were willing to take such a stand to attract a working-class following. Socialism under national control was popular in Montevideo.

In addition to the modification of their political stance, the Tupamaros continually changed their tactics and strategies, endeavoring to present a "Robin Hood" image to the Uruguayan community (Butler, 1976). Indeed, as Porzecanski (1973:19) indicates,

> Kidnapping a foreign diplomat, killing a policemen or army officer, and robbing a bank are actions that require careful evaluation with regard to the rejection or support that they might stir in the people. Violence and armed struggle help to create popular consciousness, but they can also create counter-productive effects unless used in the proper context and at the right time.

In essence, the Tupamaros took on the perspective of the generalized other (in this case, the Uruguayan people), imagining what political strategy, tactics and image would be most appealing to potential supporters among the middle and working-class masses. Adopting a more moderate approach to political change and modifying tactics illustrate how role-taking affected the Tupamaro identity.

Emergence of Self

The last component influencing the formation of identity within the members of the Tupamaros was the emergence of the self. Wieviorka (1993, p. 5) describes the role identity plays in a social movement or, as he terms it, a social anti-movement.

> The *principle of identity*, which defines the actor and the people in whose name he speaks, ceases to be a reference to any social entity—to producers or workers, for example, in the paradigmatic case of the labor movement—and rather champions some mythic or abstract entity, essence, or symbol. Deified or naturalized, the social entity is thus made out to be either meta- or infrasocial. Here, the armed insurgent expresses himself in the name of such principles as justice, morality, and freedom more often than in that of any real social entity; and he defines himself through his adherence to a community rather than in terms of his insertion into a social relationship, as he would have previously done. When social and national movements band together, the people in whose name the

activist speaks become reduced, in his discourse, to a sort of essence or a pure construct, or become defined solely in terms of obstacles to their proper existence.

For the individual member of the Tupamaros, identity became dependent upon their affiliation and participation in the movement. This collective identity became the source of self-definition, self-concept, and personal validation. Identity validation played a particularly important role in the life of the Tupamaros organization. According to Butler (1976), the group was never successful in achieving an image as a movement for the disenfranchised. Although the group gave away food and money, their inability to successfully present a "Robin Hood" persona was thought to be the principle reason for their demise. More specifically, the public at large was not opposed to the Uruguayan government's campaign to rid the country of the Tupamaros organization.

Another example of the emergence of the self at work is the process of naming or labeling oneself. As previously stated, the National Liberation Movement adopted its official name in 1963. However, "as they began to develop a revolutionary ideology and a structure for violent revolt, the group searched for a title that would identify them with the people" (White, 1998:69). Thus, a name was needed sufficient to capture the similarity of their own identities to those of the Uruguayan people. There are two explanations as to why the organization adopted the name Tupamaros. The fist of these seems to be the most well accepted (Butler, 1976; Gilio, 1972; Wilson, 1974) and is recounted by Porzecanski (1973:ix).

The name Tupamaro comes from Tupac Amaru, the famed Inca rebel who during 1780–1781 tried to free his people from the Spanish. After the defeat of his forces and his execution, the Spanish called "Tupamaros" all members of rebellious groups that sprang up throughout most of Latin America—particularly those engaged in independence movements. In Uruguay, too, the followers of revolutionary hero Jose G. Artigas received the name "Tupamaros." However, instead of rejecting the nickname, Uruguay's revolutionaries accepted it proudly and used it freely throughout the struggle for independence. The choice of the name "Tupamaro" for the guerrilla organization was meant, therefore, to have historic and symbolic meaning.

This explanation demonstrates the members' desire to reinvent their identity, consistent with a more militant group, associating their own violent struggle with that of the Inca rebels who fought the Spaniards. A second explanation is that the word "Tupamaro" is a Guarani Indian word for a large, ungainly, noisy bird whose irrepressible voice could serve the Uruguayan people much like the sacred geese who lived in Rome's Temple of Juno. The geese warned Marcus Manlius of the Gauls' attempts to scale the fortress walls (Gilio, 1972).

Taking on the name "Tupamaro" and the subsequent usage of the name in everyday social interaction established their individual and collective identities as social objects within their own psychic world and that of their environment. To the group member, the Tupamaro identity personified revolution, patriotism, and a champion of the disenfranchised. To the government of Uruguay, the Tupamaro identity was one of a violent extremist, perpetrator, delinquent, and/or criminal. Although the two perspectives might not agree upon the definitions, it is clear how the Tupamaros identity became a social object through social interaction.

CONCLUSIONS: IMPLICATIONS FOR FUTURE PRACTICE AND RESEARCH

The idea that identity plays a significant role in the behavior of terrorists is not necessarily a new one (e.g., Laqueur, 2003; Martin, 2003; Post, 1998; Whittaker, 2001). However, this article sought to provide a deeper, more robust understanding of how identity forms and influences terrorist behavior through the creation of a symbolic-interactionist model and its application to three terrorist groups. We believe that our analysis has utility for those constituencies who deal with terrorism and the interpretation of other forms of human behavior. Some provisional comments along these lines are presented below.

From a more micro perspective, the analysis works at the *contextual level* of terrorism research, as it provides a better understanding of how the terrorist identity is established and how it is significant in motivating behavior. This can be of use to law enforcement personnel who are charged with profiling, tracking, detecting, and apprehending those accused of committing terrorist acts. As a tool, law enforcement investigators will be better equipped to respond to terrorist violence with an improved understanding of the nature and cause of terrorist behavior. To be clear, our work is not to be confused with a terrorist personality; rather, it is merely an attempt to uncover one aspect of the motivation behind terrorist violence.

Another area where the preceding analysis finds utility is in the realm of law and public policy. As enumerated by Post (1998), political violence becomes an integral part of the person's identity and asking the terrorist to give up violence is like asking the terrorist to give up who she or he is. Berman (2003), too, makes a similar observation, especially in his assessment of how Muslim spiritualism has been transformed into Islamic extremism; a metamorphosis strikingly familiar to the American and European experiences centuries ago. To expand upon this implication, our inquiry offered several detailed examples of how identity is formed through one's interactions with the symbols of one's environment. This can have significant impact on peace negotiations. Those who choose to pursue peace through diplomatic relations must realize the powerful affect one's environment has in creating self and collective identity. Not only does the symbolic interactionist model allow governmental officials to understand the rationale motivating terrorist violence, it also enables them to transcend their own favored ways of thinking and understanding of the world so that they can perceive things from another perspective. This permits negotiators to see how a shared sense of identity emerges from similar perceptions of social stratification, class status, and patterns of relationships.

How military and law enforcement entities choose to respond to terrorism is another area with tremendous policy implications. This application is particularly salient in the post 9/11 climate. While heightened military force may be viewed as a necessary evil, it must be recognized that if governments continue to rely upon violence to prevent more violence, then they may inadvertently be creating the next generation of terrorists. Simply stated, an identity born in violence begets violence. Our analysis has also argued that political violence is not just a response to violence. The terrorist identity is also created and sustained through a perception of marginalization and disenfranchisement. Increasing the level of surveillance and detention of certain individuals based on racial, ethnic, or religious profiles is not only problematic from a civil rights perspective, it could also prove to be a security concern. In this instance, terrorists may continue to emerge as certain groups of people repeatedly interpret the symbols of their oppression as staples of their existence. Thus, in this context, counter-violence might be thought of as the only solution.

Identity can be seen as part of the reason why some countries have such a difficult time ridding themselves of terrorist threats, regardless of how much they are willing to compromise. The examples are salient in current affairs. For instance, just when it seems that headway is being made in the Israeli-Palestinian conflict, Hamas and other extremist groups vow to disrupt the peace process at all costs. A similar development has occurred in Northern Ireland when the PIRA finally decided to release the locations of their weapons stockpiles and to begin disarmament, splinter factions vowed to escalate their attacks against the government of Great Britain. Terrorism becomes who these individuals are and asking them to shed their identities is, perhaps, too difficult a request.

From a more macro perspective the analysis offers an interpretative and explanatory model which has utility for understanding other forms of human behavior. This symbolic interactionist model can be graphed on to such behaviors as gang affiliation, religious and political extremism, and the creation of sexual identity. By examining behavior through the symbolic interactionist framework as proposed above, researchers can get a better grasp on the impact meaning and intent have for those in various cultural and historical contexts. This type of in-depth, systematic examination of both psychological and sociological forces is needed as government officials continue to look toward the social and behavioral science community for answers to pressing problems concerning the use of political violence by various individuals around the globe.

Along these lines, future research on terrorism must operationalize, with greater precision and alacrity, the way in which such identity organizing principles as symbols and objects, acts and social acts, meaning, role-taking and role-making, and the emergence of the self function in specific contexts. As such, future investigations of terrorism must pursue more qualitative and contextual methods of analyses, mindful of how various political, economic, religious, and other social forces impact the formation of individual and collective identity. As we have argued, based on our cursory examination of three distinct terrorist groups, only in this way can we come to appreciate the emergence of a terrorist identity, the violent actions such groups commit, and the social-psychological dynamics that sustain and nurture them.

ENDNOTES

1. In the 1999 edition, the report claimed that there were 392 international terrorist attacks, 233 deaths, and 706 wounded. The 1998 edition reported 273 attacks, 741 deaths, and 5,952 wounded. In 1997, there were 304 attacks, 221 deaths, and 693 wounded. The full text of these reports are available on-line at http://www.state.gov/s/ct/rls/pgtrpt/

2. Interestingly, commenting on this phenomenon in the post–September 11 era and in relation to Arab and Islamic terrorist organizations, Berman (2003) argues that Eastern AND Western influences must be considered. As he explains, we cannot "deny or ignore for one minute the authentically Muslim and local roots of . . . Arab and Muslim terrorists organizations of recent times. Still, an amazing number of Arab and Muslim terrorists do turn out to have second and even primary identities as Westerners. It's good to glance eastward, and at the history of the Arab and Muslim world from hundreds of years ago. But in trying to make sense of these people's very strange behavior, we ought to glance westward, too. . . . " (Berman, 2003 p. 21).

3. Although the Tupamaros were disbanded in 1972, examining the events and life experiences of their group members helps to shed light on other similar terrorists that remain active or have yet to emerge.

4. The term identity will be used interchangeably with individual identity and social identity because from the perspective of symbolic interactionism no identity can exist outside the realm of social interaction (Weigert et. al. 1986; Jenkins, 1996).

5. Martin (2003, p. 34) asserts that "[p]erspective is the central consideration in defining terrorism." Thus, one's orientation to people and events is pivotal to exploring the context in which behavior is explained and/or interpreted. Kushner's (1998b) perspective is sufficiently broad enough to capture the diversity of approaches underpinning terrorism research (e.g., extremism versus mainstreamism, terrorism versus freedom fighting) and sufficiently narrow enough to focus on those issues at the core of our analysis (e.g., group identity, motives, participant roles).

6. For a comprehensive coverage of the Irish conflict and the birth of the IRA see Bell (1997) and Coogan (1994).

7. Unfortunately, sectarian violence motivated the British Government to suspend the power-sharing Northern Ireland Assembly in October 2002 causing the PIRA to curtail its own disarmament process (U.S. Department of State, 2003). This led to criticism from such groups as the Ulster Unionists, the Irish media, and the Irish Government, all of whom have now called for the wholesale disbandment of the PIRA, fearing a return to its terrorist activities and violence in the region (Wikipedia, 2003).

8. The Intifada was the name given to the Palestinian uprising which erupted over Israeli control of the occupied territories (Mishal & Sela, 2000). White (1998) describes the event as being one of the key factors that lead to the 1994 Oslo, Norway peace agreements.

9. However, we hasten to add that other activities such as the funneling of funds on behalf of Middle East terrorist groups, including al Qaeda, Hamas, and Hezballah, have taken place within the United States. When coupled with the anti-American *jihadi* sentiment in existence since the 1980s, experts acknowledge that the massive support apparatus and above-ground organizations established within several major U.S. cities may have helped to fuel the 9-11 terrorist attacks (Emerson, 2002; Martin, 2003)

10. One of the most infamous recollections of such an attack was committed on April 18, 1983 when a member of Hizballah drove a van filled with 400 pounds of explosives into the side of the U.S. Embassy in Beirut, killing 63 people. A similar attack was committed six months later when another truck filled with explosives was driven into the U.S. Marine barracks, killing 241 marines. Most recently, the attacks on the World Trade Center in New York City, the Pentagon in Washington, D.C., and the rural plains of Pennsylvania led by 13 al-Qaeda hijackers resulted in untold devastation and represented "one of the most significant single attacks in modern history because of its coordination, audacity, high death toll, and global consequences" (Martin, 2003 p. 339).

11. It is worth noting that this type of spiritual and psychological preparation is not uniformly found across all suicide bombings perpetrated by Islamic militants. For example, the al-Qaeda hijackers who initiated the September 11, 2001 attacks infiltrated the United States months before executing their plans and had their own set of rituals before martyring themselves. While the prepa-

ration may be different, the overall context in which the act is completed is the same. As Berman (2003) argues, the behavior of Islamic fundamentalists and jihad terrorists represents an old battle fought throughout the 20th century in Europe. He describes this as a confrontation between liberalism and its totalitarian enemies. Thus, as Berman (2003) observes, the Middle East and Islam are not the cause of war; rather, they are the arena in which the battle, and the ideas that constitute it, presently are being waged. These observations notwithstanding, we argue that the social act of a suicide bombing takes on rich, symbolic meaning in the formation of the terrorist identity.

12. Berman (2003) makes a similar point, arguing that the behavior of Hamas, Islamic Fundamentalism, and the Muslim culture historically mirrors extremism in the West. Thus, as he explains, "in trying to make sense of [Arab] people's very strange behavior, we ought to glance westward . . . not just to Western politics and policies, but at literature and philosophy, at the deepest of Western ideas, not just now but in the long-ago past" (Berman 2003, 21). In this context, it is not surprising that role-taking and role-making behavior helped sustain Islamic terrorists living in the United States giving rise to the 9/11 bombings (Emerson, 2002). However, this position does not itself prove an Hamas - Bin Laden link.

REFERENCES

Abrams, D., and M. A. Hogg. 1999. *Social Identity and Social Cognition.* Malden, MA: Blackwell Publishers.

Anderson, J. 2003. "Hamas at Historic Crossroads; Pressure Rises to Back Truce, End Bombings." *Washington Post,* June 28, A 16.

Anderson, J., and M. Moore. 2003. "Israeli Strike Kills Hamas Political Figure; Attack in Gaza Follows Bus Bombing; Palestinian Militant Groups Call Off Truce." *Washington Post,* August 22, A1.

Arena, M. P., and B. A. Arrigo. 2000. "White Supremacist Behavior: Toward an Integrated Social Psychological Model." *Deviant Behavior* 21, no. 3: 213–244.

Baldwin, J. D. 1986. *George Herbert Mead: A Unifying Theory for Sociology.* Beverly Hills, CA: Sage.

Barkan, S. E., and L. L. Snowden. 2001. *Collective Violence.* Boston: Allyn & Bacon.

BBC News. 2003. "Q & A: What's in the Mid-East Roadmap." July 2. Available online: http://news.bbc.co.uk/1/hi/world/middle_east/2938444.stm.

Bell, J. B. 1997. *The Secret Army: The IRA.* 3rd ed. London: Transaction Publishers, 1997.

Berger, P. L., and T. Luckmann. 1967. *The Social Construction of Reality.* Garden City, NY: Doubleday.

Berman, P. 2003. *Terrorism and Liberalism.* New York: W. W. Norton.

Best, J., ed. 1989. *Images of Issues: Typifying Contemporary Social Problems.* New York: Aldine deGruyter.

Blumer, H. 1969. *Symbolic Interactionism: Perspective and Method.* Los Angeles: University of California Press.

Burke, P. J. 1980. "The Self: Measurement Requirements from an Interactionist Perspective." *Social Psychology Quarterly* 43, 18–29.

Burton, A. 1976. *Urban Terrorism.* New York: Free Press.

Butler, R. E. 1976. "Terrorism in Latin America." In *International Terrorism,* ed. Y. Alexander, 53–59. New York: Praeger.

Cooley, C. H. 1996. "The Social Self." In *Social Deviance: Readings in Theory and Research,* ed. H. N. Pontell, 62–68. 2nd ed. Upper Saddle River, NJ: Prentice Hall.

Coogan, T. P. 1994. *The IRA: A History.* Niwot, CO: Roberts Rinehart.

Costigan, G. 1980. *A History of Modern Ireland.* Indianapolis, IN: Bobbs-Merrill.

Derfner, L., and K. A. Toameh. 2000. "Just Saying 'No' to Terror." *U.S. News and World Report,* September 18, 50–51.

Dershowitz, A. M. 2002. *Why Terrorism Works: Understanding the Threat, Responding to the Challenge.* New Haven, CT: Yale University Press.

Dobbs, M. 2003. "Palestinians Urged to Break up Terrorist Groups; Moving to Shield Peace After Bombing, U.S. Toughens Rhetoric in Pressing Abbas to Act." *Washington Post,* August 21, A14.

Dobratz, B. A., and S. L. Shanks-Meile. 1997. *White Power, White Pride! The White Separatist Movement in the United States.* New York: Twayne Publishers.

Ellemers, N., R. Spears, and B. Doosje, eds. 1999. *Social Identity: Context, Commitment, Content.* Malden, MA: Blackwell Publishers.

Emerson, S. 1998. "Terrorism in America: The Threat of Militant Islamic Fundamentalism." In *The Future of Terrorism: Violence in the New Millennium,* ed. H. Kushner, 33–54. Thousand Oaks, CA: Sage.

———. 2002. *American Jihad: The Terrorists Living among Us.* New York: Free Press.

Erikson, E. H. 1959. *Identity and the Life Cycle: Selected Papers by Erik H. Erikson.* New York: International Universities Press.

Flemming, P., and M. Stohl. 1988. "The Theoretical Utility of Typologies of Terrorism: Lessons and Opportunities." In *The Politics of Terrorism,* ed. M. Stohl, 157–170. New York: Marcel Dekker.

Garfinkel, Harold. 1967. *Studies in Ethnomethodology.* Englewood Cliffs, NJ: Prentice Hall.

Gergen, K. J. 1999. *An Invitation to Social Construction.* Thousand Oaks, CA: Sage.

Gibson, J. W. 1994. *Warrior Dreams: Paramilitary Culture in Post-Vietnam America.* New York: Hill and Wang.

Gilio, M. E. 1972. *The Tupamaros.* London: Secker & Warburg.

Goffman, E. 1959. *The Presentation of Self in Everyday Life.* New York: Doubleday.

Goode, E. 1996. "On Behalf of Labeling Theory." In *Social Deviance: Readings in the Theory and Research,* ed. H. N. Pontell, 86–96. 2nd ed. Upper Saddle River, NJ: Prentice Hall.

Guevara, E. 1968. *Reminiscences of the Cuban Revolutionary War.* New York: Monthly Review Press.

Hagan, F. E. 1997. *Political Crime: Ideology and Criminality.* Needham Heights, MA: Allyn & Bacon.

Hamm, M. S. 1993. *American Skinheads: The Criminology and Control of Hate Crime.* Westport, CT: Praeger.

Hewitt, J. P. 1976. *Self and Society: A Symbolic Interactionist Social Psychology.* Boston: Allyn & Bacon.

Hilbert, R. A. 1990. "Ethnomethodology and the Micro-Macro Order." *American Sociological Review* 55, no. 6: 794–808.

Hoffman, B. 1998. *Inside Terrorism.* New York: Columbia University Press.

Horgan, J., and M. Taylor. 1997. "The Provisional Republican Army: Command the Functional Structure." *Terrorism and Political Violence* 9, no. 3: 1–32.

Hroub, Khaled. 2000. *Hamas: Political Thought and Practice.* Washington, D.C.: Institute for Palestine Studies.

Jenkins, R. 1996. *Social Identity.* New York: Routledge.

Johnson, A. G. 1995. *The Blackwell Dictionary of Sociology: A User's Guide to Sociological Language.* Oxford, UK: Blackwell Reference.

Johnson, P. W., and T. B. Feldmann. 1992. "Personality Types and Terrorism: Self-Psychology Perspectives." *Forensic Reports* 5, no. 4: 293–303.

Katzman, K. 2002. "Terrorism: Near Eastern Groups and State Sponsors, 2002." CRS Report for Congress. Available online: http://www.fas.org/irp/crs/RL31119.pdf.

Kepel, Gilles. 2002. *Jihad: The Trail of Political Islam.* Trans. A. Roberts. Cambridge, MA: Harvard University Press.

Khalidi, R. 1997. *Palestinian Identity: The Construction of Modern National Consciousness.* New York: Columbia University Press.

———. 2003. "Can Hamas Cut a Deal for Peace?" *Los Angeles Times,* June 17, 15.

Kushner, H. W., ed. 1998a. *The Future of Terrorism: Violence in the New Millennium.* Thousand Oaks, CA: Sage.

Kushner, H. W. 1998b. *Terrorism in America: A Structured Approach to Understanding the Terrorist Threat.* Springfield, IL: Charles C. Thomas.

Lauer, R., and L. Boardman. 1971. "Role-Taking: Theory, typology, and propositions." *Sociology and Social Research* 55, no. 2: 137–153.

Lauer, R. H., and W. H. Handel. 1983. *Social Psychology: The Theory and Application of Symbolic Interactionism.* 3rd ed. Englewood Cliffs, NJ: Prentice-Hall.

Laqueur, W. 1999. *The New Terrorism: Fanaticism and the Arms of Mass Destruction.* New York: Oxford University Press.

———. 2003. *No End to War: Terrorism in the Twenty-First Century.* New York: Continuum Publishing Group.

Lemert, E. M. 1994. "Primary and secondary deviation." In *Classics of Criminology* ed. J. E. Jacoby, 287–293. 2nd ed. Prospect Heights, IL: Waveland Press.

Lifton, R. J. 1976. *The Life of the Self.* New York: Simon and Schuster.

———. 1979. *The Broken Connection.* New York: Simon and Schuster.

Livingston, E. 1987. *Making Sense of Ethnomethodology.* London: Routledge and Kegan Paul.

Marighella, C. 1985. *Manual of the Urban Guerrilla.* Chapel Hill, NC: Documentary Publications.

Marlo, F. H. 1999. "WMD Terrorism and US Intelligence Collection." *Terrorism and Political Violence* 11, no. 3: 53–71.

Martin, G. 2003. *Understanding Terrorism: Challenges, Perspectives, and Issues.* Thousand Oaks, CA: Sage.

McGuire, M. 1973. *To Take Arms: My Year with the IRA Provisionals.* New York: Viking Press.

Meltzer, B. 1978. "Mead's social psychology." In *Symbolic interaction: A reader in social psychology,* ed. J. G. Manis and B. N. Meltzer, 15–27. 3rd ed. Boston: Allyn & Bacon.

Mish, F. C., ed. 1997. *The Merriam-Webster Dictionary.* Springfield, MA: Merriam-Webster, Inc.

Mishal, S., and A. Sela. 2000. *The Palestinian Hamas: Vision, Violence, and Coexistence.* New York: Columbia University Press.

Morris, C. W., ed. 1967. *Mind, Self, & Society from the Standpoint of a Social Behaviorist.* Chicago: University of Chicago Press.

Nüsse, Andrea. 1998. *Muslim Palestine: The Ideology of Hamas.* Amsterdam: Harwood Academic Publishers.

O'Ballance, E. 1997. *Islamic Fundamentalist Terrorism, 1979–95: The Iranian Connection.* New York: New York University Press.

Pearlstein, R. M. 1991. *The Mind of the Political Terrorist.* Wilmington, DE: Scholarly Resources.

Pinto, M. D. C. 1999/1902. "Some U.S. Concerns Regarding Islamist and Middle Eastern Terrorism." *Terrorism and Political Violence* 11, no. 3: 72–96.

Pontell, H. 1996. *Social Deviance: Readings in Theory and Research.* 2nd ed. Upper Saddle River, NJ: Prentice Hall.

Porzecanski, A. C. 1973. *Uruguay's Tupamaros.* New York: Praeger.

Post, J. M. 1998. "Terrorist Psycho-Logic: Terrorist Behavior as a Product of Psychological Forces." In *Origins of Terrorism: Psychologies, Ideologies, Theologies, States of Mind,* ed. W. Reich, 25–40. Washington, DC: Woodrow Wilson Center Press.

Reich, W., ed. 1998. *Origins of Terrorism: Psychologies, Ideologies, Theologies, States of Mind.* Washington, DC: Woodrow Wilson Center Press.

Rouhana, N. 1997. *Palestinian Citizens in an Ethnic Jewish State.* New Haven, CT: Yale University Press.

Schaefer, R. T. 2000. *Sociology: A Brief Introduction.* Boston: McGraw-Hill.

Schutz, A. 1967. *The Phenomenology of the Social World.* Evanston, IL: Northwestern University Press.

Smith, B. L. 1994. *Terrorism in America: Pipe Bombs and Pipe dreams.* Albany: SUNY.

Stone, G. P. 1962. "Appearance and the Self." In *Human Behavior and Social Processes,* ed. A. M. Rose, 86–118. Boston: Houghton Mifflin.

Stone, G. P., and H. A. Farberman, eds. 1970. *Social Psychology through Symbolic Interaction.* Waltham, MA: Ginn-Blaisdell.

Stryker, S. 1977. "Developments in 'Two Social Psychologies': Toward an Appreciation of Mutual Relevance." *Sociometry* 40: 145–160.

Taithe, B., and T. Thornton. 1999. *Propaganda: Political Rhetoric and Identity, 1300–2000.* Gloucestershire, UK: Sutton.

Tajfel, H., ed. 1978. *Differentiation between Social Groups.* London: Academic Press.

Tajfel, H. 1982. Social Psychology of Intergroup Relations. *Annual Review of Psychology* 33: 1–39.

Tajfel, H., and J. C. Turner. 1986. "The Social Identity Theory of Intergroup Behavior." In *Psychology of Intergroup Relations,* ed. S. Worchel and W. G. Austin, 2nd ed. 7–24. Chicago: Nelson-Hall.

Taylor, M. 1991. *The Fanatics: A Behavioural Approach to Political Violence.* London: Brassey's.

Taylor, M., and E. Quayle. 1994. *Terrorist Lives.* London: Brassey's.

Taylor, P. 1997. *Behind the Mask: The IRA and Sinn Fein.* New York: TV Books.

Tucker, J. B., ed. 2000. *Toxic Terror: Assessing Terrorist Use of Chemical and Biological Weapons.* Cambridge: MIT Press.

U.S. Department of State. 2003. "Patterns of Global Terrorism." Washington, DC: U.S. Government Printing Office. Available online: http://www.state.gov/s/ct/rls/pgtrpt.

Weigert, A. J., J. S. Teitge, and D. W. Teitge. 1986. *Society and Identity: Toward a Sociological Psychology.* New York: Cambridge Press.

Weinstein, M. 1975. *Uruguay: The Politics of Failure.* Westport, CT: Greenwood Press.

White, J. R. 1998. *Terrorism: An Introduction.* Belmont, CA: Wadsworth.

White, R. W. 1993. *Provisional Irish Republicans: An Oral and Interpretative History.* Westport, CT: Greenwood Press.

Whittaker, D. J., ed. 2001. *The Terrorism Reader.* New York: Routledge.

Wieviorka, M. 1993. *The Making of Terrorism.* Chicago: University of Chicago Press.

Wikipedia. 2003. *Provisional Irish Republican Army.* Available online: http://www.wikipedia.org/wiki/Provisional_Irish_Republican_Army.

Wilson, M. C. 1974. *The Tupamaros.* Boston: Branden Press.

Worchel, S., F. Morales, D. Páez, and J. C. Deschamps, eds. 1998. *Social Identity: International Perspectives.* Thousand Oaks, CA: Sage.

Wright, J. 1991. *Terrorist Propaganda: The Red Army Faction and the Provisional IRA, 1968–86.* New York: St. Martin's Press.

Wright, R. 2000. *The Last Great Revolution: Turmoil and Transformation in Iran.* New York: Alfred A. Knopf.

CHAPTER 2

The Changing Face
of American Terrorism

Sarah H. Corley
University of Arkansas

Brent L. Smith
University of Arkansas

Kelly R. Damphousse
University of Oklahoma

Before the attacks on the World Trade Center on September 11th, 2001, most Americans could not identify Osama bin Laden; much less locate Afghanistan on a map. Now, ask any American about either and he or she will be able to identify both. Americans today are bombarded with countless media images of suspected terrorists. In recent years, these images have overwhelmingly included characteristics common to Middle Eastern ancestry. This stereotypical terrorist is vastly different from the demographic profile of terrorists targeting America just a few years ago. The international terrorist is a relative newcomer to American involvement with terrorism. International terrorism may have been a plague on our European allies, but the United States remained somewhat insulated until recently.

Portions of this research were funded by the National Institute of Justice (Grant Number 1999-IJCX-0005) and the Oklahoma City National Memorial Institute for the Prevention of Terrorism (Grant Number MIPT 106-113-2000-064) through the Department of Justice and the Department of Homeland Security. The opinions presented here do not represent the official position of the Department of Justice, the Department of Homeland Security, the MIPT, or the National Institute of Justice.

In the 1960s and 1970s, terrorists were categorized as young, leftist, and Marxist. By the mid-1980s, American terrorists were predominantly rightist, anticommunist, and from a lower socioeconomic background. Today, these universal descriptors seem antiquated. The face of American terrorism appears to have changed drastically. This chapter examines how.

BACKGROUND AND CONCEPTUAL PROBLEMS

While the overall number of domestic terrorist incidents has declined over the past decade, the violent acts that have occurred caused greater destruction and resulted in more deaths than ever before.[1] During the 1980s and 1990s, the FBI reported a total of 327 domestic terrorist attacks, resulting in 205 deaths and injury to more than 2,000 people.[2] While only 60 of the 327 attacks occurred in the 1990s, the 1990 terrorist incidents claimed 182 of the 205 lives that were lost.[3] Terrorism against American targets escalated as the twentieth century came to an end and a new one began. The 1993 World Trade Center bombing, the 1995 Oklahoma City bombing, and the September 11, 2001, attack brought terrorism to the forefront of American consciousness.

Although the perpetrators' acts were universally condemned as terrorist attacks, scores of other cases are not as easily defined and labeled. The subjectivity sometimes involved in determining what is a criminal act versus an act of terrorism plagues terrorism research. For instance, FBI official reports omitted the Ted Kaczynski (aka "the Unabomber") case after it became apparent that Kaczynski acted alone instead of as part of a group.[4] Consequently, varying definitions regarding what constitutes terrorism invariably affect demographic patterns of those so labeled.

Even though there is no universally accepted definition of terrorism, one general criterion for a terrorist act is that it is motivated by political or social gain and not by personal vendettas. The FBI defines domestic terrorism as "[t]he unlawful use, or threatened use, of force or violence by a group or individual based and operating entirely within the United States or its territories without foreign direction committed against persons or property to intimidate or coerce a government, the civilian population, or any segment thereof, in furtherance of political or social objectives."[5] The use of this definition is somewhat tempered by the attorney general's guidelines on terrorism investigations, which limit the opening of an official terrorism investigation to groups.

In any case, for a violent act (e.g., arson of a retail store selling fur coats) to be labeled as "terrorism" by the FBI, it must meet the FBI's threshold for designation of a terrorist act. Given the ambiguity in defining violent acts as terrorism, researchers have an enormous obstacle to overcome when examining individuals who really may or may not be considered terrorists. Substantial variation has existed regarding which persons to include in terrorism datasets.[6] In the absence of a universally accepted definition of terrorism and inconsistent operationalization, demographic descriptions of terrorists are difficult at best. Consequently, relatively few efforts have been made to even address this issue.

PREVIOUS RESEARCH

In 1977, Russell and Miller published the earliest effort to provide some demographic insight to terrorist group characteristics. Their now-classic "Profile of a Terrorist"[7] suggested that terrorists tend to be young, leftist, single males from middle- to upper-class backgrounds between the ages of 22 and 25 years old who have some university education, a college degree, or a graduate degree. Like their parents, many have some other type of professional training such as in the medical, legal, or engineering fields.[8] Since the publication of this study, researchers have realized the disparities that exist between American terrorists and the profile that resulted from Russell and Miller's research. Currently, few studies have been conducted to address this issue, the exceptions being Handler's 1990 publication of "Socioeconomic Profile of an American Terrorist: 1960s and 1970s"[9] and Smith and Morgan's 1994 study "Terrorists Right and Left: Empirical Issues in Profiling American Terrorists."[10] Ever since Russell and Miller's study on profiling, research has repeatedly turned to their findings to explain the characteristics of terrorists. It was not until Handler's study that we began to realize that as early as the 1980s, American terrorists were diverging from prevailing assumptions.

Despite the theoretical and methodological problems inherent in Handler's study, specifically due to the lack of reliable data and the ambiguity involved in defining terrorism, it contributed to the literature on profiling American terrorists by distinguishing between left-wing and right-wing terrorists and analyzing the differences between the two categories. Before discussing the demographic findings from his study, it is important to understand the ideological differences between left-wing and right-wing terrorists as defined in this literature.

Terrorists belonging to left-wing groups in the United States typically adhere to some variation of Marxist ideology; they generally believe that they are committing violent acts against the government to protect people from the harsh effects of capitalism and its exploitation of minorities and the poor. Their targets include government buildings, equipment, civil and military personnel, and prominent symbols of capitalism such as large corporations. Left-wing groups in recent history include the El Rukns, the Macherteros, the FALN (Armed Forces of Puerto Rican Liberation), the United Freedom Front, the New African American Freedom Front, the May 19 Communist Organization, and the Provisional Party of Communists. Although these groups differ in many ways, they are tied together by their common ideology, their beliefs about economics, the targets they select, their location of operation (i.e., urban versus rural settings), and the tactics they use to operate. During the late 1980s, these groups began to decline due to loss of financial support and the demise of communism in Eastern Europe and the Soviet Union.[11] Consequently, left-wing terrorism in the United States declined dramatically during the 1990s. In contrast, right-wing extremists, and members of militia groups in particular, were the target of intense federal scrutiny following the Oklahoma City bombing in 1995.

Right-wing groups that turned to terrorism have been affiliated with the Christian Identity movement, an anti-Semitic and anti-black movement based on the idea that Aryans, not Jews, are God's chosen people. Their members are white supremacists who believe strongly in the values of capitalism and abhor those of communism. They think that not only should people be rewarded for the value of their work but that minorities are not capable of and should not be allowed the same opportunities as whites. They oppose any programs that help economically disadvantaged people through welfare and education and feel no remorse for minorities who are struggling in life. Included in the right-wing category are groups such as the Aryan Nations; the Arizona Patriots; the Covenant, Sword, and Arm of the Lord; the Ku Klux Klan; the White Patriot Party; The Order; the Sheriff's Posse Commitatus; and various militia groups. By separating domestic terrorists into left- and right-wing categories, Handler's analysis revealed valuable information about terrorists.

Handler's results suggested that right-wing terrorists were predominantly white males from lower- to middle-class families. They were typically reared in Bible Belt regions of the country and had marginal educational backgrounds. His findings also revealed a disparity between the socioeconomic classes of rank-and-file members versus group leaders. Specifically, he noted that right-wing leaders tended to have higher levels of education, earn higher incomes, and hold white-collar jobs. Handler noted that, consistent with the conservative idea that "a woman's place is in the home," women did not play a tactical role in right-wing groups. In contrast, he found that among left-wing terrorists, many were African-American or Hispanic, although group membership was still primarily white. Unlike the right-wing groups, whose members shared the same religious beliefs, left-wing members came from a broad range of religious doctrines. No single religion dominated, but Catholicism and Judaism were most prominent. Furthermore, women were much more visible in left-wing groups; they held leadership positions within the group and were more likely to be involved in actual acts of violence or terror. Left-wing terrorists, whether they were rank-and-file members or leaders, were much more likely to come from middle- to upper-class families. Most had at least a college education. However, Handler found that they did not necessarily hold jobs that corresponded to their level of education. This was most likely due to the fact that being committed to the cause at hand may have impeded their ability to hold a professional job.[12]

Subsequent to Handler's study, Smith and Morgan attempted to address the methodological problems Handler faced and to provide results based on a more comprehensive database. Their study divided the terrorists into four categories: left-wing, right-wing, single-issue, and international. With the publication of the FBI's first Terrorist Research and Analytical Center report in the early 1980s, Smith and Morgan were able to access an official list of specified criminals labeled "terrorists" by the FBI. Smith and Morgan's dataset included only those persons indicted during the 1980s for "terrorism or terrorism-related activities."[13] Many of their findings regarding the demographic information of terrorists supported Handler's. However, some of Smith and Morgan's findings revealed differences between the two studies. These variations were due most likely to methodological differences that affected sample selection.

Smith and Morgan collected demographic information, case outcome, type of terrorist group, and sentencing data directly from the court case files, which were obtained either at federal district courts or from federal regional archives throughout the United

States. The Administrative Office of U.S. Courts supplied missing demographic or sentencing data. Included in this data set were 213 indicted terrorists from 21 different terrorist groups who were charged with a total of 1,363 federal violations.[14]

In general, these terrorists were considerably older than either Handler (1990) or Russell and Miller (1977) had found. The average age of indictment was 37 years, with right-wing terrorists slightly older (their average age at indictment was 39) than left-wing terrorists (whose average age at indictment was 35). Over one-third (36 percent) of the right-wing terrorists were over age 40 at the time they were indicted. Other differences included substantial variations in gender and race. Twenty-seven percent of the left-wing terrorists were female, compared to only 7 percent of the right-wing terrorists. Similarly, 71 percent of the left-wing terrorists were nonwhite, compared to only 3 percent of the right-wing terrorists.[15]

The Smith and Morgan data were similar to Handler's findings regarding educational attainment and occupational background. Smith and Morgan found that on average, left-wing terrorists were much better educated than right-wing terrorists indicted during the 1980s. They also tended to hold more professional jobs and were more likely to reside in urban areas. The right-wing terrorists predominately occupied manual labor positions or were self-employed or unemployed. They lived mostly in rural settings. Exceptions included some of the leaders of these groups, who tended to be highly educated and to have held, at least at one time, high-paying and prestigious occupations.

In addition to identifying socioeconomic and demographic factors, other studies have used psychological profiles to define terrorists. These traits may include being trustworthy, disciplined, and reasonable. However, they may also include instability, paranoia, and neuroses.[16] Some terrorist experts are skeptical about using psychological profiles, suggesting that terrorists have such a broad range of sociocultural backgrounds, goals, and contexts that it defeats the purpose of trying to create accurate and useful profiles and may even be detrimental to identifying terrorists.[17] In fact, Dingley asserted that understanding the socioeconomic factors of terrorists provides better insight into terrorist behavior than the identification of psychological factors.[18] For example, he noted that many authors suggest that terrorists have the ability to detach themselves from the violent act they commit and intellectually rationalize their behavior. He argued that this does not provide us with great insight since people in society rationalize their behavior everyday. Furthermore, he stated that while many authors characterize terrorists as being fanatical and obsessive, he suggested that those are common tendencies of many people in societies, especially individuals who are successful in life. He suggested that identifying overeducated and unemployed individuals while recognizing certain socioeconomic factors identified by Russell and Miller[19] offers a greater opportunity for understanding extremist behavior and identifying those individuals most likely to become terrorists.

In sum, efforts to compile a terrorist profile began in the late 1970s with Russell and Miller's study and eventually led to an effort to move research in this area from conclusions based on anecdotal data to more reliable findings based on empirical analysis. Consequently, research has demonstrated that it is necessary to separate terrorists into different categories (i.e., right-wing, left-wing, single-issue, and international) for the sake of accuracy and usefulness. Smith and Morgan noted that any analysis of American terrorism that does not examine left- and right-wing groups separately risks attenuating existing dissimilarities.[20] More recent findings on terrorist profiling clearly differ from initial findings. However, since Smith and Morgan's 1994 study, there have been no recent empirical studies that further address demographic profiles of American terrorists. Given the difficulty in defining terrorism and in obtaining information about terrorists, it is understandable that for many years the availability of empirical data has been virtually nonexistent. Even now, information on terrorists has often been patchy and inconclusive, making empirical analysis somewhat difficult. Despite these challenges, researchers and law enforcement officials have continued to examine individuals who choose to engage in violent acts of terrorism. The purpose of the current study was to compare demographic data of American terrorists who were indicted during the 1980s with those indicted in the 1990s to identify if changes in demographic characteristics have occurred.

METHODOLOGY OF THE CURRENT STUDY

Data for the current analysis were extracted from the files of the American Terrorism Study (ATS), a project that began in 1988 and includes demographic data on persons indicted under the FBI's Counterterrorism Program since 1980. The data include only those persons who have been identified by the FBI through a "terrorism" investigation as designated by the attorney general's guidelines.[21] Demographic information, case outcome, type of terrorist group, and sentencing data were collected directly from the court case file from either federal district courts or federal regional archives throughout the U.S. For isolated cases, the federal district courts mailed copies of the indictment, the court docket, and judgment/commitment orders to the researchers. In addition, the Administrative Office of U.S. Courts and the U.S. Sentencing Commission supplemented missing demographic or sentencing data.

FINDINGS

The FBI has categorized those individuals included in the dataset as either domestic or international terrorists. For the purpose of this study, the list of terrorists was further divided into right-wing, left-wing/environmental, and international categories. The left-wing category includes members from environmental terrorist groups. There were too few cases documented to provide reliable data solely for an environmental category. Although disputable, ideological similarities between leftist and environmental terrorists make this combination feasible. Table 2.1 shows that for the 1980s case files, there were a total of 215 individuals and 56 indictments, with a total of 1,411 violations of federal law (counts). From the 1990s, 231 terrorists were named in 63 indictments and charged with a total of 1,437 violations of federal law (counts). Of the 215 terrorists indicted in the 1980s, 48 percent (103) individuals belonged to right-wing groups, while 31 percent (67) were members of left-wing/environmental groups. In the 1990s, out of

TABLE 2.1   Type of Terrorist Group by Decade

	Right-Wing		Left-Wing/ Environmental		International		Total	
	%	N	%	N	%	N	%	N
DECADE								
1980s	48	(103)	31	(67)	21	(45)	100	(215)
1990s	45	(104)	25	(57)	30	(70)	100	(231)
AVERAGE	46	(207)	28	(124)	26	(115)	100	(446)

231 terrorists, 45 percent (104) were members of right-wing groups, while 25 percent (57) belonged to left-wing/environmental groups. The remaining offenders were international terrorists. The current study compares terrorists indicted in the 1980s with those indicted in the 1990s by gender, race, age, level of education, and income and occupation.

GENDER

Previous profiles of American terrorists have suggested that they are primarily male while acknowledging that female involvement in terrorism is higher than in traditional criminality. This study revealed (see Table 2.2) that for the 1980s right-wing cases, 94 percent (97) of members were male, and 6 percent (6) were female. For the 1990s right-wing cases, 88 percent (92) were male, while 12 percent (12) were female. Thus, for right-wing groups, female participation doubled from the 1980s to the 1990s but only increased by 6 female members. The number of males indicted remained fairly constant, with only a slight decrease from 97 to 92 individuals. For left-wing terrorist groups in the 1980s, 67 percent (45) were male, while 33 percent (22) were female. For the 1990s cases, the number of males increased to 89 percent (50), while the number of females decreased to 11 percent (6). The 1980s cases revealed that for international terrorists, 98 percent (44) were male, while only 2 percent (1) were female members. Similarly in the 1990s, 99 percent (69) of international terrorists were male, while only 1 percent (1) was female.

Overall, the analysis revealed that while there were significant differences in the 1980s between right-wing and left-wing groups regarding gender, while in the 1990s, both categories show very similar findings for gender. The 1990s data indicated that male membership slightly decreased in right-wing groups and slightly increased for left-wing groups. Female membership, which increased slightly in the right-wing groups, decreased from 33 percent (22) to 11 percent (6) in left-wing groups. Perhaps of greatest note is the finding that persons indicted for international terrorism in federal courts over the past two decades have been almost exclusively male. This variation is consistent with the ideological beliefs of these groups. The international terrorists in the

TABLE 2.2   Gender by Type of Terrorist Group by Decade

	Right-Wing		Left-Wing/ Environmental		International	
1980s	%	N	%	N	%	N
MALE	94	(97)	67	(45)	98	(44)
FEMALE	6	(6)	33	(22)	2	(1)
TOTAL	100	(103)	100	(67)	100	(45)
1990s						
MALE	88	(92)	89	(50)	99	(69)
FEMALE	12	(12)	11	(6)	1	(1)
TOTAL	100	(104)	100	(56)	100	(70)

sample are from predominantly Islamic fundamentalist groups, while the right-wing terrorists in the sample have been associated with more traditional rural American culture. These categories are to be contrasted with the more egalitarian beliefs of leftist organizations.

RACE

In Table 2.3 you can see that for the 1980 right-wing groups, 98 percent (101) of members were Caucasian and 2 percent (2) were American Indian, compared with the 1990s, in which 95 percent (97) of members were Caucasian, 3 percent (3) Black, and 2 percent (2) white Hispanic. The appearance of Black members in what has routinely been viewed as a white backlash to immigration and affirmative action deserves comment. Although 1980s right-wing groups were almost exclusively linked to the Christian Identity movement, the same cannot be said for 1990s groups. The militia movement, although retaining much of the ideological rhetoric of years past, has attracted a broader base of members. Despite this exception, race remained fairly consistent within right-wing groups.

For left-wing/environmental groups in the 1980s, 39 percent (25) were Caucasian, 26 percent (17) black, and 35 percent (23) white Hispanic. In contrast, in the 1990s, only 5 percent (3) were Caucasian, 35 percent (20) were black, and 60 percent (34) were white Hispanic. These groups experienced a significant drop in the number of Caucasian members and an increase in the number of white Hispanics primarily due to the fact that the left-wing cases from the 1990s included mainly minorities and involved a large extremist group from Puerto Rico.[22] For the 1980s and 1990s, international terrorist groups were approximately three-fourths Caucasian; white Hispanics were the second-largest race among members of this category.[23]

TABLE 2.3   Race by Type of Terrorist Group by Decade

	Right-Wing		Left-Wing/ Environmental		International	
1980s	%	N	%	N	%	N
CAUCASIAN	98	(101)	39	(25)	82	(37)
BLACK	0		26	(17)	2	(1)
AMERICAN INDIAN	2	(2)	0		0	
WHITE HISPANIC	0		35	(23)	16	(7)
BLACK HISPANIC	0		0		0	
ASIAN	0		0		0	
TOTAL	100	(103)	100	(65)	100	(45)
1990s						
CAUCASIAN	95	(97)	5	(3)	75	(51)
BLACK	3	(3)	35	(20)	7	(5)
AMERICAN INDIAN	0		0		0	
WHITE HISPANIC	2	(2)	60	(34)	15	(10)
BLACK HISPANIC	0		0		1.5	(1)
ASIAN	0		0		1.5	(1)
TOTAL	100	(102)	100	(57)	100	(68)

AGE

Since Russell and Miller's study, research has repeatedly cited their findings that terrorists are young—usually between 22 and 25 years old. However, results from the current study support Smith and Morgan's analysis that the average age of terrorists is considerably older than previously believed.[24] Results indicated (see Table 2.4) that for

TABLE 2.4   Age at Indictment by Decade

	1980s	1990s
Youngest Person Indicted	21	17
Oldest Person Indicted	69	72
Average Age of Those Indicted	37.6	38.8

the 1980s terrorists (including all categories—right-wing, left-wing, and international), the average age of indicted terrorists was 38; the youngest person indicted was 21 and the oldest was 69 years. Results for the 1990s cases (including all categories) revealed their average age to be 39 with the range of 17 to 72 years. Findings for age raise two important issues. First, although right-wing membership appears to be fairly constant, the range in age seems to be widening, with a decrease in left-wing groups and an increase in international terrorists during the 1990s. Second, the data suggest that unlike traditional criminals, terrorists appear to make terrorism a lifelong career. Considering that the crimes of the terrorists in our dataset were committed within one year of their age at indictment, the data underscore the fundamental differences between the causes of terrorism and traditional criminality.

LEVEL OF EDUCATION

Previous research has indicated that right-wing groups tend to be less educated overall than left-wing group members and that there appears to be a gap in the level of education between right-wing leaders and their rank-and-file members.[25] Results from the current study revealed (see Table 2.5) that for right-wing members of the 1980s cases, 37 percent (31) had a GED or less, 21 percent (18) had received a high school diploma, 29 percent (25) had some college or vocational training, and 13 percent (11) had either graduated from college or completed postgraduate work. These figures remained fairly consistent during the 1990s. Overall, educational levels among right-wing terrorists appear to have increased slightly—nearly one-half (49 percent) reported some college experience, while the percentage reporting only a "GED or less" declined from 37 percent to 29 percent of the right-wing terrorists.

Among left-wing groups from the 1980s, 10 percent (6) of group members had a GED or less, 37 percent (21) had some college or vocational training, and 53 percent (30) were college graduates or had completed postgraduate work. For the 1990s, results indicated that 55 percent (16) had a GED or less, 21 percent (6) had a high school diploma, 14 percent (4) had some college or vocational training, and 10 percent (3) were college graduates or had finished postgraduate work. It is important to note that unlike the data for right-wing groups, which included a total of 85 members for the 1980s and 83 members for the 1990s, there were only 57 members in the left-wing group for the 1980s and only 29 for the 1990s. Even so, the overall results for the left-wing groups in the 1980s indicated that 90 percent of all members had a minimum of some college or vocational training; 53 percent had earned a college degree or done postgraduate work. For the 1990s, the data on leftist/environmental terrorists are limited to a small number of criminal cases involving the Macheteros and environmental extremists.

The level of education among international terrorists seems to have slightly increased from the 1980s to the 1990s. Data for the 1980s cases indicated that 44 percent (16) of international terrorists had a minimum of college or vocational training. For the 1990s, 70 percent (23) had at least college or vocational experience. Although

TABLE 2.5   Level of Education by Type of Terrorist Group and Decade

	Right-Wing		Left-Wing/ Environmental		International	
	%	N	%	N	%	N
1980s						
GED or less	37	(31)	10	(6)	31	(11)
High School Diploma	21	(18)	0		25	(9)
College/Vocational Work	29	(25)	37	(21)	31	(11)
College Graduate/ Postgraduate Work	13	(11)	53	(30)	13	(5)
TOTAL	100	(85)	100	(57)	100	(36)
1990s						
GED or less	29	(24)	55	(16)	12	(4)
High School Diploma	22	(18)	21	(6)	18	(6)
College/Vocational Work	37	(31)	14	(4)	40	(13)
College Graduate/ Postgraduate Work	12	(10)	10	(3)	30	(10)
TOTAL	100	(83)	100	(29)	100	(33)

the number increased only by 7, findings still suggest that international terrorists are primarily well-educated individuals.

INCOME AND OCCUPATION

As previously discussed, collecting data on terrorists can sometimes be difficult simply because certain information is unavailable or almost impossible to obtain. Although the current dataset does include information about income and occupation, the use of income data is notoriously unreliable. Nevertheless, the data did indicate some patterns that will be discussed. These patterns are generally consistent with previous research.

Two issues exist that help to explain the difficulty in collecting data for both of these variables. First, if the terrorist's financial records are not included in the case file, that information cannot be collected. If a terrorist hires his or her own attorney and does not apply for a public defender, financial statements are typically not required to be released for the record. Second, more often than not, at the time the terrorist is arrested and taken into custody, he or she is unemployed and there is no occupation to report. Furthermore, many terrorists have reported "inmate" as what they were doing prior to arrest, which is often the case—a person is already in prison when they are charged with a terrorist crime. Finally, defendants may intentionally understate their assets so that they may qualify for a court appointed attorney.

Although data on income for the 1990s is insufficient, the 1980s data on income for right-wing terrorists is fairly complete. For the right-wing terrorists indicted during the 1980s, 85 percent (75) made less than $1,500 per month; 52 percent (46) of the 85 percent made less than $500 per month. The same pattern appears to be true for the 1990s right-wing category; 70 percent (out of 27 members) made less than $1,500 per month. Similarly, for left-wing members in the 1980s, 80 percent of the 50 members reported making less than $1,500 per month and 56 percent of the 80 percent made less than $500 per month. The results for the 1990 decade are similar to data for the right-wing income of the 1980s; 79 percent of 19 terrorists made less than $1,500 per month. Overall, there seems to be virtually no difference for income between right- and left-wing groups, and $1,500 per month (a little less than $18,000 per year) appears to be a common cutoff point. The cause at hand may require such a tremendous amount of time and dedication that the terrorist can hold only menial jobs or must forfeit employment altogether. For international terrorists, the data for income was inconclusive due to inadequate sample size.

Past profiles of terrorists often claim that left-wing members come from professional positions that include lawyers, doctors, teachers, and engineers, while right-wing rank-and-file members are predominantly blue-collar workers (with the exception of the well-educated members who fill the right-wing leadership positions). Findings for both the 1980s and 1990s are unclear and inconclusive for the occupation variable and for all group types. Both right- and left-wing terrorists reported professional occupations (i.e., attorney, engineer, accountant) as well as skilled labor (mechanic, appliance repairman, electrician). Although some variance was noted, these differences do not appear to be as clear as previous research suggested. Only among international terrorists did significant occupational patterns emerge. Occupations of international terrorists included travel agents, sales representatives for Ryder truck lines, college students, electrical engineers, cab drivers, carpenters, and airlines employees. Many of these occupations reflect job categories available to new immigrants, a characteristic of many of our international terrorists.

DISCUSSION AND CONCLUSION

If Russell and Miller's earlier findings were still true today, then the average terrorist would be a single male between the ages of 22 and 25 with a university education. He would be from a middle- to upper-class family and would hold ideologically leftist views. For many years, researchers turned to that basic terrorist profile. However, subsequent research on 1970s and 1980s terrorists has demonstrated that it is necessary to separate terrorists into ideological groups whose differences are in many ways profound but who still manage to cause the same devastating destruction. This research revealed substantial changes from Russell and Miller's profile during the 1980s.

The current study examined changes during the 1990s. Data from the 1990s are generally consistent with findings from the 1980s. Notable differences included an increase in educational attainment among right-wing defendants and the consistently older age of terrorists than was typically assumed. This age pattern was noted among international terrorists as well, as was a tendency for international terrorists to be better educated than their domestic counterparts, to be almost exclusively male, and to be from an occupational profile better than left- or right-wing domestic terrorists.

The arduous undertaking of piecing together information in order to empirically measure terrorist data will always be difficult due to the underground nature of terrorist operations. Although not perfect, the use of court case data can help fill this void. The current research corroborates both Handler's and Smith and Morgan's assertions that valuable differences are found among terrorists when groups are analyzed independently. However, according to Silke, creating an accurate terrorist profile *and* one that has a positive and substantial impact on an investigation is the most challenging obstacle of all.[26]

END NOTES

1. FBI Annual Report, *Terrorism in the United States: 1999*, 16. Available online: http://www.fbi.gov/publications/terror/terror99.pdf. This report looked at thirty years of terrorism. The name of the FBI's annual report on terrorism changed several times during the 1980s. Initially it was called *FBI Analysis of Terrorist Incidents in the United States*. In 1984, the title was changed to *FBI Analysis of Terrorist Incidents and Terrorist Related Activities in the United States*. The 1986 report reverted to the pre-1984 title. In 1987, the FBI adopted the current title: *Terrorism in the United States*.
2. Ibid., 16.
3. Ibid., 16.
4. Ibid., 26.
5. Ibid., ii.
6. See Jeffrey Handler, "Socioeconomic Profile of an American Terrorist: 1960s and 1970s," *Terrorism* 13 (1990): 195–213; and Brent Smith and Kathryn Morgan, "Terrorists Right and Left: Empirical Issues in Profiling American Terrorists," *Studies in Conflict and Terrorism* 17 (1994): 39–57.
7. Charles Russell and Bowman Miller, "Profile of a Terrorist," *Terrorism: An International Journal* 1, no.1 (1977): 17–27.
8. Ibid., 19–31.
9. Handler, "Socioeconomic Profile."
10. Smith and Morgan, "Terrorists Right and Left," 39–57.
11. FBI Annual Report, *Terrorism in the United States: 1999*, 19.
12. Handler, "Socioeconomic Profile," 211–212.
13. Smith and Morgan, "Terrorists Right and Left," 40–41.
14. Ibid., 42.
15. The two right-wing defendants claiming nonwhite status did so for ideological reasons. Claiming Native American heritage, these individuals asserted that as members of the Indian Nation in Oklahoma, the federal government had no jurisdiction over them.
16. Rex Hudson, "The Sociology and Psychology of Terrorism: Who Becomes a Terrorist and Why?" *Federal Research Division Report* (September 1999).

17. Ibid.

18. James Dingley, "The Terrorist—Developing a Profile," *International Journal of Risk, Security, and Crime Prevention* 2, no. 1 (1997): 25–37.

19. Russell and Miller, "Profile of a Terrorist," 19–31.

20. Smith and Morgan, "Terrorists Right and Left," 55.

21. Office of the Attorney General, U.S. Department of Justice, Washington D.C. *The Attorney General's Guidelines on General Crimes, Racketeering Enterprise and Domestic Security/Terrorism Investigations,* 1983; and *The Attorney General's Guidelines on General Crimes, Racketeering, Enterprise and Terrorism Enterprise Investigations,* G.P.O. 2002.

22. There is some question whether *U.S.* v. *Ramon Torres-Gonzalez et al.* (CR 90-370) should be included in the 1990 dataset. There is little or no discussion of Macheteros in the case file. This case is fairly well known and referred to by local U.S. attorney's offices as the drug "Narco Tesoro" meaning "drug treasure case."

23. Race is probably not a good mechanism for distinguishing among international terrorists. "Ethnicity" or "country of origin" may provide a better classification method. However, that coding strategy was not available at the time of this writing.

24. Smith and Morgan, "Terrorists Right and Left," 50–52.

25. Handler, "Socioeconomic Profile," 205–206.

26. Andrew Silke, "Hunting Terror: Using Offender Profiling to Catch Terrorists," *Journal of Counterterrorism and Homeland Security International* 8, no. 2 (2002): 28–30.

CHAPTER 3

Federal Programs and Their Potential to Provoke Political Violence: The Transportation Program for Yucca Mountain and Terrorist Adversaries

Lawrence Becker
Assistant Professor, Department of Political Science
California State University, Northridge

James David Ballard
Assistant Professor, Department of Sociology
California State University, Northridge

INTRODUCTION

In the near future, the federal government will begin transporting large quantities of highly radioactive wastes from nuclear power plants, research laboratories, and atomic weapon production facilities to a centralized repository in Southern Nevada (U.S. Department of Energy 2002). This "waste dump," commonly known as the Yucca Mountain repository, has a long and tumultuous political history that may influence the types of protests these transportation efforts will face and, more important, has the potential to incite violent adversaries when the shipments commence from the various production sites around the country.

To begin the story of why this program may be a target for potential terrorism and sabotage, this chapter will offer some background on the debate over Yucca Mountain and how the reality of the inventory of highly radioactive waste stockpiles at over 100 sites around the nation has led to a long-standing political fight between the state of Nevada and the federal government agencies that will control the disposal of these waste products. The chapter will first address some enduring aspects of American political culture that help place the dispute over Yucca Mountain into a relevant context. Thereafter, a brief history of the political efforts to site this particular facility is offered. This historical context leads to the development of an argument that while extraterritorial groups may target these shipments for attack, domestic groups that oppose the federal government's efforts to support nuclear power production are critical threats to assess for the overall transportation effort associated with this particular facility.

This chapter argues that the actual assessment of these groups and their risk of initiating an attack will primarily be the responsibility of local law enforcement agencies (LLEAs) and will constitute a new burden on their already strained resources. A detailed discussion on the impacts of this program on LLEAs is included.

While we do not offer any concrete solutions to the terrorism-related risks of transporting nuclear wastes across the breadth of America, our argument will suggest that an unintended yet important and underrecognized consequence of federal preemption is the increased risk of terrorist attacks. Specifically, we argue that a key potential threat is posed by those who may consider themselves patriotic but who are so passionately committed to localized political control that they are willing to resort to antigovernment violence to achieve their ends. This argument may be critically important to the future of terrorism studies and specifically to those upon whom the burden will fall—LLEAs—since the recognition of the multiple threat layers (i.e., domestic and international) offers various levels of stakeholders (i.e., policymakers, elected officials, and law enforcement administrators) the opportunity to mitigate the issues and/or the risks of various potential types of terrorist attacks.

UNDERSTANDING YUCCA MOUNTAIN IN AMERICAN POLITICAL CULTURE

Before examining the specifics of the transportation of nuclear waste, it is useful to take a step backward and understand how this policy problem fits into the larger framework of American political culture. Just as the sources of international terrorism vary, many of the sources of domestic terror are found deep in the core of the American political psyche. While Oklahoma City bomber Timothy McVeigh's actions are abhorrent and were condemned by Americans from every part of the political spectrum, the political logic that led him to his crime is a violent distortion of values that are found in mainstream American political culture. These values played an important role in the founding of the American polity and in the writing of both the Declaration of Independence and the Constitution of the United States. It is important, therefore, to examine this broader political context, because meeting the threat of domestic terror requires that police agencies and other first responders understand what motivates the militant antigovernment groups that may be a potential threat to the transport of radiological materials to Yucca Mountain.

In discussing the relationship between American political culture and domestic terror, this chapter focuses on three elements of the American founding. First, it is important to remember that the American Revolution differed from most other revolutions in the world in that it was a thoroughly political revolution and not a social revolution such as, for instance, the French Revolution. It is an important distinction because, unlike the participants in the French Revolution, Americans are not thought to be bound together by a distinctive language, culture, race, or ethnicity. Indeed, one could argue that the only thing that binds Americans together at all is their political culture. In other words, Americans are bound together by a shared set of political values and little else. As a result, Americans are particularly likely to react strongly to any perceived threat or change in the everyday ordering of political life. After all, if all that binds Americans together is a shared set of political values, any perceived violation of those values is not just unsettling, it is fundamentally un-American.

Secondly, while Americans tend to view both the Declaration of Independence and the Constitution of the United States equally as national treasures and, if one accepts the argument above, central organizing statements of American life, it is the case that these two documents contradict one another in a number of important ways. One of the important contradictions for the purposes of this discussion is that while the Declaration of Independence authorizes revolution (even violent revolution), the spirit and the letter of the Constitution deals with the establishment of order, tranquility, and stability. It is not necessary (or possible) for us to resolve the tension between these two documents in the space allotted here. For this argument, it is important to simply point out that because the Declaration of Independence remains the equal of the Constitution in organizing American political culture, the application and abuse of its logic is a reality that LLEAs must be prepared to confront when deviant groups use violence to "protect" what they perceive to be the true spirit of our political culture.

Finally, while the part of the founding generation widely referred to as the anti-Federalists lost the battle over ratification of the Constitution, as historians note, it is far from clear that they lost the battle for the hearts and minds of the population at large. For instance, Storing argues that "the political life of the community continues to be a dialogue, in which the Anti-Federalist concerns and principles still play an important part" (1981, 3).

Perhaps first among those concerns is a fear of distant and centralized political authority and a strong desire for local forms of governance (Beer 1993). The nation's long struggle with race (first over slavery, later over civil rights, and currently over affirmative action) is perhaps the best-known flashpoint for this tension between centralized and decentralized political authority. For example, both those who fought to maintain the institution of slavery and later those who sought to keep Jim Crow laws in place in the South rest their logical claims on the basis of states' rights. The point here is not to associate the Federalist or anti-Federalist vein in American political thought with any particular party or movement. Rather, the point is that the sentiment for greater local control is long-standing and even thriving in contemporary American political culture.

Pulling all three of these observations about this society together, we can more easily see how American political culture can be perverted and distorted into a justification for domestic terror. First, since all that binds Americans together is a political culture, any perceived threat to the political order as one understands it is particularly serious and threatening. Second, the logic of the Declaration of Independence authorizes the violent overthrow of a government that is perceived to trample the rights of its citizens. Finally, an enduring component of American political culture is the high value we place upon the concept of local autonomy, be it politically, economically, or socially (Skocpol 1999; Riker 1987).

In the case of Yucca Mountain, a series of decisions were made by the federal government against the wishes of the local population in Nevada to transport more than 70,000 tons of radiological waste through many communities across the United States and into a state that did not produce the waste. Viewing that process and the substance of those distant political decisions through the lens described above suggests that a potential risk of domestic terror would exist for such a program.

While an attack on radiological waste being transported to Yucca Mountain would be horrific and unjustifiable, a clear understanding of antigovernment groups and the threat they pose to the transportation of nuclear waste requires that community leaders understand these groups not simply as deviants completely out of touch with American values. Indeed, the potential threat they pose can be met only by first recognizing their self-perception as the only people "defending" the American way of life. While it is clearly a perversion of normative American political culture to engage in radiological terror, dealing with the threat requires that we see these groups as distorting, not simply ignoring, deeply ingrained parts of existing political culture.

HISTORY OF THE YUCCA MOUNTAIN PROJECT

The history of the Yucca Mountain repository is long and complicated and yields several lessons that are important in understanding the potential threats LLEAs will face in assisting with the safe transport of radiological waste to Nevada. Historically, it is critical to understand that the federal government has slowly meandered toward the construction of a single, permanent, geologic repository. It is a process that has already taken nearly fifty years and it will be decades longer before the facility is licensed, built, and filled with waste transported in from around the country.

In the 1954 Atomic Energy Act (P.L. 83-703), Congress made the Atomic Energy Commission (AEC) responsible for the disposal or reprocessing of spent fuel from the nation's commercial nuclear reactors. The act also gave the AEC preemptive power allowing it to override state or local laws and regulations that got in the way of this mission.

Despite this significant grant of power, the AEC did not immediately play a particularly active role in managing nuclear waste from the nation's nuclear-related infrastructure. There are a variety of reasons for this limited role. First, the 1950s and 1960s were merely the dawning of the age of commercial nuclear reactors. Simply put, disposal of radiological waste from the limited number of reactors around the country was not considered to be as high a priority as the development of new technologies and the construction of more reactors.

Second, and related to the first reason, there was an inherent faith that technological progress would resolve the problem at some point in the future. While waste was piling up at some sites, most policymakers believed a practical solution would emerge long before the waste became a crisis.

Finally, policymaking in the nuclear energy arena was not impervious to important institutional changes occurring in the United States. Just as there was a general decentralizing of institutional structures of various kinds in the 1970s, the nuclear infrastructure was not immune to these same social changes. As a result of the Energy Reorganization Act of 1974 (P.L. 93-438), the AEC was broken up into two parts—the Nuclear Regulatory Commission (NRC) and the Energy Research and Development Administration (ERDA) which, as a result of the Energy Organization Act of 1977 (P.L. 95-91), became the Department of Energy (DOE). At around the same time, the enactment of both the National Environmental Policy Act (NEPA) in 1969 (P.L. 91-190) and modifications in the original 1963 Clean Air Act (P.L. 88-206) in 1970 (P.L. 91-604) gave states, localities, and interest groups greater standing and authority to challenge federal agencies and their actions, even those of the AEC and its successors.

The combination of these developments essentially required that Congress would ultimately have to weigh in before any national-level radioactive waste program could become a reality. Not only were members of Congress sure to play a role in any plan to geographically redistribute the costs of nuclear power, but the creation of a nuclear waste disposal program was going to cost a lot of money, and when money is involved, members of Congress have both the tools and the incentives to play a significant role in the policymaking process. Thus, while scientists both inside and outside of DOE had been working toward the development of plans and sites for national nuclear waste repositories, it was well understood on all sides that members of Congress would not simply write a blank check.

On its face, the 1982 Nuclear Waste Policy Act (NWPA) (P.L. 97-425) seemed to put into place a process that would, on the basis of scientific criteria, select repository sites for the wastes from the nation's commercial nuclear reactors. Not only did the NWPA delegate authority to the DOE to develop criteria for site selection, it delegated authority to the DOE to narrow the list of potential sites. The NWPA also gave the state where the final site was chosen the power to veto the DOE's designation—and this veto could only be overridden by a majority in both houses of Congress.

The practical reality of the NWPA process was far different, however. The timing of the selection process the DOE had to follow was such that the NWPA really just authorized this agency to choose from among its existing inventory of sites—an inventory that included Yucca Mountain, which was considered politically attractive because the land was part of a huge federal reserve that had previously been radiologically contaminated due to nuclear weapons testing in the 1950s. Additionally, this particular site was located in a less-developed state with a relatively small and therefore weak congressional delegation.

NWPA also steered the DOE towards Yucca Mountain by including provisions that required that the final choices must be in "various geologic media" (42 USC 10133). Because many of the preexisting site selections are in salt formations and Yucca Mountain is made of a volcanic rock known as tuff, Yucca Mountain was highly likely to be one of the final choices. In sum, as Jacob points out, "NWPA was not a break with the past; it set no new administrative gears in motion but merely confirmed existing powers, priorities, and practices" (1990, 11).

Regardless of whether the NWPA process was fair, Congress stepped in again in 1987. At this time, the DOE had narrowed its choices down to Hanford, Washington; Deaf Smith, Texas; and Yucca Mountain, Nevada. Since Speaker of the House Jim Wright was from Texas, and House Majority Leader Tom Foley was from Washington state, the legislative math was not hard to calculate. Congress enacted amendments to the NWPA that explicitly named Yucca Mountain as the only site the DOE was authorized to study, delayed the search for a second repository, and cut off the development of a so-called Monitored Retrievable Storage (MRS) facility that had been considered an alternative to geologic disposal. In what Nevada Senator Reid dubbed "the screw Nevada bill," Congress had made its final decision (Garrett 2002).

In the years since the enactment of amendments to the NWPA in 1987, Nevada has fought the designation of Yucca Mountain in Congress, in the courts, in the press, and on the street. The study, licensing, authorization, and construction of the repository have been slowed, but they have not been derailed by Nevada's efforts. In February 2002, the DOE formally recommended that Yucca Mountain serve as the nation's sole repository for radiological waste, and quickly thereafter President Bush approved the recommendation (Abraham 2002; Bush 2002). As provided for in the NWPA, Nevada's governor used a veto on this decision, but Congress overrode the veto within the 90-day period provided in the NWPA and the nation's stockpile of radioactive waste appears to be headed to Nevada (Guinn 2002; Pianin and Dewar 2002).

Given the history described above, it is not surprising that even some of Nevada's most reasonable and patriotic public officials have viewed the selection of Yucca Mountain as a despotic power play by the central government over the objections of local citizens and their representatives. Highly vocal and intense opposition to Yucca Mountain was not new. At the time of the 1987 Amendments to the NWPA, Nevada Representative Barbara Vucanovich claimed that in choosing Yucca Mountain, the national government would "turn our state into a federal colony" (Congressional Quarterly 1990, 483). Nevada junior senator Harry Reid (in Congressional Record, December 21, 1987) described "revulsion at what can only be described as oppression and colonialism, directed at the people of my State by 49 other States who are supposed to be our allies in a political union" (Congressional Record 1987, 34,262).

These sentiments have not cooled over time. Just after the Senate override of Nevada's veto in 2002, Nevada assembly speaker Richard Perkins, noted that the decision was "like the whole world is falling down on top of you. That it's us against the entire country" (Morrison and Vogel 2002). Likewise, Clark County, Nevada, commissioner Myrna Williams noted that the decision was "outrageous and a travesty that the other states' senators would vote to shove this down our throats" (Morrison and Vogel 2002).

Given such deep-seated public sentiment, and from such a wide range of prominent civic leaders, the question is how radical elements in the population of this state and others will react to the large-scale and highly visible transportation program necessary to stock the Yucca repository. The chapter now turns to the policy problem created in transporting the nuclear materials destined for Yucca Mountain and what some feel will be the efforts necessary to meet potential terrorist threats to the shipments of radioactive waste destined for Yucca Mountain.

THE POLICY PROBLEM

The waste headed for Yucca Mountain includes a variety of highly radioactive wastes such as spent nuclear fuel (SNF), highly radioactive materials resulting from the reprocessing and/or treatment of SNF, mixed oxide fuel, and even inventories of weapons-grade plutonium now considered surplus (U.S. Department of Energy 1999, A-4). The official inventory of materials is estimated to weigh over 70,000 tons and will require a far larger load weight when shielding containers are used for the transport (U.S. Department of Energy 1999, A-1). For example, the GA 4 transportation cask, a legal weight container, can hold four fuel-rod assemblies from a nuclear reactor, each weighing about three-quarters of a ton, and has a total weight of 27.5 tons. Clearly, the total weight of just the radioactive wastes is not representative of the actual weight of the total shipment effort necessary to move these wastes from their point of origin to their final destination.

Other estimates of the inventory that will need transport to Yucca Mountain suggest that the actual weight of the wastes will be far greater than this number. Some critics argue that the DOE has obscured the scope of the shipments necessary to move the nation's stockpile of radioactive wastes in an effort to gain approval of this program (Berkley 2002; Halstead 2002). Critics believe that this officially sanctioned deception takes two forms; repeated misrepresentation of the total weight of the inventory that will need disposal (the mandated weight limits for the Yucca repository are the most commonly used figure) and failure to account for the actual weight of the ready-for-transport shipment containers (combined weight of the transport vehicle, shipment cask, and fuel-rod assembly). Additionally, the DOE estimates do not account for the introduction of new nuclear power generation plants being planned by the industry and fail to account for the wastes these new plants will add to the existing and future stockpile of radioactive materials in need of geologic disposal (for details on expansion, see U.S. Department of Energy 2003; American Nuclear Society 2002).

These radioactive cargos will be transported over the everyday railroad corridors and on the interstate highway systems of the United States (U.S. Department of Energy 1999). In addition, the final environmental impact statement (EIS) for the project suggests that barge shipments will become a significant transportation modality (U.S.

Department of Energy 2002). What will emerge from the transportation planning for the Yucca project will be a national system of intermodal transport and barge/rail/truck transfer facilities necessary to ship these wastes from their existing sites and to the yet-to-be-built Yucca Mountain facility.

As of this writing, the repository must still be licensed by the NRC, the actual storage facility has yet to be built, legal challenges to the program remain, and many other policy debates remain to be undertaken before shipments will begin. Considering the time, perhaps decades, it will take to license the site, the time necessary for court challenges from one or more of the transportation corridor states that will be impacted by said shipments, including a highly optimistic estimate of the time needed to transport the actual materials (DOE estimates are twenty-four years), a reasonable estimate is that it will take approximately forty to fifty years for the national government to undertake the enormous task of transporting existing and future inventories of radioactive materials.

Currently these shipments are designated for movement in shipment containers, known as casks, like those made by General Atomics (GA 4) noted earlier and/or could be shipped in what is currently designated as a multiplepurpose container (MPC), a potential transportation-cask system designed to accomplish both shipment and storage tasks. The GA 4 transportation casks are currently in use, and several other varieties are being considered for licensing or planned for use for both highway and railroad shipments (Nucleur Regulatory Commission 2002).

In the event of an accident or terrorist incident involving these materials, they may pose as large of a health hazard as any weapon-of-mass-destruction attack using chemical or biological weapons (Lamb and Resnikoff 2001; Lamb, Resnikoff, and Moore 2001). In fact, the potential use of these materials as a radiological weapon offers unique challenges for antiterrorism and counterterrorism planning professionals (Ballard 2002a, 2002b). For this reason alone, the tasks of understanding that an attack on such shipments is possible and analyzing who could create a human-initiated radiological event using these materials are critical.

As the transportation planning for such a massive shipment effort begins, and for the decades of actual shipments that will follow this planning, federal-agency transportation experts should consider these shipments potential weapons of mass radiological victimization and seek to use the typically underutilized expertise of LLEAs to counteract this threat. The release of the radioactive material would not be the only negative outcome from such an attack. The fear, dread, and social outrage created by such an attack should also drive policymakers in their efforts to offset the risk of an attack on waste shipments. Existing regulations are discussed in the next section prior to a discussion of why and how LLEAs will need to be ready to address these risks.

NRC SAFEGUARDS AND REGULATIONS

During the 1996 and 1997 legislative sessions, the U.S. Senate and House of Representatives debated various nuclear waste policy initiatives (i.e., S. 1936, S. 104, and H.R. 1270.) These policy debates reopened the controversy surrounding the safeguards and security of nuclear waste shipments in the event of a sabotage or terror-ism attack. A similar process transpired in the post-September 11 era and as a result of the 2002 decision by the DOE to recommend moving forward with the Yucca pro-posal. A brief review of the history of NRC regulatory administration should help clar-ify issues related to the large-scale transportation program necessary to stock the Yucca repository.

In May 1980, the NRC issued an interim guidance document, NUREG-0561, Rev. 1, that established regulations for the protection of SNF until such time as the reg-ulations are "rescinded, modified or made permanent, as appropriate" (iii). The sug-gested protection strategies therein are based upon the decades-old concept of safeguards and directly reflect concerns about sabotage and diversion but not the reality of con-temporary terrorism tactics such as suicide attacks similar to those used on September 11, 2001. The general requirements contained in the regulation specifically describe the rules that apply to the following areas: 1) advance transportation notification to state and local governments; 2) plans including local law enforcement in the protection of said shipments; 3) procedures for threats and emergencies; 4) advance route approval; 5) designation of heavily populated areas; 6) rules on intermediate stops; 7) escort in-structions; 8) procedures at stops while in transit; 9) communications center instruc-tions; 10) escort training in the event of an accident or sabotage; 11) requirements regarding shipping logs; and 12) periodic contact standards (NUREG-0561, 62).

In addition to these general guidance regulations, specific guidelines were included that regulate the transportation of materials through heavily populated areas (NUREG-0561, 36). These specific guidelines include two alternatives for the protection of ma-terials until local law enforcement can respond in case of a sabotage incident or accident. The first allows for a single unit escort manned by a member of a LLEA. The second option allows private security guards to escort the shipment using two escort vehicles. The goal of these escorts is to provide interim shipment protection until such time as reinforcements arrive, typically LLEA support.

In 1984, the NRC proposed modifying the protection requirements for SNF. This proposed rule change would have eased the safeguard protection measures defined in NUREG-0561. After reevaluating projections for the loss of life in the event of a de-liberate radionuclide release, the NRC attempted to alter the regulations in an appar-ent attempt to lower transportation costs associated with escorting shipments within heavily populated areas.

Currently, the status of this proposed rule change is unclear. Questions remain as to whether the proposed modifications were terminated, remain active, or are in some NRC procedural limbo (Young 1989). The NRC has proposed additional safeguards for nuclear power generation facilities, shipments of wastes, and various other related activities in the post–September 11 time frame (Nuclear Regulatory Commission 2002). These have yet to be made public as this agency and other federal agencies contend that such planning is not appropriate for public discussion.

The unclear status of the proposed NRC safety and security changes dictate that any analysis primarily focus on specific requirements as defined in NUREG-0561. In particular, four areas of concern with the regulations can be noted with respect to ship-ments to the proposed Yucca repository. First, procedures for coping with threats seem to be fundamentally documentation requirements. Second, the requirements for heavily populated areas are unclear with regard to unplanned stops within urban areas. Third, the arrangements with LLEAs assume unidirectional communication. LLEAs are seen only as providing protection and not as a valuable resource in the identification of potential threats. Last, advanced route approval procedures offer specific criteria for selection of "ideal" routes and locally appropriate response measures. In real-world applications, such "ideal" selections are very difficult. For example, the NRC and the U.S. Department of Transportation (USDOT) allow and encourage state authorities to designate preferred routes that avoid highly populated areas. Given the time frame that the transportation effort to Yucca Mountain will take, the choice of such routes may change due to road conditions, traffic patterns, population shifts, or for a variety of other reasons.

One can assume that with the elongated time frame for shipments to the proposed Yucca facility, many unforeseen problems will arise and that localized knowledge of the threats would be critical to the safe transportation of these wastes. The result is that the NRC will likely have to abandon such idealistic planning and approve routes based upon expediency rather than best-practice–based safety measures or safeguards. This could increase the risk of terrorism and sabotage as shipments are exposed to more risky geographic profiles (i.e., cities, urban interchanges, etc.) and/or shipments are made under less than ideal conditions.

Researchers working with the state of Nevada have been engaged in Yucca Mountain oversight activities for approximately twenty years (Halstead 1993, 1990; Mountain West Research 1989). One purpose of such oversight is to ensure public safety and confidence in the federal government's management of shipments to the proposed facility. A meta-analysis of relevant state contractor studies and staff reports reveals certain areas of concern with regard to terrorism, transportation, and the proposed Yucca Mountain facility. These can be summarized into five specific areas: general concerns, impact on population clusters, route-specific characteristics, countermeasure procedures, and involvement of LLEAs.

General considerations refer to those undefined or ill-defined areas relative to the proposed transportation of nuclear waste to Yucca Mountain. Four general considerations are evident. First, the duration and frequency of shipments to the proposed facility add to the risk of a terrorist attack. They do so by establishing readily identifiable routines and opportunities for terrorists to attack shipments of high-level waste. Second, the ambiguity about the percentage of rail versus truck shipments (let alone the complexity added by barge shipments) and the various methods proposed for shipping create planning problems for counter-terrorist specialists. For example, the potential for heavy-haul trucking of 125-ton containers and the potential use of specially designed tractor-trailers for legal-weight truck casks present differing security concerns. Third, the use of multiple routes will exacerbate the problems with protecting shipments. For example, we should anticipate problems with multiple jurisdictions and interagency communication. Last, the availability of access highways and rail spurs across the nation and, in particular, at some of the waste-production sites, will affect the number of nuclear waste shipments. Currently no railroad spur exists to transfer the materials to Yucca

Mountain, some production sites do not have rail access, and viable routes have yet to be determined for the construction of such a rail corridor from all waste-production sites to the Yucca facility. Until these are identified and constructed, the shipments will have to travel over the interstate highway system and in many cases over rural roadways with less-than-desirable geographic features and substandard construction.

The second major area of concern includes issues directly related to the transportation of high-level waste near or through heavily populated areas. The DOE's projections for the project seem to underestimate the growth of areas in close proximity to the most likely transportation routes that could be used for the life span of this project. The risks and consequences of an attack are underdeveloped and do not seem to account for population shifts and alterations in the demographic landscape.

The third area refers to the route-specific characteristics that increase the probability of an attack against waste shipments. NUREG-0561 identifies characteristics that may increase the vulnerability to attack or increase the impact of an attack. For example, the regulation advocates the "avoidance of tactically disadvantageous positions . . . [such as] passage through long tunnels or over bridges spanning heavily populated areas" (23). Potential highway segments that exhibit these disadvantageous characteristics are found across America and on almost every road corridor that could be used to ship these materials (Halstead 2002). Likewise, existing rail routes have significant geographic disadvantages such as tunnels, bridges, sharp curves, and steep grades (Ballard 2002a).

The fourth area that needs development by the DOE prior to the start of transportation activities is specific procedures and countermeasures for the protection of waste shipments. The logic of possible NRC reductions in safeguard procedures is questionable when one considers the post–September 11 threat of terrorism against waste shipments. In fact, the opposite reaction may be best in the face of the ever-changing terrorist threat. Potential terrorist countermeasures such as fixed motion detectors, aircraft flyovers, and helicopter escorts may be necessary and argue against cost-cutting measures such as the NRC proposal to reduce security for shipments.

The final area of concern is the role of local law enforcement. Information and intelligence are the keys to effective counterterrorism security. The DOE lacks a programmatic plan to include LLEA input on terrorism threats. The inclusion of these agencies would be critical to a proactive stance against possible terrorism. Such inclusion would also be a critical response in the advent of an emergency. Active and bidirectional communication between the DOE and LLEAs will lower the risk of an attack, since it is the local agencies that will have a better handle on the threats posed within their jurisdiction, especially the threats posed by domestic terrorists.

Additionally, increased armed security and direct involvement of LLEAs is a reasonable precaution. Other risk-reduction strategies include the use of sophisticated technology to disrupt munitions threats (e.g., missiles) or detect the presence of such weapons near a shipment corridor. Transportation planners may also want to consider the use of roadblocks to limit public access on corridor routes. Many of the potential solutions to risks found in transporting nuclear waste require LLEAs to understand the problem and provide direct input into the shipment effort. The next section offers a method of categorizing the threats and offers some exemplars for consideration.

TRANSPORTATION TYPOLOGY FOR THREATS

The transportation typology suggested in Table 3.1 is focused on potential human-initiated radiological waste events and includes three analytical types of potential attack scenarios for shipments. These types represent a spectrum of potential attacks, not a finite listing of all possibilities. To understand the typology, focus first on the upper section that offers three potential motivations for an attack. Tied to these are the consequence spectrums listed in the middle of the table, which estimate the outcomes and offer categories for labeling adversaries relative to these hypnotized attack scenarios.

The last portion of the table offers a risk profile relative to each of the three motivations noted at the beginning of the table. Details on how such an analytical tool can be used in counter and antiterrorism planning are discussed below the table in the text.

In the first type listed above—disruptions—security and safeguard professionals should recognize that the issues of nuclear power and nuclear waste will be politically contentious and could draw a significant number of protestors. Potential mass demonstrations using tactics that range from passive civil disobedience to violent confrontation should be part of the risk-related planning process for any shipment program. The type of risks posed in this category does not necessarily represent the most

TABLE 3.1   Transportation Terrorism and Sabotage Typology

Nuclear Waste Transportation Terrorism Typology		
Motivation Behind Shipment Disruption		
MOTIVATION ONE: DISRUPT SHIPMENTS WITHOUT INTENT TO RELEASE CARGO	MOTIVATION TWO: INDUCE SEVERE ACCIDENT WITH POTENTIAL RELEASE	MOTIVATION THREE: DELIBERATELY CAUSE RELEASE OF RADIOACTIVE CARGO
Consequence Spectrums		
LESS «	SEVERITY OF INCIDENT »	MORE
PROTEST «	MOTIVATION OF ATTACKERS »	TERRORISM
PROTESTER «	ADVERSARY CATEGORY OR LABEL »	TERRORIST
Risk Profile		
PROFILE ONE:	PROFILE TWO:	PROFILE THREE:
PROTESTORS	CAPTURES	RELEASERS
LOW RISK	MODERATE RISK	HIGH RISK

difficult security or safeguard challenges; thus, it is listed as a low priority. This risk profile would best be characterized by a less-severe protest-motivated adversary. While these types of protesters are capable of inducing either a deliberate or accidental release, the assumption is that they are more likely to attack the transportation infrastructure and cause delays in shipment. They will most likely increase the preventative and responsive costs for security and safety policies while representing the most viable threat shipment may face.

In the second type—inducement with potential release of materials—security and safeguard professionals should be aware that a protest group, or terrorist organization embedded therein, might attempt to cause the deliberate release of radioactive materials into the local environment. This type of attack could involve situations ranging from induced accidents to the use of explosives to attempt a breach of the shipment casks or containers. Existing safeguards address the possibility of a capture for ransom or blackmail. The recognition that perpetrators would deliberately try to release the materials and thus create a radiological incident represents a relatively new twist on existing security and safeguard policies. This in turn dictates modifications in existing security arrangements to account for this possibility. The potential use of and movement toward using WMDs by terrorists around the world should motivate such changes. In this case, increased security and safeguards of these materials is suggested because of their ability to be used as a radiological dispersion device with a highly symbolic value and enormous potential political, social, and economic impacts on society.

In the third type—direct attacks using modern ordnance—recognize that the NRC and DOE studies do not represent a most creditable attack profile given the development of modern weapons and ordnance that may well be readily available in certain official and unofficial weapon-market channels (Luna, Neuhauser, and Vigil 1999; Halstead 1993; Mountain West Research 1989). No officially available studies to date have recognized the potential use for readily available weapons such as an advanced form of antitank missile or other contemporary ordnance with enough force to crack the shipment containers. Likewise, no federal agency studies seem to exist that explore the reality of suicide attacks or other asymmetrical tactics relative to these wastes.

WHAT SHOULD BE DONE

First and foremost, transportation planners should recognize that potential threats may already exist within local jurisdictions and that domestic groups pose a potential terrorism threat to Yucca Mountain shipments. These groups may not readily fit into the preestablished categories used by federal agencies, and their tactics may not yet rise to the level of terrorism. As one countermeasure, LLEAs must develop a certain level of organized expertise prior to the onset of radioactive waste shipments to be able to identify these groups and assess the risk they pose. The typology noted in Table 3.1 is one way to begin to organize the risks.

This subsection contends that LLEAs can use known procedures to assess their organization's preparedness level in the event of a terrorist attack on waste shipments. For example, the existing management of tactical, intelligence, and strategic units by

LLEAs are a starting point in such an analysis. Riley and Hoffman (1995) report that LLEA tactical units are basically counterterrorist in design and motivation and that a self-assessment of police agencies should begin here. That is, these are ex post facto response units that are primarily designed to respond to crime incidents but can be used in other capacities. These units represent the ability of LLEAs to respond to an incident if it should occur. Critical issues include training, skills, and critical masses of offense with both.

In contrast, intelligence and/or strategic units form the basis of antiterrorism efforts. These types of units are responsible for risk identification and prevention of attacks. The tools needed for these operations are very different and are addressed below. These units will be at the forefront of prevention and represent the best hope for mitigation of risks. Next, several ways such mitigation can be accomplished are suggested.

TACTICAL SOLUTIONS

In order to plan tactical operations, LLEAs need to assess their own capacity to deal with any threat that may arise. Riley and Hoffman (1995) use several categories to conduct this capacity assessment. The first assessment area is organizational demographics, which helps identify current LLEA capacities relevant to counter and antiterrorism efforts. Second, the assessment should discover the level of terrorism training found among existing members of the agency. Next, a detailed threat/risk assessment should be conducted where the agency conducts self-assessment of its strengths/weaknesses in preparation for its support of the forthcoming Yucca Mountain shipments.

INTELLIGENCE/STRATEGIC UNITS

While such a program-specific organizational assessment is useful for response planning in the event of an incident, prevention is critical to the safety of the general public and the officers who will respond to a terrorist attack against nuclear waste shipments. In order to prevent terrorism, an agency must identify those assets which may be targets and the most likely locations for an attack, persons that pose a risk of perpetrating violence, and events that may engender terrorist attacks.

Asset identification, identification of assets and locations in this context, is the process of prioritization of existing facilities and locations with respect to their potential for attack. For local LLEAs, this may entail the on-the-fly alteration of shipment plans when faced with a large protest situation, the need to upgrade shipment protection strategies due to a threat notification, and/or many other potential real-life situations that may impact the shipment process.

The second area, identifying persons who pose a risk, is necessary but fraught with legal/civil rights problems. Many LLEAs are aware of the individuals, gangs, or organized groups that have committed violence or have the potential for violent actions within their jurisdiction. Focus on these individuals or groups offer the best opportunity for prevention.

The last area, significant events, is part preventative and part investigative in orientation. During the course of regular police activities, certain events may represent indications of problems. For example, a burglary of a pawnshop may not register on the agency radar as significant until the guns stolen are used. Likewise, incidents involving armory and armed-forces stockpiles, or specifically explosives and gun sources, should be red-flagged as potential signals that a terrorist event is forthcoming.

Intelligence units should also recognize when community sentiments run against shipments, when local economic conditions are poor, and when large-scale media events that will draw the attention of someone searching to promote their politics or their cause occur. These data-gathering activities are not the norm in policing, yet they could be critical to thwarting an attack. Prompt and decisive identification of these risks will help LLEAs in stopping terrorism and offer the support necessary for the shipment of highly radioactive wastes.

CONCLUSION

Riley and Hoffman (1995) note that LLEAs face a much larger range of behavior they can identify as terrorism than do federal agencies. In this case, LLEAs would see a larger spectrum of threats than the DOE and those (to date) that will be protecting the shipments. To address this differential in perceptions, the authors suggest that LLEAs assess their organizational capacity to address asymmetrical terrorism that includes attacks against radiological shipments and that LLEAs conduct a self-assessment of their risk of attack related to transported nuclear wastes and radiological materials. The costs of these assessments may be substantial, as may be the necessary remediation efforts they reveal. One suggestion is that a mutual aid effort between LLEAs be initiated to share information and resources. The use of fairly standardized assessment instruments and risk-evaluation techniques will help this sharing of information (see Riley and Hoffman 1995).

Regardless of the political rhetoric, the burden of the risks for terrorism against transported nuclear wastes will fall on LLEAs. The task of protecting public health and safety is made more difficult by the regulations governing the shipments, the desire for secrecy by federal agencies, the characteristics of the actual shipment campaign, its ability to incite violence, and many other factors.

This chapter started with the idea that terrorist threats to the transportation of radiological waste to Yucca Mountain is at least as likely to come from domestic terror groups as from foreign groups. This leads to the unavoidable conclusion that LLEAs will be the responsible parties that have to deal with the problems that arise. While the DOE has been part of developing plans for homeland security, the argument above suggests that the Department of Homeland Security may have serious organizational blindness in relation to the risks associated with transporting nuclear waste to Yucca Mountain. In effect, then, the burden of the actual protection of the shipments to Yucca Mountain may represent another unfunded federal mandate for LLEAs. Awareness of the program and the potential risks associated with transporting radioactive wastes is critical for these agencies. It is to be hoped that federal agencies will incorporate the expertise LLEAs have into the transportation planning, but if not, LLEAs should be prepared for the work-load that will be placed on their staffs when shipments begin and, especially, for the distinct possibility that a terrorist group will target these shipments for an attack.

REFERENCES

Abraham, S. February 14, 2002. "Letter to the President." Washington, D.C.: U.S. Department of Energy.

American Nuclear Society. May 1, 2002. "ANS Calls for Deployment of New Nuclear Power Plants." Available online: http://www.ans.org. Download date: July 7, 2003.

Ballard, J. D. 2002a. "Testimony of Dr. James David Ballard." U.S. House of Representatives, Committee on Transportation and Infrastructure. Available online: http://wwwyucca mountain.org/leg/ballard042502.htm. Download date: July 8, 2003.

———. 2002b. "Testimony of Dr. James David Ballard." U.S. Senate, Committee on Energy and Natural Resources. Available online: http://wwwyuccamountain.org/leg/ballard 052202.htm. Download date: July 8, 2003.

Beer, S. H. 1993. *To Make a Nation: The Rediscovery of American Federalism.* Cambridge, MA: Harvard University Press.

Berkley, S. April 25, 2002. "Opening Statement of the Honorable Shelley Berkley." Joint Hearing on Transportation of Spent Rods to the Proposed Yucca Mountain Storage Facility, House Subcommittee on Highways and Transit and Subcommittee on Railroads, U.S. House of Representatives. Available online: http://www.house.gov. Download date: July 7, 2003.

Bush, G. W. February 15, 2002. "Presidential Letter to Congress." Available online: http://www.whitehouse.gov. Download date: July 8, 2003.

Congressional Quarterly. 1990. *Congress and the Nation, VII, 1985–1988.* Washington D.C.: Congressional Quarterly, Inc.

Garrett, M. February 15, 2002. "Bush backs Nevada site for nuclear waste." CNN.com/Inside politics. Available online: http://www.cnn.com. Download date: July 8, 2003.

Guinn, K. C. April 8, 2002. "Statement of Reasons Supporting the Governor of Nevada's Notice of Disapproval of the Proposed Yucca Mountain Project." Available online: http:// www.yuccamountain.org/govveto0402.htm. Download date: July 7, 2003.

Halstead, R. J. 1990. Halstead, R. (1990). NWTRC 3.3 terrorism/sabotage paper. Carson City, NV: Nevada Agency for Nuclear Projects.

———. 1993. *State of Nevada nuclear waste transportation impact studies: An overview.* Document # NWPO-TN-015-93. Carson City: State of Nevada Nuclear Waste Projects Office.

———. April 25, 2002. *Testimony of Robert J. Halstead on behalf of the State of Nevada.* Joint hearing on transportation of spent rods to the proposed Yucca Mountain storage facility, House Subcommittee on Highways and Transit and Subcommittee on Railroads. United States House of Representatives. Available online: http://www.house.gov. Download date: July 7, 2003.

Jacob, Gerald. 1990. *Site Unseen: The Politics of Siting a Nuclear Waste Repository.* Pittsburgh: University of Pittsburgh Press.

Lamb, M., and M. Resnikoff, 2001. "Radiological Consequences of Severe Rail Accidents Involving Spent Nuclear Fuel Shipments to Yucca Mountain: Hypothetical Baltimore Rail Tunnel Fire Involving SNF." Document # R01-5. New York: Radioactive Waste Management Associates.

Lamb, M., M. Resnikoff, and R. Moore. 2001. "Worst Case Creditable Nuclear Transportation Accidents: Analysis for Urban and Rural Nevada." Document # R01-4. New York: Radioactive Waste Management Associates.

Luna, R., K. Neuhauser, and M. Vigil. 1999. "Projected Source Terms for Potential Sabotage Events Related to Spent Fuel Shipments to a Yucca Mountain High Level Waste Repository." Document # SAND99-0963. Albuquerque, NM: Sandia National Laboratories.

Morrison, J. A., and E. Vogel. July 10, 2002. "Nevada Politicians React: Leaders disappointed." *Las Vegas Review Journal.* Available online: http://www.reviewjournal.com. Download date: July 6, 2003.

Mountain West Research. 1989. "High-Level Nuclear Waste Transportation Needs Assessment." Document # NWPO-TN-002-89. Carson City: State of Nevada Nuclear Waste Projects Office.

Nuclear Regulatory Commission. 2002. *United States Nuclear Regulatory Commission Package Performance Study Test Protocols: Draft Report for Comment.* Washington, D.C.: Nuclear Regulatory Commission, Office of Nuclear Regulatory Research.

Pianin, E., and H. Dewar. July 9, 2002. "Senate Approves Yucca Mountain as Nuclear Waste Site." *Washington Post.* Available online: http://www.washingtonpost.com. Download date: July 8, 2003.

Reid, H. December 21, 1987. *Congressional Record.* p. 34262. Washington, DC: United States Government.

Riker, W. H. 1987. *The Development of American Federalism.* Boston: Kluwer.

Riley, K. J., and B. Hoffman. 1995. *Domestic Terrorism: A National Assessment of State and Local Preparedness.* Document # MR-505-NIJ. In Santa Monica, CA: RAND.

Skocpol, T. 1999. "How Americans Became Civic." In *Civic Engagement in American democracy,* eds. T. Skocpol and M. Fiorina. Washington, D.C.: Brookings Institution Press/Sage Foundation.

Storing, Herbert J. 1981. *The Complete Anti-Federalist: What the Anti-Federalists Were For.* Chicago: University of Chicago Press.

U.S. Department of Energy. 1999. *Draft Environmental Impact Statement for a Geologic Repository for the Disposal of Spent Nuclear Fuel and High-Level Radioactive Waste at Yucca Mountain, Nye County, Nevada.* Document #DOE/EIS-205D. Washington, D.C.: U.S. Department of Energy.

———. 2002. *Final Environmental Impact Statement for a Geologic Repository for the Disposal of Spent Nuclear Fuel and High-Level Radioactive Waste at Yucca Mountain, Nye County, Nevada.* Document #DOE/EIS-2050. Washington, D.C.: U.S. Department of Energy.

———. January 10, 2003. "Nuclear Power 2010." Available online: http://www.ne.doe .gov/infosheets/NP2010.pdf. Download date: July 8, 2003.

Young, G. 1989. *NWTRC Task 3.3.* Correspondence between contractor (Halstead and NWPO) and author.

CHAPTER 4

The Diplomacy of Counter Terrorism: Lessons Learned, Ignored and Disputed

A Special Report's Publication of the U.S. Institute of Peace

Audrey Kurth Cronin

Recent lessons learned in the diplomacy of counter terrorism included:

- the importance of consistent, long-term incremental steps taken against a phenomenon that will not disappear
- the necessity for a multifaceted policy that includes political, legal, social, diplomatic, economic, and military elements

This report is based upon a meeting of the International Research Group on Political Violence (IRGPV) held at the United States Institute of Peace to discuss national and international methods of countering terrorism. Although the original report was drafted before the September 11 attacks, it has been revised to reflect those attacks and more recent events. The IRGPV is co-sponsored by the U.S. Institute of Peace and the Airey Neave Trust of Great Britain. This report was written by Audrey Kurth Cronin, visiting associate professor in the Security Studies Program at Georgetown University and a participant in the meeting. The views expressed in this report do not necessarily reflect those of the United States Institute of Peace, which does not advocate specific policies.

The editors wish to thank the U.S. Institute of peace for their permission to reprint their Special Report of January 14, 2002.

{Editor's Note: No references are cited at the end of this article because it is the transcription of a special seminar held at the U.S. Institute of Peace in Washington, DC.}

- the need to develop realistic expectations and avoid a crisis mentality that is ultimately satisfying to terrorists, playing down military analogies that might lead to public expectations of early "victory"

- the dynamic interaction between terrorism and counter terrorism, resulting in policies that over time help shape the location, form, and methods used by terrorists

- the promise of law enforcement techniques as an effective long-term approach to fighting both national and international terrorism, not as a substitute for military action but as a complement

- the increasing dissociation of states from terrorism, and an increasing willingness of states to combine their efforts to defeat or discourage terrorist organizations

- the growing promise of international cooperation against the threat

Points of dispute that spawned lively debate included:

- the effectiveness of a law enforcement approach in situations where there is also a nascent peace process, such as Northern Ireland and Israel

- the appropriate use of military force, which tends to be effective for short-term purposes such as disrupting operations, but problematical at stopping terrorism over time

- the actual threat of attack using chemical, biological, nuclear, or radiological weapons, and the level and type of resources that should be devoted to responding to the (actual or perceived) threat

Finally, counter terrorism trends that are worrisome and need more attention included:

- the increasing globalization of the terrorist threat, resulting in shifts to new geographic areas of concern like Central and East Asia, the Balkans, and the Transcaucasus region, and the great freedom of movement by perpetrators

- the resurgence of hostage-taking as a terrorist technique, and the increasing frequency with which both governments and private companies are paying ransoms and making concessions

- the growing tendency of terrorists to use information technology, especially the Internet, to pursue their goals, and the difficulties of countering or tracking that use evidence that terrorism as a tactic may more often be resulting in strategic successes

INTRODUCTION

The September 11 attacks on the Pentagon and the World Trade Center drew into sharp focus the need to understand and counter the threat of international terrorism against innocent victims on American soil and elsewhere. As this report is being written, the campaign against the al Qaeda network is gradually unfolding; American and allied policymakers are working around the clock to develop a long-term, innovative, broad-based strategy for counter terrorism that encompasses both traditional and untraditional means. Understanding the past lessons of the diplomacy of counter terrorism has never been more important, as the coalition response is being crafted, refined, and executed, and as we brace for possible further bioterrorism and other counterattacks in the days, months, and perhaps years ahead.

The original version of this report was completed on August 30, 2001, a few days before the initial attacks occurred. It was based upon a meeting of the International Research Group on Political Violence held at the United States Institute of Peace to discuss national and international methods of countering terrorism. The distinguished members of the group represented decades of experience in studying terrorism, understanding its evolution as a tactic, and countering the phenomenon in the United States and elsewhere. Their discussions ranged from American national policy debates to philosophical arguments about optimal means of response to a fungible and almost undefinable phenomenon. Topics discussed included specific lessons learned from past experience, the challenges of building international coalitions, the effectiveness of criminal law approaches in contrast to military responses, the role of rhetoric and public diplomacy, the effectiveness of current policies, and the "new terrorism" and weapons of mass destruction. There was agreement on only a few of the points discussed; but in nearly every case, the quality of the debate was rich and new conclusions emerged from the clash of differing viewpoints.

Many of the conclusions of the group remain valid in the aftermath of the attacks and provide the opportunity to place the events into a broader historical perspective, but some of them have been altered to reflect recent events. Thus, the report that follows is not a direct reflection of the proceedings of the meeting itself, but more a selection of the counter terrorism lessons discussed there, recast in the context of the unfolding post–September 11 international campaign.

THE THREAT BEFORE SEPTEMBER 11

Even before September 11, most Americans perceived terrorism as one of the most important threats facing the United States into the 21st century (one poll said 84 percent considered international terrorism a "critical threat" to the United States). Attacks on U.S. soil had already dramatically heightened an unfamiliar sense of vulnerability at home.

Twice as many people died in international terrorist attacks in the second half of the nineties than died in the first half, even though the total number of incidents had declined overall. And high-profile incidents in the middle of the decade, particularly the Oklahoma City bombing, the first World Trade Center incident, and the Tokyo sarin gas attacks, had heightened public awareness of the threat as well as widespread worries about new tactics and targets for future assaults.

In the United States, counter terrorism efforts were already marshaling a growing part of the U.S. budget, climbing from $6 billion (fiscal year 1998) to $9.7 billion (fiscal year 2001)—an increase of almost 40 percent in those three years alone (U.S.

Office of Management and Budget, Annual Report to Congress on Combating Terrorism, August 2001, p. 100). In the weeks before the attacks, this trend was continuing, with the Bush administration putting forth a budget request of $10.3 billion in August, 2001 for the upcoming year (fiscal year 2002). International cooperation against terrorism had also increased, ranging from the United Nations' growing willingness in recent years to condemn terrorist actions, to enhanced bilateral intelligence cooperation, to the groundbreaking International Convention on the Suppression of the Financing of Terrorism, opened for signature in January 2000. The highly publicized trial of Saudi expatriate Osama bin Laden's associates involved in the 1998 bombings of U.S. embassies in Tanzania and Kenya, which killed 224 people (12 U.S.) and injured 4574 (15 U.S.), had dramatically demonstrated the global reach of the al Qaeda organization and the vulnerability of American targets overseas. And the sense of growing uneasiness was not just an American preoccupation, as demonstrated by the highly publicized warnings by Russian premier Vladimir Putin's personal protection force of a threat by al Qaeda to assassinate President Bush before the G-8 summit in July 2001.

Before September 11, no single individual had done more than bin Laden to stimulate a growing American domestic effort against terrorism and a widening international movement to meet the threat. There was general awareness even before the attacks that the geography of terrorism was changing in the 21st century. While the Middle East continued to be the locus of most terrorist activity, Central and South Asia, the Balkans, and the Transcaucasus were already growing in significance. And the use of technologies such as the Internet had increased the global reach of many organizations, for recruitment purposes as well as coordination of operations. The traditional model of the hierarchical organization dominated by a central headquarters was already considered outdated, having been replaced by transient cells often connected through cyberspace. The breakdown of barriers between countries, from NAFTA to the European Union, had further removed the traditional means to track the movements of known criminals. Globalization was making geography more of a challenge than ever for counter terrorism efforts, but it was also providing more opportunity for improved cross-border and transcontinental cooperation.

Before 1972, you rarely found the word "terrorism" in the political lexicon—it was hijackings, kidnappings, and murders. In the intervening years, describing the phenomenon as one "field" helped lead to an increasing body of research, the development of effective countermeasures to some terrorist tactics, and better communication among governmental and nongovernmental experts in counter terrorism. However, the downside to the growing community of counter terrorism experts has been the tendency to gloss over the varied political contexts that give rise to terrorist acts, exacerbating the temptation to oversimplify the means we must adopt to counter them. Different responses to terrorism can have different results, depending on the characteristics of the group or individual, the local culture, the social and economic conditions, and the motivations of the terrorists. Indeed, one participant observed that it is wrong to address terrorism as an independent variable, outside of culture and society: terrorism is always a dependent variable. There were other worrisome developments. First, there was a resurgence of hostage-taking—with, for example, high-profile cases of ransom being paid in the Philippines, concession after concession recently made by the Indian government, and an almost constant stream of ransoms being paid in Colombia—leading to a need for new means of deterrence and response by both government authorities concerned about their citizens and private companies interested in protecting their employees. Second was the frightening specter of chemical, biological, radiological, and nuclear (CBRN) terrorism attack, particularly in the United States. With arguably increased access to weapons of mass destruction, such as "loose nukes" from the former Soviet Union and potentially lethal (and poorly controlled) biological pathogens, the danger of use of these means was cause for great concern. In a world of growing religious and ideologically motivated terrorism, where terrorist incidents have in recent years aimed toward more casualties per incident with less accountability to traditional constituencies, the temptation to use CBRN weaponry was especially worrisome.

Participants grappled with the growing perception of threat of attack by CBRN weapons, and the appropriate response to the threat (and its perception). The challenge of assessing the likelihood of the use of these weapons was discussed, with some people arguing that the shift from traditional politically motivated terrorists to those motivated by open-ended religious or apocryphal aims was an important reason why these weapons might be tempting to use. More than one person mentioned that assessing the objective level of threat was not as important as the horrible consequences that would ensue if they were used. Depending upon the type of weapon, the death toll could be a matter of tens of thousands, they warned, resulting not only in nearly unimaginable carnage, but also a fundamental challenge to democratic government and civil society. We must, at almost any cost, minimize that possibility. Still others felt that the threat was grossly overstated: the technical challenges of CBRN weapons, combined with the ease with which more traditional conventional weapons can cause mass casualties, made the likelihood of their use very small. The fear that is created by public speculation, and the waste of scarce resources needed elsewhere, were much more dangerous than the threat itself, they argued.

Others countered that the question was not whether CBRN attacks would occur, but could they occur. Terrorists have unprecedented capability and access to the means of attack, particularly by biological weapons: it was not the "demand side," but the "supply side" that should be focused upon. In any case, policies that are good for humanity, such as global epidemiological monitoring, should be vigorously pursued, since their benefits would pertain even without an attack. Another participant added that he failed to see how such commonsense, needed innovations as training hospital personnel and preparing local responders would in any case be a waste.

There was no consensus reached on the question of counter terrorist efforts directed against the use of CBRN weapons, with the fault lines ultimately drawn over the question of whether we were overreacting to longstanding evolutionary changes or entering a new, more "terrifying" era of terrorism.

Finally, participants debated whether terrorism could in fact claim strategic successes. After years of study, many experts have argued that in the post-colonial world, while there have been tactical successes, terrorism has nowhere been a strategic success. Some participants argued that this no longer seemed to be true. For example, the case of Northern Ireland might be considered a strategic success, since the Good Friday accords would not have been entered into if not for the fact that the IRA's terrorism had caused a great deal of pain and brought the political situation to a new point. Likewise, Israel's retreat from Lebanon was arguably a dramatic example of the success of terrorism, also leading indirectly to the Middle East peace process.

Still, there was considerable optimism among experts about the limited extent to which terrorism could be employed as a means to an end over the long run. Internationally, an increasing dissociation of states from terrorism was already apparent, as well as an increasing willingness of states to combine their efforts to defeat or discourage terrorist organizations. Osama bin Laden was already creating an alliance of states against him and against terrorism more generally. In the United States, the Oklahoma City bombing splintered radical anti-federal government organizations by forcing consideration of the hideous extremes to which some anti-government sentiments could lead. If some terrorist organizations were increasingly achieving forms of strategic success, others were severely undermining their long-term cause by spawning increased counterterrorist activity and widespread revulsion at their methods among constituent groups that they purport to attract or to serve. In this strange world of action and reaction, major terrorist successes, rather than leading to a growing political momentum supportive of a cause, could sow the seeds of fragmentation and organized counterreaction.

Above all, generalizations about changes in the threat are fraught with pitfalls. Counterterrorist techniques are among the most complex and subtle of tools, since perceptions of the threat to which they respond can be as important as the threat itself.

COUNTER TERRORISM LESSONS LEARNED

Decades of experience indicate that the most effective counter terrorist efforts are ultimately stealthy, incremental, pragmatic, and defensive, and they may only marginally affect the terrorists' perceived pay-off. It is extremely difficult to raise the costs of terrorism significantly, since terrorists only need a few successes on the margins to make a political point. The costs of disruption and defense are much greater than the costs of opportunistic attacks. Ultimately, terrorists are spoilers—Americans and their allies cannot be safe everywhere, all the time. And the United States, while the most powerful nation on earth, has not been very effective in recent years at conducting operations against non-government actors or even, in some cases, individual terrorists. In recent years, the threat has evolved much more quickly than have U.S. political and budgetary responses, and we are forced now to learn very quickly and to make up for lost time.

Counter terrorism is typically an area of frustration because it tends to be reactive. One participant pointed to the shifting landscape of terrorist threats and the cyclical waves of counter terrorist responses, from skyjackings in the 1960s, to the hostage incidents of the late 1960s and 1970s, to the U.S. focus on state sponsors in the 1970s, to the concentration on physical security in the 1980s (after the 1983 bombing of the Marine barracks in Beirut), to the fear of attack with CBRN weapons today. This is a cause for reflection on the dynamic interaction between terrorism and counter terrorism, cause and effect, subsequently leading to cause and effect again. To what extent are the counter terrorist policies that we employ shifting the threat from one form to another, so that even "success" against one type of threat leads to mutation into another form of threat? Even when we are successful, are we merely shifting the threat "down the road" to other venues, pushing perpetrators to develop more innovative methods, and encouraging the tendency to maximize the carnage in each attack? In this regard, one participant mentioned that aviation terrorism had generally been considered an area of success in counter terrorism, with the number of skyjackings and bombings dropping precipitously in the 1990s; the events of September 11 put this observation into painful relief and were a reminder of how dangerous it can be to extrapolate from historical experience and numerical trends.

There were two other major areas of focus in discussing responses to terrorism: the use of law enforcement techniques, and the effectiveness of military responses. These will be discussed in turn. First, several participants argued forcefully for primary reliance upon law enforcement as the most effective longer term response to terrorists, asserting that it is the most intellectually consistent means of dealing with terrorists' complex political motivations or fanaticism. Law enforcement, with its focus on the illegal act itself, removes the temptation to try to judge between just and unjust motivations, legitimate and illegitimate concessions, worthy and unworthy political causes: there can be no progress toward social justice by any definition in an atmosphere of violence and insecurity. Moreover, if authorities establish the perception that these acts may be carried out with impunity, everyone suffers. This is particularly important in situations such as that in Northern Ireland, another participant argued, where officials have been tempted to downplay the criminal justice and security aspects to focus on the politics of moving the process forward. It is crucial that officials not undermine public confidence in the rule of law, for then they are actually undermining the peace process they are trying to promote, because they are not able to ensure the security of the majority of the population. Others argued that the adoption of a peace process, political and socio-economic reforms, and other prophylactic measures are desirable alternatives to the criminal law approach, because they address the root causes of terrorist activity over time. Legal inflexibility prevents the kinds of concessions that are necessary in the short run to negotiate a longer term solution. In response, proponents of the criminal law approach vigorously disagreed: if governments send signals that they are only interested in conciliatory activities, then they are taking actions that are inconsistent with the principles of democracy and very dangerous. Ultimately, national policies and laws are the building blocks to combat terrorism.

A second lively debate ignited over the use of military force. The use of military force, on the one hand, was seen as the only way to forcibly and dramatically preempt and disrupt plots and to demonstrate that you can attack terrorists' assets with speed and flexibility. Some participants argued that these measures are vitally important not only in the short run, where elaborate operations are physically destroyed, but also in the long run, since terrorists gain a healthy respect for the ability of the United States (in particular) not only to retaliate but also to preempt. Arguably this respect translates to deterrence of future activities and it also reassures the American public that the United States is not helpless in the face of asymmetrical threats. Other participants argued, however, that the record shows that the use of military force is rarely successful at stopping terrorism over time, since it tends to drive existing groups even further underground, can lock a government into an unproductive tit-for-tat escalation with terrorists, and can increase international alienation against the United States. Dramatic cruise missile attacks, for example, can inflame public opinion in some third world countries (and even among some of our allies), affirming the belief that the United States is arrogant, takes too much unilateral action, and has too much sway in the world. The ironic result can be an overall increase in political sympathy for the terrorists or their cause.

In more practical terms, moreover, the use of military force has become more difficult because of evolutions in the threat. Terrorist groups are increasingly amorphous, more likely to use evolving information technologies and to rely less upon traditional organizational structures, thus making it much harder to find targets to attack militarily. Sometimes perpetrators come together temporarily only for the purpose of attacking a target, as was the case in the first World Trade Center bombing. Furthermore, after attacks, terrorist organizations are claiming credit less often than was once the case: it is increasingly difficult to identify the perpetrators and thus to know against whom to retaliate.

Participants emphasized that terrorism is a tactic, a means, not a single perpetrator or an end in itself. This may at first seem a pedestrian observation; however, such thinking cautions against the widespread tendency either: (1) to over-personalize the threat, as, for example, an individual (Osama bin Laden) or ideology/group (religious fundamentalists); or (2) to rely overmuch on military analogies (the "war" against terrorism) that imply the possibility of a victory. Both are attractive tools to publicize the threat and gain support in a democracy, but both must be used with great care because they can ultimately serve the goals of terrorists and undermine efforts to discourage their tactics. Targeting our efforts against an individual leads to the perception that if that person is killed or captured the threat is over; and using military analogies leads to a belief that the battle or war can be effectively fought with traditional military means alone and a clear-cut victory achieved. These are dangerous illusions that work against effective counter terrorism.

The use of military force is only effective as part of a multifaceted campaign along with social, economic, legal, and political elements. Unfortunately, however, military force is often used because it is the most immediate, demonstrable way to respond to an outrageous event. When a major international incident occurs, a dramatic military response may be fully justified, but short-term fixes must not be permitted to overtake or undermine longer-term strategic interests. The often-drawn contrast to criminal law approaches, moreover, is a false dichotomy. It is hard to maintain a sustained military campaign, and law enforcement is the best way to build a foundation for international cooperation over time. The point is that both methods must be employed, and the belief that effective counter terrorism must reflect primarily one or the other is narrow, counterproductive, and reflective of bureaucratic inflexibility.

Organizational and bureaucratic factors are crucial stumbling blocks in this new environment: so much of the American counter terrorism structure is fragmented into pieces of the whole, designed to respond to a particular element of the "threat" (for example, "domestic" versus "international," "law enforcement" versus "military," "immigration" versus "intelligence") and unequipped to deal with setting broader strategic priorities. The early 20th century philosophies that were the bedrock of our bureaucracy, organized along functional lines and protective of individual turf and missions, must be replaced. An effective response must combine bureaucratic functions in a more flexible way, in the same sense that the terrorist networks that have carried out these attacks are fluid, ad hoc, and dynamic.

Past high-profile U.S. responses have tended to be cathartic, short-lived, and aimed as much at reassuring domestic audiences as at undermining the terrorist threat long-term. Longer term efforts have focused on disruption of terrorist activity, which remains mostly an invisible campaign. This problem is exacerbated in open democratic societies like the United States, where the need to build political support often takes precedence over less visible strategies. Generally, public attention rises as events occur; then there are periods of quiet. One expert spoke about the serious problems America's penchant for publicity presents for other international partners: public proclaiming of international cooperation often hurts it, and opportunistic leaks endanger sources. International partners become wary of sharing information with the United States, which ultimately hampers joint efforts to defeat common threats. And the high-profile target presented by the United States and its assets also deters potential partners from opening themselves by association to new terrorist threats.

CONCLUSION

Ultimately, the most important theme to emerge from the workshop was the need for balance, breadth, and long-term consistency in our approach to counter terrorism. The most effective measures are those that are developed in the context of a multifaceted policy, with political, legal, social, diplomatic, economic, and military elements. Experience shows that overemphasis on any one element, such as military responses, can lead to an undermining of other elements, such as political/diplomatic ties, social programs, and legal sanctions. Likewise, short-term "fixes" such as cruise missile attacks or high-profile spending initiatives must be balanced with long-term, incremental building of counter terrorism programs that establish depth of knowledge, political and social connections, language capabilities, cultural familiarity, and inter-governmental cooperation. Regardless of the level of domestic political interest over time, there is no short-cut to effective counter terrorism measures—although the political will in the United States for a sustained, effective, and broad-based response is unlikely to flag in the foreseeable future. In the aftermath of this national trauma, there is greater hope at least that the lessons of counter terrorism will be studied, expanded, and methodically applied.

RECOMMENDATIONS

We need to continually shore up our international coalition in order to anticipate, prevent, and deter terrorist attacks, not just react to them. Even if it does not yield immediate dramatic results, cooperation can help to perpetuate an international climate of condemnation of all terrorist actions.

The United States needs to make clear that it opposes terrorism no matter where it arises. International counter terrorist cooperation should be expanded, not just among traditional developed states, but also with less developed countries and even to some degree with so-called "states of concern."

The fight against terrorism should be seen as a long-term struggle, not susceptible to a "quick fix": the goal should be to manage expectations, keeping them realistic and avoiding a crisis mentality that is ultimately satisfying to terrorists.

The United States should work to enhance international and bilateral cooperation with other states, particularly in areas such as intelligence, public diplomacy, anti-terrorism measures, control of borders and territory, law enforcement techniques, and counter terrorist training. To the extent that the United States is perceived as responding unilaterally to the threat, it will also increasingly be perceived as a singular target. The United States has impressive military capabilities, but cathartic short-term attacks can boomerang into complex long-term political liabilities, unless they are carefully balanced by the full range of available counter terrorist tools.

CHAPTER 5

Implementing "Justice" through Terror and Destruction: Ecoterror's Violent Agenda to "Save" Nature

Kelly Stoner,
Director, Stop Eco-Violence

Gary Perlstein, Emeritus Professor
Portland State University

For years, a sophisticated and destructive campaign of terror and intimidation has been waged relentlessly in the shadows by a growing number of radical activists—all aiming to "save nature" by force. Frustrated by the perceived futility of effecting social and political change through legal means, these militants have instead resorted to vandalism, sabotage, harassment, and arson. Driving this call for so-called illegal direct action are a number of loosely knit, decentralized groups whose faceless followers are bound only by a common ideology. Collectively, these groups make up what is generally known as the ecoterror movement—hence the crimes committed by adherents are commonly referred to as "ecoterrorism."

The two most prominent ecoterror groups today are the Earth Liberation Front (ELF) and its cohort the Animal Liberation Front (ALF). It is estimated that in the United States alone, ALF and ELF adherents have caused in excess of $100 million in property damage through more than a thousand criminal acts. Ecoterror crimes have significantly increased in both intensity and scope over time. Both private and public property connected with perceived environmental harm and animal use have been targeted, amplifying fears that ultimately ecoterror crimes will result in the loss of human life.

HISTORY OF ECO-TERRORISM

The origins of eco-terrorism are older then many realize. In 1812, in and around the English town of Nottingham, weavers started to feel economic pressure from the use of technology (Sale 1996; Bailey 1998). For approximately 300 years, weavers had worked as independent contractors. Their lace and stockings were hand made, were of high quality, and were important items in the export trade. The industrial revolution brought changes. Factory owners began using the stocking frame and the automated power loom, and the weavers consequently lost a great deal of business.

According to legend, a young factory worker named Ned Ludd accidentally broke a stocking frame at a factory in Nottingham. Because of his youth, he wasn't punished. This gave the weavers a plan. They began breaking into factories and breaking machines. Factories were attacked in Nottingham, Wakefield, and Leeds. Parliament was so concerned that they passed an act making machine-breaking a capital crime. The government also ordered 12,000 troops into the areas where the weavers were active. The weavers formed into a guerrilla army. They would come to a factory and say they were under the orders of General Ned Ludd and threaten to destroy machines if they weren't paid reasonable compensation and given decent working conditions. Most of the factory owners complied. The Luddites, as they became known, avoided violence on any person.

On April 11, 1812, the Luddites attacked the Rawfolds Mill in Yorkshire. The owner of the factory was expecting difficulties with the weavers and had hired guards. The Luddites were unable to gain entry, and in the fighting two of the Luddites were injured and later died. A week later, they attacked another mill in the area and killed the owner. The authorities arrested and executed three Luddites for the murder, and fourteen others were executed for the attack on the mill. The attacks continued, and mills throughout England were attacked and burned. In some cases, the mill owner's homes were also burned down. The military and local law enforcement arrested many of the Luddites, who were either executed or transported to Australia. By 1817, the Luddite movement had been defeated.

The Luddites were not an environmental movement, but they were opposed to technology. Some members of ecoterrorist groups strongly identify with their movement.

MODERN GROUPS

The first significant radical environmental group was Greenpeace. Their modus operandi was using direct action to challenge nuclear weapons testers and whaling vessels (Warford 1997). Their first action took place in 1971, when about a dozen activists set sail in an old fishing boat to block nuclear tests at Amchitka, a small island in the Aleutians. They were not able to stop the nuclear tests, but they received a great amount of publicity. Greenpeace's goal was to stop the destruction of sea creatures and their habitats. In 1977, they renounced the destruction of property. A more radical group, the Sea Shepherds, however, split off from Greenpeace and continued attacks against ships involved in whaling and driftnet fishing. There were also smaller extremist groups

such as R.I.S.E., which in 1972 decided to destroy the human race using infectious diseases (Tucker 2000; Carus 2002). Group members were apprehended, but they had acquired several infectious diseases that they planned to use before they were arrested.
The present-day ecoterrorist groups can trace their origins to the organization known
as Earth First (Zakin 1995).

In 1980, five members of mainstream environmental groups went on a hike to
discuss how to save the environment. They had become frustrated by the traditional
conservation groups' lack of success in halting nature's destruction. This meeting was
the birth of Earth First, the best-known organization in the radical environmental movement. David Foreman became the spokesperson for the group. He was strongly influenced by *Ecotage* (1972) and Edward Abbey's *The Monkey Wrench Gang* (1975). Their
motto was "no compromise in defense of Mother Earth," and their tactics consisted of
tree-sitting, blockading roads to stop logging trucks, sabotaging equipment, and tree
spiking to discourage logging. As the movement developed, it adopted deep ecology
as its ideology. Arne Naess (1989), a Norwegian philosopher, first coined the term "deep
ecology" and developed the philosophy of biocentrism, which looks upon humans as
part of and not superior to nature. The radical ecologists believed that the ecological
crisis was so intense that there was no time for gradual improvement and that the work-
ings of nature must take precedence over human needs (Devall and Sessions 1986;
LaChapelle 1988; Seed 1988; Fox 1990). Throughout the 1980s, members of Earth First
engaged in "monkeywrenching," or ecologically motivated acts of sabotage, throughout the United States, and in 1985 Foreman published a book that gave specific instructions on how to commit acts of sabotage.

Foreman's rhetoric attracted anarchists, radical leftists, and pagans to the group. He
was not a revolutionary at war with western civilization, and he believed that the extreme
beliefs of the anarchists and pagans were counterproductive. In 1990, Foreman and others left Earth First because they believed it had become too radical. Viewing Earth First
as too hesitant, some of the remaining members took the name of an English organization that began in 1992, and the Earth Liberation Front was born in the United States.

THE BURNING RAGE OF A "DYING PLANET": THE EARTH LIBERATION FRONT AND OTHER ECO-DEFENDER TERRORIST GROUPS

They call themselves "the burning rage of a dying planet" (North American Earth
Liberation Front Press Office [NAELFPO] 2001b). Since the late 1990s, self-appointed
members of the Earth Liberation Front have engaged in criminal activity with the aim
of stopping perceived environmental destruction. Although such illegal "direct action"
has been claimed by a number of ad hoc eco-defender terror groups, the ELF has
emerged as the most active by far. Targets of the ELF—which range from natural resource companies to universities, developers, and car dealerships—have sustained millions of dollars in property losses. In recent years, ELF-claimed crimes have increased
significantly in magnitude and scope.

ELF'S ORIGINS, PHILOSOPHY, AND MISSION

The origins of the Earth Liberation Front are rooted in the radical environmentalist movement of the early 1980s, when environmental extremists frustrated with the perceived lack of progress being made by traditional conservation groups started Earth First (Arnold 1997). In 1992, when leaders of Earth First in England decided to decouple themselves from criminal activities in order to gain legitimacy, a group of radical members there splintered off to form the Earth Liberation Front (NAELFPO 2001c). Efforts to mainstream Earth First were also made in the United States. A key organizer in an issue of the *Earth First Journal* wrote, "England Earth First has been taking some necessary steps to separate above ground and clandestine activities. . . . If we are serious about our movement in the US, we will do the same. . . . It's time to leave the night work to the elves in the woods" (Bari 1994).

The ELF describes itself as "an international underground organization that uses direct action in the form of economic sabotage to stop the exploitation and destruction of the natural environment" (NAELFPO 2001a). One of the core beliefs of the ELF and its followers is that modern society will soon annihilate life on earth. The group's 2001 recruiting video, *Igniting the Revolution: An Introduction to the ELF,* "states that it is quite clear that life on this planet is in great danger. If we do not choose to realize this and take appropriate action immediately the Earth will no longer be able to sustain life for future generations" (NAELFPO 2001c). Underlying this apocalyptic view is an ideology known as deep ecology, which espouses that all life is equal and that humans have no right to profit from life (Naess 1989). This may explain why some ELF crimes are committed jointly with its sister organization, the Animal Liberation Front, in relation to animal-use issues. Many adherents of deep ecology extend species equity to the abiotic elements of the environment, including rocks, soil, rivers, and air. They believe that life, as well as the earth's life-support systems, are being simultaneously destroyed by human atrocities (NAELFPO 2003). Members of the ELF act out of a desire to avert an environmental catastrophe by directly disrupting those activities they perceive to be causing the destruction of the natural world.

The ELF's propaganda attributes the looming annihilation of the environment to the "very social and political ideology in operation throughout the westernized countries" (NAELFPO 2001c). That ideology, they say, is capitalism and the accumulation of wealth. To the ELF, it is the "westernized way of life" that is in "complete violation of natural law" (NAELFPO 2001c). Violating natural law, in their view, refers to the stockpiling of resources that exceed immediate individual needs of sustenance. Those entities believed to be responsible for the destruction of the environment are therefore perceived as being concerned only with "pursing profits at any cost." It is the ELF's aim to "eliminate the profit motive from the destruction of the natural environment" (NAELFPO 2001c). Actions taken by ELF adherents are intended to stop entities from making a profit from activities perceived to cause environmental harm.

The ELF is a classic example of what the FBI defines as a special-interest terrorist group in that its members forcibly seek to resolve the specific issue of perceived environmental harm rather than effect widespread political change (U.S. Federal Bureau of Investigation 1999). The basic mindset of the ELF, however, is infused with anti-government, anarchist sentiments that suggest an ultimate aim to overthrow the state, or the "system," as the ELF calls it. This call for revolution is motivated by the beliefs that the government and legal system failed to protect the environment and that the state is in collusion with antienvironmental interests. One example of this expanded ideological outlook can be found in the *Frequently Asked Questions* pamphlet issued by the ELF, which tells followers that "it is not enough to work solely on single, individual environmental issues but in addition the capitalist state and its symbols of propaganda must also be targeted" (NAELFPO 2001a).

Like many radicalized groups, the ELF justifies its criminal activities by asserting the futility and/or inability of effecting desired change through the existing legal framework. The ineffectiveness of lawful—or in their view "indirect" or "state-sanctioned"—activism is considered by the ELF to be the root cause of the perceived failure of the mainstream environmental movement to bring about proper environmental protection (NAELFPO 2003). The ELF argues that more extreme "direct" action is required. This call for extralegal measures is reinforced by the belief that the system—which both "causes and profits from the many of the various atrocities against life"—will not change unless forced to do so (NAELFPO 2001a). As stated by ELF spokesperson Leslie James Pickering, "We're not going to settle for only what the system tells us we can do. It's the system that's causing the problems we're fighting against" (Lee and Shannon 2003). ELF propaganda also contends that "every successful social justice movement throughout history has had an element of radical activism" (Lee and Shannon 2003). ELF followers are further driven to criminal activity by the rationale that perpetrators are acting out in "self-defense" to protect themselves and all life on the planet from certain annihilation (NAELFPO 2001c). The ELF uses these arguments to justify illegal direct action, or "economic sabotage."

Unlike many modern-day radical organizations, the ELF generally works toward definite, rather than symbolic, goals. Their stated aims are to cause as much immediate economic damage to targets as possible and to raise public awareness about perceived environmental atrocities (NAELFPO 2001a). The ELF's activities also appear geared to coerce targeted entities to reform out of fear of possible future attack, as evidenced by threats made following direct actions. One of the convicted perpetrators of a June 2002 incident also suggested that ELF actions are intended to directly stop activity perceived to be causing environmental harm (Barcott 2002). Statements made by ELF spokespersons also indicate a goal of creating tolerance for illegal direct action within the mainstream environmental movement and the general public at large (Hansen 2000). This strategy appears to have two objectives: 1) to add legitimacy to criminal activity so that more individuals will consider economic sabotage as a viable option, and 2) to provide cover or sympathy for those individuals who engage in direct action. Perpetrators of ELF actions appear to place the goal of launching punitive and incapacitating attacks against perceived antienvironmental entities above gaining favorable public opinion. However, swaying attitudes on specific environmental issues is nonetheless central to their mission.

ELF STRUCTURE, LEADERSHIP, AND MEMBERSHIP

The ELF is highly decentralized. There is no central leadership or formal membership. The loosely knit organization consists of an undefined number of autonomous cells that engage in economic sabotage on behalf of the group. According to ELF propaganda, these groups are not even aware of each other's existence and only become known when an illegal direct action is claimed (NAELFPO 2001a). What binds individuals to cells and cells to the movement is the ELF's ideological philosophies. As stated in the ELF's 2001 recruiting video, "If an individual believes in [the ELF's] ideology and they follow a certain set of widely published guidelines, he or she can perform actions and become part of the Earth Liberation Front" (NAELFPO 2001c). Those guidelines are as follows:

1. To cause as much economic damage as possible to a given entity that is profiting off the destruction of the natural environment and life for selfish greed and profit;

2. To educate the public about the atrocities committed against the environment and life; and

3. To take all necessary precautions to avoid harming life (NAELFPO 2001a)

ELF cells presumably follow these guidelines when engaging in illegal direct actions. Cells reportedly function without leaders, and tasks are delegated on a need-to-know basis to minimize risk of detection (Denson 1999). This tight-lipped culture, including the group's anonymous cell structure, is regarded as the chief means by which individual members evade law enforcement (NAELFPO 2001a). Persuading ELF operatives who have pled guilty to ecoterror crimes to reveal the identities of their cohorts may prove critical in solving future cases. This strategy has been successfully employed in a number of ecoterror crimes that have been solved.

There is little data available in the public record about the precise composition and operation of ELF cells or the scope of the movement's membership. What we know comes from ELF propaganda and statements from spokespersons and members convicted of crimes. It is suggested that ELF cells may consist of one to several individuals ("Meet the E.L.F." n.d.). All of the less than a dozen perpetrators arrested or indicted thus far have been male except one. Similarities in operational practices engaged in during the onset and promotion of ELF-claimed crimes suggest that perpetrators have a marked aptitude for advanced technologies. Most ELF members or suspected members are educated teenagers or young adults from the middle class, and nearly all have a known history of environmental activism. It is likely that ELF cells are formed by like-minded activists who meet while participating in aboveground activities.

The scope of the ELF movement is presumed to be generally contained to North America; the overwhelming majority of crimes claimed by the group have occurred in the United States. The ELF first made itself known in the country in 1996 with the burning of a U.S. Forest Service truck in Oregon's Willamette National Forest. Since that time, most ELF actions have taken place in the western states. Over the years, the geographical reach of the ELF has expanded, however, to encompass both Midwest and East Coast states. Because of the group's anonymous cell structure, it is difficult to determine exactly how many ELF cells exist in the United States at any given time. This is further complicated by the possibility that ELF followers may sometimes use ad hoc names such as Revenge of the Trees when claiming responsibility for an action.

Despite the lack of official leadership to organize and promote the ELF, certain organizational functions are preformed through the group's North American Earth Liberation Front Press Office in Portland, Oregon. NAELFPO states that it exists to "[expose] the political and social motives behind the direct actions of the ELF" (NAELFPO 2001a). This is arguably the group's propaganda vehicle, because it provides the media and general public with explanations for ELF actions derived from anonymous communiqués sent in from the perpetrators. The individuals who have operated the press office since its founding in 1997 profess to know nothing about the specifics of ELF crimes; they serve in their capacities because they ideologically support the movement.

The NAELFPO also aids in recruiting. This is most apparent through the ELF Web site that the press office maintains, where propaganda materials and how-to guides on committing illegal direct action (including step-by-step recipes for building incendiary devices) can be easily accessed by interested activists. A recruiting video and FAQ brochure about the ELF were also produced and distributed by the NAELFPO. Until late 2002, the ELF press office was run by self-appointed spokespersons Craig Rosebraugh and Leslie James Pickering. Although Rosebraugh and Pickering have stepped down to form a new revolutionary group known as Arissa (to be discussed later), they still actively promote the ELF. The NAELFPO is now reportedly being operated by "people working behind the scenes" (NAELFPO 2002b). The ELF Web site has remained active, and communiqués and statements continue to come out of the office.

ELF METHODOLOGY AND TARGETING

The ELF first entered the public consciousness in October 1998 after its operatives set fire to a ski resort in Vail, Colorado, and caused an unprecedented $12 million in damages. The aim of the direct action was to thwart a planned expansion of the resort, which it was believed would destroy critical lynx habitat (Weller 1998). A total of eight fires were set—in several cases miles apart—that destroyed five buildings and three chairlifts. The ELF communiqué that was issued to claim the attack triggered widespread local and national media coverage. The action was unparalleled in its scope, and it seemed to invigorate the group's use of arson as its primary mode of attack. Arson has been used by ELF operatives since the movement first formed in the United States, but it is not the only tool in the group's toolbox.

The methods and targets of the ELF appear to be primarily dictated by the group's core goals—cause maximum economic damage to targets perceived to be profiting from destruction of the environment, educate the public about such atrocities, and instill fear in targets and other like entities. Therefore, as stated in the ELFs 2001 recruiting video, "Arson has become a popular tool of the ELF for the obvious reason that it maximizes economic damage to a particular target. In addition, this tactic is very successful at getting attention" (NAELFPO 2001c).

ELF arson attacks cause much greater damage than other tactics used by the group's operatives, which include the traditional methods of monkey wrenching—such as pouring sugar in gas tanks, gluing door locks, and cutting brake lines. Perpetrators of ELF-claimed crimes often use multiple timed incendiary devices and accelerants to ensure as much destruction to their targets as possible. Acts of vandalism, such as smashing windows and thrashing equipment, also occur, both in conjunction with arsons and individually. Crop crushing—the destruction of genetically modified food crops—is another tactic of the ELF. Graffiti, including the group's initials and slogans denouncing the offending activity, is often, although not always, left at the crime site.

There have been several reported cases of fuel and other onsite materials being used in launching attacks. Operatives engage in intensive intelligence operations to scope out targets both before and after attacks. ELF followers may be fixated on preventing perceived environmental harm, but they do not shy away from using technology in their operations. Sophisticated Internet re-mailers and encryption programs are often utilized to shield communiqués and other communications from law enforcement. The ELF is also particularly security conscious. Online guides tell operatives how to create "clean rooms" so that incriminating DNA evidence is not left behind when building incendiary devices. Manuals are also available on creating a sound safety culture and what to do if law enforcement comes looking around.

Over the years since the ELF movement began, the intensity and frequency of crimes committed by its operatives has increased. This is particularly true of arsons. In the group's most recent firebombing, a 400,000 square foot, five-story condo development in San Diego, California, was destroyed, along with large construction equipment and an underground parking garage. Flames shot up nearly 200 feet in the air as about 100 firefighters battled the blaze (Green and Hughes 2003). The damages totaled approximately $50 million, making the attack the largest ever in the history of the ELF and the ecoterror movement at large. Although the San Diego development attack is atypical in that caused such massive damage, it is not an unusual ELF action. The number of crimes claimed by the group has increased over time, although the frequency of actions varies. The ELF is responsible for causing millions of dollars in property losses through the hundreds of crimes its operatives have committed. Tracking the specific number of crimes, however, is complicated because not all crimes are officially claimed or reported to authorities.

The earliest known ELF crimes in the United States tended to focus on businesses and government agencies involved in the utilization of natural resources. These targets primarily included logging companies, the U.S. Forest Service, and the Bureau of Land Management. From the late 1990s to present, however, the scope of entities in the ELF's crosshairs expanded significantly as operatives began to focus in on emerging environmental concerns. Operatives aiming to stop genetic engineering attack universities and traditional targets that are engaging in such efforts. Buildings that house research labs and experimental crops are destroyed. The issue of urban sprawl drives members of the ELF to torch and vandalize partially constructed homes and other forms of new development. "Gas-guzzling" SUVs go up in flames at auto dealerships, and personal utility vehicles are vandalized on the street and in driveways. Antiglobalization issues also trigger illegal direct action against multinational companies such as Nike. ELF actions are also occasionally committed around animal-use concerns in conjunction with its sister organization the Animal Liberation Front, with whom it declared solidarity in the 1990s. One of those attacks was launched in 2001 against a New York bank because of its ties with a company that uses animals in its drug and chemical testing. Examples of ELF crimes in the United States can be found at the end of this chapter.

ELF actions reported to date have targeted only property, and there have not been any known injuries resulting from direct actions. There have been a number of close calls, however, ranging from people stumbling onto incendiary devices that fail to ignite to emergency responders narrowly escaping burning buildings. Law enforcement and other observers have repeatedly stated that it is only a matter of time until someone is injured or killed. A direct attack has yet to be launched against an individual person by an ELF follower. There is some evidence to suggest, however, that the group's guiding principle to take all necessary precautions to protect life may become irrelevant in the future.

In September 2002, an ELF statement was issued claiming an arson attack on a U.S. Forest Service research station in Irvine, Pennsylvania. The group warned that "segments of this global revolutionary movement are no longer limiting their revolutionary potential by adhering to a flawed, inconsistent 'non-violent' ideology. . . . Where it is necessary, we will no longer hesitate to pick up the gun to implement justice" (NAELFPO 2002a). This markedly more threatening rhetoric suggests a significant shift in the targeting of at least some of the ELF's followers to include people connected with perceived environmental destruction. Additionally, in early 2003, former ELF spokespersons Craig Rosebraugh and Leslie James Pickering founded a new "revolutionary organization" called Arissa whose aim is to spur on more severe direct action ("ELF Members Spawn More Radical Group" 2003). Both ecoterror inciters said they formed the group because of personal conflicts with the ELF's "non-violence" ideology. Arissa is built on what Rosebraugh has coined "political non-violence"—the belief that lawful activism must go hand in hand with extreme actions that could potentially include physical assault (Roe 2003). Although Arissa is being billed as a separate group, it has recently published materials advocating the ELF.

COMRADES IN ARMS

A number of eco-defender terror groups have been responsible for environmentally motivated crimes both in the United States and abroad. No group compares with the reach of the ELF or the scope and magnitude of crimes claimed in its name. The ELF's parent organization, Earth First, has remained an advocate of direct action to this day, promoting monkeywrenching through its widely published bimonthly journal and Web site.

Earth First members are still known to engage in minor acts of sabotage, although the group does not actively claim them. The Night Time Gardeners are another loosely defined ecoterror group. During the late 1990s and early 2000s, they claimed a number of vandalism strikes against genetically modified crops in the western U.S. through a press office dubbed Genetix. A number of ad hoc groups have gone by a host of different names, including the Anarchist Golfing Association, The Frogs, Revenge of the Trees, and the Concerned OSU Students and Alumni. The majority of these groups have laid claim to a single direct action, but most of these individual incidents—typically vandalism strikes—have caused thousands of dollars in damages. It may be that the perpetrators of these crimes are indeed ELF followers attempting to be creative, as the names generally relate to the target's line of business. None of these groups have issued propaganda or operations manuals or have a functioning press office as the ELF does. One group within the ecoterror movement has an ideological focus that overlaps with the ELF, and its history of illegal direct action certainly compares with, if not exceeds, the ELF's record. This group is the ELF's comrade in arms and predecessor, the Animal Liberation Front.

"NO JUSTICE—JUST US" ANIMAL LIBERATION FRONT, STOP HUNTINGDON ANIMAL CRUELTY, AND OTHER MILITANT ANIMAL RIGHTS GROUPS

For more than two centuries, organized groups have concerned themselves with the welfare of animals. With the advent of the animal rights movement, numerous efforts have been launched to reduce or eliminate the suffering of animals through humane treatment. Not all of these activities, however, have transpired within the existing legal framework. Radical militant animal rights groups have taken to illegal direct action in the form of arson, vandalism, theft, and harassment to fulfill the objectives of the movement. The Animal Liberation Front has emerged as the most active of these loosely knit organizations, causing millions of dollars in property damage to targets connected with the use of animals. In recent years, the magnitude of ALF-claimed crimes has significantly increased. Additionally, some group adherents acting on the suggestion of a relatively new group, Stop Huntingdon Animal Cruelty (SHAC), are no longer drawing the line at targeting people.

ALF ORIGINS, PHILOSOPHY, AND MISSION

Organized concern for the welfare of animals dates back to late-eighteenth- and early-nineteenth-century England. Organizations such as the Royal Society for the Prevention of Cruelty to Animals and the National Anti-Vivisection Society formed at the time to address the use of animals in the growing biomedical research industry. Similar groups were established in the United States. The majority of these original animal welfare societies—many of which still exist today—aimed not to end animal research or other uses for animals but rather to ensure that animals received proper care and humane treatment. Early efforts of these groups—which were conducted within established legal channels—produced the earliest animal protection legislation in the United Kingdom and United States. Other groups such as the Society for the Suppression of Vice and later the League Against Cruel Sports formed in England at that time to abolish hunting and animal sports. These groups worked through legal channels to establish legislation that outlawed bear-baiting, cock-fighting, and similar practices. It was not until the early 1960s that interactions between the animal welfare movement and animal users took a dramatic and violent turn.

As with earlier developments in the animal welfare movement, the origins of using direct action to advance animal-rights have their roots in the United Kingdom. Frustrated with the perceived slow pace of effecting change through legal means, animal rights extremists began to attack animal enterprises with acts of sabotage, property destruction, and intimidation in the second half of the twentieth century. This shift to the use of illegal and often violent tactics was initiated by the formation of the Hunt Saboteurs Association (HSA) in 1963. Founded by 21-year-old freelance journalist John Prestige, HSA introduced the "hunt sab" tactic, or the launching of sabotage raids to disrupt fox hunts by harassing hunters and confusing hounds ("History of Hunt Saboteurs Association" 2003). Still in operation today, HSA grew from a single small group to a network of "hunt sabs" that spanned the country in just a few years. From the start, HSA has enjoyed extensive media coverage of its lively efforts to disrupt hunts. Media attention was facilitated by the open public support given to HSA from the League Against Cruel Sports (LACS), which even made available the latest know-how on sabotaging hunts to interested activists. This aboveground-belowground arrangement was effective in publicizing HSA and its cause. Ecoterrorist organizations would take advantage of this operational system for years to come (Arnold 1997).

Despite the success HSA realized in stopping hunts, blowing horns and laying hound-confusing aniseed trails seemed too tame in some of its members' minds to put a complete stop to the sport. In 1972, two hunt saboteurs, Ronnie Lee and Cliff Goodman, founded the Band of Mercy with the initial objective of attacking hunters directly. Named after an obscure nineteenth-century antivivisection group known to engage in acts of vandalism and sabotage, the small outfit significantly amplified the tenor of illegal direct action. Initial efforts carried out by the Band of Mercy generally aimed to stop hunts by disabling vehicles. What differed from Hunt Saboteur's modus operandi was that the Band's activists often left behind notes explaining their actions and urging hunters to cease their activities. After a year of operation, the Band of Mercy greatly expanded their campaign when its operatives came to "recognize their true potential for the prevention of animal suffering" ("Thirty Years of Direct Action" 2003).

In November 1973, the Band of Mercy launched its first attack on the animal research industry. The Band's activists had learned about the construction of a new medical research center by Hoechst Pharmaceutical that planned to test drugs on animals. They resolved to take action to prevent the construction of the center and decided that the only viable way to achieve their goal was arson. The activists gained entry to the half-completed facility and set it on fire, causing an unprecedented £26,000 in damages. The perpetrators returned six days later and once again set the center ablaze—this time causing an additional £20,000 in damages. A statement was sent to the local press claiming the attacks on behalf of the group. It read:

> The building was set fire to in an effort to prevent the torture and murder of our animal brothers and sisters by evil experiments. We are a non-violent guerrilla organization dedicated to the liberation of animals from all forms of cruelty and persecution at the hands of mankind. Our actions will continue until our aims are achieved. ("Thirty Years of Direct Action" 2003)

The attack on the Hoechst Pharmaceutical medical research center marked a significant turning point in the Band of Mercy's modus operandi. The group's list of targets now included an array of enterprises connected to animal use. Arson henceforth became a frequently used tool, although vandalism and sabotage were still regularly employed. The prevention of animal use continued to be one of the group's primary goals, but through its subsequent actions other aims became evident. In its second major act, the Band's activists torched boats licensed to participate in a planned seal cull. Unlike its previous arson attack, however, the perpetrators opted not to claim responsibility so that the victim and other sealers would worry that other vessels might meet the same fiery fate ("Thirty Years of Direct Action," 2003). The Band of Mercy was now seeking to terrorize its targets into compliance. The attack forced the cancellation of the seal cull and put the victim out of business. Another tactic employed by the Band of Mercy that later became a mainstay of militant animal rights extremism was "animal liberation"—the stealing of animals from laboratories and farms. The first of these raids was launched against a British farm. More than a dozen guinea pigs raised there were taken by the Band's activists. Although the economic losses from the raid were minor, the act terrorized the breeder into closing the farm.

The Band of Mercy launched an array of attacks against hunters, animal research laboratories, food-production facilities, farms, and other animal enterprises during its two and a half years of operation. Under Ronnie Lee's leadership, the outfit significantly escalated its level of violence and destruction, progressing from acts of vandalism and theft to arson. The Band's criminal exploits, however, came to a halt in 1974 when Lee and Cliff Goodman were spotted by a security guard while attempting to firebomb a medical facility. Soon after, they were arrested by the police, stood trial, and were sentenced to three years of imprisonment. The trial and jail sentence turned Lee into a martyr, and after being paroled twelve months into his sentence, he emerged from prison in 1976 to form the Animal Liberation Front.

Lee had spent his jail time plotting out the makings of a militant underground revolutionary organization dedicated to the liberation of all animals from human exploitation (Arnold 1997). He opted to drop the name of his former group, Band of Mercy, for the name Animal Liberation Front to convey a more revolutionary feel (Alleyne and Shaw 2001). Lee utilized the publicity and recognition bestowed upon him during his trail to fuel the fledgling movement. To rationalize the use of criminal tactics, the ALF was from the onset characterized as a "nonviolent" group since its actions took aim at destroying inanimate objects. Lee laid out the ALF's objectives as follows:

- To save animals form suffering here and now;
- To inflict economic loss on people who exploit animals, resulting in less profit for them to plough back into their animal exploitation business; and
- To escalate events to a point where all of these industries are under threat and can't operate (U.S. Department of Justice 1993)

Immediately following its formation, the ALF's adherents swung into action, victimizing a host of targets directly and indirectly involved with animal use. Within its first year of operation, attacks launched by the group inflicted millions of pounds in damages. As with the Band of Mercy, the actions of the ALF became increasingly violent. Petty criminal action, such as spray-painting graffiti and breaking windows, continued to be regularly used, but arson was quickly adopted as a favored tactic (U.S. Justice Department 1993). In time, ALF operatives began to use increasingly sophisticated incendiary devices that produced far more devastating fires than in previous years. A few group members were arrested for ALF-claimed crimes during its early days of operation, including Ronnie Lee in 1987 for an attempt made to burn down department stores. Most acts of "economic sabotage," however, went unanswered. It was not long before ALF activity spread across Europe. By the early 1980s, incidents of animal theft and vandalism were being claimed by the group in the United States.

    Today, the Animal Liberation Front operates in more than a dozen counties worldwide. It describes itself as a collection of "small autonomous groups of people [from] all over the world who carry out direct action against animal abuse" ("ALF Mission Statement/Credo" 2003). The widespread propagation of the ALF is believed to have been greatly facilitated by the publication of *Animal Liberation* in 1975 by Peter Singer. This influential book dramatically transformed the animal welfare movement by promoting the philosophy that animals have equal rights with humans (Singer 1975). Until this time, the animal welfare movement had espoused the view that animals are entitled to life and humane treatment unless there are overriding human interests involved. Singer interjected a radically different way of viewing animals. He argued that because animals are capable of feeling pain and suffering, they deserve the same moral consideration as humans. Hence, regardless of the reason, pain inflicted on animals should not be seen as a lesser evil just because the recipient is nonhuman. Singer argued that what he called "speciesism" was analogous to racism and sexism; he defined the term as the idea that the interests of one species can supercede the interests of members of other species. Hence, using animals to serve human needs of any kind (whether for food, clothing, the production of medicine, entertainment, etc.) is morally wrong.

    The animal-rights philosophy advanced primarily by Singer forms the basis of the ALF's ideological framework. Consequently, the ALF requires its members must at least be vegetarians, although veganism (a diet that excludes all animal products) is preferred. Further reinforcing the ALF's belief in species equity is the widely publicized principle of deep ecology. It espouses that all life is equal by putting forth the concept of biocentrism, which sees humans as a part of nature rather than being superior to it (Naess 1989). Hence, it is believed that humans are not the masters of nature and so do not have the right to use animals in servicing their needs, no matter how urgent. It is perhaps this concept of morality that leads to the widely held belief among ALF adherents that those who use animals are evil. A 2001 ALF statement claiming the firebombing of a medical research center in New Mexico said that "we intend for this act of nonviolent economic sabotage to bring an end to this truly evil institution" (North American Animal Liberation Front Press Office [NAALFPO] 2001).

The ALF, like their comrades in arms in the ELF, justifies "non-violent economic sabotage" by asserting that "crimes of enormous proportion against animals are commonly ignored by the legal system" ("Simplest ALF Action" 2003). Therefore, ALF adherents break "unjust laws" that support animal abuse. Unlike the ELF, however, it would appear that the ALF's disregard for current law does not necessarily carry with it antiestablishment beliefs. Laws relating to animal use are believed to be institutionalized, but changing them is considered possible. As stated by former ALF spokesperson David Barbarash, "animal liberation will not be achieved by illegal means alone, nor from legal protesting and lobbying alone either" ("The ALF Unmasked" 2003). Hence, the state is not necessarily considered to be in collusion with perceived animal abusers. All animal use of any kind would need to be outlawed, however, for the ALF to cease its use of illegal direct action (NAALFPO 2000a).

The ALF is categorized by the FBI as a special-interest terrorist group because its adherents forcibly seek to resolve perceived animal abuse rather than effect widespread political change. Criminal action taken by group members is geared to interfere directly with animal use and/or make associated activities unprofitable. The ALF's objectives do, however, include swaying public opinion on animal issues. This aim—"to reveal the horror and atrocities committed against animals"—is outlined in the ALF's membership guidelines ("Animal Liberation Front Guidelines" 2003). To this end, the group's adherents often videotape and/or photograph their raids for pubic release. A possible subset of seeking to end the use of animals may also be an emerging objective to prevent perceived environmental harm to habitat. As stated by former ALF spokesperson David Barbarash, "It makes no sense to fight for the lives of wildlife without also fighting for their homes (and ours)—the natural environment." ("The ALF Unmasked," 2003).

ALF STRUCTURE, LEADERSHIP AND MEMBERSHIP

The Animal Liberation Front is highly decentralized, with no traditional leadership or membership base. The loosely knit organization consists of an undefined number of autonomous cells that independently commit crimes on behalf of the ALF. What binds individuals to these cells and to the movement at large is the ALF's ideological philosophy. Adherents can earn the "right" to regard themselves as being part of the ALF only by carrying out illegal direct actions consistent with the ALF's stated guidelines:

1. To liberate animals from places of abuse, i.e., laboratories, factory farms, fur farms, etc.;

2. To inflict economic damage to those who profit from the misery and exploitation of animals;

3. To reveal the horror and atrocities committed against animals; and

4. To take all necessary precautions against harming any animal, human and non-human ("ALF Mission Statement/Credo" 2003)

ALF cells presumably follow these guidelines when engaging in criminal activity. Due to the ALF's nonhierarchical structure, cells reportedly function independent from specific direction outside of their membership. It is suggested in "The ALF Primer," one of the movement's primary online guides to illegal direct action, that cell leadership should be assumed by a single individual so that "split second decisions can be made quickly." Specific tasks are said to be delegated to cell members on a need-to-know basis to minimize the risk of detection (Denson 1999). The tight-lipped culture of secrecy that exists within the ALF movement is regarded as the chief mechanism by which adherents evade law enforcement ("Introducing the Animal Liberation Front" 2003). Hence, the practice of "snitching" on fellow cell members to law enforcement is considered unforgivable throughout the ecoterror movement (Mahonia 2003).

There is little data available in the public record about ALF cell composition and operation or the full scope of the movement's membership. What is known comes from ALF propaganda and from statements made by spokespersons and convicted followers. It is suggested that ALF cells usually consist of two to five members ("The ALF Primer" 2003). "The ALF Primer" strongly advises cells to only "use the minimum number of people needed for each action." Most of the few adherents convicted of ALF-claimed crimes have been male. Most of these followers are educated teenagers or young adults from the middle class who are raised in urban areas. A few followers have been drifters. Operational protocols typically adhered to in the commission of ALF-claimed crimes demonstrate that perpetrators have a marked aptitude in the use of technology. Nearly all of them have a prior history of involvement in the animal-rights movement and other forms of activism. It is therefore likely that ALF cells are formed by like-minded activists while participating in above-ground activities. ALF propaganda states that "starting your own cell is better than joining an existing one, since if you know of an existing one, their security obviously isn't too good" ("The ALF Primer" 2003).

The scope of the ALF movement at present is presumed to encompass about a dozen countries worldwide; crimes have been committed in Western Europe, North America, and Australia. ALF actions first occurred in England with the founding of the loosely knit organization in 1976 and progressively fanned out to other neighboring European countries. The ALF made its American debut in March 1979 after adherents, masquerading as lab workers, stole research animals from the New York University Medical Center. The global expansion of the ALF is attributable to the publicity and support the movement has enjoyed from international mainstream animal-rights groups, media coverage of crimes, and, more recently, the dissemination of propaganda via the Internet. ALF sympathizers have also advanced the terror outfit's range of operations by reaching out to potential recruits through workshops and activist meetings. Because of the group's anonymous cell structure, it is difficult to determine exactly how many ALF cells exist in those countries where criminal activity has occurred. This is further complicated by the possibility that ALF followers may sometimes use ad hoc names such as the Animal Liberation Brigade when claiming responsibility for illegal direct actions.

Despite the lack of official leadership to organize and promote the ALF, certain organizational functions are performed through a number of sympathetic above-ground groups and individual supporters. One of the most closely affiliated of these outfits is the North American Animal Liberation Front Press Office (NAALFPO), which calls itself "the voice of ALF." Its stated purpose is "to provide information to the media about the philosophy and activities of the Animal Liberation Front in the United States and Canada" (NAALFPO 2002). The NAALFPO is but one of many such press offices located around the globe where ALF activity regularly occurs. These public interfaces collectively serve as the terror unit's propaganda vehicle by providing commentary on ALF actions derived from anonymous communiqués sent in from perpetrators. Individuals operating ALF press offices have professed ignorance about the specifics of crimes committed on behalf of the group; they insist that they serve in their capacities as spokespersons because they ideologically support the movement. Aside from acting as the public representatives of the ALF, some of the better-known press officers often engage in recruiting efforts that typically take the form of road tours and appearances at major activist conferences. From the late 1990s until early 2003, self-appointed representatives running the North American ALF press office—namely Katie Fedor and her successor David Barbarash—openly discussed followers' criminal activities with reporters. Today, anonymous activists, who correspond with the media only through e-mail, operate the NAALFPO. Although the activity of the press office has markedly decreased with this management change, other supportive groups and sympathetic individuals have filled in the gaps.

Prior to the establishment of the NAALFPO in the late 1990s, adherents would sometimes claim crimes on behalf of the ALF by sending anonymous communiqués to the local press. But early ALF adherents operating in the United States did not always have to go it alone. America's largest and most well-funded nonprofit animal-rights organization—People for the Ethical Treatment of Animal (PETA)—also played public intermediary for the domestic terror outfit. PETA's involvement as media conduit for the ALF was rationalized on the grounds that the above-ground organization shared the same goal of ending animal use. One of the most high-profile cases of PETA assuming the role of ALF's press agent was the 1992 $1.2 million arson of two animal-research labs at Michigan State University. One day prior to the raid, a Federal Express package from one of the perpetrators containing details of the planned attack was sent directly to PETA (*U.S.* v. *Coronado* 1993). The information was then used by the mainstream group to issue a press release publicizing the attack on behalf of the ALF. Federal agents later discovered evidence indicating that PETA's president, Ingrid Newkirk, had made arrangements days before the MSU arson to have the attack information come directly to her though one of the group's members. A second package destined for PETA containing stolen documents and a videotape of the actual ALF raid was also intercepted by Federal Express employees.

PETA's involvement in the MSU arson did not stop at broadcasting the ALF crime. According to PETA's 1994 tax return, the group also gave $45,000 to the legal defense fund of the only ALF operative convicted of the MSU arson, Rodney "Rod" Coronado. In subsequent years, PETA has continued its practice of contributing to the legal defense funds of other individuals believed to be involved in ecoterror crime. PETA organizers, including Newkirk, have remained avid supporters of the ALF to the present day. In recent years, other sizable animal rights groups have also become vocal advocates of illegal direct action for the animal-rights cause. Chris DeRose, the president of Last Chance for Animals, whose membership is 100,000 strong, told an online activist newsletter in 2002, "I'm a firm and adamant believer in direct action. That's everything from doing civil disobedience direct action to taking over a facility to liberations" (Vaughan 2002). The Animal Defense League, another large animal-rights group that has chapters throughout the United States, also makes it a regular practice to e-mail ALF communiqués to its members.

Support from major mainstream organizations—PETA being the most prominent—has given significant legitimacy to the ALF and its practice of illegal direct action. It is widely believed by law enforcement that this favorable interface with the above-ground animal rights movement is critical in recruiting new ALF adherents. Also central to boosting exposure to the ALF's ideologies are a number of online Web sites that play a key role in disseminating propaganda and how-to guides on illegal direct action. One of the oldest and most well-known of these sites is dubbed the Animal Liberation Frontline Information Service, or ALFIS. Launched in 1994, the stated mission of ALFIS is "to provide an online information service dedicated to the activities of the animal liberation movement in Europe, North America and World-Wide" ("About Us" 2003). Until January 2002, the ALFIS site actively tracked ALF actions around the world and offered an array of primers on direct action and security protocols. Although the ALFIS site is still accessible on the Internet today, its content has not been updated in nearly two years. However, the e-mail–based information service used to disseminate ALF communiqués has been maintained by ALFIS coordinators and is in operation today. Known as the Frontline Information Service, it currently boasts more than 5,600 subscribers. The void created by the inactive ALFIS Web site appears to have filled by several other independently maintained Web sites that provide ALF-related content.

One of the more active pro-ALF portals today is *Bite Back Magazine*'s Web site, www.directaction.info. Created in 2001, the site features articles on the militant animal rights movement and provides a regularly updated listing of illegal actions committed by the ALF and other anonymous radical activists. With growing regularity, ALF communiqués and those of other spin-off groups can be found on the site. *Bite Back* also closely tracks militant activist activity associated with a relatively new hard-hitting radicalized group called Stop Huntingdon Animal Cruelty, or SHAC. Founded in the UK in 1999, SHAC has significantly fueled ALF activity in recent years. In its efforts to shut down international drug and chemical tester Huntingdon Life Sciences (HLS), SHAC has spurred activists to take forceful action against its many targets located across the globe. Routine "call to action" e-mails are sent out to hundreds of activists both in the United States and the UK, naming weekly targets that have even loose ties with HLS. SHAC's many country-based Web sites also provide extensive target lists that include the names of employees and their home address and phone numbers. While some anti-HLS activists engage in lawful protest, others have vandalized and torched property—often claiming such crimes in the name of the ALF. SHAC is highly supportive of this terrorist activity. As noted in an October 2003 e-newsletter to U.S.-based activists, "SHAC has always maintained that it whole heartedly supports the liberation of animals and the destruction of any property connected to animal cruelty" (SHAC 2003). Militant anti-HLS activists in the UK have on occasion gone beyond targeting property and physically assaulted people. Fierce rhetoric from like-minded activists in the United States has engendered fears that this violent terror tactic will become more commonplace.

ALF METHODOLOGY AND TARGETING

Since its early beginnings in the UK, the ALF has inflicted millions of dollars in damages around the globe to an array of targets connected even indirectly to animal use. Although petty criminal action is widely employed on a regular basis, more destructive tactics have become increasingly commonplace. The methods and targets of the ALF are primarily dictated by the loosely knit outfit's stated core goals—liberate animals, inflict economic damage to targets connected with animal use, and educate the public about animal harm. ALF adherents have until recently restricted their criminal activities to the theft and destruction of public, private, and corporately owned property. These actions, although certainly meant to terrorize individuals connected with animal use, have not yet resulted in physical harm. However, other clandestine militant animal-rights radicals have taken direct aim at people. This willingness to cause physical harm for the animal-rights cause signals the possible adoption of more violent tactics within the broader movement. Property crimes nonetheless remain the standard mechanism by which militant animal activists aim to force an end to animal use.

ALF operatives are known to engage in a range of criminal activities, and specific crimes often occur in conjunction with each other. The most common ALF direct actions are minor forms of vandalism that include painting graffiti (usually ALF slogans and threats), breaking windows, gluing door locks, and sabotaging vehicles. "The ALF Primer" recommends that followers should "start small, then move on to bigger things." "Animal liberation"—the stealing of animals primarily from farms and laboratories—is another commonly used tactic of the ALF. Considered the quintessential direct action, single ALF "liberations" have resulted in the release of thousands of domesticated animals. In a number of cases, scores of the animals abandoned by the perpetrators have quickly died of dehydration or were killed by cars (Schwarzen and Sullivan 2003). Perpetrators of ALF-claimed crimes have also engaged in major property destruction. These more-sophisticated direct actions range from breaking into enterprises to vandalize equipment and steal documents to setting fire to buildings. Arson, as stated in "The ALF Primer," is considered "by far the most potent weapon of direct action." Incendiary devices used by ALF followers are typically fashioned out of milk jugs filled with flammable liquid that are detonated with incense sticks or a kitchen timer. ALF arsons have caused millions of dollars in property losses to a variety of animal-based enterprises since the late 1980s.

ALF adherents invest considerable time into planning activities and are particularly security conscious. ALF operatives are cautioned to make sure they "know how to do it right" before engaging in any form of illegal direct action ("The ALF Primer" 2003). Online instructional guides direct adherents on the mechanics of specific illegal direct actions and how to evade law enforcement. It is suggested that operatives choose targets outside of their immediate area and conduct extensive surveillance to determine points of entry and security weaknesses. Individuals carrying out ALF actions are warned to wear clothing that does not have any identifiable marks and oversized shoes that will not leave incriminating footprints ("The ALF Primer" 2003). It is also recommended that clothes be purchased at a local second-hand store so that police cannot trace back hair and fibers left behind at the crime scene. ALF operatives are also advised to always wear gloves to avoid leaving behind fingerprints. Furthermore, it is cautioned that clothing and tools be disposed of properly after an ALF action is carried out. ALF adherents who want their crimes to be publicized are advised to use sophisticated Internet re-mailers and encryption programs when transmitting communiqués so that they cannot be traced to their source.

ALF operatives generally tend to target animal enterprises that are easy to access and infiltrate and offer the most potential to attract media attention and public sympathy. Operations that are readily identifiable to the general public and/or symbolic in nature stand a greater likelihood of being victimized than smaller lower-profile establishments. Animal abuse—perceived or otherwise—can also attract the interest of ALF adherents. Additionally, enterprises connected with animal use whose employees are least prepared to contend with ALF actions, namely the animal-research community, are also frequent targets. ALF activists are recommended to "get to know their local animal industry" from "the farmers, the animal transporters and the slaughterhouses to the processors and down to the retail end" ("Simplest ALF Action" 2003). "The ALF Primer" suggests that the "easiest way" for adherents to hone in on a target is through the local phone book. In general, according to former ALF spokesperson David Barbarash, "Any company or business which makes its profit from the confinement, torture, and death of living sentient animals, can expect this kind of response [illegal direct action] from the Animal Liberation Front" (NAALFPO 2000b).

The scope of ALF targets has varied over the last two decades to include both public and private establishments. Among the ALF's more frequent victims are university animal-research facilities, fur farms and retailers, food and animal feed producers, fast-food eateries, government-managed animal operations and drug and chemical man-ufactures. Perhaps the most worrisome pattern of crime to emerge within the militant animal-liberation movement is the targeting of individuals and personal property. Cases of animal-rights radicals victimizing individuals, primarily biomedical research scientists, date back to the late 1970s. In one of the more severe cases, the Animal Avengers defaced the homes, and in some cases automobiles, of five scientists working with the National Institutes of Health in April 1993. With the emergence of the SHAC campaign in the late 1990s, the willingness of animal rights extremists to repeatedly and systematically victimize people has grown dramatically. ALF adherents in Europe and in the United States have regularly vandalized the homes and property of SHAC targets while simultaneously attacking businesses. A number of the employees and companies who have come into the crosshairs—among them financial institutions and insurance providers—have never before been targeted by the ALF and hence have quickly been forced into severing ties with SHAC's primary target, Huntingdon Life Sciences.

UP CLOSE AND PERSONAL

Since the emergence of the ecoterror movement in England in the 1960s, mounting frustration has fueled the activities of radicalized activists. Militant animal extremists, in particular, have continued to escalate terror tactics used against institutions and individuals alike. Over time, adherents of various militant outfits—from the early Hunt Saboteurs Association to the present-day ALF—have splintered off to form more hard-hitting factions. Many of these spin-offs have taken direct aim at people. Among them is the Justice Department. Founded in 1993, this ALF offshoot is known for sending bombs to the employees of UK companies involved in live animal export in 1994 and threatening letters rigged with razor blades to U.S.-based research scientists in 1999 ("Justice Department Fact Sheet" 2003). Another faction is the Animal Rights Militia, or ARM, whose founders broke away from the ALF movement because it did not "go far enough with regards to direct action" ("Animal Rights Militia Fact Sheet" 2003). Adherents of the ARM perpetrate poisoning hoaxes in England and Canada and were among the first militants to target personal property. Within the present-day SHAC campaign, even more violent militant animal-rights factions are emerging.

Despite SHAC's relative youth as an organization, its intense, uncompromising terror campaign against HLS has quickly gone global. Some more radicalized anti-HLS activists in the UK have moved beyond property destruction and have physically assaulted people. In one of the more-publicized cases, a gang of masked anti-HLS activists wielding baseball bats put a seven-inch gash into the head of Huntingdon's CEO in February 2001 (Alleyne and Shaw 2001). Fierce rhetoric of an apparent ALF spin-off in the United States known as the Animal Liberation Brigade—who has to date laid claim to bombing two SHAC-targeted companies—suggests that such physical violence could become more commonplace. In one of its recent communiqués it warned, "No more will all of the killing be done by the oppressors, now the oppressed will fight back" (Chong, Pogash, and Krikorian 2003). Besieged by the intense terror tactics of anti-HLS campaigners, hundreds of companies—from janitorial services to major banks—have severed their ties with Huntingdon. It is widely feared that the success of the SHAC campaign will not go unnoticed by other militant groups with a violent bent.

REFERENCES

Abbey, E. 1975. *The Monkey Wrench Gang.* Philadelphia: J.B. Lippincott.

"About Us." 2003 Retrieved August 1, 2003, from http://www.animalliberation.net/about.

"ALF Mission Statement/Credo." n.d. Retrieved July 20, 2003, from http://www.animal liberationfront.com/ALFront/WhatisALF.htm.

"The ALF Primer." 2003 Retrieved August 19, 2003, from http://www.animalliberationfront.com/ALFront/ALFPrime.htm.

"The ALF Unmasked." 2003 Retrieved November 11, 2003, from http://www.animallib.org .au/more_interviews/barbarash.

Alleyne, R. and Shaw J. 2001. "The ALF is Known for Balaclava Clad Henchmen." *The Telegraph,* January 12.

"Animal Liberation Front Guidelines." 2003 Retrieved July 20, 2003, from http://www.animal liberation.net/library/facts/guidelines.html.

"Animal Rights Militia Fact Sheet." 2003 Retrieved June 1, 2003, from http://www.animal liberation.net/library/facts/arm.html.

Arnold, R. 1997. *Eco-Terror: The Violent Agenda to Save Nature.* Bellevue, WA: Free Enterprise Press.

Bailey, B. 1998. *The Luddite Rebellion.* Gloucestershire, UK: Sutton Publishing.

Barcott, B. 2002. "From Tree Hugger to Terrorist." *New York Times,* April 7, A56.

Bari, J. 1994. "Monkeywrenching." *Earth First* (February): 8.

Carus, W. S. 2002. *Bioterrorism and Biocrimes: The Illicit Use of Biological Agents Since 1900.* Fredonia, NY: Fredonia Books.

Chong, J., C. Pogash, and G. Krikorian. 2003. "E-Mail Says Animal Group Behind Blast." *Los Angles Times,* October 1.

Denson, B. 1999. "Ideologies Drive the Violence." *Oregonian,* September 27, A1.

Devall, B., and G. Sessions. 1986. Deep Ecology. Layton, UT: Gibbs Smith Publisher.

"ELF Members Spawn More Radical Group with 'Arissa.'" 2003. *KATU,* Mar 12. Retrieved July 20, 2003, from http://www.katu.com/news/story.asp?id=57433.

Foreman, D. 1985. *Ecodefense: A Field Guide to Monkeywrenching.* Tucson, AZ: Earth First! Books.

Fox, W. 1990. *Toward a Transpersonal Ecology: Developing New Foundations for Environmentalism.* Boston: Shambhala Publications.

Green, K., and J. Hughes. 2003. "Damage in University City Blaze May Top $20 Million." *San Diego Union Tribune,* August 2. Retrieved on June 15, 2003, from http://www .signonsandiego.com/news/metro/20030802-9999_1n2condos.html.

Hansen, B. 2000. "ELF Voice Appears Before Federal Grand Jury." Colorado Daily, March 1: B10.

"The History of Hunt Saboteurs Association." n.d. Retrieved August 1, 2003, from http://hsa.enviroweb.org/features/hist1.html.

"Introducing the Animal Liberation Front." n.d. Retrieved August 1, 2003, from http://www.animal liberation.net/library/facts/alf.html.

"Justice Department Fact Sheet." n.d. Retrieved June 1, 2003, from http://www.animalliberation .net/library/facts/jd.html.

LaChapelle, D. (1988). *Sacred Land, Sacred Sex: Rapture of the Deep: Concerning Deep Ecology and Celebrating Life.* Silverton, CO: Finn Hill Arts.

Lee, P., and P. Shannon. 2003. "Inside Base Camp: Leslie James Pickering" (Allan Myers, Director). Marsh, M. (Producer), *Inside Base Camp with Tom Foreman.* Washington D.C.: National Geographic Channel.

Love, S. and D. Obst. 1972. *Ecotage.* New York: Pocketbooks.

Mahonia. 2003. "Snitches Get Stitches?" *Earth First Journal,* (May–June): 56–58.

"Meet the ELF." n.d. Retrieved June 30, 2003, from http://www.earthliberationfront.com/about.

Naess, A. 1989. *Ecology, Community, and Lifestyle: Outline of an Ecosophy.* New York: Cambridge University Press.

North American Animal Liberation Front Press Office (NAALFPO). 2000a. "Animal Liberation Front 'Decorates' Salt Lake Meat Businesses." Courtenay, British Columbia: NAALFPO.

———. 2000b. "Animal Liberation Front Burns Fur Feed Co." Courtenay, British Columbia: NAALFPO.

———. 2001. "ALF Claims Responsibility for Coulston Fire." Courtenay, British Columbia: NAALFPO.

———. 2002. *2001 Year-End Direct Action Report.* Courtenay, British Columbia: NAALFPO.

North American Earth Liberation Front Press Office (NAELFPO). 2001a. *Frequently Asked Questions about the Earth Liberation Front.* Portland, OR: NAELFPO.

———. 2001b. "ELF Claims Credit for Fire at GE Site in California." Portland, OR: Frontline Information Service.

———. 2001c. *Igniting the Revolution: An Introduction to the Earth Liberation Front.* Portland, OR: NAELFPO.

———. (2002a). "ELF Attacks U.S. Forest Service Research Facility." Portland, OR: NAELFPO.

———. (2002b). "Statement from the Earth Liberation Front Press Office." Portland, OR: NAELFPO.

———. (2003). "ELF Torches SUVs in Erie, Pennsylvania." Portland, OR: NAELFPO.

Roe, A. 2003. "He says he wants a Revolution: A former ELF Figure Defends the Historic Role of Violence in Social Change." *Willamette Week,* Jan. 8, 2003. Pg. A1.

Sale, K. 1996. *Rebels Against the Future: The Luddites and Their War on the Industrial Revolution.* Cambridge, MA: Perseus Publishing.

Schwarzen, C. and J. Sullivan. 2003. "Thousands of Mink Released From Sultan Farm Cages." *Seattle Times,* August 26. Retrieved on August 26, 2003, from http://seattletimes.nwsource.com/html/localnews/2001620194_mink26m.html.

Seed, J. 1988. *Thinking Like a Mountain: Towards a Council of All Beings.* Gabriola Island, B.C. Canada: New Society Publishers.

"Simplest ALF Action." n.d. Retrieved July 30, 2003, from http://www.animalliberationfront.com/ALFront/ALFActs.htm.

Singer, P. 1975. *Animal Liberation.* New York: Random House.

Stop Huntingdon Animal Cruelty. 2003. "Smashing HLS is a BLAST!" *Stop Huntingdon Animal Cruelty USA Inc. eNewsletter,* October, 1.

"Thirty Years of Direct Action." n.d. Retrieved August 1, 2003, from http://www.nocompromise.org/issues/18thirty_years.html.

Thompson, D. 2003. "Activists Go To The Next Level." *Mercury News,* May 11. Retrieved on August 26, 2003, from http://www.bayarea.com/mld/mercurynews/local/5832723.htm.

Tucker, J. B. 2000. *Toxic Terror: Assessing Terrorist Use of Chemical and Biological Weapons.* Cambridge, MA: MIT Press.

U.S. Department of Justice. 1993. *Report to Congress on the Extent and Effects of Domestic and International Terrorism on Animal Enterprises.* Washington, D.C.: U.S. Government Printing Office.

U.S. Federal Bureau of Investigation. 1999. *Terrorism in the United States.* Washington, D.C.: U.S. Department of Justice.

United States v. *Rodney Adam Coronado,* No. 1:93-CR-116 (1993).

Vaughan, Claudette. n.d. "DeRose On Direct Action." Retrieved July 15, 2002 from http://www.animal-lib.org.au/more_interviews/derose.

Warford, M. 1997. *Greenpeace Witness: Twenty-Five Years on the Environmental Front Line.* London, UK: Andre Deutsch, Ltd.

Weller, R. 1998. "Environmental Group Claims It Set Fires at Vail." *Seattle Times,* October 22.

Zakin, S. 1995. *Coyotes and Town Dogs: Earth First! and the Environmental Movement.* New York: Penguin.

APPENDIX: EXAMPLES OF ECOTERROR CRIMES IN THE UNITED STATES

Over the last two decades, environmental and militant animal-rights radicals have committed criminal acts that vary widely in intensity and scope. Although these extremists have yet to kill anyone in the United States, they have committed arson, acts of sabotage, harassment, vandalism, and other similar attacks on an increasingly broad range of targets. The following is a listing of these acts drawn from numerous sources, including news articles, industry records, victim accounts, and law enforcement and government agency reports. It is intended to be a general account of ecoterror crimes rather than a comprehensive record. It indicates targets, locales, and tactics chosen by ecoterror operatives. Emphasis is placed on more serious forms of illegal direct actions; minor acts of vandalism and sabotage (such as gluing door locks, etching/smashing windows, and graffiti strikes) are underrepresented.

Date: August 1, 2003

Location: San Diego, California

Method of Attack: Arson

Incident Description: A massive 3-alarm fire levels a 5-story, 400,000-square-foot unfinished condo development in a densely populated residential area. Large construction equipment, including bulldozers, dump trucks, a 500-gallon fuel truck and a 100-foot construction crane, are lost in the blaze. Extensive damage is also done to an onsite concrete parking garage. More than 100 firefighters fight the fire, which at one point shoots up to more than 200 feet into the air. Local police evacuate about 500 residents from the Renaissance Villa Apartments located next door as grapefruit-sized fireballs land on the building. A 12-foot banner reading, "If you build it, we will burn it! The ELFs are mad" is found at the crime scene. Damage from the arson attack is estimated at $50 million, making it the most costly ecoterror crime in history.

Date: June 23, 2003

Location: Oklahoma City, Oklahoma

Method of Attack: Vandalism

Incident Description: ALF activists vandalize the home belonging to the president of SHAC target Legacy Trading, one of the remaining investment firms still trading the stock of drug and chemical tester Huntingdon Life Sciences. The residence is covered in red and black paint and the phone, DLS, and cable lines are cut. Damage is estimated at $4,000.

Date: June 4, 2003

Location: Detroit, Michigan

Method of Attack: Arson

Incident Description: Two nearly completed houses in a rapidly growing subdivision are firebombed by ELF operatives. Arson investigators indicate that an accelerant was used to hasten the spread of the fires. Embers flying from the burning homes force one family living across the street to flee. The ELF's ominous initials and graffiti reading "stop sprawl" are found scrawled on construction equipment near the smoldering homes. Upon completion, the destroyed homes would have had a combined value of $700,000. The ELF officially claims the antisprawl arsons the following month.

Date: May 18, 2003

Location: Oklahoma City, Oklahoma

Method of Attack: Vandalism

Incident Description: The main office of SHAC target Legacy Trading is broken into and vandalized. Windows are broken and red paint is poured inside the building and the sidewalk outside. The damage is estimated at $4,000. ALF activists claim the raid via a posting made to the SHAC USA Web site.

Date: April 8, 2003

Location: Santa Cruz, California

Method of Attack: Vandalism

Incident Description: Bright yellow and blue antiwar slogans—some reading "No Blood for Oil," "SUVs Suck," and "Killer"—and the ominous "ELF" initials of the Earth Liberation Front are scrawled on at least sixty trucks and sport utility vehicles in Santa Cruz, California. A local Ford and Lincoln Mercury car dealership sustains most of the damages, although at least a dozen residents living in a nearby neighborhood also take a hit. Damage totals $35,000.

Date: April 4, 2003

Location: Chicago, Illinois

Method of Attack: Arson

Incident Description: A suburban butcher shop is set ablaze by ALF operatives just one day after the owner and fifteen other individuals were convicted of trading and selling endangered tiger meat. An official ALF communiqué distributed the same day as the crime claims the action was taken to "further extend the sentence handed down by federal courts." It warned those involved in the exotic meat scandal to "Be careful, because we know who you are and where you live. Pray for extended jail time." Damage to the torched building is estimated at $100,000.

Date: March 27, 2003
Location: San Diego, California
Method of Attack: Vandalism
Incident Description: Militant animal-rights activists launch a strike against an employee of SHAC target Huntingdon Life Sciences in an attempt to force her to quit her job. Acting in the name of the ALF, the perpetrators scrawl "HLS SCUM" in red paint across the victim's garage door and slash three of the tires on the car parked in the driveway. A gallon of red paint is also dumped over the vehicle. An ALF communiqué distributed to animal-rights news groups shortly thereafter recounts the details of the vandalism attack and threatens the victim with future violence if she does not give in to their demands.

Date: March 21, 2003
Location: Ann Arbor, Michigan
Method of Attack: Arson
Incident Description: A fire ravages two nearly completed homes, causing $300,000 of damage. The blaze is not discovered until the owner of a home located between the torched houses awoke around 3 A.M. to see a "red glow" outside his window. He immediately calls 911 to report the blaze and then evacuates his family to safety as hot embers fly onto their home. Arson investigators indicate that the culprits most likely used an accelerant to hasten the spread of the fire.

Date: March 11, 2003
Location: Albuquerque, New Mexico
Method of Attack: Arson
Incident Description: Three fast-food outlets along a major thoroughfare are firebombed. Molotov cocktails and crude incendiary grenades are used in the attacks, causing varying degrees of property damage to two McDonald's and one Arby's. The hit on Arby's causes an estimated $80,000 in property losses. No group or individual claims the attack, but local investigators speculate that the crime is an act of ecoterrorism.

Date: March 10, 2003
Location: Chico, California
Method of Attack: Attempted arson
Incident Description: Employees of a McDonald's find a small fire made with combustible material that had been set outside the back of the restaurant in an

attempt to burn it down. Red graffiti reading "Liberation" and "ALF" is painted on the building's exterior wall. The perpetrators, however, did not leave any notes behind claiming responsibility for the crime, nor was an official ALF communiqué sent out. The city of Chico's planning commission had just approved a plan to tear down the restaurant and make room for a larger McDonald's on the site.

Date: March 3, 2003
Location: Chico, California
Method of Attack: Attempted arson
Incident Description: ALF activists launch an attempt to burn down a McDonald's restaurant. One of the restaurant's employees arrives at work to find two 1-gallon plastic water jugs filled with a flammable substance outside the back of the restaurant. The firebombs were each stuffed with a floating sponge that failed to light. "Animal Liberation Front" and Meat Is Murder" are scrawled in red paint across the exterior wall of the building. A typewritten note affixed to a pay phone located outside the building assigns responsibility for the firebomb attempt to the ALF, as did a letter which was sent to a local newspaper. It stated that "McDonald's has been targeted because of their prevalent connection to the farming industry."

Date: February 27, 2003
Location: Berlin, Maryland
Method of Attack: Theft
Incident Description: More than 100 chicks are stolen by ALF operatives from a research facility operated by Merial Labs. According to an ALF communiqué posted to the SHAC USA Web site, the laboratory was specifically targeted because of its connections with SHAC target Huntingdon Life Sciences. The culprits of the raid warned, "Any friend of HLS is an enemy of the ALF. We know who their clients are. We are out there, and you're next."

Date: February 10, 2003
Location: Fortuna, California
Mode of Attack: Vandalism and sabotage
Incident Description: A log loader owned by Columbia Helicopters is sabotaged. Some time after company employees left the crime site, the perpetrator(s) stuffed wood bark in the oil-fill tube, placed sticks inside the engine after taking off the valve cover, tampered with the fuel pump, removed the air filter, and stole one of the retaining straps. The engine's coverings were carefully replaced to conceal that it had been tampered with. The sabotage attack completely destroys the loader's engine, causing $20,000 in damage. Two Earth First! tree-sitters were believed to be perched in nearby trees during the time of the crime.

Date: February 2, 2003

Location: Chicago, Illinois

Method of Attack: Vandalism and sabotage

Incident Description: ALF operatives launch a sabotage attack against the Supreme Lobster seafood distribution company. A total of forty-eight refrigerated delivery trucks are vandalized during the assault. Both refrigeration and brake lines on dozens of sabotaged vehicles are cut by the perpetrators. Damage estimates exceed $50,000. Company officials discover the vehicles are sabotaged after a driver pulls out in one of the trucks and discovers the brakes are not working.

Date: January 1, 2003

Location: Erie, Pennsylvania

Method of Attack: Arson

Incident Description: The Bob Ferrando Ford Lincoln Mercury car dealership is set ablaze by ELF operatives. Sometime in the early morning hours, jugs of gasoline are ignited under three cars, engulfing them and a nearby car in flames. Two SUVs and two pickup trucks are destroyed, causing $90,000 in losses. The ELF officially claims the attack the next day. The damage could have been much worse—gasoline jugs were set under three other cars, but they failed to go off.

Date: December 23, 2002

Location: Philadelphia, Pennsylvania

Method of Attack: Vandalism and sabotage

Incident Description: A demonstration home valued at $200,000 and several construction vehicles are vandalized by the ELF. Damages sustained to the construction vehicles include broken windows, glued locks, disconnected hoses, contaminated gas tanks, and graffiti painted on the vehicles' exterior. Similar action is taken against the house. The vandalism spree causes an estimated $20,000 in damage.

Date: December 23-24, 2002

Location: Newton, Massachusetts

Method of Attack: Vandalism

Incident Description: More than a dozen sport utility vehicles parked in two separate neighborhoods in are vandalized—graffiti including "Gas Guzzler" and "I'm Changing the Environment" were spray-painted on some of the targeted cars. Two of the SUVs are donned with an anarchy symbol—an "A" with a circle around it. Other graffiti reads "No Blood for Oil." Damage is estimated at $500.

Date: November 26, 2002

Location: Erie County, Pennsylvania

Method of Attack: Arson

Incident Description: A feed barn at a 60-year-old mink farm is broken into and set on fire. Local volunteer firefighters are dispatched shortly the blaze is reported but are unable to save the barn. The arson causes an estimated $50,000 in damage. About a week after the incident, the ALF and ELF issue a joint communiqué assuming responsibility for the attack.

Date: September-October, 2002

Location: Richmond, Virginia

Method of Attack: Vandalism

Incident Description: Over the course of five weeks, more than twenty-five sport utility vehicles (several belonging to local residents), two fast-food restaurants, and heavy equipment at several construction sites are vandalized. Graffiti, notes from the perpetrators, and other indicators suggest that followers of the ELF are responsible. Damage is estimated at approximately $45,000.

Date: August 18, 2002

Location: Waverly, Iowa

Method of Attack: Theft

Incident Description: A small 30-year-old family farm is broken into by militant animal-rights activists, who release approximately 1,200 domesticated mink. Several days later, a communiqué is issued by the ALF assuming responsibility for the crime. It warns that the ALF will continue to terrorize local farms and research facilities "until every animal confinement operation is empty and every slaughterhouse is burned to the ground."

Date: August 11, 2002

Location: Irvine, Pennsylvania

Method of Attack: Arson

Incident Description: A 5-alarm fire nearly destroys an 80-year-old U.S. Forest Service research station, whose internationally recognized research includes studies on ecosystems in the Allegany Plateau region, forest sustainability, and the effects of acid deposition from air pollution. Property losses are estimated at $700,000. The ELF issues a communiqué almost a month after the blaze claiming responsibility for the crime. It states that the research station was "strategically targeted" and that "if rebuilt, [it] will be targeted again for complete destruction." The communiqué also contains a thinly veiled threat that the ELF may further escalate its violent campaign against people, saying "where it is necessary, we will no longer hesitate to pick up the gun to implement justice."

Date: July 31, 2002

Location: Long Island, New York

Method of Attack: Vandalism

Incident Description: The ALF destroys four greens and four holes at the Meadowbrook Golf Club on the eve of the PGA Lightpath classic. In addition to digging 3-foot trenches on the greens, the perpetrators remove the metal casings and flags from the holes. The ALF's sabotage attack against Meadowbrook is inflicted as part of the "direct action" campaign against SHAC target Hunting Life Sciences and its suppliers. A communiqué claiming responsibility for the crime appears on the SHAC USA Web site.

Date: July 8, 2002

Location: Louisville, Kentucky

Method of Attack: Vandalism

Incident Description: The ELF launches a vandalism strike on the construction site of a new Wal-Mart, causing $5,000 in damage. The tires of a construction-equipment trailer are slashed, its locks are glued, and four windows are smashed out. The words "Stop Sprawl" and "Respect" are painted on the wall of the unfinished building. Similar graffiti is also left on the construction trailer. A communiqué sent out by the group states that "the ELF is only beginning in the Kentucky region" and that it "will not stop until the developers and oligarchs do."

Date: March 24, 2002

Location: Erie, Pennsylvania

Method of Attack: Arson and sabotage (tree-spiking)

Incident Description: A 60-ton construction crane is torched by the ELF in an effort to halt a $31 million highway project, causing $500,000 in damage. Metal and ceramic spikes are inserted into trees scheduled for removal. An official communiqué is issued by the ELF claiming responsibility for the strike several days later. It stated that the action was taken in order to stop the construction of the new highway, which ELF members feared would threaten the biological health of the Lake Erie watershed.

Date: January 26, 2002

Location: Saint Paul, Minnesota

Method of Attack: Arson

Incident Description: A trailer and equipment at the construction site of the University of Minnesota's Microbial and Plant Genomics Research Center are engulfed in flames. A crop research laboratory working on a major prairie restoration project in an adjacent building is also damaged when the resulting fire spreads. Damage is estimated at $630,000. The ELF claims responsibility for the blaze days after it is launched on the grounds that the center would soon be serving industry interests. The center's aims, however, are to help reduce pesticide use and fertilizers in agricultural production, find renewable alternatives to fossil fuels, and identify new strategies for cleaning the environment and preserving ecosystems.

Date: November 11, 2001
Location: San Diego, California
Mode of Attack: Vandalism
Incident Description: ALF activists gain entry to a Sierra Biomedical research facility and vandalize a laboratory. Equipment is damaged, acid is poured on files, and the walls are spray-painted with graffiti, including the letters "ALF." The tires on a company van are also slashed. The raid costs the company close to $50,000. An ALF communiqué issued the day after the raid states that the lab was vandalized in "protest" of its animal-based research.

Date: October 24, 2001
Location: Long Island, New York
Mode of Attack: Vandalism
Incident Description: More than thirty windows are smashed at a Bank of America office. A communiqué is sent out two days later claiming that the "Special Operations: Huntingdon Life Sciences" cell of the ALF committed the crime against the "known terrorist organization." It warns that until Bank of America severs its ties with the drug and chemical tester, the perpetrators will continue to make the bank "pay for" its "crimes."

Date: October 15, 2001
Location: Susanville, California
Mode of Attack: Arson
Incident Description: A hay barn at a wild horse and burro facility operated by the Bureau of Land Management is leveled by a raging fire set by the ELF, causing an estimated $85,000 in damage. Losses to the corral during the attack could have been worse, however. The perpetrators had aimed to firebomb another barn, an office building, and two vehicles parked on site, but the explosives failed to ignite. There was also a failed attempt to free 160 wild horses. The ELF communiqué claiming the attack states that the raid on the facility was launched in protest of BLM's roundup of wild horses to clear public land for grazing cattle.

Date: September 8, 2001
Location: Tucson, Arizona
Mode of Attack: Arson
Incident Description: ELF and ALF operatives launch a joint arson attack on a Tucson-based McDonald's. The fast-food eatery is completely destroyed in the

resulting fire. Group initials are spray-painted on the building and the restaurant's electronic drive-through kiosk. Damage runs close to $500,000. A joint ALF-ELF communiqué is released three days later warning that the raid should be a warning to all corporations worldwide: "As long as corporations enslave workers in other countries, waste our natural resources and torture animals, we will unite and stand in opposition."

Date: July 24, 2001
Location: Sands Point, New York
Mode of Attack: Vandalism
Incident Description: An attempt is made to sink a 21-foot boot belonging to a Bank of New York employee. Holes are drilled into the boat's sides, and some of its machinery is damaged. Graffiti denouncing the bank's affiliation with drug and chemical tester Huntingdon Life Sciences is scrawled on the boat and dock. The crime is claimed by the "Pirates for Animal Liberation."

Date: July 4, 2001
Location: Detroit, Michigan
Mode of Attack: Arson
Incident Description: An executive office building of logging company Weyerhaeuser is torched. Shortly after the blaze, the ELF releases a communiqué claiming that its operatives committed the crime to protest the company's decision to fund poplar and cottonwood genetic engineering research at Oregon State University and the University of Washington. Damages total several thousand dollars.

Date: June 10, 2001
Location: Moscow, Idaho
Method of Attack: Vandalism
Incident Description: The ELF Night Action Kids for a second time attack the newly constructed Agricultural Biotechnology Laboratory at the University of Idaho. The perpetrators remove survey stakes and the exterior of the building is spray-painted with messages including "No GE" and "Go Organic." Damage to the building is estimated at more than $20,000. The communiqué issued by the ELF claims that its operatives launched the attack to force the university to end its genetics research.

Date: June 1, 2001
Location: Estacada, Oregon
Method of Attack: Arson
Incident Description: A total of eight incendiary devices are planted under logging trucks parked in front of the main office building of Schoppert Logging Company. Only four of the bombs ignite as planned. The resulting blaze com-

pletely destroys one truck and heavily damages two others, causing $50,000 in damage. Schoppert Logging was under contract to start logging at the hotly protested Eagle Creek timber-sale site the day of the attack. No official group has claimed responsibility for the crime.

Date: May 21, 2001
Location: Clatskanie, Oregon
Method of Attack: Arson and vandalism
Incident Description: One office and thirteen trucks at the Jefferson Popular Farm are set ablaze using multiple timed incendiary devices. The local bomb squad is called in to remove three of the bombs planted in the main office that did not ignite. Damage is estimated at $500,000. The ELF officially claims the attack two weeks later, stating that its operatives torched the tree farm because the hybrid poplars grown there were "an ecological nightmare threatening native biodiversity in the ecosystem" so that "greedy, earth raping corporations can make more money." ELF operatives firebomb the University of Washington's Center for Urban Horticulture the same night.

Date: May 21, 2001
Location: Seattle, Washington
Mode of Attack: Arson
Incident Description: The University of Washington's Center for Urban Horticulture is leveled by a 3-alarm fire, causing an estimated $5.4 million in damage and destroying more than twenty years of invaluable research on wetland rehabilitation, ecosystem health, and plant science. The ELF assumes responsibility for the crime after two weeks, indicating that the UW center was targeted in "protest" of its ongoing research in genetically modified popular trees. The lead scientist overseeing the research is individually named in the communiqué. At the same time the UW center is torched, ELF operatives set the Jefferson Poplar Farm ablaze in Clatskanie, Oregon.

Date: April 28, 2001
Location: Westhampton, New York
Method of Attack: Theft
Incident Description: ALF activists steal approximately 250 ducklings from a Cornell University Duck Research Laboratory that specializes in developing vaccines to fight diseases in ducks. At the crime site, workers find dead animals and graffiti messages reading "No More Animal Testing," "We Will Be Back," and the "Animal Liberation Front." The ALF officially claims the raid two days later.

Date: April 21, 2001
Location: Mount Graham, Arizona
Method of Attack: Vandalism and sabotage

Incident Description: Vandals attack the construction site of a new power line intended to feed into the University of Arizona's Mount Graham International Observatory, causing about $200,000 in damage. Sledgehammers, crowbars, and other implements are wielded against the underground power line, several construction vehicles, and other equipment. Some of the damage intentionally compromises the safety of the construction crew. Prior to the attack, local environmental groups had heatedly opposed the installation of the new power line.

Date: April 15, 2001
Location: Portland, Oregon
Method of Attack: Arson
Incident Description: Four timed incendiary devices are used to destroy three Ross Island Sand and Gravel Mack cement trucks, causing about $210,000 in damage. The ELF press office issues a communiqué a week after the arson occurred, claiming the attack. It states, "Let this be a warning to all the greedy corporations who exploit our Earth's natural resources, especially those who plan on doing it under the FTAA [Free Trade Act of the Americas] and the title of free trade."

Date: April 2, 2001
Location: Albertville, Minnesota
Method of Attack: Attempted Arson
Incident Description: An attempt is made to firebomb a retail Nike factory store by setting an incendiary device on the roof. Because of weather conditions, the fire fails to spread and the building sustains only minor damages. Nonetheless, the ELF claims the attempt several days later as an antiglobalization action and warns, "Although the roof of this Nike Outlet did not go up in flames as planned, this action is still a message to Nike they cannot ignore." Nike is given two options: shut down its overseas manufacturing operations or the "People across the globe will individually attack Nike Outlets, as well as retailers that sell Nike . . . until Nike closes down."

Date: March 30, 2001
Location: Eugene, Oregon
Method of Attack: Arson
Incident Description: A fire destroys thirty-six sport utility vehicles at the Joe Romania Chevrolet dealership, causing $1 million in damage. Perpetrators place gasoline cans under the cars to start the blaze. The ELF Press Office faxes a statement to local media claiming that an "anonymous" group was responsible for the attack. It states that "gas-guzzling SUVs are at the forefront of this vile, imperialistic culture's caravan towards self-destruction. We can no longer allow the rich to parade around in their armored existence, leaving a wasteland behind in their tire tracks."

Date: March 17, 2001

Location: Corvallis and Klamath Falls, Oregon

Method of Attack: Vandalism

Incident Description: More than 950 experimental popular trees being field-tested by a professor of forest science at Oregon State University are cut down or girdled in two separate test sites. The letter claiming the act, signed by Concerned OSU Students and Alumni, states that the action was taken because the research was found to be "a dangerous experiment of unknown genetic consequences." Losses associated with the attack are estimated at $20,000. The OSU Department of Forestry spends about $80,000 in added security measures to prevent future attacks.

Date: January 15, 2001

Location: Marblemount, Washington

Mode of Attack: Vandalism and sabotage

Incident Description: Sand was poured into oil and hydraulic parts of logging equipment owned by Pacific Logging. Damage to the equipment and the cost of related downtime total $100,000. The crime is not officially claimed but local investigators suspect an act of eco-terrorism.

Date: January 2, 2001

Location: Glendale, Oregon

Method of Attack: Arson

Incident Description: Flames roar through the 6,000-square-foot office building of Superior Lumber Company in Glendale, Oregon, after ELF operatives set it ablaze. The family-owned company's offices are nearly burned to the ground, and all of its computer equipment and records sustain considerable smoke and water damage. Property losses total about $450,000. The ELF exclaims in the communiqué sent out claiming the crime that "Superior Lumber is a typical earth raper contributing to the ecological destruction of the Northwest."

Date: December 9, 19, and 29, 2000

Location: Long Island, New York

Method of Attack: Arson and vandalism

Incident Description: An ELF cell of four teenagers launch an arson campaign against a new housing development. Four homes and sixteen units in a condominium are firebombed, causing an estimated $1 million in damage. One of the ELF's most infamous slogans, "If you build it, we will burn it," and other anti–urban sprawl graffiti is left at most of the crime sites. Each individual strike is claimed by the ELF. One of the official communiqués sent out reads, "The Earth isn't dying, it's being killed. And those who are killing it have names and addresses. What are YOU doing for the Earth tonight? No Compromise in Defense of Mother Earth! Stop Urban Sprawl OR We Will."

Date: October 18, 2000

Location: Martin County, Indiana

Mode of Attack: Vandalism

Incident Description: Logging equipment in the Martin County State Forest operated by the Indiana Department of Natural Resources is thrashed by an ELF cell, causing $55,000 in damage. The perpetrators of the crime heavily damage three skidders and one loader by cutting the fuel and hydraulic fluid lines, pouring sand the gas tanks and crankcases, and smashing glass gauges. Graffiti, including "Earth Raper," "Go Cut in Hell," and "We Are Everywhere," is spray-painted on the damaged equipment.

Date: September 7, 2000

Location: New Hampton, Iowa

Mode of Attack: Theft

Incident Description: ALF activists gain entry to a farm and set free approximately 14,000 mink. More than 10,000 of those domesticated animals released are hit by cars, preyed on by other animals, or overcome by starvation. The ALF press office issues a news release that day claiming the action, boasting that it is the largest "liberation" to date.

Date: August 10, 2000

Location: Davis, California

Method of Attack: Vandalism

Incident Description: Test plots of experimental corn at the Davis campus of the University of California are destroyed by activists using the group name "Reclaim the Seeds." The communiqué sent out by Genetix claims that the action was taken in opposition to genomics research and the university's acceptance of funding from industry sources.

Date: July 20, 2000

Location: Rhinelander, Wisconsin

Mode of Attack: Vandalism

Incident Description: Vandals hack down thousands of experimental popular trees at a U.S. Forest Service research station. During the attack, acid is spread on the windshields of ten USFS trucks and graffiti warning that the "ELF is watching the U.S. Forest Service" is scrawled on a number of the vehicles. Damage is estimated at $1 million, and the center's research aimed at curing devastating tree diseases is set back by thirty years. The attack is officially claimed the next day by the ELF. In a communiqué sent to media, the terror group declared: "In Rhinelander, the Forest Service is mapping the DNA of white pine and attempting to genetically engineer them to be resistant to pine rust. Why? To aid industry in creating disease-resistant trees suitable for tree farms that will increase their profits."

Date: July 2, 2000

Location: North Vernon, Indiana

Mode of Attack: Arson and vandalism

Incident Description: A feed truck at the Rose Acre Farm is set ablaze by militant animal activists, causing more than $100,000 in damage. The vehicle is completely destroyed in the attack. Graffiti reading "Polluter, animal exploiter, your turn to pay" is scrawled on the outside of a barn. The ALF claims responsibility for the attack.

Date: June 23, 2000

Location: Beaumont, California

Mode of Attack: Theft

Incident Description: ALF operatives break into the Sunny-Cal egg farm and steal more than 600 chickens. A communiqué sent out that day by the ALF press office warns, "Until human beings learn to take responsibility for this earth and all her creatures, it will remain necessary for compassionate individuals to act outside of the law on behalf of the innocent."

Date: June 4, 2000

Location: Canby, Oregon

Method of Attack: Vandalism

Incident Description: Experimental grass plants for putting greens on golf courses are uprooted and several greenhouses belonging to the Pure Seed Testing Company are defaced. Attackers spray-paint slogans, including "Nature Bites," on the greenhouse walls. Claimed by the Anarchist Golfing Association (AGA), the "direct action" set the research back by five to ten years and cost the company $500,000. The AGA's official communiqué states that the experimental grass is objectionable because it is "grown for profit and the pleasure of the rich and has no social value."

Date: June 1, 2000

Location: Eugene, Oregon

Method of Attack: Arson

Incident Description: Incendiary devices are used to set fire to three pickups at the Joe Romania Chevrolet dealership, causing several thousand dollars in damage. The ELF issues a communiqué claiming that an anonymous group was responsible for the blaze. The dealership is reportedly hit because the sport utility vehicles it sells cause pollution.

Date: May 7, 2000

Location: Olympia, Washington

Mode of Attack: Arson

Incident Description: A group calling itself Revenge of the Trees sets the headquarters of a small timber company, Holbrook Inc., on fire. The modular office building and all of its contents are completely destroyed, causing $150,000 in damage. In a communiqué faxed to local media, ROTT states that "Logging is just one aspect in this capitalistic industrialized system that is destroying all things wild. We will not stop until this whole stinking system rots!"

Date: February 27, 2000
Location: San Francisco, California
Mode of Attack: Vandalism
Incident Description: More than thirty windows on a Neiman Marcus store in a popular downtown shopping area are smashed, causing about $30,000 in damage. The ALF claims the vandalism attack three weeks later. Its operatives are said to have targeted the store because the chain sells fur products.

Date: February 9, 2000
Location: Saint Paul, Minnesota
Method of Attack: Vandalism
Incident Description: ELF activists destroy experimental oat crops and damage a greenhouse at the University of Minnesota with the aim of shutting down the college's plant genomics research. Phrases including "ELF" and "Free the Seed" are spray-painted on the greenhouse walls. Three of the building's locks are also glued. Damage is estimated at about $1,000, and the affected research is set back by more than three months.

Date: January 23, 2000
Location: Bloomington, Indiana
Method of Attack: Arson and vandalism
Incident Description: Arson destroys a home under construction at the Sterling Woods housing development. Investigators find spray-painted in black on a "for sale" sign near the house: "No Sprawl—ELF." Damage is estimated at $200,000. A statement issued by the ELF claims its operatives targeted the house because its construction threatens the local watershed.

Date: January 11, 2000
Location: Albany, California
Method of Attack: Vandalism
Incident Description: The so-called night time gardeners of Reclaim the Seeds launch a raid on the USDA's Agricultural Research Service's Western Regional Research Center at the University of California's Gene Expression Center. Experimental wheat is crushed and pulled out of the ground. According to an official communiqué sent out by Genetix, the hit is reportedly done in celebration of National Biotechnology Month.

Date: December 31, 1999

Location: Lansing, Michigan

Method of Attack: Arson

Incident Description: Accelerants are used to set fire to Michigan State University's Agricultural Hall. Research destroyed in the blaze is geared to fight hunger in Third World countries by developing hardier and more disease-resistant food crops. At the time of the explosion, the building's windows are blasted more then fifty feet onto the sidewalk down below. The blaze is discovered by a faculty member working late inside the facility. Damage is estimated at approximately $1 million. The ELF Press Office reports to local media that its operatives started the fire to force an end to MSU's plant genetics program because that it would push "unnatural" crops onto Asian nations.

Date: December 25, 1999

Location: Monmouth, Oregon

Method of Attack: Arson

Incident Description: The ELF sets off firebombs made using diesel, gasoline, and a kitchen timer at the regional headquarters of Boise Building Solutions. The 7,200-square-foot facility and nearly all of its contents are consumed in the three-alarm fire. Damage totals nearly $1 million. Several of the volunteer firefighters responding to the blaze came close to being seriously injured when the roof almost collapsed on them. The ELF warned in the communiqué sent out several days later, "Let this be a lesson to all greedy multinational corporations who don't respect their ecosystems. The elves are watching."

Date: November 20, 1999

Location: Puyallup, Washington

Method of Attack: Vandalism

Incident Description: Washington State University's Avian Health Lab is broken into by ALF activists, who cause thousands of dollars in damage, mostly to computers and lab equipment. The perpetrators also paint anarchist symbols on the walls and pour acid and chlorine bleach throughout the building. Damage is estimated in the tens of thousands. Several days later, the ALF press office issues a communiqué claiming the raid. It warns: "We know what you're doing to the animals. We never forget, and we will never sleep."

Date: October 19, 1999

Location: Multiple New York cities

Method of Attack: Vandalism

Incident Description: Windows at McDonald's restaurants in Jericho, Hicksville, Syosset, and Garden City are smashed. Slogans protesting the consumption of meat are written on the outside of the targeted eateries. Damage amounts to about $10,000. The ALF claims responsibility for the vandalism.

Date: October 1, 1999 through October 31, 1999

Location: Various U.S. states

Method of Attack: Harassment

Incident Description: An extreme animal-rights group calling themselves the Justice Department takes credit for mailing letters rigged with razor blades to scientists throughout the United States who used animals in their medical research. The blades are positioned to slice open the finger of anyone opening the letter. The letters indicate that those responsible are attempting to terrorize the researchers into disbanding their research.

Date: August 3, 1999

Location: Bristol, Wisconsin

Method of Attack: Theft

Incident Description: More than 3,000 domesticated mink are released from a family-owned farm. During the raid, the farm's breeding records are also destroyed. A communiqué is issued by the ALF claiming the action as part of its efforts to force the end of the fur industry. The farm is specifically targeted because it is a major supplier of pelts to retailer Neiman Marcus.

Date: April 5, 1999

Location: Saint Paul, Minnesota

Method of Attack: Vandalism and theft

Incident Description: Laboratories at the University of Minnesota are vandalized and dozens of research animals stolen by the ALF, wrecking years of invaluable medical research on Alzheimer's and cancer. Perpetrators spray-paint the walls and furniture and destroy microscopes, computers, and other laboratory equipment. Damage is estimated at $1 million. The group No Compromise issues a news release stating that the raid on the university labs was staged to force an end to animal experimentation.

Date: December 26, 1998

Location: Medford, Oregon

Method of Attack: Arson

Incident Description: The headquarters of U.S. Forest Industries in Medford, Oregon, is gutted by a fire set by the ELF, causing $900,000 in damage. The building and all of its contents are lost in the arson attack. An ELF communiqué faxed to media weeks later claims that the strike is "in retribution for all the wild forests and animals lost to feed the wallets of greedy [expletive deleted] like Jerry Bramwell [president of U.S. Forest Industries]."

Date: October 18, 1998

Location: Vail, Colorado

Method of Attack: Arson

Incident Description: An ELF cell firebombs a ski resort, causing more than $12 million in damage. Eight separate fires are set. Nine buildings and three chairlifts are consumed by the flames. Foremost is the total loss of the resort's 24,000-square-foot flagship restaurant, the Two Elk. More than 200 firefighters from eleven separate fire departments battle the blaze. Their efforts are greatly hampered by the lack of water, six inches of fresh snow, and the logistical burden of fighting multiple fires that are in some cases more than a mile apart. An ELF communiqué is issued stating that its operatives acted to stop a planned expansion of the resort in order to protect declining lynx habitat.

Date: June 21, 1998
Location: Olympia and Littlerock, Washington
Mode of Attack: Arson
Incident Description: Two U.S. Department of Agriculture research stations, miles apart, are burned to the ground. Damage to the structures is estimated at $400,000, and the value of the lost research is valued at $1,500,000. A joint ELF-ALF communiqué sent to local media claims that the attacks were done to "honor the wildlife of the great Pacific Northwest and the forests they call home by having a bonfire (or two) at facilities which make it a daily routine to kill and destroy wildlife."

Date: May 4, 1998
Location: Wimauma, Florida
Mode of Attack: Arson
Incident Description: A fire destroys a veal-processing plant, causing $500,000 in damage. The letters "ALF" are spray-painted on the outside of the plant. A communiqué from a group calling itself the Florida ALF claims the crime.

Date: November 29, 1997
Location: Burns, Oregon
Method of Attack: Arson
Incident Description: Arsonists destroy a U.S. Bureau of Land Management horse barn, chutes, pens, and equipment. Four hundred horses are released but later recaptured. Damage is estimated at approximately $350,000.

Date: July 21, 1997
Location: Redmond, Oregon
Method of Attack: Arson
Incident Description: ALF activists torch the Cavel West meat-packing plant in Redmond, Oregon, causing an estimated $1.4 million in damage. According to investigators, the perpetrators used approximately thirty-five gallons of jellied gasoline to start the fire. Hydrochloric acid was also poured into the ventilation ducts to taint any meat not destroyed by the fire.

Date: March 23, 1997

Location: Seattle, Washington

Method of Attack: Vandalism

Incident Description: The ACME chicken farm is broken into and vandalized. Forklifts and other equipment are damaged during the raid. Two offices are trashed and all of the contents are destroyed with red paint and muriatic acid. The ominous initials of the Animal Liberation Front are spray-painted on one of the office walls.

Date: March 18, 1997

Location: Davis, California

Method of Attack: Arson

Incident Description: The Bay Area Cell of the Earth X ALF takes credit for setting fire to the partially built University of California–Davis Center for Comparative Medicine. Damage is estimated at approximately $1,200.

Date: October 30, 1996

Location: Eugene, Oregon

Method of Attack: Arson

Incident Description: Perpetrators burn to the ground the U.S. Forest Service Oakridge Ranger Station, causing $5.3 million in property losses. Most of the district's records and documents on the station's environmental monitoring and research are destroyed in the blaze. The local fire department is forced to deal with hundreds of nails spread on the road at the entrance of the facility before being able to respond to the blaze. A joint ALF-ELF claim is received by local law enforcement but not published.

Date: October 28, 1996

Location: Detroit Lake, Oregon

Method of Attack: Arson and vandalism

Incident Description: A pickup is torched on the parking lot of the US Forest Service Detroit Ranger District headquarters office. The saboteurs tag the building with "Earth Liberation Front" and other graffiti. Property losses are estimated at $20,000. Damage caused in the strike could have been far worse. A plastic jug rigged as an incendiary device, found on the roof by investigators, failed to ignite.

Date: October 24, 1992

Location: Millville, Utah

Method of Attack: Arson

Incident Description: ALF operatives launch an arson attack on Utah State University's wild animal research facility. A field station manager's office at the college campus is also firebombed. Damage is estimated at $200,000.

Date: February 28, 1992
Location: Lansing, Michigan
Method of Attack: Arson and vandalism
Incident Description: Timed incendiary devices are set off by ALF operatives inside two animal research labs at Michigan State University's Agricultural Hall. The resulting fire destroys both labs—all of their contents are lost, including years of research geared to identifying toxins in the Great Lakes in order to maintain wild mink and otter populations. Two students are inside the building when the bombs go off and narrowly escape the blaze. The arson attack results in losses that exceed $1.2 million. People for the Ethical Treatment of Animals (PETA) issues a news release claiming responsibility for the firebombing in the name of the ALF.

Date: June 10, 1991
Location: Corvallis, Oregon
Method of Attack: Arson
Incident Description: Oregon State University's mink farm in Corvallis is firebombed using a timed incendiary device. Research offices were also broken into and vandalized. Damage from the attack is estimated at $62,000. The ALF issues an official communiqué claiming responsibility for the attack. It warns that the terror campaign would continue "until the last fur farm is burnt to the ground."

Date: April 22 and 23, 1990
Location: Santa Cruz, California
Method of Attack: Vandalism
Incident Description: A group of Earth Firster members calling themselves the Earth Night Action Group causes a massive power outage by toppling a transmission tower and downing power lines. Santa Cruz County residents were without electricity for ten to eighteen hours. A victim of Lou Gehrig's disease nearly dies after the emergency power pack on her respirator fails.

Date: July 4, 1989
Location: Lubbock, Texas
Method of Attack: Arson, vandalism, and theft
Incident Description: The ALF destroys records and smashes computers and equipment during a raid on a laboratory at the Texas Tech University Health Sciences Center. Lost during the raid is research on sleep disorders. Slogans are spray-painted on the walls and five cats are stolen. The total direct and indirect cost of the raid (including equipment replacement and a new security

system) is estimated at $1 million. People for the Ethical Treatment of Animals (PETA) issues a news release following the attack claiming the ALF is responsible. It states that the action was taken to force the university to discontinue animal research.

Date: September 1, 1987
Location: Santa Clara, California
Method of Attack: Arson
Incident Description: A fire at the San Jose Valley Veal & Beef Company causes $10,000 in damage. The Animal Rights Militia claims responsibility.

Date: April 16, 1987
Location: Davis, California
Method of Attack: Arson
Incident Description: A three-alarm fire rages through the John E. Thurman Veterinary Diagnostic Laboratory at the University of California at Davis, causing $4.6 million in damage. The initials "ALF" are found painted inside the burned laboratory. The laboratory, under construction at the time, was rebuilt and now provides diagnostic services and information to help control animal diseases.

Date: October 25 or 26, 1986
Location: Eugene, Oregon
Method of Attack: Vandalism and theft
Incident Description: An animal-care facility at the University of Oregon is ransacked. The perpetrators smash glass and laboratory equipment, spray-paint "ALF" and other slogans on the walls, and take more than 150 animals, including cats, rabbits, pigeons, and rats. Damage totals $120,000. A statement delivered to a local newspaper following the raid claims the ALF targeted the center in an effort to force two of the university's faculty into disbanding their animal research.

Date: April 1, 1985
Location: Riverside, California
Method of Attack: Vandalism and theft
Incident Description: A laboratory in the Life Sciences Building at the University of California at Riverside is broken into and vandalized. The intruders rip doors off hinges, smash equipment, spray-paint walls, and pour red paint mixed with glue on the computers before making off with 467 research animals. The raid causes an estimated $683,000 in losses. The ALF takes credit for the attack.

Date: March 14, 1979
Location: New York, New York
Method of Attack: Vandalism and theft

Incident Description: A medical research laboratory at the New York University Medical Center is broken into by activists masquerading as lab workers. The intruders steal five research animals; one cat, two dogs, and two guinea pigs. The ALF takes credit for the attack, marking the terror group's first known crime in the United States.

Date: Summer 1971

Location: Tucson, Arizona

Method of Attack: Vandalism

Incident Description: A group of five teenagers calling themselves the Eco-Raiders launch a two-year vandalism campaign against urban sprawl, attacking primarily new housing developments and construction equipment. Developers' homes are even hit on several raids. Damage ultimately totals close to $2 million.

SECTION TWO DISCUSSION QUESTIONS

1. Arena and Arrigo claim that the five elements of identity are observable in terrorist groups. Discuss these elements in both abstract and concrete forms.
2. Compare how the Provisional Irish Republican Army, Hamas, and the Tupamaros create their sense of identity.
3. Do you think that a group's use of violence becomes more likely if its identity formation is connected with a) other violent acts; b) a need for religious martyrs and immortality; or c) a linking of physical space with martyrdom?
4. Summarize the methods that social scientists used to profile characteristics of terrorists from 1970 through 1990.
5. Describe the profile of contemporary terrorists developed in the Corley, Smith, and Damphousse article.
6. What are the significant relationships between the variables of race, gender, age and level of education and the terrorist categories used in the Corley, Smith, and Damphousse article?
7. Becker and Ballard argue that case studies of multiple threat layers offer various levels of stakeholders (public officials) the opportunity to mitigate the risks of potential terrorist attacks. Give examples of how the Yucca Mountain case illustrates their assertion.
8. How do NRC regulations and safeguards elevate the terrorist threat connected with the Yucca Mountain repository?
9. Describe the major areas of concern with regard to terrorism, transport, and the Yucca Mountain facility.
10. List three contemporary terrorism trends.
11. Discuss what countermeasure should be taken to stop or alter the trends listed in question ten.
12. How do balance, breadth, and consistency relate to counterterrorism?
13. To which group can present-day eco-terrorists trace their origins? Describe it.
14. Describe Naess's philosophy of deep ecology and how these ideas influence environmentalists to engage in violent behavior.
15. Compare the Earth Liberation Front (ELF) to the Animal Liberation Front(ALF). Do these groups exist in countries other than the United States?

SECTION THREE

International Terrorism

LOOK FOR THESE KEY POINTS:

- Analysts of Islamic groups that choose violence as a political strategy fail to take into account their multifaceted complexity. These "New Islamic" groups rely on access to weapons, mastery of the art of public relations, access to intelligence sources, and sophisticated recruitment strategies to meet their goals.
- Intelligence agencies and terrorism scholars should engage in direct analyses of the threats that radiological weapons pose in an integrated global community.
- Steganography is an established method of hidden communication that has advanced with improvements in technology. Whether one accepts that terrorists are using steganography to communicate or one believes that such reports are overstated, the fact remains that its potential is immense.
- Although ideological sentiments on terrorism are very divided in the world of politics and diplomacy, the efforts of international police agencies such as Interpol can be based on a common ground that treats terrorism as a depoliticized crime.

Modern international terrorism is popular because states that are too weak to wage a conventional conflict use it as surrogate warfare. There are many ways in which a state may support an international terrorist group, such as:

- Recruiting group members from existing state intelligence operations
- Giving guidance as a group runs a mission
- Supporting intelligence
- Providing specialized terrorist training or basic military training
- Providing diplomatic assets and communication networks
- Providing weapons of mass destruction (WMDS), conventional weapons, etc.
- Providing use of state territory for base and/or activity
- Providing financial support—directly or indirectly
- Providing tacit support—i.e., failing to warn a target state that it is about to be attacked

- Providing rhetorical support—speeches by high government officials that approve or endorse the use of terrorist strategy, use of the state propaganda machine, etc. (Murphy 1989, 32–33).

Groups who try to terrorize populations other than their own have a goal of trying to enforce an authority they want to be all-powerful, such as a political state, a religious god, or even a type of economic power. International terrorists also develop an ideology, recruit members, select leadership, and have organizational strategies. While domestic terrorists challenge authority only in their home country, international terrorists are paid (or are financed in some fashion) to show that their sponsor is stronger than the country where they commit the violent act. Their strategic use of violence is quite different from that of domestic terrorists. Domestic terrorists accelerate to violence slowly and use it sparingly in specific situations. International terrorists accelerate quickly to violence, use a type of violence that makes it less likely that they will be captured on site, and are less likely to use strategies that might expose their leadership. If these groups are treated the same as domestic terrorists, problems in law enforcement and prevention occur.

The four chapters in Section Three are all related to the various group dynamics associated with international terrorism. The first chapter, "Islamic Extremists: How Do They Mobilize Support?" is reprinted here with permission of the U. S. Institute of Peace. Judy Barsalou, director of the Institute's grant program, wrote this report, which summarizes the presentations and discussions that occurred at an Institute's Current Briefing on April 17, 2002. Mustapha Kamai Pashs (American University), Jessica Stern (Harvard University), and Muhammad Muslih (Long Island University) presented findings from their grant-funded research projects.

The chapter discusses the recruitment and organizational strategies of "New Islamic" groups in Pakistan, South Asia, and the Middle East. Individuals join extremist groups because of a desire to achieve specific political objectives and to acquire emotional incentives. Many recruits feel they have been humiliated and treated as second-class citizens by government authorities and other elites. Other groups offer spiritual incentives; the Lashkar-eTaiba reports that they like to have recruits as young as 8 years old so that members can be trained in the spirit of sacrifice. The chapter enlightens our understanding of the commonalities between "New Islamic" groups and exposes the prime factors in the rise of religious extremism throughout the Muslim world.

Dominic Little and James David Ballard's "Analysis of Organizational Characteristics for Groups That Would Use Radiological Weapons of Mass Victimization" extends our understanding of terrorist groups through strategy classification. Although they focus specifically on which organizational strategies might lead a group to use radiological weapons, Little and Ballard's typology can be used for analysis of the risk-taking potential of all groups. Their analytical model for the study of organizational characteristics stresses six factors: ideology, knowledge, management, audience, social distance, and symbolic value. To the authors, these factors represent a collective thought process that pushes a group to choose more, rather than less, dangerous weapons/strategies. Little and Ballard suggest that it is important for terrorist experts to look at which groups could gather the organizational resources needed for a radiological attack. Their organizational analysis is both a process for developing a threat assessment and a welcome addition to the understanding of the use of radiological weapons of mass destruction.

The third chapter is an in-depth analysis and explanation of a new communication technology of which few people have even heard, much less understand. "Steganography and Terrorism: An Introduction to Data Hiding and Its Use in Terrorist Activities" by Robert Moore and Darin Walker, is a fascinating discussion of the history and current uses of steganography. The authors explain that steganography is an established method of hidden communication that has advanced because of improvements in computer software, the Internet, and other technology. The authors suggest that whether one elects to believe that terrorists are using steganography to communicate or that reports of its use are overstated, the fact remains that the potential for its use is immense. Individuals who investigate terrorist activity should make all attempts to be aware of this technology and its uses because they will be the ones who will have the best chance of developing productive countertechniques. Moore and Walker believe that the use of steganography and hidden writing are sure to see an increase in the future as individuals in the terrorist community discover its possibilities.

One of the most problematic areas associated with international terrorism is our lack of law and law enforcement at the international level. "Interpol and the Policing of International Terrorism: Developments and Dynamics Since September 11," by Mathieu Deflem and Lindsay Maybin, is a much-needed analysis of the organization of counterterrorist police strategies by the International Criminal Police Organization (Interpol). The authors argue that counterterrorism policing reorganizations have occurred throughout the world following the September 11th World Trade Center/Pentagon attack. Some of the international changes mirror the American response of making new counterterrorist agreements and legislation, but Interpol has uniquely blended its past and present ideas on counterterrorism to adjust its growing role in enforcement. It has updated its technology with a new electronic communications system, opened a specialized antiterrorist command and coordination center, begun new computerized data bases, and added a financial crimes subdirectorate.

Finally, to overcome the lack of an international definition of terrorism and differing countries' explanations of the behavior, Interpol depoliticizes terrorism and reduces it to the criminal behavior level. Authors DeFlem and Maybin analyze the implications of Interpol's reorganization and activities in their discussion of the attempts of developed nations to police terrorist activity.

REFERENCES

Jenkins, Brian. 1985. *International Terrorism: The Other World War.* Santa Monica, CA.: RAND Corporation.
Murphy, John F. 1989. *State Support of International Terrorism.* Boulder, CO:Westview Press.

CHAPTER 6

Islamic Extremists: How Do They Mobilize Support?

Judy Barsalou
U.S. Institute of Peace

BRIEFLY...

- Religious extremist groups in the Islamic world are deeply divided along ideological and sectarian lines. Stereotyped images of Islam as a monolithic religion predisposed toward violence do not do justice to the fact that most Muslims are peaceful. Such stereotypes also fail to take into account the multi-faceted complexity of those Islamic groups that choose violence as a political strategy.

Written by Judy Barsalou, director of the Institute's Grant Program, this report summarizes presentations and discussion at a Current Issues Briefing at the Institute on April 17, 2002, that featured three current grantees of the Institute: Mustapha Kamal Pasha (American University), Jessica Stern (Harvard University), and Muhammad Muslih (Long Island University). The event presented findings from their grant-funded research projects. The views expressed in this report do not necessarily reflect those of the U.S. Institute of Peace, which does not advocate specific policies.—U.S. Institute of Peace

{*Editor' Note: No references are cited at the end of this article because it is the transcription of a special seminar held at the U.S. Institute of Peace in Washington, D.C.*} Reprinted with permission of the U.S. Institute of Peace.

Special Report 1200 17th Street NW • Washington, DC 20036 • 202.457.1700 fax 202.429.6063
Special Report 89 July 2002

- The rise of religious extremism in South Asia and the Middle East has to do primarily with four factors: the absence in much of the Muslim world of democratic, accountable governments, and, indirectly related to this, disputes over contested territory; the failure of governments in some Islamic countries to address problems arising from rapid social, demographic, and economic changes in the last century; financial, logistical, and moral support provided by external actors; and the breakdown within Islam itself of *ijtihad*—the established tradition whereby religious clerics independently interpret the Koran in order to apply Koranic law to diverse and changing circumstances.

- Extremist groups in the Middle East and South Asia display a diversity of motives and methods of operation, reflecting the widely varying circumstances in which they have arisen and operate.

- Individuals join extremist groups for a number of reasons, including the desire to promote specific political goals, as well as in response to a variety of financial, spiritual, and emotional incentives. The groups also attract individuals who, regardless of their social class or economic background, feel they have been humiliated and treated as "second class" by government authorities and others.

- Successful extremist groups have clear missions, rely on a division of labor between relatively young, uneducated "foot soldiers" and better-educated elite operatives, and have developed a variety of fundraising techniques. Many groups rely heavily on the Internet to raise funds, as well as on contributions from foreign governments.

- The ability of these groups to meet their goals depends on four additional factors: access to weapons; mastery of the art of public relations, including use of the media to promote their causes; access to intelligence sources and development of counter-intelligence techniques; and the establishment of "corporate headquarters"—either in a physical area or virtually, via the Internet.

- Not all religious schools *(madaris)* in Pakistan are "factories of terrorism" as commonly depicted in the Western press. Many of the older *madaris* are long-established centers of learning that have produced serious Islamic intellectuals, while others are providing important educational and social welfare services not available from the government. Similarly, most religious schools in Lebanon, the Palestinian territories, and Egypt teach traditional religious values rather than seek to inculcate militancy among the young.

FACTORS UNDERLYING RELIGIOUS EXTREMISM IN PAKISTAN

Mustapha Kamal Pasha began his remarks with general observations about Islam and religious extremism. Muslim communities around the world and in Pakistan are deeply fractured along sectarian and ideological lines. Overlooking this, observers often make binary distinctions between "good" and "bad," "liberal" versus "illiberal," and "rational" versus "irrational" Islam that blur the complexity of the situation. Pasha argued, moreover, that the word "terrorism" is often reduced in common discourse to simplistic terms. He suggested, instead, the importance of finding a better way to characterize Islamic extremists, and to focus on terrorism as a phenomenon in its own right. Pasha stressed that terrorism is a particular form of violent activity, not simply a natural corollary of any religion.

Terrorists often seek legitimacy through particular religious idioms. But the epithet "Islamic terrorists"—often used as if this is a phenomenon requiring no elaboration —only further reinforces stereotypical images of Islam. Pasha made a distinction between "old" and "new" Islamists in Pakistan. The new Islamists generally are protagonists of political Islam; they seek to transform politics through religion and religion through politics. Unlike the old Islamists, who were willing to enjoy, at a minimum, peaceful existence with secular politics, the new Islamists are unwilling to brook such an option. Often learning the art of politics from secular modernists, especially the use of print and visual media, the new Islamists wish to transform both the state and civil society in the image of what they believe can be a truly Islamic order.

The rise of the new Islamists, Pasha argued, dates back to the era that began with the Bangladesh war of 1971 and continued with the 1973 Arab-Israeli war and the OPEC (Organization of Petroleum Exporting Countries) oil embargo. The boom of the Arab oil economies that followed led, significantly, to massive flows of workers (including Pakistan's "best and brightest") from South Asia to the Gulf in the 1970s and resulted in the weakening of the Pakistani labor movement. Some of the old Islamists became new Islamists—including the group Jama'at Islam, which started as a pro-American faction and then completely reversed itself. But many of the new Islamists emerged from political and sectarian divides reinforced by age and class and exacerbated by the circumstances growing out of the war against the Soviets in Afghanistan. New Islamists often are well-versed in the technical and scientific infrastructure of modernity and embrace modern technology but reject cultural modernity. Moreover, unlike the old Islamists, the new Islamists rely heavily on the mass media rather than on traditional political institutions to mobilize support. Nonetheless, while popular support for the new Islamists is sizable, their groups have not garnered more than five percent support at the polls, and they remain small in size.

The principal strategy pursued by new Islamists in Pakistan seeks to "capture" civil society institutions, such as educational institutions and the media, in order to eventually capture the state. This strategy recognizes that the Pakistani state and secular elite are fragile. Authoritarian and inadequate in providing even the most basic services to the neediest, the Pakistani state now focuses its resources primarily on foreign debt-servicing and military expenditures. Indeed, argued Pasha, a leading factor in the rise of religious extremism in Pakistan is the decline of the "developmental," service-oriented state. In pursuing the above strategy, the new Islamists have achieved their greatest success by redefining political discourse in Islamic terms and, in the process, have put the secular elite on the defensive. In fact, they had already begun to affect political discourse in Pakistan well before extremist religious schools were established after the onset of the war against the Soviets in Afghanistan in late 1979. In an effort to recapture lost ground, the state and secular elite have increasingly "Islamicized" their rhetoric, thus paving the way for wider support for the new Islamists. New Islamists now also dominate Pakistan's institutions of higher education.

The media have played a role in this process. While the extremist groups have achieved the greatest boost from the Urdu-language media, support for them can also be found in Pakistan's English-language media. Extremist groups have also achieved significant success in their efforts to ban alcohol consumption and confine women to the private domain of their homes, where they are subject to the authority of their male relations.

Turning to a discussion of religious schools *(madaris)* in Pakistan, Pasha argued that too often they are simplistically characterized as "factories of terrorism." In fact, there are three broad categories of *madaris.* The first are the long-established centers of learning that have produced serious Islamic intellectuals. A second category consists of those schools that have played an important role in providing educational and social welfare services to Pakistan's poorest citizens not being adequately served by Pakistan's government. Only a third set of *madaris,* largely a product of the conditions surrounding the war against the Soviets in Afghanistan, can be properly categorized as producing *jihadi* militants. The latter schools have several characteristics in common. They are run by what Pasha described as "lumpen intellectuals," mostly following a conservative Wahhabi interpretation of Islam, especially with regard to questions relating to the status of women. He noted that many of these individuals, and many leaders of extremist Islamic groups, were trained in scientific fields but have little understanding of Western culture, aside from how to manipulate the technology it has produced. In creating their own schools, these "lumpen intellectuals" took advantage of the departure in the 1970s and 1980s of some of Pakistan's best-trained citizens who sought better-paying jobs in the Gulf. They also benefited from the "kalashnikov culture" that resulted from the proliferation of arms and foreign funding (especially from Saudi Arabia and the United States) in response to the Soviet invasion of Afghanistan.

More broadly, extremist *madaris,* and the rise of religious extremism in Pakistan, reflect the breakdown of *ijtihad*—the established tradition whereby religious clerics render independent interpretations of the Koran in order to apply Koranic law to diverse and changing circumstances. Though in earlier periods a place for lively internal debate, Islamic societies today reveal a general sense of intellectual defensiveness as reflected by the extremist *madaris,* which tend to be doctrinaire in matters theological. The creation of these *madaris* also demonstrates rising frustrations marked by the widening gap between a very visible Muslim elite in Pakistan that has benefited from the globalized world economy and those left on the fringes.

MOBILIZATIONAL AND ORGANIZATIONAL STRATEGIES IN SOUTH ASIA

Turning the discussion to the broader region, Jessica Stern concentrated on two issues: key incentives for individuals to join *jihadi* groups, and organizational strategies involved in building effective *jihadi* movements. She noted that her fieldwork has found some common elements among religious extremists of different faiths around the world.

According to Stern, individuals may join extremist groups for a variety of reasons, including a desire to achieve specific political objectives such as sovereignty over disputed territory. Emotional incentives may also play an important part. Members of extremist groups often report on the "glamour" of being members of such groups, and of becoming "addicted" to the adrenaline-driven excitement of their activities, which they say becomes a way of life. Unknown, lower-class youth can become famous through their militant actions, with thousands turning out for their funerals when they are "martyred." Members also actively recruit their friends into these groups. But Stern emphasized that the single most common emotional feature among *jihadi* militants, regardless of their rank, is their feeling that they have been humiliated and treated as "second class" by government authorities and others—even those *jihadis* from relatively rich countries or advantaged backgrounds.

Spiritual incentives drive some to join these groups. Leaders of extremist groups often articulate political, economic, or social grievances—such as disputes over land—in spiritual terms. Some train their recruits from early on to focus on the "real life," that is, the next life, and on the redemptive value of membership in the group. Citing Hafez Said, a former head of Lashkar-e-Taiba in Pakistan, Stern said that the group likes to "get recruits as young as eight years old in order to train them to focus on the spirit of sacrifice." Financial incentives can also be significant. Successful groups pay their recruits well, and many members talk about the importance of money as a motivating factor. One member of Harakat ul-Mujahideen, a group based in Pakistan, mentioned, for example, that he would take a severe salary cut if he left the group for regular employment. A mid-level manager in Lashkar-e-Taiba, another group based in Pakistan, said that he earns seven times what he would in the civilian sector, and that the financial incentives for top leaders are significantly greater. Families of dead "martyrs" sometimes receive financial rewards or better housing. Group leaders also recognize opportunity costs in their salary structures. Stern noted that trial transcripts of the U.S. Embassy bombings in Kenya and Tanzania revealed that a Sudanese member of al Qaeda, Jamal al-Fadl, was furious when he learned that key Egyptian operatives were receiving up to three times as much as he was. According to al-Fadl, Osama bin Laden's response was that the Egyptians could travel and had other career options.

Stern also outlined the following organizational requirements of successful extremist movements in South Asia. First, they develop what, in essence, are mission statements in which they articulate their goals. Some, such as al Qaeda, may amend their mission statements over time to appeal to a broader audience—as Osama bin Laden did by only recently addressing the conflicts between the Arabs and Israel and in Kashmir. Groups also need access to weapons. Often they obtain them on the black market or through underworld connections. One Pakistani informant, for example, reported that over 50 percent of his group's weapons were purchased from organized-crime groups in India and from Indian military personnel.

As in other organizations, extremist religious organizations rely upon a division of labor—in this case between foot soldiers (expendable young recruits) and better-educated elite operatives. In Pakistan, the former are often plucked from *madaris*. In Indonesia, Laskar Jihad recruits young university students for the latter. When the Egyptian group Islamic Jihad merged with al Qaeda, it provided a ready-made officer corps to bin Laden. Fundraising is essential to the success of these groups, which rely on a variety of different strategies to raise money. Some, such as Laskar Jihad, which has a very sophisticated Web site, raise a substantial portion of their funds on the Internet. Others admit to smuggling drugs through Afghanistan to raise funds. Some groups display wounded members at Friday prayers to raise money. While such groups as Laskar Jihad can be seen everywhere on the streets of Jakarta raising money, this strategy has more to do with public relations—to raise their profile in the community—than with serious fundraising; most groups report that they raise only a small proportion of their budgets from ordinary people. Funding from abroad is also a significant source of support for some groups. One informant from Harakat ul-Mujahideen, for example, said that 60 percent of its funding comes from abroad—from speeches given during the *hajj* (pilgrimage) in Saudi Arabia and from wealthy donors in the Arabian Peninsula. In the past, the Saudi government has also been a source of significant funding for extremist South Asian groups.

Intelligence and counter-intelligence are also important to operations of extremist groups. Members of Pakistani groups, for example, told Stern of buying intelligence from the Indian intelligence agency known as the Research and Analysis Wing (RAW). Training manuals captured from al Qaeda teach their members how to use sophisticated techniques to disappear into enemy territory, for example. Stern acknowledged that some of the groups she interviewed mentioned significant support from Pakistan's intelligence agency (Inter-Service Intelligence or ISI). Even though the leadership of ISI has changed since the September 11 terrorist attacks against the United States, there is still much sympathy within the ISI for extremist groups.

Good public relations are key to the success of these groups. In an effort to build support, many adroitly use the media and other vehicles to create a high profile. Stern mentioned, for example, that one Pakistani group eagerly published in their newspaper her testimony to Congress about the group, even though she described them as a terrorist organization. Extremist groups also need physical space—"corporate headquarters"—within which they can organize their operations. Until recently, the failed state of Afghanistan provided such a place for al Qaeda. But when such locations are closed down to these groups, they sometimes attempt to develop "networks of networks"—leaderless networks organized through the Internet. Stern noted that efforts by the Pakistani government to limit extremist religious groups have largely been ineffectual. In the recent past, some 2,000 extremists were briefly imprisoned, but the government was able to bring charges against only a few. The government moved to close down groups' bank accounts only after many had already moved their funds. Some leaders have gone into "hiding" but were visible enough that Stern still was able to contact them. Under the pressure of outside forces, and in response to internal dissension, groups often splinter and re-form, which makes them even harder to control.

EXTREMIST GROUPS IN EGYPT, LEBANON, AND THE PALESTINIAN TERRITORIES

Turning the discussion to the Arab Middle East, Muhammad Muslih emphasized that the ideologies, agendas, methods of recruitment, and activities of different extremist groups have varied considerably from one group to the next and over time. But throughout most of the Arab world, he argued, the most important underlying cause of terrorism is humiliation and repression by authoritarian governments, or in the case of the Palestinian territories and Lebanon, the foreign occupation of land. The former problem, Muslih suggested, can best be overcome by the development of democratic, accountable governments in Muslim countries, which will help undermine the appeal of extremist groups and encourage radical Islamists to refrain from violence.

The revelations of the leaders of al-Gama'a al-Islamiyya (the Islamic Group) in Egypt confirm this point of view. A careful reading of the statements of this group's leaders in *Al-Ahram al-Duwali* (published in Cairo in February/March 2002) clearly indicates the role of humiliation and state violence in pushing the group toward violence in the 1980s and 1990s. As for the latter problem, terrorism in Lebanon and the Palestinian territories, Muslih suggested that it can only be resolved by ending occupation.

According to Muslih, all the extremist groups throughout the region have been deeply influenced by the Muslim Brotherhood, an organization established in Isma'iliyya, Egypt in 1928 by Hasan al-Banna. The works of al-Banna, particularly his letters and speeches—including, most notably *Da'watuna Fi Tawrin Jadid* (Our Call in a New Phase) and *Rasa'il al-Shahid Hasan al-Banna* (The Letters of the Martyr Hasan al-Banna)—remain among the standard references for Islamic thinkers and activists. And the works of Sayyid Qutb, particularly his revolutionary seven-volume interpretation of the Koran *(Fi Zilal al-Qur'an,* or Under the Sovereignty of the Koran) and *Ma'alim Fil-Tariq* (Landmarks on the Road), had an even deeper impact on the thought and practice of radical Islamists. Also Khalid Muhammad Khalid's earlier works, written in the early 1960s, particularly *Min Huna . . . Nabda'* (From Here . . . We Start), left a deep imprint on these movements.

Muslih emphasized that, originally, al-Banna recognized the legitimacy of the Egyptian state, accepted the notion of dialogue with the British colonial administration, and agreed to live in peace with the government even though it was not based on Islamic principles. But after Qutb and other Egyptian Islamists were tortured in Egyptian prisons, they began to advocate violence as a political strategy. Thus, argued Muslih, torture, humiliation, and violations of civil liberties went a long way toward radicalizing the Islamists' instruments of political action. Ayman al-Zawahiri, a principal leader of al Qaeda from Egypt, has indicated that the torture of Islamic activists in Egyptian jails instilled in them the belief in violence, and also made them angry and determined to seek revenge through violence, not only against the Egyptian state, but also against the major supporter of that state—the United States.

Over time, according to Muslih, the Muslim Brotherhood produced many splinter groups and factions. Among those worth mentioning are a number that emerged in the 1980s: Al-Najuna min al-Nar (Those Who Are Saved from Hell), al-Gama'a al-Islamiyya (the Islamic Group), al-Takfir wal-Hijra (Unbelief and Emigration), and Tanzim al-Fanniyya al-Askariyya (the Military Technical Organization). However, the centrist core of the Muslim Brotherhood remains largely focused on domestic issues related to the social code (such as the dress and behavior of women) and the question of governance in an Islamic state. Muslih noted that this centrist core did not hesitate to enter into political alliances with secular and even leftist groups in Egypt. A major splinter group, al-Jihad al-Islami (Islamic Jihad), itself split into two groups around the mid-1990s, with one faction seeking refuge outside Egypt, allying itself with al Qaeda, and the other remaining in Egypt. In 1995, the Egyptian Islamic Jihad, which operates outside Egypt, switched its focus from fighting "apostate" leaders and individuals in the Arab world to fighting Americans, Jews, and Christians. One of the few groups that developed a detailed frame-work for the creation of an Islamic state is Hizb al-Tahrir al-Islami (the Islamic Liberation Party). Sheikh Taqiyyu al-Din al-Nabhani established this group, which appeals mostly to merchants and other members of the middle class, in Jerusalem in 1952.

Circumstances differ in Lebanon and in the Palestinian territories, according to Muslih, and extremist groups there reflect these differences. The Lebanese group Hezbollah (which originally called itself Islamic Jihad) was initially motivated by the deprived social and political status of the Shia community in Lebanon as well as by the 1979 success of the Islamic revolution in Iran. Until the death of Iran's Ayatollah Khomeini in 1989, one of the group's main goals was to establish an Islamic state in Lebanon. Thereafter, this motive changed and like the Palestinian groups—Hamas and the Palestinian Islamic Jihad—became a national liberation movement principally interested in fighting Israeli occupation in Lebanon and extending help to the Palestinian Intifada whenever possible. Hezbollah since the late 1980s has recognized the legitimacy of the multi-cultural, multi-ethnic Lebanese state, and has transformed itself into a political party that has won representation in the Lebanese parliament. Muslih stressed that there are nuanced differences between Hezbollah and Hamas with respect to peace with Israel. For example, in its statements and published literature Hezbollah calls for the total liberation of *all* original Mandate Palestine, as well as for the recovery of the Shab'a Farms area, which it claims belongs to Lebanon, and the return of the Golan to Syria. However, the Palestinian group Hamas, according to Muslih, is predisposed to accept a Palestinian state in the West Bank and Gaza with Jerusalem as its capital, although Hamas views such a solution to be a *hudna* (truce) and not necessarily a final peace with the Jewish state. Like Hezbollah, the Palestinian Islamic Jihad insists on the total liberation of Mandate Palestine—what today is Israel and the Palestinian territories. According to Muslih, it is significant that, like the Muslim Brotherhood in its early days, Hamas has been willing to co-exist with the Palestinian Authority, and on several occasions has talked about accepting a cease-fire with Israel. In other words, unlike Sayyid Qutb, who wrote that Egypt and the Arab world were in a state of *Dar al-Harb* (the "realm of war" where governments must be overthrown because they are non-Islamic and societies must be rebuilt from scratch along Islamic lines), Hamas does not consider the Palestinian territories to be in *Dar al-Harb*. Qutb also wrote that the Koran is a "sword" that has universal application to fight infidels everywhere, but Hamas literature does not reflect this perspective. Instead, although mobilized in the name of Islam and as off-shoots of the Muslim Brotherhood, both Hamas and Palestinian Islamic Jihad remain almost exclusively focused on the national strug-gle between the Palestinians and the Israelis and on the liberation of Palestinian territory from Israeli occupation.

It is not surprising then that, from a theological point of view, the literature and the statements of Hamas and Palestinian Islamic Jihad do not expound *jihad* as a reli-gious concept to the same degree as the literature produced by the Muslim Brotherhood, Hezbollah, al Qaeda, and the Egyptian Islamic Jihad. According to Muslih, the writings of Hamas and Palestinian Islamic Jihad are not preoccupied, as were those by Sayyid Qutb, with *fiqh* (Islamic jurisprudence) or with an in-depth analysis of theological and governance questions.

While Palestinian Islamic Jihad and Hamas have important ties to Iran, both re-main within the Sunni Islamic tradition, argued Muslih. Yet Islamic Jihad is closer ide-ologically to Iran than Hamas because the latter established more direct relations with Tehran when Israel deported some 400 Hamas members and sympathizers into Marj al-Zuhur, in southern Lebanon, in December 1992 and Iran came to their political and financial aid. Overall, the *marji'iyya* (frame of reference) of Hamas is very close to that of the global Muslim Brotherhood, while that of Palestinian Islamic Jihad is deeply influenced by the *marji'iyya* of Iran. Moreover, Hamas remains privately much more critical of Iran's Shia traditions than Palestinian Islamic Jihad. (Sunni and Shia Islam are the two main branches of Islam, with Sunni Muslims being in the majority.) Compared to Hamas and Palestinian Islamic Jihad, according to Muslih, Hezbollah re-mains ideologically closer to Iran, because Hezbollah has its roots in Lebanon's Shia community. Iran, along with rich Lebanese and non-Lebanese Shia families, is the great-est source of funds for Hezbollah. Iran reportedly also provides unspecified amounts of funding for Hamas and Palestinian Islamic Jihad. In recruiting supporters, there are significant differences among the Palestinian and Lebanese groups, argued Muslih. Hezbollah draws tens of thousands of supporters annually to its religious parades mark-ing the 'Ashura celebration, and uses the parades and a wide array of social services to attract supporters. It also runs a sophisticated and influential TV station, al-Manar.

Muslih suggested that Palestinian Islamic Jihad is much more secretive in its re-cruitment and operations than Hamas. Nonetheless, the two Palestinian organizations report that since conditions deteriorated significantly with the reoccupation of many Palestinian urban centers by Israel in the first quarter of 2002, they now receive more requests from individuals who want to carry out suicide missions than they have the resources to train and equip.

Unlike South Asia, where religious schools play an active role in indoctrinating the young in extreme religious beliefs, there are no comparable schools in the Palestinian territories, according to Muslih. Palestinian Islamic Jihad and Hamas are active in schools and mosques and in providing social services to the poor, but do not invest in the full-time religious training of children. Clothed in the language of Islam, the ideological frameworks of Palestinian Islamic Jihad, Hamas, and Hezbollah remain fundamentally nationalistic and focused on the struggle against Israel. Religion is more of a garb than a guide to action.

CONCLUSION

While many religious extremist groups in South Asia and the Middle East share common organizational features, the circumstances that give rise to them and that motivate their actions vary widely from one setting to another. Among Palestinian groups, for example, the struggle against Israeli occupation is paramount. Egyptian groups, by contrast, are focused primarily on questions related to the social code and to internal governance of the country. Pakistani groups are motivated by a variety of goals, including the desire to control Kashmir. There is no single cause for the rise of religious extremism in the Muslim world. It reflects, perhaps most of all, the failure to date of secular modernism to develop good governance in most Muslim countries. All the speakers agreed that the struggle against extremism will not be won until the countries in which extremists thrive become truly democratic, and until Islamic activists are no longer humiliated and oppressed for their beliefs. In the case of the Palestinian territories, extremists groups will continue to be influential so long as the struggle against Israel continues. "Law and order approaches" to the problem of extremism generally are ineffectual because they offer no positive alternatives to the disaffected young who swell the ranks of extremist groups.

Another prime factor in the rise of extremism is the failure of many governments in the Muslim world to address the overwhelming challenges of development arising from rapid social, demographic, and economic changes over the past century. It is no accident that many of the extremist groups in Pakistan, for example, are centered in mid-sized towns whose populations have grown exponentially in recent decades because of rural-to-urban migration. Of the 140 million people living in Pakistan today, most are poor and susceptible at some level to the blandishments of extremist groups, who claim to have answers to questions that their own government has unsuccessfully addressed or simply ignored. Throughout the Muslim world, extremist religious groups tend to be most influential in locations where local governments are the least effective in addressing developmental challenges.

External forces have also played a significant role in creating extremist groups in the Middle East and South Asia. Stern pointed to the role of funding from the United States and Saudi Arabia, as well as logistical support from the ISI, in the rise of extremist groups in Afghanistan. In the Arab world, according to Muslih, the "literate class" is highly critical of the U.S. government for supporting oppressive Arab states.

A fourth, and final, factor in the rise of extremist groups relates to a deeper crisis within Islam itself. The decline of the centuries-old tradition of *ijtihad*—the ever-evolving interpretation of the Koran by religious clerics—has led to rigid and narrow interpretations of religious precepts. Muslim societies must engage in a process of genuine self-examination and grapple with the complicated question of why they have failed to build stable religious and other institutions capable of helping their societies adapt to a rapidly changing world.

CHAPTER 7

Analysis of Organizational Characteristics for Groups That Would Use Radiological Weapons of Mass Victimization

Dominic Little
James David Ballard
Department of Sociology
California State University Northridge

INTRODUCTION

In the future, terrorism tactics will continue to evolve toward the use of weapons of mass victimization (WMV), which are typically referred to in the literature as weapons of mass destruction (WMD). It takes a unique, technologically sophisticated, and particular violent philosophy within a terrorist organization to allow, or encourage, the use of such weapons. It is critically important for intelligence services, law enforcement, and policymakers to systematically sift through information collected on the numerous groups who commit political violence and separate out those "wannabes" from those who can, or will, effectively be able to employ one or more varieties of WMV. One potential assessment methodology that may help in this process focuses on organizational characteristics to understand the potential of a group to use WMV.

To help illustrate this potential, this chapter will revolve around one form of WMV, the radiological dispersion device (RDD), to facilitate the discussion of organizational characteristic analysis. By proxy, this chapter will also focus on what could be viewed as the propensity of these groups to take a social risk by using WMV and/or what factors characterize those groups who would avoid, or because of a lack of critical resources could not effectively engage in, the more risky behavior involved in using such tactics.

To accomplish these tasks, the chapter begins by offering some background and then develops a classification scheme for the organizational characteristics of groups that are capable of perpetrating such attacks. The conclusion will offer a typology and methodology for the analysis of such groups and their potential to engage in, or evolve toward using, such risk-taking tactics. Such an analytic method could be used by a variety of counterterrorism professionals as a proactive means to identify threats and hopefully prevent the use of WMV.

BACKGROUND

The term WMD was used throughout the Cold War era by Soviet forces (Steinweg et al. 1994). It is neither precise nor definitive in nature, but rather a catchall phrase that encompasses very different weapons and associated tactics that may be used by terrorists. In fact, since its inclusion into everyday political rhetoric, both the United States and the international community have begun the task of further developing or operationalizing this amorphous concept (Hogendoorn 1997; Herby 1992; Burch and Flowerree 1991).

Perhaps the most widely accepted definition of this term holds that WMD are nuclear, biological, and chemical weapons. Legally, United States Code Title 50, Chapter 40, Section 2302 notes that "weapons of mass destruction means any weapon or device that is intended, or has the capability, to cause death or serious bodily injury to a significant number of people through the release, dissemination, or impact of toxic or poisonous chemicals or their precursors; a disease organism; or radiation or radioactivity" (Legal Information Institute 2003). Similar definitions are used by law enforcement agencies such as the Federal Bureau of Investigation, international organizations such as the United Nations, and many other interested parties.

Given the common usage of this term in the literature, why alter the definition to WMV? Ballard (2000) suggests that to be proactive in addressing the threats WMD pose, it would be best to reconceptualize large-scale terrorist attacks using such weapons as incidents designed to inflict mass victimization. Accordingly, the concept WMV is more useful when identifying the outcomes of an attack, not only the tragic loss of life as emphasized by the Title 50 statute noted above but the psychological, sociological, political, and economic impacts experienced by terrorist victims, local communities, and even nation-states.

Take for example an RDD commonly referred to as a "dirty bomb." This weapon is designed to disperse radioactive material through the detonation of explosives or other dispersal means (Ballard 2002). Such methods may include the aerosolizing of radioactive material or otherwise distributing it into the environment. According to the U.S. Department of Defense, an RDD is "any device, including any weapon or equipment, other than a nuclear explosive device, specifically designed to employ radioactive material by disseminating it to cause destruction, damage, or injury by means of the radiation produced by the decay of such material" (Ferguson, Kazi, and Perera 2003, 19).

In other words, RDD devices can be constructed using almost any radioactive material. Examples may include a variety of radioactive products such as spent nuclear fuel and potentially lower-level radioactive materials, such as medical, industrial, and research waste. Weapons-grade materials such as highly enriched uranium and certain isotopes of plutonium may also be employed in RDD devices if they can be located by the terrorists, but the level of radioactivity and risk they represent is not a necessary and sufficient condition for building an effective RDD weapon (Ferguson, Kazi, and Perera 2003; Ballard 2002).

So what makes RDD so important? The answer is simple: like radioactivity, they are widely misunderstood by the general public and counterterrorism bureaucracies, they have unknown effects because of the variability of their delivery systems (i.e., explosive-induced particularization versus environmental dispersion), and it is difficult to estimate their potential impact due to the variability of the radiological material that could be used (i.e., depleted uranium versus weapons-grade plutonium).

An additional problem with an RDD is that it is not just the public that misunderstands their potential; government agencies and the international community continue to group nuclear, biological, and chemical attacks as a single weapon category and/or have a myopic perspective on how they work. This has caused great concern among terrorologists, who argue that RDDs are unique in that they will not kill an immediate large number of humans; instead, their potential impact rests more on their psychological, sociological, political, and economic ramifications. These effects are not immediately seen and may in fact transpire decades after the actual attack. Additionally, these weapons are typically mischaracterized in the literature as a singular form when in fact they could be constructed in a variety of ways other than the typical explosives wrapped with the radioactive materials configuration typically discussed (Ballard 2002).

Last, the materials needed to construct an RDD are readily available throughout the world and especially in unsecured or undersecured storage facilities located throughout the United States and parts of the former Soviet Union. These facts also suggest that terrorist organizations may be able to more easily procure radioactive material and easily assemble an RDD onsite rather than import said materials or device.

Given these types of risk factors, what would be a way to predict who could identify these types of vulnerabilities and then exploit them to their advantage? The next section of this argument will start the delineation of organizational characteristics relevant to groups that may be motivated to locate such materials, build a weapon or plan how to disperse the materials, and then use the RDD in an attack.

ORGANIZATIONAL CHARACTERISTICS

Given what some experts suggests is the changing nature of terrorism (Stern 1999; Hoffman 1999) and the reconceptualization suggested herein, the question of under what circumstances a group or terrorist organization would seek to employ a WMV should be posed. In other words, what organizational characteristics are necessary for a group to feel ready, capable, and willing to use radiological materials as a terrorism tactic?

One technique for the assessment of this risk profile is codified by the acronym IKMASS. The IKMASS analytical process uses six factors or dimensions associated with groups that could use WMV: Ideology, knowledge, management, audience, social distance, and symbolic value. Using these six factors as the analysis frame for the various types of groups who are involved in, or could become involved in, WMV terrorism may offer a chance to predict who will use certain weapons, proactively address the threat they pose, and ultimately offer nation-states a modicum of security and safety in the face of such threats.

Individually these six factors do not represent an exhaustive or mutually exclusive delineation of the characteristics that could be assigned to a terrorist organization, but they do represent a collective thought process on how such organizations need to be differentiated from the mass of groups that use political violence to gain some type of social goal. What they attempt to do is to codify a casual process some terrorism scholars use to conduct a social-scientific–inspired analysis of terrorism risks. In the next section we examine these six factors in more detail and thereafter return to the argument that they offer a chance to uncover the most likely groups who will use radiological-based WMV.

IDEOLOGY

Generally, the term "ideology" refers to the set of beliefs, values, folkways, norms, and attitudes that underlie the existing social order or an alternative to that order (Apter 1964; Mannheim 1952). Such embedded justifications for exiting structures of power and prestige help explain the existence and persistence of the dominant social order, or, in the more micro sense, justify the existence and persistence of a social organization within or opposed to that social system. Social movements that oppose the dominant culture, for example a reform movement or a resistance movement, are defined as a sustainable collective movement that seeks some degree of social change within the dominate culture (Turner and Killian 1987). These movements embody an ideology, as does the culture they reside within.

Ideology in the context of terrorist organizational analysis refers to the intellectual or theoretical structure of the violent political or terrorist organization. As is typical of social movements, this philosophy is used to gain or maintain a variety of political goals. For example, the terrorist organization could use violent rhetoric as a means to gain new members from the disenfranchised among their target recruitment population.

A variety of manifest and latent organizational philosophies exist simultaneously, each having multiple layers of meaning within the terrorist organizational context, and each organization will express these in a variety of ways. No matter the goal of the philosophy, organizations have a working set of assumptions—their philosophy, if you will—and it has a usefulness that transcends its rhetorical value for that organization. Logically, if a group advocates for nonviolent social change, the social by-products of this organization will demonstrate this nonviolent philosophy (Ackermann and Duvall 2000). Likewise, if the group exposes uncivil behavior, or violent social action, the by-products will demonstrate this propensity to violence (Bainbridge 1997; Saliba 1995).

The method associated with deciphering such an ideology is to conduct an analysis of the cultural byproducts (i.e., speeches, flyers, Web sites, etc.) of the terrorist organization and thereby reveal the dominate philosophy of the group. These oppositional by-products, what Gramsci (1971) called "counterhegemonic" social indicators, are critical to understanding the group and its propensity to commit violence, since they will embody the arguments the organization has against the governing social order.

Certain indicators of the ideological substructure of the group may emerge from such an analysis process. For example, the intercultural arguments will show the perceived disjunctions the group has from the dominant, or hegemonic, social order. Likewise, if the group is large enough, intraorganizational disagreements are likely to exist and will be identifiable as a result of this form of analysis.

In the case of these intraorganizational disagreements, the key may well be to identify the splintering of the terrorist organization along differential philosophical beliefs. For example, if one subgroup is seeking a peaceful solution to their perceived problems with the dominant social order, even after years of terrorist activity, and another subgroup within the same organization disagrees, a fracture will become visible in the organization. Such fracture lines are critical to assess since they may be the first indictors of organizational disunity and can be indicative of an increase in violence potential as the breakaway group seeks to legitimate its more oppositional philosophy, to set itself up as an alternative to the majority of the organization, and otherwise differentiate itself from the original organization's philosophy though violent actions.

None of the suggested analysis herein negates the spontaneous emergence of a terrorist group that would advocate violence, but when such an analysis is conducted in conjunction with the other factors listed below, these fractures can become a measure of the risk factors for a large-scale WMV attack. It is important to follow the developments of the philosophy within the group and its relationships to subparts of the organization and how both are reflective of antagonisms toward the dominant culture the terrorist organization opposes. In this manner, the growth or emergence of a particularly violent philosophy, one that would allow for the use of WMV, can be identified as a threat and the risk addressed accordingly.

KNOWLEDGE

Knowledge is generally understood to be what humans perceive to be real and true in the social world (Mannheim 1936, 1952; Schutz 1972). It is a socially created construct and humans depend on it for their sense of self and sense of placement in the universe, and, most important, they depend on it for a sense of reality. Knowledge allows humans to participate in social interactions, even those that are socially unacceptable or deviant such as terrorism.

The knowledge that is critical to assess for a terrorist organization is the tactical, technical, and strategic information within the group. More specifically, it is essential to try to understand if the organization can gather and comprehend the necessary information on the deployability of WMV. While this information can be obtained in many ways, we argue that three specific areas may be critical for the analysis of terrorist organizations and their ability to mount an RDD attack. The first major area of concern may well be the worldwide diffusion of weapons and knowledge of the nuclear-fuel cycle. As the list of nuclear nations expands and the proliferation of knowledge about nuclear power facilities continues, the number of scientists, technicians, and security personnel with information relevant to the production of an RDD has expanded (Center for Defense Information 2003). In short, the production of nuclear weapons and/or nuclear power requires a large and well-educated scientific, technical, and security workforce, one that could potentially be coopted by a terrorist organization.

In addition to nation-states that officially possess nuclear weapons and those who have nuclear power facilities, several other countries are known to have well-developed, albeit more surreptitious, weapons programs or are suspected of having operational weapons or are seeking nuclear power generation facilities (Slavin 2003; Cordesman 2000). These nations represent an additional source of knowledge relevant to the production of RDD that could be tapped if an organization wanted to use these types of weapons.

The problems posed by such widespread use of nuclear technology, be it for weapons or power generation, is that the minimal skill set necessary for the construction of an RDD can be augmented by expert knowledge of the types of radioisotopes that are available, which ones have the most harmful effects on humans, and many other areas of expertise that could make the difference between deploying a RDD and effectively using an RDD for mass victimization.

Understanding the strategic value of orphan and commercially available sources is a second area of concern (Ferguson, Kazi, and Perera 2003). Knowledge of where to find the most harmful radioactive materials is readily available to those who are aware of such materials. Availability of these materials may arise as the result of ineffective materials-accounting practices, insufficient inventory controls, loss of political authority/control, and many other reasons. Commercial sources pose an additional threat if they are diverted or stolen for use in RDD. Again the number of people who have knowledge of such sources, coupled with their ability to provide the raw materials for a RDD, is a significant risk factor.

Last, an understanding by someone within the terrorist organization of, and access to, high-level waste (HLW) sources such as spent nuclear fuel (SNF) may offer an additional source for potential RDD raw materials. Such insider knowledge could allow the organization to plan an attack on fixed sites (for example, a nuclear power plant and corresponding spent-fuel storage pools) or mobile transported materials (for example, shipments to a reprocessing plant or geologic repository). Some experts believe that these materials are currently an underrealized risk and may represent a significant source for RDD weapons in the future (Halstead and Ballard 1997; Ballard 2002). This argument rests on the idea that an RDD does not have to be conceptualized as radioactive materials wrapped in explosives. Rather, it is important to recognize that RDD are the result of the dispersion of radioactivity, even if that material is not located in a bomb per se but the explosive is attached to the inventory of radioactive materials (i.e., a shipment of medical or waste materials).

Knowledge of the availability and nefarious usage of inventories of radioactive materials is not the only risk factor that could be measured under this category. But if the analytical focus was to determine if an organization was intending to employ an RDD device, evidence that one or more of the members had such specialized knowledge would be critical. Put another way, it is not necessarily risky if a group says "let's use radioactive materials"; it is far riskier if they understand the value of these materials in a weapon, know how to locate the radioactive source materials, and can conceive of how to make such a weapon effective.

Assessment of this factor would entail knowing information on the backgrounds of the members of the terrorist organization. Intelligence on the types of experts familiar with radiological issues that the terrorists have contacted, how and if they have shared relevant knowledge, the presence of such information in terrorist training manuals, and other indicators would be the primary focus of such an examination.

No matter what the outcome of this analysis, effective management structures that would support the use of such weapons must be present for an attack to manifest itself. The next section looks at how to assess terrorist management structures and what characteristics of this management may be crucial to assess.

MANAGEMENT

Nonproliferation advocates and the agencies that support the goals of reducing the threat of nuclear weapons and the control of the most dangerous types of radioactive materials that could be used in an RDD attack are fairly numerous. The United Nations, the International Atomic Energy Agency, the North Atlantic Treaty Organization, the European Union, and many other well-managed bureaucracies advocate for the application of regulations, treaties, and other formal means to help control the risk these materials pose to humanity. Likewise, specific agencies such as the U.S. Department of Energy or the Nuclear Regulatory Agency seek to minimize the risk of an uncontrolled release of radioactive materials and/or the spread of weapons technology.

These formal organizations are organized along what Weber (1958) called clear lines of authority and show evidence of rigid hierarchies. They also exhibit a division of labor in their daily activities and operate based on written rules of behavior that shape how they see the world and specifically how they would seek to curb the risks of RDD attacks.

Large-scale terrorist organizations have been examined and seem to follow similar structures that, while more informal, have somewhat the same identifiable bureaucratic structures (Paz 2000; Brackett 1996). Similar to the ways that governmental and quasi-governmental bodies seek to manage the risks of radiological terrorism within an organizational context, terrorist organizations also must manage their own day-to-day activities to be effective. These groups have rules, follow procedures, and embody the idea of a division of labor within their structures. Some of the specific characteristics of terrorist organizations noted in the literature include the limited longevity of the group, the variations in the size of the group and its level of effectiveness, and its ability to gain and/or maintain funding (Stohl 1988; Pisano 1987; Adams 1986).

Research on the management of terrorist organizations may show the importance of focusing on the inspirational or charismatic leader of certain terrorist organizations (Stern 2000). For example, a detailed analysis of Shoko Asahara, the leader of the Aum

Supreme Truth organization, and his effect on the WMD aspirations of this group could be illustrative (Brackett 1996). Likewise, charismatic analysis of leaders of al Qaeda would offer insights into the motivations of the organization and rationales for its choices of tactics (Burke 2001).

This is not the only area of concern. For example, operational success for the group will rest on the ability to gather financial support from contributors (one critical area where evidence of the charismatic leader may be located) and the resultant organizational ability to provide logistic support for operations. In order to assess this aspect of the management factor, the key is what can be termed the "operations" manager. This management position is critical for the long-term survival of any organization, since it will be from here that the day-to-day operations of the organization are conducted, where the funding resulting from the charisma of the leader is allocated, where ideological control of operatives is maintained, and where many other management functions are accomplished.

The operations manager is critical to identify and analyze because he is one of the linchpins of the organization and physically represents its ability to be effective on tasks, as an operational entity, and ultimately as an organization. For example, managers such as Dr. Ayman al-Zawahiri or Muhammad Atef from the al Qaeda organization may illustrate how effective noncharismatic leaders can be in controlling the overall operations of a group and even in the perpetration of the organization after an all-out military assault designed to obliterate the leaders.

The methodology of assessing this factor will vary. It may well rest on human intelligence and/or an evaluation of the leadership qualities of the group members in position of power and/or should be considered dynamic since humans have the capacity to develop these skills over time. External organizational factors can also shape such developments. The next section offers insight into one of these external factors by focusing on the role the audience plays in an organization's ability to seek WMV as a viable tactical option.

AUDIENCE

The audience for the terrorist act is another factor that should be considered when assessing a terrorist organization's propensity to commit a WMV attack. It is important to ask and answer the question: What message is the organization communicating by planning and, even if it should come to pass, by committing such an attack? Likewise, it is critical to understand where the organization's audience is located and for what purposes the attack is being perpetrated. Purposes could include recruitment of members, solicitation of funding, and/or a variety of organizational motives and each may present a different risk or threat profile.

Organizations, just like everyday humans, exhibit behavior that they wish others to observe and/or engage in behavior that would be less than desirable if made public. Goffman (1959) refers to this role bifurcation as front stage and backstage behavior, and this idea specifically addresses what roles a social actor plays and his or her relationship to various audiences. In Goffman's dramaturgical terms, keeping the audiences ignorant of the totality of the roles you could adopt is audience segregation.

These same dynamics could apply to organizations. Typically, terrorism analysis seems to focus on territorially defined audiences where the audience resides within an identifiable geopolitical location. For example, commentators note how a terrorist group is "talking" to a subpopulation within a nation-state, sometimes trying to incite violence against a government and maybe with the intent to overthrow that government. What is emerging is the recognition that extraorganizational audiences (not necessarily defined by geographic boundaries) can be the focus. For example, these audiences could be in another country or culture or halfway around the world. The point is that terrorists have a message that is directed toward an audience that is territorially defined in some cases, extraterritorially defined in others, and even intraorganizationally defined in some cases.

One of the most important audiences may well be intraorganizational, since the message may represent a way to maintain organizational control and offset splintering within the group. Assessment of this dynamic could reveal these fractures and may be indicative of the potential to engage in more risky behaviors such as a WMV attack. Methods of assessing this dynamic could vary. The fracturing within an existing organization may show up in public debates about policies (i.e., support for a peace process or not). The fractures could be along leadership lines where two opposing leaders emerge and struggle for control of the ideology of the group. These leadership debates could find their way into the public domain by way of the media or by the ascendance of a promising leader in the organization structure.

Specifically looking for fractures within the organization or locating specific indicators that would portend a WMV attack as a symbolic gesture may be another important assessment dynamic. The connection to the next factor, social distance, and what message the terrorist organization is trying to convey to its audience(s) may well rest on how different the members of the organization feel from their fellow humans, those they are willing to use WMV against.

SOCIAL DISTANCE

Social distance is the degree to which humans seek to associate or disassociate themselves from other groups (Bogardus 1959). Analytically, it is similar to the process of social segregation, where conditions of inequality and power imbalances are perpetrated by one group and opposed by the other (Massey and Denton 1993; Bogardus 1928). Such social distancing can be based on physical distance from where the "other" lives in a different physical location, emotional distance where the separation is more internal than external, and/or on perceptions of racial or ethnic differences that allow for the dehumanization of one group by another.

Perpetrators of mass violence or mass victimization events must come to a place wherein their social distance from their target population is increased to the point where the victim's humanity is negated. The measurement of social distance is a well-defined area within the social sciences. In an effort to understand the effects of this distancing, researchers have looked at social distance and various social factors such as age (Eisenstadt 1956), nations (Grace and Neuhaus 1952), social classes (Halbwachs 1958; Kahl 1957), and race (Westie 1953).

The assessment of social distance and terrorist organizations may best be served by addressing four specific areas: potential social distance based on perceived religious differences; social distance based on perceived racial and/or ethnic differences; social distance based on perceived differences in cultures; and social distance based on perceived socioeconomic differentials. These four dimensions offer an opportunity to analyze the degree to which one organization vilifies the other and represent one dimension viable in the assessment of a group and its propensity to commit mass victimization.

The methods associated with this assessment could vary but, we argue, should follow the example set forth in the literature. For example, the analyst could use content analysis of the speeches made by leaders to uncover their social distance from the target along the four dimensions noted above. Likewise, analysis of the persistence and consistency of terrorist attacks against one group, religion, culture, or target may also reveal one or more of these factors.

The point of such an assessment is to identify the target group of the terrorist organization's aggression and violence. The degree of separation the group feels from the target may well be a measure of their potential to commit mass violence. The next section offers another measure of violence potential by focusing on the symbolic value of the attack.

SYMBOLIC VALUE OF THE ATTACK

The interactionist paradigm in sociology is a theoretical perspective that seeks to understand how humans use and interpret symbols in the process of communication and in creating and maintaining impressions. Interactionist methods focus on how we use symbols to forge a sense of identity and experience everyday life within a social system (Blumer 1969; Cooley 1964; Kuhn 1964; Mead 1934; Simmel 1950).

This process could apply to organizations who seek to use symbolic targets to convey a message of anger, dissociation, dehumanization, or any other rationale the terrorist organization could use for violence. It can apply to the victims of the organization's violence, the target site itself, or the tactic used for the attack.

The choice of a symbolic target, both human and physical, is common in terrorism attacks, but what about the RDD tactic? Would a terrorist group seek out specific targets of symbolic value for the application of this tactic? We suggest that this would be the case. For example, a domestic terrorist group could target large-scale federal projects related to nuclear power or nuclear weapons production. One example is the forthcoming Yucca Mountain project in Nevada. This program will entail tens of thousands of shipments of highly radioactive materials across the roadways, railroad corridors, and shipping lanes of America (Ballard 2002; Halstead and Ballard 1997). This transportation program has an extensive and tumultuous history and has the potential to incite political violence because of how it will be implemented.

What would make such a program viable as a symbolic target? It may well be that the program's negative publicity will attract terrorists' attention, or the actual movement of radioactive materials across the nation and to its final resting place in Nevada could be the impetus for an attack. The program's implicit support for nuclear power may draw the ire of domestic terrorists, and any number of other rationales for targeting this program may arise to inspire international groups.

The choice of an RDD attack may have symbolic value in and of itself, as suggested by an attack on such shipments. The perpetrators of such an attack could target these shipments in opposition to nuclear power or they may target perceived arrogance by the federal government. Perhaps an RDD attack would offer an opportunity to create an environmental disaster with radioactive materials, a potentially symbolic gesture in and of itself. For other adversaries, such hypothesized attacks could be used as a warning or as a means to demonstrate power to the opposition, in this case the last remaining superpower in the global community.

Regardless of the motive or the actual location of an RDD attack, the symbolic nature of choosing radioactive materials or a target such as a large-scale federal program or any other such symbolic targeting should be a pre-incident focus in any organizational analysis. The group could be assessed as to their risk-seeking potential based on what motive or symbolic gesture is behind their attack.

The assessment of this abstract concept would rest on pre-attack assessments of target selection, maybe based on pieces and bits of intelligence information. What is critical to look for is the symbolism the group is trying to use, the symbolic nature of the act itself, and the contextual nature of these choices. Alone these factors may be inconclusive; in conjunction with the others, they may be very powerful. The conclusion of this chapter suggests a methodology for accomplishing such a multidimensional analysis and how the process of using organizational analysis could be applied to other forms of WMV.

CONCLUSION

Advocates interested in terrorism risks related to RDD or other mass victimization tactics should consider how the construction of these weapons are related to the proliferation of nuclear weapons, the huge inventories of weapons-grade materials around the world, the problem posed by orphan radiological sources becoming available to terrorist organizations, and the enormous stockpiles of highly radioactive waste products that can be used for an RDD. This argument has emphasized that intelligence agencies and terrorism scholars should engage in direct analysis of the threats such materials pose in an integrated global community.

One approach to this area of analysis is to look at who could gather the necessary organizational resources for a radiological attack, what we have reconceptualized as a weapon of mass victimization. The IKMASS process suggested herein can be illustrated by the following diagram (see Table 7.1).

TABLE 7.1   Schematic

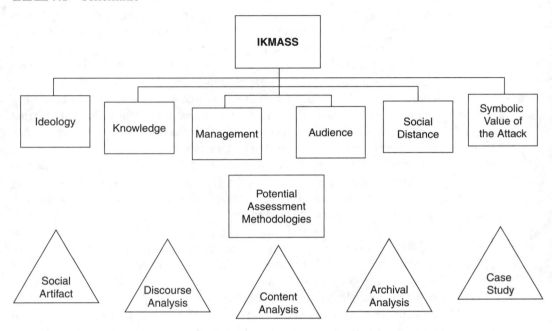

The actual assessment of the six factors or dimensions will vary depending on the group under consideration, the weapon or tactic they may be contemplating using, and/or the level of intelligence that is available on the group. Each of the six factors or dimensions should be normalized on a grading scale (i.e., a 100-point scale) so that changes in each can be analyzed. One specific suggestion is that the terrorist organization be charted over time (longitudinally) and on each of these factors (see Table 7.2). Using this quasi–time series analysis, changes in the six risk factors can be tracked. Using a trend line representing the summation of these changes over time, the risk potential for this particular organization could be assessed, updated, or downsized as appropriate.

The analysis could also focus on single indicators—each of the six factors separately, for example—but this may not be the best strategy. For example, spikes in any one indicator could be indicative of new intelligence on the group, could be the result of a temporary change in the organization, and/or could be the first indicators of a higher risk of an attack. Such singular analysis would have to be considered very carefully, and we feel that the combination of these six factors offers a better profile of the organization and thus its potential to conduct an attack using WMV.

The process suggested in this chapter would necessitate the use of knowledge of the terrorist organization that is not publicly available. Some of the material for this analysis would be from public sources, but the expectation is that such a process would best be served by the inclusion of secure data. As such, this methodology has limited potential outside the rarefied air of certain intelligence services. We offer this suggested methodology as a straw-man analysis mechanism for academic study and debate since

TABLE 7.2   Analysis Frequency

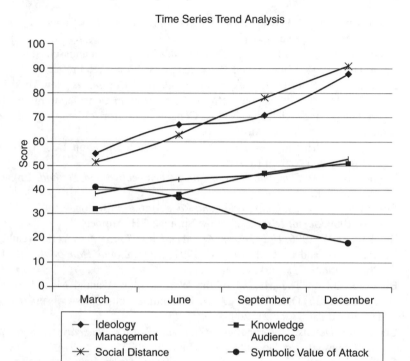

Time Series Trend Analysis

we currently do not have the potential to verify the validity or reliability of such a methodology.

At the same time, we would envision that if such a process, in modified form, was to be applied to actual public and secure data, it could represent a resource allocation mechanism for antiterrorism and counterterrorism agencies and their activities. Such a method may also act as a prediction or risk-assessment tool when considering threat remediation efforts, initiatives designed to counteract such threats, and counterterrorism-related policies.

Using a form of organizational analysis, maybe even as suggested herein, it would be possible to prioritize which threats may need the most immediate attention, and this effort could offer some semblance of order to the process of counterterrorism activity that is currently underway around the world in governments and agencies and among academics. Likewise, adjustment of the dimensions noted above could allow for a similar assessment process relative to nuclear, chemical, and biological terrorism. As noted earlier, these tactics are distinctly different from RDD and must be analyzed accordingly. If the IKMASS protocol, or variants thereof, is shown to be a viable option in assessment of the risk of RDD terrorism, such an extension of the protocol to other tactics would be prudent.

REFERENCES

Ackerman P., and J. Duvall. 2000. *A Force More Powerful: A Century of Nonviolent Conflict.* New York: Palgrave.

Adams, J. 1986. *The Financing of Terror.* New York: Simon and Schuster.

Apter, D. E. 1964. *Ideology and Discontent.* New York: Free Press.

Bainbridge, W. S. 1997. *The Sociology of Religious Movements.* New York: Routledge.

Ballard, J. D. 2000. "Weapons of Mass Victimization: Considerations for the 21st Century." Presented at the 10th United Nations Congress on Terrorist Victimization: Prevention, Control, and Recovery, Vienna, Austria, April.

———. 2002. "Hearing Testimony, May 22, 2003." Washington, D.C.: U. S. Senate Committee on Energy and Natural Resources.

Blumer, H. 1969. *Symbolic Interactionism: Perspective and Method.* Englewood Cliffs, NJ: Prentice Hall.

Bogardus, E. S. 1928. *Immigration and Race Attitudes.* Boston: Heath.

———. 1959. *Social Distance.* Yellow Springs, OH: Antioch.

Brackett, D. W. 1996. *Holy Terror: Armageddon in Tokyo.* New York: Weatherhill.

Burch, G. M. and C. C. Flowerree. 1991. *International Handbook on Chemical Weapons Proliferation.* New York: Greenwood.

Burke, J. 2001. "The Making of the World's Most Wanted Man: Part 1." *The Observer International,* October 28. Available online: http://www.observer.co.uk/international. Download date: June 21, 2003.

Center for Defense Information. 2003. *The World's Nuclear Arsenals.* Available online: http://www.cdi.org. Download date: June 20, 2003.

Cooley, C. H. 1964. *Human Nature and the Social Order.* New York: Schocken.

Cordesman, A. H. 2000. *Iran and Nuclear Weapons.* Washington, D.C.: Center for Strategic and International Studies.

Eisenstadt, S. N. 1956. *From Generation to Generation: Age Groups and Social Structure.* Glencoe, IL: Free Press.

Ferguson, C. D., T. Kazi, and J. Perera. 2003. *Commercial Radioactive Sources: Surveying the Security Risks.* Monterey, CA: Monterey Institute of International Studies.

Goffman, E. 1959. *The Presentation of Self in Everyday Life.* New York: Doubleday.

Grace, H. A., and J. O. Neuhaus. 1952. "Information and Social Distance as Predictors of Hostility towards Nations." *Journal of Abnormal and Social Psychology* 47: 540–545.

Gramsci, A. 1971. *Selections from the Prison Notebooks.* London: New Left.

Halbwachs. M. 1958. *The Psychology of Social Classes.* Glencoe, IL: Free Press.

Halstead R., and J. D. Ballard. 1997. *Nuclear Waste Transportation Security and Safety Issues.* Carson City: State of Nevada Nuclear Waste Projects Office.

Herby, P. 1992. *The Chemical Weapons Convention and Arms Control in the Middle East.* Oslo: International Peace Research Institute.

Hoffman, B. 1999. *Inside Terrorism.* New York: Columbia University Press.

Hogendoorn, E. J. 1997. "A Chemical Weapons Atlas." *Bulletin of the Atomic Scientist* (September/October): 53.

Kahl, J. A. 1957. *The American Class Structure.* New York: Rinehart.

Kuhn, M. H. 1964. "Major Trends in Symbolic Theory in the Past 25 Years." *Sociological Quarterly* 5: 61–64.

Legal Information Institute. 2003. *Legal Information.* Available online: http://www4.law.cornell.edu. Download date: June 17, 2003.

Mannheim, K. 1936. *Ideology and Utopia.* London: Routledge and Kegan Paul.

———. 1952. *Essays on the Sociology of Knowledge.* London: Routledge and Kegan Paul.

Massey, D. S., and N. A. Denton. 1993. *American Apartheid: Segregation and the Making of the Underclass.* Cambridge: Harvard University Press.

Mead, G. H. 1934. *Mind, Self, and Society.* Chicago: University of Chicago Press.

Paz, R. 2000. *Hamas's Lesson from Lebanon.* International Policy Institute for Counterterrorism. Available online: http://www.ict.orl.il. Download date: June 16, 2003.

Pisano, V. S. 1987. *The Dynamics of Subversion and Violence in Contemporary Italy.* Palo Alto, CA: The Hoover Institute.

Saliba, J. A. 1995. *Perspectives on New Religious Movements.* London: Chapman.

Schutz, A. 1972. *The Phenomenology of the Social World.* London: Heinemann.

Simmel, G. 1950. *The Sociology of Georg Simmel.* New York: Free Press.

Slavin, B. 2003. "N. Korea admits nuclear weapons." *USA Today* April 24. Available online: http://www.usatoday.com. Download date: June 20, 2003.

Steinweg, K., W. Betson, J. Matt, C. Spencer, M. Ward, R. Riccardelli, and K. H. Butts. 1994. *Weapons of Mass Destruction: Title 10 Implications for the Military.* Carlisle Barracks, PA: Center for Strategic Leadership, U.S. Army War College.

Stern, J. 1999. *The Ultimate Terrorists.* Cambridge: Harvard University Press.

———. 2000. "Terrorist Motivations and Unconventional Weapons." In *Planning the Unthinkable,* ed. P. Lavoy, S. Sagan, and J. Wirtz. Ithaca: Cornell University Press.

Stohl, M. 1988. *The Politics of Terrorism.* New York: Dekker.

Turner, R. H., and L. M. Killian. 1987. *Collective Behavior.* 3rd ed. Englewood Cliffs, NJ: Prentice Hall.

Weber, M. 1958. *From Max Weber: Essays in Sociology.* Eds. H. H. Gerth and C. W. Mills. New York: Oxford University Press.

Westie, F. R. 1953. "A Technique for the Measurement of Race Attitudes." *American Sociological Review* 18: 73–78.

CHAPTER 8

Steganography and Terrorism: An Introduction to Data Hiding and Its Use in Terrorist Activities

Robert Moore, Ph.D.
Delta State University

Darin Walker, M.S.
The University of Southern Mississippi

ABSTRACT

Following the events of September 11, 2001, the news media was flooded with reports that the terrorists responsible for the attacks upon the World Trade Center had been using the Internet as a means of communication. Within weeks it was reported that steganography, a new technology allowing for hidden communication, was used to hide their exchanges. The truth, however, is that steganography is not a new technology but is in fact an old technique that has only been improved as technology has advanced. This article examines the history of steganography in an attempt to provide the reader with an understanding of what steganography is and how the technology is currently being used by individuals in the terrorist community. The chapter concludes with an examination of where steganographic uses may be heading and what steps may be necessary to control the problem.

Once considered tools of education and research, computers and the Internet have in recent years been involved in increasing numbers of criminal acts. Today's computers are capable of accomplishing incredible tasks, but society's reliance on the devices leads to their inclusion in these criminal acts. Along with the new ideas that technology is developing, traditional activities are seeing electronic modification. The impact of this increased use was felt after the tragic events of September 11, 2001. Immediately following the terrorist attacks, news began circulating that the terrorists involved in the attacks used the Internet and e-mail as a means of corresponding during the period when they were organizing their activities. Early reports claimed that the individuals used computers from a public library to transmit these electronic messages. Other reports, however, were released that claimed the terrorists were using a new form of hidden-communication software that allowed them to hide messages inside images on Web sites across the Internet. This software, which was later identified as steganography, led to lingering questions about what the technology was and how was it used by the terrorists involved in the attacks. Before attempting to discuss how steganography is believed to have been used, it is first important to understand what steganography is and how technology has developed the technique over the years.

WHAT IS STEGANOGRAPHY?

Steganography has been defined as the practice of invisibly embedding one form of digital material within another piece of digital material (Snell 2001). This is the most common definition for steganography in the wake of the terrorist attacks of 2001; however, there is more to a definition of steganography than merely hiding information inside digital marks. Individuals active in the computer science field claim that the recent attention focused upon steganography has led to misunderstanding and that better understanding can only be reached when it is understood that the form of steganography suspected to have been used by the terrorists was in fact more akin to digital steganography (Sengupta 2001). The term "steganography" is derived from the Greek language; its literal translation is "covered writing." In essence, any form of hidden or secret communication could technically be defined as steganography. Individuals who argue that there has been a misunderstanding claim that failure to understand the difference between the two could lead an individual to believe that steganography is nothing more than an advanced form of cryptography.

Cryptography is another term for the art of encryption, which is the scrambling of information in such a manner that only the individual with a key, which is normally a password, is capable of gaining access to the information. Much like steganography, cryptography has seen increased awareness with advances in computers. With this in mind, Johnson (2000) argues that steganography should be defined as the art and science of communication that hides the actual communication in some manner or fashion. Put simply, this means that a communication is transmitted but only those who know of the communication's existence are aware of how to locate the intended message.

Cryptography, or encryption, on the other hand, is designed so that these communications may be intercepted by anyone who so desires to obtain the message. However, once intercepted, the messages remain scrambled in such a manner that they cannot be decoded and read without exhaustive work on the part of those who have intercepted the communication. This process of descrambling may require a rather significant amount of time and hard work, but with persistence almost all forms of encryption can be eventually broken. Therefore, cryptography is nothing more than a means of slowing down the interception of communications. The goal of steganography is to hide a secret communication inside a legitimate communication in a manner that prevents those who would wish to intercept a message from discovering that a hidden message even exists (Johnson 2000).

This misunderstanding of steganography is understandable, as few have probably considered that hidden communications have a formal name beyond that of "spy talk" that was made famous during childhood with spy rings, decoders, and disappearing ink. In fact, one could argue that had it not been for the terrorist attacks on the twin towers in 2001 and the subsequent revelation that this form of communication was potentially used in the attacks, the greater society would still be unaware of steganography and its existence. This awareness is not necessarily a negative thing, however, as criminals in the computer-security realm have long known about the existence of the technique. With the increased awareness, many in the law enforcement community became aware of the technology's existence. The downside to the publicity generated by the terrorist attacks is that just as law enforcement became more aware of the technique, so too did society's criminals, who may not have previously considered using the techniques in their day-to-day operations. To understand the use of digital steganography, it is first necessary to understand a bit about the history of the technique and how it has evolved over the centuries.

A HISTORY OF STEGANOGRAPHY

Researchers have traced the art of hidden writing back several thousands of years. According to Johnson (2000), the first document describing steganography and the techniques associated with its use came from the *Histories of Herodotus*. This particular writing discussed the story of Demeratus, who was an ancient Greek warrior. In a desperate attempt to hide a letter to Sparta concerning Xerxes' intention to invade Greece, Demeratus scraped the wax off several stone tablets. He inscribed a secret message on the tablet and recoated it with wax. Using this technique, Demeratus was able to escape with his message and avoid capture (Johnson, 2000).

Another method of steganography used by the ancient Greeks is detailed in the story of the Greek tyrant Histiaeus. According to Snell (2001), in an attempt to send an important and secret message to his son-in-law, Histiaeus developed what could be considered a rather ingenious method of hidden communication. Histiaeus selected his most trusted slave, shaved his head, and tattooed the message to his son-in-law on the shaved head of the slave. Then, when the slave's hair had grown back, he sent the slave to his son-in-law to deliver the message.

In the centuries since these events, there have been amazing increases in both chemicals and technology. Steganographic techniques truly began to advance during the twentieth century. During World War II, intelligence personnel discovered that secret messages could be inserted into other documents by using a special type of ink. This ink was invisible to the naked eye and could be viewed only by running a second form of ink across the message (Sengupta 2001). Spy kits and disappearing-ink kits for children appear to have developed from this communication technique.

Around this same period, another steganographic technique began to see widespread use. Individuals began to hide complex orders of information in letters that would make sense on the surface to anyone who might intercept them. Johnson (2000) provides the following example:

> News Eight Weather: Tonight increasing snow. Unexpected precipitation smothers eastern towns. Be extremely cautious and use snowtires especially heading east. The highway is not knowingly slippery. Highway evacuation is suspected. Police report emergency situations in downtown ending near Tuesday.

By taking the first letter of each word in the above writing the following phrase is revealed: *Newt is upset because he thinks he is president.* At first glance it appears that the letter is nothing more than rambling about the weather, when in fact it is a message between members of a political party.

Sengupta (2001) claims that the widespread digitization of communications is what moved steganography from the material world to the digital world. Reliance on e-mail and other forms of electronic communication motivated computer programmers to begin examining new methods of hiding data. As understanding related to the storage of data on digital media increased, it was only a matter of time until a method of compressing hidden information inside legitimate files was discovered. Perhaps steganography gained widespread notoriety among computer users not so much because of communications but because of peer-to-peer networking. The peer-to-peer network, also referred to as P2P, is the technology that allows various users to connect their computers and share files stored on other users' computers. Napster was one of the first, if not the first, peer-to-peer network program available on the market. Napster became so popular, in fact, that the Recording Industry Association of America (RIAA) took notice of the software and its users and filed a lawsuit against the company for allowing the sharing of copyrighted music.

Despite Napster's widespread popularity, the software was limited in its ability to transfer files. In order to transfer a file on the Napster network the file had to be in the .mp3 format, which refers to a special compressed audio format that was more conducive to downloading. As increasingly larger numbers of users began to use Napster, it is believed that a desire to transfer other files began to rise among users. To circumvent the Napster software, Wrapster software was developed and released. Just as the program's name implies, other file formats could be wrapped inside working .mp3 files. This software allowed users to transfer documents, video clips, and even software applications. While the software receives less consideration or attention today, likely a result of Napster's fall from glory, the program remains one of the earliest widespread steganography programs in existence. Steganographic software is less heard of today among P2P users because subsequent releases of such software have allowed for the transfer of any format of file without the need to hide the file's true format.

The existence and use of steganographic software has become well known among those in the computer science field. In fact, the software has become so commonplace that it has recently begun appearing in mainstream movies and advertisements. For example, the software made a Hollywood appearance in the film *Along Came a Spider.* In the film, two elementary school students used steganography to transfer hidden notes to each other while their computer teacher was talking. While the software in the film was not a completely accurate example of how steganography worked, the film introduced a broader audience to the possibilities of steganography.

Several different versions of steganography programs have been released in recent years. While many of these software programs must be purchased, there are just as many programs that are available for free if the user knows where to look and is willing to spend the time to locate the software. These programs are capable of hiding messages in digital mediums ranging from other documents to more complex files such as .mp3 files (music), .avi files (video), .JPEG (picture) files, and just about any other file format imaginable. With the increase in awareness of the software, there has been a growing movement for the creation of programs that are capable of scanning for files that could contain a hidden message. This scanning software is not without problems, however, as Neil Johnson, a steganography expert from George Mason University, has reported. Johnson so greatly fears that steganography could be used in terrorist activities that he has indicated that he will no longer publish his research concerning the detection of images on the Internet containing steganography. It is Johnson's belief that if people became aware of how he was able to detect images containing steganography, they would be able to develop defenses against the scanning or possibly move the images to a safer location. It should be mentioned that Johnson has released no proof that al Quada, or any other terrorist organization, is currently using steganography. However, those who believe that he has proof point to the fact that his research is financed by law enforcement, and, as such, he has indicated that it would be foolish for him to release any information he is not required to release (Kolata 2001).

HOW DIGITAL STEGANOGRAPHY WORKS

Digital steganography works by removing insignificant information from digital media and placing the hidden data in the space previously occupied by the less-important information (Wang, 2001). Steganography may best be discussed in relation to hiding text within image files. For the purpose of this discussion, the steganography tool kit known as S-tools will be examined. It is important to first understand that images are comprised of many different smaller bits of data that make up the color palette, which results from the computer's interpretation of the bit files the user sees when he or she opens an image file. Steganography software takes these images and coordinates the bits in such a manner that the colors within confined areas are as close as possible to each other. Then, the least significant bit is changed to allow the hiding of information within the image file. The modification of the bits may then change the color palette but will normally be undetectable by the human eye. If, after saving the hidden file within the image, there are less than 256 colors, which is a standard palette, the file may be saved. If the modified image contains more than 256 colors, the program will continue to restructure colors until the color palette is down to less than the required 256 colors

FIGURE 8.1   Image Containing Steganography

(Wayner 2002). Other steganography software applications work on similar premises, with differences only in the manner in which they modify the bits to hide the data. Some programs will also allow a user to hide data within music or video files, both of which work by removing unused space and replacing the gap with the hidden text.

A simplified example may better illustrate the aforementioned issues. Consider that if an individual has a 300kb Bitmap file, there is a significant amount of potential free space (the larger the file, the greater the likelihood of free space). It is possible that a text document of around 36kb, the equivalent of 6,000 words, could be hidden within the image. This hiding of information would occur without change to the file size or integrity of the original image. To provide proof of this concept examine Figure 8.1. Notice that there is no distinguishable difference between the two images, despite the fact that there is a text message hidden within the image on the right.

Another potential future steganographic technique discussed by Wayner (2002) is the spreading of information over a series of messages. Here, an individual who is attempting to send a steganographic message will hide portions of the text within multiple picture, video, or music files. The individual who receives these messages will then be responsible for reassembling the messages. Currently, there is little reference material concerning this technique, but the possibility of advancements in software design make the technique possible.

STEGANOGRAPHY AND TERRORIST ACTIVITIES

Even before the events of September 11, 2001, there had been debate among those in the law enforcement community concerning whether terrorist organizations were using steganography as a means of transmitting communications and plans to each other. However, immediately after the attacks on the World Trade Center, the level of this debate intensified when several newspapers and magazines reported that bin Laden and his terrorist followers had used the Internet to transfer commands to each other. These reports made claims ranging from evidence of messages hidden within adult sites to a report concerning an analyst's discovery of communications on an Islamic Web site. The analyst in question was tasked with the responsibility of monitoring radical Islamist Web sites, and during the course of conducting a routine examination of one of the Web sites under observation the analyst noticed that one of the sites had been changed. A portion of the Web site that had been open to the public in the past was no longer available via the regular hyperlink to the page. By using her notes, the analyst was able to retrieve the actual URL and gain access to the page, which now read "Missionaries Attack" in Arabic (Soloway, Nordland, and Nadeau 2002).

Despite instances such as the one above, there has been little in the way of absolute proof offered by the FBI or any other federal agency concerning the terrorist use of the technology. In fact, according to Carvin (2001) the only evidence to suggest that terrorist organizations use steganography relates to a story in the *New York Times* that claimed an individual named Jamal Beghal, who was known to have associated with terrorist organizations, used the technique while planning an attack on the U.S. embassy in Paris. This report, however, came from an unnamed source and little information about the use of steganography was mentioned (Cohen 200).

An article appearing in *USA Today* before the terrorist attacks of September 11, 2001, did claim that digital steganography had been used in the planning of at least three terrorist attacks. The problem with this article is that once again the source was an unnamed government employee. The article claimed that steganography has become so important to terrorist organizations that Afghani and Sudanese extremist training camps now offer courses in the use of new technology. Further, the article stated that bin Laden had an advantage over American law enforcement because he had more financial resources and better equipment (Auer 2001).

There have been other reports that argued that bin Laden was using encryption techniques and therefore could be using steganography as well. As early as 1998, Louis Freeh, then director of the Federal Bureau of Investigation, argued that terrorist organizations were using advanced levels of encryption. Freeh used the information as support for the argument that encryption should not be allowed such easy distribution. Declan McCullagh, a correspondent for *Wired News,* has argued that it is somewhat useless to debate whether terrorist organizations are using steganography and encryption. McCullagh believes that if terrorist organizations are not currently using steganography, then they will be in the near future (Carvin 2001; McCullagh 2001).

While the single example involving the discovery of a hidden message on a Web site does not involve the use of steganography software to hide information, it does show the ingenuity of terrorist organizations. There have been numerous articles discussing how al Qaeda and other terrorist organizations may be using steganography in the transmission of commands, but many of the reports have been issued on the basis of unnamed U.S. officials and experts who claim that terrorist groups have hidden maps and pictures of potential targets on pornographic bulletin boards, sports bulletin boards, and numerous other Web sites. While at first glance it may seem ironic that Muslim terrorist organizations are hiding images in pornographic images, the truth is that the use of these sites makes sense. There are two reasons for this belief: first, the large file sizes associated with pictures on pornography Web sites make it possible to hide larger communications within these images (Kellen 2001); and second, the large number of pornography sites available on the Internet creates a massive cover for their activities.

Kellen (2001) also argues that eBay and Amazon.com make attractive targets for steganographic messages because anyone may scan in a picture, encode the image with a hidden message, and place the image on the Web site for others to view. Thousands of people may view the image every day, but unless they have an awareness of steganography the hidden messages are safe from prying eyes. Individuals who are aware that the image should contain a message merely download the picture and extract the hidden message.

Other analysts now believe there are additional possibilities for bin Laden to use steganography in the conveyance of orders. Web sites that have pictures of bin Laden on the page could be used as a marker for future commands. An image of something placed to the left, a gun for example, could be a signal to followers that there is a new message for them to download and pull from the bin Laden image (Soloway, Nordland, and Nadeau 2002). Along these same lines, there is another possible use of the technology that has not been discussed in any writings discovered by the authors; this method concerns a two-way form of communication. This method of steganographic communication begins in much the same manner as that of the aforementioned example; an image could be placed to the left of bin Laden's image indicating there is a message for operatives to retrieve. However, once the message is received, the agents may respond to the commands by inputting a different message into the image and modifying the layout of the Web page. All of this can be easily accomplished using commonly available FTP (file transfer protocol) software. As an indicator that the message has been received and there is a new message waiting to be read, the image to the left of the bin Laden image could be moved to the right side. This procedure could be repeated daily, weekly, or monthly as a way for operatives to maintain constant two-way communication with leaders of the terrorist organization.

While Johnson has expressed a desire to not reveal his research on steganography scanning software, there are some in the computer science field who have been working to develop better software for locating and decrypting steganographic images who have not been hesitant to release their results. Niels Provos and Peter Honeyman were curious as to whether eBay was being used to transmit terrorist communications or if the site was being used to hide any hidden messages. The two researchers examined over 2 million images found on eBay and discovered that there was no proof that terrorist organizations were using the Internet as a means of hiding steganography (Provos and Honeyman 2001). Despite the efforts of researchers such as Johnson, Provos, and Honeyman and their willingness to discount the presence of steganography on the Internet, there are several problems with immediately declaring there is no terrorist use of the technology. Even the best technology will have limitations if it cannot locate where the images are stored. After all, it is possible that eBay is not the main depository for these images.

It is also worth noting that the use of steganography by terrorist organizations does not necessarily have to be used over the World Wide Web to communicate terrorist activities. In a recent case involving an engineering firm in Seattle, it was discovered that steganography had been used in corporate espionage. In this case, an engineer elected to sell company secrets but was unable to sneak the files out of the office through traditional means. The individual embedded the files within an image file using steganography software, then e-mailed the image to his personal e-mail account at home. Had the engineering firm not called in a professional digital forensics company to investigate the case, then the engineer selling the secrets might have gotten away with the crime (Radcliff 2002). Individuals involved in terrorist activities could e-mail images containing steganography to each other. Even if the e-mail is mistakenly delivered to the wrong place, there is little reason for concern on the part of the sender because the individual who receives the image will probably believe they have merely received the wrong e-mail and delete it.

Regardless of whether one accepts the argument that terrorist organizations are using steganography, there is little doubt that terrorist organizations are increasing their reliance on the use of computers. After each of the last three al Qaeda member arrests, the government has stated that it obtained valuable information from a computer or that investigators hope to obtain information from the computers seized during the arrest. The fact that all statements involve a computer of some type is evidence that the seizure of computers is becoming more and more commonplace during the arrest of suspected terrorists. In light of this trend, several new considerations emerge for those charged with investigating the activities of terrorist organizations. First, there is a stronger need for individuals trained in computer science and computer forensics. Even if terrorist organizations are not currently using steganography, they are more than likely using some form of encryption that will require attention during a search. If the organizations are using steganography, then the government needs individuals capable of handling investigations of computers and locating the images that are storing the hidden messages.

The use of computer experts by the government is not an important consideration as there are many in the service of the U.S. government who are skilled in computers and could conduct such investigations. However, the second consideration that arises from an increased reliance on computers and steganography is the training of soldiers who will fight the war on terrorism. The volatile nature of digital evidence, or evidence stored on an electronic media such as a hard drive, makes the proper acquisition of the evidence more important than ever before. This means that soldiers who would enter the homes of suspected terrorist operators will soon, if they are not already, be required to undergo specialized training on the proper seizure of digital evidence. As soldiers go into Iraq and other countries involved in supporting terrorism, they are potentially no longer only concerned with mission objectives and safety. These individuals are now additionally concerned with bringing back the hard drives and digital storage mediums of any computers they may encounter during raids of suspected terrorist compounds.

CONCLUSION

Steganography is not a new technique. The technique is an established method of hidden communication that has seen advancement with improvements in technology. Reports such as those of the media following the September 11 attacks and depictions of the technology in Hollywood movies have led to an increased awareness of the software, and there is sure to be an increase in its use by criminals. The rapid development of computer technology has developed a scenario where law enforcement officers are forced to work hard to stay ahead of those who would use the technology for criminal reasons.

While a thorough understanding of the technique's history may not be necessary, a cursory understanding of the technique and how steganography is accomplished today would seem to be an extremely important consideration for those involved in the criminal justice system. Specifically, individuals who are responsible for the investigation of terrorist related attacks should be interested in the use of steganography and the advancements made in the techniques and computer programs that make steganography possible.

Whether one elects to accept that terrorists are using steganography to communicate or if one elects to believe that reports of its use are overstated, the fact remains that the potential for the use of the technology is immense. Individuals who handle investigations involving terrorist activities should make every effort to be aware of the technology. Those who have taken the initiative to examine the technique and its applications will stand the best chance for developing productive countertechniques. The authors believe that steganography and hidden writing are sure to see an increase in the future as more individuals in the terrorist community discover its possibilities. Proper preparation can only make for a better response to the problem.

REFERENCES

Auer, C. 2001. "Behind the Bits." *Bulletin of the Atomic Scientists.* Retrieved on August 20, 2001, from http://www.thebulletin.org/issues/2001/mj01/mj01auer.html.

Carvin, A. 2001. "When a Picture Is Worth a Thousand Secrets: The Debate over Online Steganography." *The Digital Beat.* Retrieved on August 15, 2002, from http://www.benton.org/publibrary/digitalbeat/db103101.html.

Cohen, A. 2001. "When Terror Hides Online." *Time,* November 12, 65.

Johnson, N. 2000. "Steganography" & Digital Watermarking: Information Hiding." Retrieved on August 22, 2002, from http://www.jjtc.com/Steganography.

Kellen, T. 2001. "Hiding in Plain View: Could Steganography be a Terrorist Tool?" *Sans Info Sec Reading Room.* Retrieved August 22, 2002, from http://www.sans.org/rr/steg/plain_view.php.

Kolata, G. 2001. "The Net's Codes within Codes." *Toronto Star,* November 18.

McCullagh, D. 2001. "Bin Laden: Steganography Master?" *Wired News,* February 7. Retrieved August 15, 2001, from http://www.wired.com/news/politics/0,1283,41658,00.html.

———. 2002. "Pirate This, Go to Jail." *ZDNet,* July 29. Retrieved on August 25, 2002, from http://zdnet.com.com/2100-1107-946890.html.

Provos, N. & Honeyman, P. (2002). "Detecting Steganographic Content on the internet." *Technical Report* 01-11. Retrieved on September 2, 2002, from http://www.citi.umich.edu/techreports/reports/citi-tr-01-11.pdf.

Radcliff, D. 2002. "Steganography: Hidden Data." *Computerworld,* June 10, 1.

Sengupta, S. 2001. "A Short History of Steganography." Retrieved on August 22, 2002, from http://mail.sarai.net/pipermail/2600/2001-September/000078.html.

Snell, J. 2001. "Digital Software Makes Web More Useful for Criminals." *The Oregonian,* March 30.

Soloway, C., R. Nordland, and B. Nadeau. 2002. "Hiding (and Seeking) Messages on the Web." *Newsweek,* June 17, 8.

Tyson, J. 2002. "How Encryption Works." Retrieved on September 8, 2002, from http://www.howstuffworks.com/encryption.html.

Wang, W. 2001. *Steal This Computer Book 2: What They Won't Tell You about the Internet.* San Francisco: No Starch Press.

Wayner, P. 2002. *Disappearing Cryptography.* San Francisco: Morgan Kaufmann Publishers.

CHAPTER 9

Interpol and the Policing of International Terrorism: Developments and Dynamics Since September 11*

Mathieu Deflem
University of South Carolina

Lindsay C. Maybin
University of South Carolina

ABSTRACT

We present an analysis of the organization of counterterrorist police strategies by the International Criminal Police Organization (Interpol). Interpol has gradually developed antiterrorist activities since the 1970s and has radically expanded its strategies since the events of September 11. We demonstrate that counterterrorist strategies of cooperating police agencies at the international level are driven by concerns about efficient management and the efficient exchange of information among police. The target of terrorism is thereby (re)defined in a language that can be shared among the world's police institutions. As such, Interpol attempts to "depoliticize" terrorism and strip it of the ideological connotations that create political divisions in the world. However, these efforts in Interpol and many of its member agencies to target terrorism as a crime may

* We are grateful to Lynne Snowden for her editorial efforts and feedback on this paper.

not necessarily harmonize with the political, diplomatic, and legal activities against terrorism conducted at the level of the governments of national states.

INTRODUCTION

International terrorism has abruptly moved to the center of public attention and become a subject of intense interest at many levels of politics, law, and criminal justice. Especially since the events of September 11, 2001, there can be no rational way to deny the relevance of the study of terrorism. Much attention has already been given to counterterrorism in the scholarly community (e.g., Townshend 2002; White 2003; Deflem 2004), including contributions on the law enforcement response to the threat and reality of terrorism (e.g., Deflem 2002a, 228–231; Donnermeyer 2002; McVey 1997; Stuntz 2002). Given the contemporary climate on the global scene, especially the recent conflict between the United States and Iraq, it is clear that the complex conditions of terrorism involve many significant components. In this chapter, we will focus on the counterterrorist police response at the international level since September 11, especially the relevant changes in Interpol.

The perspective of our analysis is rooted in the sociology of social control and the transformations of social control under conditions of globalization. Based upon prior research on international policing (Deflem 2000a, 2002b), we defend the theoretical perspective that international police cooperation is enabled through a historical process by which police agencies gradually claim and gain a position of relative independence from the governments of their respective states. Following Max Weber's bureaucratization perspective, such conditions are characterized as formal bureaucratic autonomy and can be seen to have affected police bureaucracies across the western industrial world. Under these conditions, moreover, police agencies can rely on expert systems of knowledge of international crime that are shared across national boundaries to effectively form international cooperation plans on a relatively broad multilateral scale. However, despite such trends of international cooperation, nationally variable concerns of participating police remain paradoxically paramount, most distinctly in specifying shared international police objectives at the national level.

INTERNATIONAL COUNTERTERRORIST POLICING: SEPTEMBER 11 AS A WORLD EVENT

The September 11 terrorist attacks in the United States had a ripple effect that were felt across the world and that led to major reorganizations of counterterrorist policing (and other components of counterterrorism) in many countries. In the United States, among the most striking change in policing has been a sudden and considerable expansion of police powers, justified by the tragedy and devastation of the attacks. About a month after the tragedy, the PATRIOT Act (the Provide Appropriate Tools Required to Intercept and Obstruct Terrorism Act), a new federal bill to broaden police powers against terrorism, easily received congressional approval. The bill places special emphasis on foreign investigative work and the investigation of aliens engaged in terrorist activities and urges a shift in police attention toward the northern border with Canada. This expansion of U.S. police powers also brought about a refocusing of resources and a realignment of federal, state, and local police agencies. All levels of law enforcement focus more attention than ever on terrorism. In the months following September 11, for instance, the FBI assigned some 4,000 of its 27,000 agents to counterterrorist activities. Also, the former Immigration and Naturalization Service (INS) was then reorganized to separate its administrative tasks from its expanded enforcement duties, which include international and interior enforcement as well as border patrol.

The most important initiative at the federal level to secure interagency coordination in the fight against terrorism was the creation of the office of Homeland Security. The office was established on October 8, 2001 by executive order of President Bush and placed under the directorship of Tom Ridge, the former governor of Pennsylvania. On November 24, 2002, the office turned into a separate department in the executive branch when President Bush signed the Homeland Security Act of 2002 into law. The department has brought together the U.S. Customs Service, the Federal Law Enforcement Training Center, the Federal Emergency Management Agency (FEMA), the Secret Service, the U.S. Coast Guard, and the successor to the INS, the Bureau of Citizenship and Immigration Services, among many other agencies.

Counterterrorist policing reorganizations similar to those in the United States have been conducted in many countries across the world, especially in Europe, where police powers have also been expanded since September 11. The police institutions directed by the Ministry of Defense in the United Kingdom, for instance, have been given broader powers of investigation and can now arrest civilians that are suspected of terrorist involvement. Again paralleling conditions in the United States, new counterterrorist agreements and legislation have also been passed abroad. For example, the European Union has passed new antiterrorism measures, partly justified by the fact that EU nationals were among the casualties of September 11.

Thus, at the international level, the September 11 attacks have served as a powerful symbol to step up enforcement in many nations and to enhance international cooperation. Among the mechanisms that drive international cooperation against terrorism, emphasis is placed on effectiveness and speed in cooperation, especially for the exchange of intelligence information. Information on suspects and requests for information is typically transmitted directly among police (and intelligence) agencies. In the weeks after September 11, for instance, the FBI passed on information about people suspected to be involved in the attacks to Scotland Yard and requested investigations to be conducted on British soil. Typically, personal contacts are established between the representatives of police of various nations to foster swift communications. Such fostering of international police cooperation on the basis of personal contacts by police officials often takes place next to, and independent of, international diplomatic negotiations. For instance, when Attorney General Ashcroft met with German Minister of the Interior Otto Schily in October 2001 to discuss counterterrorist measures, FBI counterterrorist experts separately met with German investigators in Hamburg to discuss the profiles of the members of a Hamburg cell of the al Qaeda network. Additionally, international meetings are held to discuss international cooperation strategies of counterterrorism. For example, the meeting of the International Association of Chiefs of Police in Toronto in September 2001, just a few weeks after the attacks in the United States, was refocused to discuss the policing of terrorism. A similar adjustment of the discussion agenda took place when the Interpol General Assembly met in Budapest from September 24 to 28, 2001, the organization's first session after the September 11 attacks. In the remainder of this chapter, we take a closer look at the role of Interpol in counterterrorist policing.

INTERPOL AND INTERNATIONAL TERRORISM

Interpol is an organization that aims to provide and promote mutual assistance between criminal police authorities within the limits of national laws and the Universal Declaration of Human Rights. Originally formed in Vienna in 1923, the organization has steadily grown in membership but has never substantially changed in form or objectives (Deflem 2000, 2002b). Interpol is not a supranational police agency with investigative powers but a cooperative network intended to foster collaboration and to provide assistance in police work among law enforcement agencies in many nations. To this end, Interpol links a central headquarters, located in Lyon, France, with specialized bureaus, the so-called National Central Bureaus (NCB), in the countries of participating police agencies. At present, Interpol counts 181 participating police agencies; the police of Afghanistan were among the most recent members to join. At the Lyon headquarters, Interpol employs some 200 full-time staff and 150 seconded police officers. The objectives of Interpol have historically always been confined to criminal enforcement duties (so-called ordinary-law crimes). Since 1951, following certain politically sensitive Interpol cases that involved police from former Communist countries in Eastern Europe (Deflem 2002a), Interpol has adopted an even more explicit Article 3 to its constitution to preclude the organization from undertaking any intervention or activities of a political, military, religious or racial character" (Interpol Web site).

Interpol and Terrorism: A Brief History

With respect to counterterrorism, various resolutions were passed by Interpol to combat—at first implicitly, then explicitly—terrorism and terrorist-related activities (Anderson 1997; Bossard 1987; Interpol Web site n.d.). In 1970, the Interpol General Assembly in Brussels passed a resolution that stated that member nations would cooperate in matters of criminal acts conducted against international civil aviation. In 1971, a resolution was reached that Interpol agencies should take measures to prevent or suppress modern forms of international criminality, particularly the holding of hostages with the intention of perpetrating blackmail or other forms of extortion. The resolution clarified that this provision was valid only within the context of the Interpol resolution, which passed in Lisbon, Portugal, in June 1951, that Interpol would not concern itself with matters of a political, racial, or religious nature. In 1979, the Interpol General Assembly, meeting in Nairobi, decided to take appropriate measures against organized groups that, sometimes claiming to be ideologically motivated, had committed acts of violence, such as murder, wounding, kidnapping, hostage-taking, unlawful interference with civil aviation, arson, and bombing, that "seriously jeopardize general public safety." In 1981, the General Assembly in Nice passed a resolution to control the worldwide production, distribution, sale, and storage of explosive substances, which were often used in criminal acts of violence.

Interpol took a more explicit move toward the policing of terrorism in 1983, when the General Assembly, meeting in Cannes, France, resolved that a study would be conducted to define Interpol's position regarding criminal acts that result in many victims, are committed by organized groups, and "which are usually covered by the general term 'terrorism.'" It was also decided to organize a symposium on terrorism in 1984. That year, at the General Assembly meeting in Luxembourg, a resolution was passed on "Violent Crime Commonly Referred to as Terrorism" to encourage the member agencies to cooperate and "combat terrorism as far as their national laws permit." Referring specifically to the criminal acts of organized groups engaging in violent criminal activities that are designed, by spreading terror or fear, to attain "allegedly political objectives" and activities that are "commonly covered by the term 'terrorism,'" a new Interpol Resolution specified that "(a) [although] by virtue of the principle of national sovereignty, the political character of any offense can only be determined by national legislation, (b) it is nonetheless essential to combat this type of crime which causes considerable damage in Member States." An additional Interpol resolution of 1984 acknowledged that it was not possible to give a more precise definition of political, military, religious, or racial matters and that each case had to be examined separately.

In 1985, at the General Assembly meeting in Washington, D.C., a resolution passed that called for the creation of a specialized group, the Public Safety and Terrorism subdirectorate to coordinate and enhance cooperation in "combating international terrorism." The resolution also called for a practical instruction manual on terrorism, the organization of another symposium on terrorism, and making international terrorism an agenda item of all future General Assembly and Executive Committee meetings. In 1986, a first "Guide for Combating International Terrorism" was approved.

Following certain highly publicized terrorist incidents during the 1990s (such as the World Trade Center bombing on February 26, 1993), the Interpol General Assembly stepped up its counterterrorist initiatives. In 1998, at the General Assembly meeting in Cairo, Interpol's commitment to combat international terrorism was explicitly confirmed in a Declaration Against Terrorism that condemned terrorism because of the threat it poses "not only with regard to security and stability, but also to the State of Law, to democracy and to human rights." In 1999, at the Interpol General Assembly meeting in Seoul, it was again affirmed that the fight against international terrorism was "one of the main aims of Interpol's action in carrying out its general activities of police cooperation."

Recent Developments: Interpol After September 11

Interpol's Counterterrorism Resolutions Since September 11

A few weeks after the terrorist attacks in the United States, from September 24 to 28, 2001, the Interpol General Assembly held its 70th meeting in Budapest, Hungary. At the meeting, the Interpol General Assembly passed Resolution AG-2001-RES-05 on the "Terrorist Attack of 11 September 2001" to condemn the "murderous attacks perpetrated against the world's citizens in the United States of America on 11 September 2001" as "an abhorrent violation of law and of the standards of human decency" that constitute "cold-blooded mass murder [and] a crime against humanity." It was also decided to tackle terrorism and organized crime more effectively and that the highest priority be given to the issuance of so-called Red Notices (international Interpol warrants to seek arrest and extradition) for terrorists sought in connection with the attacks. In October 2001, Interpol held its 16th Annual Symposium on Terrorism, the first of Interpol's antiterrorism meetings to take place after September 11, at which 110 experts from 51 countries discussed new long-term antiterrorism initiatives, such as the feasibility of setting up a special aviation database, the financing of terrorism, and the expansion of anti–money-laundering measures. In October 2002, 450 representatives from 139 of Interpol's 181 member agencies attended the 71st General Assembly meeting in Yaoundé, Cameroon. Acknowledging September 11 as a catalyst in the development of global approaches to crime, the meeting paid even more distinct attention to the matter of terrorism. The Assembly attendants agreed to draft a list of security precautions for the handling of potentially dangerous materials (such as letters and parcels that might contain anthrax), while bioterrorism was specified as deserving special attention.

An online Interpol fact sheet on "The Fight Against International Terrorism" summarizes the key elements of Interpol's current policy against international terrorism (Interpol Web site). It specifies that in the aftermath of a terrorist act, member agencies are expected to inform Interpol headquarters of the particulars concerning an incident and developments of the investigation, such as details about individuals arrested and information about organizations on whose behalf the terrorist act was conducted. The Interpol offices in Lyon can then issue international notices for fugitive terrorists whose arrest is sought by a member agency. Since 1998, a formal set of "Interpol Guidelines for Co-operation in Combating International Terrorism" more explicitly addresses the relationship of terrorism to Article 3 of Interpol's constitution, forbidding Interpol to undertake matters of a political, military, religious, or racial character. The key aspect is that terrorist incidents are broken down into their constituent parts, the criminal elements of which can then be identified and subjected to police investigations (Anderson 1997, 95).

The restriction laid down by Article 3 is further clarified in an Interpol policy document outlining the "Legal Framework Governing Action by Interpol in Cases of a Political, Military, Religious or Racial character." Applying to both the General Secretariat and Interpol's member agencies, Article 3 is said to allow Interpol to check that requests from an NCB comply with the constitution. Interpol may also receive requests submitted by individuals or an NCB about cases which could potentially violate Article 3. A distinction is made between offenses that are by their very nature considered to be of a political, military, religious, or racial character, on the one hand, and offenses of which the predominant nature must be more carefully studied to determine its constituent components. In the latter case (of the so-called predominance theory), Interpol takes into account whether there are links between the aims of the accused and their victims and bases its analysis on three criteria: the place where the action was carried out, the status of the victims, and the seriousness of the offense. These principles also inform the distinction Interpol makes between requests for prevention and those for prosecution: requests aimed at prosecuting terrorists are processed in strict conformity with the above rules; but with regard to preventing terrorism, Interpol does not apply the theory of predominance.

Until recently, Interpol had a policy in place that specified that the decision to circulate information via the Interpol headquarters always had to be based on intelligence indicating that an individual might be involved in a terrorist offense rather than that the individual merely was a member of some particular group. Effective November 18, 2003, however, it was decided that a Red Notice for arrest and extradition can be issued for suspected members of a terrorist group if it provides strong evidence of such membership. The policy change has been justified because membership in a terrorist organization is considered a criminal offense in an increasing number of nations.

Interpol pays special attention to the financing of terrorist activities because it has found that the frequency and seriousness of terrorist attacks are often proportionate to the amount of financing terrorists receive. Interpol's emphasis on financing is aided by the fact that Interpol Secretary General Ronald K. Noble, the organization's chief executive (and an NYU Law School professor), has a long-standing interest in monetary crimes as president of the Financial Action Task Force, a 26-nation agency established to fight money-laundering. In 1999, the first specific Interpol resolution on the financing of terrorism was passed in Seoul, and since then, the financing of terrorism has remained a special focus of Interpol. When Secretary General Noble addressed the U.S. House Committee on International Relations in July 2003, he discussed the increasingly problematic links between intellectual property crimes and terrorist financing. Noble went as far as to argue that "intellectual property crime is becoming the preferred method of funding for a number of terrorist groups."

Finally, Interpol also sets up separate agreements to maintain liaisons with other international organizations. In November 2001, for example, Interpol signed an agreement with Europol to foster cooperation in the policing of terrorism and other international crimes, including those associated with the introduction of the new Euro currency. In December 2001, Interpol and the U.S. Department of the Treasury similarly pledged to cooperate more closely and create an international database of organizations and persons identified as providing financial assistance to terrorist groups. In March 2002, Interpol reached an agreement to cooperate closely with the Arab Interior Ministers Council to facilitate the exchange of information with the Arab police community.

Interpol's Counterterrorist Actions Since September 11

How did the terrorist attacks of September 11 fall under the authority of Interpol's ob-jectives? The clearest answer to this question came from Interpol's Secretary General, Ronald Noble, who in his opening speech to the 10th General Assembly in Budapest emphasized the global, nonpolitical dimensions of the September 11 attacks. Noble re-ferred to the fact that citizens from over eighty countries were among the casualties and argued that while the terrorist attacks took place on U.S. soil, "they constituted at-tacks against the entire world and its citizens." Therefore, Noble explained, Interpol would continue and expand its reorganization to better suit changing conditions of in-ternational crime. Likewise, the Interpol Resolution agreed upon in Budapest made ref-erence to the September 11 attacks as having been directed "against the world's citizens." And at a special session of the Financial Action Task Force in Washington, D.C., on October 29, 2001, Noble emphasized that the attacks targeted the World Trade Center, which "thus represented the world by name," indicating that the terrorists meant the attacks to "be felt worldwide . . . [and] have no geographical limits and no national boundaries."

Although Interpol recognized that the FBI was handling the primary investiga-tion of the acts of September 11, many investigative leads spanned the globe, and many of Interpol's member agencies have been involved with the investigations. Interpol mem-bers have issued Red Notices for a number of terrorist suspects through Interpol's in-ternational communication network and have published them on its Web site to give them as wide a circulation as possible. Immediately following September 11, Interpol issued fifty-five Red Notices for terrorists who had committed or were connected to these terrorist attacks. Interpol also increased its circulation of Blue Notices—requests for information about or the location of a suspect—of which nineteen concerned the hijackers who carried out the September 11 attacks. On September 25, 2001, for in-stance, Egyptian police authorities posted a Red Notice for Aiman Al Zawahry, a leader of the Al Jihad terrorist group and considered bin Laden's right-hand man. Incidentally, the first request by Red Notice for the Saudi-born militant Osama bin Laden was made by police from Libya well before the attacks on the United States (Brisard and Dasquie 2002).

International Police Arrangements and Structural Reorganization

After September 11, Interpol reorganized in several key respects, although some of these organizational changes had already begun before the terrorist attacks. Most concretely, during a press conference in Madrid on September 14, 2001, Secretary General Noble announced the creation of 11 September Task Force at Interpol's Headquarters in Lyon, France. The objective of this special task force is to coordinate international criminal police intelligence received at Interpol's Headquarters relating to the recent terrorist attacks in the United States. The creation of the task force is meant to ensure that in-formation received is processed as quickly as possible for immediate forwarding to the Interpol National Central Bureau in Washington, D.C., and through it to the FBI.

Also instituted following the September 11 attacks was a General Secretariat Command and Co-ordination Center that is operational twenty-four hours a day, seven days a week. A new Financial and High Tech Crimes Sub-Directorate was created that specialized in money-laundering. Furthermore, five new assistant director posts have been created for various regions of the world, including the Arab World, Europe, the Americas, Asia/Pacific, and Africa. The Public Safety and Terrorism Sub-Directorate became a component of the Specialized Crimes Directorate. In April 2002, Interpol announced the creation of an Interpol Terrorism Watch List, which provides police agencies with direct access to information on fugitive and suspected terrorists who are subject to Red (arrest), Blue (location), and Green (information) Notices. On June 22, 2001, Interpol established a system for member agencies to automatically enter information into and retrieve information from a database on stolen blank travel documents. And finally, at the Cameroon meeting of 2002, the establishment of a new global communications project was announced as Interpol's highest priority. This project involves the launching of a new Internet-based Global Communications System, called I-24/7, to provide for a rapid and secure exchange of data among Interpol's member agencies. The I-24/7 system allows for the searching and cross-checking of data submitted to Interpol by the organization's members over a virtual private network system that transmits encrypted information over the internet. At the 72nd Interpol General Assembly in Benidorm, Spain, in September 2003, Secretary General Noble said that a total of seventy-eight NCBs and ten other non-NCBs (among them, the New York City Police) had by then been effectively connected to the I-24/7 system. Special efforts are now under way to connect Interpol's other members. In November 2003, Interpol requested bids from equipment and service suppliers to connect the police of countries in Africa and the Caribbean to the I-24/7 system.

DYNAMICS OF GLOBAL COUNTERTERRORISM

Related to the theoretical perspective introduced in this chapter that international police developments are driven by bureaucratization trends in police agencies and that there is a remaining persistence of nationally variable concerns, two central issues emerge from our analysis. One, because of Interpol's structure as a cooperative organization, the limitations and characteristics of the various police systems of different nations continue to be revealed when they engage in border-transcending international work. Two, technological developments and concerns of efficiency are primary considerations in establishing the organizational structures of counterterrorism, oftentimes even overriding the ideological antagonisms on terrorism as a politically volatile issue.

The Boundaries of Interpol

The fact that Interpol brings together police of different nations without creating a supranational police force demonstrates that national concerns affect international cooperation among police of different nations (Deflem 2002b). By its very nature, then, Interpol serves in the "limited capacity of a communication network system to assist local law enforcement in locating terrorists" (Carberry 1999). Additionally, local developments and unilaterally executed transnational police operations typically outweigh international police work and cooperation on a multilateral scale and/or more or less prestructured basis. As a result, the famous international criminal law scholar Cherif Bassiouni (2002) argues that Interpol is simply not effective because "major powers, like the United States, do not fully trust it" (93). In the days following the attacks of September 11, FBI officials were indeed reported to "have been loathe to share sensitive information with" Interpol, instead preferring unilaterally conducted operations. Furthermore, Bassiouni argues, the fight against international terrorism is less likely to be effective when no or only limited cooperation exists with the intelligence community and instead remains restricted, as in the case of Interpol, to police agencies.

Recognizing these limitations, Interpol places most of its emphasis on the smooth coordination of and direct contacts between the various participating police agencies. Only a few days after September 11, Secretary General Noble flew to New York and Washington to meet with U.S. police chiefs and plead for international cooperation. Also, during his speech in Budapest, Noble stressed that the concrete steps that had to be taken to expand Interpol's counterterrorist role would have to begin "in each of our home countries." He added that Interpol needed "each country's commitment to use our systems and to fill our databases" but that, regrettably, "many countries consider Interpol too slow." Similarly, Willy Deridder, the executive director of Interpol, emphasized at the 16th Annual Interpol Symposium on Terrorism that information exchange is the key issue in international police work, which is in no small part influenced by cooperation between law enforcement agencies, law enforcement and intelligence services, and relations with magistrates, all issues that Deridder admitted had to be dealt with at the national level.

Police support at the national level is not self-evident, particularly when cases involve politically sensitive matters. This was clearly shown in the case of a former Chechen government representative, Akhmed Zakayev, for whom an Interpol warrant on charges of terrorism was distributed on the request of Russian Authorities. The Chechen envoy was freed by Danish authorities in early December 2002 because no evidence was found against him. Thereafter, Zakayev was also released on bail from a London prison. Another interesting instance of lack of cooperation at the national level by police agencies despite their formal participation in Interpol is the case of former Peruvian president Alberto Fujimori. An Interpol notice for Fujimori, who is now living in self-exile in Japan, was placed by Peruvian authorities in 2001. But Japanese police and justice authorities have not sought extradition for Fujimori because he has in the meantime become a Japanese citizen.

Another peculiar indication of the persistence of nationality in international policing is that sources in Arabic are always listed first on the pages of Interpol Web site and all official documents since September 11. Although Arabic was, together with English, French, and Spanish, already one of Interpol's official languages before September 11, the prominence now accorded to the language clearly shows that international police organizations and cooperative arrangements such as Interpol reflect the various characteristics of national police agencies, their relative weight on the international scene, and the focus on terrorist groups from Arab nations (Rubin and Rubin 2002). Thus, police agencies from the western industrialized world, especially the U.S. and Europe, are perceived to strongly influence the international police agenda on terrorism. Additionally, the focus on foreign terrorist groups rather than domestic groups has led to an emphasis in antiterrorist activities on citizens of certain countries, often with distinct ethnic characteristics, which has raised problematic considerations with respect to civil and human rights. Ironically, among the victims of this ethnic bias in the application of antiterrorist laws has been Interpol Secretary General Ronald Noble, who has been singled out at airport checks because he is African American. "I know that I've been searched because I look like a person who could be Arabic, if I'm traveling from an Arab country—or I could be a drug-trafficker if I'm coming from a drug-trafficking country," Noble said in an interview during Interpol's annual meeting in Benidorm.

An additional consequence of the persistence of nationality in international police work (Deflem 2002a) is the fact that international terrorism has mostly remained a matter that is regulated, policed, and prosecuted at the national level or on a more limited multilateral scale. This accounts for the development of many international antiterrorist initiatives that are independent from Interpol. In Europe, for instance, counterterrorist efforts date back to the 1970s when the TREVI (Terrorism, Radicalism, Extremism, and International Violence) was founded in the European Community (Benyon 1997; Rauchs and Koenig 2001). The group was explicitly founded because "Interpol was not considered suitable for such discussions because of a distrust of its ability to handle sensitive information" (Gammelgard 2001, 238). Since the formation of the TREVI Group, Europe's unified nations have created additional cooperative arrangements against terrorism. In 1993, the TREVI Group was, along with other European judicial, customs, and immigration organizations, united in a new structure specified by the Treaty of European Union. And since 1998, an antiterrorist unit, the Task Force Terrorism, has been set up in the European Police Office (Europol).

In multilateral antiterrorist matters, moreover, the United States has typically played a leading and dominant role. According to Ethan Nadelmann, U.S. police agencies influenced Interpol to become a more effective organization and promote U.S. law enforcement concerns, including improvement of international cooperation in Interpol and its member agencies in matters of "terrorism and the financial aspects of drug trafficking" (1993, 185). According to Malcolm Anderson, Interpol's reinterpretation of the meaning of Article 3 and its consequences for counterterrorism in 1984 was the result of "a combination of American pressure, sensitivity to sections of western public opinion alarmed by terrorism, and fear that the Organization could be marginalized" (1997, 95). And, indeed, following the reinterpretation, the Interpol communication network was, in effect, used to search for terrorist suspects. In 1985, for example, the London NCB issued about 1,000 enquiries about a bombing by the IRA aimed at killing British Prime Minister Thatcher and some of her colleagues when they were in Brighton (Anderson 1997, 95).

Relative to Interpol's increasing involvement in counterterrorism, it is important to note that police agencies at the level of national states have also gradually expanded their powers to include antiterrorist objectives. In the United States, for instance, the FBI's role in antiterrorist investigations abroad was limited until the 1970s because federal laws restricted the scope of the FBI's jurisdiction. In 1978, the deaths of a congressman and a U.S. embassy official in Guyana created an opportunity for the FBI to become involved in international investigations. In the 1980s, an increasing number of terrorist incidents and politically motivated killings of U.S. citizens created additional incentives for the FBI to become involved in international investigations (Nadelmann 1993, 157). In 1983, for example, the FBI sent forensics experts to Beirut to investigate the April embassy bombing and the October bombing of marine barracks. Federal laws then extended U.S. jurisdiction over violent crimes, such as terrorism, against American citizens abroad. The international character of terrorism has led to the passing of new laws by the U.S. Congress to protect Americans and their property from assault, regardless of where it occurs (Marx, 1997, 24; Nadelmann 1993, 157; Smith 1994). In 1984 and 1986, Congress formally passed legislation that granted U.S. police agencies wider extraterritorial jurisdiction over terrorist acts. Between 1985 and 1989, the FBI conducted over fifty investigations of terrorist actions that occurred outside American borders. From the early 1990s onward, the counterterrorist role of the FBI steadily expanded, and since September 11, the FBI has become the leading counterterrorist law enforcement agency in the United States. The case of the FBI's growing counterterrorism program shows that although Interpol's role in counterterrorism is more significant today than it ever was before, the police agencies of various countries may continue to work on a unilateral or limited cooperative basis rather than take advantage of participation in the international organization.

Toward Global Police Efficiency

A remarkable emphasis is placed on technology in formulating the proper police response to international terrorism. The centrality of technology in international counterterrorist policing is seen as a necessity in response to the use of new technologies by contemporary terrorist organizations, which are argued to be highly sophisticated in terms of scope and methods of operation and are also said to rely on high-tech means of communication and financing to recruit new members and organize attacks (Harmon 2000). Furthermore, aided by such technical developments, a relatively high degree of internationalism and cross-border activity characterizes many present-day terrorist groups. But there is also an independent technological drive in (international) police work based on the means, rather the objectives of, policing (Deflem 2002b). Indeed, language barriers, poor interagency communication, and aged equipment among police are seen as hindering police investigations. Likewise indicating the sharp emphasis on technological issues, special concern in counterterrorism goes to bioterrorism, the use of computers, and the financial assets of terrorist groupings. All these factors illustrate an emphasis on the technological means at the disposal of terrorist groups and the likewise technically sophisticated manner in which counterterrorist police strategies should respond (Deflem 2002c).

    The creation of a specialized antiterrorist command and coordination center, a new subdirectorate that specializes in sophisticated financial crimes, new computerized databases, and the newly instituted I-24/7 communications system demonstrate

Interpol's emphasis on technology. Similarly, the PATRIOT Act in the United States, much like similar legislative changes that have been introduced elsewhere in the world, places a premium on the technologies of counterterrorism. Among the surveillance tools mentioned in the PATRIOT Act, for instance, are secret search and seizure methods, the tapping of telephones, and the use of detention without charges for seven days (Whitehead and Aden 2002).

Ironically, in view of the technological focus in counterterrorism, police and intelligence agencies have been criticized for not having been efficient in curbing terrorism and for not predicting the September 11 attack. Efficiency as an aim in police operations does not necessarily equate to effectiveness in results. In the wake of the terrorist attacks of September 11, for example, there was an overload of information, as many citizens called in about all kinds of issues they thought were relevant to terrorism or because they thought they had leads on the investigations. But police officials are quick to respond that they had warned many times against the possibility of new terrorist attacks. In 1998, for instance, FBI Director Louis Freeh said that the loosely organized terrorist networks, such as the one controlled by Osama bin Laden, posed "the most urgent threat to the United States."

At the international level, Interpol head Ronald Noble admitted that the sharing of information among the police agencies throughout the world is not always easy, because national agencies do not want to jeopardize their investigations. Noble also acknowledged that Interpol's "communication system . . . is antiquated, clumsy to use." Until recently, the circulation of Red Notices occurred by regular mail. Even though a received Red Notice could be processed and translated into Interpol's four languages within a day, Interpol would then mail photocopies back to member agencies, using the cheapest and lowest-priority mail service. It could take weeks, even months, before the Red Notices would reach their destination. Changes were made after September 11 to move to an electronic communications system. During the first ten months of 2002, about half (968) of all Red Notices were transmitted electronically, albeit to only forty-two member agencies. Some NCBs are not aware of the benefits of the electronic system, while others do not have the necessary technical infrastructure.

Related to the technological emphasis in the means of counterterrorist policing is a depoliticization of terrorism as the target of police activities. The explicit nonpolitical nature of the objectives of Interpol's activities may seem problematic in the case of terrorism because terrorist activities by definition contain a political element in terms of their motive. Christopher Harmon (2000), for instance, defines terrorism as the use of illegitimate means, typically involving the exercise of violence against innocent people, to gain political power. It has therefore been argued that Interpol cannot be authorized within the parameter of its own constitution, especially Article 3, to exchange information regarding political terrorists (Bassiouni 2002). Police cooperation with respect to terrorism in the European context has been legally and formally secured in Articles K-K.9 (Title VI) of the Treaty on the European Union concerning cooperation in the fields of justice and home affairs. One of the articles provides for "police cooperation for the purposes of preventing and combating terrorism, unlawful drug trafficking and other serious forms of international crime, including customs cooperation in connection with a Union-wide system for exchanging information within a European Police Office (Europol)" (Flaherty and Lally-Green 1996, 983–984).

From a legal viewpoint it might be problematic for Interpol that there is no internationally agreed upon definition of terrorism. The plurality of terrorism definitions reflects the disagreement that exists over the politically sensitive issues of the "purposes of terrorist aims, actors, and activities . . . [and is] symptomatic of larger ideological arguments over who the 'bad guys' are" (Sabia 2000, 228). In potential terrorism cases, one country may identify an act as terrorism, while another country might label it "resistance" (Marx 1997, 33). Gary Marx cites an example in which a Pakistani religious party requested that American rock stars be tried as terrorists because, they argued, "Michael Jackson and Madonna are the torch bearers of American society [and] their cultural and social values . . . are destroying humanity" (Marx 1997, 33). Differences in definitions of terrorism across nations also shape differences in their systems of legislation, so that national laws and international conventions may often differ, making enforcement at an international level difficult. Thus, although a UN General Assembly Resolution of 1983 unconditionally condemned as criminal "all acts, methods and practices of terrorism," the only instrument of enforcement adopted by 1988 was the more restricted International Convention for the Suppression of Terrorist Bombings (Gregory 2000, 102).

From the viewpoint of international police cooperation, however, it is important to note that terrorist incidents, even when they explicitly involve political motives on the part of the perpetrators and are sensitive matters in an ideological sense, are depoliticized by police institutions to become the foundation of shared systems of information on which international cooperation can be based (Deflem 2002b; see Geraghty 2002). When Interpol was placed on high alert to respond to possible terrorist attacks that might occur during the war in Iraq, Secretary General Noble was quick to add that Interpol would not take a position on the war itself. As is the case in Interpol, politically sensitive crimes, such as terrorism, can also be broken down into several components, only the criminal elements of which (e.g., homicide, bombings, illegal weapons trade) are taken as the focus of international police investigations. Thus, while it is legally problematic that terrorism is defined differently across the nations of the world, police agencies of various countries can agree to accept their common task to focus on terrorism, whatever its more precise legal specification in any country.

From the viewpoint of a depoliticized understanding of terrorism, it becomes understandable why Interpol manages to attract cooperation from police agencies that represent nations that are ideologically very diverse and not always on friendly terms in political respects. In January 2002, for example, Interpol decided to donate communications equipment to the Cuban police to better coordinate its antiterrorist operations. According to Secretary General Noble, the technology transfer was in part the result of the cooperation agreement Interpol had signed with the U.S. Treasury Department concerning matters of the financing of terrorism. Similarly revealing the politics-transcending nature of international counterterrorist police work is the fact that shortly after the war in Iraq, authorities from France and the United States agreed to cooperate toward the development of biometric techniques to prevent the forgery of passports as part of their efforts against terrorism, despite these countries' profound disagreements over the Iraqi conflict. On the occasion of the signing of the agreement, U.S. attorney general John Ashcroft also visited the Interpol Headquarters in Lyon to attend an international conference aimed at stepping up the recovery of Iraqi works of art stolen in the aftermath of the fall of the Saddam regime. Thus, although ideological sentiments on terrorism are very divided in the world of politics and diplomacy, international efforts at the level of police agencies and organizations, such as Interpol and its member agencies, can be based on a common ground surrounding terrorism through its treatment as a depoliticized crime.

CONCLUSION

Interpol has undergone significant changes since September 11 as part of a renewed and vigorous effort to more efficiently organize international police cooperation against the terrorist threat. Most clearly, new systems of information exchange among police across the world have been instituted. Also, formal policy resolutions have been developed to offer a foundation to these new counterterrorist arrangements. Two key issues emerge that will significantly direct the shape and future of Interpol's counterterrorist activities. One, Interpol is not a supranational police force with investigative powers but instead provides a collaborative forum for cooperation among the police of 181 nations. Two, concerns of efficiency and technical sophistication in international police work are emphasized in Interpol but remain confronted with the ideological battles over terrorism on the political arena of world diplomacy.

With respect to the collaborative form of international police cooperation in Interpol, it remains unclear to what extent the organization can effectively determine the course and outcome of counterterrorist police efforts. To be sure, Interpol does aid in the fight against terrorism, and the organization is used by police of various nations. Nonetheless, relative to the activities undertaken by the police agencies of certain powerful nations across the world, Interpol's efforts are rather minimal. Particularly in matters of terrorism, these police organizations may be expected to prefer unilateral strategies and cooperative efforts on a more limited scale. Additional regional cooperation efforts (e.g., by Europol) further add to the notion that Interpol cannot readily be expected to make good on its claim to be the world's leading police organization. Potential resistance from police in Arab nations, likewise, may cause rifts in the global fight against terrorism.

As a modern bureaucratic police organization, Interpol typically institutes efficient procedures of information exchange and intelligence-gathering. In the wake of September 11, Interpol radically modernized some of its technical apparatus and built on the communications facilities it has been developing for many decades among a growing number of member agencies. Yet a key problem remains the tension between the emphasis placed in Interpol on efficiency of international police work and communications, on the one hand, and the politically sensitive nature of counterterrorist objectives, on the other. By criminalizing terrorism, Interpol seeks to develop counterterrorist programs that can be participated in by police institutions from countries across the world irrespective of the ideological justifications of and sentiments about terrorist activities. The treatment of terrorism in Interpol as a purely criminal matter reflects the impact of a professionalized police culture across nations. It remains unclear, however, how this depoliticized approach to terrorism as a crime will blend or clash with the political response to international terrorism as a matter of international diplomacy, law, and war.

REFERENCES

Anderson, Malcolm. 1997. "Interpol and the Developing System of International Police Cooperation." In *Crime and Law Enforcement in the Global Village,* ed. William F. McDonald, 89–102. Cincinnati, OH: Anderson Publishing.

Bassiouni, M. Cherif. 2002. "Legal Control of International Terrorism: A Policy-Oriented Assessment." *Harvard International Law Journal* 43: 83–103.

Benyon, John. 1997. "The Developing System of Police Cooperation in the European Union." In *Crime and Law Enforcement in the Global Village,* ed. William F. McDonald, 103–122. Cincinnati, OH: Anderson Publishing Co.

Bossard, André. 1987. "The War Against Terrorism: The Interpol Response." In *International Terrorism: The Domestic Response,* ed. Richard H. Ward and Harold E. Smith, 1–10. Chicago, IL: The Office of International Criminal Justice.

Brisard, Jean-Charles, and Guillaume Dasquie. 2002. *Forbidden Truth: U.S.-Taliban Secret Oil Diplomacy and the Failed Hunt for bin Laden.* New York: Thunder's Mouth Press.

Carberry, Jacqueline A. 1999. "Terrorism: A Global Phenomenon Mandating a Unified International Response." *Indiana Journal of Global Legal Studies* 6: 685–719.

Deflem, Mathieu. 2000a. "Bureaucratization and Social Control: Historical Foundations of International Policing." *Law & Society Review* 34, no. 3: 601–640.

———. 2002b. *Policing World Society: Historical Foundations of International Police Cooperation.* Oxford: Oxford University Press.

———. 2002c. "Technology and the Internationalization of Policing: A Comparative-Historical Perspective." *Justice Quarterly* 19, no. 3: 453–475.

———. ed. 2004. *Terrorism and Counter-Terrorism: Criminological Perspectives.* Oxford: Elsevier Science, forthcoming.

Donnermeyer, J. F. 2002. "Local Preparedness for Terrorism: A View from Law Enforcement." *Police Practice and Research* 3, no. 4: 347–360.

Flaherty, John P., and Maureen E. Lally-Green. 1996. "The European Union: Where Is It Now?" *Duquesne Law Review* 34: 923–1006.

Gammelgard, Per. 2001. "International Police Cooperation from a Norwegian Perspective." In *International Police Cooperation,* ed. Daniel J. Koenig and Dilip K. Das, 229–244. New York: Lexington Books.

Geraghty, Thomas. 2002. "The Criminal-Enemy Distinction: Prosecuting a Limited War Against Terrorism Following the September 11, 2001 Terrorist Attacks." *McGeorge Law Review* 33: 551–591.

Gregory, Frank. 2000. "Private Criminality as a Matter of International Concern." In *Issues in Transnational Policing,* ed. J. W. E. Sheptycki, 100–134. London: Routledge.

Harmon, Christopher C. 2000. *Terrorism Today.* London: Frank Cass Publishers.

Interpol Web site. N.d. http://www.interpol.int.

Marx, Gary T. 1997. "Social Control across Borders." In *Crime and Law Enforcement in the Global Village,* ed. William F. McDonald, 23–40. Cincinnati, OH: Anderson Publishing.

McVey, Philip M. 1997. *Terrorism and Law Enforcement: A Multidimensional Challenge for the Twenty-First Century.* Springfield, IL: Charles C. Thomas.

Nadelmann, Ethan A. 1993. *Cops across Borders: The Internationalization of U.S. Criminal Law Enforcement.* University Park, PA: Pennsylvania State University Press.

Noble, Iris. 1975. *INTERPOL: International Crime Fighter.* New York: Harcourt Brace Jovanovich.

Rauchs, George, and Daniel J. Koenig. 2001. "Europol." In *International Police Cooperation,* ed. Daniel J. Koenig and Dilip K. Das, 43–62. New York: Lexington Books.

Reeve, Simon. 1999. *The New Jackals: Ramzi Yousef, Osama bin Laden, and the Future of Terrorism.* Boston, MA: Northeastern University Press.

Rubin, Barry, and Judith C. Rubin, eds. 2002. *Anti-American Terrorism and the Middle East: A Documentary Reader.* Oxford: Oxford University Press.

Sabia, Debra. 2000. "International Terrorism and the United States: The Troubling Case of Latin America." In *International Criminal Justice: Issues in a Global Perspective,* ed. Delbert Rounds, 228–240. London: Allyn & Bacon.

Smith, Brent L. 1994. "Anti-Terrorism Legislation in the United States." In *International Terrorism: The Domestic Response,* ed. Richard H. Ward and Harold E. Smith, 107–118. Chicago, IL: The Office of International Criminal Justice.

Stuntz, William J. 2002. "Responses to the September 11 Attacks: Terrorism, Federalism, and Police Misconduct." *Harvard Journal of Law & Public Policy* 25 665–679.

Townshend, Charles. 2002. *Terrorism: A Very Short Introduction.* Oxford: Oxford University Press.

White, Jonathan R. 2003. *Terrorism: An Introduction. 2002 Update.* Wadsworth.

Whitehead, John W., and Steven H. Aden. 2002. "Forfeiting 'Enduring Freedom' for 'Homeland Security': A Constitutional Analysis of the USA Patriot Act and the Justice Department's Anti-Terrorism Initiatives." *The American University Law Review* 51: 1081–1133.

SECTION THREE DISCUSSION QUESTIONS

1. Discuss four factors which have led to the rise of religious extremism in the Middle East.
2. Discuss which factors enable Middle Eastern extremist groups to achieve their goals.
3. What are madaris? What characteristics do the various madaris share and how do they differ?
4. Discuss the distinction made when one conceptualizes weapons of mass destruction (WMDs) as weapons of mass victimization (WMVs).
5. Define the six factors that should be considered in a threat analysis of terrorist groups who might use radiological weapons.
6. Why do terrorism scholars argue that radiological dispersal devices are unique weapons and should not be lumped together with chemical and biological weapons?
7. Compare steganography with cryptography.
8. Describe steganography's history. What actual proof exists that terrorists such as Osama bin Laden are using steganography?
9. Other than terrorists' communications, are there additional applications for steganography?
10. What is the historical relationship between Interpol and counterterrorism?
11. What are Red Notices? Blue Notices? How are these used in international counterterrorism efforts?
12. Describe Interpol's Global Communication System and its role in counterterrorist efforts? How do the limitations and characteristics of various national police systems affect Interpol's coordination activities?

SECTION FOUR

Cultic Terrorism

LOOK FOR THESE KEY POINTS

- Intellectual extremists of the far right formed a racist cult that channeled its behavior toward showing the superiority of their own intellectualism. Rather than focusing on the overt racism, hatred, and violence of other far-right extremists, the Institute for Historical Review chose to show that they could revise history.

- Apocalyptic activism has profound effects on cultic New Age groups. One case study shows clear evidence of a fast-moving transformation in a community's millennial attitude.

- To assess today's WMD terrorism threat, we must understand the most likely types of agents to be used, identify the capabilities of the United States to respond to an attack on its homeland, and locate gaps in the current defensive system.

- Religiously based domestic terrorists use the New Testament's Book of Revelation—the prophecy of the end time—for the foundation of their belief in the apocalypse. Religious extremists interpret the symbolism portrayed in the Book of Revelation and mold it to predict that the end time is now and that the apocalypse is near.

INTRODUCTION TO CULTIC AND OTHER FRINGE GROUPS

While the Aum Shinrikyo nerve-gas attack in the Tokyo subway of spring 1995 was the major event drawing the attention of scholars and police agencies to the terrorist proclivities of extremist social, religious, and political organizations, the academic field of terrorist studies has since expanded its parameters to focus more on fringe, or cult-like, movements. The term "cult" is used in many different ways to describe a group believed to exemplify a set of specific characteristics, including social isolation; charismatic leadership authority; adherence to exotic, countercultural beliefs, and observance of a rigid worldview that promotes extreme skepticism of "outsiders." Unfortunately, journalistic and popular overuse of the term has compromised its meaning. Still, these traits fairly describe a generalized style of nonmainstream collectivity which, because of its outlook and organizational structure, maintains a self-imposed arm's length from the environing society.

It requires attention, of course, that not all cultic groups represent a threat to public order. In fact, most (including highly encapsulated groups) are not volatile and tend to follow peaceable practices. However, authorities have become more concerned over the past several years about the potential dangers posed by a minority of both religious and secular groups displaying cultic tendencies. Aum Shinrikyo's efforts to produce and deploy weapons of mass destruction in Japan represents the most ambitious terrorist action carried out by a religion-inspired cult, but additional events in the 1990s pointed to the destructive capabilities of other groups residing in the alternative ideological universe of the cultic underground. Although the group suicides by members belonging to the fringe religious groups Heaven's Gate and Order of the Solar Temple in the last decade were cases of inwardly directed violence, not terrorism, both incidents highlighted the extent to which counterculturalists observing obscure apocalyptic ideologies could mobilize for self-destruction.

Other organizations with cultic qualities do not adhere to idiosyncratic religious beliefs and millennial timetables, but take the form of secular antigovernment groups driven by a variety of extremist convictions. As with religion-inspired apocalyptic cults, secular groups with a cultic style operate as self-contained systems that, as a result of their insular character and esoteric doctrines, effectively prevent their penetration by the surrounding society. Such groups may include, for example, the most extreme and violence-prone environmental movements as well as the minority subset of militia-type organizations that adhere to bizarre conspiracy theories about government rule. The apparent efflorescence of cultic groups in recent times presents a new topic of examination for scholars working in the field of terrorist studies and a new area of potential concern for law enforcement agencies charged with countering the activism of these normally inconspicuous networks.

This section is comprised of a range of readings that underscore various aspects of cultic groups, including examples of the unusual belief structures to which they adhere. The section also includes articles that more directly identify the possible threats that some groups in this orbit may represent. David Lobb's chapter about the Institute for Historical Review (IHR) focuses on an important extremist movement that is concerned with revising conventional interpretations of the Holocaust. Founded in 1978, the IHR is an association of far-right intellectuals and amateur historians devoted to challenging the validity of the Holocaust and advancing pseudo-academic theories that seek to call into question the conventional history surrounding the Nazi regime's genocidal campaign against Jews. Lobb's article demonstrates how cultic beliefs may exist and proliferate in groups with a secular orientation. Brad Whitsel's "Catastrophic New Age Groups and Public Order" documents the unusual and underexamined episode involving the Church Universal and Triumphant in spring 1990 as its Montana-based membership prepared for a nuclear war prophesied by its spiritual leader Elizabeth Clare Prophet. While not a violent-prone group, the Church Universal and Triumphant pursued the route of apocalyptic mobilization on the basis of its leader's prediction of earthly calamity. James Ellis's "Yesterday's News? The WMD Terrorism Threat Today" deals with the pressing issue of the acquisition and use of weapons of mass destruction by terrorist groups, including Aum Shinrikyo, and offers a policy perspective on government defense against chemical, biological, radiological, and nuclear attack. Last, the Federal Bureau of Investigation's Project Megiddo report is included in this section. The report, which drew its name from the Hebrew word for "Armageddon," concentrates on those cultic and ideologically fringe groups believed to harbor apocalyptic views of the millennium.

CHAPTER 10

The Right to Revise History: The Institute for Historical Review

David Lobb,
U.S. Naval Criminal Investigative Service

A CULTURE OF FEAR

It was the day before the Thirteenth Revisionist Conference of the Institute for Historical Review (IHR) in May 2000, and participants had still not received information on the location of the event. When registering by mail, conferencegoers were told only that the meetings would be held at a hotel somewhere in southern California. Transportation from the John Wayne Airport in Orange County, California, could be arranged ahead of time. Apparently the shuttle service would simply drive participants to the undisclosed location. Having never been to a conference of the IHR, I felt anxious as I awaited an e-mail message containing a toll-free number to call that would provide me with the location for the conference. I called the number, and the man on the other end of the telephone answered simply, "Hello." After a pause I responded "I am in town for the conference and need the location." After several seconds of silence, I was given the address of the meetingplace. The next day I drove some forty miles for three days of "revisionist camaraderie."

Why would revisionist historians, intellectuals, and academics cloak their conference in a veil of secrecy? When one enters the conference room, there is no question that the historical theories of the speakers serve an ideological purpose. The IHR, founded in 1978, is concerned with revising interpretations of the Holocaust. The academics and amateur historians associated with the group attack the validity of the Holocaust and rail against world Jewry, referring to Jews as master manipulators and parasites. While in line to register for the conference, well-dressed and well-mannered conference attendees spoke of the lying and deceptive nature of the Jews as well as the myth of the "Holohoax." Literature of the IHR noted that the location of the conference was kept secret to ensure that "a congenial and untroubled Conference" was provided for all attendees. In the past, civil rights organizations, Jewish groups such as the Anti-Defamation League, and the more radical Jewish Defense League have protested the conference, picketing the hotel that booked a conference for Holocaust deniers and anti-Semites. Just in case there was any trouble, five young neo-Nazi skinheads kept a close watch from the back of the conference room. The academics associated with the IHR lament the need for secrecy and view themselves as victims of a society dominated by liberals and Jews that has unfairly declared the work they do as anti-Semitic, bad history. The academics and intellectuals associated with the IHR and the larger culture of the American racist right have become an insular group. As many of them were pushed out of or deliberately left academe, they began to construct their own institutions, where their theories denying the Holocaust and those proving the superiority of the white race were commonplace and acceptable. Since World War II, these academics of the racist right have dwelled in a self-constructed ivory tower and built a culture of fear.

In the wake of the September 11, 2001, terrorist attacks, leaders of the racist right, including those of the IHR, railed not against the Muslim extremists responsible for the acts but against the U.S. government and its support of Israel. In fact, as early as the 1970s, IHR leadership had reached out to Muslim intellectuals with ties to extremist groups united by a hatred of Israel and a fear of world Jewry. For now, the links between the two groups appear to be academic; however, the alliance of radical right-wing groups with radical Muslim groups is of concern to national security officials. Understanding the elements of the culture created by groups such as the IHR is essential in evaluating the potential for extremist violence perpetrated by the American racist right.

A FORUM FOR DENIAL

By the late 1970s, the publishing efforts of rightist Willis Carto were reaching racist anti-Semites in the United States and Britain. Carto had provided a publishing outlet for racist intellectuals since the 1950s, and by the late 1970s he was attracting the racist right in Europe as well.[1] In fact, in 1978, British racist activist David McCalden joined Willis Carto's Noontide Press and helped organize the Institute for Historical Review. McCalden envisioned the Institute as a forum for Holocaust deniers and other racist writers to publish their works. He also hoped the Institute would validate anti-Semitic and racist ideas by sponsoring conferences and printing a journal dedicated to his own form of scholarly inquiry. McCalden, who boasted that he was a graduate of the University of London and who was an active participant in the National Socialist movement in Britain, came to the United States specifically to work for Carto and Noontide Press. He often used the pseudonym Lewis Brandon (the first name of the husband of LaVonne Furr, the southerner who inherited the conservative *American Mercury* in the 1960s) and offered several ideas to make Noontide Press a more important part of the radical right movement.[2] He insisted that the racist and "cranky" book titles of the press needed to be phased out, and he told Carto that Holocaust revisionist books should become the focus of the press. McCalden explained that the only original revisionist book Noontide published was the early American Holocaust denial book by David Hoggan, *The Myth of the Six Million,* which questioned eyewitness accounts of the Holocaust and claims of German atrocities. McCalden stated that the book was "so full of mistakes it was a perpetual embarrassment."[3] Carto rejected McCalden's suggestion of doing away with the older racist books. However, he accepted the suggestion to make revisionism the focus of the Noontide Press.

Ironically, it would be the issue of revisionism, as well as accusations of embezzlement and fraud, that would lead the IHR to sever all ties with Carto in the mid-1990s. Prior to that, in 1981, just four years after he helped found the IHR, McCalden left because of a dispute with Carto over policy issues. McCalden noted that in 1980 he started to feel pressure from Carto to do things his way. By 1982, McCalden was bitter that Carto seemed to ignore the fact that before McCalden came to California there was "NO IHR, there were NO Revisionist Conventions . . . LITTLE media attention; not much of anything really."[4] Carto subsequently began publishing articles critical of McCalden in his publication *The Spotlight,* claiming that McCalden was an agent of the Anti-Defamation League (ADL).[5]

Carto often used his publications to attack enemies he had made within the movement. As early as 1970, after his split with neo-Nazi leader William Pierce, Carto published several articles in his newspaper *Statecraft* accusing Pierce of being an "FBI agent."[6] Unlike Carto, Pierce was a real academic, he had earned a Ph.D. in physics and taught at Oregon State University before devoting his life to the cause of white nationalism in the late 1960s. Carto, who would often write articles for his own publications under the pseudonym E. L. Anderson, Ph.D.," had a series of conflicts with Pierce as they both sought to corner the market of racist intellectuals.[7] By 1981, Carto had placed his own name on the IHR letterhead as sole founder of the organization. Current director of the IHR Mark Weber explained to this author in May 2000 that it had really been McCalden's idea to start the institute. As Weber put it, McCalden was the creative one, not Carto. From that point until his death in 1991, McCalden engaged in bitter legal battles with Carto.[8]

Other legal struggles would continue for Carto in the 1990s as he became further estranged from the IHR and its leadership. Tensions exploded in 1993 when Carto "suddenly decreed" that the *Journal for Historical Review,* the scholarly organ of the IHR, would abandon Holocaust revisionism. Apparently, Carto wanted to rename the journal and gradually eliminate Holocaust-related material, which he felt too narrowly focused the scope of the journal and the IHR. Carto wanted the new journal to focus on issues of race and multiculturalism. On one occasion, Carto explained to editor Mark Weber that he wanted an article to appear in *The Journal* to suggest the partial black ancestry of President Dwight Eisenhower and to call the article "Eisenhower: One Fourth Nigger"![9]

When he started the IHR, McCalden had argued that revisionism was the issue of most importance, and in fact, by the time of McCalden's death in 1991, revisionist history was being distributed by several organizations of the racist right, including Pierce's National Vanguard Press.[10] Revisionist histories denying the mass killing of Jews during World War II by the Nazis had been gaining in acceptability and importance to leaders of the far right by the early 1990s, and all of the IHR staff and editorial advisors opposed Carto's intention to alter the IHR's focus. Holocaust denial had become the bread and butter of the IHR and was helping to bring the institute wider exposure. But while the issue of Carto's desire to abandon revisionism would widen the gap between Carto and IHR leadership, the most heated battles would be about money.

In 1985, Jean Edison Farrel, a wealthy heir of Thomas Edison, died in Switzerland and designated the IHR as a beneficiary in her will.[11] In 1991, Carto obtained power of attorney to go to Switzerland and settle the Farrel bequest. IHR leaders say that it was at this point that Farrel's gift to the IHR disappeared, and in 1994 the IHR filed suit against Carto for recovery of the $7.5 million bequest. Carto refused to testify, pleading the Fifth Amendment, and then informed current IHR leaders Mark Weber and Ted O'Keefe that they were fired.[12] Carto had other reasons for disliking Weber and O'Keefe, as both had worked for his rival William Pierce in the late 1970s, helping publish his *National Vanguard*.[13] Carto's action outraged Weber and O'Keefe, considering that he had written a letter to an IHR attorney in May of 1993 explaining that he was "an officer and director of Liberty Lobby" but had "no position with LSF except that of sympathizer."[14] The LSF, the Legion for the Survival of Freedom, Inc., acts as the IHR's parent company. It was incorporated in Texas in 1952 as a nonprofit organization. When Carto became involved in the publishing of the *American Mercury* in 1966, the LSF controlled the operations of the magazine. In 1966, Carto was made treasurer of the Legion and absorbed *American Mercury* into his other publications under Noontide Press, and the content of the paper moved farther to the periphery of rightist thought.[15]

By March of 1995, police investigators from the Costa Mesa Police Department in southern California were investigating the apparent fraudulent seizure of the inheritance. On March 22, 1995, a SWAT team raided the southern California estate of Carto, seizing evidence for the investigation of the missing money.[16] Carto charged that the warrant was not valid and that the search and seizure of his property was illegal. In June 1995, a judge ruled that the search had been legal and that detectives could keep the bankbooks, guns, and photographs of Adolph Hitler for their investigation. In November 1996, a Superior Court judge in San Diego awarded the IHR $6.4 million in damages.[17] In response, Carto instigated a wave of lawsuits against the IHR and its staff. By 1998, Carto's Liberty Lobby had to file bankruptcy because of the IHR collection claims. That same year, Willis Carto and his wife Elizabeth declared personal bankruptcy because of the expense of litigation.[18]

In a 1996 interview with Swedish scholar Mattias Gardell, Carto remarked that there was a "Jewish-Plutocratic" conspiracy out to get him. He suggested that it had started with an effort to shut down the IHR, and then the conspirators had moved to "get him in person." Regarding the money, he explained, "There's no way they're going to get anything out of me. I have no bank account. So there is no way."[19] Carto had been accused of embezzlement before. In 1972, William Pierce informed readers of his newspaper *Attack!* that Carto was a "swindler." Pierce charged that Carto was mailing out donation postcards for the American Party with an address that sent contributions directly to him. Pierce labeled Carto a "shadowy wheeler and dealer," an accusation very much in keeping with charges made ten years later by David McCalden and twenty years later by the IHR.[20] Despite his call for the IHR to abandon revisionism, Carto's recent publishing venture, *The Barnes Review,* focuses on revisionist history and eugenics in an attempt to compete with IHR publications.

THE LEGACY OF REVISIONISM

Despite litigation and wars of words, the IHR has stayed alive since its 1978 founding. McCalden was right in his assessment that revisionism, specifically Holocaust revisionism, would be an important tool of the racist right in the last part of the twentieth century and the beginning of the new millennium. When the IHR was founded in 1978, Holocaust denial, or revisionism, had grown significantly in popularity and exposure.[21] Immediately after World War II, many European fascists had refused to accept the heinousness of Nazi war crimes. In their drive to salvage National Socialism, these neofascists had to downplay Nazi atrocities. As early as 1948, French socialist Paul Rassiner began publishing works that questioned the validity of the Holocaust. His 1948 work *Crossing the Line* was the first in a series of books that would question and attempt to discredit the testimonies and eyewitness accounts of Holocaust survivors. While he did not deny in his early works that the gas chambers existed in Nazi death camps or that Jews were killed, he argued that there had been no program of mass extermination, laying the groundwork for one of the basic premises that guides Holocaust revisionism today.[22]

In the United States, Holocaust denial began to take hold and find fertile soil in the extremist right of the 1950s and 60s. Early revisionists of the Holocaust concurred with Rassiner, arguing further that Jewish leaders had created the Holocaust "myth" in order to gain support for the establishment of Israel. In his 1999 work, *American Fuehrer,* Frederick Simonelli argued that American Nazi Party leader George Lincoln Rockwell was, in fact, the first postwar neo-Nazi leader to appreciate the importance of Holocaust denial as a strategy for the movement. Throughout the 1960s, Rockwell worked to popularize denial theories put forth by early Holocaust revisionists.[23]

Simonelli claimed that a German mentor, Bruno Ludtke, introduced Rockwell to the central premises of Holocaust denial and to significant writings by leading European anti-Semites such as Rassiner. Rockwell subsequently used much of this propaganda to popularize the theories of Holocaust denial. Simonelli noted further that the "endurance of the myths Rockwell fostered" about the Holocaust highlights the influence he had on the American racist right. Rockwell believed that National Socialism could be empowered by reshaping the history of the Holocaust.[24]

Many early revisionist publications in America attempted to prove that it was impossible for millions of Jews to have been killed in a Holocaust. Citing World Almanac figures that only 600,000 Jews lived in Germany during World War II, James Madole of the anti-Semitic National Renaissance Party based in New York City, argued that the figure of 6 million Jews killed was grossly overstated. This theory neglected the millions of Polish and Russian Jews placed in the camps.[25]

Benjamin H. Freedman, who donated money for the publication of the anti-Semitic work *Common Sense,* argued in the late 1950s that many of the Jews said to be killed were actually the millions of Jews who emigrated to the United States between 1939 and 1945.[26] In 1954, Freedman wrote a letter to a David Goldstein, LL.D., a Jewish convert to Catholicism who lived in Boston. In this lengthy communication, which was later published in a book titled *Facts Are Facts,* Freedman lambasted Goldstein for encouraging other Jews to convert. He explained that by converting, Jews would be able to infiltrate Christianity and the faith would be used to spread harmful lies and false facts. Freedman argued that in addition to perpetrating the myth that Jesus was a Jew, world Jewry had brainwashed American Christians, allowing them to be "duped by the unholiest hoax in all history."[27] Onetime professor of English Austin App shed light on what Freedman meant in his article "The Elusive Six-Million." App noted that the hoax Freedman had alluded to was the "propagandized myth" that the Nazis "gassed six million Jews."[28]

Freedman's letter, which was circulated widely in the circles of the racist right, was popular not only because of its attacks on Jews but also because he had exposed the "hoax." Leaders of the racist right had long believed that the hoax gave Jews power and further fed their quest for world dominance. In a 1977 book titled *Israel's Five Trillion Dollar Secret,* Curtis Dall of Willis Carto's Liberty Lobby editorial board reviewed Freedman's assertions along with Freedman's earlier work, the *Freedman Report,* written in 1946. Freedman hoped to send the pamphlet to the United Nations in an attempt to expose the dangers of Israel. In the tract, Freedman argued that the state of Israel was a Zionist plot to gain access to the rich minerals of the Dead Sea, which he estimated was worth some $5 trillion.[29]

The idea that Americans and the world had been duped by the great hoax of the Holocaust was expanded in 1976 when Arthur Butz published his pivotal *Hoax of the 20th Century.* Butz, a professor of electrical and computer engineering at Northwestern University, has become one of the most influential promoters of Holocaust denial and serves on the editorial board of the IHR. Although precursors to Butz's book existed, namely the 1974 work of British racist Richard Harwood, *Did Six Million Really Die? The Truth at Last,* and the small American book preceding Harwood's, David Hoggan's *The Myth of the Six Million,* Butz's book remains standard reading for newcomers to the movement. Willis Carto published Hoogan's book in 1963 with a forward by "E. L. Anderson Ph.D.," [Carto] and an appendix of five articles from the *American Mercury* by leading right-wing intellectuals who had various approaches to denying the Holocaust.[30]

Arthur Butz is a major icon in the movement. He grew up in New York City and received his B.S. and M.S. from M.I.T. and a Ph.D. from the University of Minnesota in Control Sciences. Like the older anti-Semitic professor Revilo Oliver, Butz is revered because he still holds his academic position at Northwestern University teaching electrical and computer engineering despite his controversial research.[31] Researchers have noted that what made Butz's book so important was the more-scholarly "veneer" he gave to the Holocaust denial movement. Butz's credentials, as well as his matter-of-fact approach to the subject, made his work appear to be objective research, especially because he is willing to question other denial scholars. After the publication of his book, Butz criticized the work of Richard Harwood, explaining that it was full of "errors of fact."[32] Butz was also willing to concede that hundreds of thousands of Jews may have actually died at the hands of the Nazis. At the IHR conference in May 2000, Butz engaged in a lively debate with prominent French denial advocate Robert Faurisson regarding the number of Jews killed during the war.[33] As Deborah Lipstadt has pointed out, Butz has added a level of scholarly appearance to the Holocaust revisionist movement, although she aptly notes that while "the packaging had changed, the contents remained the same."[34]

IHR supporters and supporters of the revisionist movement consider Butz's dense, hard-to-read book as the bible of the movement. Many denial advocates explain that it was Butz's book that "opened their eyes" to the conspiracy of the Holocaust myth.[35] As important as the book is, it was Hoggan's *Myth of the Six Million* that apparently converted David McCalden to the cause. While he felt that the book was flawed and could be expanded on, McCalden noted that it motivated him to suggest the founding of the IHR in 1978. In addition to organizing a journal to act as a sophisticated forum for Holocaust revisionists such as Butz, McCalden also initiated the revisionist conferences. McCalden wanted the conferences not only to draw attention to the growing revisionist movement but also to resemble academic conferences that are committed to legitimate research and the sharing of ideas.[36]

REVISIONIST CAMARADERIE: THE IHR CONFERENCES

The first IHR conference was held in September 1979 in Los Angles at a small technical school, Northrup University. The conference was the first of its kind, bringing Holocaust revisionist scholars together from as far away as France and Australia. Featured speakers included key figures in the movement such as Arthur Butz and Robert Faurisson, a professor of Classics at the University of Lyon-2. Faurisson seemed to sum up the theme of the conference and the premise of the IHR when he said in 1979, "There were no gas chambers at Auschwitz or anywhere else in wartime Europe. On that I stake my reputation and career."[37] At the first conference, Faurisson contended, as he does now, that the prisoners who died at Auschwitz and were photographed when the camp was freed were the sick and dying prisoners left behind as the Germans evacuated.[38] Carto's *Spotlight* newspaper pointed out that Auschwitz was an important manufacturing center for Germany, and Germans were far more interested in producing material for Hitler's war machine than in gassing potential workers.[39] The logic behind the argument of Faurisson and Carto is that if there were no gas chambers or proof of gas chambers, there could not have been a Holocaust. In fact, Faurisson has argued that his onsite inspections of the rooms at Auschwitz said to be used for the mass gassing of Jews contain no openings for the dispensing of Zyklon-B gas. "No Holes, No Holocaust" has become a movement mantra and was printed on T-shirts worn by conferencegoers at the May 2000 conference.[40]

That first IHR conference in 1979 was dedicated to the memory of Harry Elmer Barnes, who has been designated by academics of the racist right as the "greatest revisionist scholar ever produced in America."[41] The first speaker at the conference, James Martin, was a protégé of Barnes and has been called the "dean of revisionist scholars" since Barnes's death in 1968.[42] Formerly a professor at the University of Michigan, Martin served as the director at Ralph Myles publishers, a small firm specializing in revisionist works. Martin also has ties to the Cato Institute, which serves as the major research institute of the libertarian movement. In 1980, the Cato Institute published a collection of Barnes's essays with a forward by Martin.[43]

Arthur Butz also spoke at the first conference, laying out the main tenets of *The Hoax of the 20th Century*. Butz said of his detailed book that his arguments did not deal with a "complex subject at all," because he had only written "a long book on a simple subject."[44] He explained that it is easy to prove that the Jews in Europe were still there after the war, but what was difficult was getting people to accept these facts. In his confident manner, he even remarked that he had never been able to understand why Jewish and "Zionists" groups have reacted with such hostility to his book. Butz said, "Jews should be elated to discover that large numbers of their people were not deliberately destroyed."[45]

Aging right-wing scholar Austin J. App also spoke at the first conference. App claimed that no German wartime atrocities could ever compare to the Roosevelt administration's Morgenthau Plan, which App called an "official plan to starve 30 million Germans."[46] He went further, suggesting that other atrocities committed against Germans during the war went unnoticed while Zionists "blackmailed" Germany for resources to build a strong Israel. He remarked that Americans should be outraged by this extortion because "we too are captives" of Israeli aggressors, thanks to the work of "hatemongering" organizations such as the ADL.[47]

While the first IHR conference was successful in that it brought much of the intellectual leadership of the racist right together, it was remembered more for a publicity stunt orchestrated by Carto and David McCalden. At the conference it was announced that the IHR would pay $50,000 to anyone who could prove the existence of Nazi gas chambers. McCalden told conference attendees that so many Holocaust witnesses had told contradictory stories that the reward money would most likely go unclaimed for years but that in order to ensure that the reward was disseminated among "survivors of Hitler's gas ovens," word of the offer would be forwarded to all publishers of "so-called witness" books with the request that the alleged witnesses step forward to have their evidence examined.[48] The announcement for the reward was also contained in a special mailing to some 12,000 professional historians, whose names, it turned out, had been purchased by the IHR from the Organization of American Historians (OAH). The

OAH subsequently apologized to its members.[49] In 1990, Holocaust revisionists disrupted the annual meeting of the American Historical Association (AHA), calling for recognition of a book that charged Dwight Eisenhower with the murder of 1 million German prisoners during the war. In December of 1991, the AHA did issue a statement against attempts to deny the Holocaust, noting that "no sensible historian questions that the Holocaust took place."[50]

One year after the first IHR conference in 1979, the reward money had still not been claimed. Then, in 1980, Mel Mermelstein, a survivor of Auschwitz, stepped forward to claim the money. When Mermelstein learned that the judges of his evidence would be IHR associates, he filed a lawsuit against the IHR, Carto, and McCalden, who had used his pseudonym, Lewis Brandon, to offer the reward. In 1985, a Los Angeles Superior Court judge ordered the IHR to pay Mermelstein $90,000, $50,000 for the reward and $40,000 for pain and suffering, which they ended up paying.[51] Despite the loss of money for the IHR, many inside the organization were pleased with the media coverage it generated. In fact, in 1991, a TV movie about the case, *Never Forget,* starring Leonard Nimoy and Dabney Coleman, was aired.[52]

In his November 1981 *Revisionist Newsletter,* McCalden noted that the reward offer had been a publicity stunt. He commented also that the reward announcement was met with almost universal praise within the revisionist movement. Arthur Butz was the notable exception. In response to McCalden's offer, Butz wrote that if litigation followed, it could be disastrous to the IHR. Butz seemed to find the whole incident rather unsophisticated and damaging to the scholarly image he had attempted to bring to the Holocaust debate. He remarked to McCalden that he thought "such was not a scholarly way to proceed in the controversy."[53] He noted further that such "rewards" were "virtually unheard of in academe," and the only comparable project he could think of offhand was when British revisionist David Irving offered $1,000 to anyone who could prove that Hitler ordered "extermination."[54]

McCalden explained that Carto had given him the name of a Hollywood publicist to visit before the first IHR conference to discuss ways to break through the media blackout the IHR was experiencing in its early stages. McCalden noted that the publicist suggested the idea for the reward and that he took the idea to Carto, who "thought it was a splendid idea."[55] After the publicity gimmick of the reward, the IHR began to grow, in the words of McCalden, "by leaps and bounds." Revisionist book titles were published, and in 1980 McCalden created the publishing organ of the IHR, *The Journal of Historical Review.*[56] McCalden also served as editor. *The Journal* is an attractive publication that is designed to highlight the beliefs and writings of right-wing intellectuals, particularly those concerned with debunking the Holocaust. *The Journal* has attempted to give the IHR credibility as an objective research institute whose goals are merely to ferret out the truth of historical events and interpretations. The first issue of *The Journal* featured articles by leading writers in the movement, including Butz and App. The issue also featured an article attacking the validity of photos taken of the death camps.[57]

The Journal has published articles that attempt to validate revisionist arguments about World War II and the Holocaust. For example, Mark Weber, the current director of the IHR, published an article in the mid-1980s that dealt with Civil War prison camps. In that article, Weber explained that Northern claims about prisoner mistreatment in Southern camps were exaggerated and that too much emphasis has been placed on the accounts of witnesses that have been taken as historical truth.[58]

The Journal has been important to the development of the American racist right in that it has established a respectable veneer for the IHR and its subsequent academics. *The Journal* and the IHR present themselves as simply a group of researchers searching for truth. At the Third Revisionist Conference held by the IHR in 1981, Willis Carto explained that the IHR and *The Journal for Historical Review* had been founded for "honest historians to fill the vacuum that exists in historical scholarship."[59] He went farther, noting that "we are here to see that those who wish to use history to serve their own selfish ends are put down by scholarly research."[60]

Amid disputes with Carto, lawsuits, and an arson fire that destroyed the IHR offices in 1984 resulting in damages estimated at $400,000, the IHR continued holding conferences regularly until 1994, when in September, the twelfth conference was held, the last for six years. The 1994 meeting, held in Irvine, California, brought together leading Holocaust revisionists and other right-wing personalities associated with the IHR. Conference attendees heard from such prominent figures as Robert Faurisson, Bradley Smith, and David Irving. In the keynote address, Mark Weber highlighted what he called the growing impact of the IHR and its revisionism. He quoted from Deborah Lipstadt's 1993 book, *Denying the Holocaust,* and Kenneth Stern's work, *Holocaust Denial,* explaining that if mainstream scholars are talking about the IHR, it must be important.[61] Weber also noted that IHR figures such as Bradley Smith had been featured on TV magazine shows such as *48 Hours.* When asked why the IHR spends so much time on the Holocaust, he answered, "Because no one else does," and said that he found it "a pleasure to keep hammering away on this issue because, more obviously than ever, we are winning."[62]

REVISIONISM IN THE NEW MILLENNIUM

Despite Weber's words, the IHR was in serious financial trouble and was battling lawsuits as the 1994 conference was under way. In fact, by the early 1990s, the IHR had faced thirty-six suits in seven years on counts ranging from fraud to embezzlement. Another weekend of "revisionist camaraderie" would not be held until the start of the new millennium. When the Thirteenth IHR Conference was held Memorial Day weekend, May 27–29, 2000, leaders of the IHR were optimistic and talked of the rebirth of the organization and the movement. This conference was also held in Irvine, California, and was a showcase of leading revisionist scholars. The conference attracted open and ardent anti-Semites and neo-Nazis. The best example of this was the presence of Ernst Zundel as a featured speaker. Zundel, a German-born Canadian and neo-Nazi organizer, had come to the revisionist movement seeking the veneer of validity it could offer his anti-Semitism. In addition to high-profile neo-Nazis such as Zundel, several young neo-Nazi skinheads maintained a presence in the back of the room during the opening of the conference. When questioned about their presence at an allegedly academic conference, director Mark Weber commented that they were simply security.[63] A speaker at previous IHR conferences, Zundel brought the revisionist movement a measure of public exposure when he was put on trial in Canada in the 1980s. Zundel had gained notoriety in the late 1970s when he published his bizarre book *UFO's: Nazi Secret Weapons* (1977). The book argued that Hitler and a few faithful Nazis had escaped Allied troops and made it to Antarctica, where they lived in a part of the inner earth. While Zundel later admitted that he did not believe in UFOs or the hollowed-earth theory, the book brought him followers and exposure in the media. Promotion of the book even involved Zundel's attempt to charter an airplane to fly to the secret Nazi hiding spot in Antarctica.[64] Zundel runs his own publishing company, based in Toronto, which has become a main source of Holocaust denial material. In 1984, Zundel was placed on trial in Canada for disseminating false news about the Holocaust through his Samisdat Publishers Ltd. Under the Canadian Human Rights Act, the government can prosecute a person if his words or publications are thought to expose a group to hatred or contempt. Zundel faced two years in prison for disseminating such materials about Jews. Like the IHR conferences, Zundel's trial showcased the major players in the Holocaust denial movement; Robert Faurisson came to Toronto to help with the preparation of Zundel's case. Zundel was convicted in 1985 and sentenced to fifteen months in jail.[65]

By 1987, Zundel was once again on trial in Canada on similar charges. At the second trial, British revisionist David Irving flew to Toronto to assist in the defense and testify on Zundel's behalf. Zundel was able to fund his defense from the proceeds of the sale of his remarkably successful UFO book. True to his dramatic style, Zundel arrived at court during his trial wearing a bulletproof vest, and on one occasion he arrived carrying a giant wooden cross, reflecting his contention that he was being persecuted because of his beliefs. The judge hearing the case ruled that the Holocaust was a fact that could not be disputed. This would be the same decision made by a judge in London twelve years later in a case in which Irving himself was a plaintiff.[66] The May 2000 conference was well attended, by 200 people, due in large part to the attention Holocaust revisionism had received in the popular press because of the Irving trial.[67]

That trial, involving David Irving and Emory University Professor of Jewish Studies Deborah Lipstadt, had concluded just one month before the May 2000 IHR conference. The trial, which received much attention from the press, focused on Irving's suit against Lipstadt for libel. Irving claimed that Lipstadt's calling him "one of the most dangerous spokespersons for Holocaust denial" in her 1993 book *Denying the Holocaust* was libelous.[68] Irving, who has written over thirty books focusing on World War II, had gravitated slowly toward outright denial of the Holocaust by the late 1980s. As a result, Irving's reputation as a historian had been declining before the trial. Although his 1978 work, *Hitler's War,* denied that there was any evidence linking Hitler to the gas chambers or the death camps, Irving still acknowledged that the mass extermination of Jews took place. In fact, Irving challenged the work of German revisionist Ingrid Weckert who, at the Sixth IHR Conference in 1984, argued that anti-German agents and provocateurs motivated the violence of Kristallnacht (Crystal Night) in 1938. IHR literature notes that this type of academic debate among movement scholars proves the IHR's commitment to "intellectual vitality and integrity."[69]

By 1989, however, IHR publications indicated that Irving had given up belief in the "extermination" theory of the Holocaust. In fact, British historian Richard J. Evans, who has critically examined Irving's work, noted that in the 1991 reprint of *Hitler's War,* Irving omitted all references to the mass killings of Jews, reflecting Irving's shift to full-blown Holocaust denial.[70] It was the influential *Luechter Report* that converted Irving to outright denial. The report, written by American Fred Luechter, a self described gas-chamber expert, claimed that there were never any rooms at the Auschwitz or Majdanek camps capable of mass killings. Leuchter apparently spent three days at those sites collecting wall fragments and bricks, which he called forensic samples. He had the samples tested at a lab in Massachusetts and concluded that they were not part of any gas chamber capable of killing millions of people.[71] Irving reprinted *The Luechter Report: An Engineering Report on the Alleged Execution Gas-Chambers at Auschwitz, Birkenau, and Majdanek, Poland* under his own Focal Point Publications in London.[72]

When the Lipstadt/Irving trial started in January 2000, Irving repeated his assertion, like that of other prominent revisionists such as Robert Faurisson, that there were no gas chambers at Auschwitz. Irving claimed that since his interpretation of the fate of the Jews during World War II was true, it was libelous to describe him as a Holocaust denier. In his opening comments, Irving stated his belief that Lipstadt and her publisher, Penguin Press, were part of "an organized international endeavor" to destroy his career.[73] During the trial, Irving called several academics of the right to testify on his behalf, including Robert Faurisson. However, prominent British military historian Sir John Keegan also testified for Irving. While he considered Irving's notion that no Jews were killed in gas chambers at Auschwitz to be "wrongheaded," he also stated that "no historian of the Second World War can afford to ignore Irving."[74] Journalists present at the trial noted that the courtroom looked more like a history lecture than a trial. Irving, who acted as his own counsel, put up a dizzying array of maps and blueprints of Nazi death camps. Irving also held stacks of Nazi documents in his hands as he told the jury that no definite extermination program was issued by Hitler during the war.[75] In fact, defense attorneys for Penguin and Lipstadt asked the Israeli government to release the memoirs of Nazi war criminal Adolph Eichmann to assist with the defense. Israel released the documents that contained the writings of Eichmann while in an Israeli prison in 1961. The papers explained the details of the Nazi plan he helped draft to deport millions of Jews to death camps, refuting Irving's claim that no program to kill Jews had existed during the war.[76]

In April 2000, Judge Charles Gray handed down a 335-page decision that referred to Irving as an anti-Semite and a racist who "deliberately skewed evidence to bring it into line with his political beliefs." The judge concluded that no fair-minded or objective historian could examine the evidence and "doubt the existence of gas chambers at Auschwitz."[77] In addition, Irving was ordered to pay some $3 million of the defendant's trial costs. Judge Gray also noted that Irving had deliberately distorted historical evidence to make his claims. Other historians have agreed. Despite the recognition of prominent academics such as John Keegan, most historians recognize the distortions in Irving's work. In his 2001 work, *Lying About Hitler,* Cambridge historian Richard J. Evans noted that not only was Irving's work bad history, it was also bad *for* history. Evans critically examined the evidence used in Irving's most notable works to argue that Hitler had no knowledge of any plan to exterminate the Jews. In fact, Evans concluded that Irving's book, *The Destruction of Dresden,* was based on a forged Nazi document. Irving later admitted it was a fake.[78] In addition, Evans attacked Irving's book *Hitler's War,* demonstrating that Irving hid vicious statements about Jews made by Nazi leaders in footnotes and mistranslated German passages so that German comments about Jews seemed innocuous.[79] While mainstream historians continue their criticism of Irving, he has enjoyed hero status within the circles of the IHR and with other academics of the American right.

As mentioned, Irving was, in fact, the surprise speaker at the secretive IHR Conference in May 2000. An impressive figure with a dynamic speaking style, Irving has become an important spokesman for the revisionist movement. Irving told the packed conference room that he had trouble entering the United States for the conference. Jokingly, he commented that INS (Immigration and Naturalization Service) officials flagged his name, and they had to contact the Wiesenthal center in Los Angeles before they could take further action. His joke about who controlled America and her agencies received applause and shouts of praise.[80] Irving discussed his trial, explaining that he never stood a chance because powerful Jews had funded the defense. Irving argued further that Judge Gray had already made his decision before hearing the evidence. He went on to say that he understood this to a degree, considering the power and influence of Jewish groups in Britain and the world. Irving told the crowd that the trial should not be seen as a defeat, and he compared his experience to the World War I naval battle of Jutland. He explained that in that battle between the German Navy and the great British fleet, which left both navies decimated, the Germans won only because they reported it first. While he may have been beaten to the punch during the trial by a media machine he felt was out to get him, Irving still did not view the trial as a total defeat.[81]

WORKING FOR VALIDITY IN THE HALLS OF ACADEME

Certainly the IHR did not view the trial as a defeat. The trial brought the issue of Holocaust revisionism and denial into the mainstream press and to university and college campuses. Many in the denial movement had long sought to have debate about the Holocaust taken seriously by mainstream historians. In May of 1991, the American Historical Association adopted a statement into its *Standards of Professional Conduct* that explained that the AHA encourages "educational activities to counter incidents of racist, sexist, anti-Semitic and homophobic behavior (including speech) on school campuses."[82] While also noting the AHA's commitment to free speech, the statement was likely inspired by the efforts in the early 1990s of the IHR and other denial organizations to saturate college campuses with their arguments against the traditional Holocaust history.[83] The keynote speaker at the May 2000 IHR conference, Mark Weber, who is also the director of the institute, noted that the growth of the Internet has helped the movement reach younger, college-age Americans. Coverage of the Irving/Lipstadt trial on various Web sites united those adherents already involved in the moment and introduced revisionism to a new, younger audience.

Bradley Smith, also a speaker at the May 2000 IHR conference and director of The Committee for the Open Debate of the Holocaust (CODOH), had been working for years on this issue. Smith became associated with the IHR in the late 1980s, when he directed the IHR Media Project, a public-relations program to give revisionism a less objectionable tone. Smith was successful at bringing serious attention to the Institute and to Holocaust denial. Smith was profiled in a 1991 *48 Hours* news program as well as in several articles in *The New York Times* and *The Chronicle of Higher Education* that same year. Smith's main objective has been to move debate about the Holocaust story to college campuses across the country. Smith, who claims to have been influenced by reading articles by Robert Faurisson and Butz's *Hoax of the Twentieth Century,* continues to work at getting the theories of such revisionists onto the university campus by sponsoring advertisements in student newspapers.[84]

Smith started his efforts by publishing *Smith's Report* and in the early 1990s began sending ads to student newspapers. Smith would submit a copy of his ad and a check for the required amount to the advertising department of a college paper. Even if the ad was rejected, Smith still drew significant attention from the media. He has differentiated between those writers who use Holocaust revisionism to attack Jews and foster anti-Semitism and people like himself who are interested in the truth.[85] Smith insisted that the search for truth about the Holocaust is not anti-Semitic but that there are "bigots" in the movement. He did not acknowledge that he founded CODOH with Mark Weber, and he served as a contributing editor to the *IHR Newsletter* as early as 1985. This distancing himself from overt anti-Semitism is reflective of a trend that Leonard Zeskind has addressed.[86] Zeskind noted that there has been a general shift among white supremacists away from swastikas and white sheets. William Pierce, Willis Carto, and the IHR recognized the importance of this shift several decades ago. Pierce, for example, never wore the uniform of the American Nazi Party with which he was associated in the 1960s. He preferred instead to write and distribute his ideas in journals and publications of the extreme right.

In 1999, Smith began publishing *The Revisionist.* The publication prints articles that highlight the major arguments of the Holocaust denial movement, including those of notable figures such as Irving. Smith has maintained that the debate about the Holocaust is really about freedom of speech. He has noted that the persecution of those who question the Holocaust was one reason he was drawn to the movement. He argued that the fight against his ads on university campuses underscores concern about "an organized Jewish onslaught against intellectual freedom."[87] He suggested that those who would make this one issue (the Holocaust) a taboo infringe on intellectual freedom and that "no one benefits from a taboo other than those who create and manage it."[88] Smith finds this ironic, considering the participation of many Jews in the struggle for free press and intellectual freedom in America. In fact, Smith noted that as a book dealer in Los Angeles in the 1960s he was jailed for selling the banned Henry Miller work *Tropic of Cancer.* Jews from every walk of life supported his crusade against censorship. Now, because of his association with the revisionist movement, he feels persecuted by these same people.[89] Smith explains that he encourages an open debate on the "Holocaust story" because he feels that it is "filthy—psychologically, intellectually and culturally—to suppress free inquiry on any historical question."[90]

Smith's argument about free expression has won some allies outside the radical right and the revisionist movement. Many libertarians concerned with First Amendment rights and even leftists concerned with freedom of expression have shown mild support, if not for the ideas, then for the right of Smith and the IHR to write and speak.[91] The argument for free expression is also an important strategy for the racist right. Willis Carto and other rightists realized this long before Smith. Carto, present at the development of the IHR, had long claimed that attacks against his Liberty Lobby and publications such as *Spotlight* were attacks against free speech. He shifted the focus away from his anti-Semitic beliefs to being persecuted by "the" liberal media. The attempted intellectual mainstreaming of anti-Semitic rhetoric through organizations such as the IHR and figures such as Butz, Irving, and others has allowed the culture of the American racist right to grow in the new century.

NEW FRIENDS, OLD ENEMIES

Intellectualizing anti-Semitism has also allowed the American racist right to seek out new allies in their fight against Jewish influence in America and the world. Following the September 11 terrorist attacks, William Pierce referred to the terrorists as "very brave people" and praised the extremists responsible for their courage to attack a country they felt was corrupting the world. Pierce wrote the attacks were "retaliation" for the U.S. arming and financing of "Israeli aggression." Pierce stated that Osama bin Laden, the mastermind of the attacks, "exposed the treason" of the U.S. government. He argued that the attacks exposed the dangerous Jewish control of the country, stating, "In the long run that may compensate for the 3,000 American lives that were lost."[92]

Neo-Nazis in Europe also reacted positively to the attacks. In Germany and France, neo-Nazi youths took to the streets in celebration, even burning an American flag. Many students of the American right were confused by such words and actions, noting that for years Arabs had been seen as nonwhite, and thus inferior. However, support for the attacks fit well with the racist rhetoric of Pierce and leaders of the IHR. Pierce and the IHR argued that America had been attacked because of the nation's support for Israel and pandering to Jewish influence in government and society.[93]

Writing just days after the attacks, Mark Weber of the IHR noted that while shocking, the attacks were "predictable." Weber argued the attacks were not unprovoked, as so many Americans would like to believe. He stated that the terrorists who attacked America "were enraged" by America's "decades-long support for Israel and its policies of aggression." Like Pierce, Weber argued the September 11 attacks exposed a dangerous relationship between the U.S. government and Zionist Jews in and out of Israel. Weber stated that more than anything, the attacks would "encourage public awareness" of America's "perverse special relationship with the Jewish ethnostate." Weber noted that the IHR had long ago realized the extent of such a relationship and as an organization had been fighting to expose the danger involved. Weber argued that "through its educational work," the IHR has worked to prevent precisely such horrors as the attacks in New York and Washington, D.C. He went on to state that in the wake of the attacks, the IHR's work "is more important than ever."[94]

From its founding, the IHR reached out to radical Islamic organizations, offering revisionism as justification in attacking the validity of the state of Israel. Radical intellectuals of both the American far right and extremist Muslim organizations found a common bond in a hatred and distrust of world Jewry and the belief that the Holocaust had been used as a manipulative tool in the quest for a Jewish homeland following World War II. The bond between the two sides has grown stronger in the years since the September 11 attacks.

In the mid-1970s, the Pakistan-based World Muslim Congress (WMC) sent Holocaust denial literature to every member of the U.S. Congress and the British parliament. Palestinian writer Issah Nakleh, who was affiliated with the WMC, became an invited speaker at IHR conferences in the United States. Nakleh was also known to read American anti-Semitic newspapers such as Carto's *Spotlight*. Like American neo-Nazi organizations, the WMC attacked both world superpowers during the 1970s and 80s, arguing that both the United States and the Soviet Union served "Zionist interests." At the end of the 1980s, the WMC tempered its anti-American sentiment after the Soviet Union invaded Afghanistan and the United States supported Islamic freedom fighters there. However, after the Soviets pulled out of the country, the WMC again openly criticized the United States.[95]

In 1996, the IHR took pride in the growing number of Muslims around the world who had embraced revisionism in the attack against Israel and Jews around the globe. The Eleventh Annual Revisionist conference took place that year and featured among its speakers a well-known Arab anti-Semite, Ahmed Rami.[96] Rami fled to Sweden in the 1970s from Morocco after the former army general attempted a coup against the government of King Hassan II. Since the late 1980s, Rami has been an outspoken revisionist, arguing that the Holocaust never took place. Once in Sweden, Rami founded *Radio Islam* an anti-Semitic program that featured attacks on Holocaust history. In 1990, the Swedish government shut down the radio program and Rami received six months in prison. Prior to the 1996 revisionist conference, Rami was a featured speaker at the IHR conference in 1992. He eventually started his radio show again with a Web site to complement his efforts to spread the message of revisionism. Although his subsequent efforts were thwarted by Swedish authorities, his Web site still promotes Holocaust denial. In addition to articles attacking Jews as the "rulers" of America, Rami's Web site also carries the full text of the famous anti-Semitic tract *The Protocols of the Elders of Zion*.[97]

In the months before the September 11 attacks, the IHR planned a meeting of international revisionists in Beirut, Lebanon. The meeting was going to be the first of its kind; an IHR-sponsored conference held outside the United States bringing together Holocaust denial spokesmen from around the world. The fact that the conference was planned so close to Israel was no doubt intended to send a message to Jews that the Holocaust denial movement had grown and connected Arab anti-Semites with American neo-Nazis. The meeting, however, did not take place. The U.S. State Department put pressure on the Lebanese government to cancel the meeting. Lebanese newspapers argued that American officials believed that radical Islamic groups such as Hezbollah were involved in the planning of the meeting; however, such ties were never confirmed.[98]

While the connection between the American racist right and radical Islamic groups is tenuous, the American extremist culture may become fertile ground for recruitment by Islamic extremist groups. Islamic terrorists see the September 11 attacks as a strike against American society and government, both of which they believe to be corrupt and evil. The same rhetoric has come from leading American extremists such as those associated with the IHR. In addition, both sides have found common ground in their hatred and distrust of world Jewry. Holocaust denial may continue to serve as tool in the fight against perceived Jewish domination of the world. Just as Islamic terrorist organizations recruit members by preaching fear and hatred of America and its support for Israel, so too has the IHR created a culture of fear in which supporters use Holocaust denial as an intellectual justification for violent acts such as those of September 11, 2001.

ENDNOTES

1. For background on Carto and his various publishing efforts see Frank Mintz, *The Liberty Lobby and the American Right* (Westport, CT: Greenwood Press, 1985); C. H. Simonds, "The Strange Story of Willis Carto," *National Review* (September 10, 1971); and Paul W. Valentine, "Power Base for Hard Right: Wills Carto: Liberty Lobby's Unseen Boss," *Washington Post* (May 16, 1971).
2. *Revisionist Newsletter* 2 (November 1981), 2–3.
3. Ibid.; David McCalden, "A Letter from the Publisher," n.d.
4. McCalden, "A Letter from the Publisher," emphasis on the original.
5. "Carto-IHR Milestones," in *Willis Carto's Hidden Record: Behind the Spotlight/Liberty Lobby Campaign Against the Institute for Historical Review* (Newport Beach: Institute for Historical Review, 1998).
6. *Statecraft* (November/December 1970). Pierce died July 23, 2002, after a brief struggle with cancer. While the National Alliance continues to function, the fate of the "elitist" organization seemed unclear after Pierce's death as two rival leaders emerged. For information on the new leadership of the National Alliance, see Mark Potok, "Divided Alliance," *Intelligence Report* (Winter 2002).
7. Several key figures of the racist right once associated with Carto have acknowledged the use of this alias. See Mintz, *The Liberty Lobby and the American Right,* 75.
8. Mark Weber, personal interview with author, May 28, 2000, Irvine, California.
9. Mark Weber, "Willis Carto's Campaign Against the Institute for Historical Review!" *Criminal Politics* (April 1994).
10. "Carto-IHR Milestones"; David McCalden, "A Letter from the Publisher." (Partial Document, Wilcox Collection)
11. "Carto-IHR Milestones." (Partial Document, Wilcox Collection)
12. "Carto-IHR Milestones"; *Orange County Register,* April 2, 1995; Newport Beach-Costa Mesa *Daily Pilot,* April 1, 1995.
13. Mark Weber explained to the author that he left Pierce's National Alliance when Pierce moved his operations from Arlington, Virginia, to a compound in the remote area of Hillsboro, West Virginia, in August of 1985. Weber felt that Pierce's National Alliance was becoming too "cult-like."
14. Willis Carto to William Hulsy, Esq. May 20, 1993. Letter found at the Wilcox Collection, University of Kansas, Lawrence.
15. *Revisionist Newsletter* 2, (November 1981); "Carto-IHR Milestones." (Partial Document, Wilcox Collection)
16. "Police Raid Homes of Willis Carto and Henry Fischer," IHR News Release, April 4, 1995.
17. *Los Angeles Times,* June 16, 1995, November 16, 1996; Newport Beach-Costa Mesa *Daily Pilot,* June 24, 1995. (Partial Document, Wilcox Collection)
18. San Diego *Union Tribune,* November 16, 1996. *Smith's Report,* 28, December 1996. (Partial Document, Wilcox Collection)
19. Willis Carto to Mattias Gardell, December 22, 1996. Mr. Gardell is a Swedish scholar who has completed extensive interviews with major figures of the American right. He was gracious enough to share excerpts of his interview with Carto with me. See Gardell's *Gods of the Blood: The Pagan Revivial and White Separatism* (Chapel Hill: Duke University Press, 2003).

20. "Swindler Hits American Party," *Attack!* October 1972. The American Party was an attempt by rightists to continue the third-party efforts of George Wallace's American Independent Party. The party called for the abolition of the Federal Reserve and a return to the gold standard. The group also rigidly opposed welfare programs and called for criminal penalties for any "public display of homosexuality." The party's conspiratorialist philosophies attracted the support of extremists such as Carto and Pierce. See *New York Times Magazine,* November 5, 1972, 16.

21. Deborah E. Lipstadt's *Denying the Holocaust: The Growing Assault on Truth and Memory* (New York: Free Press) is the most complete discussion of the arguments presented by the deniers. See also Kenneth Stern's *Holocaust Denial* (New York: American Jewish Committee, 1993).

22. Lipstadt, *Denying the Holocaust,* 51–52.

23. Frederick J. Simonelli, *American Fuehrer: George Lincoln Rockwell and the American Nazi Party* (Urbana: University of Illinois Press, 1999), 107–109.

24. Ibid., 109, 113–14.

25. Lipstadt, *Denying the Holocaust,* 66. For information on James Madole and the American Renaissance Party, see David Harry Bennett, *Party of Fear: From Nativist Movements to the New Right in American History* (New York: Vintage Books, 1995), 324; James H. Madole, "The Program of the National Renaissance Party," *National Renaissance Bulletin* (October 1953), (May 1953). Currently, Swiss revisionist Jurgen Graf has explored the question of what happened to the Jews at Auschwitz. He argues that Auschwitz was a transit camp and that Jews were evacuated to other locations farther east rather than exterminated. See Graf's "What Happened to the Jews Who Were at Auschwitz but Were Not Registered There?," speech given at the Thirteenth Conference of the Institute for Historical Review, Irvine, California, May 27–29, 2000. In October 2004, he went to jail in Switzerland for his claims against the gassing of Jews during World War II. He commented at the May 2000 IHR Conference that Switzerland's law against challenging the 6 million figure and the gas chambers is proof that the country has been "blackmailed by Jews."

26. Lipstadt, *Denying the Holocaust,* 66.

27. Benjamin H. Freedman to David Goldstein, 1954. Letter located at the Wilcox Collection, University of Kansas, Lawrence.

28. Austin J. App, *The Six Million Swindle: Blackmailing the German People for Hard Marks with Fabricated Corpses* (Takoma Park, Maryland: Boniface Press, 1973), 1. For additional arguments used by App to discount the 6 million number, see Austin J. App, "That Elusive Six Million," *American Mercury* (June 1966). App was a prolific writer after World War II, arguing that the German people had been the real victims of the war. He served for several years as the president of the Federation of American Citizens of German Descent. He is well respected in right-wing circles not only for his academic credentials but for the fact that he maintained his academic job while championing Holocaust revisionism. For background on App, see *Autobiography of Austin J. App, Ph.D.: German American Voice for Truth and Justice* (Takoma Park, Maryland: Boniface Press, 1977).

29. Col. Curtis B. Dall, *Israel's Five Trillion Dollar Secret* (Reedy, West Virginia: Liberty Bell Publishers, 1977), introduction. Many in the movement such as Dr. William Pierce and David McCalden alluded to the fact that Dall was an alias for Willis Carto, despite the fact that there is biographical information on Dall in *Israel's Five Trillion Dollar Secret.*

30. Lipstadt, *Denying the Holocaust,* 105–106.

31. Biographical information found on the back cover of Butz's *The Hoax of the Twentieth Century* (Newport Beach, California: Institute for Historical Review, 1992). Biographical information on Oliver can be found in the end pages of the reprint of his 1966 speech, "Conspiracy or Degeneracy," given before the New England Rally for God and Country in Boston, Massachusetts. The speech was also published as *Conspiracy or Degeneracy* (Nedrow, New York: Power Products, 1967). See also the Internet Web site www.revilo-oliver.com, which is maintained by Kevin Alfred Strom of William Pierce's National Alliance; and Mintz, *The Liberty Lobby,* chapter 8.

32. Ibid., 12–13. (Partial Document, Wilcox Collection)

33. Observations made by the author who was in attendance at the Thirteenth Revisionist Conference held May 27–29, 2000, in Irvine, California.

34. Lipstadt, *Denying the Holocaust,* 124. Observations made by the author at the Thirteenth Revisionist Conference sponsored by the IHR, May 27–29, 2000.

35. Comments made to the author by anonymous attendees at the Thirteenth Revisionist Conference.

36. After his break with Carto in 1981, McCalden maintained that the founding of the IHR was his idea and suggested that there was a dire need for "an imprimatur specializing in the publishing of revisionist books." See David McCalden, "A letter from the Publisher"; David McCalden, *Revisionist Newsletter* 2 (November 1981, 2–3.)

37. Quoted in *Spotlight* (September 24, 1979), 14.

38. Ibid.

39. Ibid., 16.

40. Faurisson's arguments were laid out in his speech "Gas Chambers at Auschwitz" at the first IHR Revisionist Conference in 1979. See also Theodore J. O'Keefe, "The Liberation of the Camps: Facts vs. Lies," *The Journal of Historical Review* (July-August 1995), 18–25.

41. *Spotlight* (September 24, 1979), 14.

42. Ibid.

43. Ernest Volkman, *A Legacy of Hate: Anti-Semitism in America* (New York: Franklin Watts, 1982), 90–91.

44. *Spotlight* (September 24, 1979), 15.

45. Ibid.

46. App, *Autobiography,* 63–65.

47. *The Spotlight* (September 24, 1979), 16.

48. Ibid., 14.

49. Volkman, *A Legacy,* 90–91. Also Lipstadt, *Denying the Holocaust,* 205.

50. Quoted in Lipstadt, *Denying the Holocaust,* 204–205; *Chronicle of Higher Education* (January 8, 1992). (Partial Document, Wilcox Collection)

51. "Carto-IHR Milestones," Lipstadt, *Denying the Holocaust,* 140–141.

52. Details of the trial recounted in the *Los Angeles Times,* January 23, 1999, when Mermelstein was promoting a reprint of his 1978 book, *By Bread Alone.* For reviews of the movie, see the *Los Angeles Times,* April 5, 1991. (Partial Document, Wilcox Collection)

53. Arthur Butz to David McCalden, *Revisionist Newsletter* 3, (December 1981).

54. Ibid. The incident involving Irving occurred when he confronted Deborah Lipstadt in Atlanta, where she was speaking to a group about the danger of debating Holocaust deniers publicly. Irving apparently stood up in the audience and challenged Lipstadt's credentials as a historian. He then offered one thousand dollars to anyone who could provide documentary proof of Hitler's involvement in the murdering of Jews. For a retelling of the incident see Ian Buruma, "Blood Libel," *The New Yorker,* April 16, 2001, 83.

55. *Revisionist Newsletter* 2 (November 1981).

56. David McCalden "A Letter from the Publisher."

57. See *The Journal of Historical Review* 1, no. 1 (Spring 1980).

58. Lipstadt, *Denying the Holocaust,* 154.

59. *Spotlight,* December 14, 1981.

60. Ibid.

61. Mark Weber, "Further Progress and Renewed Commitment," adapted from the keynote address at the Twelfth IHR Conference, September 1994. Printed in *The Journal of Historical Review* (November/December 1994), 9–11.

62. Ibid., 11.

63. Observation of the author at the Thirteenth IHR Conference, May 27–29, 2000. Mark Weber to the author, May 28, 2000, Irvine, California.

64. Brad Whitsel, "Ideological Mutation and Millennial Belief in the American Neo-Nazi Movement," *Studies in Conflict and Terrorism* (Spring 2000). Mr. Whitsel interviewed Ernst Zundel on June 19, 1998, in Republic, Pennsylvania, and was gracious enough to make information on the interview available to the author.

65. "Holocaust Zundel Trial Update," flyer from Zundel's Samisdat Publishers, n.d. pg. 6. Tract located at the Wilcox Collection, University of Kansas, Lawrence.

66. For news of the trial, see *Spotlight* (August 13, 1984); "The Great Holocaust Show Trial," *Samisdat News* 1984; *Toronto Star,* June 5 and April 8, 1987 and May 14, 1988. See also *Time Magazine,* February 8, 1987. For a good analysis of the trials, see Lipstadt, *Denying the Holocaust,* 158–163. Zundel's importance in internationalizing the far right is discussed in Michi Ebata, "The Internationalization of the Extreme Right," in *The Extreme Right: Freedom and Security at Risk,* ed. Aurle Braun and Stephen Scheinberg (Boulder, Colorado: Westview Press, 1997).

67. In January 2002, Zundel was put on trial in Canada because of the content of his Internet Web site. Under Canadian law, Zundel was charged with exposing a minority (Jews) to "hatred and contempt." The charge was found unenforceable because the Web site is hosted by an American company. Zundel fled to the United States until immigration officials there arrested him in February 2003. He was then transferred to Canada, where he awaits possible deportation to Germany. As this piece was being written, Zundel had applied for amnesty in Canada, arguing that if sent back to Germany he would surely face arrest because of his Holocaust denial activity.

68. Lipstadt, *Denying the Holocaust,* 181.

69. "Spirited Twelfth IHR Conference Brings Together Leading Revisionist Scholars and Activists," *The Journal of Historical Review* (November/December 1994), 2; Ernest Sommers, "David Irving and the Normalization of Gas Chamber Skepticism," *The Revisionist* (November 1999): 10–12.

70. Richard J. Evans, *Lying About Hitler* (New York: Basic Books, 2001), 112.

71. In 1999, a documentary was made describing the efforts of Fred Leuchter. See *Mr. Death: The Rise and Fall of Fred Leuchter,* directed by Errol Morris, Channel Four Films, 1999. The PBS documentary program *Nova,* which aired on July 21, 2001, centered on the Irving trial.

72. *IHR Newsletter,* 1989. For debates Irving has had with scholars within the movement, see Robert Faurisson, " On Contemporary History and Historiography: A Challenge to David Irving," *Journal of Historical Review* (Winter, 58–70 1984); Lipstadt, *Denying the Holocaust,* 177–181.

73. *New York Times,* January 12, 2000. (Partial Document, Wilcox Collection)

74. Buruma, "Blood Libel," 82. (Partial Document, Wilcox Collection)

75. Ibid.

76. *New York Times,* March 1, 2000. (Partial Document, Wilcox Collection)

77. *The Nation,* May 1, 2000, 5. See also "David Irving and the Future of History," editorial page, *Barnes Review* (May/June 2000).

78. Buruma, "Blood Libel,"86. See Richard J. Evans, *Lying about Hitler* (New York: Basic Books, 2001), 111.

79. Evans, *Lying about Hitler,* 111–113. On the bombing of Dresden, see Evans, chapter 5.

80. Observations made by the author while attending the Thirteenth IHR Conference held in Irvine, California, May 27–29, 2000.

81. Ibid.

82. "Statement on Discrimination and Harassment in Academia," in the *1999 Statement on Standards of Professional Conduct* published by the American Historical Association.

83. Ibid.

84. For background on Smith, see his *Confessions of a Holocaust Revisionist* (Self-Published, 1988), See also Lipstadt, *Denying the Holocaust,* chapter 10; Kenneth S. Stern, *Holocaust Denial* (New York: American Jewish Committee, 1993), 14–16.

85. Lipstadt, *Denying the Holocaust,* 183.

86. Ibid., 187.

87. Smith to author, July 9, 2000, e-mail correspondence.

88. Ibid.

89. Bradley R. Smith, "Intellectual Freedom and the Holocaust Controversy," *The Revisionist* (November 1999): 13.

90. Smith to author, July 9, 2000.

91. For example, Laird Wilcox, a student of extremism in the United States and founder of the Wilcox Collection at the University of Kansas, shares this view. As an ardent defender of free speech, he is supportive of the efforts of men such as Bradley Smith even though he may not agree with their assertions. Comments made to the author, June 15, 2000. See Laird Wilcox, *The Watchdogs: A Close Look at Anti-Racist "Watchdog" Groups* (Olathe, Kansas: Editorial Research Service, 1999); Laird Wilcox and John George, *American Extremists: Militias, Supremacists, Klansmen, Communists, and Others* (Amherst, New York: Prometheus Books, 1992).

92. William Pierce, "The Big Lie," *Free Speech* (July 2002); Pierce, "Bad News Good News" *Free Speech* (May 2002).

93. Martin A. Lee, "The Swastika and the Crescent," *Intelligence Report* (Spring 2002).

94. Mark Weber, "Learning from the September 11 Attacks," Institute for Historical Review *News and Views* (September 17, 2001). The article is also available in Arabic on the IHR Web site at http://www.ihr.org.

95. Martin A. Lee, *The Beast Reawakens* (New York: Little, Brown and Company, 1997), 225.

96. "Leading Revisionist Historians and Activists to Meet in October for Eleventh IHR Conference," *IHR Update,* (July/August 1992).

97. Lee, "The Swastika"; "Poisoning the Web: Hatred Online" Anti-Defamation League online publication, available at www.adl.org. See Rami's Web site at www.radioislam.com.

98. Institute for Historical Review *News and Views* (December 18, 2001).

CHAPTER 11

Catastrophic New Age Groups and Public Order

Bradley C. Whitsel
Pennsylvania State University (Fayette Campus)
Uniontown, Pennsylvania, USA

In recent days, a particular variety of religion-inspired separatist group has begun to attract the attention of both scholars and law enforcement agencies. Two general characteristics define these groups. First, such collectivities attempt to create for themselves an internally cohesive and socially insulated style of existence which provides members with a means to psychologically and/or geographically remain apart from environing society. This attempt at "separating" from the outside world may often involve the group's adoption of communalism and the creation of a social structure defined by a high level of member solidarity and charismatic leadership.

This article examines the recent emergence of separatist, countercultural groups observing a disaster-prone view of the future shaped by variations of New Age religion. While these groups have not uniformly adopted violent strategies against outsiders, the 1995 Aum Shinrikyo case should alert authorities to the potential for violent activism that exists in some New Age collectivities during periods when the group is experiencing an episode of stress. Particular attention is given here to the psychodynamic shift, which took place in a Montana-based New Age religious movement as its visions of a forthcoming earthly disaster mobilized the membership to prepare for a cataclysmic event. It is likely that law enforcement agencies will encounter more cases of millennial excitement in catastrophic New Age groups in the near-term future as the approach of the year 2000 stimulates the apocalyptic imaginations of these countercultural movements.

Secondly, these movements adhere to varieties of religious belief which are connected to the occultic, supernatural, and mystical ideas associated with New Age philosophy. The New Age cosmology, which by the 1970s had attracted a popular following, can be traced to earlier theological doctrines. Its predecessors emphasized belief in human transcendence to the godhead through reincarnation, the possession of divine secret wisdom, and communication with evolved entities residing in a realm beyond that of earthly existence.[1] In its modern form, New Age ideology is a syncretic mix of beliefs and attitudes which often includes Eastern religious thought, occult practices, unorthodox "healing techniques," and "consciousness-raising" exercises. As a diffuse philosophical movement with neither a central organizational structure nor a commonly recognized creed, groups in the New Age orbit can vary considerably with respect to guiding tenets.[2] While New Age ideas generally convey a hopeful and forward-looking attitude about the future, a minority following in the movement perceive the days ahead quite differently. This view of the future is tied to images of sweeping terrestrial disasters, events which some New Age adherents believe will precede an expected transition in earthly history.

Since the mid-1990s, a series of incidents have occurred where social collectivities with a New Age orientation have either turned outwardly or inwardly violent. The March 1997 mass suicide of 39 members of Heaven's Gate, an apocalyptic UFO group residing in southern California, was only the most recent expression of an increasingly visible permutation of catastrophic New Ageism existing on the horizons of fringe culture. In accordance with their belief in achieving other-worldly renewal, group members took their own lives with the expectation that they would pass into the "Next Level" above human existence.[3] The group's millennial agitation was spurred by the arrival in winter 1997 of an astronomical occurrence of unusual magnitude—the spectacular Hale-Bopp Comet. Reacting to rumors spread by some UFO believers that the brilliant comet shielded "a companion object" thought to be a spaceship,[4] members of Heaven's Gate seized upon these speculations as a validation of their End-of-the-Age philosophy.

In early fall 1994, a similar event took place when the membership of the Order of the Solar Temple, a New Age group envisioning the onset of an imminent planetary catastrophe, ended their lives at sites in Switzerland and Quebec in order to "liberate" believers from a human condition thought to be corrupted and depraved. The movement, which was organized in the early 1980s as a religious secret society in France, observed an amalgamated mystical theology which integrated reincarnation, astrology, Christian symbols, and occult ritualism. Its leaders later established a survival farm in Quebec in anticipation of a future global apocalypse of uncertain origins. Believing themselves to be the victims of government and media-led conspiracies to destroy the group, 53 of the organization's most faithful followers either committed suicide or were killed as the initial step in the membership's "Transit" to another world. This ritualized journey was undertaken with the belief that the chosen would attain salvation following their earthly departure.[5]

Perhaps most startling of all, however, was the narrowly averted disaster which was played out in the Tokyo subway system on 20 March 1995. At the direction of Shoko

Asahara, leader of the Japanese religious movement Aum Shinrikyo, members of the sect released vials of a lethal nerve gas during rush hour at strategic places along the terminal's line. The attack, which killed twelve and injured 5,000, was intended to serve as a symbol of "the weird time" to come—a phrase Asahara's followers reportedly used to describe the cataclysmic war between good and evil that was believed to begin unfolding near the year 2000.[6] Aum's path to violence was dictated by Asahara's fixation on the apocalypse and its aftermath. Although the group's eclectic religion, comprised of Buddhism, Shinto, Christianity, and New Age occult beliefs, originally stressed the prevention of a prophesied calamity, by the early 1990s, the movement began to prepare for what its leader preached would be the end of civilization.[7]

The activities of the Aum sect broke new ground in that its belief system, unlike that of Heaven's Gate or the Order of the Solar Temple, led it to outward displays of violence against society. Nonetheless, there are sufficient parallels between these cases to make some general observations. First, and most clearly, Heaven's Gate, The Order of the Solar Temple, and Aum Shinrikyo all adhered to a variation of New Age religious belief that embraced a catastrophic perception of the new millennium. This vision of the future departs from the more popularly held New Age outlook. Usually identified by its association with several generic traits, including the rejection of a "repressive" Christianity, belief in reincarnation and karma, and the use of holistic healing and meditation, the New Age community is typically thought to be a philosophically flexible social movement with a peaceful perspective on the future.[8] In its "mainstream" form, the New Age millennial view is progressive and involves the expectation that a collective earthly salvation will come about through human participation in a divine plan.[9]

The concept of mankind's transformation to a higher state of existence has generally dominated popular thinking about the New Age movement. There is, however, a sometimes overlooked aspect to the concept of the millennium which has also shaped the beliefs of some New Age believers. This component of New Age thought relates specifically to its perceptions of the apocalypse and suggests the arrival of a future cleansing period which is believed will bring about sudden, catastrophic changes on earth. In this variation of the New Age vision, the unfolding of the catastrophe involves destructive and threatening scenarios, including predictions of an oncoming global war, government collapse, and the onset of natural disasters such as major earthquakes, droughts, and floods.[10]

Such ideas, of course, do not necessarily compel violent activism. Yet under ideal environmental circumstances (such as those created by the culture-defying separatist community), impressions of a future apocalypse may dominate the outlook of the group and ultimately lead it to employ violence as a means of furthering its goals. In the cases of Heaven's Gate, The Order of the Solar Temple, and Aum Shinrikyo, violence was arrived at as a group strategy because each existed in an ideological environment which blended dualistic, esoteric belief with a condition of psychological separatism from the larger society. These features of group life conform to the "cultic milieu" concept advanced by British sociologist Colin Campbell. Describing the style of mind associated with a countercultural movement's adherence to unconventional, or rejected, knowledge, the term suggests a distinctive and idiosyncratic social construction of ideas. This means of looking at the world approximates a reverse image of accepted knowledge and its sources, upon which the general society relies. Whereas conventional religion, the state, media, and institutions of higher learning "produce" information and ideas that are received and accepted by the society at large, these sources are rejected in the cultic milieu as corrupted and misleading.[11] In such a thought world the norms for orthodox knowledge are displaced by the conviction that "the truth" resides in more remote and secretive places.[12] Thus, conspiracies, the occult, and the pseudo-scientific become elevated to a level of importance corresponding to the role assumed by mainstream knowledge in general society. Gaining expression through a subculture of individual believers, groups, and a network of communication, the cultic milieu represents an "underground" culture severed from the prevailing currents of social thought.[13]

CATASTROPHE AND THE CULTIC MILIEU

Catastrophically-oriented millennial beliefs are peculiarly well suited for the cultic milieu in which they percolate. Divorced psychologically, and sometimes geographically, from the environing world, groups observing "End of the Age" cosmologies can exist as self-contained social networks in which a close knit communications framework reifies belief and promotes ideological homogeneity. The fact that the group's cosmology is often indecipherable to outsiders may also reinforce the self-imposed barrier used by the community of believers to remain apart from the encompassing culture. Doctrinal impenetrability, in this sense, allows the group to turn increasingly inward (away from the general population) and lock itself into its own information system. This psychological process, which marks the separatist group's relationship with an outside realm of existence, has become more clearly observable in cases appearing during the past few years. Both the Montana Freemen and the Branch Davidians at Mount Carmel followed theological doctrines which established clear boundaries between the Elect and outsiders.[14] While neither group embraced permutations of catastrophic New Age belief, each prophesied the coming Final Battle with cosmic forces of evil and adopted, an insular existence as a means of protecting believers against outside threats.[15]

Experts on such social movements argue that we are likely to see more cases of group-inspired millennial enthusiasm in the immediate future.[16] In part, the suggestive power of a major forthcoming date transformation will assuredly play a role in inspiring some millennialists to act on their plans to reign in their vision of the new golden age. This concept of shifting historical paradigms impacts New Age groups in one of two ways.

Those groups in the progressive New Age camp tend to harbor optimistic views of the future. Representing the dominant outlook of the worldwide New Age community, this perspective stresses the gradual improvement of human society, leading ultimately to a spiritual revolution which ushers in a period of enlightenment and bliss for all of humanity. In this vision, the approaching millennium is eagerly awaited as a time signaling the inevitable transition to a higher stage of human consciousness and a more spiritually advanced world.[17] It is the catastrophic version of New Age ideology, however, which should be seen as a cause for concern. This is especially so when the belief is coupled with factors such as a group's clear desire for societal withdrawal and its adoption of a rigid charismatic/authoritarian leadership structure.

In general, the New Age apocalypse is based on a conviction in the appearance of a near-term cataclysm which will kill off the majority of the human race, leaving the survivors to reshape the world into the millennial kingdom.[18] Such a view, for example, came to dominate the outlook of the Aum Shinrikyo sect and led the group to renounce all ties with a world seen to be degraded and beyond hope for renewal. The group's outright warfare against the environing society came as a consequence of its belief that Armageddon had to arrive before the realization of the new millennium.[19]

The symbolism attached by catastrophic New Age groups to the fast approaching fin de siècle should not be underestimated by police agencies. The past several years have provided us with a glimpse into the psychological construction of reality of at least a handful of millennial communities whose beliefs are inextricably tied to notions of a coming disaster. Some of these social collectivities, much like Heaven's Gate and The Order of the Solar Temple, will probably continue to adopt a strategy of passivity in response to the coming event. In these cases, the threat of outwardly-directed violence by the group against society is minimized since believers will seek to withdraw into the strictly-defined parameters of the community's ideational universe. Here, the greatest potential for violence is of an inward nature. As excitement builds about the salvific symbolism of the new golden age, groups having rejected the prevailing norms and values of the outside world may engage in ritual mass suicide in the furtherance of their objective to "purify" themselves from the perceived dangers of the rapidly declining world.[20]

Although the strategies of passive New Age millennialists may demand attention as a harbinger of future apocalyptic angst, these groups are not motivated to channel their energies toward striking out against the outlying culture. But, as the Aum Shinrikyo case demonstrated, not all religious sects harboring cataclysmic visions of the times ahead will remain passive about their goals. These millenarian communities bear special attention, since outbursts of apocalyptic excitation within the group carry the potential for violence aimed at outsiders.

The cultural underground of the cultic milieu provides violent-prone millenarians with a virtually impenetrable shield behind which their radically dualistic and heterodox interpretations of reality can flourish. Indeed, it is this ideological barrier separating the group from the dominant societal culture which obstructs a plain view of its beliefs and restricts an assessment of its potential for violence. As recent cases show, foreknowledge of millennial violence undertaken by cultic-style collectivities has been, at best, sketchy and limited.[21] Due to certain organizational characteristics which tend to be common among groups in the cultic orbit, including a penchant for psychological "distance" from the general society and a secretive aura,[22] the monitoring of these communities remains difficult. This is especially the case with volatile apocalyptic groups whose doctrines include society-rejecting beliefs requiring a heightened degree of insularity for the movement.

The ability of the catastrophic New Age group to comfortably exist in the cultic underground, and to blend in with the larger fringe subculture, has made its thorough scrutinization a difficult task. In fact, to this point, our knowledge about the violent proclivities of such groups is limited to after-the-fact observations. What is required is a means by which to predict the growth of apocalyptic excitement in groups whose divine imperatives may include the use of violence, or other forms of social disruption, in the furtherance of their millennial dreams.

Because New Age–inspired apocalypticism is a recent social phenomenon, there are few cases upon which to rely for comparative study. Specifically, there is little that we know about the functioning of cultic social systems operating under the strains and pressures of millennial excitement. For example, what group-perceived realities may serve as "triggers" for the community's sudden shift from a posture of patient waiting to a strategy of millennial activism? Surprisingly, few efforts have been made at investigating the in-group processes that take place within the cultic milieu thoughtworld as the perception of imminent, catastrophic change unfolds before the believer.[23] By looking for commonalities among the ways that groups in this orbit responded to millennial-inspired pressures, a predictive frame-work might be developed so as to better discern the impulses of these unusual social networks.

END TIME IN THE CHURCH UNIVERSAL AND TRIUMPHANT

In the author's opinion, the analysis of a strangely overlooked case should help in providing some measure of understanding about the effects of apocalyptic activism in catastrophic New Age groups. The author wishes to make clear that he is not proposing that a single case study of an apocalyptic movement can be used as a fail-safe blueprint for calculating the growth of sudden millennial excitement in New Age collectivities. Rather, his purpose is to examine the events associated with a brief juncture in a New Age movement's history, and to give careful attention to the group psychodynamics involved in its turn to End Time enthusiasm. Most of the same qualities of apocalyptic thought marking recent expressions of catastrophic New Ageism were present in the case under examination. As will be shown, the group's End Time belief was directly linked to the community's long-standing existence in the cultic milieu ideological universe. Like the three apocalyptic social movements mentioned previously, this case is noteworthy because there was clear evidence of a fast-moving transformation in the community's millennial attitude. It is argued that this shift, which propelled the group on a course of frenetic, chiliastic behavior, was rooted in the movement's success in achieving its desired state of psychological withdrawal from the environing world.

In early 1990, a New Age separatist group located in southwestern Montana briefly became the object of national media attention when its members began to prepare themselves to survive a nuclear war. For members of the Church Universal and Triumphant, visions of the apocalypse were not unfamiliar. Led by the charismatic New Age seer, Elizabeth Clare Prophet, the organization had been making dark predictions of the future since the early 1970s when the group was based in Colorado Springs.[24] Following a series of relocations from Colorado to southern California, in 1986 the group purchased a 24,000-acre ranch near Yellowstone National Park, upon which its utopian dream of a New Jerusalem was to be established.[25] The Church's wide-ranging use of disaster imagery became a core component of its message throughout the 1980s. Economic crisis, communism, societal degeneracy, and nuclear war were all treated, with varying fervor, as potential "triggers" for a "world emergency" expected to materialize in the near-term future.[26] Perceiving the world around it in a state of flux, the group found its separatist safe haven in the primal territory of the American northwest, a region believed to be immune from the turbulent conditions the Church thought the world would soon experience.

The organization's new property, the Royal Teton Ranch, offered a measure of group insularity unavailable in Malibu, California, where it formerly had been located. With the presence of social control reduced in sparsely-populated Park-County, Montana (pop. 13,000), and having the advantage of vast territorial holdings to separate itself from outsiders, the Church was far less bound by the regulating effects of the larger society.[27] By extension, the group's new autonomy enabled the crystallization of shared organizational beliefs to take place.

Viewed in a spatial sense, the ranch approximated a group colony where culture-defying beliefs were protected from the encroachment of mainstream ideology by the territorial limits of the Church's lands. With such geographical "barriers" in place, the pressures of social conformity which may have once weighed on the group were minimized. The relative absence of these social control forces on the group in Montana facilitated the further entrenchment of a counter cultural outlook. As a consequence of the group's increased detachment from the larger society, the organization's alternative worldview became solidified in Montana. The way in which this process took shape had to do with changes in the group's communications system. Resulting from the adjustments in the group's spatial relationship with surrounding society, the ranch community became even more reliant upon organizational channels of information. Following a pattern commonly found in utopian communities with a charismatic leadership structure, a close-knit communications framework developed which promoted ideological homogeneity.[28]

Following the move from California, the Church's thoughtworld became less encumbered by competing ideas generated by the cultural mainstream. Finally divorced from the contaminated society it feared, the movement created its separatist utopia in the Montana Rockies. As a consequence of this environmental shift, group doctrine took on a newly purified character. Removed from close contact with outsiders, the Church community became reinvigorated as an apocalyptic movement. As its leader's warnings of future catastrophe became more strident, the membership responded by psychologically preparing for the event.

The process by which the Church transformed itself from a passive survivalist sect to an agitated millennial community merits attention. This transformation was accompanied by observable changes within the group that are common to many social movements exhilarated by the prospects of life in the new millennium. It is these sudden changes in the millennial group's rhetoric and the actions they precipitate at the early stages of the community's excitation phase which should be carefully examined. In the case of the Church Universal and Triumphant, some of these signs were detectable at an early juncture.[29]

Shortly after the move to Montana, Elizabeth Clare Prophet warned her followers of a forthcoming Soviet missile strike on the U.S. that was to take place in early 1990. Prophet's prediction sparked a flurry of activity in the Church. Rushing to prepare for the calamity, members of the organization began the construction of an extensive complex of fallout shelters on and around the Royal Teton Ranch.[30] During the time leading up to the expected nuclear disaster, members exhausted their financial resources purchasing survival gear, medicine, and food supplies in order to accommodate what was anticipated to be a lengthy underground stay.[31] Encouraged by Prophet to come to the Church's ranch to survive the anticipated disaster, approximately 2,000 members of the group residing outside Montana flocked to the site during the late winter months of 1990.[32] By this period, the arrival of Church newcomers into Park County was the focus of national media attention. Press accounts of the unusual event pointed to the membership's fears of worsening earthly conditions, but emphasized particularly the group's concerns about an imminent nuclear war.[33]

The fallout-shelter construction project was undertaken secretly by the Church, which sought to conceal its plans from the surrounding community. However, the 7 July 1989 arrest of two high-ranking members of the group for their part in an illegal weapons buying plan focused immediate attention on the sect and its beliefs. As part of a strategy to provide the organization with defensive capabilities against intruders in the irradiated, post-apocalyptic era, the group's "security chief" and another official attempted to acquire, under a false name, an arsenal of high-tech, semi-automatic weapons sufficient to equip 200 Church members.[34]

Instructively, this active phase of the group's mobilization for the apocalypse was immediately preceded by a sustained period of upheaval in the movement. This interval, which began with the Church's move to Montana in 1986, was initiated by the community's gradual adoption of an increasingly countercultural outlook. Although the Church's attachment to the cultic milieu's ideational universe was established early in its existence, its attraction to conspiratorialism and rigid ideological dualism became more prominent after the resettlement to the Yellowstone region. Circulating within the group's closed information network, conspiracy thinking became pervasive in the community. Appearing frequently in the group's literature during this period, the sub currents of conspiracies operating in the Church all pointed to the existence of a shadowy league of evildoers working in league with Satan.

Bearing close similarities with the shift toward group conspiracism which occurred in the Aum sect in the time before its apocalyptic outburst, the Church's ranch community shaped a siege mentality in which group outsiders were thought to be plotting the movement's eradication. Much like Aum, whose most deeply-committed members also lived in relative isolation from outsiders on group communes,[35] Prophet's following in Montana began to see themselves as a persecuted Elect. In the two years leading up to the time of her prediction for disaster, the basis of the group's reality became grounded in luxuriant and bizarre interpretations of worldly events, all of which helped to hone the organization's catastrophic millennial outlook. Evidence that the community seemed agitated and directed toward a culminating event went curiously unnoticed until only several months before the prophesied calamity. Had outside observers been more insightful, early warning of the group's excited state would have been possible. As early as November 1986, almost immediately after the Church's move from California, group literature disseminated to the organization's worldwide membership made clear Prophet's belief that a major disaster was about to befall the world:

> *You* have every reason *to* believe, *to* be concerned, and *to* be prepared *for* a first strike by the Soviet Union upon these United States. . . . Therefore, secure underground shelters, preserve the *food,* and prepare *to* survive. . . .[36]

Other indications of the group's advanced apocalyptic condition also surfaced well before the membership's mobilization for the 1990 date. At a summer meeting held on the Royal Teton Ranch in 1988, a wide array of apocalyptic themes was addressed by visiting outside "experts" called in by the Church to help confirm its bleak outlook on society and the nearness of a divinely engineered world emergency. Drawing several thousand of Prophet's adherents to Park County, the meeting marked the onset of heightened millennial fervor in the organization. The guest speakers, who were the featured attraction at the gathering, had one thing in common—their renown was based on their appeal to "fringe" audiences thirsty for conspiratorial and heterodox interpretations of global events. Among the rejected knowledge experts delivering lectures to Church members was Antony Sutton, a one-time Hoover Institute Fellow specializing in Soviet military strategy and the alleged activities of elite secret societies believed to be plotting the erosion of American sovereignty,[37] and Linda Moulton-Howe,[38] an independent researcher and writer who produced television documentaries on UFOs and extraterrestrial visitations to earth.[39]

The group's belief structure was anchored in its recognition of threatening foes who worked to bring in the reign of world darkness. This enemy-prone cosmology included both a worldly representation of evil, which took the form of a Leftist-leaning international power elite, and incarnations of an other-worldly nature, such as malevolent aliens.[40] The consequences these thoughts had in determining the group's future actions were twofold. First, the presence (and gradual strengthening) of these ideas perpetuated the Church's sense that it was besieged by powerful enemies on all fronts. Secondly, feelings about world corruption, conspiracies, and social chaos led the group to prepare for the worst. As the Church saw it, the world had bottomed out by the turn of the 1990s, with hope for the arrival of the golden age delayed until after the occurrence of a great cleansing disaster.

The Church's brush with the apocalypse unfolded nonviolently despite its gravitation toward increasingly bizarre forms of enemy-construction and conspiracism—a shift which became potentially explosive when guns became included in the scenario. While Church leaders sought weapons for reasons having to do purely with group self-defense in the post-apocalyptic period,[41] it is unsettling to consider the potential that existed for a sudden outburst of violence. Such an occurrence might hypothetically have taken place in one of two ways. The first possibility would have been for the group to make the transition from a strategy of survivalism (a plan predicated upon weathering the apocalypse and its immediate aftermath) to a more confrontational approach of striking out against outsiders. It is improbable that the group would have arrived at a strategy of violence without the introduction of some triggering event which may have made combat with the surrounding social order seem necessary.[42] Although millennial fear had enveloped the membership, and the group sensed its besiegement by outside foes, Prophet's followers in Montana observed a fundamentally nonviolent theological doctrine which prevented the group from making the philosophical turn from passive to violent millennialism.[43]

The more likely hypothetical scenario for violent conflict on the group's ranch would have involved an intervention by either authorities or members of the surrounding community designed to quell an incident thought to be volatile. In fact, in response to the chaotic atmosphere that pervaded the region in early 1990, such a plan was at least considered. Bob Raney, a state senator from Park County who observed the "frantic behavior" in the Church's community, appealed to Governor Stan Stephans to mobilize state law enforcement agencies in an attempt to stem the group's panic about the prophesied nuclear war. Raney's greatest concern was that county-level law enforcement personnel would not have the necessary manpower to intervene if constituents from his district undertook a posse-style operation against the Church by forcing their way onto the group's property. Raney did not believe that the Church planned to initiate violence, but felt that Park County residents were "confused and scared" about the group's survivalist activities, and thought that an armed conflict could have broken out between group members and outsiders.[44]

After news had broken in July 1989 about the Church's secretive plans to amass an arsenal, the local community and law enforcement agencies kept a wary eye turned toward the activities of the survivalist sect. It is possible that the media's focused scrutiny of the organization during its frenzied apocalyptic period resulted in the Church's self-imposed efforts at arresting its millennial frenzy. At the minimum, the disclosures about the illegal gun-buying plan caused the Church to embark upon a public relations campaign aimed at allaying the fears of Yellowstone-area residents.[45] While the group's members ultimately followed the timetable for Armageddon given by Elizabeth Clare Prophet, and reported to the fallout shelters in preparation for the anticipated nuclear strike on 15 March 1990,[46] this exercise was orchestrated passively and without disturbance to outsiders.

PREEMPTING APOCALYPTIC EXCITEMENT

The Church's nonviolent response to an envisioned disaster provides us with evidence that even armed millenarians may navigate through a period of heightened chiliastic ardor without provoking or being drawn into conflict with the social order. Nonetheless, abundant opportunities for a violent encounter between the group and outsiders were present. Opportunities also existed, however, for the resolution of the episode well before it escalated to dangerous levels. It is astonishing that such an obvious psychodynamic shift in the group went without notice until events reached a near-crisis stage. The oversight appears even more prominent when it is considered that clear signals pointing to the Church's apocalyptic agitation could be seen at least two years prior to the group's attempt at fortifying its defensive capabilities. These signs included the organization's wide dissemination of literature reflecting its growing catastrophic impulses,[47] and revelations made by group defectors to the media about the survivalist program.[48]

The cultic milieu aspects of the Church's worldview, when coupled with detachment from countervailing ideas emanating in mainstream culture, gave rise to the membership's energetic End Time activism. In comparison with other recent New Age groups whose catastrophic beliefs led them to adopt extreme strategies, the Church encountered its vision of Armageddon at a relatively early stage. Believing that the catastrophic transition from the "Age of Pisces" to the "Age of Aquarius" would come as early as 1990,[49] Prophet's group represents an early example of a New Age–inspired movement which readied itself for earthly calamity. Yet, as the increase in similar cases suggests, the general characteristics associated with the Church Universal and Triumphant's catastrophe preparation stage exemplify more than the bizarre occurrences having taken place in a single New Age disaster sect.[50]

In Heaven's Gate and The Order of the Solar Temple, post-incident accounts reveal that each underwent a transformation in terms of its apocalyptic outlook in the time immediately preceding its attempted salvation.[51] With Aum Shinrikyo, the shift toward violent activism in the group's millennial strategy occurred more gradually. Asahara originally believed that he and his followers could ward *off* global disaster by prayer and meditation. But, beginning in the early 1990s, Aum embarked upon a plan of group militarization to defend itself against imagined opponents. Thus, the organization's final decision to adopt an offensive warfare strategy to rid the world of its evils was only a minor deviation from the war-footing plan the cult followed in the years immediately before its attack on the Tokyo subway.[52] During the group's period of mobilization for Armageddon, telltale signs pointing to Aum's militaristic posture and its antipathy for the surrounding social order were visible. Most conspicuously, conspiracism and rigid ideological dualism became even more pervasive in the group's construction of reality as time passed. Blending elements of strident anti-Americanism and science fiction–driven beliefs with the notion that Jewish-led secret societies were plotting against the group, Aum's outlook was shaped by a syncretic mix of heterodox ideas.[53] These beliefs, which remained largely incoherent to those outside the group, expedited Aum's descent on a path to paranoia and total isolation.

Through the detailed examination of groups that have prepared themselves for the advent of a new golden age, it may be possible to anticipate the strategies taken by cultic-style social movements during episodes of millennial enthusiasm. These insights into the unusual group dynamics of catastrophic New Age communities might facilitate the maintenance of public order in two ways. Most importantly, the further analysis of case histories should make apparent the similarities which define the escalation stage of group excitement about the future. With this knowledge at hand, authorities could better assess the prospects for violence and react to the early signs of apocalyptic mobilization before a violent confrontation transpires. In addition, specific attention to the appearance of certain recognizable features distinguishing a potentially hostile millennial cosmology could help to forestall radical outbursts of group activism. In this regard, various indications that the group is headed for a rendezvous with the apocalypse might include the community's dramatic turn to End Time rhetoric, reliance upon sweeping conspiracy theories as the motive forces of history, and evidence that the collectivity is bracing itself for some type of final conflict scenario.

Penetrating the cultic milieu in order to better understand its violent-prone mutations will be a challenging task. Certainly, not all groups in this counter cultural orbit represent threats to public order, and careful discrimination should be used to distinguish between group-held convictions which are merely eccentric from those of a more troubling variety. Furthermore, the difficulty associated with monitoring catastrophic New Age movements is compounded by their ideological detachment from society and frequent adoption of a separatist lifestyle.

The responsibility for distinguishing between passive millennial groups and End Time believers of a more aggressive character ultimately resides with the internal security agencies of the state. The task is troublesome because much remains unknown about the obscure, esoteric beliefs observed by apocalyptists. This problem is complicated since the insular social networks that act as both repositories and conduits for heterodox ideas are features of an underground society, and thus tend to be shielded from public scrutiny. These obstacles present serious problems for law enforcement groups in their efforts at preemptively countering expressions of violent-prone millennialism: The foremost danger involves the abandonment of dispassionate threat assessments and cautionary tactics by police agencies. Such a lapse occurred in the unfortunate mishandling of the Waco episode, the result of which further convinced some apocalyptists that the government sought to exterminate its opponents.[54]

The major flaw in the federal authorities' Waco strategy was that it was ill-suited for adoption against a separatist communal movement which saw validation of its End Time theology in the government's military-style operation. Based upon the use of coercive force combined with psychological warfare tactics, the strategy ignored the role that ideology assumes in groups that have adopted a counter cultural position to that of society. Having removed his followers from a surrounding world believed to be corrupted and nearing its apocalyptic denouement, Koresh readied the residents of Mount Carmel for a war with the armies of the Antichrist. Unfortunately, the actions of the authorities at Waco helped to fulfill Koresh's prophecy. Given the millennial nature of the group's belief system, the FBI's use of aggressive siege tactics and massive force resulted in the further confirmation of the community's eschatological beliefs and the strengthening of its resolve.[55]

In the fiery aftermath of Waco, federal law enforcement officials unveiled a more sophisticated plan that de-emphasized the use of force against countercultural communal movements. The new plan stressed crisis diffusion, an objective to be derived from patient negotiation, turning on-scene directional authority over to crisis management specialists, and, above all, avoiding the appearance of a military operation.[56] Even before its first implementation, which occurred in the spring, 1996 standoff between the FBI and members of the Montana Freemen,[57] it appeared that government officials had begun to consider the use of more innovative, proactive approaches in countering expressions of anti-state anger by groups in the cultic orbit. The opening of dialogue channels between representatives of the various state militias and the FBI, including a proposal made by the agency to promote diplomatic contact with right-wing protest groups,[58] comprises the central part of this proactive strategy.

Would such a strategy be useful to law enforcement officials in their attempts to quell demonstrations of apocalyptic fervor in disaster-prone New Age movements? The answer is uncertain and wholly dependent on the degree to which the group is absorbed with a catastrophic millennial outlook that might precipitate violence with outsiders. In the most extreme cases, ideological dualism, paranoia, and the construction of contrast identities (upon which the group projects the image of "the enemy")[59] become interlocked with theological doctrine. These psychological traits, however, appear to be present in an efflorescent American cultic milieu which includes both religious and secular "camps." In fact, the distinction between their respective dystopian visions of present times may be hard to discern because of the presence in each of a manichaen style which accompanies apocalyptic thought. That some catastrophic New Age religious movements, such as Aum Shiruikyo, mixed theological teachings with images of group persecution similar to those used by secular cultists in the citizen militias and Patriot movement underscores the general likeness of mindset among extreme counterculturalists.[60]

While preemptive diplomatic overtures by police agencies may succeed in defusing potentially violent confrontations with some apocalyptists, perhaps particularly with secular groups whose concerns are dominated by perceptions of their political marginalization, it is unrealistic to assume that the strategy will be universally effective. For those groups that have descended deeply into the alternative reality of the cultic milieu, there is little to be gained from engaging in dialogue with outsiders. Whereas even the most alienated elements of the citizen militias appear to share perceptions about their declining political power and freedoms in American society,[61] the more purely religion-inspired apocalyptists are not motivated by such anxieties. This difference makes proactive approaches by law enforcement a better possibility with secularists, whose antipathy toward the state may at least give police agencies a starting point from which to begin communications about recognizable issues. Finding a common framework for dialogue with religious groups in the catastrophic New Age constellation will be a harder assignment. The disaster-prone cosmologies espoused by such groups minimize any psychological investment believers have in the state or the environing world.

In order to preempt what could be an increased level of millennial enthusiasm in the near-term future, the adoption of a three-tier law enforcement strategy may be useful. The analysis of millennial group literature is an important starting point. Many separatist communities produce and disseminate literature for the consumption of members and for purposes of recruitment. By examining these tracts for evidence of particular developments within the group, including especially indications of sudden changes in its worldview, critical insights into the community's apocalyptic mindset might be achieved. In addition, revelations coming from group defectors can, in some cases, be used to expand law enforcement's knowledge about potentially volatile, catastrophic cults. Although particular discretion must be used when authorities rely on defector statements,[62] these accounts may offer a rare glimpse into the ideological core of the group and may be used to gauge whether an apocalyptic mobilization is underway. Lastly, as the author has stressed, more attention needs to be devoted to past cases of

New Age groups whose golden age visions resulted in extreme manifestations of millennial fervor.

Because we cannot estimate how counter cultural visions will be interpreted psychologically by catastrophic millenarians, it is impossible to determine precisely whether or not the end of the millennium will spark a period of growing apocalyptic excitement by groups preparing for their "rebirth" in the perfect age. However, given the recent spate of activity by New Age social movements expecting the onset of imminent disaster, it would be wise to expect more displays of catastrophic millennial behavior as the year 2000 approaches. The potential consequences of such outbursts oblige scholars and police agencies to expand their efforts at understanding the psychological worldview of disaster-prone groups in the New Age orbit.[63]

ENDNOTES

1. Among the main forebears of New Age belief is Spiritualism, a metaphysical/occult activity of the mid-nineteenth century which emphasized "communication" with the deceased through "mediums." Also included among the theological doctrines which later shaped New Age thought is Theosophy, a complex belief system assimilating aspects of Eastern religions, reincarnation, and stressing humankind's ability to become godlike. For a more comprehensive treatment of these doctrines, see J. Gordon Melton, *Encyclopedia of American Religions,* 2nd ed. (Detroit: Garland Publishing, 1989), 121–124.

2. John Saliba, *Understanding New Religious Movements* (Grand Rapids, MI: William Eerdman Publishing Co., 1995), 23–24.

3. Bill Aldorfer, "A Heaven's Gate Recruiting Session in Colorado," *Skeptical Inquirer,* July/August 1997, 23.

4. Bill Aldorfer, "Art Bell, Heaven's Gate and Journalistic Integrity," *Skeptical Inquirer,* July/August 1997, 23.

5. John Hall, "The Mystical Apocalypse of the Solar Temple," in *Millennium, Messiahs, and Mayhem: Contemporary Apocalyptic Movement,* eds. Thomas Robbins and Susan J. Palmer (New York: Routledge, 1997), 293. As Hall notes, evidence indicates that some members of the Order of the Solar Temple were executed. Those who died at the sites in Switzerland, it appears, were either murdered or otherwise assisted in their suicides. Other members also engaged in ritual suicide after the group's "Transit" in October 1994. In December 1995, 16 members committed suicide in France. This event was shortly followed by five suicides of group members in Quebec.

6. Mark Juergensmeyer, "Terror Mandated by God," *Terrorism and Political Violence,* vol. 9, no. 2 (1997): 18.

7. David Kaplan and Andrew Marshall, *The Cult at the End of the World* (New York: Crown Publishers, 1996), 85–88.

8. J. Gordon Melton, *New Age Encyclopedia* (Detroit: Gale Research; 1988), xiii.

9. Catherine Wessinger, "Millennialism With and Without the Mayhem," in *Millennium, Messiahs, and Mayhem: Contemporary Apocalyptic, Movements,* eds. Thomas Robbins and Susan J. Palmer, 49–51.

10. Melton, *New Age Encyclopedia,* xiii.

11. Michael Barkun, *Religion and the Racist Right: The Origins of the Christian Identity Movement* (Chapel Hill: University of North Carolina Press, 1995), 278.

12. Colin Campbell, "The Cult, the Cultic Milieu, and Secularization," *A Sociological Year-book of Religion in Britain* (London: SCM Press, 1972), 126–130.

13. Barkun, *Religion and the Racist Right,* 247–248.

14. For insights into the worldview of the Montana Freemen, see Jean Rosenfeld, "The Importance of the Analysis of Religion in Avoiding Violent Outcomes: The Justus Freemen Crisis," *Nova Religio,* vol. 1, no. 1 (1997): 72–95.

15. Robert S. Robins and Jerrold M. Post, *Political Paranoia: The Psychopolitics of Hatred* (New Haven: Yale University Press, 1997), 125–130. See for an account of David Koresh's apocalyptic beliefs.

16. Stephen O'Leary, "Seeds of the Apocalypse Are All Around Us," *Los Angeles Times,* 22 April 1997.

17. Melton, *New Age Encyclopedia,* xx.

18. Ibid., xx–xxi.

19. Ian Reader, *A Poisonous Cocktail: Aum Shirikyo's Path to Violence* (Copenhagen: Nordic Institute, 1996), 14.

20. For a description of this belief, see Susan Palmer, "Purity and Danger in the Solar Temple," *Journal of Contemporary Religion,* vol. 11, no. 3 (1996): 308–312.

21. Reader, *A Poisonous Cocktail,* 42–43. In the Aum case, there some indications that the group was mobilizing for an apocalyptic event several years prior to the 1995 gassing of the Tokyo subway.

22. Campbell, "The Cult, the Cultic Milieu, and Secularization," 128.

23. A notable exception is the Jonestown case. See, for example, Mary McCormick Maaga, *Hearing the Voices of Jonestown: Putting a Human Face on an American Tragedy* (Syracuse, NY: Syracuse University Press, 1998), 1–13. Also see John R. Hall, *Gone From the Promised Land: Jonestown in American Cultural History* (New Brunswick, NJ: Transaction, 1989), 175–209. The 900-member Jonestown settlement in Guyana (The People's Temple) observed a theology of apostolic socialism, which Jones derived from a mix of apocalyptic Christianity and socialist ideas. While the group believed the end of the world was imminent, and created a separatist community in Guyana as a means to protect itself from the ravages of the apocalypse, there is little documented evidence to suggest that The People's Temple movement adhered to beliefs commonly associated with New Age ideology.

24. *The History of the Summit Lighthouse,* undated pamphlet produced by the Church Universal and Triumphant. Prior to 1973, the organization was named The Summit Lighthouse.

25. *Pearls of Wisdom,* vol. 24, no. 35 (1981). Weekly publication produced by the Church. The Pearls of Wisdom typically are messages allegedly given by the group's deities, or Ascended Masters, and conveyed by Elizabeth Clare Prophet to the members.

26. Elizabeth Clare Prophet, *Prophecy for the 1980s: The Handwriting on the Wall* (Los Angeles: Summit University Press, 1980), 106–114.

27. I base this evaluation upon a personal interview I conducted with an anonymous member of the organization at the Royal Teton Ranch on 3 July 1994.

28. For a brief treatment of the boundary-control mechanism operating in closed communities with a charismatic leadership style, see Marc Galanter, *Cults: Faith, Healing, and Coercion* (New York: Routledge, 1987), 111–114.

29. "CUT Documents Show Long History of Arms Purchases," *Livingston Enterprise,* 5 March 1990. Among the most glaring signs of the organization's catastrophic millennial outlook was the attempt by two Church leaders to purchase $150,000 worth of semi-automatic weapons under false names in July 1989. Records show that prior to the attempted arms purchase, which was interrupted by federal agents, the group had amassed a weapons inventory of some 110 rifles, shotguns, and pistols.

30. These shelters were built on the Church's ranch and on a tract of Church-owned land located approximately twenty miles away.

31. *The Economist,* "Waiting for the End," 24 March 1990, 37.

32. "CUT Documents Show Long History of Arms Purchase," *Livingston Enterprise,* 5 March 1990. It should be stressed that approximately 700 of the group's most devoted members resided on the Church-owned ranch property at this time. However, the organization had a worldwide mem-

bership believed to number around 25,000. In the time immediately preceding the expected Soviet strike, about 2,000 group members responded to Prophet's call to relocate to Montana. The mass influx of Church newcomers to Park County was the source of considerable alarm among the community observing the Church's millennial activity.

33. "1990s Could be the Decade World Will End—Just Ask Guru Ma," *Chicago Tribune,* 31 December 1989.

34. "Weapons Seizure Grand Jury Probe of New Age Sect," *San Francisco Chronicle,* 17 August 1989.

35. Reader, *A Poisonous Cocktail,* 22–30. Reader indicates that Aum had approximately 10,000 members in Japan by 1995. About 1,200 of the group's most devoted followers lived a renunciate-style existence at several separatist Aum communities.

36. Elizabeth Clare Prophet, *The Astrology of the Four Horsemen* (Livingston, MT: Summit University Press, 1991), 435.

37. Antony Sutton's work on "Establishment" secret societies has attracted a following among Right-wing conspiracists for over two decades. Sutton attributes total global power to a few "insider" organizations (particularly Yale's Skull and Bones Club), and maintains that these elites intend to do away with state sovereignty in their bid for world domination. For additional discussion about Sutton's theories, see Antony Sutton, *The Federal Reserve Conspiracy* (CPA Book Publishers: Boring, OR, 1995), 33–46; and Antony Sutton, *Two Faces of George Bush* (Wiswell Ruffin House: Dresden, NY, 1988), 12–22.

38. *The UFO Connection: Alien Spacecraft and Government Secrecy* (Livingston, MT: Summit University Press, 1988). This is a Church-produced videotape of the panel presentation on UFOs and government cover-ups given at the summer 1988 meeting. Moulton-Howe electrified the Church audience with bizarre tales of extraterrestrials conducting genetic experiments on humans with the secret approval of U.S. government officials.

39. "Freedom 1988," Church promotional literature dated 1 July 1988.

40. For an early organizational statement on the dangers posed by "alien races," see Mark Prophet, *The Soulless Ones: Cloning a Counterfeit Creation* (Los Angeles: Summit University Press, 1966). Mark Prophet was the founder of The Summit Lighthouse (the predecessor to the Church Universal and Triumphant), and the husband of Elizabeth Clare Prophet. Mark Prophet died in 1973, whereupon his spouse assumed the leadership of the organization.

41. "Undercover: Delving Into the Church's Business Practices," *Calgary Herald,* 3 March 1997. Group members were motivated by fears that the community would be attacked by bands of human predators in the chaotic period of societal disruption following the nuclear war. There is no evidence that Prophet's community was planning to use the weapons as part of an "offensive" strategy.

42. Members of the group believed that they had a responsibility *to* ward off the "negative karma" they felt was leading the world to the apocalyptic event. This perceived obligation on the part of the community does not seem consistent with any strategy involving violence. This sentiment was made clear to me in the interviews I conducted with several anonymous Church members at the Royal Teton Ranch on 1 July 1994.

43. For further treatment of these millennial strategies, see Jeffrey Kaplan, *Radical Religion in America: Millenarian Movements from the Far Right to the Children of Noah* (Syracuse, NY: Syracuse University Press, 1997), 166–173.

44. Interview with Montana state senator Bob Raney, December 16, 1995. Raney's concern about the situation suggests that outsiders, responding to fears about the Church's apocalyptic mobilization, were believed to be preparing for a preemptive attack on group members.

45. "Weapons Seizure Jury Probe of New Age Sect," *San Francisco Chronicle,* 17 August 1989.

46. Kelly Smook, "Apocalypse on the Yellowstone," *Going West* (Summer 1995): 41.

47. In a pamphlet mailed to the organization's membership in early 1987, Prophet (speaking through the Archangel Gabriel) said, "The movement is accelerated on the part of the Soviets to move against Europe and to take the United States as well by a first-strike attack." Prophet made

reference to this prediction in an issue of the organization's weekly pamphlet, *The Pearls of Wisdom* vol. 32, no. 17 (2 July 1989).

48. "Weapons Seizure Grand Jury Probe of New Age Sect." *San Francisco Chronicle,* 17 August 1989.

49. Elizabeth Clare Prophet, *Prophecy for the 1980s,* 10.

50. "CUT Looks to Future," *Bozeman Daily Chronicle,* 9 March 1998. It requires attention that since the non-appearance of nuclear war in 1990 the group appears to have adopted a vision of the new millennium which is less catastrophically-inclined.

51. "Former Cultists Warn of Believers Now Adrift," *New York Times,* 2 April 1997. Also see Rodney Perkins and Forrest Jackson, *Cosmic Suicide: The Tragedy and Transcendence of Heaven's Gate* (Dallas, TX: Pentaradial Press, 1997). Although the book by Perkins and Jackson treats the group's millennial beliefs in a journalistic manner, detailed attention is given to the members' excitation as they approached their perceived voyage to the "Next Level."

52. Kaplan and Marshall, *The Cult at the End of the World,* 85.

53. Ibid., 219.

54. Mark Hamm, *Apocalypse in Oklahoma* (Boston: Northeastern University Press, 1996), 117.

55. Michael Barkun, "Reflections After Waco: Millennialists and the State," in *From the Ashes: Making Sense of Waco,* ed. James Lewis (Lanham, MD: Rowman and Littlefield, 1994), 44.

56. Barkun, *Religion and the Racist Right,* 287.

57. The Montana Freemen were an antigovernment, tax-protest group whose beliefs appear to have also been shaped by Christian. Identity, a small, anti-Semitic and racist religious movement with a North American following estimated to range anywhere from 2,000 to 50,000 adherents. Following disputes with local authorities in Montana, which culminated in charges of conspiracy, mail fraud, and threatening government officials being brought against the group's leaders, the Freemen retreated to a 960-acre ranch near Jordan, Montana, where members remained during a protracted standoff with the FBI from late March until mid-June, 1996. Throughout this period, the FBI refrained from adopting Waco-style tactics to extricate the Freemen from their place of refuge. See Rosenfeld, "The Importance of the Analysis of Religion in Avoiding Violent Outcomes," 72–74.

58. James Duffy and Alan Brantley, "Militias: Initiating Contact," *FBI Law Enforcement Bulletin,* July, 1997, 22–26. This article calls for the adoption of a "proactive dialogue" with militia groups. Duffy and Brantley are FBI Special Agents detailed to the Critical Incident Response Group's Crisis Management Unit. The proposal may be found on the internet site: http://www.fbi.gov/publications/leb/1997/july975.htm. See also, "FBI Director Faults Tactics at Sect Siege," *New York Times,* November 1995.

59. Dick Anthony and Thomas Robbins, "Religious Totalism, Violence, and Exemplary Dualism: Beyond the Extrinsic Model," *Terrorism and Political Violence* vol. 7, no. 3 (1995): 26.

60. It is interesting to note that Shoko Asahara's visions of his group's persecution involved the alleged covert efforts by the U.S. government to exterminate the movement. Adopting similar perceptions of the enemy as secular groups in the American cultic milieu, Aum believed that the U.S. government, various esoteric secret societies (such as the Freemasons), and Jews were involved in plots against Aum. See Reader, *A Poisonous Cocktail,* 62. For a brief treatment of Aum's conspiracism, see Mark Mullins, "Aum Shiririkyo as an Apocalyptic Movement," in *Millennium, Messiahs, and Mayhem: Contemporary Apocalyptic Movements,* eds. Thomas Robbins and Susan Palmer, 318. Further evidence that groups in the cultic milieu share a similar "paranoid style" (which may allow both secular and religious counterculturalists to adopt similar forms of psychological dualism) is visible in the case of Heaven's Gate. Reports coming from group defectors indicate that the membership viewed the Waco incident as a harbinger of future government tactics against marginal religious groups. The Waco episode, according to some defectors, excited the group's apocalyptic tendencies. "Secrets of the Cult," *Newsweek,* 14 April 1997.

61. Martin Durham, "Militias, the Patriot Movement, and the Oklahoma City Bombing," *Terrorism and Political Violence,* vol. 8, no. 1 (1996): 65–66.

62. There exists a small body of scholarly literature on defectors from new religious movements and the credibility of their accounts. Many scholars are justifiably skeptical about the "atrocity stories" told by apostates, particularly when financial or emotional incentives appear to be involved. However, in certain cases (especially when accounts can be corroborated by other reports), defector experiences merit serious consideration. For discussion of the veracity of such accounts, see David Bromley and Anson Shupe, *Strange Gods: The Great American Cult Scare* (Boston: Beacon Press, 1981).

63. Brad Whitsel, "The Turner Diaries and Cosmotheism," *Nova Religio: The Journal of Alternative and Emergent Religion;* vol 1, no. 2 (April.1998): 193.

CHAPTER 12

Yesterday's News?: The WMD Terrorism Threat Today

James O. Ellis, III
Memorial Institute for the Prevention of Terrorism,
Oklahoma City, Oklahoma

In the wake of the devastating attacks of September 11, 2001, the U.S. government committed American resources, personnel, and effort to a war on terrorism. In addition to these efforts to stop terrorist organizations with global reach, the United States has set out to reexamine terrorist threats to the American homeland. Among these threats remains the potential for a terrorist attack using weapons of mass destruction (WMD). The international debate on this issue had simmered for several decades prior to these attacks, but surprisingly little had been done to place the threat into context as terrorism and technology have changed over time. In the past, WMD terrorism was a low national security priority since it appeared unfamiliar, unlikely, and difficult to counteract. The issue fell victim to the "natural tendency to put it aside in favor of problems that are more comfortable."[1] The United States did not focus on countering domestic WMD terrorism in earnest until after the influential Tokyo subway sarin attack by Aum Shinrikyo in 1995. Even after this and other attacks, discussion and action have ranged and raged, but many important concerns remain to be addressed.

Uncertainty has been the hallmark of discussions regarding the threat posed by terrorist use of weapons of mass destruction. WMD acquisition and usage "is the result of a complex mix of technical capabilities, motivations, goals, and other factors whose outcome cannot be predicted with any certainty."[2] Estimates about the costs incurred for developing a WMD production capability have ranged from the tens of thousands to the lower millions for chemical and biological weapons and much higher figures for nuclear weapons. Many scholars feel this is out of reach for most terrorist organizations and lone operators, though others point out that terrorists' coffers are "filled by cash generated from enterprises that include such things as legitimate businesses, bank heists, contract assassination, drug dealing, counterfeiting, covert weapons trade, extortion, and soliciting contributions from sympathetic supporters."[3] It is clear that the technical barriers to developing chemical and biological weapons are high, though they are not as high as those for nuclear weapons. Indeed, there is a common feeling that the technical frustrations inherent in developing a nuclear capability might be the real engine behind the growing or continued interest in chemical and biological weapons.[4] The number of people required to produce an effective chemical or biological agent remains a question; Aum Shinrikyo used eighty personnel for its problematic chemical program and fewer than twenty for its failed biological one,[5] but the Alphabet bomber, Muharem Kurbegovic, was able to secure twenty-five pounds of sodium cyanide (the precursor to hydrogen cyanide and tabun nerve agent) and technical material about its weaponization by himself in 1973.[6] Nuclear weapons have proven effects, but radiological weapons appear to be less predictable. Chemical and biological weapons are much more subject to the vagaries of sunlight and ultraviolet radiation, terrain, moderate defensive precautions, weapon stability, temperature, wind speed, inversion conditions, and other meteorological factors,[7] but the nature of the target, the type of attack, and the type of agent used can reduce this unpredictability.[8] With all these variables, it is no wonder that there is a wide divergence between honest estimates of the effectiveness of and difficulties in acquiring chemical and biological weapons, especially when determining the upper limits of their destructive force.[9]

Adding to these problems is the well-known fact that "weapons of mass destruction" are not always massively destructive. "Mass destruction" implies that one weapon can accomplish large-scale, indiscriminate damage equivalent to a huge amount of conventional weapons, and a true WMD should be able to "compress the amount of time and effort needed to kill."[10] Chemical and biological weapons, however, are quite capable of small-scale, focused attacks that do not necessarily spread beyond the target or destroy infrastructure. To reflect the more limited nature of chemical and biological weapons, some feel that the label "WMD" should be dropped in favor of "weapons of mass disruption," "weapons of mass effect,"[11] "weapons of mass casualties,"[12] or simply CBRN (chemical, biological, radiological, and nuclear) weapons.[13] Since much of the current debate over WMD terrorism grew out of the debate over nuclear terrorism in the 1970s and earlier arms control regimes, the appellation "weapon of mass destruction" has subsumed chemical and biological weapons as lesser but related challenges.[14] Much more so than nuclear and large radiological weapons, biological and chemical agents do not become weapons of mass destruction without effective delivery,[15] and they may vary enormously in their destructive effects depending on which specific agent is used.[16] Indeed, simply labeling all biological and chemical weapons as inexpensive "weapons of mass destruction" and the "poor man's nuclear weapons" involves significant psychological effects and misperceptions.[17]

The debate governing the current and future risk of WMD terrorism has bifurcated into two divergent views—the alarmist and the complacent. The alarmist view considers future use of WMD a virtual certainty,[18] is driven by abstract, technology-based assessments,[19] and draws on weapon effects to reason "backward to worst-case scenarios involving their use."[20] The complacent view grounds itself in assumptions about terrorist motivations; is driven by concrete, conservative technological assessments that point out current technological barriers and difficulties;[21] and draws on past terrorist incidents to reason "forward to possibilities of future use by groups with similar resources and motives."[22] As a consequence, the risk of WMD terrorism is "exaggerated as often as it is underestimated,"[23] and there remains "no widely shared consensus accommodating the two views that balances the probability of attacks against the possibility of the consequences."[24] This bifurcation is aided and abetted by a lack of empirical data, incomplete accounts of incidents that record merely what is achieved instead of what is attempted, and the omission of attacks interdicted by law enforcement or military forces abroad.[25]

Budgetary issues now drive much of the WMD terrorism debate. Alarmists have come to view all improvements and funding increases as positive signs that the risk of WMD terrorism is being addressed; complacent analysts have become fiscally conservative and wary of each incremental increase. Alarmists feel that "the better we prepare, through a broad spectrum of antiterrorism and counterterrorism activities, the more likely we are to reach the ideal situation—the deterrence, prevention, or interdiction of any terrorist event before it occurs."[26] Complacents tend to view WMD as "weapons of mass distraction" for government leaders and the military-industrial complex and feel that the current increase in response capabilities is at best "an attempt to overcompensate for previous years of neglect and the dismissal of the domestic terrorist threat, through spending that is divorced from any rigorous appreciation or detailed understanding of current terrorist trends."[27] At worst, they see WMD an effort to exploit the fears of leaders and a public "caught up in the projections of selective media reporting, political anecdotalization, and the images of novelists, film makers, and TV programs."[28] As Congressional purse strings have loosened to improve homeland security in the wake of September 11 and the subsequent anthrax attacks, the debate continues. Dramatic increases in funding are occurring in the absence of a critical analysis, rigorous prioritization, and thorough threat assessment.[29] With so many funds flowing into efforts to counter terrorism, it is worthwhile to flesh out the current threat of WMD terrorism.

To assess the WMD terrorism threat today, we must first review a brief sample of CBRN terrorist acts and attempted acts over the past few decades, including those of Aum Shinrikyo. Second, we need to surmise the most likely types of agents to be used by terrorists in order to gauge the possibility and probability of attacks. Third, we will evaluate the U.S. capabilities to respond to such an attack on the American homeland. Finally, we will conclude by identifying gaps in the current defensive system in order to inspire institutions such as the National Memorial Institute for the Prevention of Terrorism in Oklahoma City and others about filling those needs.

Before leaping into this discussion, it is important to offer a brief word on definitions. According to Title18, United States Code, § 2332a, a weapon of mass destruction is defined as "any explosive, incendiary, or poison gas, bomb, grenade, rocket having a propellant charge of more than four ounces, missile having an explosive or incendiary charge of more than one quarter ounce, mine or device similar to the above, (B) poison gas, (C) any weapon involving a disease organism, or (D) any weapon that is designed to release radiation or radioactivity at a level dangerous to human life." In the United States, "weapons of mass destruction" can refer not only to chemical, biological, radiological, and nuclear weapons but also to large incendiary devices, massive conventional explosives, and even computers or other means used in a cyberattack. For the purposes for this discussion, however, weapons of mass destruction will be limited to chemical, biological, radiological, and nuclear weapons (CBRN) and to "potential terrorist attacks on industrial chemical facilities that do not necessarily involve an actual CBRN weapon, where the purpose is to engineer the hazardous release of a toxic gas or gases as a means to kill and injure surrounding populations" or similar attacks on nuclear reactors, biological laboratories, food, drugs, or water.[30] Despite common suppositions, there is no exclusive list of clearly identified "chemical weapons"; indeed, there are thousands of industrial and many more organophosphorus and carbamate ester candidate agents.[31] Pesticides and other substances may also be used as improvised chemical weapons. Therefore, for our purposes a *chemical weapon* is any chemical substance that is actively used to cause death, temporary incapacitation, or permanent harm to humans, animals, or plants through its chemical action or byproducts. Likewise, a *biological weapon* includes any living organism or product derived from an organism that is actively used to cause death, temporary incapacitation, or permanent harm to humans, animals, or plants, including pathogenic bacteria, rickettsia, viruses, toxins, ionophores, bioregulators, and more. A *radiological weapon* consists of radioactive material dispersed or weaponized to cause injury or damage without achieving atomic fission or fusion. A *nuclear weapon* is a weapon that relies on atomic fission or fusion to produce enormous amounts of radiation, thermal blast, radioactive fallout, and/or an electromagnetic pulse.

A Brief History of CBRN Terrorist Acts and Attempts

A survey of the terrorism literature supports many reasons why terrorists resort to CBRN weapons. A list of rationales would include:

to cause mass casualties[49]

to gain widespread publicity[50]

to gain notoriety and distinguish themselves[51]

to cause economic impact[52]

to benefit from their potency[53]

to negotiate from a position of unsurpassed strength[54]

to undermine the state[55]

to instill unique fear or panic[56]

to demonstrate technical competence[57]

to avoid traditional antiterrorist detectors[58]

to imitate others[59]

to destroy a demonized enemy[60]

to destroy an ethnic or racial enemy[61]

to mimic divine wrath out of apocalyptic belief[62]

to incapacitate rather than kill victims[63]

to assassinate a target discreetly[64]

to capitalize on the anonymity and covert nature of CBRN[65]

for financial gain[66]

out of desperation[67]

to strengthen a claim of sovereignty by taking on the trappings of a state[68]

to change core constitutive principles[69]

to indulge one's curiosity[70]

to indulge a homicidal psychosis[71]

out of fascination with military-grade weapons[72]

for personal reasons[73]

out of revenge from similar attacks[74]

out of nihilism[75]

as a religious imperative (i.e., to kill without shedding blood)[76]

There is little evidence that classically styled political terrorists sought to use these weapons,[77] but the advent of new types of terrorists interested in indiscriminate and lethal attacks makes the potential for CBRN terrorism "the most striking new development in terrorism in the years and decades to come."[78]

Many types of groups and individuals have plotted and executed attacks on chemical and nuclear facilities and with CBRN weapons.

Selected WMD Terrorism Events and Attempts

1946   Avenging Israel's Blood (Dahm Y'Israel Nokeam, or DIN) poisoned Nazi prisoners in Nuremberg, Germany, with arsenic-laced bread in retaliation for wartime atrocities, leading to a reported 2,283 casualties, 207 hospitalizations, and an unknown number of fatalities.[32]

1982   The African National Congress sabotaged two South African nuclear plants causing substantial damage but no casualties, since the reactors were not operational.[33]

1984   Mass poisoning of a local reservoir and several restaurant salad bars using *Salmonella typhimurium* bacteria by followers of the Bhagwan Shree Rajneesh sect in Oregon; there were no fatalities, though the incident did result in 751 cases of enteritis and forty-five hospitalizations.[34]

1985   Sabotage of a nuclear plant's transmission cables by Philippine terrorists.[35]

1989   Plot to blow up Arizona's Palo Verde and California's Diablo Canyon nuclear plants as well as the Rocky Flats nuclear weapons plant in Colorado.[36]

1990   Attempted release of botulinum toxin from three trucks in central Tokyo near the Diet building, near American naval installations at Yokohama and

Yokosuka, and finally at Narita Airport in April by Aum Shinrikyo; no casualties, though the ultimate effects are unknown.[37]

Release of chlorine gas by the Liberation Tigers of Tamil Eelam (LTTE, or Tamil Tigers) in Sri Lanka in June using drums of chlorine taken from a nearby paper mill; resulted in sixty-nine casualties and no fatalities.[38]

1992 German neo-Nazi attempt to pump hydrogen cyanide into a synagogue; no casualties.[39]

1993 Attempted release of botulinum toxin near the Tokyo imperial palace to coincide with the Crown Prince Naruhito's wedding celebration in June by Aum Shinrikyo; no casualties, but the ultimate effects are unknown.[40]

Attempted release of anthrax spores from an industrial sprayer attached to the roof of Aum Shinrikyo's Tokyo headquarters; despite reports of an odor and the deaths of birds and pets, there appear to have been no casualties.[41]

1994 Cyanide poisoning of champagne in Tajikistan resulting in the death of nine Russian soldiers and six civilians and requiring the hospitalization of fifty-three.[42]

Release of 20 kg of sarin nerve gas from a truck at Matsumoto, Japan, in June by Aum Shinrikyo; the attack was aimed at an apartment building housing three judges who were presiding over a trial involving Aum; all three became ill, seven others were killed, and up to 264 were injured (though figures vary).[43]

1995 Attempted release of botulinum toxin from specially designed briefcases at Tokyo's Kasumigaseki subway station on March 15 by Aum Shinrikyo; the attack could have been devastating if the toxin had been put in the briefcases.[44]

Release from eleven packages of sarin nerve gas by Aum Shinrikyo on five Tokyo subway trains during the morning rush hour to converge at the Kasumigaseki central station on March 20; the incident was supposed to generate mass casualties, though the impure sarin and poor dissemination method only killed twelve people and injured some 5,000 others.[45]

Hospitalization of more than 400 Yokohama subway riders suffering from irritated eyes, respiration problems, and dizziness on April 19 after inhaling strange fumes; attributed to Aum Shinrikyo and followed by a similar incident in a Yokohama department store two days later that injured twenty-five more.[46]

Attempted release of binary cyanide gas in a Tokyo subway restroom near a vent with a fan that pipes to a subway platform on May 5; a cleaning woman found the device and foiled the attempt, which was followed by similar incidents in July.[47]

1997 Plot to release large quantities of hydrogen sulfide gas from a Texas refinery to draw attention away from a simultaneous armored car robbery.[48]

2001 A series of anthrax-laden letters received at various government facilities and media corporate headquarters lead to in pulmonary and cutaneous infections and deaths in Florida, New York, Connecticut, and Washington D.C along with secondary infections amongst postal workers and private citizens.

These cases and others are bolstered by many more accounts of terrorists, violent extremists, and state sponsors of terrorism who have acquired or attempted to acquire CBRN weapons. This motley collection ranges all over the spectrum from Identity Christians (The Covenant, the Sword, and the Arm of the Lord), to environmental extremists (R.I.S.E.), to right-wing tax protestors (Minnesota Patriots Council), to Islamic fundamentalists (al Qaeda), to a lone wolf seeking to change American sex laws (the Alphabet Bomber, Muharem Kurbegovic). Of all the terrorist groups and individuals linked to CBRN weapons, however, the primary example is Aum Shinrikyo.

After the Tokyo subway attack in March of 1995, President Bill Clinton made "preventing and managing the consequences of a terrorist attack with a weapon of mass destruction 'the highest priority' for the United States" through Presidential Decision Directive 39.[79] He asked that the American government approach the new terrorist challenges of the twenty-first century "with the same rigor and determination we applied to the toughest security challenges of [the twentieth] century,"[80] and he stated his determination "to see that we have a serious, deliberate, disciplined, long-term response to a legitimate potential threat to the lives and safety of the American people."[81] Clearly, this attack and other events helped shape much of the American dialogue on this issue.

The chemical and biological attacks and attempts by the Japanese religious fringe group Aum Shinrikyo have been a matter of contention between terrorism commentators. The alarmist school points to Aum Shinrikyo's campaign as a dangerous harbinger of more CBRN attacks to come, while the complacency school holds up Aum as an aberration that is proof positive of the enormous technical difficulties with CBRNs. A large body of the most recent opinions rests upon some questionable lessons learned from the case of Aum Shinrikyo. These lessons have led to the view that "if Aum couldn't do it (or do it well), then no one can." After all, if a religious movement with over 50,000 members, a global network, hundreds of millions of dollars in assets, dozens of technicians, and $30 million invested in its chemical and biological programs can't carry out a successful, large-scale attack, how could any smaller group with fewer funds do better? Many have overlooked the fact that "perhaps they were merely incompetent."[82] As one observer points out, "The fact that their intentions were not realized means that we have not yet experienced [CBRN] terrorism that has brought about mass destruction and that projections about the impact of such terrorism remain speculative."[83]

The example of Aum Shinrikyo shows that a group intent on acquiring CBRN capability need not be rational. Before Aum, many terrorism experts took "solace in the belief that terrorists were fundamentally rational"[84] and felt that rationality was the best bulwark against WMD usage and mass casualty attacks. In the wake of September 11, the previous attack on the World Trade Center, the East African embassy bombings, the Oklahoma City bombing, and the case of Aum, it would appear that rational aversion to mass casualties and WMD usage no longer applies to the full gamut of potential terrorists.[85]

Despite Aum's significant investment in its weapons program, there were many factors that ultimately prevented its large-scale success. Even though Aum actively recruited scientists with high technical qualifications and supplied them with a sophisticated facility,[86] scientific life in Aum took place in suboptimal conditions.[87] Life in Aum consisted of extreme sleep deprivation, malnutrition, exhausting physical and mental rituals, putrid living conditions, and coerced, widespread use of hallucinogens.[88] A "paranoid, stressful, and fantasy-prone atmosphere" would naturally "make it difficult for personnel to perform efficiently the careful and demanding work required for a successful program."[89] Though more conventionally organized terrorists may suffer from all of the above conditions, it is doubtful that they would reach the levels seen in Aum.

The Tokyo subway attack was a bumbling affair, and it should not be taken as indicative of the power of CBRN weapons. Perhaps the next large-scale chemical assault will not be carried out eight months before the original plan and involve that which is hastily mixed the day before, diluted, small in quantity, delivered by timid assailants, and primitively disseminated by spilling out of plastic bags.[90] For these reasons, "it would be a grave mistake to assume that the limited damage caused by the Tokyo and Matsumoto attacks is representative of the effects of future attacks."[91] Aum's attempts to use biological weapons were not the best indicators of possible bioterrorism impacts. It should not be lost on observers that all of Aum's biological attempts involved "wet," nonpathogenic preparations sprayed from inappropriate aerosolizing pumps,[92] mistakes that might not be repeated by more savvy terrorists.[93]

Even more, there is little reason to assume that future groups will complicate their acquisition efforts by seeking several types of agent at once. Parallel acquisition is a folly that need not be repeated. Aum sought a host of complex and exotic weapons rather than one or two simple and effective ones.[94] It is unlikely that future groups will waste money and energy on pursuing chemical and biological programs in tandem with earthquake machines, laser weapons, magnetic weapons, and a nuclear capability built from the ground up. In this regard, Aum Shinrikyo again represents how *not* to acquire CBRN capability.

The Aum incident strikingly demonstrates that CBRN attacks do not necessarily mean immediate detection or response. It is now well known that the Tokyo sarin attack was not Aum's first use of chemical weapons against civilians. Aum's previous attack in Matsumoto, Japan, on June 27, 1994 escaped retribution and detection from both Japanese and other intelligence agencies for nine months despite the fact that the incident killed seven people, injured between 150 and 250 people, and killed several animals.[95] Aum's attempts to use biological weapons also went undetected. Despite the group's two anthrax and seven botulinum toxin attempts conducted between 1990 and 1994,[96] Japanese authorities learned of Aum's biological efforts only "after the cult collapsed and former members confessed to police."[97] Despite Aum's size, wealth, international reach, acquisition efforts, public broadcasts of their intentions, and actual attempts and uses of biological and chemical weapons, authorities failed to detect or respond to Aum Shinrikyo, making clear that "intelligence alone cannot be relied upon to provide early warning of weapons acquisition by non-state actors, at least if the groups in question are not under surveillance for other reasons."[98] As well, Aum shows that

WMD usage does not necessarily mean group extinction. Even though the Japanese government ordered Aum disbanded, had all of its assets seized on December 15, 1995, and successfully prosecuted many of its members, Aum Shinrikyo *"is apparently back in operation,* although its plans for further terrorist activity are unclear,"[99] and it retains some 2,000 members under a new leader in Japan.[100]

Perhaps the most important lesson to be gleaned from Aum experience is that unconventional threats may come from groups that have not previously been considered. We simply cannot tell who else will want to acquire a CBRN capability. Besides fringe religious groups, future CBRN terrorists may spring from organized crime syndicates, from an imploded state's security apparatus, from newly liberalizing states, from antiglobalists, from population reductionists, from antitechnologists, from idiosyncratic lone wolves, from single-issue campaigns such as antiabortionism or environmental extremism, from hitherto-unknown splinter groups of traditional terrorist organizations, or from others not on someone's list.[101] It seems clear that it is premature to limit the number and type of groups of concern at this time.[102]

LIKELY AGENTS

Many lists of potential chemical, biological, radiological, and nuclear agents have appeared in various publications, including these below:

Lethal and Incapacitating Chemical Weapons

Nerve Agents

- GA (Tabun)
- GB (Sarin)
- GD (Soman)
- GF
- VX

Vesicants

- H, HD (Mustard)
- CX (Phosgene oxime)
- L (Lexisite)

Cyanide

- AC (Hydrocyanic acid)
- CK (Cyanogen chloride)

Pulmonary Agents

- CG (Phosgene)
- DP (Diphosgene)

Riot Control Agents

- CA (Bromobenzylcyanide)
- CS (2-Chlorobenzylidenemalono Nitrile)
- CN (1-Chloroacetophenone)
- CR (dibenz (b, F)-1:4 Oxazepine)
- DA (diphenylchlorarsine)
- DC (diphenylcyanoaesine)
- DM (diphenylaminearsine)

Opioids
- Carfentanil
- Sufentanil

Anesthetics
- Chloroform
- Cyclopropane
- Ether
- Halothane

Antimuscarinics
- BX

Cholinerics
- Anatoxin A
- Epibatidine
- Nicotine

CDC's List of Restricted Biological Agents

Viruses
- Crimean-Congo hemorrhagic fever virus
- Ebola viruses
- Lassa fever virus
- Rift Valley fever virus
- Tick-borne encephalitis complex viruses
- Variola major virus (Smallpox)
- Yellow fever virus
- Eastern equine encephalitis virus
- Equine morbillivirus
- Marburg virus
- South American hemorrhagic fever viruses (Junin, Machupo, Sabia, Flexal, Guanarito)
- Venezuelan equine encephalitis virus

Bacteria
- *Bacillus anthracis* (Anthrax)
- *Burkholderia* (Pseudomonas) *mallei*
- *Burkholderia* (Pseudomonas) *psuedomallei*
- *Francisella tularensis*
- *Coxiella burnetti*
- *Rickettsia rickettsii*
- *Brucella abortus, Brucella melitensis, Brucella suis*
- *Clostridium botulinum*
- *Yersinia pestis* (Plague)
- *Rickettsia prowazekii*

Fungi

- *Coccidiodes immitis*

Toxins

- Abrin
- Botulinum toxins
- Conotoxins
- Ricin
- Shigatoxin
- Tetrodotoxin
- Aflatoxins
- *Clostridium perfringens* epsilon toxin
- Diacetoxyscirpenol
- Saxitoxin
- Staphylococcal enterotoxins
- T-2 mycotoxin

Office International des Epizooties List A Diseases for Anti-Animal Attacks

- African horse sickness
- Bluetongue
- Contagious bovine pleuropneumonia
- Highly pathogenic avian influenza
- Newcastle disease
- Rift Valley fever
- Sheep pox and goat pox
- Vesicular stomatitis
- African swine fever
- Classical swine fever
- Foot and mouth disease
- Lumpy skin disease
- Peste des petits ruminants
- Rinderpest
- Swine vesicular disease

Anti-Plant Biological Agents from Previous Biowarfare Programs

- Brown grass mosaic virus
- Karnal bunt
- Potato beetles
- Potato tuber decay
- Rice blast fungus
- Turnip weevils
- Wheat stem rust
- Brown leaf rust
- Nematodes
- Potato stock rot
- Potato virus
- Tobacco mosaic virus
- Wheat fungal
- Wheat and barley mosaic streak virus

Radiological Agents

- Americium 241, 243
- Californium 252
- Neptunium 237
- Uranium 235, 238
- Berkelium
- Cuprium
- Plutonium 238-241

Still, much can be done with chlorine and cholera. There is little reason to believe that we know everything about terrorist programs for CBRN acquisition. There are many more possible agents than the classical texts and export controls would suggest. Most of the potential agent lists inventory only agents that have been suitable for military usage. There is little reason to believe that WMD terrorists and others will have such exacting standards for stability, lethality, and predictability. Despite current planning, there are many more prospective biological weapons than anthrax, plague, and botulinum toxin. Any number of bacteria, rickettsia, viruses, toxins, ionophores, bioregulators, and others could play a role. Though technically difficult to isolate, pathogens and biological toxins are widely available in nature.[103] Of course, few biological weapons can cause thousands of casualties, but many are lethal or effective enough to cause considerable disruption and panic. As with chemical weapons, "terrorists and criminals may not use the same agents as those selected by military and biological weapons programs,"[104] so "we have, generally, fewer tools and less information to protect citizens from terrorism than we have to protect a defined military force from the classical biological warfare agents."[105]

There is a high likelihood that terrorists will avoid the problems of weaponization and procurement by using old equipment or improvised agents. Terrorists may eschew complicated aerosol attacks in favor of chemical mines, Livens projectors, smoke candles, and frangible grenades.[106] Mass casualties can also come from improvised industrial chemicals. WMD terrorists may use insecticides such as nicotine sulfate, DFP (diisopropylphosphorofluoridate), parathion, malathion, and TEPP; herbicides such as TCDD (dioxin) and benzidine; or any of the other tens of thousands of poisonous chemicals or 50,000 organophosphates.[107] Several threats to release such improvised weapons have been made to governments, including the case of Commander Nemo of Force Majerus, who tried to extort $15 million from the Cypriot government in exchange for not releasing dioxin in 1987.[108] The availability of improvised chemical, biological, and radiological weapons means that preparedness efforts must improve general response and medical capabilities in addition to countering specific agents and attack scenarios.

Some experts have pointed out that the technical difficulties of acquiring these weapons will make groups less likely to use them. Though weapons of mass destruction may appear to be high-tech, the vast majority of terrorist acts using them have and will continue to be decidedly low-tech, relying on improvised weapons such as pesticides, toxic industrial chemicals, laboratory-grade rather than weapons-grade biological agents, and detonated radiological material. The true future evolution in this area will be how and where the agents will be employed.

LIKELIHOOD OF ATTACKS

Some terrorism commentators have expected and hoped that terrorists would become disillusioned with the overall terrorist tendency to escalate the use of violence. However, terrorists have continually geared their violence for ultimate effect, including mass casualties. Many terrorists no longer want a lot of people watching; instead, they would rather have a lot of people dead. Body count may continue to grow in importance. Rather than traditional political movements, future terrorist actors and actions will increasingly emerge from impoverished and marginalized communities, single-issue causes, idiosyncratic belief systems, violent religious extremist sects, and a reactionary cultural milieu. Terrorists will imagine new methods of deployment that may not be highly lethal but will certainly be psychologically devastating. The outcome of these future events involving CBRN weapons will vary in their impact, depending on the targeting, planning, dissemination, sophistication, and luck of the terrorists. Little has been offered that would show that terrorists no longer have an interest in these types of weapons or attacks.

A peculiar development following the September 11 attacks has been the retrenchment of interest in CBRN terrorism in favor of a "return to basics" for preventing conventional terrorism. CBRN terrorism has been linked—falsely—to an assumption that it involves only mass casualties and doomsday scenarios. While this potential exists, the probability has always favored highly disruptive but still manageable crises that may become unmanageable without proper preparedness and attention to public safety and panic. In other words, a commitment to defend against CBRN terrorism means both an effort to improve capabilities against specific agents and scenarios and progressive development of general response capacity to conventional terrorism and technological or natural disasters. What September 11 and the subsequent anthrax attacks taught us was that there can be no underestimating the creativity, sophistication, or luck of terrorists and that "low probability" cannot be read "no possibility," as it has before. National security and emergency management have always dealt with unlikely eventualities. Though CBRN terrorism may not be predictable, inevitable, or imminent, it cannot be discounted as a serious possibility. Terrorism, particularly CBRN terrorism, has been labeled a low-probability, high-consequence event. September 11 reminded us that the consequences may ultimately be more important than the probability when it comes to preparing for seemingly unlikely eventualities.

Though any future CBRN attack remains "a quintessential low-probability, high-consequence event,"[109] it is possible to distinguish more probable attacks from less probable ones. There is good reason not to focus solely on high-end threats. As Brian Jenkins notes:

> [T]he scenarios projected are invariably worst cases, a fact that makes sense for planning purposes but creates another analytical problem. Because risk equals the probability of the event times its consequences, focusing on only the most horrendous events overwhelms any estimates of their likelihood. The possibility of occurrence becomes irrelevant unless the threat can be dismissed with a high degree of confidence—of course, it cannot.[110]

Smaller incidents may pose unique challenges. They will probably involve discrete uses of a CBRN weapon whose effects would be geographically limited in scope with less actual physical damage and fewer casualties. Improvised weapons and lower-consequence events, however, can still result in moderate to high casualties, disruption of infrastructure and services, and a loss of millions of dollars.[111] It is not guaranteed that preparations for large-scale incidents will necessarily guard against lower-consequence attacks, since a smaller-scale attack might require only a state and local response.[112] Federal capabilities might be of little use in these circumstances. Emphasizing the high-end possibilities might neglect, or at least fail to optimize, state and local response capabilities to deal with more probable incidents.[113]

Along with the use of improvised CBRN weapons, terrorists are more likely to attempt sabotage. Sabotage has long been a concern in the debate over nuclear terrorism. Indeed, there have been several attempts to attack nuclear facilities, including a 1982 attack by the terrorist wing of the African National Congress against two South African nuclear reactors (which were luckily not operational) and a 1985 sabotage of a nuclear plant's transmission cables by Philippine terrorists.[114] A hazardous release of toxic gases or experimental biological agents could easily result in mass casualties, and this type of sabotage bypasses the expense and difficulty in acquiring enormous amounts of toxic materials. The Bhopal, India, industrial disaster is instructive here. On the night of December 2, 1984, a disgruntled employee at the Union Carbide plant precipitated a chemical storage tank explosion simply by adding water to it, which led to a massive release of some 40 tons of methyl isocyanate, killing between 3,800 and 6,000 people and injuring some 11,000.[115] It is still not clear exactly how many people were killed or injured in the incident. There has been considerable discussion among terrorists of conducting similar attacks. One American right-wing group targeted a Texas refinery in an attempt to release large quantities of hydrogen sulfide gas, but the attack was thwarted.[116] Other groups have openly contemplated attacks involving flammable materials such as propane, hydrogen, or ethylene oxide; toxic gasses such as hydrogen sulfide or chlorine; and carcinogens such as etyhlene dibromide.[117] Mass poisoning poses similar risks.

Some of the American chemical attacks and most of the biological ones have involved poisoning to bypass the problems of weaponization. The still-unsolved 1982 Tylenol poisoning with cyanide killed only seven people but was very effective in creating mass panic, spawning copycat threats, and changing how food and medicine are packaged in the United States and abroad.[118] Biological attacks using common, food-borne pathogens have also had an impact. The best example of such an incident was the case of Bhagwan Shree Rajneesh, an international religious group in the town of The Dalles, Oregon. The religious fringe group was involved in a land dispute over the incorporation of their city, Rajneeshpuram, and it felt the outcome of the November 6, 1984 election for county commissioner would be pivotal to their case. They decided that they would attempt to poison the townsfolk to swing the election in their favor. In September 1984, the Rajneeshees proceeded to poison ten restaurants, one grocery store, and several doorknobs and urinal handles with *S. Typhimurium* to cause nonlethal cases of salmonella gastroenteritis.[119] At least 751 people were affected and forty-five people were hospitalized, ranging in age from newborn to 87 years old.[120] What is more amazing is that this was merely a test run before the larger attempt to poison the voters by tainting the town's water supply for the November elections.[121] Like Aum Shinrikyo, it took more than a year and the confessions of some commune members to link the Rajneeshees with the outbreak. Any threat assessment regarding CBRN terrorism must take into consideration the probability of sabotage and mass poisoning.

Terrorists are likely to gravitate toward the softest and most vulnerable targets, especially food, medicine, and agriculture. By shaking the population's faith in the security of the food and pharmaceutical sectors, terrorists would wreak havoc on the American economy.

Some experts have overlooked the area of agricultural terrorism in a mistaken belief that people will not be affected. Some animal and plant diseases can also cause human fatalities. The 1999 Malaysian outbreak of a swine fever, a new Nipah virus, killed over sixty people and led to the destruction of 300,000 pigs (13 percent of Malaysia's stock).[122] Terrorists who are averse to mass casualties may attempt massive economic damage by smuggling foot-and-mouth (FMD) disease or a potent swine flu into the country. FMD is a particularly pernicious viral threat that, when aimed at the 2 percent of cattle feedlots that process over 70 percent of the nation's beef, could decimate large sectors of U.S. agribusiness. FMD takes time to vaccinate against, and antibiotics are useless against it, since it is not a bacterial disease. Much of the nation's stock would have to be culled, and strict travel biosafety measures, similar to those invoked in the British countryside, would have to be put in place. The 1996 outbreak of the fungal pathogen Karnal Bunt cost the U.S. wheat industry nearly $7 billion from mandatory export restrictions, quarantines, and embargos.[123]

Terrorist attacks on critical infrastructure and associated systems would also cause tremendous damage, as much of these assets are impossible to defend with a high degree of confidence. Damaging a pipeline will not cause enormous fatalities, if any at all, but these types of attacks are pernicious and expensive. Over time, destruction of fuel depots, contamination or inactivation of critical transportation nodes, disabling of electric grids, downing of the public telephone networks, and lengthy disruption of vital commerce channels will pose great risks for American society as the costs of doing business and providing security mushroom. The variety of agents and higher-probability/lower-consequence attack scenarios translate into the need for a well-rounded, highly flexible, and robust homeland security system aimed at deterring, preventing, or mitigating the effects of different manners of terrorist attack.

U.S. CAPABILITIES TO COUNTER CBRN TERRORISM

The ability to prevent or preempt terrorist attacks presupposes good intelligence about terrorist organizations and activities.[124] Though intelligence is more important than ever, the changes in the nature of terrorism have made the collection of that intelligence exceedingly difficult. Experts across academia, business, and government sectors have indicated that terrorism is becoming more amorphous, more complex, more sporadic, more amateurish, more difficult to predict, more difficult to trace, and more difficult to observe and analyze. Therefore, the terrorist challenge, as a whole, is very tough and growing tougher. CBRN terrorism implies its own difficulties, and intelligence agencies face a tough row to hoe in this regard. John C. Gannon, chairman of the National Intelligence Council and a former deputy director for intelligence at the CIA, thinks that "the current expectation that U.S. Intelligence will be able to thwart future BCW attacks is exceedingly high."[125] He believes that terrorists' "growing ability to cloak their BCW capabilities and intentions mean[s] that the odds of a successful attack are increasing despite our vigilance."[126] Improvements in denial and deception techniques mean that "non-state actors are improving their ability to hide faster than states are improving their ability to seek."[127] Several structural problems hinder U.S. intelligence efforts against CBRN terrorism.

Perhaps the biggest hurdle remains how the American intelligence apparatus has been organized. American intelligence has been heavily oriented toward state actors, so it is still in the early stages of learning how to monitor and control nonstate actors and their WMD acquisition.[128] U.S. collection and analysis systems "were designed principally to target industrial-scale military [CBRN] programs, particularly those in the Soviet Union."[129] This is inappropriate for fighting terrorist acquisitions of CBRN weapons, which are easier to conceal than the efforts of a state. Terrorists do not require high sophistication and massive industrial infrastructure, since they will probably only seek equipment for one-time use.[130] These facilities will be much smaller and more improvised. The shrinking size and organizational self-sufficiency of potential CBRN terrorist groups and individuals has proven a challenge to the bulky machinery of intelligence agencies. Lone operators are particularly troublesome for the intelligence surveillance net;[131] because they work alone, "there will not be any communications between members of a group to intercept, nor will there be any terrorist group members to arrest and gain further information about planned operations."[132]

Another reason that American intelligence has difficulty in countering CBRN terrorism is the fragmentation of the intelligence community and its responsibilities. The United States simply "lacks a place to perform 'all-source' planning for collecting information on potential catastrophic terrorism;"[133] no principal agency has lead responsibility for detecting or identifying conventional or CBRN terrorist attacks.[134] Indeed, with the severance of responsibility between the CIA and the FBI, there can be no single authority in this matter without a fundamental reorganization of the intelligence community. Further, our overreliance on technical intelligence—information gathered using electronics, signals, satellite imagery, or other technological methods—is heavily reliant on cueing from some other sources, and without this cueing, technical means are virtually useless.[135]

The failure to prevent Aum Shinrikyo's subway attack is widely regarded as a massive intelligence failure. Many indicators should have highlighted the danger. Aum Shinrikyo made many purchases that were indicative of a large-scale effort to acquire CBRN capability. These include air-filtration media for "clean rooms"; various forms of molecular-modeling software; laser equipment; serum bottles; an extraordinary amount of peptone to cultivate bacteria (at least 2,880 liters); 400 gas masks from a company in San Jose, California; training and weapons in Russia and elsewhere; and attempts to buy export-controlled equipment related to nuclear proliferation.[136] There were also many instances that linked Aum Shinrikyo directly to chemical weapons. Examples of incidents that should have allowed intelligence agencies to predict Aum's involvement in future chemical attacks include the purchase of Banjawarn sheep station in Australia on which Aum tested sarin (allegedly killing twenty sheep and accompanied by local reports of Aum members driving around the area in white protective suits and helmets) in 1993; dozens of complaints to the police of suspicious fumes from people living near Aum facilities in Koto in July 1993; seven deaths and over 150 injuries from sarin in Matsumoto on June 27, 1994; multiple reports of mysterious gases in Kamikuishiki in July 1994; the 250 people injured from "unknown fumes" in western Japan on September 1, 1994; the discovery of sarin byproducts in Kamikuishiki in December 1994; public discussions of sarin by Aum on Russian radio, in magazines, and on the Internet; accusations by Aum Shinrikyo that one of its company presidents was leaking sarin into Aum buildings in Kamikuishiki on January 4, 1995; the twenty people hospitalized from fumes in a Yokohama underground train on March 5, 1995; and the aborted botulinum attack using three attaché cases with fans on March 15, 1995.[137] On top of all those, Aum reportedly handed out flyers in Tokyo asking "What will hit Japan next?" with a map of the Tokyo subway system below it the day before the attack.[138] It seems hard to justify this level of carelessness on the part of Japanese, American, and Russian intelligence agencies. The lack of knowledge by both intelligence and law enforcement about Aum should remind us that other groups may remain undetected and therefore unimpeded.[139]

While it is morally unacceptable to promote response capabilities over solid prevention and preemption, it is politically unacceptable to believe prevention and preemption will always work. We have recently learned that preventive and preemptive strategies are not satisfactory by themselves or in concert and that emergency management has not been satisfactorily explored as an additional mitigating component of terrorism policy. Analysts and policymakers must accept that massively destructive attacks may get through traditional antiterrorism and counterterrorism defenses. Therefore, emergency management must play a larger complementary role in the American strategy for homeland security. This includes a recommitment to CBRN capabilities for "first responders," mental health officials, and public health officials.

First Responders

The current state of the art in detection of CBRN agents hinders the abilities of emergency-response teams, especially in regard to biological agents. A reliable, robust, and rapid system to detect biological attacks remains elusive. Too many agents, too many complexities, and too many similar microorganisms that are constantly present in the environment hinder real-time detection of biological agents.[140] Unfortunately, humans and animals remain "the most sensitive, or the only, detectors of a biological attack."[141] Similar problems characterize chemical-weapon recognition. Current chemical-agent detection systems, including military models, give excessive false positives and false negatives.[142] Even basic agent-specific detectors and detection papers have been shown to register petroleum products, antifreeze, fats, solvents, and other substances as positive indications of nerve gas and mustard.[143] Obviously, some antiterrorist steps such as protecting ventilation systems, improving air filtration, and limiting access to facilities can reduce the possibility of high concentrations of a biological or chemical agent during an attack. However, sophisticated, continuous, and real-time permanent detection of chemical and biological agents is impractical even for a fraction of the sites of potential concern,[144] which include high-risk targets such as government buildings, enclosed public spaces, transportation nodes, medical facilities, and chemical factories.[145] CBRN detectors are more practical in the hands of well-trained, experienced personnel who know how to operate and maintain the equipment and are available to respond quickly. The current first-responder situation, however, leaves much to be desired.

Though Presidential Decision Directive 39 has named the FBI and FEMA as the lead federal agencies for crisis and consequence management, doubts still remain about who has authority in managing CBRN incidents. In 1998, Presidential Decision Directive 62 muddied the waters by making the Department of Health and Human Services (DHHS) the manager for "human-health-related consequences."[146] It remains unclear when FEMA hands off the baton to DHHS. Altogether, there are approximately forty federal agencies and some 150 subordinate federal offices with some level of authority and responsibility for various aspects of CBRN attacks, and all of them are expected to somehow coordinate their actions with other law enforcement, fire, paramedic, and public health organizations within each of the fifty states.[147] This is not an ideal situation for creating a smooth and cooperative response. Let us hope that the new Office of Homeland Security will address this confusion.

Activities to improve WMD response capability have also been incorrectly prioritized. Under the Defense Against Weapons of Mass Destruction Act of 1996, the process of domestic preparedness focused primarily on two activities: creating and reorganizing elite chemical and biological weapons (CBW) response teams and training local "first-responders."[148] There are numerous military response teams, including the army's two Technical Escort Units (TEU), which are trained to disable and transport CBW;[149] the marines corps's Chemical-Biological Incident Response Force (CBIRF), which has sophisticated detection, decontamination, and medical stabilization gear for a few hundred victims, though it is intended for protecting overseas installations and requires up to four hours to deploy an advance party;[150] the marine corps's Chemical-Biological Emergency Response Team (CBERT), which is similar to the CBIRF but is meant for domestic CBW terrorist incidents;[151] the U.S. Army Medical Research Institute of Infectious Diseases' Aeromedical Isolation Team, which can deploy worldwide with twelve hours' notice but can only accommodate two patients at a time;[152] and various special National Guard units that are meant as rapid responders, though there appears to be few and conflicting accounts on their capabilities.[153]

Civilian teams include FEMA's Emergency Response Teams (ERT), which are meant to provide administrative, logistical, and operational support to activities in the field;[154] FEMA's Rapid Assessment and Initial Detection (RAID) teams that were last reported deployed in only ten designated areas;[155] the FBI's Hazardous Materials Response Unit (HMRU), which is specially trained in WMD evidence recovery;[156] four National Medical Response Teams (NMRT), which are intended to provide "on-scene extraction, decontamination, antidote administration, and other primary care services";[157] several dispersed Metropolitan Medical Strike Teams (MMST), which consist of fire, police, and other public safety and health personnel tailored to each high-risk city and are on-call twenty-four hours a day to provide pre-hospital treatment and mitigation within thirty to ninety minutes of an incident;[158] twenty-one Disaster Medical Assistance

Teams (DMAT) out of the sixty primary response teams of the National Disaster Medical System, which are composed of health and administrative personnel and capable of providing self-sufficient emergency care onsite for 200 victims per day but usually require from twelve to twenty-four hours to mobilize.[159] Despite the valuable skills possessed by these various teams, most of them are too slow, too dispersed, and too focused on chemical attacks to be of much use outside of their immediate areas.

Few of the teams are capable of truly merging and assisting with a local response effort during an emergency. Therefore, the critical initial phase of any response "will still have to be carried out by non-specialist local responders."[160] Local and state responders will shape the outcome of any incident much more than elite but removed federal response teams. For the most part, these responders are the only assets capable of reducing casualties, minimizing economic impact, and maintaining critical infrastructure during the crucial first hours.[161] "Local responders" include more than just police, fire, and emergency medical technicians. A CBRN incident could involve personnel from departments of public safety, state and local emergency management, fire marshals, environmental quality, transportation, agriculture, water, health, mental health, human services, commerce, the Red Cross, and voluntary organizations. Though not all of these departments require funding and training for CBRN incidents, they all need some level of awareness about their likely involvement in such a disaster.

The current overemphasis on federal capabilities is inappropriate for the CBRN threat. Federal units are too large, too few in number, too far away, too varied in capabilities, and too slow to be of use in the most important stages of a response.[162] Though many of these assets claim to be skilled in both biological and chemical response, they are in fact almost solely equipped and trained for a chemical disaster. Chemical incidents are the ones that demand the most rapid of responses, so there is little likelihood that these units can address these emergencies without predeployment. Some feel that "because all incidents are local, and Federal government response is significantly time-distance delayed, this has essentially resulted in a U.S. version of the 'Maginot Line,' lending a false sense of security to those responsible for the nation's welfare."[163] Federal teams may have the resources and expertise to answer most types of chemical weapon attacks, but they do not have the essential proximity to most locations, making them of very limited usefulness in saving lives. The federal government's primary objective should be to assist state and local governments by providing resources, expertise, training, equipment, and pharmaceuticals.[164] State and local assets are the only ones capable of immediate, on-scene response for the vast majority of scenarios and locales. They are the only teams that can intervene in an unfolding chemical attack during the "golden hour"—the window of opportunity for preliminary medical treatment that turns victims into patients.[165] Federal dollars and time could be better placed by meeting disasters with the lowest-level and most immediate actors. In the end, "the only real option for improving the quality of national planning and coordination is to work with, not against, the existing 'community-based' approach,"[166] and "a true national strategy must have a 'bottom-up' approach."[167]

Another obstacle in the current state of emergency management of CBRN terrorism is the very limited training coverage in the United States. The Federal Domestic

Preparedness Program brought in with antiterrorism legislation of 1996 was aimed only at the country's 120 largest cities, which constitute only a modest percentage of the combined American population. Though intended as a "train-the-trainer exercise"—teaching small groups that in turn instruct more people from other locations, the Domestic Preparedness Program has not led to the spread of CBRN training outside the targeted cities. Focusing efforts solely on large cities could displace attacks, so "the threat is no less significant to smaller communities."[168] After all, since larger municipalities already have much greater capability, equipment, training, and experience than smaller ones, there is good reason that a terrorist might target a more vulnerable locale.[169] States also vary greatly in their individual levels of response readiness. More than half of twenty-two states surveyed by the National Governors' Association indicated that they "did not have the equipment necessary to detect a nerve agent release or sufficient medical resources to treat its effects."[170] There was even less capability for addressing biological attacks. Overall, the federal commitment to train state and local responders has not provided adequate defensive coverage.

The Bush administration is to be commended for its $3.5 billion budget request for first responders; however much remains to be seen as to how this money will be apportioned and distributed. Many other technical issues must be sorted out if CBRN response is to achieve its full potential. These diverse issues involve patient and technical decontamination, environmental protection, legal liability, media and public relations, evacuation techniques, scene control, equipment interoperability, interagency communication, personal protective equipment, standardizing treatment of CBRN injuries, computer tools, and dealing with volunteers. It is beyond the scope of our discussion to cover these matters with an appropriate level of detail.

Mental Health

Many practitioners have been consumed with the physical effects of CBRN terrorism and have neglected the psychological effects. The threat of panic seems the most likely result of any CBRN attack or attempt, regardless of the casualties or damage. An attack with these agents, especially biological agents, is frightening, since people are threatened by disease every day without terrorists or others helping it along. For most individuals, the microbial world is a mysterious place filled with colorless, tasteless, and odorless enemies, evoking strong negative emotions.[171] Everyone experiences illness, and fear of infection is often as big a problem as the actual risks and consequences of the infection.[172] A fear of contagion or contamination could have direct and dangerous implications for any response to a CBRN incident.

Very few plans or exercises take into account the psychological reactions among surviving victims, emergency workers, and the public in the aftermath of a CBRN attack or campaign.[173] The public reaction to a CBRN incident can make or break a successful response. Public panic can lead to self-evacuations of entire neighborhoods and cities, indirect fatalities of rescue workers or fellow citizens, overload of the communications systems, clogging of roads, and other problems.[174] The entire medical system can be overwhelmed by uninfected people who are acute psychiatric casualties presenting autonomic arousal from rumors or misleading media announcements.[175] This is what appears to have happened during the Tokyo sarin attack. Some studies estimate that up to 80 percent of the 5,510 casualties were suffering from panic-induced symptoms.[176]

The stress of seeing responders in gas masks and "space suits" or having to disrobe in public for decontamination could easily cause heart attacks, shock, or unexpected reactions. Inattention to the threat of public terror jeopardizes the efficacy and efficiency of response and mitigation efforts,[177] and a failure to anticipate psychological effects could lead to virtual paralysis of response assets.[178] A small incident or even a credible threat can produce psychological casualties, even if there are no physical ones. CBRN terrorists will likely seek to maximize the psychological impact of an attack by negating the aura of governmental preparedness and by overwhelming existing response capabilities.[179] A resilient and accurate public information campaign will have to be waged if these types of panic reactions are to be minimized (though they cannot be eliminated). As with natural disasters, credible response efforts will have to include teams of physicians, psychologists, social workers, chaplains, and other mental health specialists to counsel victims and families.[180] The threat of public panic is the element most likely to escalate a manageable event into an uncontrollable one.

These types of issues became apparent during the October anthrax mailings. As some observers have lamented, "One of the big mistakes is that we didn't give people things to do. We left them on their own to go buy gas masks and stock up on Cipro."[181] The limited nature of the anthrax mailings may have been a saving grace. One insightful account put it this way:

> We are not significantly closer to biological doomsday after September 11 and the anthrax mailings. If anything, we are closer to an effective biodefense policy. . . . Paradoxically, as unsettling as it was, the post-September 11 and anthrax scare had a reassuring aspect. It may not have occurred to many Americans in the anxiety of the moment, but the events of October gave the country a chance to learn some of the scientific facts, cope with the fears, and think about the threat without the far greater disruption and panic that would have occurred if its first biological episode had been a truly catastrophic one. Instead of having to learn on the job while dealing with mass casualties, government, public security, and public health authorities had an opportunity to weigh their actions—including missteps—and consider what might be done to better manage a future attack, if one occurred."[182]

Much work remains to bring the problems of mental health into sharper relief for CBRN response and recovery efforts.

Public Health

Biological incidents can require different types of responses than other WMD events. Chemical attacks are usually localized in time and space, have a linear chain of events, offer a very limited period to save lives, are easier to detect, and require different levels of personal protection than biological ones.[183] Biological attacks, on the other hand, may be more widely dispersed, last much longer, involve parallel and recursive response activities, be more amenable to medical intervention, spread more easily to affect others, be more difficult to detect, and create more public panic.[184] Some existing response systems are built on the erroneous assumption that biological attacks will be similar to Aum's sarin attack, but there will be no first responders rushing to a scene of a covert biological release.[185] Instead, detection of a biological attack rests almost solely on the decisions of a multitude of individual clinicians, epidemiologists, veterinarians, and medical examiners.[186]

There may always be toxicological and epidemiological questions about whether or not a biological attack has in fact occurred, and early warning or detection remains a difficult proposition.[187] After all, it took thirteen years to get the story behind the Sverdlovsk anthrax release. It is wrongly assumed that health agencies will be able to quickly and easily determine whether an epidemic is natural or artificial in nature. Biological attacks do not necessarily produce a clear signature,[188] and agents may present incubation periods far exceeding the estimates gathered from very limited data on human exposure.[189] Epidemiological intelligence—monitoring unusual patterns or cases in health reporting databases—represents one useful avenue for uncovering CBRN indicators.

Epidemiological information could point to possible CBRN programs, weapons tests, or accidents by highlighting cases of pulmonary or cutaneous anthrax, plague, radiation, or organophosphate poisoning along with other illnesses involving unusual means of transmission, high fatality rates, and odd distribution patterns.[190] Efforts should be made to augment existing domestic surveillance systems by strengthening the Emerging Infections Program (a grant-awarding body for improving state and local health department epidemiology), the Epidemic Intelligence Service (the Korean War–era rapid investigative unit for biological attacks), the Data Elements for Emergency Department Systems (an emergency department–based system meant to standardize electronic reporting across clinical care systems), the active reporting of the Sentinel Surveillance Networks, and the passive National Notifiable Disease Surveillance System.

The government should improve international disease surveillance by backing the epidemiological efforts of the World Health Organization along with the DoD's Global Emerging Infections Surveillance and Response system (which conducts antibiotic resistance surveillance), the U.S. Air Force's Global Surveillance Program (which integrates several other surveillance efforts), and the Federation of American Scientists' Program for Monitoring Emerging Diseases (which facilitates communication among global sentinel stations). It is also important to invest in food security and monitoring assets such as PulseNet, which links the Centers for Disease Control, the U.S. Department of Agriculture, and the Food and Drug Administration to state laboratories and which may help to warn about and reduce the thousands of deaths each year from food contamination in the United States.

There should be more communication between the medical community and other organizations, especially intelligence agencies. There must be a formal contact network between the medical and intelligence communities that distributes clinical data and allows health departments to receive information on suspected and potential terrorist activity, because such communication could shorten identification time, improve responses, and lower mortality. Eventually, a system should be designed that brings together all of these assets into a coherent whole. All health-related federal departments should seek to develop an integrated, limited-access, Internet mechanism for the distribution of relevant clinical CBRN data based on rapid reporting, best practices, and exchanged ideas. While it is possible that epidemiological intelligence can warn of preincident CBRN activity, it is not a certain warning system. At the end of the day, all efforts to improve the detection of biological agents should be complemented by general improvements in the health care system.

Biological attacks must be covert to achieve massive casualties, since precautions greatly limit most deaths and injuries.[191] Therefore, improving public health enhances national security. Emergency medical technicians, nurses, and primary health care physicians deal with emergencies every day,[192] so building on these existing capabilities is more practical than inventing more at the federal level. There is an overwhelming consensus that the medical community is the weakest link in CBRN preparedness and that no response will be successful without some major reinvestment in the biosciences and the existing health infrastructure. The current health system is incapable of dealing with incidents that overwhelm its limited capacity, as demonstrated by the flu outbreaks in the winter of 1999–2000. Managed health care and the conversion to just-in-time inventories leave little to no surge capacity to deal with any marked increase in patients, let alone a mid- to large-scale disaster.

The current program to stockpile medications and equipment could be made more sophisticated. Medications could be stockpiled in the public hospital system by creating inventory "bubbles" in supply lines; this way they are used and replaced regularly, efficiently maintaining an available cache and protecting citizens from both natural and intentional disasters. The National Disaster Medical System, a system that coordinates the disaster medical response activities of FEMA, the DoD, Veterans Affairs, and DHHS, should be further streamlined to supplement the lack of surplus medical capacity and to act as the strategic positioning agent and mobile supplier of support ventilators and other expensive equipment.

There are also huge gaps in overall health coverage and communication. A 1993 survey confirmed that twelve states had no professional position for the surveillance of foodborne and waterborne diseases,[193] and a 1997 survey showed that fewer than 50 percent of local health departments had any Internet access.[194] It is vital that policymakers shore up the existing health infrastructure to help with CBRN preparedness. Unlike investments in other antiterrorism and counterterrorism sectors, improvements in health infrastructure would combat all disease and poisoning and improve the lives of average citizens beyond terrorist events. There is already significant overlap between the daily suppression of disease outbreaks and poisonings and CBRN terrorism, so it would be a serious strategic mistake to ignore long-neglected health mechanisms by building a new system focused only on low-probability, doomsday-type terrorist events.

We must strengthen existing bodies that deal with hazardous chemicals and agriculture. Since organophosphate pesticides are widely used throughout the United States regional poison control centers are quite used to dealing with poisoning that is identical to that of nerve agents, but they need more stocks of medication and better education about military chemical weapons to become nodes for data collection and central resources for large-scale disasters. Veterinarians must also be brought into CBRN defense programs. After all, most military biological warfare agents are veterinary pathogens that rarely infect humans in nature; therefore, veterinarians have greater familiarity, rapid confirmatory assays, and alternative antibiotics along with large stocks of atropine to treat organophosphate pesticide poisoning of livestock. These capabilities are already present, but they need to be included in the planning to be successfully utilized. Limited capability exists for dealing with agricultural crises in terms of adequate stocks of vaccines, carcass disposal capacity, or psychological preparedness to accept a devastating agricultural disaster.[195]

Further efforts must also be directed at technical aspects of a medical response, including detectors; decontamination technology; psychological-effect reduction techniques; new drugs, treatments, and vaccines; managing patient flow; "hardening" of the health infrastructure; mass triage; disposition of human remains and personal effects; vaccination and prophylaxis; and quarantine laws. MIPT's widely cited Dark Winter exercise uncovered a number of questions with regard to smallpox:

- Who controls release of the vaccine?
- How do leaders prioritize vaccination and isolation?
- What vaccination strategy should be implemented, ring vaccination or mass immunization?
- How much vaccine should be reserved for military personnel?
- How much vaccine should be reserved for first responders (who are the first responders?)?
- How does government create surge capacity in vaccine production?
- What civil liberties will be affected if forcible constraints and limits on movement are the only options?

The Dark Winter exercise pointed out major fault lines between different levels of government (federal, state, and local), between government and the private sector, among different institutions and agencies, and within the public and private sector. These "disconnects" could impede situational awareness and compromise the ability to limit loss of life, suffering, and economic damage. In addition, the lack of surge capacity in the health care, pharmaceutical, and vaccine industries could result in hospitals being overwhelmed, could impede analysis of an epidemic, and could limit the ability to educate and reassure the public. Reassuring the public also entails better attention to information management and strategic communication—dealing with the press effectively, communicating with citizens, and maintaining the information flows necessary for command and control at all institutional levels.

FILLING THE GAPS AND THE PATH TO A MORE SECURE HOMELAND

The United States needs a serious recommitment to antiterrorism and counterterrorism that is realistic, economical, and acceptable. We have learned that we cannot treat security the way we have treated our health care. Security does not generate revenue, and for this reason government and industry have treated it as a luxury or a "black hole" for money better spent elsewhere. Much like a person's health, we do not realize the basic importance of security until it has failed us. Security is a basic prerequisite for doing the business of governance and commerce, not an afterthought to minimize loss. The American security system of relying on the lowest bidder to provide minimal coverage of liabilities and risks cannot stand. We must move past the managed-care equivalent our homeland security has become. As with most everything, we will get what we pay for when it comes to our security. Like the technology behind CBRN weapons, our organizational techniques and response capabilities should be dual use; much more thought is needed on how to superimpose responses to terrorism on systems already in place to deal with nonterrorist events. Prudent policy initiatives and strategic reorientation of capabilities are the keys to minimizing CBRN terrorism dangers.

As the Office of Homeland Security creates a national budget for counterterrorism equipment and research and development, there are many areas for government, nonprofit, commercial, and university partners to fill the gaps in the current system. Findings and recommendations from many studies and groups show that these include:

General Needs

Communication and Coordination

- Development of coherent decision-making protocols
- Plans on how to better coordinate operations in rural areas
- Interoperable communications systems
- Better strategic communications
- Templates for public education and public information prior to and following a CBRN attack

Law and Law Enforcement

- Studies of the legal issues in quarantine, containment, isolation, mandatory vaccinations, and other prescriptive activity
- Clarification of CBRN legal authorities, including the interface between the Federal Response Plan and the National Oil and Hazardous Substances Pollution Contingency Plan and the Federal Radiological Emergency Response Plan
- Rigorous legal clarification on CBRN homeland security roles and missions for the military
- Improved financial tracking capabilities

- Integration or increased sharing between intelligence and law enforcement databases

Terrorism Preparedness

- More research on the causes and effects of terrorism
- Periodic assessments of risks and trends in terrorism
- Evaluations of types and quantities of medical stockpiles, mass decontamination resources, general guidelines for mass-casualty incidents, and current CBRN detectors
- Clarification of continuity of government functions
- Assessment of critical infrastructure protection and how best to protect privately owned infrastructure
- Methods for improved information sharing from government to private sector

General Equipment Needs

- Improved airline and airport security, including feasibility studies of biometric identification cards and high-tech detection and screening for baggage
- Enhanced border sensors and screening
- Feasibility studies of a universal identification card
- Better understanding and testing of air quality after building collapses and explosions, along with measures to protect against toxic particulates

First Responder Needs

Training

- Consideration of a national training curriculum grounded in the "golden hour" concept, stressing civilian panic and psychological casualties, offering standardized care for certain injuries, focusing on situations with a minimum of information and no warning, and emphasizing cooperation, coordination, and communication
- Sophisticated training and planning on dealing with the "worried well"
- Development of force-protection training for civilian response personnel
- Training for missed audiences, including psychologists, pathologists, medical examiners, poison control officials, veterinarians, and others

Personal Protective Equipment

- Higher protection factors for respirators
- Protective equipment that is less bulky, lighter, and causes less heat stress
- Studies of standards and the impact of occupational regulations on protective equipment use
- Development of guidelines for the selection and use of personal protective equipment, especially for hospitals
- Evaluation of alternatives to respirators for general public use

CBRN Detection

- Broad-based detection technologies that are not too expensive or technically demanding for most users
- Evaluations of current HazMat and EMS chemical detection equipment for ability to detect military chemical weapons
- Better, field-deployable detection, identification, and monitoring devices for biological agents
- Devices to detect radiological and nuclear weapons in transit
- Miniaturized, multipurpose, and less-expensive gas chromatography/mass spectrometry technology for environmental monitoring of fixed medical facilities and patient transport vehicles
- Methods to pool surplus gear, ensure compatibility, and promote integrated response
- Standard Operating Procedures for passing detection information from first responders to Hazardous Materials teams, EMS teams, and hospitals
- Faster, cheaper, and easier patient diagnostics for CBRN exposure
- Scenario-specific testing of assay and detector performance

Decontamination

- Guidance on physical layout, equipment, and supply requirements for performing mass decontamination for patients of all ages and health in the field
- Methods for performing patient decontamination, including decontamination of mucous membranes and open wounds
- Benefit versus risk assessment of removing patient clothing for decontamination and the effectiveness of removing agent from clothing by showering
- Determination of showering time necessary to remove CBRN agents and methodology to verify if patient is "clean."
- Evaluation of high pressure/low-volume or low pressure/high-volume spray superiority for patient decontamination
- Studies of the psychological impact of undergoing decontamination on all age groups
- Feasibility studies of technical and environmental decontamination technologies such as high-power ultraviolet beams

Software and Other Technical Needs

- Development of an unclassified, Internet-accessible collection of lessons learned and best practices
- Better Web site and computer software for CBRN symptomology and toxicological information with methods to report to public health authorities
- Further testing of atmospheric dispersion and vector models, including water, food, and transportation
- Customizable and interactive simulation software

- Modeling of CBRN environmental impact to support recommendations on decontamination and facility reoccupation

Mental Health Needs

Research

- Development of coherent decision-making protocols
- Research on long-term mental health and psychological issues associated with terrorism
- Psychological screening methods for differentiating adjustment reactions from more serious psychological illness
- Research and methodologies for critical incident stress debriefing
- Techniques for preventing or limiting psychological trauma of emergency workers, survivors, and near-victims
- Research on children's responses to terrorism
- Psychologically sensitive public information on risk assessment/threat perception for use by public officials

Training

- Training for educators and mental health professionals on how to speak with children exposed to terrorism
- Guidance for parents, day care workers, and others responsible for caring for children during these times
- Resource materials on CBRN agents that can be integrated into mental health professional training

Public Health Needs

Research

- Basic research on pathogenesis and microbial metabolism
- Additional research on how to thwart potential genetic modifications and mutations in biological weapons
- Standardized patient assessment and triage process for evaluating patients of all ages and health conditions, including the immunosuppressed
- Research on legal and procedural problems in public health terrorism response

Epidemiology

- Development of a formal communication network between the intelligence and public health communities
- National mechanism for clinical data distribution to both communities after events or exercises
- Improved information-sharing and syndromic surveillance through pharmacies, hospitals, primary care physicians, and others for early warnings

- Faster and more complete methods for expert access to electronic disease reporting, from the health care provider level to global surveillance
- Symptom-based, automated decision aids to help clinicians in early identification of CBRN exposure

Forensics

- Standards and protocols for laboratory methods and reporting
- Pathogen "fingerprinting" of microbes and a database to distribute to regional laboratories
- Rapid and innovative methods for determining agent attribution and provenance
- Improved physical security standards for research laboratories and specimen storage facilities

Treatments and Antidotes

- Study of the optimal antidote stockpiling and deployment system for fast-acting chemical and biological agents
- Methods to screen for, limit, and repair airway injuries
- Research into "scavenger" molecules for prophylaxis and post-exposure therapies
- Improved, safer vaccines for anthrax and smallpox
- Creation of new specific and broad-spectrum antibiotic and antiviral drugs
- Recombinant vaccines, monoclonal antibodies, and antibody fragments to counter botulinum toxin
- Study of universal vaccines and detection devices against all pathogens

Training

- More general awareness training on CBRN terrorism for health practitioners
- Training aids for medical examiners and others missed in traditional CBRN training

Agricultural Needs

Research

- Enhanced comprehension of plant and animal disease etiology
- Development of disease-resistant plants through genetic enhancements or other modifications
- Research into agricultural techniques that offer greater protection against disease and sabotage
- Development of broad-spectrum vaccines that are effective against multiple animal and plant diseases

Epidemiology

- Improved national and international surveillance of agricultural disease outbreaks
- Rapid diagnostic capabilities for specific pathogen and strain identification

- Advanced microbial forensics
- Comprehensive tracking of nonindigenous animal and plant diseases

Infrastructure

- Study into more specific threats to food, water, and agricultural sectors
- Improved security of drinking-water systems and food-processing facilities
- Enhanced laboratory capacity and safety for USDA labs

Training

- Disease outbreak awareness training for veterinarians, farmers, and extension agents

The National Memorial Institute for the Prevention of Terrorism in Oklahoma City stands ready to assist in many of these areas. Ongoing and future research efforts at the Memorial Institute have and will continue to address several of these gaps in the nation's homeland security system. Many of these concerns cropped up in the MIPT-sponsored Dark Winter exercise and Bioterrorism: Knowing the Agents, Preventing the Terror, a joint conference with the New York Medical College. Sooner Spring, a state-level version of Dark Winter, will likely shed light on more concerns at the more-immediate levels of emergency response. A provider for first responders and a center for lessons learned, the Memorial Institute remains committed to improving the country's ability to prevent and deter terrorism or to mitigate its effects through sound planning, policy, and preparedness efforts.

By enacting a national strategy that is systematic, dynamic, and cost effective, the United States can diminish the terrorists' ability to achieve their ultimate goal—the induction of terror.[196] Though the risk from CBRN terrorism may appear ambiguous at times, the nation's preparedness for and response to that risk must be certain.

ENDNOTES

1. Richard Danzi and Pamela B. Berkowsy, "Why Should We Be Concerned about Biological Warfare?" in *Biological Weapons: Limiting the Threat,* ed. Joshua Lederberg (Cambridge, MA: MIT Press, 1999), 10.

2. Michael Moodie, "Introduction," in *Hype or Reality? The "New Terrorism" and Mass Casualty Attacks,* ed. Brad Roberts (Alexandria, VA: Chemical and Biological Arms Control Institute, 2000), xiii.

3. James K. Campbell, "On Not Understanding the Problem," in *Hype or Reality? The "New Terrorism" and Mass Casualty Attacks,* ed. Brad Roberts (Alexandria, VA: Chemical and Biological Arms Control Institute, 2000), 39.

4. Bruce Hoffman, "The Debate over Future Terrorist Use of Chemical, Biological, and Nuclear Weapons," in *Hype or Reality? The "New Terrorism" and Mass Casualty Attacks,* ed. Brad Roberts (Alexandria, VA: Chemical and Biological Arms Control Institute, 2000), 212.

5. *Assessing the Threat: First Annual Report to the President and the Congress of the Advisory Panel to Assess Domestic Response Capabilities for Terrorism Involving Weapons of Mass Destruction* (December 15, 1999), 47.

6. Jeffrey D. Simon, "Lone Operators and Weapons of Mass Destruction," in *Hype or Reality? The "New Terrorism" and Mass Casualty Attacks,* ed. Brad Roberts (Alexandria, VA: Chemical and Biological Arms Control Institute, 2000), 78.

7. *Assessing the Threat,* 27; Randall Forsberg, William Driscoll, Gregory Webb, and Jonathan Dean, *Nonproliferation Primer: Preventing the Spread of Nuclear, Chemical, and Biological Weapons* (Cambridge, MA: MIT Press, 1995), 35.

8. Edward M. Spiers, *Chemical and Biological Weapons: A Study of Proliferation* (New York: St. Martin's Press, 1994), 158.

9. Stansfield Turner, *Caging the Genies: A Workable Solution for Nuclear, Chemical, and Biological Weapons* (Boulder, CO: Westview Press, 1999), 47, 49.

10. Forsberg et al., *Nonproliferation Primer,* 11, 14–15.

11. Paul M. Maniscalco and James P. Denney, "Public Safety Agencies: Trying to Define Readiness While Surviving the Rhetoric," in *Hype or Reality? The "New Terrorism" and Mass Casualty Attacks,* ed. Brad Roberts (Alexandria, VA: Chemical and Biological Arms Control Institute, 2000), 256.

12. *Assessing the Threat,* iii.

13. *Assessing the Threat,* ii.

14. Brad Roberts, "Has the Taboo Been Broken"? in *Terrorism with Chemical and Biological Weapons: Calibrating Risks and Responses,* ed. Brad Roberts (Alexandria, VA: Chemical and Biological Arms Control Institute, 1997), 125–125.

15. Richard A. Falkenrath, Robert D. Newman, and Bradley A. Thayer, *America's Achilles' Heel: Nuclear, Biological, and Chemical Terrorism and Covert Attack* (Cambridge, MA: MIT Press, 1999), 33.

16. Spiers, *Chemical and Biological Weapons,* 3–4.

17. Wendy Barnaby, *The Plague Makers: The Secret World of Biological Warfare* (London: Vision Paperbacks, 1997), 14.

18. Falkenrath, Newman, and Thayer, *America's Achilles' Heel,* 47.

19. Joseph F. Pilat, "The New Terrorism and NBC Weapons," in *Hype or Reality? The "New Terrorism" and Mass Casualty Attacks,* ed. Brad Roberts (Alexandria, VA: Chemical and Biological Arms Control Institute, 2000), 225.

20. Paul De Armond, "Right-Wing Terrorism and Weapons of Mass Destruction: Motives, Strategies, and Movements," in *Hype or Reality? The "New Terrorism" and Mass Casualty Attacks,* ed. Brad Roberts (Alexandria, VA: Chemical and Biological Arms Control Institute, 2000), 50–51.

21. Falkenrath, Newman, and Thayer, *America's Achilles' Heel,* 27.

22. De Armond, "Right-Wing Terrorism and Weapons of Mass Destruction," 50–51.

23. Falkenrath, Newman, and Thayer, *America's Achilles' Heel,* 97.

24. De Armond, "Right-Wing Terrorism and Weapons of Mass Destruction," 50–51.

25. W. Seth Carus, "Unlawful Acquisition and Use of Biological Agents," in *Biological Weapons: Limiting the Threat,* ed. Joshua Lederberg (Cambridge, MA: MIT Press, 1999), 211; Brad Roberts, "Conclusion: The Prospects for Mass Casualty Terrorism," in *Hype or Reality? The "New Terrorism" and Mass Casualty Attacks,* ed. Brad Roberts (Alexandria, VA: Chemical and Biological Arms Control Institute, 2000), 268.

26. *Assessing the Threat,* 51.

27. *Assessing the Threat,* 36.

28. Paul Schulte, "Motives and Methods of Future Political Violence: Landscapes of the Early Twenty-First Century," in *Hype or Reality? The "New Terrorism" and Mass Casualty Attacks,* ed. Brad Roberts (Alexandria, VA: Chemical and Biological Arms Control Institute, 2000), 185.

29. *Assessing the Threat,* 2–3; Roberts, "Conclusion," 263.

30. *Assessing the Threat,* ii.

31. Hugh D. Crone, *Banning Chemical Weapons: The Scientific Background* (Cambridge: Cambridge University Press, 1992), 3.

32. Ehud Sprinzak and Idith Zertal, "Avenging Israel's Blood," in *Toxic Terror: Assessing Terrorist Use of Chemical and Biological Weapons,* ed. Jonathan B. Tucker (Cambridge, MA: MIT Press, 2000), 17.

33. Walter Laqueur, *The New Terrorism: Fanaticism and the Arms of Mass Destruction* (New York: Oxford University Press, 1999), 72.

34. George W. Christopher, Theodore J. Cieslak, Julie A. Pavlin, and Edward M. Eitzen, Jr., "Biological Weapons: An Historical Perspective," in *Biological Terrorism and Weapons of Mass Destruction,* ed. Gary E. McCuen (Hudson, WI: Gary McCuen Publications Inc., 1999), 38; Bruce Hoffman, *Inside Terrorism* (London: Indigo, 1999), 121; Laqueur 69.

35. Laqueur, *The New Terrorism,* 72.

36. Laqueur, *The New Terrorism,* 203.

37. Robert Jay Lifton, *Destroying the World to Save It: Aum Shinrikyo, Apocalyptic Violence, and the New Global Terrorism* (New York: Metropolitan Books, 1999), 39, 187–188; Falkenrath, Newman, and Thayer, *America's Achilles' Heel,* 20.

38. Hoffman, "The Debate over Future Terrorist Use," 216, 223–33.

39. Falkenrath, Newman, and Thayer, *America's Achilles' Heel,* 43.

40. Lifton, *Destroying the World to Save It,* 188; Falkenrath, Newman, and Thayer, *America's Achilles' Heel,* 20.

41. Lifton, *Destroying the World to Save It,* 188; Falkenrath, Newman, and Thayer, *America's Achilles' Heel,* 20.

42. Falkenrath, Newman, and Thayer, *America's Achilles' Heel,* 34.

43. Laqueur, *The New Terrorism,* 54; Lifton, *Destroying the World to Save It,* 39–40; Falkenrath, Newman, and Thayer, *America's Achilles' Heel,* 20.

44. Lifton, *Destroying the World to Save It,* 39, 188.

45. Hoffman, *Inside Terrorism,* 121, 126.

46. Ron Purver, "The Nature of Chemical Terrorism," in *Biological Terrorism and Weapons of Mass Destruction,* ed. Gary E. McCuen (Hudson, WI: Gary McCuen Publications Inc., 1999), 78; Leonard A. Cole, *The Eleventh Plague: The Politics of Biological and Chemical Warfare* (New York: W. H. Freeman and Company, 1997), 155–156.

47. Cole, *The Eleventh Plague,* 156; Purver, "The Nature of Chemical Terrorism," 78.

48. De Armond, "Right-Wing Terrorism and Weapons of Mass Destruction," 52–54.

49. *Assessing the Threat,* 11; Dean A. Wilkening, "BCW Attack Scenarios," in *The New Terror: Facing the Threat of Biological and Chemical Weapons,* ed. Sidney D. Drell, Abraham D. Sofaer, and George D. Wilson (Stanford, CA: Hoover Institution Press, 1999), 101.

50. Spiers, *Chemical and Biological Weapons,* 169; Ron Purver, "Understanding Past Non-Use of CBW by Terrorists," in *Terrorism with Chemical and Biological Weapons: Calibrating Risks and Responses,* ed. Brad Roberts (Alexandria, VA: Chemical and Biological Arms Control Institute, 1997), 69; Jerrold M. Post, "Psychological and Motivational Factors in Terrorist Decision-Making: Implications for CBW Terrorism," in *Toxic Terror: Assessing Terrorist Use of Chemical and Biological Weapons,* ed. Jonathan B. Tucker (Cambridge, MA: MIT Press, 2000), 277.

51. Purver, "Understanding Past Non-Use of CBW by Terrorists," 69.

52. Wilkening, "BCW Attack Scenarios," 101–102; *Assessing the Threat,* 12; Brad Roberts, "Terrorism and Weapons of Mass Destruction: Has the Taboo Been Broken?" *Politics and the Life Sciences* 15, no. 2 (September 1996): 217.

53. Spiers, *Chemical and Biological Weapons,* 160.

54. *Assessing the Threat,* viii.

55. Falkenrath, Newman, and Thayer, *America's Achilles' Heel,* 207; Roberts, "Terrorism and Weapons of Mass Destruction," 217; *Assessing the Threat,* viii.

56. Jessica Eve Stern, "Weapons of Mass Impact: A Growing and Worrisome Danger," *Politics and the Life Sciences* 15, no. 2 (September 1996): 222; Thomas Stock, "Fighting CBW Terrorism:

Means and Possibilities," *Politics and the Life Sciences* 15, no. 2 (September 1996): 225; *Assessing the Threat,* viii, 11.

57. Falkenrath, Newman, and Thayer, *America's Achilles' Heel,* 210; Wilkening, "BCW Attack Scenarios," 101.

58. Stock, "Fighting CBW Terrorism," 225.

59. Jonathan B. Tucker, "Lessons from the Case Studies," in *Toxic Terror: Assessing Terrorist Use of Chemical and Biological Weapons,* ed. Jonathan B. Tucker (Cambridge, MA: MIT Press, 2000), 265; Wilkening, "BCW Attack Scenarios," 101.

60. *Assessing the Threat,* viii; Tucker, "Lessons from the Case Studies," 260.

61. Stern, "Weapons of Mass Impact: A Growing and Worrisome Danger," 224; Falkenrath, Newman, and Thayer, *America's Achilles' Heel,* 205; Roberts, "Terrorism and Weapons of Mass Destruction," 217.

62. David Claridge, "Exploding the Myths of Superterrorism," *Terrorism and Political Violence* 11, no. 4 (Winter 1999): 141; Tucker, "Lessons from the Case Studies," 261, 265; Roberts, "Terrorism and Weapons of Mass Destruction," 217; Jonathan B. Tucker, "Bioterrorism: Threats and Responses," in *Biological Weapons: Limiting the Threat,* ed. Joshua Lederberg (Cambridge, MA: MIT Press, 1999), 298–299; David C. Rapoport," Why Does Religious Messianism Produce Terror?" in *Contemporary Research on Terrorism,* ed. Paul Wilkinson and Alasdair M. Stewart (Aberdeen: Aberdeen University Press, 1987), 85; Falkenrath, Newman, and Thayer, *America's Achilles' Heel,* 205.

63. Carus, "Unlawful Acquisition and Use of Biological Agents," 226; Stock, "Fighting CBW Terrorism," 225.

64. Stock, "Fighting CBW Terrorism," 225; Wilkening, "BCW Attack Scenarios," 101; Tucker, "Lessons from the Case Studies," 267.

65. Spiers, *Chemical and Biological Weapons,* 160; Stock, "Fighting CBW Terrorism," 225; *Assessing the Threat,* 11–12.

66. Simon, "Lone Operators and Weapons of Mass Destruction," 73; Wilkening, "BCW Attack Scenarios," 102.

67. Purver, "Understanding Past Non-Use of CBW by Terrorists," 69.

68. Wilkening, "BCW Attack Scenarios," 101; Falkenrath, Newman, and Thayer, *America's Achilles' Heel,* 207.

69. Falkenrath, Newman, and Thayer, *America's Achilles' Heel,* 207.

70. Falkenrath, Newman, and Thayer, *America's Achilles' Heel,* 210.

71. Falkenrath, Newman, and Thayer, *America's Achilles' Heel,* 205; Roberts, "Terrorism and Weapons of Mass Destruction," 217.

72. Tucker, "Lessons from the Case Studies," 266; Falkenrath, Newman, and Thayer, *America's Achilles' Heel,* 211.

73. Gavin Cameron, "Lone Actors as Perpetrators of Incidents with CBRN Weapons," 12, presentation at the conference Terrorism and Beyond: The 21st Century, Oklahoma City, OK, April 17–19, 2000.

74. Tucker, "Lessons from the Case Studies," 265; Falkenrath, Newman, and Thayer, *America's Achilles' Heel,* 205; Roberts, "Terrorism and Weapons of Mass Destruction," 217.

75. Bruce Hoffman, *Responding to Terrorism across the Technological Spectrum* (Santa Monica, CA: RAND, 1994), 11; Purver, "Understanding Past Non-Use of CBW by Terrorists," 69.

76. Claridge, "Exploding the Myths of Superterrorism," 141; Falkenrath, Newman, and Thayer, *America's Achilles' Heel,* 205.

77. Tucker, "Lessons from the Case Studies," 266; *Assessing the Threat,* 37.

78. Laqueur, *The New Terrorism,* 271.

79. Simon, "Lone Operators and Weapons of Mass Destruction," 71; Barnaby, *The Plague Makers,* 45–46.

80. Ashton B. Carter and William J. Perry, *Preventive Defense: A New Security Strategy for America* (Washington, D.C.: Brookings Institution Press, 1999), 153.

81. Hoffman, "The Debate over Future Terrorist Use," 218.

82. Roberts, "Conclusion," 274.

83. Joseph F. Pilat, "Prospects for NBC Terrorism After Tokyo," in *Terrorism with Chemical and Biological Weapons: Calibrating Risks and Responses,* ed. Brad Roberts (Alexandria, VA: Chemical and Biological Arms Control Institute, 1997), 3.

84. *Assessing the Threat,* 40.

85. Falkenrath, Newman, and Thayer, *America's Achilles' Heel,* 51.

86. Lifton, *Destroying the World to Save It,* 23.

87. Pilat, "Prospects for NBC Terrorism After Tokyo," 9.

88. Pilat, "Prospects for NBC Terrorism After Tokyo," 24.

89. *Assessing the Threat,* 24–25.

90. Barnaby, *The Plague Makers,* 34; Falkenrath, Newman, and Thayer, *America's Achilles' Heel,* 21; Jonathan B. Tucker, "Policy Approaches to Chemical and Biological Terrorism," in *Terrorism with Chemical and Biological Weapons: Calibrating Risks and Responses,* ed. Brad Roberts (Alexandria, VA: Chemical and Biological Arms Control Institute, 1997), 95.

91. Falkenrath, Newman, and Thayer, *America's Achilles' Heel,* 22.

92. Milton Leitenberg, "The Experience of the Japanese Aum Shinrikyo Group and Biological Agents," in *Hype or Reality? The "New Terrorism" and Mass Casualty Attacks,* ed. Brad Roberts (Alexandria, VA: Chemical and Biological Arms Control Institute, 2000), 165.

93. *Assessing the Threat,* 49.

94. Falkenrath, Newman, and Thayer, *America's Achilles' Heel,* 24.

95. *Assessing the Threat,* 22; Cole, *The Eleventh Plague,* 152; Anthony Fainberg, "Debating Policy Priorities and Implications," in *Terrorism with Chemical and Biological Weapons: Calibrating Risks and Responses,* ed. Brad Roberts (Alexandria, VA: Chemical and Biological Arms Control Institute, 1997), 83.

96. *Assessing the Threat,* 47n166; Leitenberg, "The Experience of the Japanese Aum Shinrikyo Group and Biological Agents," 159; Ehud Sprinzak, "On Not Overstating the Problem," in *Hype or Reality? The "New Terrorism" and Mass Casualty Attacks,* ed. Brad Roberts (Alexandria, VA: Chemical and Biological Arms Control Institute, 2000), 8.

97. Carus, "Unlawful Acquisition and Use of Biological Agents," 215–216.

98. Falkenrath, Newman, and Thayer, *America's Achilles' Heel,* 22.

99. *Assessing the Threat,* 11–41, emphasis added.

100. Lifton, *Destroying the World to Save It,* 229.

101. Moodie, "Introduction," xvi; Schulte, "Motives and Methods of Future Political Violence," 174–175; Hoffman, *Responding to Terrorism,* 15; Roberts, "Conclusion," 273.

102. Pilat, "The New Terrorism and NBC Weapons," 229.

103. Barnaby, *The Plague Makers,* 41; Forsberg et al., *Nonproliferation Primer,* 59.

104. Carus, "Unlawful Acquisition and Use of Biological Agents," 228.

105. David Franz, "The Nature of Biological Terrorism," in *Biological Terrorism and Weapons of Mass Destruction,* ed. Gary E. McCuen (Hudson, WI: Gary McCuen Publications Inc., 1999), 40.

106. Crone, *Banning Chemical Weapons,* 48.

107. Purver, "The Nature of Chemical Terrorism," 77; Spiers, *Chemical and Biological Weapons,* 170–171; Seymour M. Hersh, *Chemical and Biological Warfare: America's Hidden Arsenal* (Indianapolis, IN: Bobbs-Merrill, 1968), 8 note.

108. Simon, "Lone Operators and Weapons of Mass Destruction," 75.

109. Falkenrath, Newman, and Thayer, *America's Achilles' Heel,* 2; Tucker, "Policy Approaches to Chemical and Biological Terrorism," 96.

110. Brain Michael Jenkins, "The WMD Terrorist Threat—Is There a Consensus View?" in *Hype or Reality? The "New Terrorism" and Mass Casualty Attacks,* ed. Brad Roberts (Alexandria, VA: Chemical and Biological Arms Control Institute, 2000), 247.

111. Campbell, "On Not Understanding the Problem," 40.

112. *Assessing the Threat,* 21.

113. *Assessing the Threat,* 21.

114. Laqueur, *The New Terrorism,* 72.

115. Laqueur, *The New Terrorism,* 29; Crone, *Banning Chemical Weapons,* 75; Spiers, *Chemical and Biological Weapons,* 170–171.

116. De Armond, "Right-Wing Terrorism and Weapons of Mass Destruction," 52–54.

117. De Armond, "Right-Wing Terrorism and Weapons of Mass Destruction," 64.

118. Simon, "Lone Operators and Weapons of Mass Destruction," 70.

119. *Assessing the Threat,* 19; Carus, "Unlawful Acquisition and Use of Biological Agents," 222; Thomas J. Torok, Robert V. Tauxe, Robert P. Wise, John R. Livengood, Robert Sokolow, Steven Mauvais, Kristen A. Birkness, Michael R. Skeels, John M. Horan, and Laurence R. Foster, "A Large Community Outbreak of Salmonellosis Caused by Intentional Contamination of Restaurant Salad Bars," in *Biological Weapons: Limiting the Threat,* ed. Joshua Lederberg (Cambridge, MA: MIT Press, 1999), 172, 179.

120. Torok et al., "A Large Community Outbreak of Salmonellosis," 172, 180.

121. Torok et al., "A Large Community Outbreak of Salmonellosis," 172; Jean-Francois Mayer, "Cults, Violence and Religious Terrorism at the Dawn of the Twenty-First Century: An International Perspective," 3, presented at the conference Terrorism and Beyond: The Twenty-First Century, Oklahoma City, OK, April 17–19, 2000.

122. Floyd Horn, "Agricultural Terrorism," in *Hype or Reality? The "New Terrorism" and Mass Casualty Attacks,* ed. Brad Roberts (Alexandria, VA: Chemical and Biological Arms Control Institute, 2000), 114.

123. Horn, "Agricultural Terrorism," 114.

124. Jonathan B. Tucker, "Chemical/Biological Terrorism: Coping with a New Threat," *Politics and the Life Sciences* 15, no. 2 (September 1996): 175.

125. John C. Gannon, "The US Intelligence Community and the Challenge of BCW," in *The New Terror: Facing the Threat of Biological and Chemical Weapons,* ed. Sidney D. Drell, Abraham D. Sofaer, and George D. Wilson (Stanford, CA: Hoover Institution Press, 1999), 132.

126. Gannon, "The US Intelligence Community and the Challenge of BCW," 132.

127. Falkenrath, Newman, and Thayer, *America's Achilles' Heel,* 176; Gannon, "The US Intelligence Community and the Challenge of BCW," 128.

128. Gannon, "The US Intelligence Community and the Challenge of BCW," 133; Bruce Hoffman and Jennifer Morrison Taw, *A Strategic Framework for Countering Terrorism and Insurgency,* A RAND Note Prepared for the U.S. Department of State (Santa Monica, CA: RAND, 1992), 138.

129. Falkenrath, Newman, and Thayer, *America's Achilles' Heel,* 287–288.

130. John Gee, "CBW Terrorism and the Chemical Weapons Convention," *Politics and the Life Sciences* 15, no. 2 (September 1996): 204; Rolf Ekéus, "UN Biological Inspections in Iraq," in *The New Terror: Facing the Threat of Biological and Chemical Weapons,* ed. Sidney D. Drell, Abraham D. Sofaer, and George D. Wilson (Stanford, CA: Hoover Institution Press, 1999), 254; Barnaby, *The Plague Makers,* 118–119.

131. Tucker, "Lessons from the Case Studies," 268.

132. Simon, "Lone Operators and Weapons of Mass Destruction," 72.

133. Carter and Perry, *Preventive Defense: A New Security Strategy for America,* 160.

134. Falkenrath, Newman, and Thayer, *America's Achilles' Heel,* 281.

135. Francis H. Marlo, "WMD Terrorism and US Intelligence Collection," *Terrorism and Political Violence* 11, no. 3 (Autumn 1999): 57, 61; Tucker, "Chemical/Biological Terrorism," 176.

136. Lifton, *Destroying the World to Save It,* 187; David E. Kaplan, "Aum Shinrikyo," in *Toxic Terror: Assessing Terrorist Use of Chemical and Biological Weapons,* ed. Jonathan B. Tucker (Cambridge, MA: MIT Press, 2000), 215; James K. Campbell, "Excerpts from Research Study 'Weapons of Mass Destruction and Terrorism: Proliferation by Non-State Actors," *Terrorism and Political*

Violence 9, no. 2 (Summer 1997): 36; Marlo, "WMD Terrorism and US Intelligence Collection," 60; Falkenrath, Newman, and Thayer, *America's Achilles' Heel,* 22.

137. Frank Barnaby, *Instruments of Terror: Mass Destruction Has Never Been So Easy* (London: Vision Paperbacks, 1996), 129, 131; Lifton, *Destroying the World to Save It,* 39–40, 184; Falkenrath, Newman, and Thayer, *America's Achilles' Heel,* 22; Cole, *The Eleventh Plague,* 155–156; Alex P. Schmid, "Terrorism and the Use of Weapons of Mass Destruction: From Where the Risk?" *Terrorism and Political Violence* 11, no. 4 (Winter 1999): 125; Taiji Miyaoka, "Terrorist Crisis Management in Japan: Historical Development and changing Response (1997–1997)," *Terrorism and Political Violence* 10, no. 2 (Summer 1998): 30; Laqueur, *The New Terrorism,* 54.

138. Marlo, "WMD Terrorism and US Intelligence Collection," 69.

139. Roberts, "Conclusion," 273.

140. Committee on R&D Needs for Improving Civilian Medical Response to Chemical and Biological Terrorism Incidents, Health Sciences Policy Program, Institute of Medicine, and Board on Environmental Studies and Toxicology, Commission on Life Sciences, National Research Council, *Chemical and Biological Terrorism: Research and Development to Improve Civilian Medical Response* (Washington, D.C.: National Academy Press, 1999), 5.

141. David R. Franz, Peter B. Jahrling, Arthur M. Friedlander, David J. McClain, David L. Hoover, W. Russell Byrne, Julie A. Pavlin, George W. Christopher and Edward M. Eitzen, Jr., "Clinical Recognition and Management of Patients Exposed to Biological Warfare Agents," in *Biological Weapons: Limiting the Threat,* ed. Joshua Lederberg (Cambridge, MA: MIT Press, 1999), 77.

142. Committee on R&D Needs and Commission on Life Sciences, *Chemical and Biological Terrorism,* 46.

143. *Chemical and Biological Terrorism,* 55; Ulf Ivarsson, Helena Nilsson, and Johan Santesson, eds., *A FOA Briefing Book on Chemical Weapons: Threat, Effects, and Protection* (Stockholm: FOA, 1992), 68.

144. Committee on R&D Needs and Commission on Life Sciences, *Chemical and Biological Terrorism,* 5.

145. Tucker, "Policy Approaches to Chemical and Biological Terrorism," 106.

146. Thomas P. Monath, "Introductory Remarks," in *The New Terror: Facing the Threat of Biological and Chemical Weapons,* ed. Sidney D. Drell, Abraham D. Sofaer, and George D. Wilson (Stanford, CA: Hoover Institution Press, 1999), 332; Richard A. Falkenrath, "Chemical/Biological Terrorism: Coping with Uncertain Threats and Certain Vulnerabilities," *Politics and the Life Sciences* 14, no. 2 (September 1996): 202.

147. Turner, *Caging the Genies,* 109–110; Tibor Tóth, "Negotiating a Compliance Protocol for the Biological Weapons Convention," in *The New Terror: Facing the Threat of Biological and Chemical Weapons,* ed. Sidney D. Drell, Abraham D. Sofaer, and George D. Wilson (Stanford, CA: Hoover Institution Press, 1999), 233.

148. Tucker, "Bioterrorism: Threats and Responses," 314.

149. Falkenrath, Newman, and Thayer, *America's Achilles' Heel,* 298, 310.

150. Carter and Perry, *Preventive Defense: A New Security Strategy for America,* 145–147, 158; Jonathan B. Tucker, "Measures to Fight Chemical/Biological Terrorism: How Little Is Enough?" *Politics and the Life Sciences* 15, no. 2 (September 1996): 240; Committee on R&D Needs and Commission on Life Sciences, *Chemical and Biological Terrorism,* 26; Tucker, "Policy Approaches to Chemical and Biological Terrorism," 107; Falkenrath, Newman, and Thayer, *America's Achilles' Heel,* 310, 310n64.

151. Tucker, "Policy Approaches to Chemical and Biological Terrorism," 107.

152. Falkenrath, Newman, and Thayer, *America's Achilles' Heel,* 312.

153. Maniscalco and Denney, "Public Safety Agencies," 254.

154. George Buck, *Preparing for Terrorism: An Emergency Services Guide* (Albany, NY: Delmar Publishers, 1998), 175.

155. Committee on R&D Needs and Commission on Life Sciences, *Chemical and Biological Terrorism,* 27.

156. Falkenrath, Newman, and Thayer, *America's Achilles' Heel,* 298–299.

157. Robert F. Knouss, "The Federal Role in Protection and Response," in *The New Terror: Facing the Threat of Biological and Chemical Weapons,* ed. Sidney D. Drell, Abraham D. Sofaer, and George D. Wilson (Stanford, CA: Hoover Institution Press, 1999), 350.

158. Knouss, "The Federal Role in Protection and Response," 353; Committee on R&D Needs and Commission on Life Sciences, *Chemical and Biological Terrorism,* 240; Tucker, "Measures to Fight Chemical/Biological Terrorism," 240; Tucker, "Chemical/Biological Terrorism," 179; Tucker, "Bioterrorism: Threats and Responses," 316–317.

159. Knouss, "The Federal Role in Protection and Response," 350; Robert A. De Lorenzo and Robert S. Porter, *Weapons of Mass Destruction: Emergency Care* (Upper Saddle River, NJ: Prentice Hall, 2000); Tucker, "Chemical/Biological Terrorism," 179; Committee on R&D Needs and Commission on Life Sciences, *Chemical and Biological Terrorism,* 25–26; Buck, *Preparing for Terrorism,* 26.

160. Falkenrath, Newman, and Thayer, *America's Achilles' Heel,* 310.

161. Maniscalco and Denney, "Public Safety Agencies," 256–258.

162. Falkenrath, Newman, and Thayer, *America's Achilles' Heel,* 310; De Lorenzo and Porter, *Weapons of Mass Destruction: Emergency Care,* 24; Knouss, "The Federal Role in Protection and Response," 358.

163. Maniscalco and Denney, "Public Safety Agencies," 254; Buck, *Preparing for Terrorism,* x; Falkenrath, Newman, and Thayer, *America's Achilles' Heel,* 274–275.

164. Buck, *Preparing for Terrorism,* x.

165. Frank J. Cilluffo and Jack Thomas Tomarchio, "Emergency Response Teams Can Mitigate the Effects of a Chemical or Biological Attack," in *Weapons of Mass Destruction,* ed. Jennifer A. Hurley (San Diego, CA: Greenhaven Press, 1999), 99.

166. Falkenrath, Newman, and Thayer, *America's Achilles' Heel,* 275.

167. *Assessing the Threat,* 54.

168. Maniscalco and Denney, "Public Safety Agencies," 258.

169. Maniscalco and Denney, "Public Safety Agencies," 258.

170. Buck, *Preparing for Terrorism,* 296.

171. Harry C. Holloway, Ann E. Norwood, Carol S. Fullerton, Charles C. Engel, Jr., and Robert J. Ursano, "The Threat of Biological Weapons: Prophylaxis and Mitigation of Psychological and Social Consequences," in *Biological Weapons: Limiting the Threat,* ed. Joshua Lederberg (Cambridge, MA: MIT Press, 1999), 252; De Lorenzo and Porter, *Weapons of Mass Destruction: Emergency Care,* 4.

172. Cole, *The Eleventh Plague,* 219; Lena Norlander et al., eds., *FOA Informerar: Biological Weapons* (Umea: FOA, 1995), 6.

173. Jeffrey D. Simon, "Biological Terrorism: Preparing the Meet the Threat," in *Biological Weapons: Limiting the Threat,* ed. Joshua Lederberg (Cambridge, MA: MIT Press, 1999), 244.

174. Sprinzak, "On Not Overstating the Problem," 15; De Lorenzo and Porter, *Weapons of Mass Destruction: Emergency Care,* 5.

175. Holloway et al., "The Threat of Biological Weapons," 252, 254; Falkenrath, Newman, and Thayer, *America's Achilles' Heel,* 6; Jenkins, "The WMD Terrorist Threat—Is There a Consensus View?" 249.

176. Tucker, "Bioterrorism: Threats and Responses," 317n108; *Assessing the Threat,* 48; Tucker, "Policy Approaches to Chemical and Biological Terrorism," 96.

177. Tucker, "Policy Approaches to Chemical and Biological Terrorism," 260.

178. *Assessing the Threat,* 19.

179. *Assessing the Threat,* 19.

180. De Lorenzo and Porter, *Weapons of Mass Destruction: Emergency Care,* 7.

181. Critical Incident Analysis Group, "Public Responsibility and Mass Destruction: Facing the Threat of Bioterrorism," 102, presented at the 4th Annual Conference of the Critical Incident Analysis Group, Charlottesville, VA, April 2–3, 2001.

182. Critical Incident Analysis Group, "Public Responsibility and Mass Destruction," 104.

183. Committee on R&D Needs and Commission on Life Sciences, *Chemical and Biological Terrorism,* 27, 184; Falkenrath, Newman, and Thayer, *America's Achilles' Heel,* 303; Tucker, "Chemical/Biological Terrorism," 178.

184. Falkenrath, Newman, and Thayer, *America's Achilles' Heel,* 154; Joshua Lederberg, "Introduction," in *Biological Weapons: Limiting the Threat,* ed. Joshua Lederberg (Cambridge, MA: MIT Press, 1999), 8; Tucker, "Bioterrorism: Threats and Responses," 312; Tucker, "Measures to Fight Chemical/Biological Terrorism," 242; Michael Osterholm and Luther L. Fincher, Jr., "A Public Health Response to Terrorism," in *Biological Terrorism and Weapons of Mass Destruction,* ed. Gary E. McCuen (Hudson, WI: Gary McCuen Publications Inc., 1999), 28; Committee on R&D Needs and Commission on Life Sciences, *Chemical and Biological Terrorism,* 27, 184; Alan P. Zelicoff, "Preparing for Biological Terrorism: First, Do No Harm," *Politics and Life Sciences* 15, no. 2 (September 1996): 235–236.

185. Osterholm and Fincher, "A Public Health Response to Terrorism," 28; Committee on R&D Needs and Commission on Life Sciences, *Chemical and Biological Terrorism,* 78–79.

186. Committee on R&D Needs and Commission on Life Sciences, *Chemical and Biological Terrorism,* 65; Osterholm and Fincher, "A Public Health Response to Terrorism," 28.

187. Crone, *Banning Chemical Weapons,* 1, 7.

188. Graham S. Pearson, "Biological Weapons: Their Nature and Arms Control," in *Non-Conventional Weapons Proliferation in the Middle East: Tackling the Spread of Nuclear, Chemical, and Biological Capabilities,* ed. Efraim Karsh, Martin S. Navias, and Philip Sabin (Oxford: Clarendon Press, 1993), 108.

189. Matthew Meselson, Jeanne Guillemin, Martin Hugh-Jones, Alexander Langmuir, Ilona Popova, Alexis Shelokov, and Olga Yampolskaya, "The Sverdlovsk Anthrax Outbreak of 1979," in *Biological Weapons: Limiting the Threat,* ed. Joshua Lederberg (Cambridge, MA: MIT Press, 1999), 206.

190. Marlo, "WMD Terrorism and US Intelligence Collection," 70; Falkenrath, Newman, and Thayer, *America's Achilles' Heel,* 292–292, 124–125; Cole, *The Eleventh Plague,* 208–209.

191. Falkenrath, Newman, and Thayer, *America's Achilles' Heel,* 240.

192. Critical Incident Analysis Group, "Public Responsibility and Mass Destruction," 34.

193. Committee on R&D Needs and Commission on Life Sciences, *Chemical and Biological Terrorism,* 67.

194. Committee on R&D Needs and Commission on Life Sciences, *Chemical and Biological Terrorism,* 71.

195. Jonathan Ban, *Agricultural and Biological Warfare: An Overview* (Washington, D.C.: Chemical and Biological Arms Control Institute, June 2000), 5.

196. Holloway et al., "The Threat of Biological Weapons," 261.

CHAPTER 13

Project Megiddo

II. INTRODUCTION (PART ONE DELETED)*

Are we already living on the precipice of the Apocalypse—the chaotic final period of warfare between the forces of good and evil signaling the second coming of Christ, as forecast in the New Testament's Book of Revelation? Or, will life on earth continue for another 1,000 years, allowing humans to eliminate disease and solve the mysteries of the aging process so they can live as long as Methuselah, colonize space, commune with extraterrestrials, unravel the secrets of teleportation, and usher in a golden age of peace and productivity?[1]

At first glance, some of the predictions compiled in *Prophecies for the New Millennium* that claim to foretell how the millennium will affect the United States seem

* The following *excerpt* was taken from a report entitled Project Megiddo, which was an FBI strategic assessment of the potential for domestic terrorism in the United States undertaken in anticipation of or response to the arrival of the new millennium. The entire report may be found at *http://permanent.access.gpo.gov/lps3578/www.fbi.gov/library/megiddo/megiddo.pdf*. The authors thank the FBI for the use of this document.

benign. In fact, those predictions capture some of the countless ways that domestic terrorists view how the millennium will affect the world. The threat posed by extremists as a result of perceived events associated with the Year 2000 (Y2K) is very real.

Numerous religious extremists claim that a race war will soon begin, and have taken steps to become martyrs in their predicted battle between good and evil. Three recent incidents committed by suspects who adhere to ideologies that emphasize millennial related violence illustrate those beliefs: Buford O. Furrow, Jr., the man charged in the August 1999 shootings at a Los Angeles area Jewish day care center, told authorities "its time for America to wake and kill the Jews"; Ben Smith, who committed suicide after shooting at minorities in Indiana and Illinois, killing two and injuring ten, over the July 4, 1999 weekend, was found to have literature in his home that indicated the year 2000 would be the start of the killing of minorities; and John William King, the man convicted in the dragging death of James Byrd, Jr., a black man in Jasper, Texas, believed that his actions would help to initiate a race war. Each of these men believed in the imminence of a racial holy war.

Meanwhile, for members of the militia movement the new millennium has a political overtone rather than a religious one. It is their belief that the United Nations has created a secret plan, known as the New World Order (NWO), to conquer the world beginning in 2000. The NWO will be set in motion by the Y2K computer crisis.

Religious motivation and the NWO conspiracy theory are the two driving forces behind the potential for millennial violence. As the end of the millennium draws near, biblical prophecy and political philosophy may merge into acts of violence by the more extreme members of domestic terrorist groups that are motivated, in part, by religion. The volatile mix of apocalyptic religions and NWO conspiracy theories may produce violent acts aimed at precipitating the end of the world as prophesied in the Bible.

When and how Christ's second coming will occur is a critical point in the ideology of those motivated by extremist religious beliefs about the millennium. There is no consensus within Christianity regarding the specific date that the Apocalypse will occur. However, within many right-wing religious groups there is a uniform belief that the Apocalypse is approaching. Some of these same groups also point to a variety of non-religious indicators such as gun control, the Y2K computer problem, the NWO, the banking system, and a host of other "signs" that the Apocalypse is near. Almost uniformly, the belief among right-wing religious extremists is that the federal government is an arm of Satan. Therefore, the millennium will bring about a battle between Christian martyrs and the government. At the core of this volatile mix is the belief of apocalyptic religions and cults that the battle against Satan, as prophesied in the Book of Revelation, will begin in 2000.

An example of the confrontational nature and belief system of religiously motivated suspects illustrates the unique challenges that law enforcement faces when dealing with a fatalist/martyr philosophy. It also illustrates the domino effect that may occur after such a confrontation. Gordon Kahl, an adherent to the anti-government/racist Christian Identity religion, escaped after a 1983 shootout with police that left two Deputy U.S. Marshals dead. He was later killed during a subsequent shootout with the FBI and others that also left a county sheriff dead. In response to the killing of Kahl, Bob

Mathews, a believer in the racist Odinist ideology, founded The Order. After The Order committed numerous crimes, its members were eventually tracked down. Mathews escaped after engaging in a gun battle and later wrote,

> "Why are so many men so eager to destroy their own kind for the benefit of the Jews and the mongrels? I see three FBI agents hiding behind some trees. . . . I could have easily killed them. . . . They look like good racial stock yet all their talents are given to a government which is openly trying to mongrelize the very race these agents are part of. . . . I have been a good soldier, a fearless warrior. I will die with honor and join my brothers in [heaven]."

Exemplifying his beliefs as a martyr, Mathews later burned to death in an armed standoff with the FBI.

In light of the enormous amount of millennial rhetoric, the FBI sought to analyze a number of variables that have the potential to spark violent acts perpetrated by domestic terrorists. Religious beliefs, the Y2K computer problem, and gun control laws all have the potential to become catalysts for such terrorism. The following elements are essential to understanding the phenomenon of domestic terrorism related to the millennium:

BLUEPRINT FOR ACTION: *THE TURNER DIARIES*

Many right-wing extremists are inspired by *The Turner Diaries,* a book written by William Pierce (under the pseudonym Andrew Macdonald), the leader of the white supremacist group National Alliance. The book details a violent overthrow of the federal government by white supremacists and also describes a brutal race war that is to take place simultaneously. To date, several groups or individuals have been inspired by this book:

- At the time of his arrest. Timothy McVeigh, the man responsible for the Oklahoma City bombing, had a copy of *The Turner Diaries* in his possession. McVeigh's action against the Murrah Federal Building was strikingly similar to an event described in the book where the fictional terrorist group blows up FBI Headquarters.

- The Order, an early 1980s terrorist cell involved in murder, robberies, and counterfeiting, was motivated by the book's scenarios for a race war. The group murdered Alan Berg, a Jewish talk show host, and engaged in other acts of violence in order to hasten the race war described in the book. The Order's efforts later inspired another group, The New Order, which planned to commit similar crimes in an effort to start a race war that would lead to a violent revolution.[2]

- Most recently, *The Turner Diaries* provided inspiration to John William King, the man convicted for dragging a black man to his death in Jasper, Texas. As

King shackled James Byrd's legs to the back of his truck he was reported to say, "We're going to start the Turner Diaries early."[3]

During the year 2000 and beyond, *The Turner Diaries* will be an inspiration for right-wing terrorist groups to act because it outlines both a revolutionary takeover of the government and a race war. These elements of the book appeal to a majority of right-wing extremists because it is their belief that one or both events will coincide with Y2K.

INTERPRETATIONS OF THE BIBLE

Religiously based domestic terrorists use the New Testament's Book of Revelation—the prophecy of the endtime—for the foundation of their belief in the Apocalypse. Religious extremists interpret the symbolism portrayed in the Book of Revelation and mold it to predict that the endtime is now and that the Apocalypse is near. To understand many religious extremists, it is crucial to know the origin of the Book of Revelation and the meanings of its words, numbers and characters.

The Book of Revelation was written by a man named "John" who was exiled by the Roman government to a penal colony—the island of Patmos—because of his beliefs in Christ.[4] While on the island, he experienced a series of visions, described in the Book of Revelation. The writing in the Book of Revelation is addressed to churches that were at the time experiencing or were threatened by persecution from Rome because they were not following the government. For this reason, some believe the Book of Revelation was written in code language, much of which was taken from other parts of the Bible.

One interpretation describing the essence of the message contained in Revelation is that God will overcome Christianity's enemies (Roman Government/Satan) and that the persecuted communities should persevere.[5] For right-wing groups who believe they are being persecuted by the satanic government of the United States, the Book of Revelation's message fits perfectly into their world view. This world view, in combination with a literal interpretation of the Book of Revelation, is reflected in extremist ideology, violent acts, and literature. For this reason, it is imperative to know the meaning of some of the "code words" frequently used:

- Four (4) signifies the world.
- Six (6) signifies imperfection.
- Seven (7) is the totality of perfection or fullness and completeness.
- Twelve (12) represents the twelve tribes of Israel or the 12 apostles.
- One-thousand (1,000) signifies immensity.
- The color white symbolizes power and can also represent victory, joy and resurrection.
- The color red symbolizes a bloody war.
- The color black symbolizes famine.

- A rider on a pale green horse is a symbol of Death itself.
- "Babylon" is the satanic Roman Government, now used to describe the U.S. government.[6]

Black Hebrew Israelites, a black supremacist group, typify the use of numerology from the Book of Revelation. They believe group members will comprise the 144,000 people who are saved by God in the second coming that is outlined in Revelation (7:1–17). In the Book of Revelation, John is shown a vision of 144,000 martyrs who have survived and did not submit to Satan. This number is derived from the assertion that the twelve tribes of Israel consisted of 12,000 people each.

Groups not only use the Bible to interpret the endtimes, but use it to justify their ideology. Phineas Priests, an amorphous group of Christian Identity adherents, base their entire ideology on Chapter 25 of the Book of Numbers. The passage depicts a scene where Phineas kills an Israelite who was having relations with a Midianite woman and God then granted Phineas and all of his descendants a pledge of everlasting priesthood. Modern day followers of the Phineas Priest ideology believe themselves to be the linear descendants of Phineas and this passage gives them biblical justification to punish those who transgress God's laws. Therefore, the group is ardently opposed to race mixing and strongly believes in racial separation. The number 25 is often used as a symbol of the group.

APOCALYPTIC RELIGIOUS BELIEFS

To understand the mind set of why religious extremists would actively seek to engage in violent confrontations with law enforcement, the most common extremist ideologies must be understood. Under these ideologies, many extremists view themselves as religious martyrs who have a duty to initiate or take part in the coming battles against Satan. Domestic terrorist groups who place religious significance on the millennium believe the federal government will act as an arm of Satan in the final battle. By extension, the FBI is viewed as acting on Satan's behalf.

The philosophy behind targeting the federal government or entities perceived to be associated with it is succinctly described by Kerry Noble, a former right-wing extremist. He says the right-wing "envision[s] a dark and gloomy endtime scenario, where some Antichrist makes war against Christians."[7] The House of Yahweh, a Texas based religious group whose leaders are former members of the tax protesting Posse Comitatus, is typical: Hawkins (the leader) has interpreted biblical scripture that the Israeli Peace Accord signed on October 13, 1993, has started a 7-year period of tribulation which will end on October 14, 2000, with the return of the Yeshua (the Messiah).[8] He also has interpreted that the FBI will be the downfall of the House of Yahweh and that the Waco Branch Davidian raids in 1993 were a warning to The House of Yahweh from the federal government, which he terms "the beast."[9] Similarly, Richard Butler, leader of the white supremacist group Aryan Nations, said the following when asked what might have motivated the day care shooting by Buford O. Furrow, Jr., one of his group's followers: "There's a war against the white race. There's a war of extermination against the white male."[10]

VI. BLACK HEBREW ISRAELITES

As the millennium approaches, radical fringe members of the Black Hebrew Israelite (BHI) movement may pose a challenge for law enforcement. As with the adherents of most apocalyptic philosophies, certain segments of the BHI movement have the potential to engage in violence at the turn of the century. This movement has been associated with extreme acts of violence in the recent past, and current intelligence from a variety of sources indicates that extreme factions of BHI groups are preparing for a race war to close the millennium.

Violent BHI followers can generally be described as proponents of an extreme form of black supremacy. Drawing upon the teachings of earlier BHI adherents, such groups hold that blacks represent God's true "chosen people," while condemning whites as incarnate manifestations of evil. As God's "authentic" Jews, BHI adherents believe that mainstream Jews are actually imposters. Such beliefs bear a striking resemblance to the Christian Identity theology practiced by many white supremacists. In fact, Tom Metzger, renowned white supremacist, once remarked, "They're the black counterpart of us."[11] Like their Christian Identity counterparts, militant BHI followers tend to see themselves as divinely endowed by God with superior status. As a result, some followers of this belief system hold that violence, including murder, is justifiable in the eyes of God, provided that it helps to rid the world of evil. Violent BHI groups are of particular concern as the millennium approaches because they believe in the inevitability of a race war between blacks and whites.

The extreme elements of the BHI movement are prone to engage in violent activity. As seen in previous convictions of BHI followers, adherents of this philosophy have a proven history of violence, and several indications point toward a continuation of this trend. Some BHI followers have been observed in public donning primarily black clothing, with emblems and/or patches bearing the "Star of David" symbol. Some BHI members practice paramilitary operations and wear web belts and shoulder holsters. Some adherents have extensive criminal records for a variety of violations, including weapons charges, assault, drug trafficking, and fraud.

In law enforcement circles, BHI groups are typically associated with violence and criminal activity, largely as a result of the movement's popularization by Yahweh Ben Yahweh, formerly known as Hulon Mitchell, Jr., and the Miami-based Nation of Yahweh (NOY). In reality, the origins of the BHI movement are non-violent. While the BHI belief system may have roots in the United States as far back as the Civil War era, the movement became more recognized as a result of the teachings of an individual known as Ben Ami Ben Israel, a.k.a Ben Carter, from the south side of Chicago. Ben Israel claims to have had a vision at the age of 27, hearing "a voice tell me that the time had come for Africans in America, the descendants of the Biblical Israelites, to return to the land of our forefathers."[12] Ben Israel persuaded a group of African-Americans to accompany him to Israel in 1967, teaching that African-Americans descended from the biblical tribe of Judah and, therefore, that Israel is the land of their birthright. Ben Israel and his followers initially settled in Liberia for the purposes of cleansing themselves of bad habits. In 1969, a small group of BHI followers left Liberia for Israel, with Ben Israel and the remaining original migrants arriving in Israel the following year. Public source estimates of the BHI community in Israel number between 1500 and 3000.[13] Despite promoting non-violence, members of Ben Israel's movement have shown a willingness to engage in criminal activity. For example, in 1986, Ben Israel and his top aide, Prince Asiel Ben Israel, were convicted of trafficking stolen passports and securities and forging checks and savings bonds.[14]

BHI in Israel are generally peaceful, if somewhat controversial. The FBI has no information to indicate that Ben Israel's BHI community in Israel is planning any activity—terrorist, criminal, or otherwise—inspired by the coming millennium. Ben Israel's claims to legitimate Judaism have at times caused consternation to the Israeli government. BHI adherents in Israel have apparently espoused anti-Semitic remarks, labeling Israeli Jews as "imposters."[15] Neither the Israeli government nor the Orthodox rabbinate recognize the legitimacy of BHI claims to Judaism. According to Jewish law, an individual can be recognized as Jewish if he/she was born to a Jewish mother or if the individual agrees to convert to Judaism.[16] At present, BHI in Israel have legal status as temporary residents, which gives them the right to work and live in Israel, but not to vote. They are not considered to be Israeli citizens. While BHI claims to Judaism are disregarded by Israeli officials and religious leaders, the BHI community is tolerated and appears to be peaceful.[17]

While the BHI community in Israel is peaceful, BHI adherents in the United States became associated with violence thanks to the rise of the NOY, which reached the height of its popularity in the 1980s. The NOY was founded in 1979 and led by Yahweh Ben Yahweh. Ben Yahweh's followers viewed him as the Messiah, and therefore demonstrated unrequited and unquestioned obedience. Members of the organization engaged in numerous acts of violence in the 1980s, including several homicides, following direct orders from Ben Yahweh. Seventeen NOY members were indicted by a federal grand jury in Miami in 1990–91 on charges of RICO, RICO conspiracy, and various racketeering acts. Various members were convicted on RICO conspiracy charges and remain imprisoned.

While the overwhelming majority of BHI followers are unlikely to engage in violence, there are elements of this movement with both the motivation and the capability to engage in millennial violence. Some radical BHI adherents are clearly motivated by the conviction that the approach of the year 2000 brings society ever closer to a violent confrontation between blacks and whites. While the rhetoric professed by various BHI groups is fiery and threatening, there are no indications of explicitly identified targets for violence, beyond a general condemnation and demonization of whites and "imposter" Jews. Militant BHI groups tend to distrust the United States government; however, there are no specific indications of imminent violence toward the government.

VII. APOCALYPTIC CULTS

For apocalyptic cults, especially biblically based ones, the millennium is viewed as the time that will signal a major transformation for the world. Many apocalyptic cults share the belief that the battle against Satan, as prophesied in the Book of Revelation, will begin in the years surrounding the millennium and that the federal government is an arm of Satan. Therefore, the millennium will bring about a battle between cult members—religious martyrs—and the government.

In the broadest meaning, cults are composed of individuals who demonstrate "great devotion to a person, idea, object or movement."[18] However, using that definition, many domestic terrorist groups could be characterized as cults, including Christian Identity churches, Black Hebrew Israelites, and some militias. For law enforcement purposes, a narrower interpretation of groups that qualify as cults is needed. A more useful definition of cults incorporates the term "cultic relationships" to describe the interactions within a cult.[19] Specifically, a cultic relationship refers to "one in which a person intentionally induces others to become totally or nearly totally dependent on him or her for almost all major life decisions, and inculcates in these followers a belief that he or she has some special talent, gift, or knowledge."[20] This definition of cults provides important distinctions that are vital for analyzing a cult's predilection towards violence.

The origin of the cult, the role of its leader, and its uniqueness provide a framework for understanding what distinguishes cults from other domestic terrorist groups that otherwise share many similar characteristics. These distinctions are: (1) cult leaders are self-appointed, persuasive persons who claim to have a special mission in life or have special knowledge; (2) a cult's ideas and dogma claim to be innovative and exclusive; and (3) cult leaders focus their members' love, devotion and allegiance on themselves.[21] These characteristics culminate in a group structure that is frequently highly authoritarian in structure. Such a structure is a sharp contrast to the rapidly emerging trend among domestic terrorist groups towards a leaderless, non-authoritarian structure.

While predicting violence is extremely difficult and imprecise, there are certain characteristics that make some cults more prone to violence. Law enforcement officials should be aware of the following factors:

- **Sequestered Groups:** Members of sequestered groups lose access to the outside world and information preventing critical evaluation of the ideas being espoused by the leader.

- **Leader's History:** The fantasies, dreams, plans, and ideas of the leader are most likely to become the beliefs of the followers because of the totalitarian and authoritarian nature of cults.

- **Psychopaths:** Control of a group by charismatic psychopaths or those with narcissistic character disorders.

- **Changes in the Leader:** Changes in a leader's personality caused by traumatic events such as death of a spouse or sickness.

- **Language of the Ideology:** Groups that are violent use language in their ideology that contains the seeds of violence.

- **Implied Directive for Violence:** Most frequently, a leader's speeches, rhetoric, and language does not explicitly call for violence, rather it is most often only implied.

- **Length of Time:** The longer the leader's behavior has gone unchecked against outside authority, the less vulnerable the leader feels.

- **Who Is in the Inner Circle:** Cults with violent tendencies often recruit people who are either familiar with weapons or who have military backgrounds to serve as enforcers.

Apocalyptic cults see their mission in two general ways: They either want to accelerate the end of time or take action to ensure that they survive the millennium. For example, Aum Shinrikyo wanted to take action to hasten the end of the world, while compounds in general are built to survive the endtime safely. An analysis of millennial cults by the FBI's Behavioral Science Unit describes how rhetoric changes depending on whether the leader's ideology envisions the group as playing an active role in the coming Apocalypse or a passive survivalist role:

> A cult that predicts that "God will punish" or "evil will be punished" indicates a more passive and less threatening posture than the cult that predicts that "God's chosen people will punish. . . ." As another example, the members of a passive group might predict that God or another being will one day liberate their souls from their bodies or come to carry them away. The followers of a more action-oriented group would, in contrast, predict that they themselves will one day shed their mortal bodies or transport themselves to another place.[22]

A cult that displays these characteristics may then produce three social-psychological components, referred to as the "Lethal Triad," that predispose a cult towards violence aimed at its members and/or outsiders.[23] Cults in which members are heavily dependent on the leader for all decision making almost always physically and psychologically isolate their members from outsiders, the first component of the triad.[24] The other two components interact in the following way:

> "—**isolation** causes a reduction of critical thinking on the part of group members who become entrenched in the belief proposed by the group leadership. As a result, group members relinquish all responsibility for group decision making to their leader and blame the cause of all group grievances on some outside entity or force, a process known as **projection.** Finally, isolation and projection combine to produce pathological **anger,** the final component of the triad."[25]

Of the nearly 1000 cults operating in the United States, very few present credible threats for millennial violence. Law enforcement officials should concentrate on those cults that advocate force or violence to achieve their goals concerning the end time, as well as those cults which possess a substantial number of the distinguishing traits listed above.[26] In particular, cults of greatest concern to law enforcement are those that: (1) believe they play a special, elite role in the end time; (2) believe violent offensive action is needed to fulfill their end time prophecy; (3) take steps to attain their beliefs. Those factors may culminate in plans to initiate conflict with outsiders or law enforcement.

The violent tendencies of dangerous cults can be classified into two general categories—defensive violence and offensive violence. Defensive violence is utilized by cults to defend a compound or enclave that was created specifically to eliminate most contact with the dominant culture.[27] The 1993 clash in Waco, Texas at the Branch

Davidian complex is an illustration of such defensive violence. History has shown that groups that seek to withdraw from the dominant culture seldom act on their beliefs that the end-time has come unless provoked.[28]

Cults with an apocalyptic agenda, particularly those that appear ready to initiate rather than anticipate violent confrontations to bring about Armageddon or fulfill "prophecy" present unique challenges to law enforcement officials. One example of this type of group is the Concerned Christians (CC). Monte Kim Miller, the CC leader, claims to be one of the two witnesses or prophets described in the Book of Revelation who will die on the streets of Jerusalem prior to the second coming of Christ. To attain that result, members of the CC traveled to Israel in 1998 in the belief that Miller will be killed in a violent confrontation in the streets of Jerusalem in December 1999. CC members believe that Miller's death will set off an apocalyptic end to the millennium, at which time all of Miller's followers will be sent to Heaven. Miller has convinced his followers that America is "Babylon the Great" referred to in the Book of Revelation. In early October 1998, CC members suddenly vanished from the United States, an apparent response to one of Miller's "prophecies" that Denver would be destroyed on October 10, 1998. In January 1999, fourteen members of the group who had moved to Jerusalem were deported by the Israeli government on the grounds that they were preparing to hasten the fulfillment of Miller's prophecies by instigating violence.[29]

Ascertaining the intentions of such cults is a daunting endeavor, particularly since the agenda or plan of a cult is often at the whim of its leader. Law enforcement personnel should become well acquainted with the previously mentioned indicators of potential cult violence in order to separate the violent from the non-violent.

VIII. THE SIGNIFICANCE OF JERUSALEM

The city of Jerusalem, cherished by Jews, Christians, and Muslims alike, faces many serious challenges as the year 2000 approaches. As already evidenced by the deportation of various members of the religious cult known as the Concerned Christians, zealotry from all three major monotheistic religions is particularly acute in Israel, where holy shrines, temples, churches, and mosques are located. While events surrounding the millennium in Jerusalem are much more problematic for the Israeli government than for the United States, the potential for violent acts in Jerusalem will cause reverberations around the world, including the United States. The extreme terrorist fringes of Christianity, Judaism, and Islam are all present in the United States. Thus, millennial violence in Jerusalem could conceivably lead to violence in the United States as well.

Within Jerusalem, the Temple Mount, or Haram al-Sharif, holds a special significance for both Muslims and Jews.[30] The Temple Mount houses the third holiest of all Islamic sites, the Dome of the Rock. Muslims believe that the prophet Muhammad ascended to Heaven from a slab of stone—the "Rock of Foundation"—located in the center of what is now the Dome of the Rock. In addition, when Arab armies conquered Jerusalem in 638 A.D., the Caliph Omar built the al-Aqsa Mosque facing the Dome of the Rock on the opposite end of the Temple Mount. The Western (or Wailing) Wall, the last remnant of the second Jewish temple that the Romans destroyed in 70 A.D., stands at the western base of the Temple Mount. The Western Wall has long been a favorite pilgrimage site for Jews, and religious men and women pray there on a daily basis. Thus, the Temple Mount is equally revered by Jews as the site upon which the first and second Jewish Temples stood.

Israeli officials are extremely concerned that the Temple Mount, an area already seething with tension and distrust among Jews and Muslims, will be the stage for violent encounters between religious zealots. Most troubling is the fact that an act of terrorism need not be the catalyst that sparks widespread violence. Indeed, a simple symbolic act of desecration, or even perceived desecration, of any of the holy sites on the Temple Mount is likely to trigger a violent reaction. For example, the Islamic holy month of Ramadan is expected to coincide with the arrival of the year 2000. Thus, even minor provocations on or near the Temple Mount may provide the impetus for a violent confrontation.

The implications of pilgrimages to Jerusalem by vast numbers of tourists are ominous, particularly since such pilgrimages are likely to include millennial or apocalyptic cults on a mission to hasten the arrival of the Messiah. There is general concern among Israeli officials that Jewish and Islamic extremists may react violently to the influx of Christians, particularly near the Temple Mount. The primary concern is that extreme millennial cults will engage in proactive violence designed to hasten the second coming of Christ. Perhaps the most likely scenario involves an attack on the Al-Aqsa Mosque or the Dome of the Rock. Some millennial cults hold that these structures must be destroyed so that the Jewish Temple can be rebuilt, which they see as a prerequisite for the return of the Messiah. Additionally, several religious cults have already made inroads into Israel, apparently in preparation for what they believe to be the end times.

It is beyond the scope of this document to assess the potential repercussions from an attack on Jewish or Islamic holy sites in Jerusalem. It goes without saying, however, that an attack on the Dome of the Rock or the Al-Aqsa Mosque would have serious implications. In segments of the Islamic world, close political and cultural ties between Israel and the United States are often perceived as symbolic of anti-Islamic policies by the Western world. Attacks on Islamic holy sites in Jerusalem, particularly by Christian or Jewish extremists, are likely to be perceived by Islamic extremists as attacks on Islam itself. Finally, the possibility exists that Islamic extremist groups will capitalize upon the huge influx of foreigners into Jerusalem and engage in a symbolic attack.

IX. CONCLUSION

Extremists from various ideological perspectives attach significance to the arrival of the year 2000, and there are some signs of preparations for violence. The significance of the new millennium is based primarily upon either religious beliefs relating to the Apocalypse/Armageddon, or political beliefs relating to the New World Order conspiracy theory. The challenge to law enforcement is to understand these extremist theories and, if any incidents do occur, be prepared to respond to the unique crises they will represent.

Law enforcement officials should be particularly aware that the new millennium may increase the odds that extremists may engage in proactive violence specifically targeting law enforcement officers. Religiously motivated extremists may initiate violent conflicts with law enforcement officials in an attempt to facilitate the onset of Armageddon, or to help fulfill a "prophecy." For many on the extreme right-wing, the battle of Armageddon is interpreted as a race war to be fought between Aryans and the "satanic" Jews and their allies. Likewise, extremists who are convinced that the millennium will lead to a One World Government may choose to engage in violence to prevent such a situation from occurring. In either case, extremists motivated by the millennium could choose martyrdom when approached or confronted by law enforcement officers. Thus, law enforcement officials should be alert for the following: 1) plans to initiate conflict with law enforcement; 2) the potential increase in the number of extremists willing to become martyrs; and 3) the potential for a quicker escalation of conflict during routine law enforcement activities (e.g. traffic stops, issuance of warrants, etc.).

ENDNOTES

1. Cliff Linedecker, *Prophecies for the New Millennium* (Lantana, FL: Micromags, 1999), 3–4.
2. Charles Bosworth Jr., "Illinois Man Sought Start of Race War," *St. Louis Post-Dispatch,* March 15, 1998.
3. Paul Duggan, "From Beloved Son to Murder Suspect," *The Washington Post,* February 16, 1999.
4. While he never claimed to be the book's author, the Apostle John was identified as such by several of the early church Fathers. Authorship is generally ascribed to him today.
5. This interpretation of the Book of Revelation is according to the Catholic Bible and a Catholic scholar that was consulted on the matter. However, there are other varying interpretations of the Book of Revelation within Christianity.
6. All symbolism was taken from *The Catholic Bible: New American Bible*
7. Kerry Noble, *Tabernacle of Hate: Why They Bombed Oklahoma City* (Prescott, Ontario, Canada: Voyageur Publishing, 1998).
8. Robert Draper, "Happy Doomsday," *Texas Monthly,* July 1997, 74; Evan Moore, "A House Divided: Tensions divide Abilene-area cult," *The Houston Chronicle,* March 24, 1996.
9. Evan Moore, "A House Divided: Tensions divide Abilene-area cult."
10. John K. Wiley, "Profile of Attack Suspect Is Familiar and Frightening," *Miami Herald,* August 12, 1999.
11. See Fall 1997 edition of the Southern Poverty Law Center's *Intelligence Report,* "Rough Waters: Stream of Knowledge Probed by Officials."
12. Linda Jones "Claiming a Promised Land: African-American Settlers in Israel are guided by idea of independent Black Hebrew Society," *The Dallas Morning News,* July 27, 1997.
13. Ibid.
14. See Fall 1997 Southern Poverty Law Center's *Intelligence Report,* "Rough Waters: Stream of Knowledge Probed by Officials."
15. Jones, *Dallas Morning News,* July 27, 1997.
16. Ibid.
17. Ibid. In fact, in the community of Dimona where the BHI community resides, the Dimona Police Chief spoke in complimentary terms as to the group's discipline, leadership, and integrity.
18. Frederick C. Mish, ed., *Merriam Webster's Collegiate Dictionary, 10th ed.* (Springfield, MA: Merriam-Webster, Incorporated, 1997), 282

19. Margaret Thaler Singer and Janja Lalich, *Cults in Our Midst: The Hidden Menace in Our Everyday Lives* (San Francisco, CA: Jossey-Bass Publishers, 1995), 7.

20. Singer and Lalich, *Cults in Our Midst,* 7.

21. Singer and Lalich, *Cults in Our Midst,* 8–9.

22. Carl J. Jensen, III, Rod Gregg and Adam Szubin, "When a Cult Comes to Town," accessed from Law Enforcement Online.

23. Kevin M. Gilmartin, "The Lethal Triad: Understanding the Nature of Isolated Extremist Groups," accessed at www.fbi.gov/publications/leb/1996/sept961.txt.

24. Carl J. Jensen, III and Yvonne Hsieh, "Law Enforcement and the Millennialist Vision: A Behavioral Approach," accessed from Law Enforcement Online.

25. Ibid.

26. B.A. Robinson in "Factors Commonly Found in Doomsday Cults," (*www.religioustolerance.org/cultsign.htm*) identifies traits that provide a framework for analyzing cults. They include the following: 1) The leader preaches end of the world/Armageddon in 2000 or within a reasonable time frame before and after 2000; 2) the cult expects to play a major elite role at the end-time; 3) the cult has large numbers of firearms, explosives, or weapons of mass destruction; 4) the cult has prepared defensive structures; 5) the cult speaks of offensive action; 4) the cult is led by a single male charismatic leader; 5) the leader dominates the membership through physical, sexual, and emotional control; 6) the cult is not an established denomination; 7) cult members live together in a community isolated from society; 8) extreme paranoia exists within the cult concerning monitoring by outsiders and government persecution; 9) and outsiders are distrusted and disliked. These factors are designed to leave out cults that have unique end-time beliefs but whose ideology does not include the advocacy of force or violence.

27. Jeffrey Kaplan, *Radical Religion in America: Millenarian Movements from the Far Right to the Children of Noah* (Syracuse, NY: Syracuse University Press, 1997), 57.

28. Ibid., 165

29. Lisa Beyer, "Target: Jerusalem," *Time Magazine,* January 18, 1999.

30. Arabs refer to this site as Haram al-Sharif, which is Arabic for "Noble Sanctuary." Israelis refer to it as Har HaBayit, which is Hebrew for "Temple Mount." American news organizations almost always refer to it as the Temple Mount. Therefore, for the sake of simplicity and continuity, the term Temple Mount will be used in this report when referring to this section of Jerusalem.

SECTION FOUR DISCUSSION QUESTIONS

1. Describe the beliefs of the Institute for Historical Review.
2. Did the IHR fulfill the aspirations of its founders?
3. What are some problems that the IHR experienced in the early 1990s? What organizational changes occurred at that time?
4. Discuss two general characteristics that define cultic groups.
5. Describe New Age theology. How does it increase the likelihood of violence in cultic groups that practice it?
6. What is millennialism? How does it increase the likelihood of violence in cultic groups that practice it?
7. How were millennialism and New Age theology manifested in the Church of the Universal Triumphant?
8. Review the Aum Shinrikyo chemical attack that occurred in Tokyo and compare it to earlier chemical attacks in other countries.
9. Agree or disagree with the following statement and support your answer with examples: Most terrorist groups will continue to rely on improvised weapons such as pesticides and laboratory grade biological elements.
10. What are the biggest hurdles to responding to a CBRN terrorist attack?
11. Explain how religious groups use the New Testament Book of Revelations for the foundation of their belief in the Apocalypse.
12. Define the term cult and give some examples that are discussed in Project Megiddo.
13. What are some characteristics that make certain cults more prone to violence?

SECTION FIVE

Atavistic Terrorism

LOOK FOR THESE KEY POINTS–

- The Christian Identity movement is one of the largest and most long-standing members of the modern extremist right in the United States. It developed out of two early religious traditions: Anglo-Israelitism and charismatic Christianity.

- To understand the white supremacist movements in the United States, we must be able to identify their beliefs and organizational characteristics.

- Leaderless resistance (also called lone wolf terrorism) is characteristic of a particular stage of terrorist groups, not a separate type of terrorism.

- The Basic Christian Community and the Covenant Communities of right-wing Christian organizations are primarily based on scriptures applicable to both evangelical and fundamentalist Christians as well as Christians in the Identity movement.

- A case study of two racially motivated murders in Fayetteville, North Carolina, can help you to understand the reaction to racial and ethnic extremism in the U.S. Army.

INTRODUCTION TO ATAVISTIC TERRORISM: HATE GROUPS AND THE TERRORISM OF THE FAR RIGHT

Atavistic groups wish to return to some earlier time when someone or something was not present in their social or physical environment. Atavistic terrorist groups form when a number of people feel their vested interests are threatened by a group of strangers. They aggressively deny the stranger's civil and social rights through defamation, avoidance, threat, coercion, segregation, colonization (enslavement), relocation, or annihilation (Rose 1990, 111). Animosity toward these strangers can occur through economic competition, authoritarian attitudes, personal frustration, in-group conformity needs, poor or discriminatory education, or any combination of the above factors. Atavistic groups form to achieve a goal that the individuals cannot reach alone. The goal of the atavists is to defend their "space" from those they blame for creating the threat, no matter what interests they see in danger. That a group forms to defend against some enemy implies that they are at the point where they will consider using violence as an immediate defense tactic. In other words, while most terrorist groups will take days, months, years, or even decades to merely approach this point in time, an atavistic group begins there. This is why, from a law enforcement perspective, atavistic groups can be as dangerous as the most violent terrorists on the planet.

Atavistic violence is not the typical tactic that Gamson describes as a successful strategy of challenging groups (Gamson 1997). It is the melding of goal and strategy into one entity. The Atavist belief system spurs them to violence by legitimating their goal of eradication. Gurr (1989) calls it organized opposition to social change, but it is also social regulation without law. It is the explosive reaction of hate, sometimes illogical but always violent, even if the group reacts only with words instead of deeds (Gurr 1989, 20). However, make no mistake; an atavistic group is very unlikely to achieve its goal with just words. More than likely, actions, possibly heinous, will be used. Publicly acceptable motives aid both normal and hate-driven members to link their self-interest to the group's social requirements.

For almost thirty years, the competition model of ethnic conflict has reigned supreme in explaining why atavistic groups develop. This model states that ethnic conflict occurs as part of the social modernization process when jobs, housing, and other valued resources become scarce. If the society is composed of more than one cultural entity, the competition between these ethnic groups becomes so intense that conflict (violence) occurs (Barth 1969; Olzak 1993). Belanger and Pinard (1997) have reformulated this model through a critical historical review and survey research on interethnic competition between the French and English Canadians in Quebec, Canada. They concluded that the competition holds only under very limited circumstances, which include the presence of discriminatory acts, the failure to punish such acts, and the perception that the group is relatively deprived in comparison to its competitors (Belanger and Pinard 1997, 21). Several theorists suggest that social deprivation frustrates individuals and the atavistic groups they form, leading them eventually to the use of violence (McPhail 1971; Gurr 1989).

At least some, if not all, members of atavistic groups experience relative deprivation vis-à-vis the despised group. In other words, the members feel that the despised ones have deprived them of a job, government benefits, or other substantial rewards. They may be members of the majority group, but they behave as if they are not. This is why atavistic groups are so volatile, why they hate, and why they develop violent goals from the inception of their group.

All the chapters in the Section 5 investigate various group processes that differentiate atavistic terrorism from the other types discussed in this book. First is an article by Adam Silverman, "Zealous Before the Lord: The Construction of Christian Identity Theology." Christian Identity has been one of the leading ideologies of American extremists for over thirty years. Dr. Silverman, a leading authority on both religion and extremism, treats us to an insightful history of the Identity belief system. This article also explains why Christian Identity is a strong motivator of violence and how the motivation is perpetuated.

The second chapter describes the beliefs and organizational characteristics of the white supremacist movement in the United States. Lieutenant Etter, who has personally encountered many terrorists, including Timothy McVeigh, in the course of his work, explains how white supremacists recruit members and gather financial resources. He then outlines various violent strategies they prefer, including bombs, sabotage, and assignations. Numerous examples are included with each strategy.

Next is a chapter on leaderless resistance, a type of organizational leadership often used by atavistic groups. After discussing the exact meaning and use of this technique, the paper debunks several myths connected to the term "leaderless resistance." Data collected by organizations that do research on terrorists forms the foundation for the author's analysis.

The fourth chapter in this section is a case study of extremist activity in the U.S. Army. Colonel Reed describes the Burmeister case, in which soldiers allegedly committed two racially motivated murders in Fayetteville, North Carolina, on December 7, 1995. The case study is followed by a discussion of how the army is a tempting target for recruitment by extremist groups. The author concludes that the army cannot escape the growing impact of extremist, racist organizations from society at large. However, he stresses that it must identify and address all extremist behavior that occurs in order to maintain the sacred bond of trust that exists between the army and the American people.

The last chapter, "Rural Radical Religion: Christian Identity and Covenant Community Militias" by Chester L. Quarles, shows us how atavistic groups merge their beliefs with their organizational goals. This merger accelerates their ability to mount violent activities as soon as group formation occurs. This article also discusses one of the newer trends among atavistic terrorist groups, namely their desire to create isolated compounds known as covenant communities. Similar to cultic communities, these are often linked to apocalyptic Identity beliefs.

REFERENCES

Barth, Frederik. 1969. *Ethnic Groups and Boundaries.* Boston: Little, Brown, & Company.

Belanger, Sarah, and Maurice Pinard. 1997. "Ethnic Movements and the Competition Model: Some Missing Links" in *Social Movements,* ed. D. McAdam and D. Snow. Los Angeles, CA: Roxbury Publishing Company, 13–22.

Gamson, William. 1997. "The Success of the Unruly" in *Social Movements,* ed. Doug McAdam and David Snow. Los Angeles, CA: Roxbury Publishing Company, 356–364.

Gurr, Ted Robert. 1989. *Violence in America, Vol. 2.* Newbury Park, CA: Sage Publications.

McPhail, Clark. 1971. "Civil Disorder Participation: A Critical Examination of Recent Research," *American Sociological Review* 36: 1058–1073.

Olzak, Susan. 1993. "Theories of Ethnic Conflict and Subnationalism," presented at the Annual Meeting of the ASA in Washington, D.C., August 1993.

Rose, Peter. 1990. *They and We.* New York: McGraw-Hill Publishing Company.

CHAPTER 14

Zealous Before the Lord: The Construction of Christian Identity Theology

Adam L. Silverman, Ph.D*
Visiting Asst. Professor Temple University (adamsilv@temple.edu)

The Christian Identity movement is one of the largest and most long-standing members of the modern extremist reactionary[1] right in the United States. Christian Identity developed out of two early religious traditions: Anglo-Israelitism and charismatic Christianity (Barkun 1994). This racist fusion has spawned a very large and organized movement, the Aryan Nations, as well as the motivating theology and ideology behind the terrorism and criminal acts of Gordon Kahl, Bob Mathews and the Order, Buford Furrow, Randy Weaver, and Eric Robert Rudolph.

The ability of the leaders of Christian Identity to use their racist, separatist, and xenophobic theology to motivate extralegal forms of political behavior and the interconnections between Christian Identity and other extremist reactionary movements in the United States make it an excellent case for examination. Gordon Kahl, the 1970s tax dissenter who died in a shootout with federal authorities, was a founding member

* I wish to thank Ronald L. Akers and Kenneth W. Wald for reading successive drafts of this chapter. Their assistance was invaluable. I would also like to dedicate this chapter to my Dad, Mitchell Silverman, 1940-2003.

of the Posse Comitatus, an extremist tax dissenting, anti–U.S. government organization (Aho 1990). Bob Mathews, the founder and leader of the Order, started his journey into extremist politics in the John Birch Society and had ties with a number of other extremist groups including the National Alliance (Flynn and Gerhardt 1989), the largest neo-Nazi group in the United States. Eric Robert Rudolph, the alleged Olympic Park Bomber, has been linked to several extreme antiabortion movements ("Running with Rudolph" 2001).

Christian Identity theology has provided all of these actors with ideational motivations and justifications for their activities. In essence, they have learned that it is not only acceptable but that it is theologically preferred to attack Jews, blacks, Asians, Hispanics, homosexuals, the U.S. government, and all others that Identity teaches are evil, deviant, and responsible for the declining status, power, and position of white Christians in America. In this chapter, I will review social learning theory, which provides the most coherent explanation for the effects of ideational motivation on behavior, especially deviant behavior. I will then present a brief history of Christian Identity and several examples of how Identity's definitions favorable to terrorism have been learned by advocates who promote violence.

SOCIAL LEARNING, VIOLENCE, AND TERRORISM

Social learning (Akers et al. 1979; Akers 1985, 1998), one of the most powerful social science explanations for human behavior, posits that behavior in general, and delinquent, deviant, and violent behavior in specific, is learned from one's associational milieu through differential association. The theory of differential association asserts that the primary associations—family, religious affiliation and other identity markers, and peer groups—provide stronger support for behavior than secondary associations. Through associational interaction, individuals are exposed to definitions that promote and justify some behaviors while retarding others. These definitions—teach the individual how to behave. When the individual receives reinforcement (directly or indirectly) for his or her associationally based behavior, he or she will continue until stopped. Other potential offenders with the same primary association(s) will perceive this reinforcement as types of definitions that are favorable and neutralizing, leading them to imitate this type of behavior.

Wieviorka's (1993) research into terrorist groups leads him to posit that terrorists differentially associate with other terrorists in what he refers to as an antimovement. The antimovement is the violent antithesis of the movement it claims to represent. Wieviorka's understanding of the terrorist subculture is an image of a subcultural doppelganger. While the antimovement claims to be striving for the same goals as the movement that it developed out of, it is really not interested in achieving the movement's goals. Rather, it has redefined the movement's objectives into unyielding principles that cannot be compromised. As a result, the antimovement, and the violence that its members use, often cause as much damage to the movement itself as it does to the social or political regime that it seeks to change.

The traditional definitions of terrorism come in a wide variety. Schmid and Jongman (1988) counted and collected over 100 different ones in their survey of terrorism research. These include "official" law enforcement descriptions such as that of the Federal Bureau of Investigation:

> The use of serious violence against persons or property or the threat to use such violence, to intimidate or coerce a government, the public, or any section of the public in order to promote political, social or ideological objectives. (*www.fbi.gov*)

Other definitions take a more academic and research-oriented approach:

> The systematic or threatened use of violence by non-state actors in pursuit of political, social, religious, or ethno-linguistic objectives where the psychological impact of the event considerably surpasses the physical results and the victims are not necessarily the targets. The actions are intended to bring about socio-political change through fear and intimidation. (Schmid and Jongman 1988)

These conceptualizations, however, fail to get at a unique aspect of terrorism that differentiates it from other types of criminal or violent behavior. Unlike rape and theft, which are "predatory" or immediately enriching forms of behavior, terrorism is "moralistic" (Black 1976; Cooney 1998; Senechal de la Roche 1996). That is, it is used to seek redress of perceived grievances and to enforce the norms of the groups and causes with which the terrorists identify against those perceived to have violated them. Terrorists' identities are shaped around strongly held ideologies that define their violence as fully justified acts in service of political, social, religious, or ethnolinguistic ideals and objectives. In this mode, terrorism is:

> the systematic or threatened use of violence by non-state actors attempting to bring about social and political change through fear and intimidation. Terrorism is one way that subcultural actors attempt to resolve the disputes between themselves and the larger culture or between themselves and other subcultures. Acts of terrorism are committed with the intent to assert the subcultural norms and world view of the actors onto the larger culture and/or other subcultures Thus, terrorism is both an "identity-based" and "strategic/utility-maximizing" behavior. (Silverman 2002).[2]

As a result, it is important to understand terrorism in regard to Weber's (1968) notion of value rationality. The terrorist's identity is so strong that it limits the choices of behavior to those permitted by the group context. Moreover, it overcomes the problem of collective action (Olson 1971). Terrorists take actions with high personal costs because of, not despite, their identity. The identity and the context it provides reduce the cognitive costs of terrorism for the terrorist. The narrow identity of the terrorist provides a logic of consequences bound within a logic of appropriateness.

As part of their subcultural identities, terrorists learn an ideology that asserts that the ends justify the means; violence for political ends is accepted and rewarded. Terrorism becomes a way of life and a means for at least some of the members of the subculture to pursue the conflicts that they perceive between themselves and out-groups. In essence, the "framing" of the conflict as a moralistic struggle teaches the terrorists definitions of the situation—when, where, and how often it is morally right or justified to engage in political violence. It is important to note that not every member who participates in or identifies with such a subculture or collectivity will engage in terrorism. A major external determining factor is the availability for action. Even those who have completely learned a set of definitions favorable for terrorism will become terrorists only if there is an opportunity to do so.

Terrorism is a type of instrumental behavior available to members of groups, movements, and subcultures. Terrorists, like other political actors, differentially associate by adopting an identity (Wald 1992). As noted above, the terrorist's identity provides definitions that are favorable and neutralizing through the promotion of a set of definitions that justify killing, destruction, and injury. The extremist subculture provides identity, ideational and physical resources, and a more or less coherent understanding or perspective on the disputes and grievances that are so important to the promotion of violent struggle is an integral type of political behavior. These definitions are transmitted through a variety of media: books, videos, magazines, comic books, and the Internet. The terrorist learns that violence is permissible and rewarded by political outcomes and the approbation of both leaders and members of the group. Certain groups, like al Qaeda, directly transmit definitions that are favorable and neutralizing for specifically planned terrorists attacks on identified targets. In other groups, the learning of violence and appropriate targets is less direct, and the harsh and uncompromising political language used by some leaders and members encourages, without specifically endorsing or planning, violent actions. These may be extreme expressions of religious and political values that the terrorists ostensibly share with others who do not engage in violence. They refrain because they have not adopted the self and group identity of the terrorists and subscribe to countervailing nonviolent definitions that the terrorists do not endorse. This suggests that the concept of "identity" found in political science, sociology, criminology, and religious studies is linked to the social learning concepts of differential association and definitions and may provide linkages between social learning theory and other perspectives on terrorism (Silverman 2002).

CHRISTIAN IDENTITY

Christian Identity, the guiding force behind a large portion of the extremist and racist right in America, is based on a fusion of Anglo/Israelitism, the insurrectionist interpretation of the second amendment, and a belief in the organic constitution (the Ten Commandments, the Articles of Confederation, and the Bill of Rights). Anglo/Israelitism is in the most general sense the belief that the descendants of the Anglo-Saxons are the descendants of the ten lost tribes of Israel and that England is the promised land of milk and honey (Kaplan 1997). This theological trend originally developed in Victorian England and was partially used to justify both Britain's imperial behavior (Barkun 1994) and a patronizing attitude towards Jews. Anglo/Israelitism eventually crossed the Atlantic to the United States, where it was reconceptualized. The American incarnation reworked certain portions of the theology; specifically, America replaced Britain as the promised land. Anglo/Israelitism became entrenched in a number of theological and academic centers, including the Ivy League. In fact, the most prominent Anglo/Israelite in America was President Wilson (Barkun 1994).

In the years between the end of World War II in 1945 and the middle of the 1970s, Anglo/Israelitism, as presented in successive incarnations of American Christian Identity, became infused with a virulently intolerant ideology with regard to race and religion. Adherents also developed the belief that the federal government was illegitimate and was conspiring with Jews and communists to take over and destroy whites and the United States. Christian Identity theologians developed the theory that Satan, in the avatar of the serpent in the Garden of Eden, and Eve had sexual relations and that the ensuing offspring, sometimes identified with Cain, are the Jews (Barkun 1994). The leaders of the modern Christian Identity movement include several "ministers": Richard G. Butler of Aryan Nations, the late Pastor Bob Miles of the Mountain Kirk, Pastor Pete Peters, etc. These leaders dispense religiously inspired hatred from their pulpits.

At the core of Christian Identity theology is the belief that only whites—the descendants of the Anglo-Saxons and other northern Europeans—are really human. The reason for this is that the Hebrew word *Adam,* the first man, means "red man."[3] Christian Identity teaches that if you smack a white person's face, the blood rushes to it in a blush. Identity members believe that since it is not possible to see nonwhites blush, they are not humans (Ridgeway 1991). If you cannot see the blood in the face, then the person is obviously not human. This understanding of who is a human (whites) and who is not—Jews, Africans, Asians, Hispanics, indigenous peoples, and people of mixed ethnicity ("mud people")—provides a theological set of definitions favorable for Christian Identity–based violence. If members of these groups are not really human, then sanctions against killing them do not apply. This definition neutralizes the normal prohibitions against homicide.

The largest group within the Christian Identity movement, the Aryan Nations, has been led until recently by Pastor Richard Girnt Butler from his compound in Couer d'Alene, Idaho. Aryan Nations constitutes one of the largest Christian Identity communities, and includes Butler's Church of Jesus Christ Christian. Aryan Nations has given rise to some of the most violently racist literature, ideology, and behavior in the United States. In September 2000, Pastor Butler and his followers lost a civil suit (*Keenan* v. *Aryan Nations*) that forced them to surrender their compound in order to pay for the judgment against them. Since losing his property, Pastor Butler has appointed several successors to the leadership of Aryan Nations.

Butler, a former engineer at Lockheed Martin and follower of Christian Identity leader Wesley Swift, founded the Church of Jesus Christ Christian in Couer d'Alene in 1973 (Barkun 1994). Aryan Nations grew out of Butler's church and became the political wing of Butler's movement. Butler held annual Aryan Nations World Congresses at his compound for a number of years. These meetings, attended by a variety of racialists and white supremacists, came close to approximating an umbrella organization. Many of the most violent white supremacists have ties to Butler's Aryan Nations.

In the early 1980s, the Order, led by an Aryan Nations follower of Pastor Butler by the name of Robert Mathews, was involved in several major violent incidents (Barkun 1994). Mathews, galvanized into action by the shoot-out death of Gordon Kahl, a tax dissenter, took an oath to G-d as an Aryan warrior to deliver his people from the Jew. After several high-profile armored-car heists, the assassination of Jewish talk-show host Alan Berg in Denver, and several lesser bias-motivated crimes, Mathews died in a stand-off with federal agents in Smugglers Cove, Washington.

More recently, in August 1992, federal law enforcement engaged in a violent stand-off with the Weaver family in Ruby Ridge, Idaho (Wessinger 2000). The Weavers had ties to Pastor Butler's Aryan Nations and his Church of Jesus Christ Christian in Coeur d'Alene. Randy and Vicki Weaver, their children, and family friend Kevin Harris held the U.S. marshals and the FBI at bay for several weeks. The confrontation began when Deputy Marshal William Degan and another marshal attempted to serve a warrant and apprehend Randy Weaver on weapons violations. Degan shot the family dog and shot and killed Sammy Weaver; he was shot and killed in return.

The nearly 2-week standoff ended after FBI sharpshooter Lon Horiuchi shot and killed Vicki Weaver (Wessinger 2000). Horiuchi was following rules of engagement that had been modified onsite by Deputy Director Larry Potts. Randy Weaver and Kevin Harris were subsequently acquitted of murder and conspiracy charges. Involuntary manslaughter charges against Agent Horiuchi were dropped, Deputy Director Potts and others were disciplined, the federal government made a multimillion-dollar settlement with the Weaver family, and both the House of Representatives and the Senate held numerous investigations into the incident.

In the summer of 1999, another major Christian Identity–related incident occurred. On August 10, Buford Furrow, a follower of Pastor Butler and the second husband of Vicki Mathews (Robert Mathews's wife), entered a Los Angeles Jewish Community Center and began shooting. He wounded five people, including several children, and then killed a U.S. postman of Filipino descent while attempting to flee. Furrow's stated reasons for the shooting was to initiate an overly harsh response from the authorities that would galvanize white Christians into action and herald the apocalyptic battle between the forces of G-d (white Christians) and those of Satan (the Jews and their minions: blacks, Asians, Hispanics, and people of mixed ethnicity; Silverman 2003).

As noted, Pastor Butler and the Aryan Nations lost their compound in Couer d'Alene as the result of a civil suit in September of 2000. Morris Dees and the Southern Poverty Law Center brought the lawsuit against Aryan Nations on behalf of Victoria and Jason Keenan (Hellwege 2001). The Keenans' vehicle was pursued and forced from the road by Aryan Nations security after it backfired while they traveled near the Aryan Nations compound. After they were pulled from the vehicle, they were both beaten by the Aryan Nations security guards. It remains to be seen whether or not Pastor Butler's Aryan Nations can survive the $6,330,000 judgment against it.

Christian Identity has gotten even more recent press as a result of the 2003 capture of alleged Olympic/Centennial Park bomber Eric Robert Rudolph. Rudolph was exposed to the anti-Semitic and racial religious message of Christian Identity at an early age ("Running with Rudolph" 2001). Eric's mother, a lapsed Catholic, took Eric and his brother to live in Identity minister Dan Gayman's compound in 1984. Upon their return to North Carolina, Rudolph began to associate with Nord Davis, another Identity minister ("Running with Rudolph" 2001). Given the anti-Semitic, homophobic, antigovernment theology of Christian Identity, it should not be surprising that Rudolph is suspected of bombings at Centennial Olympic Park, two Atlanta-area homosexual nightclubs, and an abortion clinic in Birmingham. A law enforcement officer and a clinic worker were killed in the Alabama bombings (Warner 2000).

Rudolph never directly accepted credit for any of these bombings. Instead, credit was taken by the Army of G-d, a nebulous, extremist antiabortion group (CNN 2002). Forensic inquiry, however, eventually tied Rudolph to all four bombings. Rudolph's former sister-in-law, who was recently interviewed by the Southern Poverty Law Center, indicates that several factors probably contributed to Rudolph's bombing campaign ("Running with Rudolph" 2001). These include his belief that whites were becoming an endangered minority (the clinic bombing), finding out that his younger brother was gay (the nightclub bombings), and his antigovernment views and lingering hostilities over his failure to make it into the Special Forces (the Olympic Park Bombing). Other than his ties to the Christian Identity movement, it is unclear exactly how Rudolph is tied to the Army of G-d. One of the more interesting links that seem to tie Rudolph to the Army of G-d is found on Neal Horsely's Web site, the Nuremberg Files. Horsely had dedicated an entire section to Eric Robert Rudolph and the Army of G-d (*www.christiangallery.com*).

DISCUSSION: CHRISTIAN IDENTITY, SOCIAL LEARNING, AND TERRORISM

Christian Identity theology provides those who adopt it with a set of definitions favorable to engaging in acts of terrorism against the U.S. government and minority groups within the United States. The theological and dogmatic assertion that minorities are not really human is an excellent example of a definition that neutralizes societal conventions and restraints. By reconceptualizing the Genesis story of the temptation of Adam and Eve into the seduction of Eve by Satan (as the serpent), Christian Identity theologians have been able to get around the legal and moral prohibitions against homicide. In their view, killing minorities is not the same as killing human beings. By killing Jews one is actually doing something positive—destroying Satan's children.

The Christian Identity movement also provides a number of excellent examples for imitation, a mechanism critical to the social learning process. Bob Mathews's motivation for his actions was the treatment of Gordon Kahl by the IRS and Kahl's death as a result of a shoot-out with federal law enforcement. Buford Furrow was following in Matthew's steps when he attacked the Jewish Community Center in Los Angeles. Even non-Identity adherents have found inspiration and motivation in the previous activities of Identity followers. For instance, Timothy McVeigh was galvanized into action by two events: the disastrous U.S. confrontation with the Branch Davidians at Waco, Texas and the earlier confrontation between federal authorities and the Weaver family (Identity adherents) in Ruby Ridge, Idaho.

Christian Identity followers who engage in terrorism also demonstrate the principle of reinforcement, repeatedly offending until one is stopped. Mathews and his followers in the Order committed a number of armored car heists, numerous hate crimes, and an assassination until he was stopped in a violent conflict with federal authorities outside Seattle, Washington. Mathews's inspiration, Gordon Kahl, also engaged in more that one act of terrorism and violence against federal authorities before he too was stopped in a violent standoff. Some of Mathews's followers and supporters within the Christian Identity movement and the Aryan Nations even reconstituted his terrorist group, calling it The Order II. Eric Robert Rudolph bombed three different locations before he was forced into hiding in the rural and mountainous areas off the Appalachian Trail. In each of these examples, the offenses continued until the Identity adherents were stopped.

Christian Identity and its adherents make excellent examples of the components of social learning theory. The theology and dogma of Identity—that whites are the chosen people; that Jews are the children of Satan; that Africans, Asians, Hispanics, indigenous people, and people of mixed ethnicity are "mud people"—are definitions that are neutralizing and favorable for terrorism. By promoting the belief that nonwhites are satanic, do not have souls, and are not really human, Christian Identity provides definitions that neutralize prohibitions against homicide and favor a range of violent and terrorist activities against members of these groups. The most famous and well-known of the individuals to differentially associate as Identity adherents have been recycled into examples of true white, Aryan, and Christian heroes. These human examples, often referred to as Phinean Brothers in reference to the ancient Israelite priest Phineas (Pinhas), who was zealous before the Lord, have served as motivation for new actors to engage in violence and terrorism. One of the reasons that Identity-motivated terrorists continue to offend is the belief that they have not been caught because G-d has blessed their actions. The ability of the theology and dogma of Christian Identity to motivate, influence, and promote violence through the process of social learning will continue to make it a major source of terrorism, hate crimes, and low-level political violence.

Christian Identity has been one of the preeminent ideologies/theologies within America's extremist reactionary right wing for over thirty years. It has provided theologically and dogmatically based definitions that are favorable and neutralizing to the use of terrorism ever since Gordon Kahl's violent confrontation with federal law enforcement in the early 1970s. The most successful and highly publicized activities of Identity adherents have also served as a source of imitation for other Identity followers and their fellow travelers on the extreme right. Moreover, Identity theology's stark, Manichaean view of the world seems to serve as reinforcement for those who use it as the ideational basis of their violent political and criminal behavior. While it does not appear that Christian Identity is going away, it remains to be seen if it will be as strong a motivator for violence now that its premier organization, the Aryan Nations, seems to be foundering after the loss of the Hayden Lake, Idaho, compound and the semiretirement of Pastor Butler.

ENDNOTES

1. I am using the term "reactionary" instead of "radical" for groups on the extreme right of the political spectrum. "Reactionary" correctly describes any ideology that seeks to return to a perceived golden time period for the select members of the group. "Radical" refers to the attempts to quickly institute "progressive" and inclusive social change. For further information, see Baradat (2003).

References 301

2. In this aspect, I am differentiating between terrorism and state terror. State terror occurs when the threat and/or actual use of force by the state against its populace is used to intimidate the populace into certain types of behavior. While the end result, the fear and terror, may be the same, the process is different because states possess much greater resources than the movements, groups, and networks that engage in terrorism.

3. This is an inaccurate translation. The Hebrew word *Adam* is derived from *Adamah,* which means "earth." *Adam* is traditionally defined as "earthling."

REFERENCES

Akers, Ronald L. 1998. *Social Learning and Social Structure: A General Theory of Crime and Deviance.* Boston: Northeastern University Press.

Akers, Ronald L., Anthony J. La Greca, John Cochran, and Christine Sellers. 1989. "Social Learning Theory and Alcohol Behavior among the Elderly." *Sociological Quarterly* 30: 625–638.

Akers, Ronald L., Marvin D. Krohn, Lonn Lanza-Kaduce, and Marcia Radosevich. 1979. "Social Learning and Deviant Behavior: A Specific Test of a General Theory." *American Sociological Review* 44: 635–655.

Baradat, Leon P. 2003. *Political Ideologies: Their Origins and Impact.* Upper Saddle River, NJ: Prentice Hall.

Barkun, Michael. 1994. *Religion and the Racist Right.* Chapel Hill: University of North Carolina Press.

———. 1976. *The Behavior of Law.* London: The Academic Press.

———. 1984. "Social Control as a Dependent Variable." In *Toward a General Theory of Social Control, Volume I: Fundamentals,* ed. Donald Black, 1–36. London: Academic Press.

CNN. 2002. *CNN Presents: Eric Robert Rudolph.* February 17.

Cooney, Mark. 1998. *Warriors and Peacemakers: How Third Parties Shape Violence.* New York: New York University Press.

Flynn, Kevin and Gary Gerjardt. 1989. *The Silent Brotherhood: Inside America's Racist Underground.* New York: The Free Press.

Hellwege, Jean. 2001. "Hate in the Crosshairs: Lawyers, Legislators Battle Hate Crime." *Trial* 37 (January): 1, 14–19.

Kaplan, Jeffrey. 1997. *Radical Religion in America: Millenarian Movements from the Far Right to the Children of Noah.* Syracuse: Syracuse University Press.

Olson, Mancur. 1971. *The Logic of Collective Action: Public Goods and the Theory of Groups.* Cambridge: Harvard University Press.

Ridgeway, James. 1991. *Blood in the Face: The Ku Klux Klan, Aryan Nations, Nazi Skinheads, and the Rise of a New White Culture.* New York: Thunder's Mouth Press.

"Running with Rudolph." 2001. *Southern Poverty Law Center The Intelligence Report.* (Winter): 35–39.

Schmid, Alex P., and Albert J. Jongman. 1988. *Political Terrorism: A New Guide to Actors, Authors, Concepts, Databases, Theories, and Literature.* Amsterdam: North-Holland Publishing Company.

Seneschal de la Roche: Roberta. 1996. "Collective Violence as Social Control." *Sociological Forum* 11 (1996): 97–128.

Silverman, Adam L. 2002. "Just War, Jihad, and Terrorism: A Comparison of Western and Islamic Norms for the Use of Political Violence." *The Journal of Church and State* 44, no. 1 (Winter): 73–92.

————. 2003. "The Aryan Nations." In *The Encyclopedia of Religion and Politics in America,* ed. Paul A. Djupe and Laura R. Olson. New York: Facts on File.

Wald, Kenneth D. 1992. *Religion and Politics in the United States.* Washington DC: CQ Press.

Warner, Jack. "Rudolph Indicted in Four Bombings." in *The Atlanta Journal and Constitution,* 11/16/2000, 3A.

Weber, Max. 1968. *Economy and Society: An Outline of Interpretive Sociology.* Trans. Ephraim Fischoff. New York: Bedminster Press.

Wessinger, Catherine. 2000. *How the Millennium Comes Violently: From Jonestown to Heaven's Gate.* New York: Seven Bridges Press.

Wieviorka, Michel. 1993. *The Making of Terrorism.* David G. White (trans). Chicago: University of Chicago Press.

CHAPTER 15

Security Threat Groups: The Threat Posed by White Supremacist Organizations

Lt. Gregg W. Etter, Sr., Ed. D.
Sedgwick County Sheriff's Department Wichita, Kansas

INTRODUCTION

Terrorist attacks may come from either internal or external sources. The most recent terrorist attacks by the Muslim extremist group, al Qaeda, against targets in the continental United States in New York and Washington D.C. showed that the United States was vulnerable to external threats. These attacks were applauded by many white supremacist groups, including the head of the American Nazi Party. Several of these white supremacist groups have seen these attacks as a call to action against the government of the United States and minorities. This has elevated that danger of domestic terrorism attacks against the government and people of the United States as well. While the danger of terrorism can come from both the left and right wings of the American political spectrum, the right wing extremist groups have been the most vocal over the past

Note: Earlier versions of this paper were presented at the 54th Annual Meeting of the American Society of Criminology, Chicago, Illinois, November 13–16, 2002 and in the *Journal of Gang Research*, Vol. 10, No.2. Winter, 2003. Used with permission of National Gang Crime Research Center.

twenty years. Comparing the philosophies of the left and the right and their potential
for terrorism, Simonsen and Spindlove (2000) found that right-wing extremist groups
generally adhere to an anti-government or racist ideology. Many of these right-wing
recruits" feel displaced by rapid changes in the U.S. culture and economy, or are seeking some form of personnel affirmation. As American society continues to change, the
potential for escalating hate crimes by extremist right wing groups is an increasing concern" (Simonsen and Spindlove 2000:279).

DEFINING TERRORISM

In the report of the Vice President's Task Force on Combating Terrorism, Vice President
George Bush (1988) noted that some extremist groups that were unable to rally sufficient political support for their causes resorted to terrorism to attempt to achieve their
goals. Bush stated: "Mostly small, tightly knit, and politically homogenous, such groups
are incapable of developing popular support for their radical positions and therefore
resort to terrorism to gain influence" (Bush 1988:1). Although at the time, Bush was
discussing international terrorist groups, such as Hezbollah, the observation is equally
true for the radical political and racial agendas advocated by the White supremacist
groups and the domestic terrorist tactics that some of these groups have either attempted
or actually carried out inside the United States. Riley and Hoffman (1995) observed
that the Federal Bureau of Investigation defined terrorism as: "the unlawful use of force
or violence against persons or property to intimidate or coerce a government, the civilian population, or any segment thereof in furtherance of political or social objectives"
(Riley and Hoffman 1995:3).

THE NATURE OF THE THREAT

Most domestic terrorists have a grievance with the government or industry over a single or multiple issues. The issues that motivate these groups come from historical, political, and religious reasons. These groups feel that the normal channels of government
are ineffective and that change can be better brought about by revolutionary conflict
or violence. The notion that conflict is inevitable is central to the belief system of all
extremist groups. Sargent (1995) observed that no matter what the form of extremism
(radical, political, religious, or economic) there was a common belief that the particular members of these groups were engaged in a struggle with those that were opposed
to their views. These people were viewed as enemies in this conflict by the extremists.
It was the presence of this "enemy" that was a "common thread" throughout all extremist groups. Sargent [observed that an enemy can take many forms, "but the presence of a clear-cut ideological foe is an intrinsic component of extremism" (Sargent
1995:1).]

It is the combination of a grievance, a perceived enemy, and the view that the
problem can only be solved through conflict that turn the extremist groups into a warrior culture. White extremists see themselves as soldiers in the upcoming race war.

Their self concept is that of a hero that is tasked to save America and the White race. They view that armed conflict is inevitable, even if they have to start the war themselves.

Simonsen and Spindlove (2000) noted that political groups' usage of terrorism was a means to an end. Because of this, targets were often selected for maximum political effect rather than their military value. For example, the target list of a terrorist group might be in the opposite order of priority than that of rebels or conventional military forces: Civilians unconnected in any way with the continuance of the policy against which the group was fighting.

GOVERNMENT OFFICIALS: MILITARY PERSONNEL

This seemingly illogical order is very logical for terrorists because maximum fear and anxiety can be generated by attacks against noncombatants. This demonstrates to the populace as a whole that the targeted regime is unable to protect them. Such actions are generally a far safer technique for the terrorist group than trying to prove that the regime cannot protect itself. Terror groups frequently have to outrage and cause revulsion in their target audience in order to maintain the required level of terror and anger at the government.

We now have an understanding that while strategies incorporating acts of terrorism in the past centuries have changed somewhat in delivery and methods, the basic purposes of terrorist acts have generally remained constant. They are:

- To bring attention to a perceived grievance or cause by some act or acts that are shocking and attention getting.
- To use media by getting coverage of such acts in order to get the widest possible dissemination of their message.
- To contain reaction by the public at large through fear and intimidation and
- To coerce change and destabilize opponents through the threat of further and continued acts until these grievances or causes are recognized and acted upon (Simonsen and Spindlove 2000 p. 18).

In his *White Resistance Manual,* white supremacist, Axl Hess (2001) stated that there were four short and long term goals of their revolutionary struggle:

a. To exacerbate existing racial tensions to the point where a situation of open conflict exists between Whites and non-Whites.

b. To smash Jewish power and influence both in our own respective nations and worldwide.

c. To destroy the legitimacy of current government and to offer legitimate government in it's place, and

d. To punish those Whites who have committed treasonous acts against their own people.

Advocating the leaderless resistance, Hess went on to state:

> "The usage of selective assassination, arson attacks, bombings, sabotage and vandalism against non-Whites must be employed with the goal of creating a maximum amount of animosity, outrage and fear within the hearts of our enemies. High profile targets, such as non-White entertainers, sport figures, religious and political leaders must be targeted for selective assassination. Non-Whites must also be attacked anywhere they can be struck in large numbers, such as in high-rise apartments, subways, shopping malls or packed nightclubs in order to produce maximum causalities. The symbols of the non-White presence on our land: Churches, temples, Mosques, businesses and political institutions must be considered as well. The idea is to drive them into the streets in outrage. To force them to retaliate. Because our movement is underground and leaderless they will be unable to strike back against us directly so their rage will be leveled against White society in general and law enforcement and authority figures in particular" *(http://members .odinsage.com/white88/4_TheGoalsOfOurStruggle.htm).*

Among terrorists groups, the reasons for attacking a target are more likely to be symbolic or political rather than military. Mullins (1997) observed that terrorist operations are usually well planned events to ensure that they successfully achieve the individual and organizational goals.

Safety and escape are other reasons for planning as well as the terrorist's desire to deliver a specific message to his target audience and government. Successful operations are necessary because they are the only way to produce fear in the public and guarantee political change. If operations are not successful, the terrorists are perceived as incompetent and ineffective, and the organization will lose support. "Planning of an operation typically involves three phases: target analysis, intelligence gathering, and development of an operational plan" (Mullins 1997:257–258).

CHARACTERISTICS OF TERRORIST GROUPS

Terrorists groups have many common characteristics that define the culture of the terrorist group and affect their actions. These characteristics include:

- A belief that their political or economic goals cannot be achieved through conventional and/or legitimate means.
- A belief that armed conflict is inevitable and necessary to achieve their goals.
- A clearly defined "enemy" that is viewed as the cause of the group's failure to achieve success through legitimate means.
- The philosophy of the group is influenced by historical, political, or religious reasons.
- The groups set up training camps or compounds to teach their followers terrorist techniques.
- Violence is seen as a legitimate tactic to achieve the group's goals.

- Targets are often selected for symbolic rather than military reasons.
- Crimes are often committed to support the terrorist activities of the group.

White supremacist groups have engaged in criminal activities that are typical of other terrorist organizations including arson, assassination, bank robberies, bombings, sabotage, sedition and other crimes of disorder.

RELIGION AS A FACTOR

For many white supremacist groups, religion is a motivating factor. Because of the pseudo-warrior culture of the white extremists, the religions often practiced by these extremists tend to bolster their racial and political beliefs. Hate is thus rationalized by religion. White supremacist groups in the United States often practice one of four basic religions: Christian Identity, World Church of the Creator, Satanism, or Germanic/Norse Paganism. Each of these faiths share the common belief of an apocalyptic vision of a race war in America and that their members will be called upon to be warriors in that battle.

Agreeing that religion has the potential to stir terrorist violence, Simonsen and Spindlove (2000) stated that: "Terrorism motivated by religious imperatives is growing quickly, increasing the number of killings and reducing the restraints on mass, indiscriminate murder" (Simonsen & Spindlove 2000:325). So great is this change according to terrorist experts, that we may have to revise our notions of the stereotypical terrorist organization. Traditional terrorist groups could be characterized as groups that engage in conspiracy as a full-time avocation, living underground and constantly planning and plotting terrorist attacks, perhaps under the direct control or at the behest of a foreign government. A model of a new kind of terrorist group might be a more or less ad hoc amalgamation of like minded individuals, who merely gravitate toward one another for a specific, perhaps even one-time, operation. This new breed of part time terrorists may represent an even greater threat than its predecessors have.

"Holy terror" and the so-called "secular terror" have radically different value systems, mechanisms for justifying their acts, and concepts of morality. For the religious terrorist, violence is a divine duty. Whereas secular terrorists generally regard indiscriminate violence as immoral and counterproductive, religious terrorists view such violence as both morally justified and necessary. Also, whereas secular terrorists attempt to appeal to a constituency composed of sympathizers and the aggrieved people they claim to speak for, religious terrorists act for no audience but themselves. This absence of a constituency, combined with an extreme sense of alienation, means that such terrorists can justify almost limitless violence against virtually any target who is not a member of their own religious belief or sect.

It has been suggested that religion and ethnic fanaticism allow terrorists to overcome any reluctance to mass murder that they might experience. For example, some white supremacists actually welcome the prospect of nuclear war or terrorism because they see it as an opportunity to eliminate their avowed "enemies" and to reach their goal of creating a new world order peopled exclusively by the white race. "Any doubts about the seriousness of such hate groups were dispelled when police and federal agents raided a white supremacist compound in rural Arkansas in 1984, and discovered a stockpile of some thirty gallons of cyanide to be used to poison the water supplies" (Simonsen and Spindlove 2000:325-326).

Morgan (2001) observed that religions practiced by white supremacist groups often preach violence, advocate racial war and have started prison ministries to recruit followers. Speaking of Christian Identity she said:

> "Identity was organized in 1946 by Klan organizer and former Methodist minister Wesley Swift. Identity adherents will tell you that Christ was an Aryan, not a Semite, that the Jews are descended via Cain from Eve's mating with Satan, that the lost tribes of Israel are really Anglo-Saxon, and that the United States is the Promised Land—to be purged of all non-Aryans. From his Ministry of Christ Church in Mariposa, California, William Potter Gale, an Identity pastor, preaches: "Damn right I'm teaching violence! God said you're gonna do it that way! It's about time somebody is telling you to get violent, Whitey." But Gale is regarded as a bit of a wimp by Keith Gilbert, who served five years in San Quentin on conspiracy to explode 1,400 pounds of dynamite during a speech by Martin Luther King. Gilbert, who founded the Restored Church of Jesus Christ in Post Falls, Idaho, preaches that the prophet Elijah was reincarnated in the person of Adolph Hitler and that *Mein Kampf* is actually the last book of the Bible" (Morgan 2001: 94).

Coates (1987) observed that many different right wing radical groups had united under the banner of Christian Identity. Prior to the Christian Identity movement, students of the radical right described the occurrence of the "circular firing squad" phenomenon whenever such groups tried to join forces: each special-interest group was so utterly obsessed with its own cause—tax revolt, racism, anti-Semitism, fluoride in the water supply or whatever—that it was unwilling to collaborate with groups that otherwise would have been natural allies. "Indeed, single-cause right-wingers usually took as many shots at fellow radicals with a different cause as they took at those on the left. The violent early Survivalists in the Minutemen feuded with the John Birch Society for being Milquetoasts eager to curl up in some Jewish-controlled conservative's political pocket, while the Bircher's castigated the Posse for being anti-Semitic when it should have been anti-Zionist instead" (Coates 1987:80).

In keeping with their neo-Nazi traditions, some white supremacists practice Satanism. The link between National Socialism (Nazis) and the occult has been the object of much literature (Goodrick-Clarke 1992). Many view Adolph Hitler as some type of "Occult Messiah" and look forward to the day that he rises from the dead to lead the forces of darkness against the forces of light in the battle of Armageddon. Many of the symbols of Satanism are interchangeable with those of Nazism. Most of the white supremacists that practice Satanism do not belong to any of the traditional organized Satanic sects (Church of Satan, Temple of Set, or the Church of Satanic Liberation). They are self-taught Satanic "dabblers." The practice of Satanism is particularly popular among prison inmates including the Aryan Brotherhood and with some skinheads. Leet, Rush, and Smith (1997) found that there are Skinheads who identify with Satanism and a belief in racial purity. This gives them a self defined approval from Satan to "cleanse the earth." They look forward to an Armageddon that combines a racial blood-bath with a salvation from hell (Leet, Rush, and Smith 1997:143).

Many Nazis and neo-Nazis have embraced the revival of the old Norse/Germanic pagan religions: Asatru, Odinism, and Wotanism. These are warrior based religions that envision a final battle called Raganarok that will bring about the end of the world. The Germanic Volkish philosophies that are central to theoretical Nazism embrace many of this religion's beliefs on the relationship between blood, honor, and soil. Some white supremacists prefer to be known as Wotansvolk and feel that WOTAN stands for Will of the Aryan Nation.

On the role of religion in the white supremacist movement, Axl Hess (2001) stated that the movement had to have a complete alliance between all Aryans to achieve their goal of survival. After advocating attacks on their true enemies, he said "Creator, Christian, and follower of Odin must all work together to achieve this goal. We must take any required action to destroy our enemies and remove from power whether it is by McVeigh style or as a member of the WOTC. Any time spent attacking each other is time we could be attacking ZOG. Time is valuable and our Race is dying right before our eyes. All efforts should be directed towards our survival."

DEFINING THE "ENEMY"

With extremist groups there is always a perceived enemy (Sargent 1995). The leaders of the extremist group use the hatred of this enemy to focus the actions of their follower towards the goals of the group. Paranoia is intentionally fostered by the leaders as an aid to motivate and thus control the actions of their members. This perceived state of emergency also serves as a call to action to recruit new members to aid in the struggle. Propaganda from white supremacist groups is explicit in defining the perceived threat to the race and outlines the proposed solution advocated by the group. Justifications for this hatred are often based on religious grounds.

Founded in the late 1860's the members of the Ku Klux Klan have opposed minorities, Catholics, and Jews throughout their long history. In the 1930s, William Dudley Pelley's Silver Shirts advocated anti-Semitism and support for the cause of Nazi Germany (Lipset and Raab 1978, p. 162–164). The enemy thus became the Jews.

Since 1969, the Posse Comitatus has held the position that the United States federal government is the real enemy. Ridgeway (1990) explained: "Like other constitutional fundamentalists, the Posse Comitatus thinks that the federal government has far exceeded the limits prescribed in the Constitution, and that by means of a coalition of lawyers and judges, the government has violated the basic terms on which the country was founded" (Ridgeway 1990:111).

The Aryan Nations view nonwhite races and Jews as a threat to the survival of the White race. As is common in Christian Identity type religious movements, an alternative version of Genesis and creation is advocated. Aryan Nations leader Richard

Girnt Butler (1995) explaining the dual seed theory of his Church of Jesus Christ Christian, advocated that the Bible was written for the White race and stated that:

> "WE BELIEVE that the true, literal children of the Bible are the 12 tribes of Israel which are now scattered throughout the world and are now known as the Anglo-Saxon, Celtic, Scandinavian, Teutonic people of this earth. . . .
>
> WE BELIEVE that there are literal children of Satan in the world today. These children are the descendants of Cain, who was a result of Eve's original sin, her physical seduction by Satan. We know that because of this sin, there is a battle and a natural enmity between the children of Satan and the Children of the Most High God" (Butler 1995:147).

On 06/01/01, Richard Butler's named successor, Pastor Ray Redfeairn of the Church of the Sons of YHVH (True Church of Israel) praised Hamas and the Islamic Jihad for killing Jews in Israel (Redfeairn [2001]).

The leader of another White Supremacist group, World Church of the Creator leader Matt Hale, argued that racial hatred is necessary to save the white race. Hale (2001) stated that:

> "One of the many particulars that distinguish our World Church of the Creator from other White racial organizations is the fact that we Creators refuse to shun what has been a negative emotion: hatred. On the contrary, we Creators recognize that in order to create, one must first often destroy, the emotion of hatred must be involved. To think otherwise is folly. To think and express the idea that we don't hate the Jews and mud races (minorities) but we only love our own is a flight from reality—one which many in the White race struggle all too often chose to indulge in. Perhaps these well-intentioned comrades believe that the masses will like us better if we say such things. Perhaps they truly have become convinced the feel-good propaganda that hatred is not present in our struggle. Perhaps they have told others so much that they don't hate that they themselves have come to believe it. In any case, it is not the truth, and it is so obviously such that the masses are actually less sympathetic towards the White racial struggle as a result. No, it would be better to say, "Yes! I hate!" and earn the respect of one's listeners than to insult their intelligence by denying the obvious" (Hale 2001:121)

The National Alliance's founder, the late William Pierce, described an alleged upcoming racial war and their effect on other potential terrorists in *The Turner Diaries,* a terrorist manual. For example, this novel deeply influenced a man named Robert Mathews, another Christian militant. During the 1980s, Mathews built up a fund of over three million dollars from bank holdups and armored car robberies. Mathew's followers in The Order became involved in robberies, assassinations, and bombings from Washington to Colorado. One of Mathew's followers was David Lane. Lane was convicted in participation in many of the group's crimes and now is serving a 150 year prison sentence at FCI Florence, Colorado. Lane is credited with authoring the infamous "14 words" that have become a center piece of the philosophies of many white supremacist groups. Lane stated: "We must secure the existence of our people and a future for white children!" The enemies of this Silent Brotherhood included Jews, non-whites, bankers, and the United States government (Flynn and Gerhardt 1989). Although he managed to bomb a mere two buildings before he barricaded himself and had a shoot-out to the death with FBI agents, Mathews left evidence of detailed plans to attack and immobilize the infrastructure and support systems of a major U.S. city (Morgan 2001: 96).

For many militias, the enemy is the United State government and the United Nations. Militia of Montana leader John E. Trouchmann and M.O.M. attorney Bob Fletcher (1996) described their view of why the United States government and the United Nations is the "real enemy".

- a. The high office of the Presidency has turned into a position of dictatorial oppression through the abusive use of executive orders and directives thus leaving Congress stripped of authority. When the President overrules Congress by executive order, representative government fails.

- b. Government now defines human beings as a biological resource under the United Nations ecosystem management program, maintaining that the state and local laws are barriers to the goals of the federal government.

- c. Government now allows our military to be ordered and controlled by foreigners.

- d. Under presidential order, our military labels "caring" patriots as the enemy, then turns their tanks loose on U.S. citizens to murder and destroy or directs a sniper to shoot a mother in the face while holding her infant in her arms, and

- e. Government refuses to hold hearings on government sanctioned abuses, then white-washes those hearing(s) that are held.

- f. Government tampers with or destroys evidence needed to solve a crime, then considers the very idea of infringing upon the people's rights of freedom of speech, assembly and the right to redress after having destroyed the Second and Fourth Article (Fletcher 1996: 67–69).

Touchmann and Fletcher cited the government's alleged abuses of power in the sieges at Waco and Ruby Ridge. They also expressed dissatisfaction with the lack of "objective" government hearings to investigate those alleged abuses. The land use policies of the Clinton administration and their attempts to comply with United Nations treaties (some of which had not been ratified by the Senate) was also under fire by M.O.M. leadership. Another issue was the policy of the United States military under the Clinton administration, to court-martial members of the United States military who refused to wear UN patches on their uniforms or to wear the blue beret of the UN peace keeping forces (SFOR) while engaged in operations in the territory of the former Yugoslavia.

TRAINING COMPOUNDS OF WHITE SUPREMACIST GROUPS

Extremist groups often establish compounds where their adherents live, study ideology and train for the imagined upcoming fight with society. Residents are expected to maintain a similar philosophy with the group and adhere to their code of conduct. Ideological deviation from the "norms" established from the leader is not tolerated.

Paramilitary and survivalist type training is conducted. These compounds often have firing ranges and are usually located in remote rural areas. Security is maintained and entrance to the compound area is often restricted to members of the group. Weapons and explosives are often stockpiled in these compounds so they represent a clear danger to law enforcement officers attempting to serve warrants or civil process.

Louisville, Illinois, August, 1961

John R. Harrell founded the Christian Conservative Church and established a compound with four guard towers at his estate. Anti-Zionism, tax protests and survivalist training were among the group's activities. Harrell invented the term "Zionist Occupational Government" or ZOG to describe his conflicts with the government. Harrell was arrested in a raid on his compound and sentenced to serve four years in a federal penitentiary for tax evasion and harboring a federal fugitive. Raiding law enforcement officials captured four bunkers filled with weapons, canned water and food. Harrell still holds annual "Freedom Festivals" at this site for like minded Identity groups (Coates 1987:147–152). Coppola (1996) noted that Harrell felt that the Jews enjoyed their "victim" status and often "staged" attacks against themselves to gain sympathy for their cause. Members of the Aryan Nations and the KKK often attended and spoke at Harrell's Freedom Festivals. Coppola quoted Harrell as having said, "Zionists paint a lot of their own swastikas and tip over their own tombstones. They like being victims" (Coppola 1996:148).

Mark Twain National Forrest, Licking, Missouri & Smithville, West Virginia, 1984

Christian-Patriot's Defense League leader, John R. Harrell, established compounds for survivalist training sessions. Harrell's group practices a Christian Identity type of philosophy. Coates (1987) observed that "While only an estimated twelve Harrell followers are full-time residents at the Missouri compound, federal investigators have observed as many as a thousand people passing through military training sessions and other events held there each summer" (Coates 1987:145).

Rulo, Nebraska, 1985

In two different raids, Richardson County Sheriff's deputies, Nebraska State Patrol, and the FBI arrested Michael Ryan for the murder of two followers and possession of a machine gun. Ryan also had outstanding felony warrants from Brown County, Kansas. The items seized showed the types of activities in which the group was involved: five truckloads of stolen farm machinery, more than thirty semiautomatic and assault rifles, thirteen fully automatic pistols and rifles, a sawed off shotgun, camouflage gear, 150,000 rounds of ammunition, and one bunker stocked with food and water. They also found quantities of Christian Identity and Posse literature, along with tapes of Jim Wickstrom (Ridgeway 1990:139–140).

Lake Bull Shoals, Three Brothers, Arkansas, April 19, 1985

Local and federal authorities raid the rural compound of the Covenant, Sword and Arm of the Lord (Jones and Israel 2001 p. 175–176). BATF agents recovered firearms, explosives, and 33 gallons of cyanide ("Downside Legacy at Two Degrees of President Clinton" n.d.). In an effort to hasten the revolution, CSA members were allegedly plotting to poison city water supplies and to bomb federal buildings (The Nizkor Project n.d.). CSA used their compound to conduct paramilitary training for their adherents and those of a like mind. Describing the CSA compound, Stern (2000a) observed that members built several factories where they manufactured grenades, silencers, and other firearm accessories. These weapons were sold at gun shows. CSA also has a publication business which has printed books, including *Witchcraft and the Illuminati; Christian Army Basic Training Manual; The Jews: 100 Facts;* and *Prepare War (Stern 2000a, 141).* The group also sells racist, anti-Semitic, and survivalist literature as a part of its official book list, including *The Protocols of the Learned Elders of Zion; The Negro and the World Crisis; Who's Who in the Zionist Conspiracy; The Talmud Unmasked;* and *A Straight Look at the Third Reich (Stern 2000a, 141).* They also have a printed manual, the C.S.A. *Journal,* which provided instructions for "spiritual and physical survival," including how to use guns and double-edged knives to kill one's enemies. CSA also built a sophisticated shooting range called 'Silhouette City,' which was modeled after the FBI Academy shooting range in Quantico, Virginia. "Whereas the FBI version has mockups of armed criminals surrounded by women and children, the CSA version had mockups of prominent Jews and federal agents. One wooden cutout of a state trooper wore a Star of David instead of a badge. CSA members used Silhouette City for target practice at their Endtime Overcomer Survival Training School, which was established to provide training in 'Christian martial arts.' Outsiders paid $500 or more to go through the training course" (Stern 2000a:141).

Phoenix, Arizona, 1996

The Viper Militia held training sessions to carry out planned bombings of government installations. The Viper Militia regularly held 2 types of training sessions: A-shoots and B-shoots. During A-shoots, the members only brought legal weapons and often invited family members and friends to join them. For B-shoots however, only members of the militia could attend, and during these sessions, they would detonate test bombs and train with illegal automatic weapons. The group trained so extensively and so often that one of the members bragged to undercover informants that the Viper Militia was so well trained and equipped that it could take on any SWAT team (Snow 1999, 72).

In 1994, the Viper Militia made a training video to show members how to blow up buildings. Their video bragged: "Today's date is May 30, 1994. This is a reconnaissance tape for American Patriots. What you are looking at now is the Phoenix, Arizona Treasury Building, which houses Alcohol, Tobacco, and Firearms. . . . Notice the structure. These pillars support the entire building. Take out the pillars, simultaneously, with explosives, and the building will collapse" (Snow 1999:73). The video went on to explain how to booby trap mailboxes near the facility to injure workers and how to disrupt water supplies to hinder firefighters.

Hayden Lake, Idaho

Aryan Nation's leader Richard G. Butler developed a compound at Hayden Lake, Idaho for his Church of Jesus Christ group. The compound served as a training and meeting place for the Aryan Nations, Christian Identity groups, KKK, skinheads, and other White extremist groups. Bushart, Craig and Barnes (1998) observed that: "Charles Lee and other Klansman have attended meetings and are frequent visitors to Aryan Nations at Hayden Lake, Idaho. In fact, Hayden Lake has been visited by a veritable "who's who" among the radical right. Aryan Nations is a center for many organizational activities focused upon the development of a New America, an Aryan America" (Bushart, Craig and Barnes 1998:5).

On June 26, 1983, the founder of The Order, Robert Mathews, acted as security for an Aryan Nation's rally at Riverfront Park in Spokane, Washington. The service was being held by Butler to eulogize Posse Comitatus leader Gordon Kahl. Kahl had killed two law men and wounded four others in North Dakota. Kahl was tracked down to a farmhouse near Smithville, Arkansas and died in a firefight with law enforcement officers attempting to capture him. Mathews confronted counter demonstrators and gained favor with Butler for his actions. Mathews attended the Aryan World Congress the following month at the Aryan Nations compound with Louis Beam (KKK & Kingdom Identity Ministries), Jim Ellison (C.S.A.) and David Lane (The Order) (Flynn & Gerhardt 1989:88–90).

In 2001, a successful lawsuit filed by the Southern Poverty Law Center on behalf of victims assaulted by Aryan Nations compound guards forced Butler to surrender the compound to the court as a part of the damages awarded to the victims.

BOMB MAKERS

Many of the threats posed by white supremacist groups involve bombs or bomb threats. The FBI Bomb Data Center stated that: "Two thousand, two hundred and seventeen (2,217) bombing incidents were reported to the Bomb Data Center in 1997" (Gadson, Michael, Perrin and Walsh 2001:5). Anarchist William Powell (1989) advocated the use of bombs as a terrorist weapon. Powell stated that as a terrorist weapon, bombs were going to kill and maim more people than all the rest put together, because people just refuse to take things seriously (Powell 1989:112). Powell further observed that "explosives, if used with care and all the necessary precautions, are one of the greatest tools any liberation movement can have. Ninety percent of all sabotage is based upon some sort of demolitions, or booby traps" (Powell 1989:112). Mullins (1997) agreed as he stated: "Bombings are one of the terrorist's most effective tools. The terrorist may bomb to scare or frighten, to kill several innocent victims, to kill a particular victim, to destroy a particular facility, or to enter a bank, business, or military establishment to obtain money, equipment, weapons or other supplies. . . . Bombings are one of the safest of all terrorist operations. Bombing operations draw attention to the terrorist cause and are virtually risk free" (Mullins 1997:252).

Most of the extremist bombers are self taught in the manufacture and usage of explosives. Many books and references are available at meetings and on the internet. Examples include: *The Anarchist Cookbook, The Poor Man's James Bond; The White Resistance Manual,* various publications from Palidan Press and military manuals from surplus stores and at gun shows. McGuckin (1997) felt that extremists in America adhered to a "bomb culture" and that explosives were often the weapons of choice for these groups. He stated that:

> "A significant factor in the increase in bombings is that the dissemination of bomb know-how has become a minor industry. The past few decades have produced the rise of mail-order publishing companies that serve the so-called gun aftermarket, including the gun fanciers, survivalists, wannabe cops and closet anarchists who like to shop for such products as laser sights, camouflage, fake badges and fake FBI and ATF hats. Some of the most popular offerings are "burn-and-blow" books that describe in detail how to make landmines, booby traps and bombs" (McGuckin 1997:11).

Bath, Michigan May 17, 1927

Fifty-five year old Andrew Kehoe was the owner of a failing farm in Bath, Michigan in 1927. Kehoe blamed property taxes from the local school levy for most of his financial problems. Kehoe got himself elected to the school board in Bath to protest the rate of taxation. According to Gado (2000):

> "On the board, Kehoe campaigned endlessly for lower taxes which, he claimed, were causing him financial hardship. His creditors tried to work out an agreement with Kehoe but were unsuccessful. Soon, he stopped paying his mortgage altogether. To complicate matters, his wife Nellie was chronically ill with an undiagnosed illness. She required frequent hospital stays, which depleted the family savings further. Kehoe envisioned losing his farm and plunging into debt. In his mind, he blamed higher taxes for all his financial woes. He couldn't understand the need for bigger and better schools. He saw many of the town expenditures as wasteful and ill conceived. But above all and without respite, without any valid reason or logic, he blamed the Bath Consolidated School Board for his troubles" (Gado 2000, chapter 2).

Gado (2000) noted that Kehoe felt that taxes were unjust. Therefore, any increases in taxes were "illegal and unfair." Kehoe blamed the president of the school board, Emory E. Huyuck, for these tax increases because of his influence on the other board members. Kehoe began to believe that taxes were "the ruination of his life" (Gado 2000, chapter 3).

Kehoe became a maintenance employee of the school board. This granted him unlimited access to the school building. Kehoe developed a plot to blow up the school. He began to gather a military surplus explosive called Pyrotol, which he began placing throughout the school building under the floor and into the rafters. Over 1,000 pounds of Pyrotol and dynamite were planted in the school building. Kehoe arranged for the charges to fire electrically using a timing device fashioned from a clock. Kehoe also plotted to blow up his farm. He planted multiple homemade incendiary devices in each building of the farm. The devices consisted of a gasoline bomb to be ignited via an automobile spark plug and a car battery. Kehoe then painted a plaque that stated "CRIMINALS ARE MADE, NOT BORN" (Gado 2000, chapter 5). Kehoe then turned his automobile into a car bomb by packing it with explosives and scrap iron for shrapnel. On May 17, 1927, Kehoe killed his wife and set off the explosives at his farm. He then drove to the school at Bath in his explosives filled car. During the drive, the timers detonated the explosives secreted in the school, starting fires and collapsing most of the building. As Kehoe pulled in front of the collapsed school, he observed Huyuck and other officials standing there. Kehoe pulled his car beside them and set off the explosives using a rifle he had brought along for the purpose.

In the resulting explosions, Kehoe was killed along with Huyuck, 7 teachers and 38 school children. Sixty-one others were injured and the buildings were a total loss. This was the worst school disaster in the nation's history. Many of Kehoe's beliefs and attitudes about taxes, government, and banks echo in the beliefs of the modern day tax protesters and the Posse Comitatus, Gordan Kahl and Kehoe shared many beliefs and circumstances. The idea of using explosives to collapse a government building as a tax protest would resurface in 1980 in Andrew MacDonald's (aka Dr. William Pierce founder of the National Alliance) book, *The Turner Diaries* and again in 1995 with Timothy McVeigh's bombing of a federal building in Oklahoma City.

Birmingham, Alabama September 15, 1963

The bombing of the Sixteenth Street Baptist Church by members of the KKK left four African-American girls dead. Killed in the bombing were Addie Mae Collins, Denise McNair, Carole Robinson, and Cynthia Wesley. The victims were attending a Sunday school class in the church building at the time of the bombing. The bombing touched off a race riot that left several others dead or injured ("Bombing of the Sixteenth Street Baptist Church," n.d.). In two separate trials, former KKK members Bobby Frank Cherry (2002) and Thomas E. Blanton (2001) were convicted of participating in the bombing almost forty years after the original incident occurred. Fellow conspirators Robert E. Chambliss died in prison in 1997 after being convicted of an unrelated murder and Herman Cash died without having been charged ("Witnesses Recall 1963 Church Bombing" n.d.). This church bombing was typical of church bombings throughout the South during the civil rights struggles from the 1950s to the 1980s.

Tacoma, Washington July 20, 1993

Skinheads from the American Front explode a pipe bomb at the NAACP headquarters. The skinheads were members of the Church of the Creator which was the predecessor to the W.C.O.T.C.

Tacoma, Washington July 22, 1993

Skinheads from the American Front exploded a second pipe bomb in Tacoma (FBI 1999, 24).

Oklahoma City, Oklahoma, April 19, 1995

Timothy McVeigh and Terry Nichols detonate a homemade truck bomb parked in front of the Alfred P. Murrah Federal Office Building. The explosion destroyed the building, killing 168 people and injuring over 500 others (Michael and Herbeck 2001). Dees and Corcoran (1996) reported McVeigh's alleged association with contacts with the Michigan Militia and the fact that McVeigh sold copies of William Pierce's *The Turner Diaries* at gun shows (p. 161–162). Cash and Charles (2001) alleged that McVeigh and Nichols had connections with the Aryan Republican Army in Pittsburg, Kansas and may have participated in some of the bank robberies that the ARA was involved in (p. 58–63). Timothy McVeigh, Terry Nichols, and Michael Fortier were convicted on felony charges stemming from this crime. McVeigh received the death sentence and was executed. Nichols and Fortier both received lengthy federal prison sentences.

Spokane, Washington April 1, 1996

Members of the Phineas priesthood are involved in a bombing and bank robbery.

Phoenix, Arizona July 2, 1996

Twelve members of the Viper Militia are arrested by federal authorities for plotting to bomb local, state, and federal government buildings; illegal possession of explosives and illegal possession of fully automatic firearms. Firearms, machine guns, explosives, gas masks and bullet proof vests were seized in the search of militia members' residences. Large amounts of ammonium nitrate and nitromethane were recovered in the search by federal agents. These are the same types of materials used by McVeigh and Nichols to construct the bomb used in Oklahoma City. Snow (1999) found that:

> "They also charged six of the militia members with conspiracy to furnish instructions in the use of criminal explosives as a way of promoting civil disorder. In the criminal conspiracy complaint, authorities claimed the group had been plotting to blow up a number of buildings in Phoenix, including the offices of the Bureau of Alcohol, Tobacco, and Firearms, offices of the Internal Revenue Service, offices of the Immigration and Naturalization Service, the Phoenix Police Department, and an Arizona National Guard Center. According to the indictments, the group had been plotting these bombings for two years, and during this time had also been training extensively in the use of automatic weapons and explosives, setting off several test bombs. The government infiltrators claimed the group conducted this training in order to be prepared to fight either the New World Order when it came, or the federal government, if it should decide to declare martial law and begin confiscating weapons from private citizens" (Snow 1990: 74).

Spokane, Washington, July 12, 1996

Members of the Phineas Priesthood are involved in a second pipe bombing and robbery.

Atlanta, Georgia July 27, 1996—Centennial Park

Eric Rudolph is accused of planting a bomb filled with nails and contained in a knapsack in the Olympic park area. The bomb killed Alice Hawthorne and wounded over 100 others. Rudolph is under federal indictment for this crime. He was captured by local police in Murphy, North Carolina on May 31, 2003 after being a fugitive for over 5 years. According to Wyatt (June 1, 2003), Rudolph was a practitioner of Christian Identity and a survivalist. He allegedly sent letters claiming responsibility for at least two of the bombings and signed them "Army of God."

Clarksburg, West Virginia October 11, 1996

Seven members of the Mountaineer Militia were arrested on charges of plotting to blow up the Federal Bureau of Investigation's Criminal Justice Information Services (FBI/CJIS) facility. "General" Floyd Raymond Looker, leader of the militia group had obtained blueprints of the federal fingerprint identification facility from James "Rich" Rogers. Rogers was a member of the militia group and was employed by the Clarksburg Fire Department. Looker had obtained explosives and blasting caps to conduct the operation. A militia member turned government informant and warned the FBI about the plot. A FBI agent posed as an interested terrorist and wanted to purchase plans and explosives from Looker. During the execution of the search warrants that resulted from this investigation, blueprints, explosives, and weapons were recovered. Looker and 6 others were charged in federal indictments. Looker pleaded guilty in a plea bargain with the federal government (Militia watchdog n.d.)

Atlanta, Georgia January 16, 1997—Atlanta Northside Family Planning Service

Eric Rudolph is accused of bombing an abortion clinic injuring 54 people. Two bombs were used in the attack. Rudolph is under federal indictment for this crime. Rudolph was captured by local police in Murphy, North Carolina on May 31, 2003 after five years on the run (Wyatt 2003).

Atlanta, Georgia February 21, 1997—Otherside Lounge

Eric Rudolph is accused of bombing a gay and lesbian bar. Again, two bombs were used in the attack, however only one exploded, injuring five people. Rudolph is under federal indictment for this crime. (CNN November 15, 2000). Rudolph was captured in Murphy, North Carolina on May 31, 2003 after five years on the run (Wyatt 2003).

Birmingham, Alabama January 29, 1998—Sandy Spring Professional Building

Eric Rudolph is accused of again bombing an abortion clinic. The explosion at the New Woman's Health Care Clinic killed Robert Sanderson, an off duty law enforcement officer and wounded Emily Lyons, a nurse. Rudolph's pickup truck was spotted near the scene of the bombing. (Covenant News n.d.). This far, the federal government has spent over $30 million dollar searching for Randolph (CNN March 20, 2002). Rudolph was captured on May 31, 2003, by local police in Murphy, North Carolina on the outstanding federal indictment for his alleged participation in this and other bombings (Griffin June 2, 2003).

Battle Creek, Michigan, March 18, 1998

The leader of the North American Militia, 23rd Resistance Group, 1st Battle Group, "Colonel" Ken Carter was arrested along with Randy Graham and Brad Metcalf for plotting to take over Battle Creek in a military style coup. The plot included planned sniper attacks on police and informants; explosion of propane tank bombs at major intersections to cause chaos; kidnapping of state and federal judges; bomb attacks on natural gas supplies, on electrical transformers and on high voltage power lines; disruption of water supplies; disruption of rail lines and bomb attacks against federal agencies. The BATF was able to place an undercover agent into the group and raid the compound before the group could execute their plans. The militia group had informants inside the local sheriff's department and tipped the group off about the upcoming raid, but federal agents from BATF, the U.S. Marshall's Service and local agencies were able to successfully conduct the raid. Carter, Graham and Metcalf were all convicted on federal charges (Stampenhouse 2003).

Dyson (2001) cited examples of terrorist bombing activities by white extremist or militia groups:

> Rex Levi Rabou, 25, of Cheyenne Wyoming and Carl Carlson, 24, of Kimbal, Nebraska, were arrested on charges of selling illegal pipe bombs to an undercover agent. The men thought they were joining a super-secret white-supremacist organization known as the "National Militia" (Dyson 2001a)

Fort Worth, Texas, August 2, 2000

Four Aryan Circle members—Robert Cliff Massey, 25; Heather Petree, 27; Todd William Tucker; and Ryan Throne, 24—were arrested at a local hotel for narcotic violations, possession of explosive devices (two booby-trapped cigarette packages), weapons violations and outstanding warrants (Dyson 2001a).

Tallahassee, Florida September 15, 2000

White Supremacist Lawrence Lombardi received a sentence of life in prison plus 30 years for his involvement in two PVC pipe bombings on the campus of historically black Florida A & M University in 1999 (Dyson 2001a).

Reno, Nevada January 1, 2001

Jewish Temple Emanu El was set on fire shortly after 12:00 Midnight. The culprit sprayed fuel onto the synagogue's front door and set it ablaze, charring the entryway and door but not seriously damaging the structure. A Molotov cocktail was previously thrown at the same synagogue on November 30, 1999. The five skinheads responsible for that attack were sentenced to lengthy prison terms on December 1, 2000, in federal court in Reno (Dyson 2001b).

Golden, Colorado January 10, 2001

Colorado State Defense Force leader Paul Giovanni Graham was convicted of selling 130 illegal explosive devices (Dyson 2001b).

Sandy, Oregon February 9, 2001

Four individuals were arrested by the Clackamas County Sheriff's Department in a raid on a rural residence. Seized in the raid were ammonium nitrate, fuel oil, homemade C-4 explosives, homemade hand grenades, blasting caps, primers, fuses, black powder, and white supremacist literature. Propaganda from the extremist anti-abortion groups, Army of God, was also seized in the house. Arrested were: Anthony D. Huntington, 28; Jennifer J. Williams, 27; and Forest E. Bateman Jr., 29. In 1992, Bateman had formerly appeared on the Oregon State Police's ten most wanted list on accusations of felony, possession of a firearm, and second degree assault related to skinhead activities (Dyson 2001b).

Illinois, Iowa, Nebraska, Colorado, and Texas, May, 2002

A college student in a grunge rock band named Apathy planted homemade pipe bombs in a smiley face pattern across the center of the United States. Over 15 pipe bombs were planted by Luther Helder in mailboxes across five states. Helder was captured near Reno, Nevada. Helder's e-mail address was *dirdjew@hotamil.com*. According to Pina (2002), Helder had sent letters to his parents in Minnesota and to the University of Wisconsin *Badger* newspaper outlining his fatalistic views, out of body experiences, and attacking the government (p. 1–3).

ASSASSINATION

Assassination has always been a favorite tool of the terrorist. It fits in nicely with the "lone warrior" or "lone wolf" philosophies of most white extremists and other terrorists. The victims are usually selected for the maximum political impact that their deaths will cause. Enemies of the group are eliminated and this causes terror among those that oppose the group and serves as a reminder that discipline will be maintained inside the group. In his *White Resistance Manual*, Axl Hess advocated the consideration of "selective assassination" as a tactic (Hess 2001, "Selective Assassination").

Jackson, Mississippi June 13, 1963

Civil rights advocate Medgar Evers is shot to death by Bryon De La Beckwith. It took three trials and over 30 years to convict Beckwith of the crime of murder. After his 1994 conviction for murder, Beckwith was sentenced to life imprisonment and died in prison on 01-22-01. Beckwith was associated with the Ku Klux Klan and had boasted that he had killed Evers at a KKK rally (Lyons n.d.).

Glendale, California 1965

Neo-Nazi and Identity minister Keith Gilbert is sentenced to serve five years in San Quentin for conspiracy after he is found with 1,400 pounds of dynamite at his home. Gilbert planned to use the explosives to kill the Reverend Dr. Martin Luther King Jr. (Flynn and Gerhardt 1989, p.63).

Homochitto National Forrest, Mississippi June 10, 1966

In an unsuccessful attempt to lure the Reverend Dr. Martin Luther King Jr. to Mississippi so they could assassinate him, Ku Klux Klan members Claude Fuller, James Jones and Ernest Avants kidnapped and murdered Ben Chester White because they believed that the grotesque killing of a black man would cause King to come to Mississippi where they would attempt to kill him (June 17, [2004]). King did not take the bait. Two of the murderers confessed to the police. During their trial in Mississippi state court, Jones and Avants were acquitted. Fuller was never charged. However, Avants was convicted in 2003 of federal charges of aiding and abetting the killing of Ben Chester White as Avants' defense in state court had been that while he had shot White, White was already dead from the gunshot wound administered by Fuller. Neither Fuller nor Jones could be tried on federal charges as they had both died prior to the commencement of the new federal prosecution. (CNN February 28, 2003).

Memphis, Tennessee April 4, 1968

Convicted felon James Earl Ray shot and killed civil rights leader Reverend Dr. Martin Luther King Jr., setting off racial riots and disturbances in 125 cities across the United States. Ray was captured by British law enforcement authorities in London, England after he robbed a bank there. Ray confessed to the assassination after the FBI found his fingerprint on the rifle that was recovered near the scene of the assassination (*www.comspire.com/curren.28html*). Ray pled guilty to killing King in 1969 and is sentenced to life imprisonment. Ray later recants his confession and states that King's assassination is a part of a larger conspiracy. The FBI and subsequent investigations showed that Ray acted as a lone wolf sniper. While not a documented member of any specific racist group, Ray was associated with J. B. Stoner of the National States Rights Party and Stoner visited Ray in jail in 1968 (Weisberg 1971, p. 45). McKinley (1977) noted that Ray had also been known to make overtly racist statements prior to the King assassination (p. 181). Ray died in prison in 1996.

Denver, Colorado June 18, 1984

Jewish radio talk show host, Alan Berg is murdered by members of The Order. Berg had denounced right wing groups on his radio show. The killing had been ordered by Order leader Robert Mathews (Dees and Corcoran 1996, p. 144). Mathews died in an armed confrontation with the FBI in Washington. David Lane and Bruce Pierce were convicted of violating Berg's civil rights and were sent to federal prison. The MAC-10 .45 cal. weapon used in the shooting had been modified to be fully automatic in the workshops of the C.S.A. compound in Arkansas prior to the assassination of Berg.

Alexandria, Minnesota August 12, 1994

Four members of the Minnesota Patriot's Council, a tax resistance group, were arrested for conspiring to assassinate local and federal officials with the poison Ricin. Ricin is made from castor beans and the group mail ordered the poison from a right-wing publication (Stern 2000c, p. 159–183).

Waco, Texas 1995

Convicted bomber Timothy McVeigh told FOX News reporter Rita Cosby that before he decided on making the bombing attack against a federal building, he considered "a campaign of individual assassination" against federal officials. Named as possible targets were: Attorney General Janet Reno, Judge Walter Smith (who presided at the Waco trial), and FBI Agent Lon Horiuchi (a sniper at Ruby Ridge) (FOX NEWS April 26, 2001).

Boise, Idaho 1999

Members of the San Joaquin County Militia had plotted to assassinate Federal District Court Judge Edward Lodge in Boise, Idaho. The plot fell apart when members of the group were arrested for conspiracy charges stemming from a plan to bomb a propane plant in Elk Grove, California (ADL October 18, 2002).

Chicago, Illinois January 8, 2003

World Church of the Creator leader, Matt Hale was arrested by Federal authorities of the Joint Terrorism Task Force on charges of soliciting someone to kill Federal Judge Joan Humphrey Lefkow who had presided in a civil trial that the W.C.O.T.C. was a litigant in and had ruled against Hale in the lawsuit. Hale had accused Judge Lefkow as being biased against him because she was married to someone Jewish and had grandchildren of mixed race (Wilgoren 2003).

SABOTAGE

Historically, sabotage has been a traditional tactic of terrorist groups. Sabotage offers many advantages to the terrorist group. Among these advantages are: Sabotage produces a maximum effect for a minimum effort by the saboteur, It is inexpensive and it involves a minimum of risk to the saboteur from law enforcement or military authorities. Sabotage by terrorist groups serves three purposes:

1. Sabotage damages property and thus interferes with the operations of business or government. Sabotage demonstrates to the public the inability of the government to protect them from this type of attack.

2. The threat of sabotage instills fear in the population and affects actions in their daily lives.

3. Acts of sabotage bring publicity to the terrorist group.

4. As white supremacist Axl Hess (2001) stated in the *White Resistance Manual:*

"A significant amount of damage can be inflicted against government and corporate interests with the use of sabotage. Denial of services such as electrical power, fuel supplies, water, food supplies, communications or transportation will encourage the kind of civil unrest that we require in order to carry out more of our program. A sustained campaign of even minor sabotage can inflict serious financial damage upon our government and corporate enemies. It will be nearly impossible for law enforcement to protect all of these infrastructure targets" (Hess 2001, "Sabotage").

Harney, Nevada August 12, 1939

A Southern Pacific passenger train named "The City of San Francisco" was derailed in a deliberate act of sabotage. Spikes were removed from the rails and a section of rail was removed. An electrical connection was wired over the missing link of track to foil the safety system and show that the track was intact. As a result of the derailment, several railcars plunged into the river and 24 persons were killed and 114 were injured. Members of William Pelley's Silver Shirts were suspected, but the crime was never solved (Denevi, 1977).

Lancaster, Ohio May 12, 1995

Larry Wayne Harris is arrested at his home and three vials containing the bubonic plague virus *Yersina pestis* were seized by the Lancaster Police Department and public health officials. Harris was allegedly planning a biological attack on the New York City subway system using the bubonic plague. Federal prosecutors surmised that Harris had hoped the federal government would be blamed for the attack. The plot modeled itself after the March, 1995 attack by Aum Shinrikyo on the Tokyo, Japan subway system when the toxic Sarin gas was released by the group in the subway killing 12 and injuring over 1,000. Harris had mail-ordered the plague virus from a legitimate laboratory (ATCC) by faking paperwork to show that he ran a licensed laboratory and could legally possess the virus. Stern (2000b) described the raid on the Harris dwelling:

"While the police were inspecting the Harris's home, they found weapons and explosives in addition to the plague bacteria. They also found a certificate stating that Harris was a lieutenant in the neo-Nazi organization Aryan Nations, based in Hayden Lake, Idaho. The group's leader, Richard Butler, initially denied that Harris belonged to his organization but later admitted that Harris had been a member from the early 1990's until 1995" (Stern, 2000b:237).

Harris pled guilty to wire fraud in obtaining the plague virus. He was fined, given 18 months probation and 200 hours community service by Judge Joseph Kinneary.

Hyder, Arizona October 9, 1995

A neo-Nazi group calling themselves "The Sons of the Gestapo" took responsibility for the derailment of an Amtrak train named the "Sunset Limited" near Hyder, Arizona. A typewritten note was recovered at the scene of the wreck. The note criticized the government and mentioned the sieges at Ruby Ridge and Waco. The derailment was caused when saboteurs removed a section of rail on a trestle by taking out the spikes. The saboteurs then connected a wire between the missing links to complete the circuit and not set off the railroad electronic warning system. As a result of the derailment, two locomotives and four of the ten railcars crashed over 30 feet into a dry creek bed killing one and injuring 70. There have been no arrests (Agency for Nuclear Products n.d. and Stern, 1996:252–253).

Wise County, Texas April 23, 1997

FBI agents arrest white supremacist militia members Edward Taylor, Shawn Dee Adams, Catherine D. Adams and Jay Waskom for plotting to bomb hydrogen sulfide storage tanks at the Mitchell Energy Company. The bombing was to serve as a diversionary action for the planned robbery of an armored car that was scheduled to deliver approximately $2,000,000 to a bank located in Chico, Texas. The FBI was made aware of the group's plans by former KKK member Robert Leslie Spence Jr. who was acting as an inside informant for the FBI. Spence had told the FBI of other plots by white-supremacist groups to bomb the Bridgeport Texas Police Department and the JFK museum at the Texas School Book Depository in Dallas (Vozzella April 30, 1997; May 21, 1997; October 8, 1997).

Tampa, Florida July 28, 2000

A member of the 77th Regiment Militia of Pinellas County, Don Beauregard pled guilty to violation of 18 USC, T371, conspiracy to commit an offense against the United States for plotting terrorist attacks on power plants and government buildings (Dyson, 2001a).

THE CYBER-THREAT

White supremacist groups use the internet for training their followers, to communicate and to spread their ideas. They have extensive expertise in the use of this medium. Pitcavage and Terry (2000) observed that:

"Since as early as the 1980's and the creation of Louis Beam's white supremacist computer bulletin board, right-wing extremists have used the digital electronic media to recruit members, exchange information, and propagate their ideas. In the late 1980's, they branched out into the Internet, and in the mid-1990's, discovered the possibilities presented by the World Wide Web (WWW). As of 1997, communication via computers has become one of the most important means of information exchange and outreach for the entire patriot movement" (Pitcavage and Terry, 2000:1).

White supremacist groups maintain web pages to spread their views, recruit new followers, and communicate with their members (Kushner 1998). Perlman (2002) sees terrorist scenarios where the computer hacking of government computers could cause chaos within society. Perlman noted that "30,000 websites are dedicated to hacking, and that the types of tools are becoming more sophisticated" (Perlman, 2002:22). Possible targets for cyber-sabotage included:

- Computer operated controls of municipal water supplies being tampered with.
- Corruption of the criminal justice data base causing prison inmates to be improperly released.
- Destruction of data bases in government computers through the usage of viruses resulting in computer shutdowns caused by cyber-terrorism (Perlman, 2002).

Recognizing the possible terrorist threat, Perlman (2002) observed that:

"Previous incidents have showcased how someone with a mission can exploit holes in computer systems. An inmate in a Key West, Florida jail was able to hack into a jail computer system and delete text files. A young computer hacker in Massachusetts was able to disable a key telephone company computer that provided service for the Worcester airport, disrupting and disabling vital service to the control tower for six hours" (Perlman, 2002:22).

SUMMARY

Some right wing white extremist groups have historically resorted to terrorism to attempt to gain support for or accomplish their goals. White supremacist groups that participate in terrorism to accomplish their goals use historical, political, and religious reasons to justify their actions. Terrorists may act in groups or as "Lone Wolves" as theorized by Coates (1987). The ability of some terrorists, such as Eric Rudolph, to elude capture for long periods of time, emboldens other aspiring terrorists to follow in their footsteps. The potential for further terrorist actions by members of white supremacist groups remains a threat to American society. The prospect of future terrorist actions by white supremacist groups has been increased by the efforts of the Aryan Nations to reach out to Islamic terrorists in their common fight against the United States government, Z.O.G. and the Jews. Their website stated that:

"Aryan Nations' Ministry of Islamic Liaison is an outreach of Identity believers who work to establish further discourse and working relationship with the Muslim world (who we believe are Ishmaelites, our cousins through Nahor). As the world wide attack against the Yehudi-Shataan intensifies we, the watchers on the wall, know full well that the "enemy of our enemy is our friend" and that any cause which further undermines the United States government (Z.O.G.) is a worthy cause" (Aryan Nations).

REFERENCES

ADL October 18, 2002. "Militia Assassination Plot Uncovered in Idaho." Available online: *http://www.adl.org/learn/news/idaho_militia.asp.*

Agency for Nuclear Products. N.d. "Nuclear Waste Transportation Security and Safety Issues." Available online: *http://www.state.nv.us/nucwaste/trans/risk12.htm.*

Aryan Nations. N.d. "Aryan Nations: Fighting Jewish Takeover for over 25 Years." Available online: *http://www.aryan-nations.org.*

"Bombing of the Sixteenth Street Baptist Church." N.d. Available online: *http://useekufind.com/peace/summary.htm.*

Bush, G. 1998. *Terrorist Group Profiles.* Washington, D.C.: GPO.

Bushart, H., J. Craig, and M. Barnes. 1998. *Soldiers of God: White Supremacists and Their Holy War for America.* New York: Kensington Books.

Butler, R. G. 1995. "This Is Aryan Nations." In *Extremism in America: A Reader,* ed. L. Sargent. New York: New York University Press.

Cash, J., and R. Charles. 2001. "OKC: From Bank Robbers to Bombers?" *Soldier of Fortune* 26, no. 10 (October): 58–63.

CNN. November 15, 2000. "Grand Juries Indict Suspected Bomber Eric Rudolph." Available online: *http://www.cnn.com/2000/LAW/11/15/eric.rudolph.indict.*

_____. March 20, 2002. "FBI Cuts Search for Accused Olympic Bomber." Available online: *http://www.cnn.com/2002/US/03/20/rudolph.search/index/html.*

_____. February 28, 2003. "Jury Convicts 27-Year-Old Man in 1966 Slaying of Black Sharecropper." Available online: *http://www.cnn.com/2003/LAW/02/28/avants.trail.ap.*

Coates, J. 1987. *Armed and Dangerous: The Rise of the Survivalist Right.* New York: Hill and Wang.

Coppolla, V. 1996. *Dragons of God: A Journey through Far-Right America.* Atlanta, GA: Longstreet Press.

Covenant News. N.d. "The Search for Eric Rudolph." Available online: *http://www.covenantnews.com/eric/rudolph.*

Dees, M., and J. Corcoran. 1996. *Gathering Storm: America's Militia Threat.* New York: HarperCollins Publishers.

Denevi, D. 1977. *Tragic Train: The "City of San Francisco."* Seattle, WA: Superior Publishing Co.

"Downside Legacy at Two Degrees of President Clinton." N.d. Available online: *http://www.alamo-girl.com/103.htm.*

Dyson, W. 2001a. "Calendar of Terrorist and Criminal Extremist Events in the United States," *BJA State and Local Anti-Terrorism Training (SLATT) Program,* 1, no. 1. Tallahassee, FL: Institute for Intergovernmental Research.

_____. 2001b. "Calendar of Terrorist and Criminal Extremist Events in the United States," *BJA State and Local Anti-Terrorism Training (SLATT) Program,* 1, no. 2. Tallahassee, FL: Institute for Intergovernmental Research.

_____. 2001c. "Calendar of Terrorist and Criminal Extremist Events in the United States," *BJA State and Local Anti-Terrorism Training (SLATT) Program,* 2, no. 1. Tallahassee, FL: Institute for Intergovernmental Research.

FBI. 1999. *Terrorism in the United States 1998.* Washington, D.C.: Counterterrorism Threat Assessment and Warning Unit National Security Division.

Flynn, K., and G. Gerhardt. 1989. *The Silent Brotherhood: Inside America's Racist Underground.* New York: The Free Press.

Fox News. April 26, 2001. "McVeigh's Apr. 26 Letter to Fox News." Available online: *http://www.foxnews.com/story/0,2933,17500,00.html.*

Gado, M. 2000. *Hell Comes to Bath: America's Worst School Violence Ever.* Available online: *http://www.crimelibrary.com/serial_killers/history/bath/index_1.html?sect=6.*

Gadson, L., M. Michel, R. Perrin, and N. Walsh. 2001. *FBI Bomb Data Center General Information Bulletin 97-1: 1997 Bombing Incidents.* Washington, D.C.: GPO.

Goodrick-Clarke, N. 1992. *The Occult Roots of Nazism: Secret Aryan Cults and Their Influence on Nazi Ideology.* New York: New York University Press.

Griffin, A. June 2, 2003. "Rudolph's Past Strewn with Anger, Extremism." *The Wichita Eagle,* 1A.

Hale, M. 2001. "Racial Hatred Is Necessary to Save the White Race." In *Extremist Groups: Opposing Viewpoints,* ed. T. Roleff, H. Cochran, and J. Torr. San Diego, CA: Greenhaven Press.

Hess, A. 2001. *The White Resistance Manual.* Available online: *http://dawino6260 .no-ip.com/White&20Resistance%20Manual%20v2_4/MainPage/WRMMainpage.html.*

Jones, S., and P. Israel. 2001. *Others Unknown: Timothy McVeigh and the Oklahoma City Bombing Conspiracy.* New York: Public Affairs.

Kushner, H. 1997. *Terrorism in America: A Structured Approach to Understanding the Terrorist Threat.* Springfield, IL: Charles C. Thomas Publisher, Ltd.

Leet, D., G. Rush, and A. Smith. 1997. *Gangs, Graffiti, and Violence: A Realistic Guide to the Scope and Structure of Gangs in America.* Incline Village, NV: Copperhouse Publishing Company.

Lipset, S., and E. Raab. 1978. *The Politics of Unreason: Right-Wing Extremism in America, 1790–1977.* 2nd ed. Chicago, IL: University of Chicago Press.

Lyons, Jennifer. N.d. "Justice Delayed: The Ghost of Medgar Evers." Available online: *http://clioseye.sfasu.edu/ghostschron.htm.*

McGuckin, F. 1997. *Terrorism in the United States.* New York: H. W. Wilson.

McKinley, J. 1977. *Assassination in America.* New York: Harper & Row.

Michael, L., and D. Herbeck. 2001. *American Terrorist: Timothy McVeigh & the Oklahoma City Bombing.* New York: Regan Books.

Militia Watchdog N.d. "The Mountaineer Militia's Long, Slippery Slope." Available online: *http://www.adl.org/mwd/mountain.asp.*

Morgan, R. 2001. *The Demon Lover: The Roots of Terrorism.* Rev. ed. New York: Washington Square Press.

MSNBC. June 18, [2004]. "Reputed Mississippi Klansman Avants Dies in Prison." Available online: *http://www.msnbc.com/id/5235798.*

Mullins, W. 1997. *A Sourcebook on Domestic and International Terrorism: An Analysis of Issues, Organizations, Tactics, and Responses.* 2nd ed. Springfield, IL: Charles C. Thomas Publisher.

The Nizkor Project. N.d. "Paranoia as Patriotism: Far-Right Influences on the Militia Movement." Available online: *http://www.nizkor.org/hweb/orgs/american/adl/paranoia-as-patriotism/ covenant.html.*

Perlman, E. 2002. "Digital Nightmare: What if Terrorists Break into Critical State and Local Networks and Wreak Havoc?" *Governing* 15, no. 7 (April): 20–24.

Pina, P. May 13, 2002. "Few along His Route Were Quiet: Smiling Man as Pipe Bomber." *Wichita Eagle.*

Pitcavage, M., and J. Terry. 2000. "A Guide to Right-Wing Extremism on the World Wide Web." In *BJA State and Local Anti-Terrorism Training (SLATT) Program,* ed. W. Dyson. Tallahassee, FL: Institute for Intergovernmental Research.

Powell, W. 1989. *The Anarchist Cookbook.* New York: Barricade Books.

Redfeairn, Ray. [2001]. "More Jewish War Crimes." Available online: *http://www .churchoftrueisrael.com/red/red5.html.*

Ridgeway, J. 1990. *Blood in the Face: The Ku Klux Klan, Aryan Nations, Nazi Skinheads and the Rise of a New White Culture.* New York: Thunder's Mouth Press.

Riley, K., and B. Hoffman. 1995. *Domestic Terrorism: A National Assessment of State and Local Preparedness.* Santa Monica, CA: RAND.

Sargent, L. 1995. *Extremism in America: A Reader.* New York: New York University Press.

Simonsen, C., and J. Spindlove. 2000. *Terrorism Today: The Past, the Players, the Future.* Upper Saddle River, NJ: Prentice Hall.

Snow, R. 1999. *The Militia Threat: Terrorists among Us.* New York: Plenum Trade.

Stern, J. 2000a. "The Covenant, the Sword, and the Arm of the Lord (1985)." In *Toxic Terror: Assessing Terrorist Use of Chemical and Biological Weapons,* ed. J. Tucker. Cambridge, MA: MIT Press.

_____. 2000b. "Larry Wayne Harris (1998)." In *Toxic Terror: Assessing Terrorist Use of Chemical and Biological Weapons,* ed. J. Tucker. Cambridge, MA: MIT Press.

Stern, K. 1996. *A Force upon the Plain: The American Militia Movement and the Politics of Hate.* New York: Simon and Schuster.

Stumpenhouse, R. 2003. "The Role of an Undercover Officer." Presented at the meeting of the 9th Annual Midwest Law Enforcement Conference on Gangs & Drugs, Wichita, Kansas, May.

Trochman, J., and B. Fletcher. 1995. "Militias Are Patriotic Organizations." In *The Militia Movement and Hate Groups in America,* ed. G. McCuen. Hudson, WI: Gary E. McCuen Publications, Inc.

Tucker, J., and J. Tate. 2000. "The Minnesota Patriots Council." In *Toxic Terror: Assessing Terrorist Use of Chemical and Biological Weapons,* ed. J. Tucker. Cambridge, MA: MIT Press.

Vozzella, Laura. April 30, 1997. "Suspect in Plot Cites Ties to KKK: Defendant Ordered Held without Bail." *Fort Worth Star-Telegram,* 1.

_____. May 21, 1997. "Klansman Depicted as a Snitch in Bomb Plot." *Fort Worth Star-Telegram,* 1.

_____. October 8, 1997. "KKK Trio Plead Guilty: Trial Averted in Plot to Blow Up Gas Plant." *Fort Worth Star-Telegram,* 1.

Weisberg, H. 1971. *Frame-Up: The Martin Luther King–James Earl Ray Case.* New York: Outerbridge & Dienstfrey.

"Witnesses Recall 1963 Church Bombing." N.d. Available online: *http://wwwblacknewsweekly .com/bin122.html.*

Wyatt, K. June 1, 2003. "5-Year Hunt for Bombing Suspect Ends: Police Nab Fugitive in Grocery Parking Lot." *The Kansas City Star,* 1.

CHAPTER 16

Leaderless Resistance: Are Terrorist Groups a Thing of the Past?

Dr. Lynne L. Snowden
Dept. of Sociology, Anthropology & Criminal Justice
Univ. of North Carolina at Wilmington

Prior to the September 11th World Trade Center and Pentagon attacks, prestigious experts such as the U.S. Federal Bureau of Investigation, prominent criminologists, and the international media argued that terrorists had abandoned the group as their preferred method of social organization in favor of a new style of terrorism that they dubbed "leaderless resistance." The following chapter debunks several myths that surround the concept of leaderless resistance. It then analyzes a government dataset to see if the data supports the claim that leaderless resistance has become the predominant terrorist structure throughout the world. Finally, it concludes with more suitable analytical frameworks that can help researchers understand how and when terrorists are coordinating their efforts.

THE DEFINITION OF LEADERLESS RESISTANCE:

Myth #1:

Leaderless resistance consists of uncoordinated violent acts committed by individuals or very small groups who operate on their own, taking their cues from hints and messages that flow along [a] movement's elaborate communications system.

Reality:

Leaderless resistance is a strategy for the protection of a movement's leaders and well-known involved parties (sponsors) who wish to disassociate themselves from extremely violent people who are dedicated to the same goals leaders promote. It has been used throughout history with varying degrees of success and varying degrees of intensity in many political protest movements, but when one looks at terrorist events in total, leaderless resistance is relatively rare. In addition, today's Internet/World Wide Web has provided a new and more effective venue for the leadership to disassociate itself from violent members while still remaining in constant contact.

Far from being a type of lone wolf terrorism, leaderless resistance is a method of organizing deep-cover groups that have been labeled as negative by powerful state or media forces. Over the centuries, a few groups have adopted the strategy in order to remain in operation. Such disparate groups as the colonial Sons of Liberty, the Irish Republican army, and the USSR Communist counterintelligence organizations have used it.

The term became popularized after Louis Beam, a leader in the Aryan Nation and KKK movements, wrote a widely quoted essay suggesting that it could be used by his groups to fight off "ever-increasing persecution and oppression" from U.S. government agencies such as the United States Federal Bureau of Investigation (FBI), Bureau of Alcohol, Tobacco, and Firearms (BATF), and the U.S. Marshals Service (Beam 1999). His chief concern was that hierarchical organizations such as the KKK could be easily infiltrated by U.S. government agents, even at the highest levels. In his essay, he expanded on the concept of leaderless resistance, which was perfected by international intelligence organizations during the 1950s and 60s when Soviet/Sino communists mounted deep undercover operations in the highest levels of the U.S. government. Beam claimed he learned of the method from a former intelligence officer, Col. Amoss, who taught that the cell system completely isolated one agent from another; neither agent had any knowledge of each other's identity (Beam 1999). The cell "leaders" held very low social positions and were only known to one person in each cell, but in general, all direction (including funding) came from the home country. Beam acknowledged that the strong central direction and state-funded terrorism model would not work for his Klan or the new Patriot movement, so he proposed a system of cell organization (Phantom Cells) in which all individuals and groups would mimic the intelligence operations but would raise their own funds, operate independently of each other, and never report to a central headquarters or depend on it for permission to act (Beam 1999, 3). In general, Beam felt that the key to success of a movement organized in this way was the initial training and recruitment process. Only like-minded individuals would be recruited and then trained to react in the same way, thereby acquiring the appropriate skills and information about what was to be done on their own. They would be like a group of voluntary Manchurian candidates who, when they encountered tyranny, would all have the same button pushed and respond in an identical manner.

If one reads Beam's essay carefully, one notes that he really did not envision that an entire movement would adopt this type of organization, only the most violent sections. He states that "those who join organizations to play 'let's pretend' or who are 'groupies' will be quickly weeded out" (Beam 1999, 4). While this strategy has succeeded for short periods of time, as in the case of the colonial patriots, it is extremely difficult for the cell endure. Especially today, it is extremely difficult, and sometimes impossible, for individuals and groups to obtain adequate funding and other resources needed to carry out terrorist operations without attracting a great deal of attention from neighbors, community, or higher-level officials.

Luckily for America, Beam was not a very good social movement student. If he had been, he would have realized that the literature on political and social activism, especially in the United States, shows that political challengers and members of hate group's are unlikely to react to anything in the same way. We know from cult studies that members often require constant brainwashing or indoctrination, as well as isolation from mainstream society, to keep even a modicum of new, or disparate, ideas from infiltrating the group. In addition, it turns out that activists come and go frequently, so infiltrating a small group is almost as easy as infiltrating a large one, especially when one does not have a large organization to do a background check on the new members.

Some analysts have suggested that leaderless resistance is thriving via the World Wide Web. For example, Barkun suggests that our country is at high risk from "individuals or very small groups who operate on their own, taking their cues from hints and messages that flow along the movement's elaborate communications system through fringe publications the Internet, faxes, and other alternative media" (Barkun January 1997, 1). While the Internet is certainly a boon to those protestors who want semi-anonymous communication, anyone who takes orders (cues) is involved in organizational behavior, no matter how the message is delivered. Also, the use of computers, fax machines, alternative media publications, and so forth suggests the presence of large amounts of movement resources, a situation that is not compatible with Beam's lone wolf idea. In this scenario, the Internet acts as a facilitator for groups claiming leaderless resistance as a tactic rather than a replacement for group affiliation itself. Leaderless resistance has been erroneously portrayed in the media as lone wolf terrorists whose only goal is to create chaos in the world. It is actually a strategy for organization rather than disorganization. Finally, media sources such as *Newsweek* have picked up a buzz word the "new terrorism" developed by terrorism scholars such as Walter Laqueur and have used it interchangeably with the concept of leaderless resistance. There are two major problems with this. First of all, the terms are not interchangeable. Laqueur and others have used the term "new terrorism" to refer to the "emergence of new kinds of terrorist violence, some based on ecological and quasi-religious concerns, which consider as strategy, the possibility that weapons of mass destruction may be employed" (1999, 4–5).

LONE WOLF VIOLENCE:

Myth #2:

Most terrorist acts are now committed by lone wolf terrorists whose only goal is to create chaos in the world. In 1999, the U.S. Federal Bureau of Investigation declared that the more traditional terrorist organization was dead as the general trend in domestic extremism and that terrorists now disavow "traditional, hierarchical, and structured terrorist organizations" (U.S. FBI 1999, 3) in favor of leaderless resistance.

Reality:

When we look at the actual violence throughout the world, we find almost no evidence that these episodes are being performed by "lone wolf terrorists whose only goal is to create chaos in the world." An analysis of all violent terrorist events that occurred during 1998 showed that lone wolf terrorism is the exception rather than the rule (see Appendix 1).

Two very clear patterns were found: almost all events are connected with a particular cause or causes, and events not attributed to specific groups tend to have minimal injuries and deaths compared to those directly traced to particular groups. Ninety-five percent of all terrorist violence throughout the world was connected to specific groups with a defined leadership. Even suicide bombers are usually linked to particular terrorist organizations. Five percent of the terrorist events that were only possibly attributed to leaderless cells (some were blamed on "angry mobs," etc.) occurred mainly in the African and Middle Eastern regions where record-keeping is minimal. In addition, there was only one event in the world where deaths were attributed to leaderless groups, a restaurant bombing in Kampala, Uganda, where there were five deaths and six people injured. In 1999, 1,634 deaths and 6,363 injuries resulted from terrorist incidents recorded throughout the world. Of those, five deaths and fourteen injuries were not attributed to known terrorist organizations. If leaderless resistance exists at all, it was not active during 1999.

NO MORE TERRORIST GROUPS:

Myth #3:

"The general trend in domestic extremism is [one] whereby terrorists disavow traditional, hierarchical, and structured terrorist organizations" (FBI 1999:3).

Reality:

It is impossible to generalize from the fact that all types of terrorists have traditionally used hierarchical and structured organizations or argue that most terrorists have abandoned this behavior in favor of leaderless resistance.

This myth has spread so easily because it is quite difficult to keep abreast of contemporary terrorist organizations, mainly because most terrorist groups gain the attention of law enforcement agencies only after they have attempted, practiced, or threatened to commit violence. In addition, it often takes years of intelligence-gathering to develop a realistic picture of a particular organization. Osama bin Laden is an excellent example. When he first came into the public eye following the embassy bombings, he was thought to be a lone wolf, then a financier of several lone wolf terrorists, and now the world press speaks daily of his leadership of the largest and most deadly international terrorist organization.

DATA ANALYSIS (DATASET IN APPENDIX 1)

To see if leaderless resistance had become a general trend, I analyzed profiles of more than forty-seven present and past terrorist organizations that had formed from 1970 to 1990 to see if they had moved toward leaderless resistance as their characteristic strategy. The analysis of groups listed by the U.S. Government as the most common international terrorists during the 1980s shows that most of these terrorists were associated with groups that had a defined leadership and some type of hierarchical organization, such as several funding sources, a history of merging with other terrorist organizations, and a sustained period of activity (more than a decade).

In fact, many of these groups identified by Vice President George Bush's Task Force on Combating Terrorism are still active today. Our analysis showed that 17 percent (eight of forty-seven) of the analyzed groups might be classed as using leaderless resistance. The remainder of the groups had a sharply defined leadership and, often, specific procedures for the selection of new leaders if the old ones were to be captured or incapacitated.

Seventy-nine percent (thirty-seven of forty-seven) of the terrorist organizations were still active during the 1990s, and many still exist today. Others listed as terrorists by the U.S. government in 1990 still exist but have gained respectability, such as the ANC of South Africa. Some groups, such as the Basque Fatherland and Liberty (ETA) have experienced periods of inactivity, only to return to bombings and other violent methods as recently as the summer of 2000. Sixty-six percent (thirty-one of forty-seven) showed evidence of one or more outside funding sources, an indicator of their ability to gain international attention and publicity, while 43 percent (twenty of forty-seven) had more than one international funding source, showing the ability to solicit and distribute funds from a number of countries, sometimes with organizational structures that would be the envy of volunteer organizations everywhere. Finally, 32 percent (fifteen of forty-seven) of the terrorists showed evidence of mergers, having anywhere from one to five different names, an indicator that a group has become an umbrella for people with several different issues or grievances.

SUMMARY AND CONCLUSION

There are many reasons why the myths surrounding the term "leaderless resistance" have circulated and grown so rapidly. First, new technologies have helped reduce the necessity for terrorists to meet face to face in order to maintain their organizational structures. Many groups now use the Internet and the World Wide Web extensively. Second, terrorism scholars were hard pressed to explain why cultic/religious groups were using weapons of mass destruction and why two men with no terrorist ties committed the Oklahoma City bombing. Finally, counterterrorist organizations and theoretical analysts committed what social scientists call "an ecological fallacy," which means that they collected data on terrorist groups but used it to make assertions about terrorists as individuals. For example, a 1988 report issued by Vice President George Bush gave profiles of the fifty-one most violent terrorist groups in the world. Yet Bush's list of government responses focused on strategies that would be more appropriate for individuals. These included tracking individual terrorists, developing watch lists for border guards, and tightening extradition treaties. None of these efforts would be improved by accumulating group-level data. Finally, the data collected was mainly limited to geographical facts and political ideology, leaving most of the group processes that occurred out of the equation.

In conclusion, you would most likely learn more about terrorism if you asked a social movement expert to explain something called "collective violence." This is the study of violent group behavior. It you asked that expert to look at Louis Beam's description of the process of leaderless resistance, he or she would probably tell you that all social movements begin with this type of organizational structure. Goal formation is the first, and may be the only, joint action of the group if the goal is quickly achieved. Ideology typically follows, and then some form of rudimentary organization, or division of labor, develops. A small group may function for some time without a leader. Is that the case with the Ku Klux Klan, the Irish Republican Army, or the Aryan Nations? Definitely not. These groups have existed for long periods of time with large horizontal organizations. It is also possible that groups who are in imminent danger of suffering a mortal blow from social control agents may return to their nascent form of organization in a last-ditch attempt to survive. We cannot be sure, but it is to be hoped that sociological research will systematically examine this suggestion in the near future.

One thing is sure, however. Terrorist groups are always in a state of organizational flux, just as are the more benign social movements. The existence of one or two events, such as the Oklahoma City bombing, where we only suspect but cannot find evidence of group association does not mean that we should indulge in "terrorism paranoia" by imagining that most terrorists have abandoned their contacts to become lone wolves bent on using violence to destroy everything that surrounds them. Even individuals and small groups cannot act, especially effectively or violently, if they do not have a goal in mind.

Second, leaderless resistance is not used regularly by people who want to send society into chaos. Even anarchist groups, who typically espouse this goal, are frequently quite organized and usually wish to disrupt only one part of society, such as its economic system. For example, a group of anarchists currently operating in the United States disrupted the World Trade Organization protest in Seattle, Washington (Denson 1999). To accomplish this feat, they began to plan their participation almost six months prior to the event, as rumors began to circulate that environmental, labor, and human rights activists would mount a large demonstration in Seattle. In June, the group, complete with its national spokesperson John Zerzan, provoked a police riot in Eugene, Oregon, by breaking some windows in downtown businesses and stopping traffic (Denson December 11, 1999, A10). Before this, the group had mostly used nonviolent strategies such as handing out leaflets on street corners and setting up information tables at the local library. Buoyed by their success, the group's hard-core activists blended in with the peaceful protestors at the World Trade Organization Meeting in Seattle and began vandalizing stores when the police appeared to control the crowd. "They hit mostly large corporations, spraying graffiti on buildings and smashing windows" (Denson December 11, 1999, A10). Their strategy worked again and violent clashes between police and protestors were photographed and sent around the world. Although the anarchists met their goal of causing a slight disruption in the capitalist system of trade, their actions were not indicative of the organizational cell system known as leaderless resistance. In fact, the group publicly states its goals, uses typical movement organizational characteristics and has a spokesperson who does news interviews.

SUGGESTING A FRAMEWORK FOR UNDERSTANDING CONFLICT AND TERRORISM

How can we better understand the Oklahoma City bombing or the Eugene, Oregon, anarchists? 1) We can use a framework to compare each actor's behavior to see whether they are involved in rational—"goal seeking"—behavior or behavior somehow induced or influenced by some other irrational source such as drugs, alcohol, disease, and 2) we can ascertain whether these people are engaging in such organizational behaviors as a defined leadership, membership recruitment, the establishment of a set of beliefs, and some type of hierarchical organization. If any of these is occurring, then a terrorist group is mimicking a social movement organization that can be understood and analyzed by techniques developed by social and behavioral scientists.

REFERENCES

Barkun, Michael. January 1997 Remarks prepared for delivery at the session on Changing U.S. Domestic Threats, International Conference on Aviation Safety and Security in the 21st Century, Washington, D.C. Available online: *www.gwu.edu/~cms/aviation/track_ ii/barkun.html.*

Beam, L. R. 1999. "Leaderless Resistance." Available online: *http://www.crusader.net/texts/ bt/bt04.html.*

Denson, Bryan. December 11, 1999. "Eugene Man Speaks Up for Northwest Anarchists," *The Oregonian,* A1–A10.

Laqueur, Walter. 1999. The New Terrorism. New York: Oxford University Press.

U.S. Department of Defense. 1990. *Terrorist Group Profiles.* Washington, D.C.: GPO.

U.S. Federal Bureau of Investigation. 1999. "Project Megiddo." Report Prepared for the Senate Special Committee on the Year 2000 Technology Problem. *WWW.FBI.GOV/*

TABLE 16.1   Appendix I–Chart of Terrorist Acts Throughout the World in 1998 by Region

Region 1- Asia

City/Country	Group Associated	Action	Deaths	Injuries
Kandy, Sri Lanka (Temple of Tooth)	Yes—LTTE	Suicide vehicle bombing	16	23
Mandano, Sri Lanka	Yes—LTTE	Vehicle bomb	36	250
Jaffina, Sri Lanka	Yes—LTTE	Political assassination	1	
		Mine bombed	5	
		Govt. building bombed	12	Unknown
		Power plants bombed	0	0
		Vessel seized (hostages)		21
Jaffina, Sri Lanka	Yes—Sangilian Force	Mayor assassinated	1	
Phnom Penh, Cambodia	Yes—Khmer Rouge	Vietnamese attacked	12	
Kashmir, India	Yes—Kashmiri Militia	Villagers attacked	28	
Coimbatore, India	Yes—Islamic Militia	Series of bombings/attacks	50	200
Karachi, Pakistan Punjab Province Pakistan	Yes—Sunni and Shia Sects	Assorted attacks	900	Unknown
Mindano, Phillipines	Yes—ASG	Clash with government agents	1	Unknown
	Yes—MILF/ASG	Kidnappings		5

Region 2-Africa

City/Country	Group Associated	Action	Deaths	Injuries
Ebangan, Angola	Yes—UNITA	Kidnapping		2
Calandula, Angola	Yes—UNITA	Mortar attack	1	2
Cabinda, Angola	Yes—FLEC-FAC	Kidnapping and hostages		3+
Yetwene, Angola	Yes—UNITA	Diamond mine attacked	8	22+
Central African Republic	No	Small bomb— minor damage		

Region 2-	Africa			
City/Country	**Group Associated**	**Action**	**Deaths**	**Injuries**
Monda National Park, Chad	Yes—UDF	Kidnapping		4
Tibesti, Chad	Yes—NFRC	Hostage taking		8
Ruwenzori Mountains, Congo (DRC)	Yes—PALR	Hostage taking (abduction)		6
Gode, Ethiopia	Yes—ONLF	Hostage abduction		1
Somalia	Yes—Al-Ittihad al-Islami	Kidnapping		6
Nairobi, Kenya	Yes—Al Qaeda	U.S. Embassy bombed	291	5,000
Bayelsa, Nigeria	No—Mob of angry youth	Shell workers abducted		8
Komalo, Sierra Leone	Yes—RUF	Kidnapping		1
Capetown, South Africa	Yes—MAGO	Restaurant bombed	1	25
Somalia	Yes—Somalian clansmen	Hostages		9
Dar es Salaam, Tanzania	Yes—Al Qaeda	Truck bomb	10	77
Kampala, Uganda	??—ADF	Two bombs in restaurant	5	6
Northwestern Uganda	Yes—UNRF	Rocket grenade thrown at UN vehicle		1
North Uganda	Yes—RLRA	Convoy attacked	7	28

Region 3-Latin America

Columbia	Yes—FARC	U.S. Citizen Kidnapped		7
Columbia	Yes—ELN	Kidnapping		3
		Bombing	71	Unknown
		Pipeline bombing		77
Peru	Yes—Sendero Luminoso	Police station attacked	4	

Region 4-Europe

Belgium	Yes—GIA	Found with explosives	–	–

TABLE 16.1   Appendix I–Chart of Terrorist Acts Throughout the World in 1998 by Region (*cont.*)

Region 4-Europe

City/Country	Group Associated	Action	Deaths	Injuries
Germany	Yes—PKK	Violence threatened	–	–
Athens, Greece	Yes—17 November	Firebombings against U.S. buildings (6); property damage only		
Turin, Italy	Yes—Osama Bin Laden	Weapons violations		
Milan, Italy	Yes—GIA	Forgery—counterfeiting		
Spain	Yes—GRAPO	Bombing/extortion letters		Unknown
SE Turkey	Yes—PKK	Bombing		7
Istanbul, Turkey	Yes—PKK	Bombing	3	25+
		Kidnapping		1
Karakose, Turkey	Yes—PKK	Kidnapping		1
Omagh, Ireland	Yes—Real IRA	Car-bombing	29	330+
Banbridge, Ireland	Yes—Real IRA	Bombing		35

Region 4-Middle East & Eurasia

City/Country	Group Associated	Action	Deaths	Injuries
Side Hamed, Alg.	Yes—GIA	Massacre	100+	Unknown
	Yes—GIA	Isolated incidents	Unknown	Unknown
Algeria	Yes—Salafi Group for Call and Combat	Assassination	1	
Egypt	Yes—Al-jihad as Gama'at	Assorted terrorist attacks	47	
Tel Aviv, Israel	Yes—Hamas	Car bombing and shootings		13
Israel	Yes—PIJ	Suicide car bomb		
Hebron, Israel	Yes—Hamas	Grenade attack	2	25
Beersherd, Israel	Yes—Hamas	Grenade attack		50
Gaza, Israel	Yes—Hamas	Car bomb	1	5+
Amman, Jordan	Yes—The Reform and Defiance Movement	Bombings		
Beirut, Lebanon	No	Rocket grenade attacks		
Beirut, Lebanon	Yes—PIJ	Car bomb		3
Saudi Arabia	Yes—Osama bin Laden	Threats against U.S. businesses		

Region 4-Middle East & Eurasia

City/Country	Group Associated	Action	Deaths	Injuries
Yemen	Yes—Yemeni Tribe	Kidnapping		60
Yemen	Yes—Islamic Army of Aden	Kidnapping	4	12
Sonaa, Yemen	Yes—Islamic Army of Aden	Car hijacking		1

Eurasia

Armenia				
Georgia				
Kazakhstan				
Russia	Violence in this	Assignations		
Tajikistan	unstable area is	Abductions		
	intertwined with	and minor attacks		
	ethnic and political	are more common		
	unrest, revolution,	than bombings and		
	and war	other random		
		violence		

Region 5-North America

No incidents of international terrorism were reported in North America during 1998.

Source: US Dept. of State, *www.state.gov/www/global/terrorism.html*

Total of all regions

Group Assoc.	Deaths	Injuries
Yes = 53 No = 4	1,634	6,363

Source: U.S. Department of State, USIS Stockholm, Sweden, *www.state.gov/www.usis.usemb.sc/terror/rpt1998*

Key of Terrorist Groups (In Order Presented)

Africa

UNITA   -National Union for Total Independence of Angola

FLEC-FAC   -Cabinda Liberstion Front-Cabindan Armed Forces

UDF   -Union of Democratic Forces

NFRC   -National Front for Renewal of Chad

PALR   -People in Action for the Liberation of Rwanda

ONLF   -Ogaden National Liberation Front

RUF   -Revolutionary United Front

MAGO   -Muslims Against Global Opression

ADF   -Allied Democratic Forces

UNRF   -Uganda National Rescue Front II

RLRA   -Rebels of the Lord' Resistance Army

Latin America

FARC   -Revolutionary Armed Forces of Colombia

ELN   -National Liberation Army

Europe

GIA   -Armed Islamic Group

PKK   -Kurdistan Workers' Party

GRAPO   -First of October Anti-Fascist Resistance Group

Real IRA   -Splinter Irish Republican Army group

Middle East

PIJ   -Palestine Islamic Jihad

GIA   -Armed Islamic Group

HAMAS   -Harakat al-Muqawamah al-Islamiyya (courage and bravery)

CHAPTER 17

Extremism in the Military: The Burmeister Case and Policy Response

Col. George E. Reed,
U. S. Army War College

For over 220 years, the U.S. Army has been the defender of the nation and the values embodied in our Constitution. That sacred bond of trust between the army and the American people was brought into question on December 7, 1995, when soldiers allegedly committed two racially motivated murders in Fayetteville, North Carolina. The army is a reflection of American society and has a 21 percent annual turnover of personnel. It cannot escape the growing impact of extremism and racist organizations in our society at large, but clearly it must identify and address indications of extremist behavior when it occurs (U.S. Department of the Army 1996, i).

In December 1995, the hate-motivated murders of Michael James and Jackie Burden, an African-American couple, near Fort Bragg, North Carolina, by three Caucasian soldiers assigned to the elite 82nd Airborne Division raised questions about the extent of racial and ethnic extremism within the army (Clifford December 13, 1995; Fields and Johnson December 11, 1995; Harrison December 17, 1995). High-profile bias crimes occur infrequently in the armed forces, but they are not unknown. In 1986, service members were implicated in the stockpiling and sale of weapons to the White Patriot Party (Flesher July 25, 1986; Schmidt April 15, 1986). In 1992, a joint federal

The views expressed in this article are those of the author and do not necessarily reflect the official policy of the army, Department of Defense, or the U.S. government.

investigation uncovered soldier involvement in the theft of U.S. government weapons, ammunition, explosives, and other property for a white supremacist group (United States Army Criminal Investigation Command 1992). Incidents of racial and ethnic extremism occur despite the fact that the army is recognized as an example of healthy race relations.

Examination of the 1995 case is a useful case study not only as an example of extremism in practice but also for the organizational response it engendered by a large and complex public-sector organization. This essay begins with some context about the nature of the army at the time of the Burmeister case. The policy before and after the murders is explored in some detail with an eye to identifying a model of policy change that is descriptive of the army's approach to the problem. The essay concludes with a cautionary note against depicting extremists as fringe actors unconnected to mainstream society. The lessons learned in this process are many, and it is hoped that through their examination some good may come from what was otherwise a senseless tragedy.

Sociologists Moskos and Butler (1996) characterize the army as an institution that achieves a high level of racial integration, including interracial intermingling and intermarriage. They observed that the army is also promoted as a place where African Americans are successful and where African-American culture is an integral part of the institutional culture. They noted that the army is one of the few places in American life where blacks routinely supervise whites. It is an institution where failure to embrace the principles of equal opportunity can result in career failure, if not criminal charges and discharge. The army invests unit commanders with a broad array of powers to ensure good order and discipline, and they are accountable for establishing a leadership climate that facilitates respect and dignity. Incidents of racial intolerance clearly undermine these principles.

RAND analyst Carl Builder (1989) identified the enduring personality of each of the military service branches and concluded, in part, that the army is the branch that is perceived as closest to the American people. It sees itself as the loyal servant of the nation, its institutions, and its population. In such an organization, racial and ethnic extremism is viewed as anathema to group effectiveness. Racial and ethnic extremism exacerbates friction between groups, an outcome that soldiers are expected to subordinate in favor of higher patriotic ideals. How the public at large thinks about the army is important not only to its self-image but also for recruitment and retention as well. Builder (1989) noted that the army has historically relied on conscription of the male citizenry at large to fill its ranks, but since the early 1970s the army has been an all-volunteer force. It uses a population calculus to determine its readiness to fight. Instead of basing readiness on the number of ships or aircraft, the army tends to count people as its major asset.

Former chief of staff of the army General Eric K. Shinseki highlighted the importance of focusing on people in his vision of the future army. In a public speech after assuming duties as the 33rd army chief of staff, he said, "I think it's important for me to point out that we should recognize that in that vision statement it begins talking about people and it ends talking about people. And we should not miss the importance of this construct. People are central to everything else we do in the Army" (Shinseki 2001).

For the army, which lacks a profit motive, the currency of the realm is the faith and confidence of the American people, a reservoir filled by the patriotic and selfless acts of soldiers for over 200 years of service to the nation. Incidents of racial and ethnic extremism diminish public faith and confidence, as indicated by congressional hearings by the House Committee on National Security after the 1995 murders near Fort Bragg (U.S. Congress, House Committee on National Security 1997). Katzenstein and Reppy observe, "When a military culture promotes violent behavior that spills over into civilian society, its effects cannot be ignored—not only because such behavior runs counter to normative societal practice but also because the military's own standing in society is seriously jeopardized" (1999, 11–12).

Despite proclamations in support of racial tolerance, it is apparent that military personnel and installations present lucrative recruitment targets for organized hate groups. Soldiers have access to weapons, explosives, training, and expertise. Army barracks are populated by large numbers of impressionable young soldiers living in close association. Soldiers serve throughout the United States and the world, and they are exposed to a broad array of cultures and ideologies, including those of neo-Nazi skinheads. According to the Anti-Defamation League, skinhead groups are present in thirty-three countries (Anti-Defamation League 1995, 1). The skinhead movement serves as just one example of a problematic ideology that is most obvious in Western Europe, where large numbers of young soldiers have been stationed since the end of World War II. Soldier involvement in an organized hate group is a worst-case scenario for the army because it represents a total failure of the basic and advanced individual training processes. This type of training is designed to imbue values relating to teamwork and cohesiveness that are essential to combat effectiveness. Involvement with extremist groups reflects negatively on unit leaders who may have failed to observe or act decisively despite signs of extremism such as the presence of tattoos, graffiti, or racist literature. The following case is an example of how racist skinhead ideology can erupt in one of America's most integrated institutions.

On December 7, 1995, three young soldiers assigned to the famed 82nd Airborne Division, James Norman Burmeister, Malcolm Wright, and Randy Lee Meadows, Jr., set out with a 9-millimeter semiautomatic pistol to look for victims. Wright sported a spiderweb tattoo on his elbow, a symbol that to some racist groups indicated an act of violence against a minority. Burmeister apparently wanted to earn his tattoo. Randy Lee Meadows, Jr., drove the trio to a number of bars in Fayetteville, North Carolina, before finding 27-year-old Jackie Burden and her companion Michael James, age 36. After spotting the couple in a predominantly black neighborhood, Burmeister and Wright exited the vehicle while Meadows waited nearby. Upon hearing a series of pistol shots, Meadows fled the scene, leaving his two companions to make their escape on foot. Meadows later stated that he didn't believe the others would actually shoot anyone and that he panicked. Afraid and despondent, he remained near the scene of the crime, where he was later stopped and questioned by Fayetteville police. He provided information to the police that led to the arrest of Burmeister and Wright. He also became the star witness for the prosecution, providing much of the information we know about the specifics of the murder.

During searches of a mobile home that Burmeister rented in the local community, police found the pistol used to kill Burden and James. They also found an assortment of white supremacist literature, a book about how to make bombs, and materials on the Third Reich (Harrison December 17, 1995). Burmeister was known as a racist in his unit. He came to the attention of his commander after hanging a Nazi flag in his barracks room. On the heels of this encounter with his commander, Burmeister moved out of the barracks and into the trailer.

The murder received widespread media coverage that questioned the extent of a racist subculture in the military in general and at Fort Bragg in specific. Unit commanders were criticized for failing to see the signs of extremist involvement, and the post commander, Lieutenant General John Keane, admitted that leaders "were not sensitive enough to the signs and manifestations and symbols of extremism" (Galvin December 9, 1996).

Fort Bragg and Fayetteville are not unfamiliar with crime. The fort is one of America's largest and most active military installations with a population of over 75,000. It is also the location where special forces captain and physician Jeffrey MacDonald allegedly murdered his family, a case made famous in Joe McGunniss's book *Fatal Vision*. The adjacent city of Fayetteville has a reputation as a boisterous GI town that is largely overstated but is perpetuated by highly publicized incidents and ubiquitous tattoo parlors, strip clubs, and bars that cater to concentrations of young males between the ages of 18 and 25. The city was rocked by the knowledge that soldiers were implicated in the hate crime, while army spokespersons were quick to indicate that there was no link to an organized extremist group.

The Army Criminal Investigation Command conducted an investigation in tandem with local authorities that implicated twenty-one soldiers in extremist activities. All were either discharged from the army or were barred from reenlisting, which results in termination of service at the end of the contracted enlistment period. The investigation failed to substantiate association with known hate groups. One soldier was accused of paying for a billboard that advertised a toll-free number belonging to the National Alliance. While Burmeister and others implicated in extremist activity were not members of a specific hate group, it is apparant that they were influenced by readily available hate literature and maintained a loose association characteristic of neo-Nazi skinheads. During the trial, Burmeister's attorney admitted skinhead involvement but stated that he was only associated with them for a 9-month period preceding the murders. Burmeister and Wright received life sentences for two counts of first-degree murder and conspiracy to commit murder. Meadows received credit for time served pending trail and for his role as a state witness and three years' probation.

The Burmeister case illustrates that it is not enough for those intent on countering extremism to focus solely on group membership. We know that most perpetrators of hate crimes are not members of organized hate groups (Ferber, Grattet, and Jenness 1999). Many are simply influenced by the readily available ideology of hate groups facilitated by the rise of low-cost access to the Internet. E-mail, unregulated electronic mailing lists that cater to the supremacist community, and sophisticated Web pages that broadcast information to vast audiences provide new and powerful tools to extremists who wish to distribute hate propaganda (Kessler 1999). The case of Timothy McVeigh is another example of why a focus on hate group membership is insufficient. McVeigh, a former soldier recently convicted of and executed for the single most devastating act of domestic terrorism in the United States, the bombing of the Murrah Federal Building in Oklahoma City, Oklahoma, was not a member of a specific hate or antigovernment group.

Retired Special Forces Noncommissioned Officer Steven Barry successfully concealed the extent of his association with extremist groups from authorities while on active duty. His activities as the publisher of an unauthorized underground newspaper, *The Resister,* were well known and resulted in at least one letter of reprimand, but since retiring from the army as a sergeant first class in 1997, he has become more openly racist and anti-Semitic. According to the Southern Poverty Law Center, he has become "a key figure at the crossroads of right-wing extremism and the paramilitary underground," and affiliates with the neo-Nazi organization The National Alliance (Walker 1999, 6). Barry was able to successfully serve in the army for twenty years, long enough to become eligible for retirement. Despite racist views (which we must assume were part of his makeup before he left military service), he was able to keep his behavior within a range of acceptability that would not justify a stronger command response. Thus, we discover an important aspect of army policy on extremism; the policy is based less on attitudes and modes of thought than on highly observable intolerant behaviors.

The Burmeister and Barry cases indicate that the presence of racist behavior alone does not guarantee effective command action in an organization that has typically gauged its perception of race and ethnic relations based on representation. In other words, the army tends to view its racial health in terms of the extent to which racial and ethnic groups are represented at various levels of the organization. This equal opportunity view focuses more on diversity and less on the nature of interaction between those different racial groups until racist behavior reaches a level that necessitates an organizational response.

MILITARY POLICY ON EXTREMISM

Those outside the army would be hard pressed to locate its policy on extremism. There is no single policy so entitled. Instead, the policy directly on point resides as two and one-half pages in a subchapter of a 130-page regulation entitled *Army Command Policy.* This document prescribes policy on basic responsibilities of "command, military discipline, and conduct" (Department of the Army 1999). The regulation covers a wide array of topics ranging from the responsibilities of noncommissioned officers to family care plans, fraternization, and the Army Equal Opportunity Program. Army regulations serve as the primary means of implementing department of defense policy contained in department of defense directives and instructions. Whereas department of defense directives and instructions are often narrowly focused on a particular issue, Army regulations tend to incorporate several in a single document. This is the case with Army Regulation 600-20, which implements seven directives and one instruction, including the one that addresses the department of defense policy on extremism, Directive 1325.6,

"Guidelines for Handling Dissident and Protest Activities Among Members of the Armed Forces." The army regulation identifies participation in extremist organizations and activities as inconsistent with the responsibilities of military service.

The army regulation reiterates the policy of equal treatment for soldiers without regard to race, color, religion, gender, or national origin and places the responsibility for good order and discipline squarely on unit commanders. It directs soldiers to reject participation in extremist organizations and activities defined as those "that advocate racial, gender, or ethnic hatred or intolerance; advocate, create, or engage in illegal discrimination based on race, color, gender, religion, or national origin or advocate the use of or use force or violence or unlawful means to deprive individuals of their rights under the United States Constitution or the laws of the United States, or any State by unlawful means" (Department of the Army 1999, 33).

The regulation identifies specific prohibited activities that include penalties ranging from administrative to criminal sanction. A soldier who engages in prohibited activities may face penalties ranging from an oral reprimand to prosecution under the Uniform Code of Criminal Justice. Specifically prohibited activities include participation in public demonstrations or rallies; attending a meeting or activity known to involve an extremist cause; fund-raising activities; creating, organizing, or taking a visible leadership role; and distributing extremist literature on or off a military installation when the literature presents a clear danger to the loyalty, discipline, or morale of military personnel or the distribution materially interferes with the accomplishment of a military mission. The regulation specifically states that commanders may prohibit any activity they determine will adversely affect good order, discipline, or morale within the command. The regulation reflects consideration of lessons learned from the Burmeister case because it clearly authorizes the removal of symbols, flags, posters, or other displays that are contrary to good order and discipline or morale or pose a threat to the health, safety and security of military personnel or a military installation.

Also in response to the murders, the secretary of the army launched a task force to determine the scope and impact of extremist activities in the army and to make recommendations. The task force visited twenty-eight installations in twelve states, seven sites in Germany, and five sites in Korea. It concluded that soldier participation in extremist activities or organizations was minimal while acknowledging that 3.5 percent of those surveyed reported having been approached to join an extremist organization since joining the army, 3.1 percent reported having been approached to participate in an extremist activity, and 7.1 percent said that they knew of another soldier whom they believed to be a member of an extremist organization (U.S. Department of the Army 1996). The task force reported that the existing army regulation was confusing and noted that assessment tools did not adequately address extremism. It made twelve recommendations, including clarification and expansion of the army's regulation on extremist activity and clarification of chain-of-command responsibilities for soldier quarters.

Most the recommendations were adopted, with the exception of a Department of the Army pamphlet on extremist activity that is yet to be published. The 1999 regulation stipulated that any soldier's involvement in extremism, whether a prohibited action or not, could threaten the good order and discipline of a unit. It further stated that at the very least, commanders must take positive actions to educate soldiers and inform them of the consequences of violation of the army policy. Hudson (1999, 40) observed that the policy directed commanders to aggressively combat extremism, focusing on what soldiers do. Command actions in response to extremism could include education about the army's equal opportunity policy, advising that any participation could be taken into consideration on personnel evaluation reports when positions of leadership and responsibility are assigned, possible removal of security clearances, and reclassification or prohibiting reenlistment actions. Commanders were reminded that they have the authority to prohibit demonstrations and deny requests for the use of military-controlled facilities by groups that engage in discriminatory practices or activities. The section on extremism wisely concluded with the recommendation that commanders seek the advice and counsel of legal advisors when acting pursuant to the policy.

The 1995 murders obviously had something to do with the revision of Army Regulation 600-20. The tragedy served as a watershed event that sparked policy change for the entire department of defense. It issued a new directive, number 1325.6, in October of 1996. Although the army delayed publication of a new AR 600-20 until 1999, the secretary of the army quickly amended the existing regulation by electronic message in October 1996. Actual publication of the new regulation was delayed by other events, including a sex scandal involving fraternization between drill instructors and recruits assigned to Aberdeen Proving Ground, Maryland. We must recall that the army regulation covers a broad range of activities resulting in an involved staffing procedure that can delay changes based on unfolding events. When the Aberdeen sex scandal occurred, publication of the regulation was delayed in order to incorporate lessons learned from that incident that were applicable to the army's fraternization policy. A review of recent history will show that changes in Army policy on extremism occur in the wake of high-profile political events.

BRIEF HISTORICAL OVERVIEW OF POLICY

Department of Defense Directive 1325.6 is the fountain from which military extremism policy flows. In order to obtain a more comprehensive overview of policy changes over time, it is to this document that we must turn our attention. Secretary of Defense Melvin Laird signed the first Department of Defense Directive 1325.6 in 1969. It was, and remains, entitled "Guidelines for Handling Dissent and Protest Activities Among Members of the Armed Forces" (Department of Defense 1969). The policy was published in an era of antiwar protest and under the specter of movements to establish servicemen's unions. The policy clearly recognized a tension between a desire to safeguard service members' rights of expression and the necessity to control actions that would be injurious to unit effectiveness. In a trend that continues today, the directive recognized the importance of the unit commander when it stated, "The proper balancing of these interests will depend largely on the calm and prudent judgement of the responsible commander" (Department of Defense 1969).

The 1969 directive addressed the possession and distribution of printed materials and the authority to place establishments off limits to military personnel when people in those establishments counsel service members to refuse to perform their military duties or desert or involve acts with a significant adverse effect on member's health, morale, or welfare. It further prohibited the publication of underground newspapers if they contained utterances punishable by federal law. The directive also reflected concerns about demonstrations by servicemen, noting that commanders shall prohibit demonstrations that could hamper the orderly accomplishment of the installation mission or present a clear danger to the loyalty, discipline, or morale of the troops. It prohibited members of the armed forces from participating in off-post demonstrations when they were on duty or when in a foreign country when those activities constituted a breach of law and order, when violence is likely to result, or when they are in uniform. It specifically prohibited commanders from recognizing or bargaining with servicemen unions, a provision deleted in a change posted in 1977. The directive did not address membership in organizations, civil rights, or discrimination. It did not distinguish right-wing from left-wing activities, nor did it use any language indicating specific concern with what we would today recognize as extremism.

The instruction remained essentially unchanged until 1986, when Deputy Secretary of Defense William H. Taft, IV, signed Change Number Two. This change represented the first inclusion of antidiscriminatory language, reflecting an attempt to apply the tools developed to counter antiwar protest and unionization to combat hate-group membership. The watershed event for this change was the alleged participation of soldiers and marines from two military installations in North Carolina (Fort Bragg and Camp Lejeune) in training activities of the White Patriot Party, a group headed by Frazier Glenn Miller, Jr. Miller was an army veteran of twenty years and while on active duty served as a member of the elite Special Forces. At a trial that convicted Miller of operating a paramilitary organization in violation of a federal court consent decree, an ex-marine admitted receiving $50,000 in exchange for arms, ammunition, and explosives stolen from military installations.

When law enforcement officials told the press that some soldiers and marines attended rallies or other activities of the White Patriot Party, an army spokesman commented, "We cannot restrict their freedom of expression in as much as it does not interfere with their military duty, or violate civilian or military law" (Schmidt 1986). A marine corps spokesman observed that under rules in effect at that time, military personnel could not be barred from joining the Klan or other activities such as those of the White Patriot Party. The Southern Poverty Law Center (SPLC), a watchdog group that monitors hate-group activities, called upon Secretary of Defense Weinberger to take action. Morris Dees, the executive director of the SPLC, stated, "It is simply intolerable that members of the U.S. armed forces, sworn to uphold and defend the Constitution of the United States, be allowed to hold membership in an organization which seeks to overthrow the Federal Government through violent means" (Schmidt April 15, 1986).

The defense-policy response to the publicity from the incident was the addition of the following paragraph in DoD Instruction 1325.6:

Military personnel must reject participation in organizations that espouse supremacist causes; attempt to create illegal discrimination based on race, creed, color, sex, religion, or national origin; or advocate the use of violence, or otherwise engage in efforts to deprive individuals of their civil rights. Active participation, such as publicly demonstrating or rallying, fund raising, recruiting and training members, and organizing or leading such organizations is incompatible with Military Service, and is therefore prohibited. Commanders have the authority to employ the full range of administrative procedures, including separation or appropriate disciplinary action against military personnel who actively participate in such groups. (Department of Defense 1986)

The paragraph reflected a concern with soldier involvement in groups such as the White Patriot Party as well as a focus on specific acts or behaviors encompassed in the distinction between active and passive involvement.

The language describing active participation proscribed specific acts of participation while avoiding prohibitions against membership and nonactive support of discriminatory or violent groups. By failing to prohibit passive involvement, the policy tacitly approved membership in extremist groups. It did not include the term "extremist," a word that entered the American lexicon in the 1990s. The 1995 bias-motivated murders highlighted weaknesses of the active-passive dichotomy.

The Burmeister case touched off a firestorm of press activity that included articles and national media stories that questioned the extent of a white-supremacist culture within the armed forces. Secretary of the Army Togo West, also an African American, directed a blue-ribbon panel to assess the extent of extremism activities in the army. The House of Representatives Committee on National Security also convened hearings on Extremist Activity in the Military. The Department of Defense initiated a worldwide assessment of the status of equal opportunity in the military. A flurry of initiatives were implemented at various levels, including tattoo inspections for racist and gang symbols of all soldiers assigned at two major installations: Fort Bragg, North Carolina, and Fort Lewis, Washington.

At many installations some military law enforcement personnel, equal opportunity officers, inspectors general, and chaplains received additional training on recognizing and responding to the presence of extremist symbols. Additional equal opportunity training was mandated for all soldiers that emphasized the incompatibility of extremism and military service. Commanders received prepared presentations designed to standardize and quickly disseminate information on antiextremism policy and were required to certify that soldiers received the instruction. In October 1996, Deputy Secretary of Defense John P. White signed the revised Department of Defense Directive 1325.6 that remains in effect. The revision eliminated the active versus passive participation language, thereby giving commanders license to act before involvement in extremist causes reaches the stage of active participation.

A MODEL OF POLICY CHANGE

On the one hand, the directive changes represent responsiveness to a shifting environment that is less permissive regarding extremist inclinations of some service members. On the other hand, the fact that major policy change did not occur in this area without highly publicized failures suggests a reticence or inability to take a proactive stance in this policy area. Kier (1999, 47) suggests that because of the strength of military culture and the consistency of beliefs that prevent the development of different viewpoints, there is little reason to expect any more than incremental change to come within a military organization. It is arguable whether the evolution of Department of Defense Directive 1325.6 represented incremental or major policy change. It is clear, however, that those changes were episodic in nature and occurred on the heels of traumatic events covered in detail by the mass media.

Political scientist John Kingdon recognized the importance of focusing on events such as crises and disasters in bringing problems to the attention of government officials. His framework for explaining the reasons why some issues reach the governmental agenda and others do not is applicable to the case of extremist policy in the army. Kingdon observed that the rational decision-making process does not always describe the realities of public-sector decision making. The actual policy process does not always involve linear development consisting of a) clear identification of goals along with levels of achievement that satisfy them; b) a listing of feasible alternatives; and c) selection of the most cost-effective alternatives (Kingdon 1995). Instead, a random convergence of factors often informs the policy process. In his framework, the streams of problems, policies, and politics operate independently until focusing events cause them to couple, opening a window for policy change for a limited amount of time.

When the policy window opens, policy entrepreneurs have an opportunity to push a readymade solution forward for authoritative decision making. In this light, we can see how the media coverage of soldier and marine involvement with the White Patriot Party served as a focusing event in 1986 leading to a policy entrepreneur's (Southern Poverty Law Center) request to the secretary of defense to tighten policies addressing dissident activities in the military. Kingdon (1995) observed that crises, disasters, symbols, and focusing events only rarely carry a subject to policy prominence in isolation. However, they do serve to reinforce perceptions of an existing program that can combine with similar events to prevent dismissal of the incident as a fluke. Thus, we can see why the murders in 1995 resulted in a more sweeping policy response than in 1986.

CONCLUSION

The Burmeister case was a tragedy for the James and Burden families, the community of Fayetteville, North Carolina, and the U.S. Army. It is a case wherein some who were sworn to protect the Constitution of the United States against all enemies rejected the espoused values of the most successfully integrated institution in American society. The warning signs were missed, and the policies were inadequate to the needs of those charged with maintaining good order and discipline. The institutional response included sweeping policy change, large-scale training initiatives, and studies to reassure the public.

Defense officials wanted desperately to convince the public and themselves that the events at Fort Bragg were an anomaly associated with a small segment that did not represent the military at large. Within this approach, however, lies a danger. Ferber et al. (1998) sounded a caution against relegating the white supremacy movement to the racist fringe because such designations tend to absolve the mainstream population of its role in its creation and maintenance. They permit mainstream society to reject incidents such as the 1995 murders near Fort Bragg as not worthy of connection to the ostensibly non-racist majority. It would therefore be a mistake for the army to address incidents such as the Burmeister case as aberrant leadership or training failures without addressing the underlying behaviors or structures that may lead to recurring extremist incidents. This path leads to an episodic and symbolic mode of crisis response.

Organizations intent on addressing extremism would do well to expand the search for indicators of extremism beyond that of spectacular incidents of violence and threats of harm to include discursive acts that are not necessarily prima facie components of extremism. They would take note of the pernicious nature of the racist subculture in America and be alert to signs of its manifestations. If the Burmeister case can happen in an organization as successful in terms of equal opportunity and cohesiveness as the U.S. Army, it can happen anywhere.

REFERENCES

Anti-Defamation League. 1995. *The Skinhead International: A Worldwide Survey of Neo-Nazi Skinheads.* New York: Anti-Defamation League.

Builder, C. 1989. *The Masks of War: American Military Styles in Strategy and Analysis.* Baltimore: Johns Hopkins University Press.

Clifford, T. December 13 1995. "G. I.s, Hate Groups Eyed." *Daily News,* New York, NY 49.

Department of Defense. 1969. Department of Defense Directive 1325.6: *"Guidelines for Handling Dissident and Protest Activities Among Members of the Armed Forces."* Washington, D.C.: United States Department of Defense.

————1986. Department of Defense Directive 1325.6: *"Change 2: Guidelines for Handling Dissident and Protest Activities Among Members of the Armed Forces."* Washington, D.C.: United States Department of Defense.

Department of the Army. 1999. Army Regulation 600-20: *"Army Command Policy."* Washington, D.C.: Headquarters, Department of the Army.

Ferber, A. L., R. Grattet, and V. Jenness. 1999. *Hate Crime in America: What do We Know?* Washington, D.C.: American Sociological Association.

Ferber, P. T., E. D. Kirkpatrick, K. Melcher, G. Mowrey, T. Chen, S. Chen, T. Chen, B. Zhang, J. La Barbara, and A. L. Ferber. 1998. *White Man falling: Race, Gender, and White Supremacy.* Lanham, MD: Rowman & Littlefield.

Fields, G., and K. Johnson. December 11 1995. "Killings Prompt Army Probe of Roots in Racism." *USA Today,* 3A.

Flesher, J. July 25 1986. "Jury Convicts White Patriot Party Leader." *Associated Press.* Retrieved December 5, 2001, from LexisNexis database.

Galvin, R. December 9 1995. "A Better Fort Bragg." *Army Times,* 14.

Harrison, E. December 17 1995. "N.C. Killings Expose Racism Lurking in Army." *Chicago Sun-Times,* 37.

Hudson, W. M. 1999. "Racial extremism in the Army." *Military Law Review 1,* no. 159, 1–88.

Katzenstein, M. F., and J. Reppy, eds. 1999. *"Beyond Zero Tolerance: Discrimination in Military Culture."* Lanham, MD: Rowman & Littlefield.

Kessler, J. 1999. *Poisoning the Web: Hatred Online.* New York: Anti-Defamation League.

Kier, E. 1999. "Discrimination and Military Cohesion." In *Beyond Zero Tolerance: Discrimination in Military Culture,* ed. M. F. Katzenstein and J. Reppy, Lanham, MD: Rowman & Littlefield.

Kingdon, J. 1995. *Agendas, Alternatives, and Public Policies.* New York: Harper Collins.

Moskos, C. C., and J. S. Butler. (1996). *All That We Can Be: Black Leadership and Racial Integration in the Army.* New York: Basic.

Schmidt, W. E. April 15 1986. "Soldiers Said to Attend Klan-Related Activities." *New York Times,* 14.

Shinseki, E. K. 2001. *"CSA Remarks (As Prepared) AUSA Seminar, 8 November 2001."* Department of the Army. Retrieved from: http://www.army.mil/leaders/csa/speeches.htm, December 5, 2001.

United States Army Criminal Investigation Command. 1992. *Report of Investigation 0715-90-CID033-31340.* Fort Campbell, Kentucky: U.S. Army.

U.S. Congress. House Committee on National Security. 1997. *Extremist Activity in the Military.* Washington, D.C.: U.S. Government Printing Office.

U.S. Department of the Army. 1996. *The Secretary of the Army's Task Force on Extremist Activities: Defending American Values.* Washington, D.C.: U.S. Army.

Walker, G. A. 1999. "Special Forces Underground: A Defector in Place." *The Southern Poverty Law Center's intelligence report. Summer 1999:* 6–11.

CHAPTER 18

Rural Radical Religion: Christian Identity and Covenant Community Militias

Chester L. Quarles, Ph.D., CPP
Professor of Criminal Justice
Department of Legal Studies
The University of Mississippi

INTRODUCTION

There is more than just one America according to the far-right advocate. . . . Writer David Neiwert declares a "new" reality in America and asks if America is a homogeneous society today, as north, south, east, and west merge with urban and rural. Heartland Americans are watching their way of life disintegrate. Many are embittered as family farms fail, businesses are foreclosed, factories are abandoned as Big Business transfers manufacturing to developing nations, and small towns shrink through neglect, economic adversity, and malaise. Many rural towns are abandoned, much like the Old West "ghost" gold, silver, and railroad towns.

Identity followers and members of the Patriot movement claim the basic fabric of society is disintegrating. Criminals are unpunished, families divorce, girls abort, drug use spirals, homosexuality multiplies, churches close, and school prayers are prohibited by secular judges citing grave constitutional issues. Farmers and ranchers—far away

From: *Christian Identity: The Aryan American Bloodline Religion* copyright Chester L. Quarles by permission of McFarland & Company Inc., Box 611, Jefferson, NC 28640. www.mcfarlandpub.com

from the convenient response and assistance of law enforcement officers—fear anti-gun initiatives will seize their guns, as the Australian government did recently, and with it their right to protect their rural homes from predators, both animal and human. Hunters are afraid they will loose the right to harvest wild game in a land of plenty.

The population explodes as huge hordes of legal, as well as illegal, immigrants flood the countryside, crossing borders as easily as water through a colander, from Mexico and its Gulf or the southeastern Atlantic seaboard as Cubans, Haitians, and other Caribbean refugees sail to our shores in small, illegal craft. More rural Americans are failing economically than are succeeding. As they are displaced from their farming and ranching operations, they find many aliens have taken the only jobs left. First atavists were fearful, and then antipathy replaced fear. Hatred towards those who manage our government and its economy is increasing exponentially.

Our government gives away jobs to developing nations under complex agreements. Nations without fair labor laws, near servility or outright slavery, get work contracts, while American jobs are disappearing, the economy is faltering, and the international business interests and one-world government are heralded as the economic promise to a rich future.

The Patriot movement was founded as a commitment to America, to reclaim our heritage, rather than to accept the future planned by our politicians who patriots claim sold our economic birthrights for their silver coins. Patriots are obsessively fearful of tyranny and government abuse. Frequently, they exhibit a formidable hatred of Federal authorities, especially those living and working in the "Beltway."

As contemporary as "God, Country, and Apple pie," many of these groups have worked through political, civic, and social organizations, always seeking change. Then a more militant "patriot" appears, and Americans are asked to join the "unorganized militia" of their state. Some of the patriot and militia organizations are secular, but many are "ethno-religious" and believe in the superiority of the white race over other racial groups.

CHRISTIAN IDENTITY: THE SOLDIERS OF GOD

Christian Identity is a name given to a complex, highly varied, unorganized movement. The most fundamental teaching pivots on the belief that Anglo-Saxons, are the direct descendants of the Ten Lost Tribes of Israel, and thus, are the "true chosen people" of God.[1]

> The Soldiers of God know their identity. Their race is white and they believe race is in the blood. Their national identity is American. Their religious identity is Christian. Their Christian identity is the servant nation, the true Israel, America. The [Soldiers of God] are the inheritors, enforcers, and protectors of Yahweh's laws.[2]

Christian Identity is the bloodline religion of the radical-white-right in America and several other majority-white western nations. Called Identity because its converts claim they have finally realized their identification as descendants of the lost tribes of *"white"* Israel, "they are by far the most prevalent racist religious movement in

America."[3] In the United States, its believers accept a conservative or radical worldview, both in politics and theological perspective.

"Identity is a name given to a complex, highly varied, and not well-organized movement. The most fundamental teaching pivots on the idea that Anglo-Saxons are the direct descendants of the Ten Lost Tribes of Israel, and, thus, are the true chosen people of God."[4] Many Identity believers also include all Aryans, or those of Germanic descent.

Dr. Brent Smith wrote *Terrorism in America: Pipe Bombs and Pipe Dreams*. In his study of American terrorism during the 1980s, he says:

> Of the 170 individuals in our study who were named in indictments for domestic terrorism or terrorism-related activities during the 1980's, 103 were members of or associated with, a loose coalition of right-wing groups frequently referred to as being part of the Christian Identity Movement.[5]

These people believe that God's family, "the race of Yahweh," the true Israelites, are Caucasian.[6] David A. Niewert, in writing *In God's Country: The Patriot Movement and the Pacific Northwest,* called these people "the dwellers of the "otherworld" [sic]."[7] Bloodline Christianity and Christian Identity is the religion of the Ku Klux Klan, the Aryan Nations; the Covenant, the Sword, and the Arm of the Lord, Elohim City, and many other white racist groups. Bloodline Christianity influenced the first martyrs of the white-right cause, including Gordon Kahl of the Posse Commitatus, Robert J. Mathews of the Order, and Wayne Snell of Elohim City.

GOD'S PATRIOTS

True Believers and God's Patriots, (as defined by the Patriot movement, not an individual's value system) don't look at the positives of contemporary society. They look at the negatives. This is especially true of theocracy-based Identity advocates. They maintain that our way of life, our government, and our economy is so faulty that it can't be fixed. They assert that the Zionist Occupied Government (ZOG) of the United States and the Satanically influenced international tribunals of the New World Order, whatever that description means–and it means different things to various Identity and bloodline Christianity advocates—are keeping our country from its Godly destiny. They believe that the United Nations is inherently evil and that it will assist Satan in the development of the One World Order, or the "New" World Order.

Because the world has turned away from God and has turned to Satan, these "Soldiers of God" believe that the government needs to be destroyed. A theocracy can be established within our republic, replacing the secular humanistic government. Theocracy will return our early constitutional values. The Soldiers of God believe that our government must be destroyed along with the United Nations and the New World Order because these entities are hopelessly entwined with the evils of darkness. The Soldiers of God want to build a worldwide, centralized theocracy for Christ to return and claim His earthly Kingdom and reward the white Anglo-Saxon-Celtic remnants of the original tribes of Israel.

They maintain they are the only ones who represent truth, virtue, and God's will here on earth. They claim that they are the only people, (God's people), who see the real world and are not affected by its depravity. Many of these believers have joined Patriot groups, militias, and Christian communes called Covenant Communities in order to "retire from America." Many are surrendering their American citizenship in a government they believe to be evil. Posse Commitatus named this process *"severation,"*[8] and they surrendered their citizenship, tore up their drivers' licenses, Social Security cards, and other government identifiers. By the same token, many of these are "good" people, "good" neighbors, and "good" folks are called your friends, although some, most certainly, are not.

If you are not a member of Identity or if you cannot be led to believe as they do, then you are "spiritually blinded by evil." Hence, you are part of the problem, not part of the solution, insofar as the unjust peoples of the world are concerned. God's Army wants to reestablish Theocratic order on our planet, returning to the Old Covenant rules and regulations, and re-establishing God's law on our planet. Some of the bloodline neo-Nazis even believe that the final order will be the New Reich. They believe that they are armed with the right kind of knowledge, and God allows them to be armed with the right kind of weapons, which they have the moral obligation to use for His Kingdom's service.

In this perspective, America's "Army of God" shares the destructive attributes of the anarchist and the nihilist, who seek to destroy society as we know it. The soldier in the Army of God believes that he or she has the right to destroy America because America—with its topless clubs, nude beaches, child pornography, adult book shops, abortion-on-request, capitalistic usury, and the U.S. Government's "Satan tithe," the individual income tax of every wage earner—no longer deserves the right to exist. We no longer hold "in God we trust" as any reasonable value except for the religious hyperbole embossed on our coins.

The American Patriot, joining the Army of God, maintains terrorism is acceptable because people who are not "right" are "wrong." And the Army must destroy those who are not a component of theocratic solutions to the political, social, economic, and moral problems facing America. Those citizens of our population, who not part of the solution, are inherently a part of the problem they say and "have no right to live." Moshe Amon notes in his terrorism book:

> Opposing groups are viewed as representatives of the adversary power, that is, the devil. Terrorism thus serves both as a means to fight Satan . . . and a way to find fraternity and solidarity.[9]

ARMAGEDDON SURVIVALISTS

> Armageddon survivalists consist of some ultra-conservative Christians and Mormons [sic] as well as other religious groups who have adapted parts of the Bible as their religious belief system. The end result is that this group of survivalists believes they may have to fight against the Biblical Anti-Christ in the near future.[10]

Other conservative patriots believe that the third American Revolution is imminent. Thomas W. Chittum, author of Civil *War II: The Coming Breakup of America,* penned these thoughts:

> America's current economic decline must be halted, or else one day the crime that is rampant in the streets of New York and Washington, D.C., may develop into low-intensity conflict by coalescing along racial, religious, social, and political lines, and run completely out of control.[11]

COVENANT COMMUNITIES

Right-wing religious survivalists and separatists are creating new neighborhoods, communities, towns, compounds, and farms. In the United States, these religious developments are often named Covenant Communities (CC), in respect to their religious orientation. Worldwide, liberation theologists call their separatists Christian communities, Basic Christian Communities (BCC). Covenant Community spokesman Robert K. Spear wrote the book entitled *Creating Covenant Communities,* an insightful look at the subject. While he did not impress his political or scriptural values upon his reader, Spear provided several insights into "how to select a place of his or her own."

> Like-minded people need to come together and covenant with one another to share talents and resources in order to survive and even flourish. A covenant is a contractual exchange of promises based on a law more powerful than any man might generate. A covenant is an exchange of promises based on a law more powerful than any man might generate. It implies a legal structure related to spiritual considerations. Its courts and judges are not of this earth but are of a Heavenly nature. This coming together will then become a Covenant community, one that is based on spiritual commitments.[12]

The Basic Christian Community and the Covenant Community of right-wing Christian organizations is primarily based on scriptures applicable to both evangelical and fundamentalist Christians, as well as those of Identity. II Corinthians 6:14 reads "Be ye not unequally yoked together with unbelievers." and the 17th verse of that same chapter says, "Wherefore come out from among them, and be ye separate, saith the lord, and touch not the unclean thing; and I will receive you."[13]

Some are called Armageddon Survivalists.[14] Christian survivalists believe that the world will end in a catastrophic event preceded by years of fighting. The economy will fail, society will collapse, and our government will fail. Because we now have international agri-businesses dependent on imports, there will be mass starvation within the cities. There will be food and race wars in most urban centers. Only in rural developments will citizens still have the ability to survive. In the event of nuclear war or a cataclysmic event, a great portion of the world's population will perish within a short time, leaving the elect of God to rebuild society and to usher in the millennial rule of Jesus Christ.[15]

ELOHIM CITY

One strong example of a Covenant Community is the one located at Elohim City, Arkansas. Of Christian Identity perspective, it was run by Robert Millar, who called Elohim City a "kind of family-oriented monastery."[16] Kerry Noble said Millar was called "Grandpa" by his followers. One source stated that Elohim City was founded by Jim Ellison, a polygamous Christian Identity preacher who was later convicted of federal racketeering and conspiracy charges[17] and who also started the Covenant, the Swords, and the Arm of the Lord (CSA) in an Identity-oriented communal settlement near the Arkansas-Missouri border,[18] but this is very unlikely. The Anti-Defamation League says the primary founder was Millar, not Ellison, a former Mennonite who once had ties to the Covenant, the Sword, and the Arm of the Lord.[19] These men were closely associated under any circumstances. When Jim Ellison left prison on April 23, 1995, he moved to Elohim City, Oklahoma, and on May 19, he married one of Millar's granddaughters, 26-year-old Angie.[20]

Ellison's name will come up often in the far-right literature. A vitriolic white supremacist, separatist, and anti-Semite, he, too, began hating the U.S. Government, which he calls the Zionist Occupied Government (ZOG). Ellison was assigned the Patriot nickname "Warlord," by the former Texas Ku Klux Klan Dragon Louis Beam, Jr.[21] A helicopter gun ship tail gunner in Vietnam, Beam returned from the Vietnam War with an intense hatred for our government. Frequently in the national news, Beam was connected to the Baytown Vietnamese fishermen's assaults, but it was his association with Christian Identity and the development of the "Warrior" status for the Patriot movement which has gained him the most recognition. He proposed a point system to achieve Aryan Warrior status. To become an Aryan Warrior, the convert must attack the enemies of the Zionist Occupied Government (The United States).

> This approach awards fractions of points for assassinations [of personnel representing the United States, and sometimes state or local government]. Members of congress are worth one-fifth of a point each. Judges and the FBI director are worth one-sixth of a point. Journalists and local politicians are worth one twelfth of a point each. **The President of the United States is worth one full point!** Upon achieving one full point, the rank of Warrior is given to the Aryan National.[22]

The residents of Elohim City "do not think of themselves as white supremacists but as a 'chosen people' charged by God with the responsibility of serving and leading others."[23] Elohim City is quite unusual among far-right Christian Identity separatists. While residents live apart from society, they are still allowed to watch TV, unlike many other separatist communities. What is most unusual about Elohim City is that the children and all of the adults are receiving instruction in the Hebrew language and are observing the rigid dietary laws of ancient Israel.[24]

As federal agents retraced the time period between Timothy McVeigh leaving the military and blowing up the Murrah Building in Oklahoma City, they claim he had placed a telephone call to Elohim City, Oklahoma, and told the followers there that he hated the federal government because of the atrocities at the Waco Branch Davidian Compound and Ruby Ridge.[25] While Elohim City is restrictive and is not perhaps the "standard" exclusivist, survivalist, separatist, racialists, or "covenant" community, other Americans claiming to accept the gospel of Jesus Christ are becoming militant and confrontational. The author first heard of "militant, "conspiratorial," and "confrontational" Christianity when he researched the Ku Klux Klan for a Masters thesis in 1970. That militancy is now spiraling rather than deescalating. Many of the right-wing activists and militias are secular humanists and do not purport Christian idealism of any sort.

THE ARYAN NATIONS

One of the oldest active right-wing Identity organizations in America, the Aryan Nations has been on the scene several decades. Its founder was Pastor Richard G. Butler, who had preached on occasion at the Church of Jesus Christ, Christian founded by Dr. Wesley Swift. Butler, who continued Swift's work at his death, calls himself a "White Nationalist and a "long standing warrior in the Struggle for the preservation of the Aryan Nation."[26] The warrior description is appropriate for Butler, who publicly has vowed "that a racially pure nation [the Aryan Nations], needs an army."[27]

The Aryan Nations development was pioneered by Butler and Robert Miles of The Mountain Church of Jesus Christ [also known as Mountain Kirk]. Miles also had held the position of the Grand Dragon of the Michigan Realm of the United Klans of America. Their Covenant Community was a planned beginning for a new Aryan State, composed of Oregon, Washington, Montana, and Wyoming. The Aryan Nations compound was moved from California to Hayden Lake, Idaho, in the 1970s, to "expand the Kingdom Identity program and form the foundation for a 'Call to the Nation' or Aryan Nations."[28] This group was to have great influence, and hybrid splinter groups, such as "The Order," were to come from Hayden Lake.

Race is always on the agenda at Aryan Nations, and Butler called for a theocracy, a government led under the "Law of God, for your Race is your Nation."[29] The Fidelity of Aryan Nations follows:

> That for which we fight is to safeguard the existence and reproduction of our Race, by and of our nations, the sustenance of our children and the purity of our blood, the freedom and independence of the people of our Race, so that we, a kindred people, may mature for fulfillment of the mission allotted to us by the Creator of the universe, our Father and God. Hail His Victory![30]

Aryan Nations use the Nazi Swastika Cross behind their pulpits, instead of the traditional cross of Calvary. This is widely publicized in all of their published materials and on their internet website. While primarily an Identity group, Aryan Nations advocates virulent anti-Semitism and disassociating "people of color, or other races" from the promises of God. Members believe that all non-whites are "mud people" and have the status of animals, rather than human, and they believe that all Jews are the "children of Satan" and maintain in all of their progeny the "seedline of Satan."

The Anti-Defamation League web site on Aryan Nations quotes Dennis Hilligoss, the group's state coordinator in Oregon, as saying: "The Jew is like a destroying virus that attacks our racial body to destroy our Aryan culture and the purity of our race."[31] Rev. Butler was once indicted on a sedition charge, but the Fort Smith, Arkansas federal jury did not find him guilty of the government's allegations. Aryan Nations, however, cannot separate itself from The Order, which was formed from many of the Aryan Nations' membership. The Order was the group which robbed several armored cars in the northwestern United States, to begin a "funding effort" for organizations of the radical right. The Militia leader, Col. "Bo" Gritz attended Butler's Aryan Nations Congress at least three times.[32]

THE COVENANT, THE SWORD, AND THE ARM OF THE LORD

CSA was a paramilitary unit formed out of a recent Covenant Community commitment to Christian Identity. Originally this group lived at Cherith Brook near Elijah, Missouri. Cherith Brook was where the prophet Elijah sojourned and was fed by the ravens. When the Brook dried up, the prophet traveled to Zarephath, where a widow shared her sustenance with him. When financial hard times hit the Cherith Brook group, they moved to the Arkansas-Missouri border near a town called Mountain Creek. Later members pooled their resources and purchased a 224 acre property from Campus Crusade for Christ. Constructed at the new location, the church was named the Zarephath-Horeb Community Church.

At first, the Zarephath-Horeb Community Church was an off-shoot of conservative fundamentalist Christianity, oriented somewhat toward a Pentecostal-like, charismatic fellowship. "Zarephath emphasized prophecies, speaking in tongues, healings, visions, dreams and miracles."[33] Members called the Christian-community living arrangement "body-life" which was the highest ideal God had for his people.[34] They emphasized corporate fellowship under a patriarchal system, "where the men were in charge."[35]

At the beginnings of this church, members shared what they called a "plural ministry," the belief that a one-man ministry was dangerous and unscriptural.[36] "We believed in the checks-and-balances of more than one elder."[37] Later on, Ellison became more dynamic, insisting upon his own revelations. Under this influence, CSA became more closed from outside influences, more militant and more revolutionary. When The Order was investigated for armored car robberies in the northwestern United States, the FBI visited CSA.

Two of the fourteen indictments registered against members of The Order were ex-CSA members. Four more Order members were hiding on the CSA properties on April 18, 1985, when Gene Irby of the Arkansas State Police Criminal Investigation Division came by to arrest CSA founder James Ellison. Irby wanted a CSA spokesman to tell Ellison to surrender himself at the entrance to their compound. Ellison refused, and the next afternoon FBI Hostage Rescue Team leader Danny Coulson surrounded the CSA properties. Negotiations settled the siege and Ellison surrendered.

COVENANT CHURCHES

Called Covenant Churches because they claim the promises [covenants] of God made to Abraham, Isaac and Israel, bloodline Identity groups differ from both evangelical and fundamentalist Christianity on many basic doctrines. Many, if not most, bloodline

Identity groups choose to worship on the Sabbath, rather than on a Sunday. Some Covenant Churches claim that "Sunday worship is a mistake, or a corruption of scripture."[38] They also reject Christmas and Easter as pagan celebrations, "held on the wrong day, anyway."[39] The Covenant Church members claim the promises of God made to the Israelite people. Many of them are called Covenanters[40] or Covenanteers. This term comes from Nehemiah when he read the law of Moses to the people. Certain Hebrews made a commitment to the ranks of the righteous God and they signed their names in this Covenant Book.

Most Covenant Churches are not of the seedline approach, that being the belief that there is a miscegenated "satanic" race in constant conflict with the people of God. However, the more bizarre beliefs of the seedliners tend to gain more news coverage than the kinder-gentler versions of Anglo-Israelism.

At the Zarephath-Horeb Community Church on the Arkansas-Missouri border (later to become known as the Covenant, the Sword, and the Arm of the Lord [CSA]), the members celebrated the Israelite Feast of the Passover, Weeks, and Tabernacles."[41] At one point, the Covenant, the Sword, and the Arm of the Lord accepted the practice of polygamy,[42] and they sold all of their hogs because they wanted to practice the ancient Israeli tribal laws of cleanliness.[43]

Bloodline Identity groups also emphasize the Old Testament more so than does the average Christian. Identity beliefs depend on Old Testament rather than New Testament themes. Some Identity adherents also accept the warlike concepts of the ancient Israelites, rather than the loving, gentle Savior who wants us to turn to Him from our sins. There is nothing "tender" about [Seedline] Identity. "It is a religion that few traditional Christians would recognize as that of Jesus, the God of Righteousness and love,"[44] say the authors of *Soldiers of God*.

At the Aryan Nations Headquarters, Identity preachers anoint those who accept Identity tenets. Preachers approach the convert/initiate and using oil, draw a cross on their foreheads, saying "I declare you a soldier in the Army of God."[45] Randal Rader of Zarephath-Horeb, who later became the military training officer for the Covenant, the Sword, and the Army of the Lord (CSA), prayed "Lord, teach our hands to war and our fingers to fight. Teach us to love and teach us to hate, in Jesus Name."[46] Pastor August B. Kreis III, who accepted the leadership reins of Aryan Nations, includes these lines in his web site prayer, "We, as your elect, will carry out your wrath against your enemies, in this, the great battlefield called earth. . . . We look forward to the destruction of your enemies on this earth and to the establishment of your Kingdom."[47]

Their emphasis is on militancy, fighting Satan's forces, and doing battle with the anti-Christ, rather than referring to the positive satisfiers of forgiveness from sin, accepting the love of Christ, and reflecting that love toward other peoples. In referring to the Seedline belief, Morris Dees and James Corcoran also state "it is a religion that few traditional Christians would recognize as that of Jesus, the God of righteousness and love."[48]

Pastor August B. Kreis III of Aryan Nations takes a strong stand as he leads the Aryan Nations away from Hayden Lake, Idaho. Here are his remarks from a web-site message he titled "Sitting On The Edge of Our Seats" [the capitalized and bold-print words are Pastor Kreis's]:

I say to you kinsman out there. **YOU** are either with **YHVH our Father** *or* you are against Him! Soon you will be forced into making a decision. . . . You will be forced to choose sides. . . . There will be no more *fence sitting!* You will be identified by your willingness to do whatever it is that the New World Order will want you to do OR like myself, by your opposition to it. Those that have *faith, knowledge, belief,* and *understanding* in their place in this world, will **soon** be forced to **take up the sword** in a **Holy Jihad** against the enemies of our Almighty Father. This does not mean just those who identify themselves as Identity Christians but all those that realize that if they don't **take up the sword,** they, their children and their children's children will become slaves and pawns of the New World, Jew World, Order.[49]

We **firmly** believe that until every last yehudi-shataan (Jew) is dead, there will be no peace on earth. There is no room for negotiation, we want no peace with them, there is no living with them, we will accept nothing less for Edom/Esau jewry than explained in Matthew 13.[50*]

Butler did not become more tolerant with age; rather he became more vehement and intensified his racist pejorative. After his wife passed away, and in deteriorating health, he decided to step down from Aryan Nation's leadership role. In 2001, Butler appointed "Pastor Ray Redfeairn of Ohio as National Director and successor of the Aryan Nations and Pastor August B. Kreis III was named Director of Information."[52] At the time of these appointments, it was announced that the Aryan Nations Office and church grounds would be moved to an area near Ulysses, Pennsylvania. Pastor Redfeairn complimented the 84 year old Butler on his service to his race, announcing that "the advancement of our Racial Nation is also my goal, my only goal. I am humbled by the fact that Pastor Butler has put his confidence in me to direct the Aryan Nations to realize that goal. Any decision that I make will be made with the single question in mind— is this good for our Race"?[53]

On January 28, of 2001, however, there was already significant strife and fragmentation. Stiff opposition arose over moving the Aryan Nations Headquarters from Hayden Lake to Pennsylvania. Likewise, the status of Pastor Butler, in spite of his advanced age and health problems, continued to be a widely reported issue, both within and without the Aryan Nations organization.

THE THIRD AMERICAN REVOLUTION

Pastor George Udvary of the New Harmony Christian Crusade in Mariposa, California, immigrated from war-torn Hungary. He witnessed communist atrocities and believed they could occur here as well. The strong-minded militarist has this to say about what he calls the Second Civil War in America and what others call the Third American Revolution:

I firmly believe that the **Second Civil War** is not only inevitable, but very near. The forces of evil are working around the clock to reduce this great and Christian nation that has been

* Author's note: Matthew 13 pertains to several "mysteries"[51] revealed to the disciples about several parables.

especially superior, strong, and rich into a weak, inferior, bankrupt, and corrupt nation, peopled by a low grade mixture of coffee-colored people. The record speaks for itself; we are becoming more divided each day.[54]

Anything and everything appropriate to stop government policies, procedures, and conditions who they consider to be sinful and thus unconstitutional. Violence and revolution will be their response. Many Patriots claim the new American Revolution will take place between 2003 and 2005. The bloodline Identity advocates, Patriots, and militias claim they will not tolerate foolhardy government for another generation.

THE GUNS AND GOSPEL APPROACH

Oftentimes, the Christian far right also accepts the "gun and gospel approach." This philosophy has recently been called Christian Identity. Identity members believe that they are especially chosen by God and believe that the Twelfth Chapter of Romans is written exclusively for Anglo-Saxon Christians—the Anglo-Israeli—the remnant of the Lost Tribes of Israel.

Thomas W. Chittum, who wrote *Civil War II: The Coming Breakup of America,* anticipates racial and ethnic community wars, especially from the illegal immigrants along the Mexican border, as well as in the African-American communities throughout our nation. He believes families and other groups will set themselves apart from others, just as the American Indian tribes did some centuries ago. Then the tribes will go to war, he said, protecting their own turf. Here is a powerful quotation in his "Prepare Yourself" chapter:

> First, realize that areas with mixed tribal populations will experience the most fighting, employment of heavy weapons, and general devastation of life and infrastructure. Regardless of which side wins, these areas will look like the Yugoslavia we've all seen on TV. If you currently live in such an area, you must move out. Likewise, you must sell all non-moveable assets in such areas or risk losing them, either by destruction or confiscation by the new government, a certainty if the new government is not of your tribe.[55]

Chittum recommends hideouts, hideaways, and defensible rural communities. He also suggests that guns purchased "off the books (from an individual and not a licensed dealer)" should be hidden or even buried in accessible locations, along with sufficient ammunition for the coming war.

ENDNOTES

1. "Christian Identity Movement," available online: http://religiousmovements.lib.virginia.edu/nrms/identity.html.
2. Howard L. Bushart, John R. Craig, and Myra Barnes, *Soldiers of God: White Supremacists and Their Holy War for America* (New York: Kensington Books, 1998).
3. Benjamin Radford, "Hating in the Name of God," available online: http://www.secularhumanism.org/library/aah/radford_10_3.htm.

4. "Christian Identity Movement."

5. Brent L. Smith, *Terrorism in America: Pipe Bombs and Pipe Dreams,* (New York: State University of New York Press, 1994), 32.

6. Pastor George Udvary, *Identity Bible Reference Manual: Volume I, Revised,* (Mariposa, California: New Harmony Christian Crusade Identity Ministry, 1994), B-1.

7. David A. Neiwert, *In God's Country: The Patriot Movement and the Pacific Northwest,* (Pullman, Washington: The Washington State University Press, 1999), 22.

8. Morris Dees with James Corcoran, *Gathering Storm: America's Militia Threat,* (New York: HarperCollins Publishers, 1996), 87.

9. Amon Moshe, "The Unraveling of the Myth of Progress," in *The Morality of Terrorism: Religious and Secular Justifications,* ed. David C. Rappaport and Yonah Alexander (New York: Pergamon, 1982), 69.

10. Danger: Extremism—The Major Vehicles and Voices on America's Far Right Fringe (New York: Anti-Defamation League, 1996).

11. Thomas W. Chittum, *Civil War II: The Coming Breakup of America,* (Show Low: Arizona: American Eagle Publications, 1996), 112–113.

12. Robert K. Spear, *Creating Covenant Communities,* (Leavenworth, Kansas: Universal Force Dynamics Publishing, 1993), 4.

13. Spear, *Creating Covenant Communities,* 4.

14. Long, *Apocalypse Tomorrow: The Survival Scene,* 45.

15. Danger: Extremism—The Major Vehicles and Voices on America's Far Right Fringe (New York: Anti-Defamation League, 1996).

16. Vincent Coppola, *Dragons of God: A Journey Through Far-Right America,* (Atlanta, Georgia: Longstreet Press, Inc., 1996), 11.

17. Coppola, *Dragons of God,* 11.

18. Anti-Defamation League, *Danger: Extremism,* (New York: Anti-Defamation League, 1996), 210.

19. Anti-Defamation League, *Danger: Extremism,* 210.

20. Noble, *Tabernacle of Hate,* p. 219.

21. Howard L. Bushart, John R. Craig, and Myra Barnes, *Soldiers of God: White Supremacists and Their Holy War for America,* (New York: Kensington Books. 1998), 117.

22. James Stinson, "Domestic Terrorism in the United States," *Police Chief Magazine,* (September 1987), 2.

23. Anti-Defamation League, *Danger: Extremism,* 212.

24. Coppola, *Dragons of God,* 137.

25. Lou Michel and Dan Herbeck, *American Terrorist: Timothy McVeigh and the Oklahoma City Bombing* (New York: HarperCollins, 2001), 205.

26. http://www.nidlink.com/~aryanvic/index-E.html, accessed February 5, 2002. 3.

27. Charles P. Cozic, ed., *The Militia Movement,* An "Opposing Viewpoints" Series, (San Diego, California, Greenhaven Press, 1997), 71.

28. http://www.nidlink.com/~aryanvic/index-E.html, 2/5/2002, 4.

29. http://www.nidlink.com/~aryanvic/index-E.html, 2/5/2002, 4.

30. http://www.nidlink.com/~aryanvic/index-E.html, 2/5/2002, 5.

31. http://www.adl.org/presrel/neosk_82/aryan-nations-82.asp, 2/5/2002, 1.

32. Weis, Philip, "Off the Grid," *New York Times Magazine,* January 8, 1995, 24–33.

33. Noble, *Tabernacle of Hate: Why They Bombed Oklahoma City,* 29.

34. Noble, *Tabernacle of Hate: Why They Bombed Oklahoma City,* 29.

35. Noble, *Tabernacle of Hate: Why They Bombed Oklahoma City,* 77.

36. Noble, *Tabernacle of Hate: Why They Bombed Oklahoma City,* 123.

37. Noble, *Tabernacle of Hate: Why They Bombed Oklahoma City,* 123.

38. Alan W. Bock, *Ambush at Ruby Ridge: How Government Agents Set Randy Weaver Up and Took His Family Down,* (Irvine, California: Dickens Press, 1995), 35.

39. Bock, *Ambush at Ruby Ridge,* 35.

40. The American Institute of Theology, *Bible Correspondence Course* (Harrison, Arkansas: The American Institute of Theology, 1994), 80.

41. Noble, *Tabernacle of Hate,* 93.

42. Noble, *Tabernacle of Hate,* 117.

43. Noble, *Tabernacle of Hate,* 92.

44. Dees and Corcoran, *Gathering Storm,* 22.

45. Bushart, Craig, and Barnes, *Soldiers of God,* 196.

46. Noble, *Tabernacle of Hate,* 80.

47. Kreis III, August B. (Pastor of Aryan Nations), "Sitting On the Edge of Our Seats," as found in http://www.aryan-nations.org/indexpagenews/sitting_on_the_edge_of_our_seats.htm, 2/6/2002, 1.

48. Dees and Corcoran, *Gathering Storm,* 22.

49. August B. Kreis III, (Pastor of Aryan Nations), "Sitting On the Edge of Our Seats," as found in the Aryan Nations Website: http://www.aryan-nations.org/indexpagenews/sitting_on_the_edge_of_our_seats.htm, 2/6/2002, page 1 of 2.

50. http://www.aryan-nations.org/indexpagenews/further_clarification.htm, 2/6/2002, 1.

51. The "mysteries" refer to a subheading approach used by the Reverend C.I. Scofield in his Study Bible in the King James Version.

52. http://www.aryan-nations.org/indexpagenews/greetings_from_national_director.htm, page 1 of 3 pages.

53. http://www.aryan-nations.org/indexpagenews/greetings_from_national_director.htm, page 3 of 3 pages.

54. Pastor George Udvary, *Identity Bible Reference Manual: Volume I, Revised,* (New Harmony Christian Crusade Identity Ministry, 1994), B-i.

55. Thomas W. Chittum, *Civil War Two: The Coming Breakup of America,* (Show Low, Arizona: American Eagle Publications, 1996), 163.

SECTION FIVE DISCUSSION QUESTIONS

1. What is an anti-movement? How does this concept help us to understand terrorism?
2. Describe how Anglo-Israelitism merged with intolerance and racism to become the Christian Identity theology.
3. Use some examples of American terrorism to show how social learning theory can help us understand how hate groups turn Christian ideology into a belief system that supports the use of violence.
4. What are some methods that white supremacists use to recruit members and obtain other resources?
5. Give examples of various violent strategies used by white supremacist groups?
6. What are the long and short term goals of the supremacist terrorists movements?
7. Define "leaderless resistance" and discuss the frequency of its use.
8. How did leaderless resistance become popularized?
9. Describe the typical life span of a terrorist group.
10. How did the tragic Burmeister case spark a change in the U.S. Army policy?
11. What was the Army's initial response to the Burmeister case?
12. Why is the military sector a good recruitment medium for racists?
13. Discuss the difference between the Christian Identity religion and Covenant Communities.
14. Compare the belief of Elohim City, Aryan Nations, and The Covenant, The Sword, and The Arm of the Lord.
15. What are the apocalyptic aspects of the groups who espouse the Christian Identity religion?

SECTION SIX

Conclusion

LOOK FOR THESE KEY POINTS

- The need to provide reasonable campus security now must be redefined to include the possibility that college campuses could be the target of terrorism.
- Most people derive their sense of fear and safety not from the actual incidence of crime or from being personally victimized by crime rather from the frequency and attention paid to crime in media reports. In short, if there is considerable media attention on crime, viewers will feel scared.

THE AFTERMATH AND THE FUTURE

In addition to understanding the group dynamics of terrorism, researchers have also written about the consequences of the September 11 attack. Actions that resulted from the terrorist attack on September 11 include the invasion into Afghanistan, war with Iraq, and a reorganization of the U.S. government. Both countries and small towns began to think about something called homeland security. Some responses were mandated by law. For example, the federal government, through passage of the PATRIOT Act in 2001, set up new safety requirements for institutions, such as colleges and universities, that have labs or other facilities containing chemical and biological agents. The first chapter in this section takes a nuts-and-bolts approach as it explains how a university developed a plan to respond to future terrorist events.

  The second chapter explores what has been done at the federal level to ensure our future safety. It also develops a theoretical background that helps us to understand the responses that occurred. Finally, it briefly outlines how federal, state, and local governments responded and reviews some of the key accomplishments in the "War against Terror."

CHAPTER 19

Planning for Campus Security After September 11: One University's Experience

Max L. Bromley
University of South Florida

INTRODUCTION

The tragic events of September 11, 2001 have resulted in changes in many facets of life in America.[1] Virtually all major institutions of private enterprise and government have had to evaluate their potential as targets of future terrorist attacks. This, of course, includes institutions of higher education. While securing college and university campuses has been a topic of growing concern for several decades (Smith 1998; Fisher and Sloan 1995; Bromley 1995; Fisher et al. 1998), the focus must now widen to include the possibility of terrorist attacks (Nelson 2001; Mojica 2001). There have already been a number of well-documented domestic terrorist attacks on American universities by groups such as the Animal Liberation Front (Burke 2000).

Over the last fifty years there has been unprecedented growth in the number of students attending institutions of higher education in the United States. Between 1960 and 1990, the number of college students increased form approximately 4 million to 16 million (U.S. Department of Education 1991). New colleges and universities have been built to meet the demands of increasing student enrollment, and existing campuses have been expanded in physical size and complexity. Some authorities have suggested that college campuses share many of the characteristics of a typical urban community (Sloan 1994). Others have suggested that universities may be seen "cities within cities" (Bromley and Territo 1990). However one chooses to conceptualize the modern American college, the need to provide reasonable security for campuses must now be redefined to include the possibility of being the target of terrorism.

While there is no shortage of potential targets for terrorists throughout the United States, institutions of higher education should not be considered as immune from such attacks. As early as the 1980s, one author noted the importance of campus public safety directors being prepared for possible terrorist activities (Nichols 1987). The need for campus security decision makers to be aware of potential international terrorist activities was also noted in the 1990s (Powell, Pander, and Nielson 1994).

WHY COLLEGE CAMPUSES MAY BE ATTRACTIVE TARGETS TO TERRORISTS

Colleges and universities may be considered as potential targets for future terrorist attacks for a number of reasons. While not inclusive, the following list is meant to provide a starting point for consideration.

1. Most college campuses take pride in allowing relatively easy public access to campus grounds and many on-campus facilities. Campuses usually have multiple public entrances that are open twenty-four hours a day, seven days a week. In addition to having the normal complement of students, faculty, and staff, colleges and universities frequently have numerous vendors, service providers, and visitors on their campuses on a daily basis. Brantingham and Brantingham (1995) have suggested that one useful way to categorize campuses is to determine the proportion of major, moderate, and minor users of campus grounds and facilities. One could argue that the higher the proportion of minor users present on campus on a daily basis, the easier time a terrorist would have in blending in on campus and not appearing suspicious.

2. The academic tradition of most campuses places a high premium on the freedom of movement and general accessibility to campus buildings and other facilities. This freedom must be balanced with the need to provide a reasonable level of security. Given the present threat of terrorism throughout the world, campus decision makers face a significant challenge when developing policies that must take into account both the general openness of an academic community and the need to provide security. Those who might commit terrorist attacks are no doubt aware of the relative vulnerability of American colleges and universities with regard to these issues.

3. Given the public nature of many universities, terrorists may be well aware of the vast number of ongoing chemical and biological research projects being conducted on campuses throughout the United States. Many of these projects are funded by the U.S. government and could be very attractive to potential terrorists. Research facilities might be subjected to theft of biohazardous materials or chemical agents. These same research facilities could also be targeted for destruction by terrorists.

4. Some universities may be considered attractive targets based on the sheer size of their student enrollment. On a given day when classes are in session, many large universities may have on-campus populations in excess of 50,000 people. Many of these persons on campus are youthful students between the ages of 18 and 24. It has been well documented that when a single serious crime of violence such as murder, rape, or robbery occurs on a college campus, there is often a sense of shock and disbelief on the part of not only the campus but also its surrounding community. The level of shock following a terrorist attack on a college campus that resulted in thousands of youthful casualties would be significant and long lasting. Large crowds in attendance at high-profile on-campus athletics events or concerts could also be very attractive as targets to potential terrorists.

In the next section, the manner in which one large state university reacted to various security issues post–September 11, 2001, will be discussed. It is intended to provide a general framework for discussion of campus security in these very difficult times. While most experts agree that it is almost impossible to predict when or how terrorists may attack, it seems prudent to take the steps necessary to provide reasonable security for a college community.

DESCRIPTION OF THE UNIVERSITY

The University of South Florida (USF), located in Tampa, Florida, opened in 1960 and had an enrollment of 37,500 students in 2001. The University has 200 degree programs at all levels; bachelors, masters, specialty, doctoral, and doctor of medicine. It is considered the principal public university for the Tampa Bay region. In 2001, USF research generated more than $186 million in grant funding. The student population is quite diverse. The students come from every state in the nation and from more than 100 foreign countries. African Americans, Hispanics, and students from other minority groups constitute 29 percent of the student population. Approximately 60 percent of the students are women. International students are numbered at 1,724. Located on over 1,700 acres, USF has a major outpatient clinic, two hospitals, an elementary school, a hotel, and a 10,000-seat multipurpose facility in addition to its traditional academic and general-purpose buildings. This university has twenty-five miles of roadway within its boundaries and nine public entry points (Staehle 2003).

CAMPUS SECURITY DECISION MAKING AFTER SEPTEMBER 11, 2001: THE UNIVERSITY OF SOUTH FLORIDA EXPERIENCE

Shortly after the terrorist attacks of September 11, the president of the University of South Florida established a Task Force on Safety and Security. The provost, the deans of each of the colleges, and university vice presidents had input into the selection of the task force members. The chairman of the task force was an associate professor from the criminology department who had previously served as the assistant chief of university police and had considerable practical and academic experience with campus security issues. The other members of the original task force included the director of the university counseling center, the director of International Student and Scholar Services, an assistant professor from the College of Public Health, an associate librarian, the director of the student center, the director of the physical plant division, a student resident assistant, a doctoral student, a student director of the University Safe Team, the second in command from the University Police Department, the director of university housing, an associate dean in the College of Business Administration, and a faculty member from the Department of Environmental and Occupational Health. Special assistance was given to the task force by the faculty assistant to the president. This individual served as a direct link between the president's office, the task force, and other appropriate departments through the year. The decision to include this individual on the task force, allowing access to the president's office and assuring cooperation from all facets of the university, was later judged to be critical to the success of the Task Force.

The president gave the Task Force on Campus Safety and Security a very specific charge. The charge was as follows:

> To fulfill its mission, the University must maintain a teaching and learning environment in which inquiry and civil discussion can flourish. Therefore, the Task Force on Safety and Security will review university policies, procedures and practices intended to ensure the safety and security of all USF students, faculty, staff and property and make appropriate recommendations for improvements. The Task Force will advise the president on whether steps are needed to protect the rights and reaffirm the responsibilities of all members of the university in maintaining the safety and security of the learning environment. A report will be submitted by December 2001. (USF Task Force on Safety and Security 2001)

STEPS TAKEN PRIOR TO THE FORMAL MEETINGS OF THE TASK FORCE

The chair of the safety and security task force developed a list of questions relevant to the various security policies and procedures at the university. The chair had prior experience in this regard as he had previously written a manual entitled *Departmental Self Evaluation: A Guide for Campus Law Enforcement Administrators* that had been published by the International Association of Campus Law Enforcement Administration.

This document was used as a source for the questions that were developed to evaluate USF's current level of security. The task force chair also asked the regional director of the Florida Department of Law Enforcement (the state's equivalent to the FBI) to review and comment on the list of proposed questions. Once this was accomplished the final list of questions was prepared for later distribution to task force members and the university department heads with responsibility for various areas of inquiry.

The questions were grouped under six areas of general inquiry:

1. General crime prevention
2. Facilities security
3. Residential security
4. Emergency operations
5. Fire, bomb, and hazardous materials threats
6. Counseling services

TASK FORCE MEETINGS

The first meeting of the task force was devoted to a presentation of the group's charge, time line, and report format by the president of the university. In addition, an overview of the process, assignments, invitees, and scheduled presentation was provided by the president. Following the president's presentation, the chair presented the agenda, introduced task force members and guests, and presented a detailed outline of the approach to be used and the assigned tasks. At that point comments and questions were entertained and date and time frames were established for subsequent meetings.

Also at the first meeting a detailed list of issues related to physical security, personnel security, and the major areas to receive focused consideration was made available to members and discussed. Each member of the task force was made responsible for addressing a number of questions related to campus safety and security on campus. In general, assignments were made on the basis of departmental responsibilities, but they often included questions that required collaboration between departments to adequately address the issues. Task force members were also asked to provide three suggestions for improving campus safety and security as part of their written responses to the questions.

A report from the University Police Department entitled "Overview of the University Police and Campus Crime" was made at the time of the first meeting. This assignment had been previously made in the interest of time. Remaining assignments were made at the initial meeting within the respective areas identified earlier. Presentations were made by task force members and other subject-matter experts and were organized around responses to the previously assigned questions that specifically related to campus safety and security. Both formal and informal task force discussions took place around each topic. On numerous subsequent occasions guests were invited to take part in meetings on the basis of their expertise and their potential to enhance the effectiveness of the committee process and, ultimately, the report to the president. In addition to their oral presentations, each task force member provided detailed written responses to all questions asked.

At the conclusion of the individual reports, the task force devoted three extended meetings to review and input on final recommendations. The chair of the task force formed a subcommittee consisting of himself, the faculty assistant to the president, and the director of the counseling center to develop a format for the task force report and to ensure that all recommendations were written to reflect the actions required.

A written copy of the task force report was presented to the president of the university in December of 2001. An oral overview of major points within the report was also made at that time. The task force report presented a total of thirty-five recommendations and included an evaluation of each recommendation with respect to importance, time frame for action, the type of recommendation it was (high, medium, low priority), the current status of any initiative, fiscal implications, vice presidential area of responsibility, and specific university unit responsibility. Additional comments were provided with each recommendation to address issues that need to be considered in the actual implementation of the actions recommended. The recommendations were the product of The President's Task Force on Safety and Security and represented a sense of immediacy associated with the initial charge. Copies of the report were also made available to various university governance groups. It is believed that this report represented the most detailed and current inventory of USF's security policies ever assembled.

GENERAL RECOMMENDATIONS

The task force made four general recommendations as overarching considerations. These included:

1. Identify and expand current university positions that require fingerprint checks of prospective employees.

2. Improve safety and security of individuals and facilities to include air, water, utilities, and building docks.

3. Update University Emergency Operations plan to include an improved comprehensive communications system in the event of disaster.

4. Develop a comprehensive hazardous materials management system.

A SECOND TASK FORCE

After briefing the president of the university, a series of additional presentations of the task force report were made to the Council of Deans, the President's Cabinet, and other interested parties. As recommended by the chair and the members of the original safety and security task force, the president agreed to appoint a second task force comprised of liaisons from each of the vice presidential areas to ensure adequate follow-up on the task force's recommendations. The chair of the task force was asked to continue to serve as chair and to oversee the completion of Phases II and III of what would become a yearlong project. Phase II was titled "Developmental/Action" and Phase III "Implementation." Vice presidential liaisons were charged with developing and implementing a plan to systematically follow up on the recommendations made in the initial December 2001 task force report. In February 2002, each university vice president identified a liaison to work on the second phase of the safety and security project.

The chair of the task force, the faculty assistant to the president, and the director of the counseling center met and developed three general questions to guide the developmental stage of the safety and security project. These questions were as follows:

1. What can we do with regard to the individual recommendations?

   Input would be solicited from the vice presidential areas after involving key staff.

2. What are the estimated costs associated with the recommendations?

   Realistic estimates for all costs involved in implementing the recommendations would be developed where possible.

3. When can we act on the recommendations?

   This would involve the development of realistic time frames and a specific time line for periodic follow-up briefings by the liaisons.

4. Who is accountable for the recommendations?

   Some of the recommendations would clearly fit within a single presidential area but others involved other vice presidential jurisdictions.

During April, May, and June of 2002, the second task force formally met on six occasions to prioritize the initial recommendations, establish time frames for implementation, and to study the budget implications for each action. In order to maximize its efficiency, the task force was further organized into several small work groups with the intent of assuring interdivisional communication and planning. This resulted in additional meetings that included the chair and select members of the task force. Additionally there were numerous phone calls, e-mails, and exchanges of faxes between members working on various parts of the project. During the remainder of the summer the implementation phase began, as numerous less-costly recommendations were acted on. The president had made it clear from the beginning that practical, necessary actions did not need to await the final task force report for implementation.

At the final meeting of the second task force, each member submitted a two-part document that included an abstract of individual recommendations and a recommendation status report. The former provided an executive summary, time line, and estimated cost for the implementation of each action. The latter paralleled the framework of recommendations found in the initial December 2001 report. The formal written report for Phases II and III was presented to the president in August of 2002. A briefing of the highlights of the final report was presented at that time as well.

HIGHLIGHTS OF THE SECOND TASK FORCE'S
FINAL RECOMMENDATIONS

In the area of general crime prevention, the task force recommended that additional training and education in crime prevention be provided for various university staff and faculty. This was intended to provide additional eyes and ears to enhance security on campus. Implementation of these actions began prior to the final task force report.

The next set of recommendations made by the task force dealt with the complex issue of campus facility security. Included were a variety of recommendations dealing with issues such as after-hours use of campus facilities, control of access, a review of labs considered to be "at risk," consideration of various security surveillance systems, and additional security for the numerous utility supply locations on campus. One of the more important recommendations dealt with the development of a comprehensive university facility space-use policy that would better reflect the security needs of the twenty-first century. The assessment of "at risk" university labs and other facilities focused on identifying the activities and locations that may be considered high-risk areas due to chemical, biological, and radiological materials usage. As the final task force recommendations were being written, a comprehensive assessment of these locations had already begun.

With regard to on-campus residential security (dorms), the major recommendation by the task force was to continue a program wherein two university police officers were assigned full time to the residence halls areas on campus. During the time of the task force deliberations, the University Police Department was organizationally transferred to the Division of Student Affairs that also had responsibility for the residence halls program. The popular residential police officer program was to be continued and expanded as annual budgets were further developed.

One of the major recommendations made by the task force dealt with a review and update of the university's Emergency Operations Plan. During the course of the year, the plan was reviewed and appropriate changes were made and implemented. In addition, a new university Crisis Communications Plan was developed that included a protocol to address emergency procedures during a crisis event and to identify the appropriate spokesperson and management leaders who would constitute a response team. In addition, the personnel evacuation procedures for the various university facilities were updated to encompass the various types of emergencies that are now covered by the university Emergency Operations Plan.

The next set of recommendations dealt with fires, bombs, and hazardous materials management. Recommendations in this critical area included a variety of actions ranging from providing additional training to university staff members on appropriate steps to take upon receiving a bomb threat to the development of a university-wide hazardous materials database inventory. The development of a comprehensive Hazardous Materials Management Program emphasizing safety, control, and security at every operational level beginning with the original receipt and purchase of material through to its final disposal was started. It was recommended that a database be developed in order to maintain individual inventories of hazardous materials of each of the university's principal investigators. This included devising a method to flag and record purchases of hazardous materials, limiting the receipt of hazardous materials to specific areas on the campus; developing designated specific hazardous material storage and use areas, and requiring background checks for individuals with access to select agents.

In addition, prior to the final report of the task force, an ongoing inventory of chemicals present in the chemistry and biology departments was conducted. A subcommittee comprised of representatives from Information Technology, the University Police Department, Environmental Health and Safety, the chemistry department, and the research compliance department met on a regular basis to define developmental needs in this area. Costs associated with the development of a customized hazardous material database were estimated at $500,000, making this the most expensive recommendation of the Task Force. An additional recommendation was made to add new staff to the Department of Environmental Health and Safety and the Office of Research Compliance in order to conduct quarterly reviews of hazardous materials stored in restricted areas for the purpose of security, possible leakage, and/or needed disposal. Finally, while the task force was still at work, the recommendation to reactivate and merge the chemical safety oversight and biohazard committees in order to better evaluate the need for additional hazardous materials precautions and monitoring was implemented.

A final set of recommendations dealt with available on and off campus counseling services in the event of a major emergency. It was recommended that the university's Counseling Center establish closer relations with the Crisis Center of Tampa Bay and the Hotline of Hillsborough County. It was also recommended that the Counseling Center facilitate access to the Hotline and the university police through telecommunication enhancements. The recommendation was acted upon almost immediately in order to further strengthen the University Counseling Center's professional alliance with the Crisis Center of Tampa Bay and the Hotline of Hillsborough County. They established a multilevel community network of professional service providers that would be mobilized to provide assistance in time of local or national crisis.

CONCLUSIONS AND IMPLICATIONS

The potential threat of a terrorist attack on an American college or university has implications for campus executives and security decision makers as the first decade of the twenty-first century unfolds (Ryan 2001). While it may be impossible to predict where or when such an attack may occur, preparation for such an event has considerable merit. It is therefore necessary to take all reasonable steps to ensure an adequate level of security on campus.

The leadership necessary to provide guidance with regard to campus security in the post–September 11 era can come from sources external to the colleges and universities as well as those internal to these institutions. For example, the federal government, through the passage of the PATRIOT Act in 2001, mandated new requirements for institutions such as colleges and universities that have labs or other facilities containing chemical and biological agents. As one authority suggests, institutions of higher education should now determine current safety and security procedures, consider all "agents at issue and be diligent in adding security to research procedures" (Harrison 2001, 24). Likewise national-level higher education associations such as the National Association of College and University Attorneys have recently conducted seminars on the legal issues facing colleges and universities as a result of the war on terrorism. This association recommended that colleges and universities conduct a thorough evaluation of their campus emergency plans and review their current level of campus security (White et al. 2001).

While it is beneficial to meet federal requirements and to use guidelines suggested by national-level associations, it is also critical that institutional-level leadership play a major role in shaping campus security policy post-September 11. Top campus executives must be proactive in seeing that there is an evaluation of the current campus security efforts, that security enhancements are recommended after that evaluation is conducted, and that there is adequate followup to the recommendations. These functions can best be managed at the institutional level.

Only top-level campus executives can assure that newly enacted policies and procedures will be adhered to. These same executives are also the ones to assure that the necessary fiscal and human resources are in place to support enhanced security programs. This leadership challenge with regard to providing an adequate level of campus security today exceeds those facing university presidents at the height of the Vietnam War era, when many university presidents saw the need for a more professionalized approach to campus security issues.

In the past, it has been suggested that at campus-wide team approach should be developed in order to adequately address campus security issues. It was recommended that this team should include the following areas in addition to the university police or security department: the provost, the chief student affairs officer, the physical plant director, the student residence life administrator, the general counsel, and the vice president for administration (Bromley 1995, 225). In order to provide a comprehensive approach to campus security issues post-September 11, that team should be expanded. Additions to the existing team should include representatives from the following areas, depending upon the needs and resources of a particular campus: a representative from the office of the president, the university counseling center, the department of research compliance, the media relations department, the computer center, the department of environmental health and safety, the office of international student affairs, and any other appropriate department whose input would be necessary in a security policy area. In addition, it is essential that regular contact be made with local, state, and federal law enforcement officials to ensure ongoing communication.

Providing a comprehensive, well-integrated security program for a college campus is a very taxing endeavor that will become more challenging in the near future. A successful program would combine principles and practices from the fields of community policing, industrial security, risk management, and environmental health and safety. The present case study described one institution's attempt to begin the process of enhancing campus security after the fateful day of September 11, 2001. A process of continuous evaluation and improvement is necessary to meet the goal of providing an adequate level of campus security.

ENDNOTES

1. The author wishes to thank Dr. Josue Cruz, dean of the College of Education, Bowling Green University, and Dr. William Anton, director of the Counseling Center for Human Development, University of South Florida, for their significant input on an earlier version of this chapter.

REFERENCES

Brantingham, P., P. Brantingham, and J. Seagrave. 1995. "Crime and Fear of Crime in a Canadian University." In *Campus Crime Legal, Social, and Policy Perspectives,* ed. B. Fisher and J. Sloan. Springfield, IL: Charles C. Thomas.

Bromley, M. 1995. "Factors Associated with College Crimes: Implications for Campus Police." *Journal of Police and Criminal Psychology* 10, no. 3: 13–19.

Bromley, M. L., and L. Territo. 1990. *College Crime Prevention and Personal Safety Awareness.* Springfield, IL: Charles C. Thomas.

Burke, R. 2000. *Counterterrorism for Emergency Responders.* Boca Raton, FL: Lewis Publishers.

Fisher, B., J. Sloan, 1995. *Campus Crime: Legal, Social, and Policy Perspectives.* Springfield, II: Charles C. Thomas.

Fisher, B., J. Sloan, F. Cullen, and C. Lu. 1998. "Crime in the Ivory Tower: The Level and Sources of Student Victimization." *Criminology* 36, no. 3: 671–710.

Fisher, B. S. 1995. "Crime and Fear on Campus." *Annals of the American Academy of Political and Social Sciences* 539: 85–101.

Harrison, D. 2001. "Higher Education Issues After the USA Patriot Act." Division of Legal Affairs, the University of North Carolina.

Lizotte, A., and A. Fernandez. 1993. *Trends and Correlates of Campus Crime: A General Report.* Albany, NY: Consortium of Higher Education Campus Crime Research.

Mojica, S. 2001. "Putting the Pieces Back Together." *Campus Safety Journal,* 9, no. 10: 14–15.

Nelson, T. 2001. "Incident Management." *Campus Safety Journal* 9, no. 10: 11–13.

Nichols, D. 1987. *The Administration of Public Safety in Higher Education.* Springfield, IL: Charles C. Thomas.

Powell, J., M. Pander, and R. Nielsen. 1994. *Campus Security and Law Enforcement, 2nd Edition.* Boston, MA: Butterworth-Heinemann.

Ryan, S. 2001. "Preparing for the Unthinkable." *Campus Safety Journal* 9, no. 10: 10–11.

Sloan, J.J. 1994. "The Correlates of Campus Crime: An Analysis of Reported Crimes on University Campuses." *Journal of Criminal Justice* 22(1): 51–62.

Smith, M.C. 1998. *Coping with Crime on Campus.* New York: Macmillan.

Staehle, R. 2003. Captain, University of South Florida Police Department, personal interview, October.

USF Task Force on Safety and Security. 2001. *University of South Florida Task Force on Safety and Security Report,"* Tampa, FL.

U.S. Department of Education. 1991. *Digest of Educational Statistics.* Washington, D.C.: Government Printing Office.

White, W., M. Michaelson, P. Virtue, and D. Ashford, 2001. *The War Against Terrorism: Legal Issues for Higher Education.* National Association of College and University Attorneys.

CHAPTER 20

Post 9/11: Are We Really Safer Now?[1]

Jeffrey Ian Ross, Ph.D.
Associate Professor
Division of Criminology, Criminal Justice and Social Policy
Fellow, Center for Comparative and International Law
University of Baltimore

INTRODUCTION

Since the devastating terrorist attacks of September 11, 2001, the government, media, and general public are finding it difficult to put the tragedies completely behind them—and for good reason.

While the United States declared war on terrorism and sent troops overseas to hunt down those responsible for the attacks, has life in America really changed? The public has been faced with bomb threats, breaches of airline security, videotapes of bin Laden celebrating the attacks, and other intimidating threats since September 11.[2] These events have certainly caused many to question the current state of national security.

Are we really safer now? How sufficient are the new security measures enacted across the country? Is the public right to criticize the inconvenience of heightened airport measures, especially in light of ongoing news reports about lapses in such security? Is it safe to once again go to the tops of tall buildings, such as the Empire State Building and the Sears Tower? How much of a presence do terrorists still have in our country, and are we a target for future attacks? What, if anything, should we still fear? Can we feel more at ease? Will it ever be safe to go back to how we used to be?

The short answer to the provocative question "Are we any safer?" is maybe. But you probably already knew this. Maybe this means there is no need to read any further. Not so fast. Although some may feel safer and others may want to head for the hills, I want to help contextualize our current state of preparedness in the United States. In the context of this chapter, I want to develop a theoretical background; outline what federal, state, and local governments have done; and review some of the key accomplishments in the "War Against Terror." I will not enter into a discussion of what terrorism is. Nor will I look specifically at the events of September 11, at who is to blame for the incidents, or how operations are unfolding in Afghanistan and Iraq. In short, I want to encourage readers as much as possible to avoid simplistic responses. Why? Because many of these kinds of answers led to the needless expenditure of resources, and some are actually quite dangerous.

THEORETICAL BACKGROUND

Although much has been written on the effects of terrorism (e.g., Wardlaw 1983; Hewitt 1984; Weinberg and Davis 1989: Chapters 5-7; Sederberg 1989, Chapter 6), particularly counterterrorism efforts (e.g., Livingstone and Arnold 1986), few comprehensive models of responses have been developed.[3]

Ross and Miller (1997) created a series of relatively comprehensive actor-based models that outline the responses to (i.e., effects of) terrorism. In order to accomplish this task, the stimulus-response conflict model (Holsti, Brody, and North 1964) served as a framework to sketch these responses and to specify some of the more important hypotheses. This work provides a tool for exploring and testing the responses, causes, and, ultimately, cycles of terrorist-target interaction.[4] Five basic actors are involved in the reaction: terrorists, victims, the general public, businesses, and government. These serve as the framework for the discussion in this chapter.

Additionally, I would like to call attention to the phenomenon of crime-reporting waves that partially informs our perception of terrorism. During the 1980s, Mark Fishman (1980) introduced and documented the phenomenon that became known as crime-reporting waves. He said that the crime rate, which we already know to be an inaccurate indicator of actual crime, bears little relationship to the frequency with which the media report on crime. More important, most people derive their fear and safety not from the actual incidence of crime or from being personally victimized by crime but rather from the frequency and attention paid to crime in media reports. If there is considerable media attention on crime, then viewers will feel scared.

Building on Fishman's work, others, such as Joel Best (1989, 1999) and Philip Jenkins (1998, 2003), have sensitized us to the fact that although there may be a very real problem with child molesters or serial killers, the media attention and the public fear that it engenders is way out of proportion to the actual amount of these types of crime in society.

The public's fear and safety is directly connected to what they read about in the press or hear in the media. So—although it sounds simplistic—if you don't want to feel scared, don't read the paper and don't watch television. This leads to another point: in some places in America, there is no fear at all.

HAS LIFE REALLY CHANGED?

Introduction

As a result of September 11, in some quarters, life has changed drastically, while in others it appears as if it is business as usual. These divergent reactions are dependent on a number of factors, including the proximity to the attacks, the pervasiveness of existing fear in the population, and the susceptibility of the actor. Let me talk about the first two aspects, and then I will concentrate the balance of the discussion on the actors.

Proximity and General Level of Fear in the Population

In 2001, the University of Houston conducted a poll. The results, which should not be surprising, indicated that those closest to the September 11 attacks experienced the highest levels of anxiety. Thus, residents of New York City—even though they did not know someone who perished in the incident—experienced disruption in some shape or form because of job loss, transportation route delays, the massive cleanup, or the debate over what to do with the Twin Towers site.[5]

Perhaps some people are in a state of denial, blocking out the shocking reality of what transpired. As an attempt to deal with the horror, Americans may have become numbed or have numbed themselves. In some rural communities out West, however, it is business as usual. The local sheriff or small-town police officer still does his or her rounds without a glimmer of hope that they are going to stumble upon a terrorist cell plotting to blow up the local grain elevator.

Perhaps more important, the events of September 11 have had both structural and psychological effects. These broad explanations will be analyzed using the five broad categories of terrorists, victims, public, businesses, the public, and government.[6]

Terrorist Level

It appears that, at last count, there are something like 300 al Qaeda and Taliban detainees at Gauntanamo Bay (Cuba). This does not include the numerous individuals in foreign jails and prisons, some of whom are being held at the request of the United States. Apparently, when the detainees are captured, regardless of the place, Federal Bureau of Investigation officers or other representatives of U.S. national security organizations interrogate them. There is some speculation that a significant blow has been made against the al Qaeda organization. A phenomenon called the "tipping point" suggests that once you capture or kill about half of an organization, then the group goes downhill toward failure from there (Gladwell 2002). In an attempt to achieve this objective, at the end of March 2002, Abu Zubaida, a senior al Qaeda member, and several of his subordinates were captured in Pakistan. During the raid, all sorts of relevant intelligence documents and materials were found.

This operation, it was alleged, "could lead to other al Qaeda leaders and disrupt planned future terrorist attacks" (Pincus 2002). It appears that all pertinent information from these raids has been distributed around the world to relevant national security and policing agencies. In sum, particularly after the American invasion of Afghanistan, numerous al Qaeda members have been arrested or killed.

Victims (including family and friends)

The number of people who died as a result of September 11 is close to 3,000. Countless others were injured and will have permanent physical effects from the tragedy. Some people may have experienced psychological outcomes such as anger, anxiety, insomnia, and post traumatic stress disorder (PTSD), especially because so many innocent lives were lost, and confusion because they did not know the best way to respond. Most people did not believe that a foreign-based terrorist group had the capability to carry off an operation of that magnitude. Many Americans previously thought that the country was invincible. Now many individuals are more alert about their surroundings, security, and safety. Others may shy away from large populated places or events (e.g., transportation hubs, sporting events, fireworks displays, etc.). Some victims responded positively by expressing their grief and turmoil through creating makeshift memorials that were set up throughout locations in New York City.

Public Level Response

Among the community there were several noticeable effects, including the loss or temporary absence of a family member because they were called up for active duty, an increase in the fear of flying, criticism of the government because it failed to protect citizens, and antipathy toward Arab- or Muslim-looking individuals in the United States.

In the immediate aftermath of the attacks, members of the public stepped up to the plate and made donations to victims' funds. Large public assistance organizations such as the Red Cross and the Salvation Army increased their aid programs.

Some suggest that the attacks somehow brought the country closer together and have led to an increase in nationalism and patriotism made visible in expressions such as "these colors don't run." Whenever a crisis strikes, there is always the possibility of unintended consequences. Commentators and pundits have gloated about how September 11 has made us more brotherly, claiming that if we fail to take part in normal every day activities, "surely the terrorists have won." This attitude exhibited itself in the countless acts of generosity and kindness spurred by the atmosphere, including more tolerance of others.

In some quarters, faith in government has been questioned. September 11 pointed out the shortcomings of our crime-prevention and security apparatuses. The perception of a nationalistic surge is buttressed by the numerous displays of flags on cars and houses. Slogans such as "United We Stand" were displayed on postage stamps, posters displayed in shopkeeper's windows, and bumper stickers on pickup trucks and SUVs. But, by the same token, September 11 has probably led to an increase in prejudice toward foreign-born Americans, immigrants, and visitors, particularly those of Islamic, Arabic, or Middle Eastern backgrounds.

In the immediate aftermath, some investigative reporters (e.g., Emerson 2002) went on a search for "the smoking gun." Many people are trying to understand why our national intelligence agencies missed the signs and signals of September 11. After the fact, it became apparent that some FBI agents either had prior knowledge of the possible attacks or were restricted in their efforts to detect them. Many reporters, experts, and pundits concluded that there must have been a failure in communication. Other individuals developed a new sense of respect for our nation's first responders: the police, firefighters, and paramedics.

Business Community

The events of September 11 prompted a number of reactions by business interests. The airline and hospitality sector was economically affected, security-protection firms did a brisk business, defense-related contractors' business increased, some companies (particularly those that were housed in the Twin Towers) were relocated, and terrorism insurance was sold at alarming rates.

Initially, the airline and hospitality industry experienced a financial setback. In the wake of the event, the federal government bailed out the airline industry. The stock market was temporarily shocked; prices plummeted, especially those of businesses connected to the travel industry. Many businesses went bankrupt, which caused thousands of people to loose jobs. Thus, we had an increase in unemployment and perhaps in homelessness.

Government Level

In order to combat terrorism, local, state, and federal government law enforcement agencies have implemented a number of measures. By far, the most dramatic responses have come from the federal government. These initiatives are listed from least to most important. Some of the more dominant have been hardening of targets and new policies, practices, and laws, especially the passage of the *Patriot Act*.

As in previous eras, there was considerable target hardening at particular places. Those that felt vulnerable changed policies and practices. This was particularly prominent at transportation hubs and around government buildings and facilities. New and more concrete barriers have been placed at airports and critical infrastructures. On the other hand, some targets that you would think would be hardened are not. The Saudi Arabian embassy in downtown Washington does not appear to be any more protected than any other targets of opportunity,

In the middle of October 2001, Congress passed sweeping legislation against terrorism embodied in what is now referred to as the *Patriot Act*. Some of the more important highlights include so-called roving wiretaps on people rather than on particular telephones; nationwide search warrants instead of those limited to specific jurisdictions; searches of electronic mail; and the power to detain foreigners for extended periods of time. Part of the *Act* includes longer and more severe sentences and the extension of the "statute of limitations on terrorism cases" ("House Committee Approves Anti-Terrorism Measure," October 4, 2001). The bill gives "authorities the ability to hold immigrants suspected of terrorist acts for 7 days without filing charges."

The Treasury Department closed or tightened the reigns on the *hawalas,* the Islamic money exchanges, believed to be critical in the transfer of money to terrorists and their supporters in the United States. The Immigration and Naturalization Service (INS) separated into two divisions, one concerned with administration and another with enforcement. The INS was then moved out of the Department of Justice and into the Office (now called Department) of Homeland Security. The organization has also cracked down on visitors that have overstayed their visas. This has resulted in the detention of numerous individuals suspected of being part of terrorist groups or having knowledge of them. There has been increased surveillance on the Canadian/American border. One of the issues that has come up here is what the proper role of the National Guard in airports and along the 49th parallel is.

Perhaps the biggest changes have been in the field of transportation. Those who have taken an airplane, a train, or a Greyhound bus in the last six months know that with some means of transportation, extra security precautions have been implemented. I'm not sure that any new changes have occurred with Greyhound bus travel or in their stations. In the immediate aftermath of September 11, there was an incident where a mentally disturbed individual attacked a bus driver while the vehicle was en route. As a result of this event, Greyhound started talking about installing geopositioning satellite technology (or GPS) tracking devices on their buses. The use of this tool probably would not have prevented the attack, but it may have aided in locating the bus if it was hijacked.

Things are slightly different if you take an Amtrak train. There are now more Amtrak police patrolling the platforms; before, they were simply walked around the station. Although you need to show your identification now to purchase a ticket from a window, you can still buy one anonymously through an automatic ticket machine conveniently located in most stations. This procedure would be secure if you were also required to show your identification once on board, but this is not the case. In Washington, D.C., for example, before they let you out of the waiting area, you need to show your ticket and identification. However, the Amtrak gate person does not compare the two. In Baltimore, a similar safeguard procedure does not even exist. You don't even need to show your identification to the conductor. It appears that the authorities do not view trains as a serious threat to public safety. This seems odd considering the derailments in Florida, California, and Maryland, all of which occurred in 2001.

In most of the big airports, security procedures have become more rigorous. Picking up and dropping off passengers is now more of a time-consuming and expensive hassle because you can't really pick up or drop off at the curbside anymore. And although you are still asked a number of questions—which are easy to lie about—when you check in at the ticket counter, such as "Has anyone helped you pack your bag?" or "Has your bag been in your possession at all times?" airlines are now restricting carry-on luggage to one item.

Baggage handlers/screeners have been federalized and integrated into a new government agency, the Transportation Safety Administration (TSA), which is part of the

Department of Transportation. In general, passenger and baggage screeners (there are now 30,000 of them) are doing a more thorough job instead of having pleasant chats with each other. Checking baggage is more onerous. New legislation is designed so that those responsible for baggage handling and inspection will be better trained and will be required to have more experience.

One of the new programs that is being used is Computer Assisted Passenger Screening (CAPS), which is a program that examines passengers' travel history to determine if there are any unusual patterns. CAPS "uses airline reservation computers to identify passengers who may pose a higher risk of being terrorists and subjects them to additional scrutiny" (Levin and Morrison 2001). CAPS "examines 26 aspects of a passenger's travel history," but we don't know exactly what they are because "details are classified" (Leven and Morrison, 2001).

Because of its close proximity to the Pentagon, flights out of Ronald Reagan National Airport (Washington, D.C) were initially suspended after the September 11 attacks, then scaled back. Sky marshals were placed on all flights in and out of the airport. In addition to the heavily scrutinized baggage, you cannot get up from your seat for the first half hour after the plane takes off or after it lands at the airport.

When you are finally about to board the plane, certain passengers can be taken aside to have themselves and their carry-on items completely searched. A number of changes have occurred with respect to on-board procedures as well. Airplane pilots are now allowed to carry guns, and cockpit doors have been reinforced. The airlines no longer serve food on so-called short-haul trips. Ostensibly, this last precaution is because your utensils can be potential weapons and because not providing food defrays the immediate loss of income incurred from the low ridership as a result of September 11. Even so, this probably lessens airline liability and adds to your safety because this omission means that the risk of getting a stomachache or food poisoning from airline food is reduced. Even so, many people are scared to travel long distances, especially if the trip involves flying.

In November 2001, two air travel security bills were debated in Congress. While this was occurring, a number of security breaches and incidents with passengers bringing weapons on board planes were discovered. One took place in Chicago, where a man was discovered with several weapons in his bags.

Secretary of Transportation Norman Mineta has mentioned a National Travel Card that would "verify proof of citizenship and provide photo identification, generating a national database" (Levin and Morrison 2001). Since September 11 there have been other suggestions for national identity cards. If we had these pieces of identification, advocates argue, it would be easier for law enforcement authorities to share information and detect known terrorists and criminals. It would also mean one more item to forge; in the long run, the identification cards are probably just like drivers licenses. You can get a fake one and hold on to it long enough to commit a number of crimes. It does not seem wise to burden society with more rules and regulations; we just need to properly implement the ones we have and not be complacent about enforcement.

Increased cooperation and sharing of data among law enforcement agencies and between the United States and our allies is always needed. Better coordination among Customs, the Immigration and Naturalization Service, the Federal Bureau of

Investigation, and the Central Intelligence Agency has been proposed. This was the intent of the creation of the Department of Homeland Security.

Because of increased security, primarily through the stepped-up efforts of the INS, those working illegally in the United States will be deported. This might have a negative effect on the already beleaguered service and on agricultural, construction, and service industries, where many illegal aliens have found work.

On November 6, 2001, the inspector generals of the U.S. Department of the Justice released a report that said "Hundreds of foreign nationals who came under suspicion during immigration inspections were allowed into the country under a special program and then disappeared, ignoring requirements to return with missing information" (Sheridan November 7, 2001). "The report called on the INS to establish a better system to track deferred foreign nationals" (Sheridan, November 7, 2001).

In the fall of 2002, Congress authorized the construction of the Office of Homeland Security. In essence, it is supposed to coordinate national policy and security on terrorism, bringing these functions out of the hands of the Federal Bureau of Investigation. Needless to say, there are a number of potential difficulties, including the increasingly complex communications needs that result from developing one more layer of bureaucracy. In the meantime, a number of new appointments of capable-sounding individuals are at the helm of counterterrorism agencies.

Currently very comprehensive antiterror legislation is being considered in Congress. This has been dubbed the Patriot Two Act. Both the House and the Senate are developing separate terrorism bills that would "enhance domestic surveillance powers, stiffen penalties for terrorism and make it easier for law enforcement and intelligence agencies to share information" (Lancaster October 9, 2001). In order to mount a successful terrorism campaign, the organization needs financing (Adams 1986). Currently banks are only required to report to the federal government transfers and withdrawals that are over $100,000. Perhaps banking legislation needs to be changed. This would undoubtedly slow down the pace of international capitalism, though.

Since the attacks, the local, state, and federal government has increased security around significant holidays and parades, such as those on Memorial Day, July 4th, and New Year's Eve. Many of the new policies and practices considered and implemented as a reaction are in development. To be certain, the federal government has increased the number of military patrols over Washington.

The Office of Homeland Security, in a scene reminiscent of the old Cold War nuclear threat days, came up with a color code that would enable the public to judge the seriousness of terrorist threats. It was easily dismissed as ineffective, a joke, which prompted an irreverent *Saturday Night Live* spoof on the issue. These announcements have become a little like the little boy who called wolf. The warning gets offered, but then no terrorist event takes place. In the meantime, the public becomes desensitized and lets its guard down. But the government is in a "damned if you do, damned if you don't" position. It must issue these warnings because it wants to maintain legitimacy. The government must err on the side of caution.

Many people believe that Thomas Ridge, the former Pennsylvania governor who now directs the Department of Homeland Security, does not instill confidence. He appears awkward in public and is considered to have minimal impact. The Department of Homeland Security is a good example of poorly thought out reasoning by the government. Do you think this will help or hinder things? Basic public administration theory will teach you that when you add another layer of bureaucracy, there are advantages and disadvantages (Ostrom 1976).

If you want better oversight where calm, cool, and collected reasoning is valued, then adding more levels is a good suggestion. However, if you want a body to make decisions and act quickly, then having another government bureaucracy is counterintuitive. Traditionally in government, when there is a policy issue or crisis, we establish a lead agency. Before September 11 there was some (albeit attenuated) coordination between the Federal Bureau of Investigation and the Central Intelligence Agency. It is only now that we are starting congressional investigations to see if there was a so-called intelligence failure.

Then there is what I call the "threat of the week" syndrome. Shortly after the attacks, there were numerous rumors, facilitated by increased public access to the Internet, about bomb-laden rental trucks (e.g., U-Haul, Ryder, etc.) that were missing or were unaccounted for that could be carrying explosive materials ready to be parked almost anywhere. The message was that the public needed to be on guard. The truth of the matter is that at any given time, a small percentage of the fleets of truck rental companies are unaccounted for.

Approximately a month after September 11, our family made what now appears to be our annual pilgrimage to New York City. My wife typically has business to take care of during the day and I hang out with the children. The Statue of Liberty was closed. This closure was probably because New York City counterterrorist planners thought that the building and other tourist locations would be targeted next. In November, there were a series of threats of terrorist attacks against bridges, especially in California, that were later downplayed. Many Californians knew better and feared more from earthquakes than some foreign terrorist threat.

Then on April 20th, 2002, there were reports that banks and financial institutions in the mid-Atlantic and Northeast region of the United States would be hit by a terrorist attack. It appears that the federal government has now placed a disclaimer on these warnings, saying that they are "being issued out of an abundance of caution." This, among other expressions, will form the lexicon of turn-of-the-century idioms.

By the same token, you have to realize that the public and government agencies have limited attention spans. Perhaps the focus on al Qaeda is leading to less national security and a minimal intelligence focus on other potentially threatening terrorist groups. In Spain during the fall of 2001, there was a major attack by the Basque separatist group ETA in which ninety-five people were injured. The draconian antiterrorism legislation, which few literate Americans have seen or read (and that includes a handful of Congresspeople who passed the bill), is something to be watchful of. In short, we need to be afraid of an emerging "big brother" attitude.

In February 2003, after so-called credible threats of terrorism, the federal government issued its highest security threat. This was almost coterminous with a tape of bin Laden exhorting his followers and those sympathetic to al Qaeda to launch suicide attacks against the United States if it bombs Iraq. This was the first time the federal government had suggested so-called practical measures that Americans could take in order to protect themselves beyond simply being vigilant. In the event of a nuclear, chemical, or biological attack, Americans were advised to use duct tape and plastic on their doors and windows and have on hand three days' supply of food. Many commentators and pundits thought this was a little unrealistic, but it did serve as a wake-up call for some Americans, who do not do anything in light of these sorts of warnings.

CONCLUSION

Many Americans fail to realize that the federal government, at the behest of the current Administration, may be using the September 11 disaster to strengthen and expand the national security state. Several of the proposals that are being hastily considered and passed have been "on the table," hidden in file cabinets, for a considerable period of time, only to be dusted off and put into place now. We need to avoid panicky or knee-jerk responses. In sum, "we must develop countermeasures to fight terrorism and to actively seek out terrorists. But let us do so in an intelligent and rational manner—we owe this much to ourselves and the country. If we do not act slowly, and wisely, the terrorists have already won" (Yepez 2002).

ENDNOTES

1. Special thanks to Bridgette Mueller and Jose Yepez for comments.
2. It also did not help that there were a handful of yet-unsolved anthrax threats and a youth who went throughout the American West leaving pipe bombs in mailboxes in rural locations.
3. The effects of terrorism have been covered in the literature dealing with counter- and antiterrorism and is subsumed by the conflict literature on consequences, implications, outcomes, reactions, and responses. Gurr (1988) points out that this area is extremely neglected in the study of terrorism.
4. See the literature on symbolic interactionism for a more detailed explanation.
5. This discussion categorizes what does, and not what could, happen.
6. To the best of my knowledge, no similar studies were done of Washington (actually Arlington, Virginia) and rural Pennsylvania, the other sites of the attacks.

REFERENCES

Adams, J. 1986. *The Financing of Terrorism.* New York: Simon & Schuster.

Best, Joel., ed. 1989. *Images of Issues: Typifying Contemporary Social Problems.* New York: Aldine de Gruyter.

————1999. *Random Violence: How We Talk about New Crimes and New Victims.* Los Angeles, CA: University of California Press.

Emerson, Steven. 2002. *American Jihad.* New York: The Free Press.

Fishman, Mark. 1980. *Manufacturing the News.* Austin: University of Texas Press.

Gladwell, Malcolm. 2002. *The Tipping Point.* Back Bay Books.

Gurr, Ted Robert. 1988. "Empirical Research on Political Terrorism: The State of the Art and How it might be improved," in R. O. Slater and M. Stohl (eds.) Current Perspectives on International Terrorism. London: Macmillan, pp. 115–154

Hewitt, Chris. 1984. *The Effectiveness of Anti-Terrorist Policies.* Lanham, MD: University Press of America.

Holsti, O. R., R. A. Brody, and R. C. North. 1964. "Measuring Affect and Action in International Reaction Models: Empirical Materials from the 1962 Cuban Crisis." *Journal of Peace Research,* 1: 170–89.

"House Committee Approves Anti-Terrorism Measure." 2001. *USA Today,* October 4, 5A.

Jenkins, Philip. 1998. *Moral Panic.* New Haven, CT: Yale University Press.

———2003. *Images of Terror: What We Can and Can't Know about Terrorism.* Hawthorne, NY: Aldine de Gruyer.

Lancaster, John. October 9, 2001. "Hill Is Due to Take Up Anti-Terror Legislation," *Washington Post.* A1

Levin, Alan, and Morrison. "Security Plan proposed years Ago." *USA Today,* October 5, 2001, 2A

Livingstone, Neil C., and T. Arnold, eds. 1986. *Fighting Back: Winning the War Against Terrorism.* Toronto: Lexington Books.

Ostrom, E. 1976. "Size and Performance in a Federal System," *Publius* 6, no. 2 (Spring): 33–74.

Pincus, Walter. April 22, 2002 "Seized Materials May Help Thwart Future Attacks," *Washington Post,* A 14.

Ross, Jeffrey Ian, and Reuben J. Miller. 1997. "The Effects of Oppositional Political Terrorism: Five Actor-Based Models," *Low Intensity Conflict and Law Enforcement* 6, no. 3: 76–107.

Sederberg, Peter C. 1989. *Terrorist Myths: Illusion, Rhetoric, and Reality.* Englewood Cliffs, NJ: Prentice Hall.

Sheridan, Mary Beth. 2001. "Report: Some INS Targets Disappeared," *Washington Post,* Wednesday November 7, p. A10.

Skinner, B. F. 1938. *The Behavior of Organisms: An Experimental Analysis.* New York: Appleton-Century-Crofts.

Wardlaw, Grant. 1982. *Political Terrorism: Theory, Tactics, and Counter-Measures.* New York: Cambridge University Press.

Weinberg, Leonard, and Paul B. Davis. 1989. *Introduction to Political Terrorism.* New York: McGraw Hill Publishing Co.

Yepez. This is personal correspondence I had with an individual named Jose Yepez.

SECTION 6 DISCUSSION QUESTIONS

1. List the reasons why colleges and universities are potential targets for future terrorist attacks.
2. How did the University of South Florida act to ensure the safety of its students?
3. Why was their response done in phases?
4. Explain how the concept of crime-reporting waves helps us to understand the 9/11 terrorist attack.
5. List three factors that have caused people to have divergent responses to the 9/11 event. Explain.
6. Compare the five social categories that have experienced both structural and psychological effects after 9/11.
7. Are we really safer now?

Index